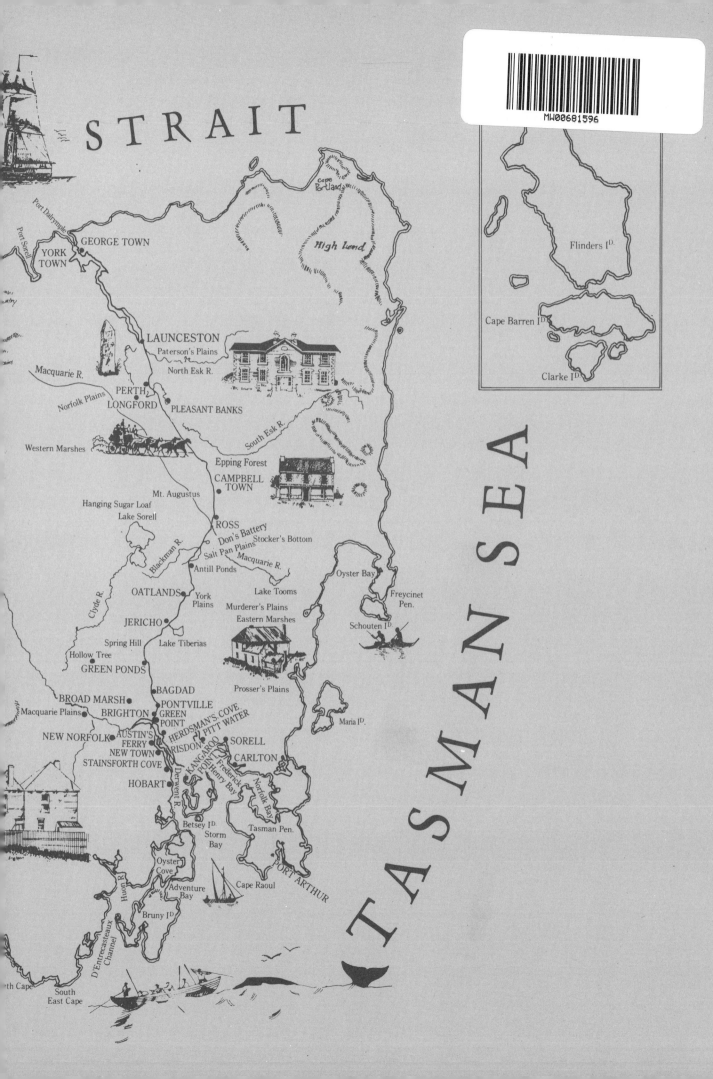

STRAIT

TASMAN SEA

Flinders I.D.

Cape Barren I.D.

Clarke I.D.

Cape Portland

High Land

Port Dalrymple

Port Sorell

GEORGE TOWN

YORK TOWN

Macquarie R.

LAUNCESTON

Paterson's Plains

North Esk R.

PERTH

Norfolk Plains

LONGFORD

PLEASANT BANKS

Western Marshes

South Esk R.

Epping Forest

CAMPBELL TOWN

Mt. Augustus

Hanging Sugar Loaf

Lake Sorell

ROSS

Don's Battery

Stocker's Bottom

Salt Pan Plains

Blackman R.

Macquarie R.

Antill Ponds

Oyster Bay

OATLANDS

York Plains

Lake Tooms

Freycinet Pen.

Clyde R.

Murderer's Plains

Eastern Marshes

Schouten I.D.

JERICHO

Spring Hill

Lake Tiberias

Hollow Tree

GREEN PONDS

BAGDAD

Prosser's Plains

BROAD MARSH

PONTVILLE

Macquarie Plains

BRIGHTON

GREEN POINT

HERDSMAN'S COVE

PITT WATER

Maria I.D.

NEW NORFOLK

AUSTIN'S FERRY

RISDON

KANGAROO POINT

SORELL

NEW TOWN

CARLTON

STAINSFORTH COVE

Frederick Henry Bay

HOBART

Derwent R.

Norfolk Bay

Betsey I.D.

Tasman Pen.

Storm Bay

Oyster Cove

PORT ARTHUR

Huon R.

Adventure Bay

Cape Raoul

Bruny I.D.

D'Entrecasteaux Channel

th Cape

South East Cape

Convicts Unbound

Convicts Unbound

The Story of the *Calcutta* Convicts and their Settlement in Australia

Marjorie Tipping

Marjorie Tipping

VIKING O'NEIL

For Paul

PREVIOUS PAGE:
H.M.S. Calcutta, *tallest of the tall ships that transported convicts to Australia, ended its days in the Bay of Biscay off Rochefort, destroyed in battle against the French in September 1804.*

Viking O'Neil
Penguin Books Australia Ltd
487 Maroondah Highway, PO Box 257
Ringwood, Victoria 3134, Australia
Penguin Books Ltd
Harmondsworth, Middlesex, England
Viking Penguin Inc.
40 West 23rd Street, New York, N.Y. 10010, U.S.A.
Penguin Books Canada Ltd
2801 John Street, Markham, Ontario, Canada L3R, 1B4
Penguin Books (N.Z.) Ltd
182-190 Wairau Road, Auckland 10, New Zealand

Published by Penguin Books Australia Ltd 1988
Copyright © Marjorie Tipping, 1988

Produced by Viking O'Neil
56 Claremont Street, South Yarra, Victoria 3141, Australia
A division of Penguin Books Australia Ltd

Designed by Sandra Nobes
Typeset in Garamond by Bookset Pty Ltd, Victoria
Printed and bound in Hong Kong through Bookbuilders Ltd

National Library of Australia
Cataloguing-in-Publication data

Tipping, Marjorie, 1917– .
    Convicts unbound.

    Bibliography.
    Includes index.
    ISBN 0 670 90068 0.

    [1]. Convicts – Australia. 2. Calcutta (Ship).
    [3]. Transportation of convicts. [4]. Convict
    ships. I. Title.

365'.994

CONTENTS

CONVERSION TABLES

Money values below show theoretical conversion rates from sterling to decimal currency. To get a better idea of comparative values, readers should allow for the huge inflation of the currency which has occurred in recent decades.

CURRENCY
One halfpenny (½d) = ½ cent approx.
One penny (1d) = 1 cent approx.
One shilling (1s) = 10 cents
One pound (£1) = $2
One guinea = $2.10

LENGTH
One inch (1 in) = 2.54 cm
One foot (1 ft) = 30.5 cm approx.
One yard (1 yd) = 0.914 metres
One mile = 1760 yards = 1.61 km

AREA
One acre = 0.405 hectares approx.
One square mile = 640 acres = 259 hectares

CAPACITY
One gallon = 8 pints = 4.55 litres
One bushel = 8 gallons = 36.4 litres

WEIGHT
One ounce (1 oz) = 28.3 grams
One pound (1 lb) = 454 grams
One stone = 14 lb = 6.35 kg
One hundredweight (cwt) = 112 pounds
One ton = 20 cwt = 1.02 tonnes

Camp at Sullivan Cove Derwent, Van Diemens Land

This topographical sketch by the surveyor George Prideaux Harris provides strong evidence that Harris was the artist of the watercolour Sullivan Cove, Tasmania, 1804. First Settlement at the River Derwent (see cover illustration). Although unsigned, the painting has been attributed to several persons including Lieutenant John Bowen, James Grove and the settler Robert Littlejohn. No works, however, of these three artists appear to have survived and, stylistically, the painting is not unlike other known Harris watercolours. Apart from its similarity to the sketch, the painting could be attributed to Harris on several grounds. First, he was present at the unloading of the stores from the Ocean and the erection of the tents to house them, while Bowen and Grove were not. Secondly, the snow near the top of Mount Wellington does not necessarily indicate that the sketch was drawn in winter, as there is frequently snow on the summit in summer time. Thirdly, the smaller ship in the painting looks very much like the brig Lady Nelson which, with the Ocean, moved anchorage from Risdon Cove to Sullivan Cove beside Hunter's Island, landing the settlers and stores between 20 and 22 February. On 27 February the Reverend Robert Knopwood noted that convicts were employed making store houses on the island. The sketch must therefore have been taken before this date and the painting probably soon afterwards. The Lady Nelson left for Port Jackson on 6 March. Four days later the American captain Amaso Delano arrived in his little schooner Pilgrim with Bowen on board, but this boat would have been too small to be the second ship in the painting. Grove did not arrive until the Ocean's return on 22 June by which time the stores had long been housed in a wooden store house which replaced the tents. Grove's voluminous letters tell much of his activities but never mention that he sketched or painted in Hobart Town.

INTRODUCTION

'Father, what can there be in those wagons?'
Jean Valjean answered:
'Convicts.'
'And where are they going?'
'To the galleys.'
. . .

Cosette trembled in every limb. She continued:
'Father, are they still men?'
'Sometimes,' said the wretched man.

Les Misérables.[1]

MIDWAY THROUGH HIS saga about his convict hero, Victor Hugo reflected that where the telescope ends the microscope begins. He pondered over which one had the grander view. He halted his narrative at a critical moment to contemplate things of intellect and things of matter as he perceived them in relation to the wild garden where Valjean had been living in obscurity, and where the gate to the garden always remained closed. 'Jean Valjean', wrote Hugo, 'had left the garden uncultivated, that it might not attract attention.'[2]

Some seeds of Australian history have long remained uncultivated, hidden behind a closed gate. There have been telescopic images of what might lie beyond, but the microscope has been used sparingly. Similarly microscopic studies appear to display ignorance of the telescope. Yet one needs more than scientific instruments when seedsearching. One needs practical implements such as rakes and spades and hoes, which may give 'to airy nothing,/A local habitation and a name'.

Without prejudice, my microscope has had to examine 308 detailed lives of a particular group of convicts who sailed from England in 1803 in H.M.S. *Calcutta* to settle a little-known land. Their story varies somewhat from accepted views. For my part it has been tempting to go on and on, readjusting the lens to probe more clearly. But as the shape of a complex society began to formulate, I knew it was time to cast off the microscope and bring on the telescope. I have found that too many histories have compounded errors of the past and presented the same interpretation, often with little variation in language. The dead hand of nineteenth-century histories, bound by tradition, gullibility and often shallow assumptions, still weighs heavily on those who have unquestioningly accepted oral communications as fact.

Until recently historians have ignored the role that individual and lesser known convicts played in the development of Australia. Even more importantly they have neglected the human flotsam and jetsam that floated in directions other than Botany Bay. By exposing the lives of a large group, I hope to correct some distortions. My methodology may sometimes exclude what was formerly believed important, but on balance I have found it advantageous to draw on many untapped strengths from original sources. Of those 308 prisoners who embarked from England in the *Calcutta* (including one Joseph Myers whose name does not appear on the earliest official lists, although there is other evidence that he was a *Calcutta* convict) this study traced the crimes of 303, as five were impossible to trace. Where court and gaol records do not exist, court reports in early county newspapers have provided valuable information.

The results at first surprised me because I discovered that, contrary to popular belief, the convicts in my study were not at all too old or useless as Lieutenant-Governor David Collins had at first reported.[3] There is evidence that they were hand-picked, almost all with trades suitable to begin a new colony;[4] unlike the First Fleeters who had set out for Botany Bay, among whom, Governor Phillip complained, there was no experienced farmer except for his own servant.[5] Yet most had earned sentences for crimes more serious than one might have imagined, committed in an era when crimes were multiplying because wars had brutalised, and peace had disillusioned, many who were not the stereotypes of a criminal class.

Despatching petty criminals to populate a new colony was no new venture, but the system had its critics. Two centuries earlier Francis Bacon had taken the view that it was 'a shameful and unblessed thing to take the scum of people and wicked condemned men, to be the people with whom you plant . . . for they will ever live like rogues, and not fall to work, but be lazy, and do mischief, and spend victuals, and be quickly weary . . .'[6] But convicts had already proved their suitability to pioneer a new land, in Virginia and Maryland, where the arrow could be as deadly and fearsome as a gunshot, and where convicts had learned to work under discipline in a place where lives were expendable.

Any idea that settlement of the Great South Land had its origins in matters little related to convict-dumping gains credence when one examines the situation in England at the end of the eighteenth century. Those espousing the theory that England sent the First Fleet to Botany Bay for mercantile reasons might well strengthen their case by recognising the later significance of that other 'first fleet' which comprised H.M.S. *Calcutta* (Captain Daniel Woodriff) and its storeship the *Ocean* (Captain John Mertho). These two ships brought convicts to Port Phillip — some with families. There were also free settlers, often with their families, and a civil and military force. The conception of this settlement was more explicit, even though the gestation period was much shorter, than that of the better known settlement at Botany Bay.

Notwithstanding the overcrowding of gaols and the loss of the American colonies, or any other arguments supporting reasons for the decision to settle New South Wales, there is substantial proof that plans to expand into Bass Strait were certainly embedded in mercantilist policy. British trade and commerce demanded that sea routes should be free and that prospective foreign outposts should not endanger British interests. The rising merchant class, as exemplified by the British East India Company, depended upon naval strength and continuous naval supplies, which in turn denied other nations, particularly the French, territories claimed as British. The settlement planned in 1803 was never meant to be a prison, but if transportation could act as a deterrent to crime, and wrong-doers undergo rehabilitation while providing the necessary labour, so much the better.[7] The chronicler of the voyage of H.M.S. *Calcutta*, Lieutenant James Tuckey, even called his published work *An Account of a Voyage to establish a colony at Port Philip {sic} in Bass's Straits* — a colony, not a penal settlement.

In Tuckey's mind and in that of his commander, Captain Daniel Woodriff, a major purpose of the voyage was to fill the *Calcutta* with suitable naval timber to replenish supplies that had been cut off during the years of war. The examination of possible supplies of flax for the Navy was also an important consideration. Traditional secrecy surrounding the activities of the Silent Service is understandable, but the swiftness with which decisions were made and the part played by the Admiralty have been understated by most historians. There were strong arguments why British naval ships should be participating in peace-time activities such as helping to establish a new colony: by transporting convicts the Royal Navy was underplaying the real purpose for its presence in Antipodean waters.[8]

Actual plans for settlement were consistent with proposals that James Matra had placed before the government some twenty years earlier. He was a loyalist from New York whose origins appear to have been Corsican. Matra claimed to have the support of Sir Joseph Banks, and was probably one of several lobbyists. His memo and a further submission from Admiral Sir George Young comprised contemporary evidence of the commercial possibilities promulgated in government circles. In it he gave strategic and economic reasons as to why Britain should act to take advantage of the many benefits of New Holland, which he had visited with Captain Cook. He also envisaged the place initially as a refuge for loyalists fleeing the lost American colonies.[9]

Matra suggested radical methods to provide the necessary labour force. He did not rule out the use of convicts, but believed that they should be treated humanely and given free land as soon as they arrived. He believed that the importation of cheap Chinese labour and the 'procurement' of Pacific Island women for the use of the men would make the colony economically viable. Sir George Young's scheme and Lord Sydney's Heads of Plan for Settlement of New South Wales had retained these recommendations.[10] Lord Sydney even allowed £2 19s 6d each for the clothing of Island women 'as companions for the men'.

But neither Chinese coolies nor island maidens were to be among the founding parents of white Australia, where the climate and soil were reportedly adapted to provide products especially needed by the maritime powers of Europe, such as the excellent New Zealand hemp and flax-plant and, with considerable perspicacity, the *great probability of finding in such an immense country metals of every kind* [my italics].[11]

•   •   •

By the time Governor Phillip arrived in January 1788 to settle New South Wales, the *ancien regime* in France was tottering. The British lion was rampant, girding its loins for the inevitable thunderclap that rocked Europe a year later. It was a shock to all when it came with such suddenness, such finality. England's own destiny was at stake. The mother country neglected to sustain and develop the new colony for several hungry and frustrating years. By 1802, when the Treaty of Amiens brought a temporary peace, it was difficult to convince those who had made England their home to move on again. Lord Sydney, for one, did little to encourage the American loyalists to migrate. Few did. Even the American wife of the appointed Lieutenant-Governor of Port Phillip, David Collins, chose to remain in England. Nor was it easy to convince other worthy persons to settle in one of the furthest corners of the earth. But the American widow of a naval lieutenant, Ann Hobbs, together with her American-born daughter and her family, comprising in all eight persons, would travel in the *Ocean* to Port Phillip. Two half-Americans, sons of Captain Daniel Woodriff, would serve their father in the *Calcutta* as midshipmen.

If a garrison were needed to defend the territory from the French and if settlers were needed to plant and produce or, alternatively, to harvest from the sea, the need for a supportive labour force was obvious. The success of any nation whose prosperity stems from trade has always depended on cheap, perhaps forced, labour. The abduction of black Africans, the press-gang and black-birding were perhaps more iniquitous than transportation, but the encouragement of poor emigrants and refugees has often worked for the mutual good of all concerned.

But the transportation system, conceived in the minds of those who governed, and born of evil like the spirit that always denies, was still slavery of some magnitude. It could only have been invented by a nation of shopkeepers expecting good recompense for their investment. The French, whose new tricolour was already flying over plantations in debilitating and disease-riddled climates, discovered that the labour of the indigenous people was less expensive than digging white men's graves. The English had heeded Edmund Burke's Miltonic grandiloquence when he declaimed in Parliament against transportation to a place such as Gambia, where 'all life dies and all death lives'. By comparison, Port Phillip appeared to be ideal and, according to European rules, it was *terra nullius*.

The prisons and hulks were bulging with the oddest mixture of idle humanity, costing money and earning nothing, but which fortuitously was available for cheap export. Donkey work on the hulks had provided a few with some useful discipline and experience suitable for a new colony's needs. Some were engaged in dredging the Thames and others in quarrying and excavation work for the dockyards. There were some 100 000 confined at the beginning of the nineteenth century. The Tyburns of England had fewer wretched customers as the hangman's noose pricked the conscience of august justices with eyes severe and beard of formal cut. They were becoming inclined to reprieve many who had been capitally convicted. Transportation for life or for a set period would be the answer to many of the contemporary problems. The assignment of convicts to those settling a distant land for the glory of King and country was a more refined system of slavery than that known on the American plantations, where the master himself wielded absolute power.

The men who sailed in the *Calcutta* were luckier than the felons who settled at Port Jackson. They were also more fortunate than those later governed by men who were used to autocratic rule. There was a chance to redeem themselves and make a new and prosperous life for their immediate families and their descendants. In many cases they fared better than the indifferent lot of settlers whom they were sent out to serve. There were of course failures and disappointments. Some were destined to become recidivists, although overall most succeeded in grasping opportunities presented to them. It was the later arrivals in Van Diemen's Land who tarnished the image of the Eden that they had the chance to create. Their standard of living was much superior to the pauperism and poverty that most had known, whether it was, apart from the British Isles, in Holland, Germany, Poland, Portugal, France or America, in the Jewish ghettoes or anywhere else whence the *Calcutta* convicts originated. For them, early freedom and land grants as Matra had suggested were the prizes awaiting those who could prove their worth. The provision of food, clothing and shelter for the first few years was some guarantee against want until a free economy emerged.

From the first moment they came together, these convicts had the capacity to make an indelible if not generally recognised mark on history. Even Queen Victoria would not have been amused had she known how much she owed her later existence to a bunch of drunken soldiers. Mutineers all, these Irish and Dutch members of the garrison at Gibraltar helped cause the man who became her father to lose his job and change his domestic arrangements. Within a year these men would be rehabilitated and entrusted with the protection of part of the Empire that one day would bear the Queen's name.

The Old Lady of Threadneedle Street should have been grateful to James Grove for suggesting a method to prevent the forgery of notes. Richard Kidman would warn the Governor of a plot against his life. William Buckley would live for thirty-two years among the blacks and the knowledge he gained from them would be more acceptable to present-day anthropologists than to his contemporaries.

There would be some extraordinary successes. Some who attracted notice from the beginning would be granted privileges which set them apart from the rest. William Thomas Stocker, with an eye for the main chance, was always ready to take a risk in any undertaking — even marriage to the intimidating Mary Hayes after her widowhood. James Grove believed his salvation lay in the prayers he could offer to his newly found Creator; his reward was Collins' close friendship. James Lord and David Gibson achieved great wealth, the former by occasionally taking advantage of his fellow men who had succumbed to alcohol, and the latter by Scottish thrift and highly successful farming. On the distaff side the widowed Catherine

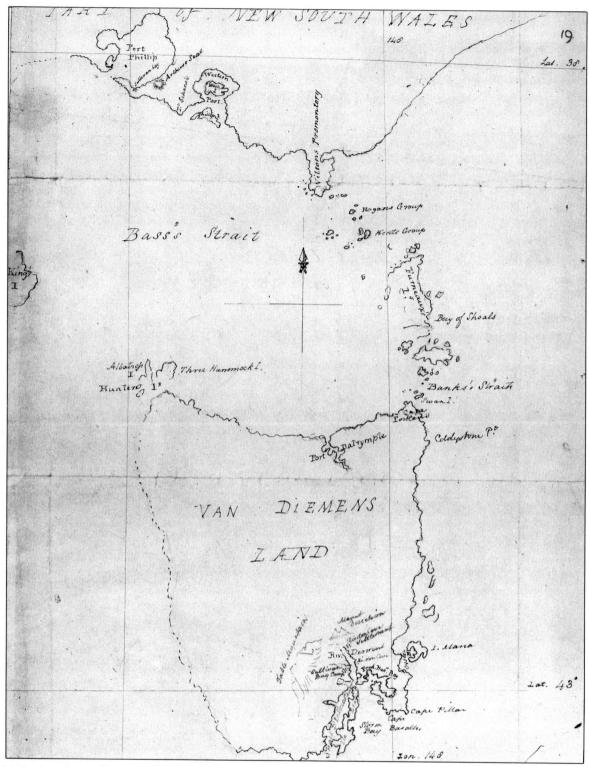

This sketch (indicating the Yarra and Tamar Rivers) which
G. P. Harris probably sent to England by the Ocean in August
1804, is the first known map of Bass Strait and its surrounding
islands to note Sullivan Bay in Port Phillip and Sullivan Bay
(Cove) in Hobart Town. It proves that Lieutenant-Governor
Collins must have had access to Ensign Barrallier's Combined
Chart of Bass's Straits, published by Alexander Dalrymple in
January 1803, and to Grimes' chart made when he discovered the
Yarra. Harris also had at least some knowledge that the French

had circumnavigated French Island in Western Port and was with
Lieutenant Tuckey during the survey of Port Phillip in October
1803.
Although a very simple effort, the sketch shows a more defined
course for the river at Port Dalrymple and also some small islands
not shown in the Barrallier and early Flinders charts. This
suggests that William Collins and his exploring party also made
some contribution to Harris's sketch.

Wade showed she could be as tough as any man when it came to farming and disciplining her children. (One of her descendants is an internationally-known feminist.) Mary Ann Peters, Fanny Anchor, Susannah Grove, Hannah Power, Martha Whitehead, Janet Gunn, Hannah Fawkner and Mary Fitzgerald all showed initiative while their husbands were still servants of the Crown.

Several literate men would become attached to the administration, including six clerks, and fourteen police who effectively employed their former skill in the use of force and arms to better advantage. Those who remained in the colony on the expiration of their sentence, or after a conditional or absolute pardon, succeeded to some of the richest lands. For a long time the origin of the *Calcutta* convicts — and indeed of most convicts sent to Australia — was a taboo subject. Legends grew up within families who had flourished and who were anxious to ensure that the evil men do would *not* live after them. Land sharks had spawned a materialistic culture. Children of rich convicts aspired to become colonial gentry, some moved away from the colony that had nurtured them, hoping to evade the convict 'taint'. Great wealth and prosperity, fame, power, high honours and social acceptance were to them the way, the truth and the life. Dames and knights, chief justices, the wife of a lieutenant-governor, ministers of state, churchmen and other dignitaries, politicians and, even today, some of the largest landowners in Australia, are among the many thousands of descendants of *Calcutta* convicts and their kin. The sons of John Fawkner and John Wade were closely connected with the beginnings of two large cities — Melbourne and San Francisco.

There were others whose taste for adventure exceeded any desire to hold on to the land and fortune they might have acquired. Some descendants include Bass Strait Islanders, the last links with the lost Tasmanian race. Probably hundreds more are the result of fleeting unions in the Pacific Islands, where many of those who sailed before the mast dallied betwixt the capture of the wild pig or the gathering of the trochus shell. Some spread out as far south as Macquarie Island, as far north as China, or disappeared into India or America. Some settled in Sydney, others returned to England. At least two of the latter decided life in the colony was preferable and organised their later return as guests of His Majesty.

However, there were others who were highly disreputable and unsuccessful. Some, including the notorious Robert Stewart, were pirates, while others became bushrangers, sheep stealers and pilferers, adding variety to the new social structure. There were

several unnatural deaths — execution was the punishment for six of these scoundrels. Bushranger Michael Howe would account for the shooting of William Drew. Natives killed four, while one would not venture to guess how many *Calcutta* convicts killed natives; there were those who might have been considered pillars of society, yet exhibited many cruelties towards the native race. There were many drownings, and a number of inquests indicated that alcoholic excess contributed to a decline in health and the death of some *Calcutta* men in later life. The greatest survivor of them all, escapee William Buckley, would end his days in what one might describe as a traffic accident when his gig overturned in Arthur Circus, Hobart.

The purpose of this work has been to reconstruct the lives of the *Calcutta* convicts, to discover what patterns emerge and how such patterns contributed to social history or even influenced the wider course of Australian history. Although it is specifically their story, it has been impossible to detach them entirely from their fellow settlers and officials. Their importance both as individuals and as a group is easily recognisable when the relevant facts come together. In the early years there was scarcely an event with which one, and often several or many, of the colourful *Calcutta* convicts were not connected. Their lives are as firmly woven into the fabric of those years as that of Collins and the racy chaplain and diarist, Robert Knopwood, and other officials who accompanied them. Together with their wives and families they lived and loved, developing a communal spirit that overcame many of the problems of a pioneering society.

Domestic relationships and families were encouraged, however irregular, because early governors had tried to humanise the situation of their motley people, both bound and free. Affection, respect and self-sacrifice were qualities that flourished alongside violence and exploitation based on race, wealth and sex. When Van Diemen's Land became a separate colony under the lieutenant-governorship of George Arthur, it lost some of the more commendable aspects of the earlier days. He was a hard man for times when hardened convicts, who had, strangely, committed lesser crimes than the *Calcutta* convicts, began infiltrating the society which had previously survived with few laws and a laxity unknown in other penal colonies. The transportation of convicts had worked up until this point because so many people, both free settlers and those who had gained their freedom, became dependent upon it and dependent upon each other.

PART I
At Home

Young boys spent their long days loitering along the Thames, always on the lookout for an unguarded boat, which they could then board and fill their pockets with stolen goods.

1 THE 'LUXURY' OF PEACE

URING THE LATTER part of the eighteenth century when most of the *Calcutta* convicts were born, England was a country of little more than seven million persons. About eleven per cent lived in London, that is, in the city (part of the old Roman Londinium), Southwark and Westminster, the seat of government. Beyond these areas, traversed by the King's Highways, were the fields linking the pleasanter villages and prosperous seats of the nobility and gentry.

By 1802 the population of London was 641 000, of whom at least 20 000 men were unemployed and as many as 50 000 women were living on prostitution.[1] The increased population in both London and the bigger towns created worse problems than in the country. There were not enough police to safeguard the property and person of the city-dweller, whereas in the country the well-to-do classes had trusted servants to safeguard them, although that was no guarantee when temptation came their way.

From Greenwich to Chelsea settlements hugged the River Thames, which received the British East India Company ships filled with cargoes from many countries. They sailed away to distant and exotic lands loaded with British merchandise. 'Heart of oak are our ships, heart of oak are our men' was as wholeheartedly sung by the merchant sailors as those of the Royal Navy guarding the sea lanes. The eighteenth century had seen many wars, with almost every European country embroiled in conflict, for or against the colonies across the Atlantic, or to gain the riches of India and the spices of the East.

In the Navy the lower ranks, in particular, were badly paid and fed, and during the years of revolutionary war with France, morale had deteriorated owing to the heavy loss of life and of ships. When Spain and Holland joined with France against the British, the position seemed hopeless. As a result of the mutinies at Spithead and the Nore in 1797 the Admiralty was obliged to overhaul conditions in the Navy.

Across the channel a 'whiff of grapeshot' had quietened the terror-stricken streets of Paris. Napoleon was consolidating the gains of the Revolution and reconstructing the institutions of La Belle France. After the humiliation and overwhelming destruction of Napoleon's fleet at the battle of the Nile and other reverses, it was confirmed that, for the time being, Britannia would continue to rule the waves and guard her shipping lanes. But everyone knew it was only a matter of time before Napoleon would use all the forces at his command in an attempt to invade his adversary. The Treaty of Amiens of 1802 would be, as both England and France feared, little more than a truce. Both countries had suffered badly on land and sea. The Revolutionary war of the 1790s had drained the two nations of manpower, naval facilities and money to pursue the imperial stakes.

Fleets needed to be built up again in readiness for the possible renewal of hostilities. England was short of the right kind of timber for mastheads, spars and decking, while rigging and sails needed large quantities of flax. Transatlantic supplies had been halted by the loss of the American colonies, and Swedish sources had been cut off when the Dutch became allied to the French and patrolled the seas between England and Sweden. Therefore, what better use of naval vessels than to allow the Admiralty to send them during peace, as Home Secretary Lord Pelham suggested, to collect large quantities of timber and flax from New South Wales.[2] The ships would then be in a position to show the British flag in the Pacific, both to warn off any designs by the French and to protect an infant fishing industry, while at the same time carrying human ballast to add strength to the colonial labour force and defences. Besides, the men and ships of the Royal Navy needed employment.

The Reverend Samuel Marsden, corresponding with the Board of Transport on the possible supplies of timber useful to the Navy, received a letter from Transport official Ambrose Serle, who was somewhat sceptical about sparing two naval ships 'for the cutting out and preparing and bringing home *naval* timber . . . none which will repay the *time* and expense which must be laid out in procuring it . . .'[3] Yet Sir Joseph Banks himself had seen and identified the tall timbers of the eastern coast, and artists accompanying the earlier voyages had sketched them. There were other reports on the hardness of the timber and the luxuriousness of the flax. Governor Hunter, reporting favourably on the timber of N.S.W. in March 1802, had found by experience that it was more durable than oak or teak, did not readily decay, and contained so much resinous gum that it appeared impervious to water. He strongly recommended its use for naval timber, particularly for gun-carriages, masts and planking because of its hardness and accessibility.[4] The authorities had no reason in 1803 to believe that Port Phillip might not yield as good if not better supplies. The Admiralty's instructions to the captains of ships sent to collect timber made it quite clear that one of their major duties was to return with the quantity already ordered, through the Governor of New South Wales, Philip Gidley King, to be cut down and prepared to be sent to England for use in His Majesty's dockyards.[5] The long list of instructions regarding the care of the convicts has overshadowed the less publicised motive for directing a naval presence to the Pacific.

•   •   •

The ratification of the Peace of Amiens brought gaiety to the cities of London and Westminster and a hope that there would be some stability and restoration of trade. At midnight there were general illuminations and pealing of church bells in every part of the kingdom. It was almost impossible to pass in the crowded streets. In the metropolis alone there were about half a million people celebrating.[6] One can picture the scene by day's-end as money that most could ill afford to part with poured into the coffers of the 5 000 public houses. A noisy and boisterous rabble crowded the streets and the Horse Guards had to help police from Bow Street curb the violence that ended in broken windows and bloodshed, vividly described by William Cobbett from his newspaper office in Southampton Street.[7]

In the country they celebrated differently. The squire of Aston Hall, Staffordshire, for example, gave his poor neighbours an ox, two sheep and a quart of ale to each man and a pint to each woman, according to *Aris' Birmingham Gazette*. The same newspaper reported the fall in the price of wheat in Mark Lane by 14s a quarter, whereupon very little grain was sold in the market.[8]

King George III had lived in and ruled from London since 1760, but by this time he had already shown signs of mental derangement. He had been the first of the House of Hanover to gain some respect from his subjects, as his mother tongue was English instead of German. But during his reign England had lost the American colonies, the Tory party under William Pitt had consolidated and overthrown the supremacy of the old Whig families, and the union of England and Ireland had become a formality if not a reality. The King's sons were siring the children of numerous women and the Prince Regent himself was renewing his alliance with Mrs Fitzherbert, with some support from the Pope, who recognised her as the Prince's only wife. At this time William Wilberforce had not yet won his fight against slavery, but John Howard had seen some advancement in prison reform when he died in 1790. F. M. Eden had completed his extensive survey on the state of the poor just before the worst of the famines which raged in England around the turn of the century. T. R. Malthus had attacked parents for bringing children into the world without adequate support. He recommended that all relief be withdrawn from the children!

With wars and preparations for wars, Georgian England was, during this Age of Enlightenment, a place of inconceivable contrasts: of rich and poor, justice and often injustice, of degradation, ignorance and despair. It was the mother country of an incredibly rich empire from which its merchant princes, such as those associated with the East India Company, drained all the wealth possible from the vassal states. It was a place of learning where universities flourished, where literature and the arts and sciences received encouragement, and patronage was rarely surpassed, if ever, in all history. The luxurious country homes of the nobility and the wealthy were ornamented with the artistic achievements of all ages. Architecture and landscape reflected the refined taste that epitomises eighteenth-century England, a taste that, ironically, owed as much to the French and sometimes the Chinese, as to the Greeks and Romans, while the people remained unquestionably English.

The Industrial and Agrarian Revolutions had relied heavily on applied scientific research which produced inventions and machinery in England that no other country could generate. They were to affect, if not immediately benefit, rich and poor alike. The natural sciences of botany, zoology, geology and astronomy were for the leisure and pleasure of learned scholars and wealthy patrons. There was a certain self-indulgence in such studies which fostered the creation of the Royal Society and the Lunar Society, both influenced by the indefatigable Sir Joseph Banks. Such personages as Omai from the Hawaiian Islands and Bennelong from New South Wales were among the exotica to appear as dainty dishes set before the King.

But out there in the streets of England there

3

Arts, Sciences, and the Muses, drove with
furious hands from the Continent of Borelia
just on the point of expiring are saved by Maecenas.

*This vignette showing Sir Joseph Banks as Maecenas illustrates
how the enlightened ones viewed the New World in the south.
While at Port Phillip Lieutenant Tuckey was to contemplate the
future possibilities of 'a second Rome, rising from a coalition of
banditti . . .'*

seemed to be so much crime in a land that was in
many ways richer, better governed and more civilised
than most other parts of the world. The wealth and
luxury, the education, artistry and science, the trade
and commerce, were part of a society that spawned
depraved rogues and thieves, little more than beasts,
dissipated with debauchery and stupefied with 'strip-
me-naked', a euphemism for gin. Human beings eked
out a miserable existence in the vermin-ridden caverns
of vice that were the lanes and alleyways of London,

and many persons lived in the shadow of those 'dark
satanic mills' where already children worked for long
hours in appalling conditions, the legacy of eighteenth-century England. Emaciated, bleary-eyed,
toothless beings were the prey of bludgers mature in
vice, cunning and treachery, who provided the gin
that was mother's milk to them and used them as
harlots, pick-pockets and fencers. To paraphrase
Dickens, it was still the best of times and yet the
worst of times. It was an age of wisdom and an age of
foolishness: 'the spring of hope, the winter of despair
. . .' and if some had everything before them, others
had nothing.

Sailors on leave gravitated to 'flash' houses and low
lodgings in the most iniquitous part of London which
was situated eastwards from St Giles' Church and the

4

Seven Dials to Moorgate Street, where pedlar's French and the 'flash' language screamed out twenty-four hours a day. The adjoining alleys and courts were particularly crime-ridden, harbouring many of those 'Gentlemen of the three Ins: In gaol, Indicted, and In danger of being hanged.'[9] Sailors with money to spend soon found they were without it after succumbing to the licentiousness and depravity of life in the densely populated areas such as that between Fore and Chiswell Streets, a favoured refuge for criminals, prostitutes and the demoralised poor. Sometimes they brought with them virulent diseases which, emerging from the badly drained and foetid alleyways that neither sun nor fresh air reached, spread like wildfire through whole families. Perhaps the stricken sailor, welcoming death, would have agreed with Polly Peachum that

To die a dry death at land
    Is as bad as a wat'ry grave.[10]

Death could pass unnoticed when life was cheap and could be snuffed out like a candle.

Not only was death ever-present, but life itself was unstable during the great changes wrought by the Industrial Revolution and the ensuing uncertainty of employment for a rapidly increasing population. Sometimes families in the city were dependent on the meagre pennies that a child of six might bring in from employment. For instance, there was work for chimney sweeps who needed to be as small as William Blake's 'little black thing among the snow' in order to squeeze inside the chimney. It was fashionable to make some sort of protest against this custom, although it took many more years before the employment of young children received notice in the Statute Book.

In May 1799 Mrs Elizabeth Montagu, queen of the London 'bluestockings' and friend of Dr Samuel Johnson, gave her annual entertainment of roast meat and plum pudding in the courtyard of her palatial house in Portman Square to the chimney sweepers of the metropolis. In reporting the event the correspondent for the *Gentleman's Magazine* attributed her benevolence to 'her having once had a child of her own kidnapped, and afterwards discovered among the sooty tribe . . . Her compassion for the little urchins that often undergo cruel hardships was, we believe, the only motive to this little anniversary feast'.[11] It was unfortunate that this occasion was the last she would give. It may well have been attended by sweeper William Roberts, a *Calcutta* convict from Spitalfields, and his mate Billy who, the next year, broke into an ironmongery shop, soon after the death of Mrs Montagu.

Sydney Smith viewed such acts of beneficence as harmful and condemned organisations such as the

'St Giles' breed / Better hang than seed.' (An old saying.) The St Giles' rookery, or Seven Dials, was said to have provided more felons than the rest of England, as well as a large number whose final march was to Tyburn.

Society for the Suppression of Vice, popularly formed at the beginning of the nineteenth century. He saw them as busybodies who feared that the poorer classes might get out of hand, as they had in France. 'Men', he wrote, 'whose trade is rat-catching, love to catch rats; the bug-destroyer seizes on his bug with delight; and the suppressor is gratified by finding his vice.'[12]

He satirised the do-gooders who had noted the misfortunes of the underprivileged by picturing the scene of an excellent and well-arranged dinner with rank, wealth, wit and beauty surrounding the meats:

everything of sensual and intellectual gratification which a great nation glories in producing. In the midst of all this, who knows that the kitchen chimney has caught fire half an hour before dinner! — and that a poor little wretch, of six or seven years old, was sent up in the midst of the flames to put it out?[13]

Evidence had been given before Parliament on the plight of these boys and the apparent frequency with which chimneys caught fire when preparations were in hand for a grand celebration. Smith asked 'But what matter acts of Parliament, when the pleasures of gen-teel people are concerned? Or what is a toasted child, compared to the agonies of the mistress of the house with a deranged dinner?'[14]

Years later one elderly sweeper described to Henry Mayhew his 'printiceship' as a climbing-boy from the time he was seven until fourteen. He considered it a good job because he got twopence or threepence a day, enough to gamble with among his mates. He told how he would climb the wide flues with elbows and legs spread out, his feet pressing against the side of the flue. But in narrow flues, sometimes only nine inches, he had to slant his sides in the angles to make himself smaller. 'I niver got to stay stuck myself, but a many of them did; yes, and were taken out dead. They were smothered for want of air, and the fright, and a stayin so long in the flue . . .'[15] Occasionally there was justice such as in a case brought before the Sessions at Westminster in October 1802. One employer was declared guilty and sentenced to six months imprisonment for assaulting and ill-treating his eight-year-old sweep by goading him and sticking pins into him.

The effects of the Agrarian Revolution were begin-ning to be felt by the community at large. The increased population was demanding more food at a time when years of poor harvests had depleted stocks. Labour was cheap and plentiful. Around the turn of the century the open fields were enclosed and agricul-tural methods became less labour-intensive creating an even wider division between the wealthy land-owner who could buy up the smaller properties and the smaller tenant who, losing the security of the lord of the manor, was rapidly on the way to becoming a pauper. For the latter, England was no green and pleasant land.

War had become a way of life and had provided employment. The luxury of peace did not extend to those without a job, but was fraught with more prob-lems for those who had found there was no bread to strengthen the hearts and bodies of men and women. Neither would there be any more circuses for the thousands of discharged soldiers who wandered aim-lessly around the countryside looking either for work or some means of obtaining food and sustaining life itself. An ungrateful society had been unable to evolve a means to rehabilitate those who had saved, at least temporarily, their country from the ambitions of Napoleon Bonaparte. Many took to the countryside, assaulting and robbing their fellow countrymen, often in as violent a manner as practised in war. The worst of these received the death sentence. Others were capi-tally reprieved and some with less violent crimes were to sail in the *Calcutta*.

In 1800 some soldiers addressed their commanding officer, Lieutenant-General Rookes, with the kind of

anonymous threat that was quite common among those who were literate: unless prices dropped to what they were in 1790 they would not only lay down their arms, but would 'Scour the Country & hang up a farmer In Every Parish'. Not only that, but there would no longer be a Parliament, a 'tyrant and a Dam'd Infernal Imposing Lords & Commons, a Republic must Ensue, and we will fight for our rights & liberties to the Last moment'. They reminded the General of French success in making 'every Article Cheap and Reasonable and we will follow her Example'.[16]

What had become known as the 'crime of anonym-ity' was not uncommon. For most of the century protesters had been threatening their exploiters, such as the wheat hoarders, farmers and middlemen in the community who had kept the cost of provisions beyond what the poor could pay. They would place their warnings on whipping posts and church doors. In Petworth, Sussex, some social protesters had decreed that 'We had better be lanched [*sic*] into Eter-nity at Once than submit to your Diabolical Imposi-tion and starve by Inches'.[17]

A glimpse at contemporary county newspapers depicted a sad and uncaring world, containing accounts of the small riots and disturbances due to unusually high prices and the brief reports of those committed for trial or sentenced as a result. The *Royal Cornwall Gazette* began its life in 1801 and immedi-ately struck an overly distressed and poverty stricken period in an area that was already among the most impoverished in England. The miners in Cornwall rose against their miserable state and conditions in the mines but there were no trade unions then and nobody cared. In retaliation they descended upon the ports to try and stop the exportation of the corn for which they hungered.

In Southampton, where five *Calcutta* convicts received sentences in 1801 and 1802, the *Hampshire Chronicle* reported a bread riot in Romsey in 1799 followed by disturbances in 1800 over the price of food in Winchester, Romsey and New Aresford. Social unrest became rife throughout the land. People *were* hungry and were prepared to manifest their des-perate plight in some form of violence or, in despera-tion, they were driven to steal. Animals, themselves like skeletons, had been turned loose to graze on the commons and were dying for want of food.[18] During times of peace the countryside was a pleasant place for those who knew little of the economic effects of the poor harvests and unemployment. One John Britton rediscovered the beauties of Wiltshire, where the boundless Salisbury Plains were no longer covered with hundreds of tents. Gone, too, were the thou-sands of blood-stained soldiers who had breathed fear into the 'humble solitary shepherd and the whistling ploughman', and the poor cottager could retire to his straw bed 'undisturbed by the marauding warrior.'[19] The aesthetes did not realise that wealth was accumulating and men were decaying in a country that was alive with a different type of marauder, which preyed upon the innocent who were out of work and starving.

Sometimes the ordinary people showed some sympathy towards the miscreants and forgave them their sins, while the wealthier landed people were much more inclined to charge wrong-doers. Whereas two-thirds of the persons charged in London received acquittals, two-thirds charged in the rural areas were convicted and sentenced. When a man was to be executed in 1800 in Leicester and escaped from gaol with ironed feet, the locals liberated him, changed his clothes, gave him money and sent him on his way.[20] People generally sympathised with the more romantic offenders such as the smuggler or the highwayman, but few would shelter a sheep stealer because sheep and wool for textile manufacture provided employment.

There were rumours that the harvests were not as bad as had been imagined, and that rapacious persons were taking advantage of the distressed time to conceal grain until it reached a higher price. The price of a loaf of bread was increasing and the adverse situation was aggravated by the suppression of riots throughout the country. One Mr Thorn, a silk broker in Spital Square, was so troubled by the misery around him that he petitioned the King in 1800 on the subject of the high price of provisions. He believed this was due to the horrors and calamities of war, the spirit and practice of monopoly, the machinations of rich mealmen, of opulent and overgrown farmers and to the 'increased circulation of country bank paper, which gave speculators a facility of engrossing more of the articles than they could otherwise do.'[21] Coming from an ordinary man who saw the misery before his own eyes, this was a good summation of the causes. He knew of many families with nine or ten children with little hope of obtaining even a morsel of bread. One who was more unfortunate and weary of breath, was a soldier's wife he had known in Cambridge who had hanged herself and her two children to avoid the more lingering death by starvation. Those who did manage to earn a weekly pittance were living on 'scanty meals of offals mixed with beans, greens and perhaps for luxury, a little oatmeal.'[22] Butcher's meat was shamefully and exorbitantly dear (which explains why sheep stealing was one of the commonest crimes).

Newspapers were full of ideas and advice to readers (but how many of the poor could read or buy a newspaper?) on how to stretch their food a little further.

Lord Townshend had been responsible for introducing turnips as a food crop for animals, a revolutionary idea in conservative England, so that sheep and cattle could be fed in the winter instead of being killed for market prices. One publication was quick to see turnips as a possible substitute for human consumption and gave the recipe for turnip bread, much used in Essex in the sixteenth century. One had to boil the turnips, then mix them with an equal amount of wheatmeal, add salt and water, then bake in the oven.[23]

In spite of the rumours that there was artificial inflation on the grain market, there is enough evidence that unfavourable soil conditions had produced poor quality grain, especially in 1799. Critics, however, continued to point out that comfortable gentlemen farmers had been guilty in 1795 and 1796 of concealing large quantities, declaring that they would not sell until the price rose — they preferred to let it rot on the ground.[24]

Is it any wonder then that so many 'sweet Auburns' had altered by the end of the eighteenth century? Many had become prey to hastening ills, full of the misfortunes and distresses of life, more often than not through no fault of their own but often through the greed of their neighbours. There was a new breed of old and infirm mendicants who could not wander far from the neighbourhood in which they had always lived. They wore 'picturesque attire as ornamental as the Signs of old London' according to Charles Lamb.[25] Rags were their insignia. There were 'calling' days on which they might receive alms or provisions at the houses of those better off than themselves. And the saddened eyes of foresaken children begged to be freed from the cold and hunger that corroded the flesh and exposed the skeletal bones.

But there were also professional beggars, men who had spent a lifetime earning a living, sometimes as a fake cripple or blind person, and often in the employment of a 'captain', such as the well-known 'Copenhagen Jack' of the 200-odd Pye Street beggars who haunted Westminster during the French wars. One young beggar turned to begging as a child when his father had been killed in Egypt. Years later he told Henry Mayhew that he had worked for 'Copenhagen Jack' for much of his life, living well on geese and turkey, dressing in a red coat and top-boots while he waited on his master, and his jealous colleagues attempted to murder him. He was never anything else but a beggar: 'How could I? It was the trade I was brought up to. A man must follow his trade.'[26]

2 THE INEQUALITY OF MERCY

*B*OTH OFFICIAL ATTITUDES in Europe and the general callousness of the populace had supported excessive punishments and terror as deterrents to crime. But the moral need for reform had been the subject of heated debate ever since the appearance of Cesare Beccaria's work *Dei Delitte e delle Pene* (On Crime and Punishment) in 1764. Man was morally responsible for his acts, Beccaria wrote in his argument against capital punishment and torture: 'Men as slaves are more sensual, more unmoral, more cruel, than other men'. He was the first person to advocate education as a means of lessening crime and urged that a regular police force was an essential deterrent.[1]

In England some more concerned thinkers had helped develop a public conscience agitating for the repeal of much barbaric legislation such as the Waltham Black Act. Originally passed in 1722, this Act was

for the more effectual punishing wicked and evil disposed persons going armed in Disguise, and doing Injuries and Violences to the Persons and Properties of His Majesty's Subjects and for the more speeding bringing the Offenders to Justice.[2]

The Act was named because the Roberdsmen of Hampshire were followers of Robert (or Robin) Hood who disguised themselves by blackening their faces and committing local crimes in the area of Waltham. The naturalist Gilbert White had noted as early as the 1760s that 'The Waltham blacks at length committed such enormities, that government was forced to interfere with that severe and sanguinary act called the Black Act, which now comprehends more felonies than any law that ever was framed before'.[3] The controversial Bishop of Winchester, Dr Benjamin Hoadley, a 'goodly' man, had refused to restock Waltham Chase with deer, replying that the Act 'had done mischief enough already'.[4]

It came as a shock to a few persons to find that 160 crimes listed by the celebrated jurist, Sir William Blackstone, were capital offences.[5] Almost all were against property, and capital statutes were increasing

every year at the whim of a parliament that really only represented the interests of the wealthy and the powerful. Jeremy Bentham, a long-time critic of Blackstone's Commentaries, argued, along with others, that the punishment should be proportional to the crime, and that deterrence rather than prevention was important. He introduced a plan by which he could reduce the cost of maintaining prisoners confined to the hulks, by twenty-five per cent.[6] In more recent times the twentieth-century criminologist Leon Radzinowicz has found that the perpetrators of as many as 350 different crimes could receive capital punishment under the Waltham Black Act — including crimes like cutting down a tree — and he doubted whether 'any country possessed a criminal code with anything like so many capital provisions as there were in this single statute'.[7]

By the 1790s, Patrick Colquhoun, who was well versed in Bentham's theories and had had years of practical experience as a London police magistrate, was searching for the causes of crime rather than moralising over the punishments.[8] Samuel Romilly had also begun his work on the mitigation of sentences as a means of cleansing the uncivilised laws which blotted the statute books.[9] But Lord Chief Justice Ellenborough was one who repeatedly opposed his efforts and even created new capital felonies, bullying juries into facing up to their responsibilities. It would not be until 1806, when Romilly became Solicitor-General, that he would make much headway; in 1808 Parliament began to repeal some of the harsher and more obsolete laws.[10]

But life and liberty, the catch-cry in the latter part of the eighteenth century in England, primarily referred to the life and liberty of the master rather than of the servant class, even though England, having had her revolution in 1688, did not deny the right of the individual to justice. But the chief end of such a society was the preservation of property, the sole *raison d'être* of civil government as expounded more than a century before by John Locke.[11] The prerogative of mercy allowed to the judiciary alarmed the men of property, who wholeheartedly supported the death sentence and made sure that Parliament continued to enact legislation that would provide for the ultimate penalty when their own interests were jeopardised.

The judiciary was the only lawful body that might have influenced Parliament had it tried. Justices of the Assizes, particularly at the Central Criminal Court in London, known as the Old Bailey, became averse to pronouncing the death sentence for social crimes, believing that the awesome gibbet, apart from its inhumanity, was no longer effective as either a warning, an example or a preventative.

But there were times when the law would extend no mercy and that involved crimes against a person rather than property. Of these, treason was among the worst. Lord Ellenborough passed sentence on one famous inmate of Newgate at that time, the Irishman Colonel Edward Marcus Despard. Lord Nelson gave evidence of his past character and courage when they served together in a perilous expedition at Fort San Juan in 1779. Despard was found guilty of conspiring in 1800 to assassinate the King and to seize Parliament House, the Tower and the Bank of England. He had, for several years, been influenced by the principles of the French Revolution. His Irish nationalism and the troubles among his native people had not encouraged him to retain much loyalty to England, even as a former professional soldier of some note in the service of the King.

Held captive in the same gaol and at the same time as many *Calcutta* convicts, Despard was brought to trial in February 1803, together with his fellow conspirators. He heard Ellenborough's sentence in severe and solemn tones, describing all the condemned men as sad victims of Despard's seduction and example. They had no chance of receiving the royal mercy, in spite of the jury's plea and Lord Nelson's intervention. Ellenborough reminded the victims in strong language that the sentence was according to the law as it stood, and 'involved all the abominable particularities about hurdles, hanging by the neck, but not till dead, ripping out of bowels and burning them before the faces of the living sufferers, and cutting off heads and quartering of bodies'.

'This is the head of a traitor, Edward Marcus Despard', cried the executioner beside the scaffold erected on the top of the gaol. The large crowd had heard his last words declaring the 'final triumph of liberty, justice and humanity over falsehood, despotism and delusion, and over everything else hostile to the interests of the human race'. Their cheers turned to groans as the blood streamed from the grey-haired veteran.[12]

•   •   •

In the main, the convicts who sailed in the *Calcutta* were, as throughout the whole history of transportation to this country, city born and bred, and though the majority had trades they were largely unemployed; the members of a convicted, if not criminal, class. They mostly committed crimes of theft, in one form or another, in London and the larger cities where the multitudes had congregated and whose business was crime.

Most London transportees were remanded in custody at Newgate, pending their trial and ultimate removal to the hulks. Designed by George Dance junior, it was a massive and forbidding construction built between 1770–78 to a plan incorporating three courtyards, with a long elevation to the Old Bailey where the trials of 107 *Calcutta* convicts took place. But it was out of date almost as soon as it was built, for John Howard's movement towards prison reform was just beginning.[13] Although gaol conditions, as one would expect, varied from county to county, most of them were charnel houses of horror. But new gaols were beginning to appear in the counties according to Howard's specifications, with more attention being paid to health and cleanliness.[14] Several reforms had been effected by the turn of the century so that some Port Phillip convicts were more fortunate than those who first set sail for Port Jackson.

It is surprising that some of these prisons have had few changes since then. For instance, if the five *Calcutta* convicts confined at Shrewsbury gaol were to return there today they would probably recognise it. Outwardly little has changed, although it has been altered within. It was new when they were on trial there, a very modern and model prison built to Howard's satisfaction in consultation with the architect. Howard's bust still has pride of place over the main door.

A few prisons tried to give their inmates some form of occupational therapy. Dorset county gaol served as a hat factory, where at least prisoners had something to do other than clanking their chains in prison yards during their dreary incarceration. Some gaolers' bills give indications of some kindness to sick prisoners who may have needed special diets. Those in the county gaol and bridewell at Winchester returned special thanks to the Dean of Winchester for a dinner on Christmas Day 1800; according to the *Hampshire Chronicle* the prisoners of the gaol thanked the Dean and Chapter for two guineas.[15] Other gaols were still full of filth and fever, still the miserable, unventilated and profligate places that Howard had described. In outmoded county gaols or behind cold and dark castle bars, men and women on remand were herded with little, if any, distinction between class or crime. Indolence and free living went hand in hand with ignorance and disease.

Marshalsea Prison was typical of the older type of prison which John Howard loudly condemned.

Some prisoners were housed in 1802 at the ruinous and notorious Marshalsea prison in Southwark at the time when part of it fell in.[16] Others were better off at Clerkenwell, the House of Detention, of which investigations in January 1799 showed that of 5 000 persons imprisoned over a period of four years, only seventeen had died from natural causes, and two had suicided. The doctor examining the prisoners found that, out of 200–300, only one was ill. He had asthma.[17] Nevertheless there were still complaints to be made against prisons in the London area. The Grand Jury of the county of Middlesex at the Clerkenwell Sessions of December 1800 stated that it wished to visit the House of Correction in Cold Bath-fields because of all the general complaints it attracted. The chairman declared he had no right to grant their wishes but that he would refer the complaint to the Committee of Magistrates.[18]

Registers of the number of felons and trespassers committed to Newgate for a twelve-month period beginning on 28 September 1800 are a guide to the punitive measures at the time *Calcutta* convicts were being held there. Of 319 in residence 240 were males and seventy-nine were females. Of the latter, only ten were sentenced to life and eight for fourteen years, leaving 106, having committed relatively minor offences, with a seven-year sentence. Two had been sentenced to hard labour on the Thames, fourteen were discharged after a public whipping and fine of one shilling. One received a capital reprieve while two were sent to sea and twenty remained on committal. Of the thirty-nine sentenced to death, seven were executed in the twelve month period, two were reprieved and were awaiting transportation for life, two were sent to serve in the Army and one was pardoned on a good behaviour bond.

One hundred and three prisoners registered at Newgate in 1800 were imprisoned for various periods ranging from one week to five years, two were sent to the House of Correction for one year and ten others for six months. Eighty-one transportees were delivered to the hulks, thirteen transportees reprieved and removed to the House of Correction, one to Lancaster gaol and one to Bethlehem Hospital. Of those committed, 129 were discharged either on commitment, proclamation, according to sentences, pardons, trials and acquittals, or bailed out.[19]

Most of the *Calcutta* convicts tried at the Old Bailey spent some time in remand at Newgate before being tried at the Middlesex Sessions by justices commissioned to deliver prisoners held in gaol on indictable offences. After being sentenced the convicts were returned to gaol before removal to the hulks and transportation. Many of these would have been guests of His Majesty in January 1802, a momentous time in the history of the prison when the execution of Governor Wall took place. He had been tried at the Old Bailey for a murder committed years before on the island of Goree off the Senegalese coast. On the eve of his execution his fellow prisoners, who would have included some of the *Calcutta* convicts gaoled there, heard him singing psalms.

J. T. Smith, a former keeper of the Print Room at the British Museum, witnessed the hanging outside the gates of Newgate. Crossing the press-yard as a cock crowed he found the 'solitary clanging of a restless chain was dreadfully horrible' and the prisoner 'was death's counterfeit, tall, shrivelled, and pale; and his soul shot so piercingly through the port-holes of his head'. The hangman misplaced the rope, Wall must have been tortured for nearly half an hour before he expired. Some locals were quick to make the price of a meal out of the harrowing event when, outside the prison, one began selling what he claimed was part of the hangman's rope for a shilling an inch, and further along the street another was selling pieces of identical rope for sixpence an inch. J. T. Smith added that on the north-east corner of Warwick Lane the reputed wife of the yeoman of the halter, 'Rosy Emma', had buyers for a third noose different from

One third of the trials of the Calcutta *convicts took place in the Old Sessions House at the Old Bailey.*

that of the butterman from Epping, who had come only that morning to Newgate market![20]

At the turn of the century one finds that many prisoners who had been sentenced to death were reprieved and their sentences altered to life imprisonment. In some cases it might be a conscience-stricken judge who might seek the royal pardon. The prerogative of mercy might also extend to those sentenced to transportation for life, reducing it to seven years if witnesses had produced character references for first offenders. Juries, the enemies of the conservative class, might even bring in verdicts of 'not guilty'. At the Old Bailey it was common practice for the value of stolen goods to be underestimated (Blackstone called it 'pious perjury') because more enlightened persons called up for jury service were beginning to revolt against the severity of sentences, especially when young children could be hanged for trivial offences. Also the privilege of benefit of clergy was extended to some cases of petty crime.[21]

Justices of the Peace had come into being during the reign of Edward III. Their commission to keep the peace and hear and determine charges of felonies and trespasses against the peace gave them particularly wide powers which they often appeared to have abused more in rural than in urban areas. If they wished they could manipulate the law, having both the power to arrest and the power to judge. Many cases might be dealt with inquisitionally and summarily in the home of a single magistrate, especially when the offender was heard on minor charges or pleaded guilty. If he pleaded not guilty to indictable offences and hopefully could produce witnesses, the accused would stand trial before two or more magistrates at the Sessions of Peace, held quarterly in the county where the alleged crime took place. But bills of indictment were often ignored, the trial brief and the evidence of the magistrate who committed the felon usually being enough to satisfy his colleagues.[22]

Prior to 1842, Sessions of Peace (also known as Quarter and sometimes General Sessions) were as much a social and political exercise as a judicial one. As justices, the magistrates would make decisions on diverse matters affecting the county, especially in those counties where law and order might be threatened by the new industrialism and more effective local government. The aristocracy and landed gentry were still trying to hold on to their powers. Only in a rare instance would a manufacturer or rich merchant be co-opted on to the Bench.[23]

Some felonies needing further investigation, such as perjury, fraud and uttering base money, would be referred to the Justice of the Assize acting under a commission of *Oyer et Terminer*.[24] More serious crimes were held over until the Justices of the Assizes visited on circuit from London. Prisoners who were ignorant of their right to put themselves before a jury were often detained in gaol for years. They had been neither convicted nor acquitted.

Rural magistrates had little hesitation in pronouncing judgment, even a sentence of transportation for seven years, rather than risk committing the accused for trial in the higher Court of Assize and the possibility of acquittal. It was often in the interests of persons of property not to lay capital charges even when justified so that their local friend at court might deal with the accused and at least ensure there would be a verdict of guilty and some punishment. Local justices were over-zealous in interpreting the common law to suit those of power and wealth.

A study of some cases held in Quarter Sessions show just how far some might go to pretend they were meting out justice. One such case is that of John Jory, a seventeen-year-old Cornish boy, who eventually died at Port Phillip, but was convicted at the Truro Quarter Sessions in April 1801 and sentenced to transportation for seven years by what appeared to be twelve good men and true.[25]

It is difficult at any time to track down these records in the counties, if they still exist, and in Cornwall they are largely defective because a clerk in the office burnt most of them in 1931. But the rolls do reveal that John Jory was from the mining parish of Gwennap and that he was a labourer, almost certainly a surface worker, employed at the mines. At the Truro Sessions of 14 April 1801 he was indicted, tried *and* convicted for feloniously taking two pounds weight of candles, value sixpence, from William Hichens, probably the chief adventurer in the mine concerned. It was not uncommon for candles to be stolen from the mines and a public flogging was the normal punishment. Candles were becoming common barter where French sailors who knew the isolated indentations of the rugged Cornish coast would smuggle brandy in exchange.

In this case the sentence was passed by a dozen justices of the peace, all local landowners exercising their right to attend the sitting and probably attending to some of their other business at the same time. Contrary to the generally accepted view, this particular case (and several others of that time) indicates that persons could be convicted for minor offences by justices in minor courts and punished by as much as transportation for seven years, rather than acquittal for a first offence, a warning, a fine or a flogging. The result of the case of John Jory, heard before so many justices, also confirms that some importance was attached to the principle that justice must appear to be done. Of course if a person pleaded guilty the case was clear-cut. Detained persons must have also feared that if they appealed their sentences might be greater than that pronounced in Sessions. One even wonders how many, believing themselves prejudged, might have been innocent or at least judged 'not guilty' had they appealed. Comparatively few of the accused could call, or knew enough about the law to attempt to call, witnesses who could attest to the soundness of their character or advise that they should appeal to the higher court of law.

Justices of the High Court visited the counties bi-annually to try serious criminal charges at the Assizes. Prisoners were held in the county gaols, from where they were delivered to march in chain gangs through the streets to court. When on circuit the justices had the authority to try every person already committed to the county gaol for an alleged crime. This standing authority, known as gaol delivery, also gave justices the right to acquit and deliver a person from custody. They could then review a sentence of death and pardon the prisoner by proclaiming the King's mercy and remitting his sentence to transportation. Rural newspapers made much of the fate of the unfortunate prisoners awaiting execution, but also the justices' occasional reprieves.[26]

In London they did not have far to go to cross from the forbidding Newgate to the Old Bailey, and might have taken in an execution such as that of Governor Wall in front of Newgate on route to their destination. Trials held there were for offences committed in the City of London and county of Middlesex. Those with the jurisdiction to pronounce sentences on those proven guilty were justices of the High Court, the Recorder of London, the Common Sergeant, the Lord Mayor and Aldermen of the City and occasionally other judges. One little custom which has survived over a long period of time is the presentation of nosegays of herbs to the justiciary, a reminder of the days when the judicial noses needed protection from the stench exuded by the accused and his confrères.

Although there were many more acquittals at the Old Bailey than convictions, the trials were often hurried. But there seemed to be more justice at the beginning of the century than in later years. Only one-third brought to trial received sentences, however short the trial might be.

Some judges at the turn of the century openly expressed compassion for the 'labouring poor' and their contempt for those who would exploit them. There was, therefore, a tendency towards greater leniency. For instance, when the sheriffs of London met at the Guildhall to report the election of Chief Magistrate for 1801, their choice of Sir William Staines, who had served a term as Lord Mayor, was a humane one. Sir William confessed that he was a friend to the poor and that he would

exert his utmost abilities to alleviate their distresses; and in virtue of his office, should any Forestaller, Regrater, or Monopolizer . . . come before him, he would exercise the law against him in its fullest extent.[27]

There is no record that he carried out this promise in pronouncing sentence against anyone who sailed in the *Calcutta*, however, he certainly tried several *Calcutta* men, including James Fossett[28] and Richard Leonard,[29] the former for stealing 170 pounds of tea (he was already facing a capital charge for sheep stealing) and the latter for stealing a pocket-book.

One cannot help but reflect on how some of the judgments came about when often witnesses could not be produced, even at the Old Bailey where the punishment was likely to fit the crime according to the letter of the law, more justly than in the rural courts. But William Vasey's trial would have lasted no more than a minute. Charged with stealing a pocket-book, value two shillings, from a William Newhouse, Vasey heard Newhouse swear that he was robbed in Leadenhall Street, looking at a print-shop near the corner of Cree Church. He chased the prisoner who hurled the pocket-book across the road. The constable who took possession of the pocket-book swore that he knew nothing of the transaction. Vasey's defence was that he was

going down Fenchurch Street, and heard a *sing* out of stop thief . . . I am quite an innocent man, it is a malicious piece of business; my uncle and aunt are now lying bad of a fever; I very lately came from sea.

Newhouse insisted he was the man and that he had told him he had 'sworn his life away'.[30] Many gave no such excuses or could produce witnesses to give them good characters. If the law decreed that the guilty one should hang, mitigating circumstances did not normally arise.

The accused rarely had any status in the community, few would have owned or even rented property, and education, if any, would have depended on what was available in their place of birth and whether the parents had bothered to send the son to a dame's school. There are, however, indications that some had had considerable education, at least to grammar school level, and in some cases beyond, while others had been trained in the armed services. There is evidence that at least seventy-two could write and more than that number would have had some capacity to read. A few would become self-taught in the colony.

In the city the most frequent form of stealing was petty larceny, for which seven years' transportation was the punishment. Those convicted usually included the pickpockets, mostly teenage boys, who often picked no more than a pocket handkerchief or a pocket-book worth sixpence, sometimes with nothing in it. They were known as 'gallowsbirds' or 'St Giles Breed'.

In general terms, if the article robbed was worth more than a shilling, the charge was grand larceny and the guilty sentenced to transportation for life. If the amount were considerable or the offence committed on the King's Highway, accompanied by assault, it was a capital offence because 'blood money' was involved. So many different types of crimes were listed and distinctions were made between burglariously, privately and feloniously stealing, stealing from a dwelling house or a lodging house, or stealing from a person.

Generally, the sentences were fairly consistent in the city — seven years' transportation for petty felonies and life sentences, usually after a capital reprieve, for more serious ones. Those sentenced to fourteen years were mostly forgers, embezzlers, or receivers of stolen goods. Embezzlement was only classified as a crime towards the end of the eighteenth century, as a result of an upsurge in common law crimes.[31]

There was often great drama, and to us some humour, in the language used in these courts. At the Kent Summer Assizes of 1802 one rather venomous female who was a witness, was arraigned as being

moved and seduced by the instigation of the devil and contriving and intending to pervert the true course of justice and wickedly and wrongfully and unjustly trying to cause a verdict to pass against [the named prisoner] . . .[32]

A sample of jurors taken at random in one of the more conservative counties, shows that very little sympathy was shown to the person in the dock. In some rural courts, juries consisted of the most prominent persons of the town or borough and were very often friends of the accuser.

For instance at the Southampton Midsummer Assizes of July 1802 three *Calcutta* convicts were sentenced by either Justices Sir Giles Rooke or Sir Robert Graham to transportation for life after capital reprieves: John Avery, for stealing a grey mare; William Jacobs, for stealing a cow; and William Cooper for sheep stealing.[33]

The juries at these trials consisted of members of the oldest families of Hampshire, including two baronets, Sir Henry Mildmay and Sir Nathaniel Holland. Some families such as that of Bigg Wither could trace their place in the county back to the Middle Ages as tenants of the Dean and Chapter at Manydown. Mildmay of Dogmersfield came to prominence in Tudor times, Hulse of Braemore acquired estates in Hampshire in the 1740s, the Stares family had been yeoman of Botley from very early times. James Amyatt, who came from Southampton, and E. B. and Elias Arnaud from Portsmouth were probably prosperous merchants whose economic position justified their alignment with the old ruling class. How different from today

when you find prominent persons get exemptions from jury service!

Inconsistencies in the county courts also related to sentences. Seven prisoners heard the death sentence read out, only to hear it later replaced by seven years' transportation. Eight had it commuted to fourteen years. There is little evidence of mitigating circumstances playing any part, but such practice does suggest that the royal mercy could be extended if some influence prevailed, perhaps even corruption, especially in the provinces. Yet every capital sentence pronounced at the Old Bailey on a prisoner who ultimately embarked in the *Calcutta* had been replaced by transportation for life.

When guilt had been declared and sentence passed, the prisoner awaiting transportation was returned to gaol until such time as a space on the hulks became available. Gaolers and constables often sent in huge bills for their expenses and one wonders whether the sick prisoner Joseph Pendridge ever did receive the 'mutton broth and other nourishments' for which his gaoler billed the prison authorities. Others were known to have received bread, cheese and beer.[34] An itemised account for April 1802, during the period when the *Calcutta* forger James Grove was imprisoned at Warwick, comes to £71 9s 4d and embraced such items as 'Horse and expenses attending the execution of the men at Washwood Heath — 12s 6d', 'Relief of vagrants — £1 3s 5d', 'Paid for repairs to prison — £2 3s 7d', and 'Handcuffs — £1 9s 0d'.[35] Grove was fortunate to escape the noose; four of those executed had been forgers.[36]

Once removed to the hulks the prisoner could remain there for days, months or even years before being placed in a transport. Some of the *Calcutta* convicts, however, managed to escape time in the hulks and were placed directly in the *Calcutta*. The hulks and all the problems arising from them had been in existence for some twenty years when, in September 1800, Jeremy Bentham submitted proposals to the Lords of Treasury developing his Panopticon scheme for the employment and reformation of convicts. He suggested that the government should employ those confined in the hulks, housing them instead in a building which would provide work, clothing, education, hygiene and spiritual care, bedding, food, security, old age benefits and rehabilitation at a cost of twenty-five per cent less than it was then costing the government to transport them. Spirituous liquors would be forbidden. The colony of New South Wales might then become a training ground for soldiers and sailors engaged in the East India service.

But conditions in the hulks and transports were as bad as if not worse than the gaols. Those sentenced to hard labour while in the hulks might be engaged in cleansing the Thames, considered an extreme form of punishment in which only the physically strong could participate. It was a cheap and effective way of keeping the river free from sand, gravel and refuse. The *Calcutta* transportees were mostly accommodated in the *Prudentia* and some in the *Stanislaus* and *Minorca* hulks at Woolwich, on the Thames, and the *Captivity* at Portsmouth. Others were in hulks at Langston, near Portsmouth. Death was not unusual while waiting in hulks or in transports ready for sail. Conditions were particularly bad for the children of convicts, as shown in a report in the *Hampshire Chronicle*:

On Thursday morning there were found buried in a field between Alverstoke and Fort Monckton eight small children, the oldest not more than two years old. It is supposed they were brought from on board some transport. [37]

The inhuman confinement in the prisons, the hulks and the transports, rather than life in the new land, was undoubtedly the real punishment. Homosexuality was rife among those awaiting transportation. One *Calcutta* convict, George Lee, informed the Hampshire baronet, Sir Henry Mildmay, M.P., that he and the surgeon in the *Portland* hulk had been threatened with assassination for trying to prevent 'the horrible crime of sodomy'. [38] Often young boys were the victims of those who set out to bastardize the new arrivals. Conditions led to frequent riots, such as that during August 1802. At Woolwich the overcrowding in the hulks created an inflammatory situation: one hundred and seventy convicts scheduled to leave for New South Wales grouped themselves in the yard of a building near the waterside where they were working. They made a sudden rush on their keepers, seizing them while the ringleader, brandishing a knife, threatened the sentinel to let them through the outer gate. The soldier swiftly shot the ringleader through the head. He died immediately, while another soldier shot one of the convicts attempting to scale the wall. They had intended to seize the boats waiting to take them on board the hulks. Many would have got clear but for the arrival of a few dragoons who, together with the artillery, subdued them all and returned them to custody. Some of those must have been men who sailed in the *Calcutta*. [39]

It might well be that this attempted escapade, which almost succeeded, sowed the seeds of an adventurous escape in the mind of Robert Stewart who was to become the most persistent person trying to evade the completion of his sentence, and, after many attempts, finally succeeded when he escaped in command of the brig *Harrington* from Port Jackson. [40]

The bulks, known as 'floating Hells', were even more demoralizing
than the prisons.

PART II
Crimes of the Calcutta Convicts

3 LAND THIEVES AND WATER THIEVES

THE CHOICE OF those convicts sent with Lieutenant-Governor Collins in H.M.S. *Calcutta*, leaving Portsmouth on 17 April 1803 and arriving at Port Phillip on 9 October, was not such a bad one. Although many of them had committed serious, but mainly non-violent crimes, most of these convicts did not appear to be members of a criminal class. Here they came, from the rolling downs of Sussex, from the hills and dales of Yorkshire, from the sleazy wharves of Liverpool, from the foetid alley-ways of London. Some were from Shakespeare's town and some had seen, perhaps, Wordsworth's daffodils and the forest of Robin Hood and the stately towers of Oxford and Cambridge. Others had known only an orphanage or the workhouse. There were a few from Scotland, several from Wales and Boglanders from Ireland, all charged after crimes committed in England.

There were some who did not even speak the tongue that Shakespeare spoke, and interpreters were needed at trials by juries that normally included six foreigners in their number. There were sailors, marked with weird tattoos and gunshot wounds, who must have seen many strange lands and learnt many strange customs. There were soldiers who were out of work after their discharge from regiments that had fought in India and Egypt; there were seven young mutineers, victims of a hushed-up 'court martial' at Gibraltar.

Half of the *Calcutta* convicts came from a London Thomas Rowlandson was trying to recapture in his caricatures. It wasn't unlike the London that Hogarth had pictured many years before. They knew the same evil streets that Oliver Twist was soon to know, and the kind of London that Henry Mayhew later wrote about. They haunted the gambling dens and the riotous drinking houses and the vile-smelling wharves. They had lived among decay and dregs and destitution; among the whining children of sluttish females whose future was at best the workhouse. In the dirty hulks, those already speckled with pock were tickled by vermin, and they stank. Transportation to a world away was hardly a sentence. To many it was a kindness. And for them, distance was not a tyranny. It was an indulgence.

But there were others — and in some ways these were the saddest of them all — who, as the well-bred Lieutenant James Tuckey wrote, had come from a rank in life equal or superior to his own.[1] The degradation of those from a less lowly situation in life being thrust among such evil and destitution must have been appalling. Collins himself preferred the company of some of the more educated ones to that of his own officers, and did all he could to rehabilitate the worthy ones. There were contrasts between the types of prisoners and the environment from which they came: the good-humoured Yorkshire tyke or the rustic yokel charged with sheep stealing or the drunken sailor stealing clothes were worlds away from the suave embezzlers of London city. There were vast differences in ages. William Appleton was only nine when he stole an apron and seven shillings from a milkman and William Steel, also nine, stole a cloth from a linen draper. The oldest *Calcutta* convict was Robert Cooper, a gypsy, aged fifty-seven who hailed from Dorset.

One learns many quaint facts as one browses through the records of the trials, discovering much about the persons who brought the charges against them and those who adjudicated. One also understands just how little chance the poor and the ignorant had if they could not produce (as they rarely could) any witnesses or defence. This was a shipload of persons whose crimes were not, on the whole, violent, nor, in many cases, supposed to be very grave. But the majority were of such a nature that, if they were truly guilty, the sentences even today would be severe, though not perhaps as severe as transportation to a distant unknown land. All these were the men who, through their own misfortune, had been sent to this country as prisoners but who remained to become pioneers; men who were given the opportunity in a new land and a new environment to rehabilitate themselves and contribute something to the early history of the several Australian States in which they later settled.

Could it have been coincidence that the large majority of embezzlers and forgers among the *Calcutta* convicts committed their crimes — crimes of literate men — soon after the publication of the Prologue to a Botany Bay theatrical? When pickpocket George Barrington spoke the famous lines which he might have written himself at the opening of the theatre in the new colony, attention was drawn to the pleasantries of life for those patriots who had supposedly left their country for their country's good. The verses were not only an invitation to those who could read, but also those who heard of the 'honest way' in which they could pick pockets in Botany Bay.[2]

John Whitehead was among those who had been transported previously, having served time in New South Wales where he was known as 'Country Jack', and who had no qualms about opting for a second sentence if the chance arose. He was one of the crowd who hung around the Seven Dials, the haunt of a brawling lot of noisy pedlars, fish women, bird and birdcage sellers and domestic pets. Receivers of second-hand clothes sold their wares with no questions asked. The Seven Dials mob was said to have furnished America with more persons than the rest of England, as well as many who went on their last march to Tyburn. Whitehead was a gardener from Beverley in Yorkshire who might have been typical of many who had strayed into the big city and finished up in this area; intent, it would appear, on receiving a second sentence of transportation.

In October 1800 Whitehead was committed to Newgate for stealing two salt fish and received a public whipping before discharge. With his wife Sarah, a blue-eyed Shrewsbury girl, he appeared four months later at the Old Bailey charged with stealing two pairs of breeches from a clothes shop at Russell Court and a pair of leather breeches from a clothes shop at the Seven Dials. In the first instance Whitehead spent two hours trying on clothes while Sarah hid the chosen breeches under her cloak. Swearing that he had offered money in return for the goods, he received a comparatively light and welcome sentence of transportation for seven years. Sarah, guilty of the first charge but innocent of the second, was sentenced to seven years transportation, gaoled briefly at Newgate, then delivered on board the *Nile* in June 1801; six months later she arrived at Port Jackson. John Whitehead had already left Newgate and joined first the *Minorca* and then the *Prudentia* hulk at Woolwich, where he was to remain for nearly two years before sailing in H.M.S. *Calcutta*. After arriving in Hobart Town, Whitehead died of scurvy in September 1804.[3]

James Carrett, who would become one of the char-acters in the colony, was another who had previously served time at Botany Bay. His crime was that he had returned from transportation before his term expired.[4] History does not relate how, but his later career shows that he was an experienced sailor and he would have been a useful crew member. William John Leach, a watchmaker, had made several attempts to steal before being sentenced to seven years, the same sentence as he had received in 1791 when he sailed to Port Jackson in the *Albermarle*.[5] Another prisoner, William Pope, was sentenced to transportation for seven years to the West Indies in 1795. However, he never left England but spent many years before the courts on minor offences, trying his best to be transported; the magistrate dubbed him 'a very old offender'.[6]

Others known to have convictions and appearing to have hoped for a sentence of transportation were John Birchall, who had escaped from gaol, Joseph Bradley who had served six weeks in the House of Correction, James Coward for stealing, William Drew, another old offender who had served two months in Newgate and received a public whipping, and John Gwynn, who had been whipped for stealing. William Roberts (Middlesex, January 1802) served six weeks in gaol and was publicly whipped. John Smith (May 1800) served two years in the House of Correction as Henry Williams. John Cole had been 'detained', Michael Michaels was a 'common' utterer, William Moore spent one year in Newgate as William Stone, and Joseph Rose had previous convictions. Joseph Hedford received a sentence of seven years transportation in December 1797, was at Woolwich, but pardoned. George Brewer, William Appleton, Thomas Arnott, Daniel Crawley, Samuel Gray, Daniel McAllenan, Matthew Nelson and Thomas Page had all been before the courts but had been acquitted of previous charges.

The *Calcutta* convicts were a good cross-section of men to pioneer a new colony. Their crimes may be divided into four groups: petty pilferers mostly from London and other cities, often with a trade; rural thieves, including some highway robbers, who mostly pleaded hunger and poverty; literate criminals who committed premeditated crimes, such as forgery and embezzlement; and those who committed miscellaneous crimes such as mutiny, bigamy or perhaps had prematurely returned from transportation. The trial records show that 125, or forty per cent, of the *Calcutta* convicts were sentenced in London. Dr Robson found in a sampling of one in twenty of the total transported to Australia, that only seventeen per cent came from London, although the proportion was higher in the earlier years.[7] All but nine of the London trials took place in the Justice Hall at the Old Bailey, and the black cap was placed on the head of the eminent presiding justice in sentencing twenty-seven criminals — about a quarter of all those tried — who were later reprieved and sentenced to transportation beyond the seven seas for the term of their natural lives. Within the cold forbidding walls of the county courts, where justice was harsher, 101 out of 190 received the death sentence before they were reprieved in favour of transportation.

What, then, constituted the crimes of the *Calcutta* convicts? Larceny in one form or another accounted for most of the convictions — 252 in all. The sentence for petty larceny was seven years and for grand larceny, life. Among the records one finds that at least seventeen of those convicted of larceny used force and arms, yet in tracing their later career in the colony one finds that several of the more law-abiding and respected citizens were those in this category. Some of them for obvious reasons became constables. Twenty-seven of those who stole were charged with burglariously stealing, and sixteen offences were classed as highway robbery. There is one description of a violent crime when Richard Wall, who later settled down quietly in the *Calcutta* as a sailor, was found guilty of forcibly entering a dwelling house with fellow conspirators. Armed with bludgeons and with blackened faces, they mercilessly beat up their victim.[8]

Because of the high prices of all items of food, the 'village Hampdens' who stole to keep hunger at bay were numerous. In one court on one day alone, one hundred cases dealt with the problems of starving people, breadwinners who could not feed their large families unless they stole. Yet among the *Calcutta* convicts only two stole the proverbial loaf of bread. James Duff, a baker boy, stole four quarter loaves, while Henry Pizzey stole not only a loaf of bread but also a pair of shoes and a pair of breeches. Of those twenty-six who stole food, items specified ranged from bacon, cheese and butter to honey and apricots. Many others, from country areas, stole poultry and animals, twenty-six of whom were sheep stealers. Sheep stealing was a major capital offence. After all, a loaf of bread is a loaf of bread, a sheep has the potential to provide many more sheep. Fortunately for the *Calcutta* convicts, it had become customary for justices to obtain the royal mercy, reprieving most of these capital offences and sentencing a period of transportation instead.

In defence those who stole food declared they were hungry, and others who stole blankets said they were cold. Several walked into clothing shops, tried on clothes and came out with some of them on. Others stole furniture, two or three beds, and several Londoners who had a roof to call their own, but which was in need of repair, stole lead from the roofs of others' houses; such thieves were known as 'blue pigeons'.

The original car thieves stole twenty-three horses.

Eighteen stole cloth, or pieces of linen, and forty-two stole clothing ranging from those who pick-pocketed a handkerchief in the hope of finding money, to those who stole a trunkload of clothes. Two persons stole books and one a writing desk but there is no indication that any of these three might have been literate. Twenty-three stole unnamed goods, six stole tools or instruments, fifteen stole jewellery or silver plate, fourteen others preferred watches. Thirty-one stole varying amounts of money. There were only three charged with pickpocketing, although the crime was common among the young people who had been trained by their elders to nip in and out among the crowds in a manner popularised by William Gay:

Here dives the skulking thief, with practised sleight,
And unfelt fingers make thy pocket light.
Where's now thy watch, with all its trinkets, flown?
And thy late snuff-box is no more thy own.[9]

There were nine embezzlers who had been charged under the Act of 1799 (39 Geo.3.C85) which created a special classification for those who were receivers of trust money in the course of employment, such as clerks, bankers or brokers. These were educated and literate men, in most cases a little higher in status than the forgers and utterers of counterfeit money. Crimes of such magnitude against property had increased as England's trade, commerce and industry had expanded. However, despite the seriousness of their crimes, these convicts proved to be of inestimable value when several of the twenty-five offenders received appointments to government office. The first two schoolmasters, George Samuel Warriner[10] and Thomas Fitzgerald, were former clerks who had embezzled money from their employers.[11] One of Lieutenant-Governor Collins' closest associates was Hannah Power (she was to become his mistress), who had been acquitted of the same charge of forging and uttering for which her husband Matthew Power was sentenced, but she came in the *Calcutta* with her husband.[12] Collins became friendly with another forger, James Grove, whose unusual story is told elsewhere.[13]

The case of Thomas Salmon is an example of how lucky some prisoners could be when the law was interpreted in their favour. He received a sentence of seven years, the same as the sentence for those who stole articles for a few pence, when his crime was the theft of a £200 Bank of England note, a crime for which some before him had even received the ultimate punishment. In his case the learned justices quashed the capital part of his indictment on their reading that stealing a bank note was no felony at common law.[14] Likewise, Timothy Hurley's sentence at Ayr (he had uttered false and counterfeit money) was reduced to seven years and a public whipping.[15]

There were a few crimes which do not fit into the categories so far discussed. The charge against Robert Holdham, for instance, was for bigamy. It was sad that neither wife followed him to this country, for his fate in the colony was to have one of the unhappiest endings. Another disparate offender was transported for mixing with common thieves (Archibald Campbell); another because he had returned from transportation before he'd served his time (James Carrett); another for perjury (Joseph Richards); another for aiding prisoners to escape from gaol (John Jones).

Ten of the *Calcutta* convicts were apprehended while stealing from ships or barges, mostly on the River Thames, the scene of many crimes. Sailors from ships that had returned from British Guiana, Bengal, the East Indies, America and India, thought nothing of stealing from their officers' cabins when in port. Many barges and lighters were moored in the Thames, particularly at Millbank and near Blackfriars and Waterloo Bridges, close to the haunts of both criminals and upholders of the law where according to lawyer James Smith:

In Craven Street, Strand, ten attorneys find place,
And ten dark coal-barges are moored at its base;
Fly, Honesty, fly, seek some safer retreat:
For there's craft in the river, and craft in the street.

To which another wit, Sir George Rose, replied:

Why should Honesty seek any safer retreat,
    From the lawyers or barges, odd rot 'em?
For the lawyers are just at the top of the street,
    And the barges are just at the bottom. [16]

After their convictions were passed at the Canterbury Midsummer Sessions, Urias Allender, who would become the old ferryman from Kangaroo Point, and David Wakefield, a successful meat contractor in Van Diemen's Land, were brought before the same sitting of the Assizes at Maidstone, Kent, as Matthew and Hannah Power. Wakefield broke into a vessel on the River Medway and stole slops clothing and Allender received some of the goods. [17]

Many offences were committed during alcoholic binges often at taverns of ill-repute. There were 5 000 public houses in London alone at this time. The Blue Boar Inn at Aldgate was the scene of Robert Armstrong's crime and the Pea Hen Inn near Gray's Inn Lane the scene of William Bowers' crime. The Sign of the Standard in Whitechapel (John Cole), the Salisbury Arms at Smithfield (James Dowsing), the Commercial Treaty (John Isaacs), the Plough in Tothill Street (Robert Walsh), and the Glazier's Arms, Blackfriars (John Williams) were others.

One, who later served the Reverend Robert Knopwood, was Daniel McAllenan. He stole a silver butterboat and a tablespoon from the George and Blue Boar. He was lucky to get only seven years because only two months previously he had been tried, also at the Old Bailey, for stealing a mare and saddle, which he had ordered in the name of Captain Lynn. The first trial was fascinating and for those days a long one, lasting five hours, in which one learns quite a lot about the prisoner, who must have been a plausible character to the jury, for he was acquitted. [18]

Other crimes took place at more high-sounding places such as Lincoln's Inn (Jeremiah Emblin), Temple Bar (Valentine Henley), Caius College, Cambridge (Richard Kidman), Lord Mulgrave's stables at Hartley Mews (William Williams) and Lady Dacre's estate at Belhus Aveley (Richard Godwin). John Dinham, who unfortunately finished his life in Australia at Newcastle, in a gaol for secondary prisoners, was sentenced for life for stealing three wether sheep in Somerset in 1802. One of the sheep belonged to the Rt Hon. Hester, Countess Dowager of Chatham and mother of William Pitt, whose loss of the American colonies was one reason given for the development of Botany Bay as a prison. [19] The person who brought the charges against John Maggott, who stole a check brace in London's West End worth tenpence and was sentenced to seven years, was George, the second Marquis of Townshend, a nephew of Viscount Sydney whose part in planning the transportation of felons to New South Wales is commemorated in the name of the mother city. [20]

There is some knowledge of the parentage or family in England of twenty-eight *Calcutta* convicts while thirty-two were married at the time of their trials and between them had thirty-three children. Some of the prisoners were related. It is well known that James Austin and John Earle, who became ferrymen on the Derwent and later publicans and wealthy landowners, were cousins. They came from Somerset after stealing honey and beehives from their Uncle Peter Higgens. [21] Higgens must have been a tough character to help cause his own nephews to be transported. But younger members of the Austin family migrated and inherited much of the fortune their rather strange Uncle Jim had amassed. He must have been the original skeleton in the family closet, the rich uncle in Australia who was sent out for his country's good and did very well for his own and his family's good — and the good of all those other Somerset family friends who followed him out here, the Clarkes, the Millears and others who ultimately settled in Victoria.

There were two sets of brothers. Charles and John Brown were convicted at Reading Assizes on two counts of breaking and entering houses and stealing thirty pounds of bacon, cheese, bread and wearing apparel. There was a third Brown, Richard, also of Berkshire, in the *Calcutta*, two years older than John

Brown, who might have been related.[22] The two Everitts could have been brothers, Charles and John, who were both known as Everard. Almost certainly Charles was a brother of another Everitt, alias Everard, whose name was James and who arrived at Port Jackson in the *Coromandel*. He had been a party to the same crime as Charles when they used a ladder from a barge on the Thames to climb through the window of a house into which they broke. John, however, was convicted in Wiltshire for forging and uttering. The ages of the three are close, the names and aliases the same. Crimes were often committed deliberately so that one might join a relative who had been convicted.[23]

There were others who had stolen valuable jewellery and silverplate, who would become among the most successful and wealthy settlers. It appeared that one had a much better chance to be a really successful colonist if one's stakes were high. This was the case with both Thomas Peters and David Gibson, whose later success bestowed great wealth and status on their descendants. Although his crime was not as great, James Lord belongs to this group, for his success and that of his immediate descendants was at least equal to theirs.[24] Coincidentally, these three were all tried at the Yorkshire Assizes.

Unfortunately some history has to be rewritten about some of these *Calcutta* men. The father-in-law of George Armytage, one of the best-known squatting names in the history of Victoria's Western District, was not, as Henderson's *Victorian Families* and other authorities tell us, a lieutenant in the Duke of York's Regiment stationed in Van Diemen's Land. He was the aforementioned Thomas Peters of Bagdad, wealthy farmer and one-time licensee of the Duke of York public house in Hobart. He was sentenced to life transportation for grand larceny — the theft of ten silver cups.[25]

David Gibson was convicted at the same sessions as Peters. Contrary to family tradition he was not living at his farm near Perth, where he was said to have shot a bull that was devouring his barley. Although it is possible that there was some truth in the story — perhaps the Perth Court of Justiciary *had* convicted him earlier for such a crime. In Scotland his sentence might have been banishment, which would explain why this red-headed Scots lad was living at Kingston-on-Hull where he robbed the portmanteau of a William Coles at the Neptune Inn. Coles was a jeweller who had just arrived from London. His portmanteau contained a large quantity of gold watches, lockets, gold coins and other notes, and silver jewel-

lery. A servant at the inn chased Gibson to Beverley where he was arrested. His papers noted he was to be hanged, but he was reprieved.[26]

Augustus Morris was almost certainly never educated at a military college in England nor did he fight at the Battle of Aboukir — another legend from Henderson who omits the fact that, as a convict labourer, Morris was transported for seven years. Using force and arms, he stole six shirts, stockings, pantaloons and other clothing from his master James Hughes, of the 16th Light Dragoons. A check with army records does show that a James Hughes was cornet with the 16th Light Dragoons between 1800 and 1803. Augustus Morris was not listed as a member of any of the troops in the regiment, which at that time was stationed variously at Canterbury, Croydon and Southampton and not at all in Egypt.[27]

One of the more unusual cases in the history of transportation created much publicity in England. Thomas Scott Smith, at the age of twenty-three, poisoned himself in the *Calcutta* while still at Spithead. In London he became known as the 'sham parson'. Obviously a well educated and wealthy eccentric, he had posed as a nephew of Lord Eldon, had graduated with a Bachelor of Arts degree at Queen's College, Cambridge and had been in Orders for twelve months. He actually officiated for the curate of St Martin's-in-the-Fields for a month, was said to be very attentive to duty and read prayers morn and afternoon. He also administered the sacrament, attended christenings, burials and marriages. He had been convicted of forging a signature after ordering a set of canonicals. Lieutenant Pateshall of the *Calcutta* related that he'd had every indulgence on board and that had he arrived in New Holland he would have found that his unhappy father had purchased for him an estate already cultivated and stocked, presumably at Port Jackson.[28]

Another destined for Port Phillip but who suicided during the voyage was a young forger of fourteen, John Henry Cashman. He was literate, had served with a London legal firm, and would have had a good future in the colony. But he jumped overboard at the Cape of Good Hope after a charge that he'd stolen a watch from the ship's surgeon.[29]

After their experiences in the hulks and their removal to even more confined quarters in the *Calcutta*, one can readily understand that death was preferable to those like Cashman and Scott Smith whose previous environment and social contacts were far removed from the overwhelming majority of ill-educated creatures who left England.

Others who had been in a position of trust and became embezzlers, were employed by barristers and business houses. One, John Clarke, had worked as a clerk for James Yarraway, a leading timber merchant

OPPOSITE PAGE:
Old inns like these in Southwark were the scene of many crimes of the Calcutta *convicts.*

at Blackfriars, for six years without a mark against his character but, uncharacteristically, he embezzled nearly £150.[30] Likewise John Benjamin Fell, collecting clerk for some London shipbrokers for ten years, embezzled £25 12s 9d.[31]

George Samuel Warriner was clerk to a perfumer in Cockspur Street and he was apprehended at Liverpool in possession of a banker's draft of £11 1s 6d he had embezzled. He died in Hobart Town in 1813 having been the Governor's clerk.[32] Andrew Whitehead received seven years for embezzling a £40 bill. While employed as a collecting clerk, he had failed to enter it in the wharfage book. He was already on the American ship *Industry*, about to sail for New York, when he was apprehended.[33] These men and other forgers and embezzlers did well in Van Diemen's Land because they were literate, mostly clerks, and their services were most useful in the administration of the new colony.

The trial of John Fawkner at the Old Bailey has to be read in conjunction with the trials of Thomas Collett, and Henry and Mary Hayes.[34] Thereby hangs an intriguing tale, worth relating in some detail because the many Hayes and Fawkner descendants include some who achieved great fame.

Proceedings of the trials inform us that a soldier of the Third Regiment of Guards, Thomas Collett, had called at the Bell Inn in the notorious Red Lion Market in Whitecross Street. Mary Hayes, formerly Denight, was the licensee and helped Collett upstairs with a red leather trunk containing jewellery valued at £1200. The trunk and its contents belonged to a wealthy Jamaican planter, John Christian Weppler, who was looking for lodgings when Collett stole the trunk from a cart. After some bargaining, Collett received some six guineas and a pound in halfpennies from Mary Hayes for most of the goods. As Collett still had to dispose of his booty, he persuaded Mrs Hayes to introduce him to a refiner, whereupon John Fawkner who lived in Whitecross Street joined the party at the Bell Inn. He took Henry Hayes and Collett with him to his refinery and Fawkner took two crucibles and melted down the gold and silver, separating the precious stones.

The police appeared from Bow Street after Weppler had advertised a reward of 150 guineas and a servant girl of the Hayes family, Elizabeth Smith, later described in court what she knew:

I went into the tap-room, and saw some silver and other articles lying upon her lap; there was a diamond necklace and a pearl necklace, they were lapped in wool or fine cotton; I made the observation to my mistress when I was drawing the beer, I said, Lord, Ma'am, what a handsome diamond necklace that is, and she bid me go out of the tap-room, and mind my business; the child was looking over them while her mother was in the bar; when they came in again, the child had the pearl necklace in her hand, and a pair of ear-rings, a pair of pearl ear-rings and diamond drops . . . the next morning, Mrs Hayes sent the pearl ear-rings and the pearl drops to Mrs Hinton, which she returned again in a few minutes, saying none of them would suit her; then Mrs Hinton came to our house soon after, she was looking the goods over upon my mistress's knee, in the bar . . .[35]

Although the daughter, Martha was implicated in the crime, she was not charged. Apart from Elizabeth Smith's evidence, one of the police officers, when searching the Hayes family, discovered Martha had possession of some of the Spanish coins belonging to Weppler. Collett received a sentence of transportation for seven years and Mary for fourteen years. Henry Hayes was judged 'not guilty', although it was suggested in court that he was 'as great a sinner as ever lived' and had often been charged for similar offences. While remanded at Newgate he gave his occupation as a calico glazier, from Ledbury in Gloucestershire, aged thirty-nine.

In a separate trial John Fawkner was charged with receiving a gold snuff box set with diamonds worth £400; a diamond necklace, £20; a pair of shoe buckles, £11; two silver tablespoons, £1 10s; and five silver teaspoons, £2; all of which Collett had stolen, but considerably less than the amount Hayes had received. Fawkner declared that Henry Hayes had sworn very falsely against him because 'he had come forward under a promise of getting his wife's pardon if he will appear against me'. Fawkner was sentenced to transportation for fourteen years.[36]

Mary Hayes was not destined to sail in the *Calcutta* but would arrive at Port Jackson as a convict in the *Glatton* several months earlier with her daughter Martha.[37] The purpose of sending the *Glatton* to New South Wales was for the same reasons as the *Calcutta*: to utilise a naval ship in a time of peace, to deliver convicts to the colony and to return with a large supply of timber suitable for naval purposes. Giving his occupation as a carpenter, Henry Hayes successfully applied to Lord Hobart to proceed as a settler to New South Wales.[38] As Hannah Power had been acquitted of assisting her husband in his crime, so Henry Hayes had been acquitted of assisting his wife.

4 EXILES AND EX-SERVICE

THE 1790s HAD seen changes in legislation that did little to alleviate the harshness of the penalties for many offences, especially those relating to foreigners. Also the effects of the French Revolution exposed a weakness in British law in another area that had been virtually overlooked. The government was alarmed that the legislation to penalise political agitators was inadequate and needed revision. Consequently a number of laws were hurriedly enacted.[1]

Statutes now determined what were treasonable and seditious attempts and practices. They controlled the more effective prevention of seditious meetings and assemblies, the prevention and punishment of mutineers or insubordinates in the armed forces and more effectually prevented the administration of unlawful oaths. They covered the suppression of societies established for seditious and treasonable practices, the consideration of daring outrages offered to His Majesty's sacred person, the control of seditious pamphlets and speeches, as well as the renewal of laws against riotous assembly. These were directly aimed at supporters of the United Irishmen, United Scotsmen and other organisations within England itself.[2]

Most of these statutes were in force by the time of the Irish rebellion of 1798. Anticipating an insurrection in Ulster, the Government had arrested leaders there while the peasantry of Leinster engaged in a formidable struggle, culminating in the rising of the Irish peasantry and the storming of Vinegar Hill in Wexford.[3] The English subjugated the insurgents during a cruel and bloody campaign that added a further deep scar to Anglo-Irish relationships. One immediate result was the abolition of the old Irish Parliament, composed entirely of Protestants, under the Act of Union in 1800. Other plans for Catholic emancipation fell by the wayside as Prime Minister Pitt tried to convince George III of the urgent need for reform. But the King lapsed into one of his fits of insanity; the Protestants remained in the ascendant; promises were broken; Pitt resigned. The Irish question continued to produce hatreds and fears between the two peoples, which have never been entirely eliminated.

Although none of the *Calcutta* convicts were sentenced in Irish courts, there were at least seventeen Irishmen among them. They had been arrested in England and charged for a variety of crimes, mostly concerned with petty larceny. England had become the home for many Irish searching for work. It has been common practice for historians to suspect that some Irishmen were in England for motives other than those of the crimes for which they were convicted. Others believed they were scapegoats held on spurious charges because they were suspected of being associated with the rebellion of 1798.[4] A close scrutiny of what evidence is available in the *Calcutta* and other contemporary trials, does seem to vindicate the judicial system. Had there been any suggestion of treason they would probably have been hanged, for 1798 was too fresh in the memory of English judges. Some of the prominent and influential rebels such as Joseph Holt, were transported.[5] However, it does appear that all the *Calcutta* Irish, except perhaps Robert Walsh, were guilty of the crimes with which they were charged.[6] Robert Walsh, in a letter secreted at Port Phillip and sent to Holt at Port Jackson, indicated that he had been associated with prominent rebels at Vinegar Hill, some of whom were already serving at Port Jackson. It is a document which suggests that Walsh's lengthy trial at the Old Bailey in December 1801 could be a fabrication, as he was unable to provide witnesses for his defence. Writing that he was tried for sedition in London may indicate that he hoped to ingratiate himself with Holt. In either case, the text shows that he was on intimate terms with Holt, Phil Cunningham and other prominent rebels.[7]

Walsh was a printer by trade, he hailed from Wicklow and, in fact, was charged with stealing various articles of clothing from a sailor whose wife, Mary Thompson, kept the Plough in Rochester Row, Tothill Street. Two men, Walsh and Thomas Blake, had arrived in a coach and went up to the dining room and

'Who fears to speak of '98?' The artist, James Gillray, viewed the Irish rebellion of 1798 as French-inspired.

drank brandy. She believed Blake was the captain of a ship. Walsh, who said he had leased a house at Bristol for £500, was the mate of his ship. Walsh asked her to take care of his house for £200 but she refused as she was a married woman with a family. That, however, made little difference to Mary when she took Blake up to her bedroom for 'only two minutes', denying she'd ever met him by agreement. After all, her husband had been away for a year in the *Kent*. All the evidence seems to indicate that Walsh was little more than an accessory to the crime. The stolen goods were supposed to be for the use of Blake's pregnant wife. Walsh gave evidence that Mary had called Blake 'her dear husband' and had put the articles under his coat. Whatever the crime, whatever the truth, Walsh was sentenced to transportation for seven years.

Other Irishmen who sailed in the *Calcutta* included William Cormack, Michael Lawler and Denis Kennedy, all from Tipperary; Matthew Power and Thomas Quin from Dublin; Daniel Crawley and John Williams from Cork; Patrick McCarthy, one of the Irish from the 25th Regiment at Gibraltar; Stephen Byrne, who had been living in Liverpool; Daniel McAllenan from Ballimoney; Patrick Duff from Monrath; Henry Rice, possibly from Armagh; and Valentine Henley. Among others known to have been Catholics and probably Irish were John Dawson and Henry Robinson. A few such as Patrick Plunkett had Irish names but nothing further is known of their origin. John Pascoe Fawkner referred to George Lee (convicted at Worcester Assizes for passing forged banknotes) as an Irish gentleman.

At least eight convicts were of Scottish origin: Thomas Brown of Aberdeen; Archibald (or James) Campbell (Glasgow?); Adam Carmichael of Aberdeen; David Gibson, the son of a small farmer, from a village near Perth; Robert Hay of Alyth; Timothy Hurley (Ayr?); Andrew Whitehead of Stirling; and Robert Stewart. Their activities were far removed from those earlier educated men known as the Scottish martyrs, found guilty of sedition and transported in 1795.

One whose claims to Welsh origin are suspect is Augustus Morris. At his trial he gave his birthplace as Salisbury, Wilts. However, there were at least eight definitely known to have been born in Wales, four of whom received sentences in Welsh courts and four in English. These were Jeremiah David from Newton, Thomas Price from Llanwyde, John Jones from Steviouk, John Price from Llanhew, William Lewis from Llandyssul, and Thomas Williams from Llanvillo. From the shires of Caenarvon and Montgomery came William Williams and John Gwynn respectively. The first five had little chance to redeem themselves; four died during the voyage and one died at Port Phillip, an indication perhaps that the Welsh had suffered more deprivation than other prisoners.

They had all committed larceny in one form or another but only one Taffy had stolen food, a piece of beef, although John Price had tried to drive away two head of oxen valued at £20 each. Owen Keogh, whose trial at Southampton is one of the least documented, probably came from Wales, and the origins of any one of the other four Joneses, two of whom were living in London, might also have been Welsh.

However, the success stories of men such as Gibson, Power, Williams, Morris and Whitehead, the further misdemeanours of John Gwynn, and the lively histories of Stewart and Campbell, will be related in later chapters.

. . .

But the Irish, Scots and the Welsh were not the only nationals who had gravitated to England. At least fourteen other *Calcutta* convicts had come to England to look for work knowing that the British had traditionally harboured the poor, the destitute and refugees from harsh regimes. Others might have served British officers in time of war and escaped as refugees or from custody. Several had been sailors, convicted in England of crimes committed while on leave or after having deserted ship.

The origin of the six or possibly seven Jews who set out unwillingly for an unpromised land presents a different problem from that of any other non-Anglo-Saxon-Celtic convicts. All appear to have been English-speaking and as far as one can tell were literate. They were all urban dwellers living in the East End of London, three had been born in provincial cities. They were victims of persecution even within the impoverished and crime-ridden areas in which they dwelt. They were also outcasts of society even among the closely knit Anglo-Jewish establishment which had evolved from the wealthy Sephardic Jews who had arrived in England more than two centuries earlier.

From the seventeenth century the long drawn out effects of the Inquisition had driven large numbers of Jewish merchant classes away from Spain and Portugal. Many settled at first in central Europe where they found entry into trade and guilds impossible, while a few prominent families came to England. Eastern Europe became at first a haven for about one million Jews, most of whom set up business because they could not practise their trades or professions. They lived in urban areas which members of the aristocracy found unattractive and far removed from their landed

life style. As the Jews increased in numbers, waves of anti-Semitism forced them to live in ghettos. By the end of the eighteenth century Jews seeking refuge in England from the ensuing pogroms numbered more than 60 000. Within the next sixty years the number would increase threefold.

Most had settled in London, particularly in Chelsea or in and around Middle Row in Holborn and Field Lane. Second-hand stalls thrived there and Jews peddled their goods, crying out the few English words they knew such as 'Old clothes for sale'. Rosemary Lane was known as 'Rag Fair' because many of the wares were dirty and ragged, as were many of the newcomers who kept arriving from poorer and dirtier countries. Racism was rife and local louts who had never heard of Shylock kicked at them, spat at them, and pulled their beards in full view of the police, crying out 'Go to Chelsea'.[8] Often they had no fixed abode but peddled and wandered from the slummiest areas of London into the countryside and back again, strange and unfamiliar characters who fast became the butt of the insensitive and the young.

Prejudice against the Jews as a race rose strongly when the first execution of Jews took place at Tyburn in 1771. Even when Magistrate Colquhoun wrote in 1796 of the 100 000 criminals in London (about ten per cent of the population), he made a point that along with the 50 000 prostitutes and 8 000 thieves there were 2 000 itinerant Jews:

wandering from street to street, holding out temptations to pilfer and steal, and Jew boys crying Bad Shillings, who purchase articles stolen by Servants, Stable Boys, etc. etc. generally paying in base money.

He believed that they existed

chiefly by their wits, by living upon the industry of others. Educated in idleness from their earliest infancy, they acquire every debauched and vicious principle which can fix them for the most complicated acts of fraud and deception. From the orange boy, and the retailer of seals, razors, glass and other wares in the public streets, to the shopkeeper dealing in wearing apparel or in silver and gold, the same principles of conduct too generally prevail.[9]

The author of *The Newgate Calendar* thought the Jews generally were a set of cheats and that the

lowest order are to be found lurking in every street lane and alley, pretending to buy old clothes, old metal, glass, hares' and rabbits' skins, old hats and shoes, but their real object is to corrupt servants to pilfer from their masters . . . they seldom give the thief more than a third of its value. They also carry about base money . . . they seldom scruple at committing perjury . . .[10]

Except for Michael Michaels who was guilty of uttering counterfeit money, the *Calcutta* Jewish convicts

27

were not found guilty on any of these counts. Nor were they found to be receivers of stolen property. Rabbi Levi found that contrary to the observations of Colquhoun, only fifteen Jews among his sample of 436 adults were transported for receiving stolen goods and only five were in possession of counterfeit money.[11]

Levi also found that the Jewish convict population reflected a similar pattern of transportation as that of other convict statistics, at least in the early years.[12] Jewish convicts, in that time, represented about one per cent of the total number of convicts, whereas two per cent of the total number of convicts who came in the *Calcutta* were Jews (possibly seven out of the total of 308). One was a tailor and one a brickmaker while the others were in some way connected with dealing and peddling, occupations which two of them followed very successfully in the colony. Their crimes were relatively minor thefts, although Joseph Raphael's crime was classified as highway robbery and accompanied, characteristically for him but rarely for Jews, with assault.[13] The unemployed Henry Lazarus uttered counterfeit money.[14] The *Calcutta* sample of Jews is too small to relate it to most of Levi's findings. Their average age at the time of trial was only 20.1 years (twenty-three if we accept the older William Jacobs as Jewish) while Levi found the average age of his sample of Jews as 24.76 and Robson estimated the overall average age of convicted Jewish persons to be 25.09 (23.9 in London).[15]

Those children of Israel who sailed in the *Calcutta* were mostly an industrious and, except for Joseph Raphael, orderly lot with no crimes in the colony apart from an attempted escape or two in common with many others. But there was one horrible incident before they sailed which was completely out of character with the later history of the person we know of as Michael Michaels. He was imprisoned at Newgate after a life sentence pronounced at the Old Bailey for selling a watch to the master of a coastal vessel and offering two counterfeit seven shilling pieces to buy it back (an old trick and the downfall of many convicted persons). His brother, D. Michaels, visited him in gaol and presented him with a half-guinea. For some unknown reason, Michaels, a notably mild-mannered man, savagely attacked his brother and, according to *The European Magazine and London Review*, the 'villain in confinement ripped open his belly with a knife. He was immediately confined in his cell and his brother was taken to St Bartholomew's Hospital'.[16]

Was it possible that this outrage was because he, Michael Michaels, might have been the innocent party, mistakenly apprehended and convicted in place of his brother and thereby provoked by an injustice? He had earlier served a twelve months' sentence for common uttering. Perhaps the two brothers were

equally guilty — who knows? Anything was possible in the strange and haphazard manner in which justice was often meted out in Georgian England. What happened to his poor brother is not on record but Michaels' later behaviour in the colony was exemplary.

Henry Lazarus was well named because it seemed that he kept returning to life. As a pedlar from Houndsditch, he was convicted the second time he was charged in London, perhaps because he wished a sentence of transportation, when he stole a napkin and handkerchiefs from linen-drapers in Oxford Street. He was married with one child, living in Gravel Lane, Houndsditch, in a distressed condition: 'their child is sleeping naked'.

John Isaacs was a thirteen-year-old Jewish boy from Newcastle and might well have been caught while stealing for a Fagin-like character when he boarded a ship at the Berwick and Leith wharf in the Thames. In his defence he said that he had won the stolen silver watch in a raffle and that a boy had given him other goods, including a gold chain and seal as well as clothes to sell.[17]

Samuel Jacobs was a tailor who came from Norwich, also lured by the lights of London — he stole shoes from a shop on Tower Hill.[18] But it is doubtful whether another convict by the same name, William Jacobs, was a Jew, in spite of his surname. The name Jacobs was well known in both Cornwall and Scotland among Gentiles. Jewish persons would not normally be called William, were not normally agriculturalists, and were unknown to steal animals.[19] This man, whatever his origins, had probably been a farm labourer in England. He had stolen a fat cow at Southwark and was lucky to escape the rope.[20] Joseph Rose, alias Sadler, who stole a horse in Leicester, might also have been Jewish. He barely survived the long journey to Australia and died of scurvy in Hobart in October 1804.[21] Joseph Myers appears to have been tried at Cambridge but little is known of his origins.[22]

Some of the trials involving foreigners were quite lengthy. If witnesses appeared there would be a considerable amount of cross-questioning, such as in the trial of Raphael. With three associates, he was accused of assaulting a foreigner, Peter Theodory, on the King's Highway between Wapping and Whitechapel and robbing him of a silver watch and chain as well as clothes. Being a foreigner, an interpreter was provided. What makes this trial interesting is the uncommonly close relationship between Raphael, a colourful London Jew, and his Gentile colleagues, as well as the persistence with which the counsel Mr Knapp cross-examined the witnesses, especially a thirteen-year-old lad said to have been leading the foreigner. It seemed that it was more important to instil the moral code into the mind of the young boy than to ask him straight out whether he was accompanying the defendant and did actually witness the crime. Two of the four accused received the death sentence from Lord Ellenborough, noted for his sarcasm and intellect. This trial must have been one of his first appearances as Lord Chief Justice. Among *Calcutta* convicts whom he tried apart from Raphael were Thomas Peters at York and James Taylor at Lancaster.

One record shows that Raphael was a hatter by trade, another that he was a dealer. Of all those of Jewish origin his is the only description that shows he was dark with black hair and black eyes. Many years later G. T. W. B. Boyes was to describe him as 'rather stout and not too tall'.[23] The others were all fair to medium in colouring, indicating northern European origins. But whatever their origin, they continued to wear the badge of all their tribe.

Although some forty per cent of Jews who came to Australia in the early days were originally from Poland, it is more likely that John Potaski, who stole a shawl, was Catholic (as were ninety-five per cent of his countrymen).[24] He had married an Irish woman from Connaught, who was allowed to sail in the *Calcutta*, and he might well have arrived in England in the early 1790s as a refugee after Russia, Prussia and Austria partitioned Poland. He was never naturalised in England and his name was more probably spelt Potoski or Potowski. As he was an illiterate man his name was spelt as he pronounced it. Many Poles who had migrated to England were political refugees and freedom fighters, mostly belonging to the Polish *szlachta* or nobility. Potaski obviously was not of this class and would appear more likely to have arrived as a minor merchant or seaman, perhaps from Danzig, which belonged to the Polish crown until 1793, when Prussia seized it as a result of the second partition of Poland.[25]

It is likely that John Hoberman, who had a tobacco business in Hamburg, sought refuge because he feared the danger of a power rising in the east which might prove as formidable as Germany's traditional enemy in the west. The Treaty of Luneville in February 1801 had expanded French hegemony over the western German states. Hoberman spoke good English and probably brought his wife to England with him. Evidence at his trial indicated he had a child. If true, they showed some foresight, for their native soil would soon be stained with blood and ravaged with long years of war that would cripple Europe. Hoberman was to bring no family to Australia.[26]

Nicholas Piroelle was a French confectioner, formerly of Burgundy, who brought his wife with him. He might well have lived in London for several years, perhaps a refugee from sansculottism. The name of his wife, Sarah, suggests that she was English. He had stolen a large number of ingredients from the firm of

Lord Ellenborough, a stern and conservative judge who strongly opposed Bentham and his proposed reforms, passed judgment on several Calcutta *convicts.*

confectioners which employed him. A half English and half foreign jury was empanelled to try foreigners. Piroelle had to conduct his defence through an interpreter.[27]

Joseph Fernandez hailed from Portugal, Britain's oldest ally. He was a sailor who had arrived in London after leaving his ship at St Catherine's on the Isle of Wight. He had stolen gum from an American schooner berthed in the River Thames.[28]

There were at least two who had originated from Holland, England's European ally in the recent wars. They had served the allied cause in Egypt in the 25th Regiment of Foot with some seventy-odd other disenchanted fellow Dutchmen. They had not been repatriated to Holland at the end of hostilities but became part of the garrison stationed at Gibraltar and, as will be revealed, played a significant part in the mutiny there. Their names were Sander van Straten and John Sculler (perhaps Schuyler). Two others from Gibraltar whose names suggest Dutch origin were Christopher Cronbury (Croenburgh?) and John Crute or Cruitt.[29]

William Thomas was known to have been an American and there may have been others among the seamen. He had been stranded in London and had sought work as a lumper in a ship on the Thames. Unfortunately he was tempted to steal sugar from his employer, pleading that a Customs House officer said he could take a little for his seastock. He said he was starving and offered to work for victuals to evade conviction.[30]

There could have been other national or ethnic groups represented and their origin not recorded. Why, for instance, was Robert Cooper classified as a gypsy?[31] This appellation suggests a more colourful background than the homely Anglo-Saxon origin of the surname. But many had chosen a gypsy-like existence in preference to living in the slums of the cities. Born near Warminster, Wiltshire and charged at Dorchester in Dorset, Cooper's territory embraced the ancient Roman fortification of Maiden Castle. He was probably part of a well known family of gypsies named Cooper. They roamed around the dry chalk lands of these counties renowned for their wonderments of primitive man and the ruins of Roman occupation in which they saw their origin. Here in the mysterious and rather isolated region Cooper had lived for some fifty-seven years. He certainly looked and acted like a gypsy; the Dorchester gaol register describes him as having 'black hair, dark complexion, hazel eyes and a cut on left eyebrow and another on forehead (left), high cheek-boned, high forehead. Lusty'. He was let off lightly, perhaps because of his age, receiving a sentence of seven years for a crime he and his fellow gypsies probably committed over and over again: 'on suspicion of stealing nine he-asses and four blind halters', useful equipage for persons who idly wandered the countryside with the caravanserai, casting keen-edged spells and curses, hatred and contempt, on those in authority.

·   ·   ·

Calcutta convicts known to have fought for King and country, however unwillingly, included one who had been an officer: William Thomas Stocker, a lieutenant in the Dragoons who was sentenced to death at the Old Bailey in April 1802 for being in possession of forged and counterfeit notes. His sentence was later reduced to transportation for fourteen years. Although it is not known how he obtained his commission, it was possible for a recruiting sergeant to save enough to buy an ensign's commission or occasionally to receive promotion as a reward for bravery.[32]

But Stocker who had married Ann, the daughter of a Captain Pemberton of the Royal Navy, might well have been in a position to gain further promotion had he not succumbed to the common temptation of the time among persons placed in positions of trust. Stocker certainly was capable of leadership as his later history in the colony confirms. Ann had also been charged, with her husband, of being in possession of counterfeit notes, and both were tried and pleaded guilty, and committed to Newgate in April 1802. In the end charges against Ann were dropped, but she chose to exile herself with her husband. But while in the *Calcutta* she 'died of a broken heart', reported

Lieutenant Pateshall, soon after leaving England: 'Her fine feelings and delicate constitution, added to her being at the time in a far state of pregnancy, were ill-calculated to endure so great a change in life'.[33]

According to surveyor George Prideaux Harris, two others had served as Army officers, George Lee[34] and Thomas Fitzgerald.[35] They too had been convicted of forgery, the former sentenced to fourteen years and the latter to seven years. But if they had served as officers in the Army, they were certainly not soldiers at the time of their conviction when both were working as clerks.

Several others served in the ranks. A former biscuit maker, Adam Carmichael, had been a lance-corporal in the Fifth North British Militia and was convicted at the Aberdeen Court of Judiciary in April 1801 for the theft of cheeses, tea and tobacco.[36] William Richardson, a private in the Third Regiment, stole money from the person in whose Westminster house he was billetted.[37] Born in Monrath, Ireland, Patrick Duff had been discharged at the age of thirty-two from the Army (regiment unknown) in which he had been three times wounded in battle. He was probably one of many who, disillusioned with life after the wars, were unemployed and committed highway robbery.[38]

Thomas Riley, a stocking weaver by trade, had joined the Royal Artillery and was living with his wife Isabella at Berwick-upon-Tweed. He stole some poultry at Tynemouth, Northumberland. His wife and son accompanied him in the *Calcutta*.[39] John Reynolds was a private in the 18th Regiment, Light Dragoons, who incurred a sentence of seven years for stealing handkerchiefs at Beverley, Yorkshire.[40]

Best known of all the ex-soldiers was William Buckley, the wild white man, who had served in the Fourth or King's Own Regiment of Foot in Holland, where he had been wounded. Buckley had received rolls of cloth known to have been stolen, together with two pieces of Irish linen from a shopkeeper at Warnham, Sussex. His parents were farmers at Marton, Macclesfield in Chester, where the name Buckley was a respected one, known in the area for hundreds of years. He had been a bricklayer by trade before his army service.[41]

Francis Barnes, a printer by trade, became one of the more successful colonists. He was serving in the 60th Regiment in 1801 when he was wounded. At the time of his arrest, Barnes was living at St Bride in London. His was one of the more interesting crimes, reminiscent of those circumstances in which the pickpocket George Barrington had been discovered some years before. Whereas Barrington had contrived to be seated in a box at Covent Garden next to the wealthy Russian, Gregory, Count Orlov, whose valuable gold and jewelled snuffbox he tried to steal, Barnes was sharing a box with a Nathaniel Swan at the Drury Lane Theatre, watching the fascinating Dorothea Jordan, 'the muse of comedy', appearing (in between producing children for the Duke of Clarence) in a performance of *The Country Girl*. Barnes picked the pocket of his friend to the tune of £172 and actually sat out the performance. Unlike Barrington, who was acquitted of his first offence, Barnes received a sentence of transportation for life. It was revealed that he had previously been convicted as William Barnes in 1795 and sentenced to seven years, but had been pardoned, whereupon he joined the Army.[42] The first of the *Calcutta* convicts to be convicted was Joseph Pendridge who gave his occupation as soldier at his trial. In March 1799 his death sentence was commuted and replaced by seven years' transportation, one year of which he served in the county gaol at Bedford and three long years in the *Prudentia* hulk at Woolwich before transferring to the *Calcutta*. He is one of several who received short sentences of transportation but served almost half that time in the teeming prisons and verminous hulks before they arrived at their destination.[43]

Although many of the *Calcutta* convicts were experienced seamen, few appear to have served in the Royal Navy. The early life of Robert Stewart, the pirate, remains obscure. According to officers' lists at the Greenwich Museum he was not a former captain in the Navy as some had suggested, but Captain Woodriff noted R. N. against his name, and events would show that he had considerable maritime experience.[44] The delusions of grandeur which Stewart acquired and his obvious qualities of leadership led others to put their trust in him implicitly when he planned numerous escapes in the colony.

Stewart appeared at the Old Bailey on several charges of forging bills of exchange. He had posed as Michael Seymour and claimed he was captain of the frigate *Prudentia* and had come to Thomas Boote's shop to buy stores for the ship. He said the army officer who had given him the bill had gone to Minorca. Mr Justice Graham passed sentence of death on Stewart and, while awaiting execution at Newgate, he heard of his reprieve and his new sentence of transportation for life. He was transferred from Newgate to Woolwich, coincidentally to the hulk *Prudentia*. At the time of committal, Stewart had several aliases. He was also known by the name Michael Stewart, alias Seymour, alias Robert Seymour.

Samuel Gunn had been a sailor on board a man of war for some three years and was at the Battle of Copenhagen.[45] Urias Allender claimed in 1826 that he was 'an old man of wars, wounded twice, and eighteen years on board a King's ship either fighting or trying to fall in with some, has often been engaged and fought the battles of his country . . .' One source suggests he was a captain on the foretop in H.M.S. *Formidable* under Lord Rodney but his name does not appear on the naval lists searched.[46] However, both these men were experienced seamen and one does not doubt that they had seen much battle.

But of all those who wandered far afield, whether to or from England, and for whatever reason, none made their mark in history as auspiciously (although since completely forgotten) as the mutineers from Gibraltar.

5 THE MUTINY AT GIBRALTAR

*T*HE LOWER CLASSES felt more affinity with the British royal family than one might have expected. Radical thoughts which may have floated across the Channel did not necessarily reach the poor and the petty thieves of London who would be more likely to accept one of their own being hanged than their monarch being guillotined. The English had had their revolution more than a century ago. They had opted for royalty, however deranged their King, or however degenerate his offspring might be. One must remember George III was the first ruler since Queen Anne who spoke English without a foreign accent. God save any king who appeared to be a buffer against harsh landowners and the grasping *nouveau riche* created by the Industrial Revolution.

There are several links with the royal dukes in the *Calcutta* story. Convicts who had served in the Army had the Duke of York as their Commander-in-Chief. William Buckley had served in the Netherlands in the King's Own (4th) Regiment of Foot and had been wounded. Soldiers stationed at Gibraltar were in close, if not happy, contact with the Duke of Kent, Governor of Gibraltar and his younger brother, the Duke of Sussex. Ex-Royal Navy convicts were in the service headed by the Duke of Clarence, Admiral of the Fleet and later King William IV, the 'sailor king'. When ex-soldier Francis Barnes committed his crime at the Drury Lane Theatre it could well be that the same Duke was in the royal box applauding his mistress, the actress, Dorothea Jordan, before accompanying her to their home in Bushey Park.[1]

The Reverend Robert Knopwood's reputed escapades with the Prince of Wales were said to have been given as a reason for his transfer from the Royal Navy, and away from England where he could no longer participate in the high jinks of the young blades. The huntin', shootin' and fishin' career in which he followed his royal patron, not to mention the boudoir antics of most of the royals, was a common pursuit.[2] The string of mistresses and children born out of wedlock set the pattern of living from the Palace to the poorhouse. What was good enough for His Grace was good enough for the lowest citizen of London. But out there in the countryside, among the respectable working class, the colliers, yeomen, artisans, factory workers and agricultural labourers hovered the ghost of John Wesley, guiding the would-be sinners along the straight and narrow furrow which alone might lead them to salvation. They were more likely to be the 'labouring poor' idealised as those 'Village Hampdens' than the wretched thieves and ne'er-do-wells of the profligate cities.

The King's sons appeared to give some public service for which, in May 1802, two bills brought successfully before the House of Commons ensured annuities of £20 000 to two of the royal dukes — Sussex and Cambridge. There were times when the dukes were more useful than they have been given credit. But on several occasions they were dismissed in strange circumstances, as in the case of the Duke of Kent at Gibraltar. History appears to have maligned him greatly. He became a scapegoat of ambitious and corrupt army officers and later a victim of Creevey gossip and Greville memories. Yet he appears to have been an able and incorruptible administrator. He suffered from being a younger royal prince without much chance to show his worth. He could almost be forgiven for two well-known faults: he could not live within his relatively meagre income and he thought he could not live without Madame St Laurent.[3]

But he was also closely associated with Robert Owen, to whom he was to confide that there 'were no titles in the spiritual spheres into which he had entered . . . to benefit, not a class, a sect, a party, or any particular country, but the whole of the human race . . .'[4] Prior to his interest in the Owenites, which was enough in itself to earn the displeasure of his brothers as well as the Tory faction, he had gained the reputation of being unduly severe in carrying out his military duties. He had to be put on the mat without the whole world knowing.

What transpired must rank as one of the great

'cover-ups' of the British Army and Establishment. A certain incident at Gibraltar concerned seven of those transported in the *Calcutta*. After a court martial which was apparently held in secret, just after Christmas 1802, the seven were swiftly taken to England and put aboard just before the ship sailed. The cover-up was probably aided by the diversion of public interest created by the case of the Irish conspirator Edward Despard, who was awaiting execution for attempting to assassinate the King. The soldiers whom Captain Woodriff received on board were Christopher Cronbury, John Crute, John Haynes, Patrick McCarthy, John Sculler, James Taylor and Sander Van Straten.

•   •   •

At the time, England was primarily a naval power, as was proved by her victories during the eighteenth century against the other major powers. But in the Army there had long been an anti-militarist tradition through which the sovereign had supreme command of his lord-lieutenants. They in turn appointed subordinate officers — members of the gentry who were prepared to pay for the privilege of becoming a commissioned officer — who commanded a voluntary militia of serving soldiers who were billetted among the people. The system was financially favourable to the government which could then evade responsibility for retirement pay.

Frederick Augustus, Duke of York, the second son of George III, had become British Commander-in-Chief in 1795, in spite of an unimpressive performance while commanding an expedition to the Netherlands two years previously. He had inherited a motley assortment of undisciplined regiments, officers and men of the worst type. During the seven years of his first term of office they did convert to a remarkable army which would ultimately make England as strong on land as she was on sea. An Act of 1799 empowered the King to offer bounties to army volunteers who might enlist for service in Europe, but they were not obliged to fight in Egypt or elsewhere. By 1801 the strength of the united forces of England, Scotland and Ireland was 140 000 soldiers.[5]

The Duke set up a staff college in 1798, and the Royal Military College for professional soldiers opened with one hundred gentlemen cadets in a rented house at Great Marlow in 1802.[6] The health of the men was an increasingly important consideration; the 85th Regiment and the Coldstream Guards, for example, were among the first to become guinea pigs for Dr Jenner's vaccination against smallpox.[7]

Like most of the King's sons, the Duke had his weaknesses. It was his current mistress, Mrs Mary Ann Clarke, who caused his downfall when it was discovered that she was using her influence to traffic in army promotions. Even a wealthy merchant could obtain his son's entry into a society of which the ordinary person had formerly only dreamed he might attain. The Duke was forced to resign although he had shown considerable aptitude in his role and introduced many innovations which formed the basis of the British Army today.[8] The Duke of York had also begun a Rifle Brigade which trained in Windsor Forest, drawing members from each of the fifteen regiments of line under the command of Colonel Coote Manningham. One of these regiments was the 25th line of foot which saw service in Egypt in July 1801 and later Malta.[9] After the signing of the Peace of Amiens it became part of the garrison at Gibraltar. In May 1802 the King's fourth son, Edward Augustus, Duke of Kent, arrived at Gibraltar as Governor, where he was to open up a Pandora's box of problems and corruption. There a gypsy prophesied that in spite of all the losses and crosses he would have to bear, he would die in happiness and his only child would one day become a great queen.[10]

The uneasy peace had created tension among the soldiers confined to a fortress close to an inimical people. The Duke found they had become completely undisciplined. They were perpetually drunk and licentious. The situation was accentuated by a system whereby the income derived from the sale of wine house licences largely contributed to the Governor's salary. Apart from other sources, a predecessor, General O'Hara, had encouraged the proliferation of public houses and other licensed premises, receiving as much as £7 000 per annum from this practice.[11] Although always in debt, the Duke of Kent was not corrupt. He closed half of the ninety drinking houses and sacrificed some £4 000 in licence fees. He forbade all but commissioned officers to enter the wine shops. The Duke's own troops resented his interference with what they regarded as a curb on their freedom. The authorities at home were loath to support him when even the subordinate officers did not.

There were continual minor riots until, on Christmas Eve 1802, a mutiny against the Duke's disciplinary measures broke out in the Second Battalion of the Royals.[12] They had expected the other regiments to rebel and planned to put the Duke on a ship-of-war. But the ordinary soldiers, flush with money from their sojourn in India, had other ideas for celebrating Christmas Eve. Most had become incensed with the unnecessary severity of a newly appointed adjutant, but Christmas pay had arrived, the men were off duty and liquor was flowing freely in the barracks. The adjutant ordered the gates of the barracks to be locked, whereupon 250 armed men escaped through windows to link up with a wholly Irish, 34th Regiment. They marched on the Governor's house crying

33

'Liberty! Liberty! We want two heads!' The artillery planted cannon to defend the entrance while General Barnet appeared to hear their demands.

'We wish you to be the Governor, and that the Prince should go away,' they told him. The General replied:
  'Be peaceable, and tomorrow I will give you an answer.'

Although they retired, the Grenadiers of the 54th Regiment opened fire, killing and wounding several men.

Back at their barracks they expressed repentance and fidelity to their officers. The Duke of Kent reprimanded them in forcible terms, warning them of the fatal consequences of their conduct. Christmas Day passed without further incident. The following evening forty or fifty of the more riotous members of the 25th Regiment were extremely drunk and rolled down the streets, firing muskets in the air. The Royals went forth to drive them back but the artillery unwittingly mistook them for the troublemakers. *The Times* reported that the Prince himself advanced at the head of his regiment and all was in a state of insurrection. The discharge of cannon and musketry went on for nearly two hours and it was believed eighty men were killed and two hundred wounded.[13]

The following day the leaders of the mutiny were reportedly brought before a court martial where drunkenness was judged to be the chief cause of most of the trouble. Seventy discontented Dutchmen in the regiment, who had expected to be discharged at the end of the war, were considered to be the chief instigators of the riot, inevitably supportd by the Irish. It transpired that the wine-sellers who had had their licences suppressed had supplied the men with buckets of wine, in fact more than they could drink.

The Times reported that a sentence of death was passed on three of the ringleaders as an example to others. Two Dutchmen and one Irishman were shot on 4 January by protesting fellow members of the 25th Regiment whose names were drawn by lot.[14] The troops filed past the dead bodies and peace returned to the fortress. A further report stated that ten others of the 25th Regiment were condemned to death but the Duke pardoned them and they embarked for England in the *Cynthia*.[15] Seven of these joined the *Calcutta*, transported for life; but who passed that sentence remains a mystery.[16] The Duke was recalled to England the following March. He demanded, and the Government steadfastly refused, a formal investigation of his conduct.[17]

There was, however, one informer, Henry Salisbury, a mutineer. Although sworn to secrecy, he allegedly confessed all from the prison ship *Dedham* in November 1804. He confirmed that the first ranking officers of the garrison had held a court martial and

formed a committee to pay off the ringleaders; that the Duke of Kent was to be taken from the grand parade during divine service and put on a ship-of-war, not to return on pain of death; that an officer had made the scheme known to the Duke; that three of the mutineers who knew of the plan swore they would never tell and received a letter (since burnt) containing money to allow them to embark; that the plan was known to the captain of the ship and officers of the Royals and the garrison.[18]

The disciplinary measures the Duke had tried to institute were set aside by his successor. Laxity and demoralisation returned for the time being to Gibraltar. Nevertheless, much of the discipline and reforms he had tried to introduce later became basic army principles. The Duke was aged thirty-six and it was almost the end of his service.

Probably the most conscientious and certainly the least profligate of the royal sons, Kent spent the next sixteen years of his life in exile with his mistress. Then it became obvious that he was the only possible Royal who could produce an heir to the throne, provided he made a suitable marriage. The Duke reluctantly gave up Madame St Laurent, dutifully married the Princess of Saxe-Coburg, and became the father of Queen Victoria.

• • • •

In unusual circumstances therefore, two royal soldiers had mysteriously lost their jobs which they had carried out in a manner one accepts as standard practice in any defence force today. In Kent's case, it was probably desirable to make a scapegoat of him when, after all, he would have to take the blame for so much blood on his hands. But why omit the names of the mutineers (except those executed) from reports and records? Why omit the crime and place from contemporary lists of the *Calcutta* convicts? Charges of rape, theft and murder all appear in the War Office (Gibraltar) records at that time.[19] They omit the courts martial for mutiny, as though these men never existed. (One may ask if ever there *was* a court martial in which these men had a chance to plead their case.) And why did *The Times*, after taking long reports from the *Moniteur*, suddenly play down the whole affair.

The Home Office convict transportation register also ignores their names, although someone has added five of them to a duplicate list in the Mitchell Library without any information on where they were tried and for what reason.[20] Likewise, the shipping indents add only the seven names, nothing else, at the end of the list.[21] The Tasmanian archives has a comprehensive register of convicts recording that John Cruit [*sic*] tried at Gibraltar in 1802 and sentenced to transportation for life, was ultimately executed in 1826 for sheep stealing.[22]

At the end of Captain Woodriff's personal list of convicts received from the hulks at Langston the seven elusive names appear as a 'list of soldiers received for mutiny', and it would appear that they were put aboard the *Calcutta* at the last minute. There is nothing to indicate their ages, or place and time of conviction except in the columns indicating 'offences' and 'sentences'. There Woodriff has written 'mutiny' and 'life' against each name. During the voyage Woodriff noted that John Crute served Lieutenant Donovan. The rest remained in irons.[23]

In January 1804 George Prideaux Harris wrote to his brother Henry from Sullivan Bay that the soldiers from the Gibraltar mutiny were 'fine fellows whom you might trust your life with'. They were, he wrote, behaving 'extremely well' in their responsible role as members of the night association.[24]

How fortunate they were they had yet to learn. Their exile allowed them to begin life afresh as a more privileged group. It also freed them from long years of war, or an equally devastating epidemic at Gibraltar in August 1804; 5 733 out of 15 000 of their former fellows would die of yellow fever. Australian records show that most were very much alive.[25]

The 'court martial' of these mutineers falls into a different category from the trials of the other *Calcutta* convicts. The latter were more related to the changing times when an industrial economy was largely superseding that of a rural economy. Mutiny under circumstances such as at Gibraltar might happen at any time. Boredom on an island fortress and provocation from those who were losing the perquisites of their office had incited the act that led to their fate. They were social protesters rather than petty offenders. They were also martyrs in a corrupt system which succeeded in using them to perpetuate itself, at least for the time

being, and rid itself of the one dubbed a royal martinet.[26]

It was nearly fifty years before a biography of the Duke, by Erskine Neale, made a belated attempt to set the record at Gibraltar straight. He quoted the Duke of Sussex who alluded to a 'mystery' hanging over the mutiny at Gibraltar,[27] but even then, only the three executed were known by name. Neale feared that it would never be cleared up because the surviving parties were 'keeping it in shadow'. The Duke's family shunned reference to it, though he considered several of the officers of the garrison 'most culpably mixed up with it — some more to blame than their men'.[28] Authorities were afraid to be quoted. Neale unearthed a few forgotten references and interviewed some old soldiers who had been at Gibraltar at the time.[29] He discovered that it was the Duke's humanity that really saved him from assassination; for instance it was his custom to visit the sick soldiers, taking medicine and other comforts.[30] While visiting the hospital he chatted on several occasions to one of the most turbulent men in the regiment who warned him of a plot to seize him on parade and eject him.

Even though the Duke of York tendered some support, it did little good — 'You send a man out to control a garrison all but in a state of mutiny', he said; 'He goes out. He finds matters infinitely worse', acknowledging how his brother quelled an outbreak thoroughly, 'By way of reward you disgrace him!'[31] Yet history takes strange turns. But for the mutiny at Gibraltar there might have been no Queen Victoria — no state of the Commonwealth named Victoria, nor would the name have appeared anywhere else to inspire the jingoism that refused to allow the sun to set on the empire. The incantations of the prophet Isaiah might well be invoked when one considers this side issue which had emerged from the 'shadow of a great rock in a weary land'.

6 CAMBRIDGE CAPERS

OF THE TWENTY-SEVEN *Calcutta* men who had the death sentence commuted after 'burglariously stealing' no criminal was more audacious than one whose hunting ground was Cambridge University. For several years burglaries had occurred in King's and Caius Colleges, where nimble burglars left no trace of their crime. Silver plate including strainers, snuffers, skewers, ladles, a waiter, spoons, cream pot, pint mugs, tankards, medals, coins and valuable candlesticks disappeared. Even the Mayor of Cambridge as well as the Vice-Chancellor became involved as searches took place in the houses of local inhabitants.

In March 1801 the actual trial of Richard Kidman for a burglary and robbery in the Colleges of Caius and King's on the nights of 13 October and 5 May 1799, took no more than a minute.[1] He pleaded guilty, although Mr Justice Grose suggested to him that he had the right to retract. This appears to have been because a barrister, Mr Alley, appeared briefly at Kidman's trial. Alley declared that he had an interest in Kidman's plea because he had 'the misfortune to be called upon to defend a man [Henry Cohen], who is charged as accessory to this burglary and robbery'. (Cohen's trial did not occur until March 1801.) Mr Justice Grose declared that Alley's appearance was quite irregular because 'he was neither counsel for the man, or called upon by the court. Call the prisoner for his plea'.

The prisoner appeared. The clerk of arraigns called: 'Are you guilty of this felony or not guilty?' Prisoner: 'Guilty'.

The Justice, turning to Mr Alley, informed him that if he were counsel for the accessory he would have the opportunity of controverting the guilt of the principal, just as if the principal were on his trial.

There was a further indictment, a similar trial lasting a few seconds, and a similar verdict when Richard Kidman assented with a nod that he was guilty of the second burglary, robbery and sacrilege.

It is largely from the lengthy trials of William Grimshaw and Henry Cohen that we learn more of the weird and intriguing process of the law as well as the happenings in Cambridge in these years.[2]

Richard Kidman was born about 1761, at Waterbeach, a village in the neighbourhood of Cambridge, where his working-class parents had him apprenticed to a gardener in Cambridge. In his spare time he engaged in the sport of cock-fighting, which was even then condemned as a barbarous pastime. After committing a robbery in his employer's garden, he was committed to the local bridewell but his master forgave him and he returned to his service. He robbed him again, along with other neighbours, of some game fowls. After appearing at the Quarter Sessions he received a public whipping in the market place. He then became apprenticed to a shoemaker but disliked the work and entered the plumbing and glazing trade. His new master recognised that he had considerable talent and would remark that 'there were but two clever fellows in Cambridge, and this man Dick Kidman was one of them'.[3] His employer died and left Kidman his tools, mechanical instruments and other equipment, whereupon Kidman became his own master. He acquired a good reputation for making and maintaining clocks, while at the same time he continued his plumbing and glazing trade. This took him into the butteries and private apartments of several of the University colleges. At night he frequented the fields behind the colleges where he set traps to catch birds, thereby gaining some knowledge of the terrain under the cloak of darkness. He could hardly have had much sleep.

Some time before 1796, while cleaning the windows of a private room in King's College, he met Richard Grimshaw who was sweeping the chimney.[4] Grimshaw had ideas well beyond his station, which included the need for more money to satisfy his sexual appetite. During the friendship that followed between the two men, Kidman observed 'how easy it would be to rob colleges in the summer, when the gentlemen are gone down into the country'.[5] While on frequent walks they planned robberies which the police were unable to solve for nearly four years. There was alarm throughout the whole community when families lost confidence in their long-time servants.[6]

In August 1796 at the treasury of King's College, Kidman made a model key from a piece of wood covered with tinfoil. He then made a key from the model and they were able to secure their booty undisturbed. The robbery was not discovered until the Provost's return from vacation, when the College offered 100 guineas' reward for the return of the stolen silver plate, by which time Kidman had converted it into shillings and sixpences.[7]

Sometimes Grimshaw committed the robberies singly while Kidman was planning the next, which included a daring exploit at Trinity College needing several sets of keys. He had filled a five-bushel sack with plate and staggering under its weight he hid it in a dry well pit he had artfully bricked up behind his cellar. Magistrates came from London, runners were stationed at the turnpikes to search suspicious carts, and even Kidman allowed constables into his house to search unsuccessfully. They had been able to melt down much of the plate and sell it to Henry Cohen, who provided the crucibles, allegedly for 44s a pound.[8]

The nightly visitors continued their robberies in rooms, halls and chapels at Caius College, King's College, Emmanuel College and Trinity College. After several attempts, Kidman had acquired on his own a valuable collection of gold and silver medals held in the King's College Chapel. Five hundred guineas' reward was offered for their return; even the *Gentleman's Magazine* gave the mystery some coverage.[9] Kidman managed to off-load some of his booty, with which he bought some land, giving rise to suspicions that he might be the culprit. Yet before his apprehension the two plotted the most ambitious robbery of all. They laboured each night for six weeks at Caius College, including almost an entire night when Grimshaw spent hours unscrewing the lock of one of the gates, taking it to Kidman to fit a key, and then replacing it. Kidman had to make two trips with a sack, but as dawn broke he decided not to risk returning a third time. By this time Cohen was suspected of receiving the plate Kidman melted down. The comings and goings between the houses of the three men and the parts played by the wives add to the incredible story that so much crime could go undetected for so long.

The amount stolen from Caius College alone was judged to be about 400-500 pounds in weight, but Cohen was anxious to obtain more and more, raising the price he would pay and encouraging Kidman in

Richard Kidman would have passed through the King's College gateway to commit one of his many robberies, including the booty stolen from King's College Chapel.

particular to keep up his nightly depredations. Cohen was known as an itinerant pedlar. Locals believed some of the boxes containing the wares he was peddling held the stolen goods.

Kidman was the first to be charged and made his voluntary confession before the mayor, John Forlow, of the parish of St Giles, Cambridge, on 19 February 1801, which was given at the instigation of his wife, Sarah.[10] Sarah Kidman stood up splendidly, as a witness, to a lengthy cross-examination during the trial of Cohen.[11] There was a long discussion as to whether the evidence of the wife of a convicted man who was a party to the crime would be admissible during which the counsel for the prosecution, Mr Wilson, averred that Kidman was 'dead in law'[12] and counsel for the defense, Mr Alley, invoked the wisdom of Lord Chief Justice Hale:

A woman is not bound to be sworn or give evidence against her husband, in case of theft, etc., if her husband be *concerned*, though it be material against another, and not directly against her husband.[13]

He argued that as Kidman had already been convicted her evidence could not even *collaterally* affect him. The decision to allow her to be a witness took hours of legal argument before Sarah appeared in the box. Mr Alley thought the gentlemen were 'blowing hot and cold' until Mr Justice Grose intervened believing that she would be a competent witness because 'no judgement in this case can ever avail to set aside the judgement in the former, by which he [Kidman] is said to be a felon convict.'[14]

During the cross-examination of Sarah Kidman it transpired that she was intelligent, could read and was obviously truthful and helpful until the moment she learnt that her husband had been sentenced to death the previous day. There is no indication that the news upset her but she refused to answer a number of questions thereafter, finally admitting that she did persuade her husband to plead guilty. In this summing up Mr Justice Grose indicated that he believed she understood that her examination would probably have the effect of saving her husband's life.[15] This turned out to be correct. Kidman received a reprieve from the death sentence. Cohen was surprisingly acquitted of procuring Kidman to commit the robbery; a number of witnesses had given him a good character. A further indictment against Cohen produced a much shorter trial at which Sarah Kidman again appeared as a witness,[16] but she was accused of perjury and taken into custody.[17] Again Cohen was acquitted through lack of reliable evidence against him.

Sitting in judgment, Baron Hotham left no doubt that he was unhappy with the jury's verdict and addressed himself to Cohen:

We are, as you know, only an earthly tribunal, and can only be guided by the evidence which is brought before us. Upon the evidence that has been now adduced, the Jury have, as they ought to do, thought fit to acquit you, . . . whether you are guilty of it or not is between God and your own conscience; and I have only to remind you, that though you are acquitted here to day, another day will come when you must stand before another Judge, and that Judge cannot be imposed upon, by any art or concealment of yours. If you should be found guilty by Him, you have added to your guilt, by not only having been the means of execution of one fellow subject, the conviction of a second, but probably of the transportation of a third . . .[18]

Grimshaw was 'launched into eternity, amidst the cries and lamentations of a vast concourse of people'.[19] Richard Kidman escaped with the sentence of transportation for life. After further imprisonment at the Castle he spent a short time in the *Prudentia* hulk at Woolwich before sailing in the *Calcutta*.[20]

To date his life had been full of incident. It was to take even more extraordinary turns, yet to be related, before his death, at the age of seventy-one in, of all places, Cambridge. He actually returned there to follow his old vocation as a cleaner and mender of clocks.

7 A THREAD OF THREADNEEDLE STREET

THE FORGERY OF coins had long been a common practice, particularly in Birmingham, where counterfeit copper halfpence sold at twenty per cent less than the mint coin. They were often notoriously passed as the meagre pay of workmen who barely earned the necessities of life. They in turn found that the only persons who would accept the base coins were the alehouse keepers, who perpetuated the crime by passing the coins on to the unwary.[1] Matthew Boulton's engineering works at Soho on the outskirts of Birmingham and some fifteen other smaller manufacturers were responsible for designing and minting tons of exquisite copper penny and halfpenny tokens used throughout Britain in the 1790s. Employers issued these extensively to workers and tradesmen and they became a form of currency. It is not difficult to imagine that some of the many employed in the trade would have acquired the technology needed to produce base coinage, and that the counterfeiting of banknotes would be an even more ambitious pursuit.

James Grove was a Birmingham man who had not only the motivation but was also a reasonably good craftsman with the ability and technical knowledge to commit his crime.[2] Born about 1769 in Birmingham, he carried on a business as a die-sinker in Church Street. Grove was a skilled tradesman, and by education was a man who could apply his knowledge, such as chemistry, in the manufacture of very useful products. He and his wife Susannah had a four-year-old son, Daniel, and her family were persons of some fortune. Why should he, with a good job and good prospects, succumb to the temptation of engraving a set of plates for forging a quantity of Bank of England notes which were easily traced to Birmingham? The bank had its spies who found the likely culprit with forged plates on his person. Grove was arrested and confined to Newgate in December 1801 where, through a chance meeting with a well known printer, Thomas Bensley, he was able to discuss his crime with officers of the bank whom he advised on measures they

could take to prevent forgeries in the future. He planned a mould for an improved banknote paper which the bank at first rejected. He then suggested the introduction of a coloured mark in the banknote paper. Again his idea was rejected. But he was persistent. Several bank officers eventually called on him at Newgate to listen to his ideas, but there is no evidence that the bank used any at that time.[3]

Bensley remained Grove's friend, and from his business in Fleet Street he would stroll up to the prison to console the prisoner during his confinement.[4] Bensley's own pious adherence to a religious sect led by William Lushington, known as the 'Coal-haven Saint', undoubtedly influenced Grove whose spiritual meditations in prison, which he put to paper, indicate a seemingly sincere atonement for his crime.

Grove was delivered to the gaol at Warwick in March 1802 to await his trial at the Spring Assizes held at Warwick where he was found guilty and sentenced to death.[5] His letters to Bensley, written after the trial, are among the more illuminating reports available of confinement in a county gaol at that time. They also show that he was treated with a respect that was unusual for a prisoner with a death sentence hanging over his head.

While in Newgate he had heard of the horrors of a county prison. Apart from some trifling inconvenience such as the iron chain on his leg and intrusive visitors he thought Warwick gaol preferable to Newgate. He found plenty of restraints on the outwardly profane, the drunkard kept under control, and the slothful made to walk some hours during the day for exercise. Prisoners arose at six o'clock. Grove had a room to himself where he had two eggs and a glass of wine for dinner and 'a crust of bread and a glass of wine finish the gluttony of the day'; surely this was not typical prison fare.[6]

His uncle sent a clerk to Warwick with a report containing three large sheets of *lies* (presumably the

The Bank of England was as solid as its genuine currency.

indictment) which Grove insisted be laid aside and wrote fifteen half-sheets himself, stating the whole business as well as he could.[7]

Bensley's friendship with Grove extended to his lodging Susannah and Daniel in his own house in London. Grove kept writing to him, begging him to prevent his wife, a small and delicate woman, from visiting him, because he felt so ill that the shock might agitate her unduly; her health was impaired enough already and their son had measles. She was also experiencing trouble with her 'miserly' parents who were 'on the brink of the grave'. Should she survive them Grove expected her to inherit £400–£500 a year to settle on their child.[8]

The letters continued to pour out Grove's religious feelings with a fervour of the newly converted. His wife did visit him. He noted her wretched appearance, while she was shocked to see his cell with a notice printed over the fireplace: 'Transportation for life' and declared that she would not let him go alone.[9] His finances were good and by June Susannah must have become reconciled to her parents who promised her £3 000.[10] Grove's brother visited him

and it was hoped that members of the family would at least be able to ensure the Groves a more comfortable voyage.[11]

In September he was taken to Portsmouth in the Governor's gig and placed in the *Captivity* hulk, a 'floating hell', in which his 'ears are ringing with the bitterest imprecations of some, whilst others are singing the most obscene songs'. He did not want to see his wife, who was staying at a local inn, or anyone else, attired as he was in 'this wretched, disgraceful garb my country has thought right to furnish me with'. He asked for his books, including David Collins' history, a few yards of flannel, a pair of worsted stockings, a few quires of paper, pens, wafers, pencils and penknife.[12] He bought a bed and blanket for a hammock and a pair of stockings from the boatswain's mate for £1. He asked his brother to send 300–400 red herrings so he could sell them to repay the money. Grove remarked on the complexions of the crew and wrote that he was taking boiled barley and trying not to eat the ship's provisions to avoid blotchiness and continuous itching.[13]

He was, however, ill for a time and begged his brother not to come again. On a more cheerful note he found that prisoners were, in a recent ship that sailed,

allowed to take boxes with them and as he had been able to arrange for the use of the carpenter's cabin in the *Calcutta*, he and his wife had enough room for trunks.[14] He felt fortunate that they were not on their way to the West Indies for he had heard more reasonable reports of Botany Bay from a returned prisoner (probably James Carrett) who had thought fit to get himself re-transported.

Once on board the *Calcutta*, the Groves found themselves in relative comfort. At Portsmouth the newly married missionary William Crook and his wife, who were to sail in the *Ocean*, befriended them and the Groves in turn entertained them with a

Even when attending service in the Newgate chapel prisoners were hemmed in behind bars.

meal.[15] Other prisoners deferred to Grove as 'Mr Grove'. The Groves also became friendly with the prisoner Samuel Gunn, a carpenter by trade, who had fought at the Battle of Copenhagen.[16] The captain and the officers were extremely polite and treated the family with humanity and respect. Susannah Grove managed to endure the queasiness she was to feel with every roll of the ship on a journey that was to provide, at least for a few years, a rosier future for them than they could have believed possible.[17]

George Harris' sketches are the only detailed illustrations of the camp site at Sullivan Bay in 1803–04.

PART III
The Camp at Sullivan Bay

8 A FISHY STORY

THE 1803 EXPEDITION led by David Collins did not, however, have its origin in matters directly related to easing pressure on the prisons of England. Not only was the Navy in dire need of a fresh source of supplies, but British commercial interests were becoming aware of the potential value of a fisheries industry in the south seas and Bass Strait, a treacherous and later infamous stretch of water discovered in 1798 by George Bass. Both seals and whales abounded in the south seas. Off the western Australian coast, as early as 1699, William Dampier had noted the largest whales he had ever seen. Yet Captain Cook never remarked on them, therefore the development of a whaling industry rated no mention in the plans for the settlement at Botany Bay submitted by James Matra and Sir George Young. However, the House of Enderby and others based in London had already established major interests in the Pacific. Sperm oil as developed since the 1770s provided an important economic commodity essential for British industrialists. Oil was used not only for lighting but also in the manufacture of soap, as dressings for wool and leather, and above all for lubricating the increasingly important wheels of industry. The loss of the American colonies had exposed Britain's dependence on regular supplies of oil formerly provided by the whalers from Nantucket. Many of the colonists who were loyal to England had fled America with their skills, benefiting from the trade concessions of the East India Company. The Company expected protection for its trading interests and some aid to develop industries that would encourage trade with the East, but it would not welcome competition. While on leave in 1791 Captain Philip Gidley King had become friendly with the Enderbys and invested a little money in their company.[1] He firmly supported their commercial interests in Asia and the Pacific, which the East India Company monopolised.

That same year Captain (later Governor) John Hunter was impressed with the number of spermaceti whales reported off the coast of New South Wales and in his *Journal* quoted a letter from the *Britannia*'s captain, Thomas Melville, to Messrs Enderby and Sons. Melville had seen more whales around his ship within a few days than in the entire six years he was off the coast of Brazil. He

saw a very great prospect in making our fishery upon this coast . . . Our people were in the highest spirits at so great a sight, and I was determined, as soon as I got in . . . to make all possible despatch on the fishery on this coast . . .

Captain King used all his interest in the business . . . The secret of seeing whales our sailors could not keep from the rest of the whalers here, the news put them to the stir . . . we were the first ship ready for sea . . . in less than two hours we had seven whales killed . . .[2]

Governor Phillip had mixed feelings about the report. He expressed great anxiety that such an industry would tempt prisoners, especially the more useful ones, to escape from Port Jackson. He was also worried that it could be perceived to be in competition with the East India Company and create fresh problems.[3]

While England was at war with Spain and France there was little chance of sustaining a whaling industry in the Pacific Ocean. But the Americans were confidently able to send their ships sperm whaling because they had access to Spanish ports on the west coast of South America, which were open to them to refit and replenish their supplies.[4] British whalers presented a memorial to the Board of Trade in 1797 demanding the development of a new port for sperm whale fisheries projected off islands adjacent to New Holland, such as the New Hebrides and New Caledonia, and as far to the south-west as Kerguelen Island and north to the Philippines and even Formosa.[5] Port Jackson was already an important stopping place for British ships on the way to China, saving them from entering the Dutch controlled seas of the East Indies. As they learnt of the new British possession, Spanish, American and French crews had begun to make contact and received hospitality.

Although not developed to service whaling vessels, Port Jackson was becoming a regular place for whalers to replenish their stores. David Collins, formerly Judge Advocate in New South Wales, was in England at that time and backed up by reports from Hunter, he urged Messrs Champion, Enderby and others engaged in the industry to establish a repair depot or warehouse at Port Jackson, well supplied with naval stores and try-pots near the entrance to the harbour, in order that British whalers would not have to risk seizure by calling at Peru, where there was a well established station.[6] In 1799 the Spanish Navy had captured fifteen British whalers. Not surprisingly, a number of British whalers turned privateers and captured several Spanish prizes. On one occasion enough grain was salvaged to afford some relief to the near-starving colonists at Port Jackson where, by necessity, a small shipbuilding industry had begun.[7]

While delayed in Sydney awaiting repairs to his own boat, George Bass explored the coastline and its harbours in a locally built whale-boat owned by Governor Hunter, sighting Western Port and its islands as well as the Strait named after him.[8] The south-east coast of the continent had been a land unknown to Europeans, although Cook had sighted Point Hicks in 1770, and it had been a haven for convict escapees along with shipwrecked convicts in 1797 from the *Sydney Cove*. Bass' later discoveries with Matthew Flinders of the river harbours of the Tamar and the Derwent proved how vulnerable the British hold over such widely spaced territory would be if some foreign power appeared on the horizon.[9]

Although sealing before this time had not been very productive the British companies believed it would soon become part of the worldwide chain of trade movement. Sealers were already visiting the Furneaux Islands prior to the departure of Hunter and the discovery of the Strait had raised hopes that there were great sealing grounds awaiting exploitation.

Prior to the expansion of wool production, the people of New South Wales could give little aid to the mother country in her attempts to balance her trade with China. Ships arriving in Sydney, filled with provisions as well as human beings, might conceivably pick up cargoes of skins, which would find a ready market in the thickly populated northern China, a market which a thinly populated Siberia could not satisfy. Oil for the lamps of China as well as Europe was an equally valuable commodity. The busy Chinese merchants would be only too eager to load the holds of the ships with large quantities of tea, to satisfy the recent English addiction, or with the silks and lacquered wares prized greatly in Georgian England.

In 1798 Captain Bishop of the brig *Nautilus* landed fourteen men on Cape Barren Island. Within two months they had clubbed 9 000 seals.[10] By 1802–03 Kable and Underwood had a near monopoly on King and Cape Barren Islands, employing up to 200 men in sealing groups.[11] Small vessels based in Sydney and owned by individuals such as Samuel Rodman Chase conducted a lucrative trade. Selling or bartering with the masters of ships heading for China always depended on whether or not the market there was glutted.

In June 1802 William Campbell, the opportunist owner–master of the brig *Harrington*, had collected a cargo of 5 200 seal skins as well as 500 gallons of oil from elephant-seals before rushing off to grab prizes off the South American coast. But Campbell left thirteen men on King Island where their slaughter of many young seals greatly depleted their numbers.[12]

King sailed for Port Jackson in November 1799 in one of Enderby's whalers, the *Speedy*, arriving the following April to take command as governor. Within two years he reported that three ships had left for England loaded with spermaceti oil, six more were on the coast and off the north end of New Zealand and whales were plentiful. Even in a time of peace it would be preferable to encourage the industry in the south seas rather than rely on the waters off South America, where the wear and tear of ships in the vicinity of Cape Horn was more destructive than the run by Van Diemen's Land. Moreover King stressed that whalers could be used to bring prisoners and stores.[13]

King was farsighted enough to know that economic benefits derived from the development of any industry would provide a *raison d'être* and staple for the colony. From the earliest days he had envisaged, as did Governor Phillip, that the colony would prove to be one of the greatest acquisitions Britain had ever made. This was not the opinion of one who had been sent out merely to purge the prisons and hulks of the refuse of humanity. It was rather the utterance of the naval officer Phillip upon his recognition of the potential riches in the surrounding seas as well as in the land of opportunities.[14]

•　　　•　　　•

H.M. brig *Lady Nelson*, sailing on its maiden voyage from England under the command of Lieutenant James Grant, entered Western Port on 21 March 1801. She had been specially designed with sliding keels to allow exploration of unsurveyed harbours and shallow river estuaries. Grant found excellent deep water while Ensign Barrallier surveyed the southern coast towards Wilson's Promontory. King was anxious to know what potential harbours might lie beyond Western Port when he sent Acting Lieutenant John Murray in the *Lady Nelson* to make further explorations later that year. Murray raised the newly designed Union Jack at Point Paterson on 8 March 1802, proclaiming the territory of Port King in the name of King George III. (Governor King renamed Port King as Port Phillip and Point Paterson became Point King.) He sounded the waters near the Heads and along the eastern coast a little beyond Arthur's Seat, but regrettably left only a sketchy map and a guess at the rest of the coastline. For one who had spent four weeks in the bay his report was superficial and was unlikely to give much encouragement to prospective settlers.

Murray found no adequate water supply, nor did he investigate the surrounding land, beyond climbing Arthur's Seat to examine whether it might be suitable for agricultural or pastoral purposes. However, he did elaborate on the grave difficulty for ships entering the Heads at Port Phillip.[15]

A French scientific expedition led by Nicolas Baudin had sailed along part of the coast and named some features between Western Port and Encounter Bay, many of which had been discovered earlier and named by Grant. In the meantime, Flinders had returned to Australia in H.M.S. *Investigator* and met Baudin at Encounter Bay, where they had an amiable conversation. Unaware that Governor King had sent Murray down from Port Jackson to explore the southern coastline, Flinders sailed on to Port Phillip and anchored off present-day Sorrento on 26 April 1802.

The first known sketch taken in Port Phillip, inscribed: '30 April 1802. Looking to south-west {probably meant north west}. Distant view of the west arm of Western Port'. The artist, William Westall, accompanied Matthew Flinders in the Investigator.

Within a week he had charted its waters much more thoroughly than Murray but he also failed to discover the fresh water river at the head of the harbour.[16]

In all the published results of Baudin's voyage few references hint at any thoughts held by the French other than an interest in science. François Péron, designated anthropologist of the voyage, found that all the phenomena of New Holland

baffles all our analogies, and shakes those scientific opinions which are the most scrupulously admitted. In short, whatever we may have to say of this singular country . . . we shall state many other natural phenomena equally strange and incomprehensible.[17]

In a private letter to King (who spoke fluent French), Baudin professed his ideals of human equality and of the rights of man, including the original inhabitants of Van Diemen's Land and its islands, with an eloquence rarely surpassed on that subject. He reminded King that Tasman and his heirs did not bequeath him those territories and that 'sooner or later they may say to you *"Sic vos non vobis nidificatis"!*'

To my way of thinking, I have never been able to conceive there was justice and equity on the part of Europeans in seizing . . . when it is inhabited by men who have not always deserved the title of savages or cannibals which has been given them, whilst they were but the children of nature and just as little civilised as are actually your Scottish Highlanders or our peasants in Brittany, who, if they do not eat their fellow men, are nevertheless just as objectionable.[18]

Baudin admitted that his remarks were 'no doubt impolitic, but at least reasonable from the facts' and

that had Britain adopted these principles she would never have needed to found a colony

by means of men branded by the law, and who have become criminals through the fault of Government which has neglected and abandoned them . . . not only have you to reproach yourselves with an injustice in seizing their land, but also in transporting on a soil where the crimes and the diseases of Europeans were unknown all that could retard the progress of civilisation, which has served as a pretext to your Government . . . [19]

Baudin also lamented that such an inhospitable place as King Island bore the Governor's name. It had no suitable harbour or anchorage and he warned King that the surrounding seas already indicated that resources such as the sea-wolf and sea-elephant (seals) were becoming scarce. [20]

Péron conducted dynamometrical experiments, developed by Edmé de Regnier (who had studied medicine), on the physical strength of the people in Van Diemen's Land, New Holland and Timor, comparing them with the English and the French, but he had little time to further his study of the native race. [21]

It was too early in the study to be searching for a 'missing link'. The 'child of nature' was still very much an illusion of the French scientists. But Péron claimed to be the first to observe in distant parts that physical strength is neither diminished by civilisation nor does it constitute a natural consequence of a savage state. He set out to disprove the 'dangerous opinion so generally promulgated and believed, *that the physical degeneration of man is in proportion to his state of civilisation!*' [22]

Péron did not live long enough (he died in 1810) to complete the classification of 100 000 zoological specimens collected. This number included 2 500 new species which he claimed to be more than those discovered by all contemporary naturalists. His ethnological and zoological observations were to form a basis for Jean-Baptiste Lamarck's publication *Besoins des Choses*, which was to shake the creationist doctrines of Calvinist and Catholic Europe long before Charles Darwin's concept of natural selection.

Was there, however, any significance in the more political observations Péron made on 'savages', principally on their uncivilised condition, their lack of physical strength as compared with other native populations, and his conclusion that they were weaker in every respect than the English? Was it possible that he was there to report on the kind of opposition one might expect from the indigenes if those Gallic intruders chose to occupy any part of the Great South Land? The St Domingue affair had indicated that Napoleon's policy was to crush any native population which showed signs of strength. [23] The early years of

British occupation unfortunately bear witness to the fact that it was the superiority of technological strength, not physical strength, that would be more significant in the long run.

Péron was also to report back to his *Institut* with some important observations on the British use of convicts to colonise, those 'redoubtable brigands, who were so long the terror of the Government of their country . . . have, under happier influences, cast aside their anti-social manners . . .' He found that, having 'expiated their crimes in hard slavery', most of the convicts became 'bound to a state of citizenship'. The acquisition of land and perhaps a family obliged them to maintain order and justice. [24]

Governor King suspected French motives and suggested further settlements in Bass Strait to the Duke of Portland in May 1802, after considering Murray's and Flinders' reports. [25] They had believed that the soil and climate of Port Phillip made it more eligible for raising wheat than Port Jackson. The security and spaciousness of the harbour made Port Phillip a more desirable location than Western Port. In anticipation that greater numbers would be sent to the colony after the peace, King considered that occupation was urgent. Otherwise, when they received Baudin's and Péron's reports, the French could well contemplate early settlement; King could not help 'thinking it a principal object of their researches'. [26]

King's concern could hardly fall on deaf ears when caricaturists James Gillray and Thomas Rowlandson were rudely lampooning Napoleon and his grandiose ideas, while the comics blasted the French from the London stage:

With lantern jaws, and croaking gut,
See how the half-starved Frenchmen strut,
   And call us English dogs!
But soon we'll teach these bragging foes,
That beef and beer give heavier blows
   Than soup and roasted frogs. [27]

King too was the subject of crude lampoons because of his relatively minor financial interest in Enderby & Co., very minor compared with the corrupt commercial ventures of the New South Wales Corps. [28] He had managed to provide himself and his *two* families with some of the plums of office, but he had not been as successful as other officers in exploiting his colonial position for financial gain and therefore had little to invest in the breed of fine-wooled Spanish sheep that Sir Joseph Banks had extolled in the corridors of power. King was watching his colleagues grow rich and powerful, causing divisions within the ranks of the small society. But trading in rum was anathema to him and he fought against its evils during his entire governorship. Spurred on by Enderby's successes, it

Sealing, the main reason for British, American and French interest in Bass Strait, is here portrayed by the French artist Charles Lesueur, a member of the Baudin expedition during its sojourn at Sea Elephant Bay, King Island.

may well be that, after the discovery of Bass Strait, the thought of building his own small fishing empire was uppermost in King's mind: a nice venture with a future. But he was not so blatant as to use this as a major pretext in promoting occupation of the Strait. It might have been a case of honest graft, more honest or rather more subtle than that employed by the Macarthurs of the colony. But he was over-sensitive to criticism and changed his emphasis on the reasons for a southern settlement. He seized the opportunity when William Paterson, his newly appointed Lieutenant-Governor, breathed doubts about French intentions.[29] He now had a new motive for extending the British domain that would also include the fisheries. It was a good ploy to frighten those at Whitehall into action.[30] A memorandum, inspired by King, specifically mentioned both the advantages of a port and the fear of the French. The unknown official who wrote the memo at the end of November 1802 anticipated that the French must be aware of the British discovery

of the more important prizes within the Strait, that is, Port Phillip and King's Island. They may be 'stimulated to take early measures for themselves in positions so favourable for interrupting in any future war the communication . . .'[31]

Supporting immediate establishment of a settlement at the 'capacious and secure harbour' of Port Phillip, the memorandum stressed the additional advantage that would be accorded to the valuable fishing industry in the 'Straights [*sic*] where the seal and seal elephant abound'. It also specified the need for moral improvement in the future colony which would not take place unless a certain number of settlers would form part of the settlement together with the selected male convicts. If the wives and children of some of them were sent it would be an 'added incentive' for their good behaviour.[32]

Lord Hobart, who succeeded the Duke of Portland as Secretary of State for War and the Colonies, thought it was essential to disperse the convicts away from Port Jackson: 'If you continually send thieves to one place it must in time be supersaturated. We must let it rest and purify it for a few years and it will be again in condition to receive.' These were the sentiments of which Sir Joseph Banks approved.

9 THE GOVERNOR AND THE CHAPLAIN

TWO NAVAL VESSELS chosen to collect timber in New South Wales were H.M.S. *Glatton* (Captain James Colnett) which left for Port Jackson with a large contingent of male and female convicts in September 1802 and H.M.S. *Calcutta* (Captain Daniel Woodriff) carrying a complement of 150 men and 308 male convicts along with civil officers, marines and some wives and children. The *Calcutta* sailed from Portsmouth in April 1803 for Port Phillip, accompanied by the *Ocean* (Captain John Mertho). The *Ocean* was under contract to carry supplies as well as settlers and other civil officers and their families. Lieutenant-Colonel David Collins of the Royal Marines was commissioned Lieutenant-Governor of the new settlement. In all, more than 600 persons bravely set out for a little known part of the world.[1]

Collins had been an obvious choice to command the new settlement. He was, one might say, born to rule but had usually to serve, a role which he had discharged without rancour and with much distinction. He was born in London in 1756, son of Major-General Arthur Tooker Collins and his wife Harriet (née Fraser) of Pack, King's County, Ireland, a grandson of the noted author of the *Peerage of England*, Arthur Collins. His mother's ancestors were Highland Scots. David was the third child of a family of eleven. He was to inherit both the military and intellectual abilities of his ancestors. On completing his formal education at Exeter grammar school at the early age of fourteen, he joined the marines as an ensign in his father's division. He fought conspicuously in the American War, including the battle of Bunker Hill. While stationed at Halifax, Nova Scotia, he married Maria Stuart Proctor, daughter of a loyalist leader, Captain Charles Proctor, one of the founders of Halifax. The only child of the marriage died in infancy.[2]

After participation in the bloody siege of Gibraltar Collins was retired from active service on a captain's half-pay. He and his wife made their home at Rochester in Kent. There were financial difficulties until the opportunity arose to accompany Governor Arthur Phillip (dubbed 'that Romulus of the South Pole' by the Reverend Sydney Smith) as Secretary and Judge Advocate of the new colony of New South Wales. Collins' knowledge of the law was then limited to courts martial. Legal duties during his eight years' absence from England meant imposing heavy punishments for what may appear trivial matters, for he lacked discretionary powers. Theft of food, for instance, during periods of starvation, warranted the severest of floggings, sometimes the death sentence. Such severity was alien to his nature, but notably approved when he reprimanded and punished convicts who had robbed or harmed the natives. On one occasion, after the destruction of a native canoe and the resultant spearing of the convict who was guilty of the action, he asked who had the 'greater claim to the appellation of savages . . . the wretches who were the cause of this, [or] the native who was the sufferer?'[3] He expressed 'great pleasure' when he heard of the steps taken to prosecute the master of the transport *Neptune* for the neglect of and cruelty towards the convicts in his care during the voyage in 1790.[4]

Collins was Phillip's closest friend and confidant. The Lieutenant-Governor, Major Robert Ross, whose hatred of Phillip, Collins and the colony was intense, complained of Phillip that 'he communicates nothing to any person here but his secretary'.[5] As a result, Collins' *An Account of the English Colony in New South Wales* remains the most authentic first-hand report of the first eight years of European settlement, even if one critic did believe it bore a striking resemblance to the *Newgate Calendar*.[6]

Phillip was not the only person with whom Collins had a close relationship. Like many of his colleagues David Collins had taken a convict, Ann Yeates ('a very fit person', according to Lieutenant William Bowes Smyth, 'having uniformly behaved well') as his mistress and companion.[7] They had a son and daughter, both of whom were to become known in later years in Hobart Town. The little family bound him to the colony for longer than most of the original founders.

Lieutenant-Governor David Collins 'was remarkably handsome and his manners extremely pre-possessing . . .' (Joseph Holt).

Perhaps the disrespect of Collins shown by 'that devil Ross', as Collins' wife Maria called Ross after he visited her in England, was related to this behaviour.[8]

But eventually Collins did return to his lawful wife in England in 1797 on half-pay, with little hope of advancement from his promotion the following year to the rank of lieutenant-colonel. Four years later the chance came to lead the expedition to Port Phillip. It was during these four years that he wrote his two-volume history which was a success. After he left England for the second time, Maria Collins, a person of considerable literary ability (she was later to write several novels, in spite of continual ill health due to epilepsy) produced a good single-volume edition. Collins wrote privately of her to Sir Joseph Banks with some concern as he prepared

with the utmost cheerfulness in an arduous and hazardous enterprize . . . I leave behind me a wife, who has been elegantly and delicately brought up, and whose Constitution has been much impaired by my former long Absences abroad, and subsequent Disappointments; but who will now, I trust, during my Life, be enabled to live with Comfort, but who, should anything happen to me while abroad, would be left destitute, not having . . . even the Widow's Pension to support her . . . if you Sir, would interest yourself in the cause of the Widow and the friend-

less Woman . . . My expenses on this Occasion far exceed my Means . . . wholly out of my Power to make any Provision for her myself . . .[9]

Even his mother had realised that he probably looked forward to his return to the colony for some sort of reunion, at least with the children he had fathered years before.[10] But just before his departure he did make out his will, bequeathing all his effects, such as they were, to his beloved wife, and his soul 'into the hands of my Creator hoping for a remission of my sins through the Merits of my Redeemer'.[11] He obviously, as history suggests, had made some separate arrangements for the upbringing of the children by Ann Yeates.

The second volume of his book, based on information obtained from several sources, appeared shortly before he sailed in the *Calcutta*. He would surely have seen Sydney Smith's review in the latter's newly established *Edinburgh Review*, in which Smith expressed the pompous belief that 'To introduce an European population and consequently the art and civilisation of Europe, into such untrodden country as New Holland, is to confer a lasting and important benefit on the world . . .'[12]

But Smith took to task the policy of the government in settling the continent with convicts, even though he agreed that 'with fanciful schemes of universal good we have no business to meddle'. He queried the wisdom of erecting 'penitentiary houses and prisons at the distance of half the diameter of the globe and to incur the enormous expense of feeding and transporting their inhabitants to, and at such a distance', believing that it would encourage further offences.

When the history of the colony has been attentively perused in the parish of St Giles, the ancient avocation of picking pockets will certainly not become more discreditable from the knowledge that it may eventually lead to the possession of a farm of 1 000 acres on the River Hawkesbury. Since the benevolent Howard attacked our prisons, incarceration has become not only healthy, but elegant . . . transportation will be considered as one of the surest roads to honour and to wealth.[13]

Worst of all, he could foresee the terrible calamity that would befall the mother country, which, after all the capital expended on the colony, might one day be humbled again before a 'fresh set of Washingtons and Franklins'.[14]

Collins himself had played down any censure of government policy he himself might have had, especially in this second volume of his work. After all, he was a servant of the Crown who had aspired to further appointment in the colony. There is a hint of reprobation in his first volume, published some four years earlier, no doubt the source of Smith's criticism, that the wonderfully fertile valley of the Hawkesbury, the 'Nile of New South Wales', should fall into the hands of unworthy persons who might become opulent farmers.[15] As a man who was ill-rewarded for his own honest labours during fifteen years colonial service, he must have wondered at the fairness of wrong-doers being the recipients of so much.

Sydney Smith also predicted that the time might come when

Some Botany Bay Tacitus shall record the crimes of an Emperor lineally descended from a London pick-pocket, or paint the valour with which he has led his New Hollanders into the heart of China. At that period, when the Grand Lahma [*sic*] is sending to supplicate alliance; when the spice islands are purchasing peace with nutmegs; when enormous tributes of green tea and nankeen are wafted into Port Jackson and launched on the keys [*sic*] of Sydney, who will remember that the sawing of a few planks and the knocking together a few nails, were such a serious trial of the energies and resources of the nation?[16]

The situation, for Collins, would recur at Port Phillip and again at Hobart Town, drafting whatever labour was available to him. In his exhausted mind the men were usually old and useless, hardly capable of building a settlement from scratch — the habitations for his people as well as for himself, a place for stores, a hospital, a gaol and all the necessary accoutrements of a town. Of course there would be dramas unappreciated by Smith, as when the stores failed to provide any necessary nails for the First Fleeters. It would be impossible even to imagine Collins' reaction when he read Smith's review of his work, written from the comfortable study of a vicarage and with the solid traditions of centuries behind him. The invasion of China could well wait for the millenium, while every possible grain of wheat had to be watched, sown, grown, harvested and safely stored, every animal protected even more than a human being, rags of clothing scavenged and mended and reshaped. The drama at their own back door, the drama of survival, was to be as basic in the early years of Collins' reign as it had been during the hungry years of Arthur Phillip.

•   •   •

If the appointment of Collins was sound, albeit somewhat dull, the transfer of the highly adaptable Reverend Robert Knopwood from naval duties in the West Indies to sail in H.M.S. *Calcutta* as chaplain was an inspiration. The First Lord of the Admiralty, the Earl of Spencer, was probably the person responsible for obtaining his chaplaincy aboard H.M.S. *Resolution* in 1801.[17] Knopwood served in the West Indies under Captain the Hon. Allen Hyde Gardner. He then

began to keep his daily diaries in a thick volume with a blue and red-brown watered cover, half-bound with calf. His quaint style, wayward spelling and the triviality of most of his diary entries for more than thirty years of his life in the colony all contrast with the first class education he had enjoyed. Yet from the human weaknesses that breathe life into every page one can reconstruct the social history of his time more faithfully than by reproducing the official version of how Governor King's plans for settlement in Bass Strait were achieved.

Knopwood hailed originally from Threxton in Norfolk, a village on the edge of the area known as Breckland, south-west of Norwich and extending into Suffolk. Born in June 1863, he was the son of Robert, High Sheriff of Norfolk, a prosperous farmer who had acquired the whole parish of Threxton and adjacent lands. Another son and daughter had died in infancy and Robert junior shared his childhood days with an older and younger sister.[18]

From his earliest years he had fostered a lifelong love of the horse and outdoor life. He would have had his own pony to attend primary school a few miles away from home at Wymondham, on the road to Norwich. The flat terrain, dotted with odd windmills, presented a peacefulness and beauty that sat incongruously with its history of Roman, Viking and Anglo-Saxon invasions. Blood had spattered the fens for centuries, blood as red as the poppies that added colour in high summer to the sweeping cornfields.

Not far from Threxton the haunting Peddar's Way, built by a prehistoric people long before the Romans arrived, inspired legends of a more distant past. It belonged to an age of flintstone and had become a way for pilgrims, dividing the marshy Breckland from the farms. Birds nested in the sedge from the sandy approaches where bracken and heather ran wild. It was a land of colour which had inspired a distinct school of painting, the Norwich school, for generations. Here Bobby Knopwood spent his formative years surrounded by natural beauty and bird life of great variety.

He was only eight when his father died in debt. Part of the family estate had to be sold to pay off £10 000 still owing. However, Threxton Hall itself remained in the family. By the time Knopwood was twenty-three he had inherited what was left (some £18 000) and he was expected to add to the support of his mother and sisters. But life at boarding school at Bury St Edmund's, and at Newport in Essex, followed by studies at Caius College, Cambridge, were expensive.[19] When he graduated as a bachelor of arts in 1786 he had already begun to dissipate his inheritance. Before furthering his studies to gain his master's degree in 1790 Knopwood was ordained at Norwich Cathedral, first as deacon and later as priest. He went

51

further into debt, the result of an association with young Viscount Clermont, one of the set surrounding the loose-living Prince of Wales. He ultimately had to sell Threxton to cover his debts, becoming private chaplain to Clermont and later to the Earl of Spencer.[20]

Already his interests, both sportive and sporting, were far removed from those of a near contemporary who had also taken holy orders, Gilbert White. The latter despised the country squire and country parson whose horizon 'was bounded by their rod, their gun, their hounds, and their dinner'.[21] Knopwood's whole life, even in the Antipodes, was to remain unbound by convention. In that respect he was the archetype of an eighteenth-century English parson, complete with his cry of 'Yeoix, yeoix! Tantivy, tantivy!'.[22] Yet it was his spirits rather than his spiritualism that made him an all-too-human and genial parson, rather well-suited to the position thrust upon him, aware of his own frailties, when he advised his flock to 'do as I say, not as I do'.[23] He gave hospitality and received even more from all who would drink or share a pipe with him, stipulating if necessary that 'Where I dine I sleep'.[24]

In Norwich the young bucks used to carouse into the small hours at the King's Head and many other places, particularly at the inn where Mother Dilly-water and her 'lovely fair crew' reigned.[25] While he was sowing his wild oats he had fathered a child in Norwich, but there is little known about any further relationship he might have had with the mother, Hannah Cook.[26] They were giddy days, nurturing a band of somewhat worthless youths who contributed very little to life. In his own way, Knopwood was to contribute far more than most.

He served in the West Indies during a relatively calm period of hostilities when British naval vessels were safeguarding British interests instead of engaging in hostilities. The greater action was then at Copenhagen, where Admiral Nelson subdued the Danish fleet, and in the Mediterranean, where Lord Keith landed General Abercromby's army in Aboukir Bay. Life in the *Resolution*, according to Knopwood, amounted to a series of pleasant interludes, not least of which was going ashore at Barbados for a large ball in March 1802, perhaps a preliminary celebration of the anticipated peace.[27] This was a very different naval experience from that of the officers and men in H.M.S. *Calcutta*, most of whom had survived great battles during their confrontations with the French. But it set the pattern for Knopwood's social life. Sojourns ashore during the voyage to Australia were among the highlights of his life. Entertainments aboard visiting ships and reciprocal functions ashore would be among the few indulgences in the colony to gratify his gregarious nature.

10 A LONG SEA VOYAGE

*T*HE *EUROPEAN MAGAZINE and London Review* of May 1803 reported the departure of the *Calcutta* and *Ocean* and credited Captain Daniel Woodriff with having only one death (Smith, the 'sham parson') during the first three months he had care of the convicts and three on the sick list, because of the

unremitting exertion of officers to have them clean; at five every morning their hammocks are carried up on the booms, and the decks washed and scraped; and as many are admitted in turn, as is consistent with safety, upon deck for two hours every day . . . fifty-nine healthy young women to go out with them; and these, doubtless, will form not the least important part of the stock taken out for the eventual colonisation of this hitherto unexplored region, certainly situated at the farthest limits of the known world.[1]

At first it was not intended to send the wives and children of convicts in the same ship as their husbands. Reunion itself in the colony would be an incentive for those who were expected to be regarded as indentured servants. But Lord Hobart allowed a few families to sail in the *Calcutta* in answer to Governor King's letter stressing the need to send wives and children with any men, including convicts, who might comprise the contingent establishing the new colonies. Families would be an incentive to good behaviour and improve the moral tone of the colony.[2]

Seventeen wives left England with their convict husbands (including two de facto) together with six sons and five daughters. The wives of nine marines together with three children set off, alongside the wives of eight male settlers and two women settlers together with eighteen children, the wives of two civil officers and four children as well as the wife of a missionary. At least eleven of the twenty-four children of free persons were girls. The convict wife and daughter of one settler, Henry Hayes, and de facto convict wife and two sons of another, John Blinkworth, already at Port Jackson, would later join their partners in Hobart Town.[3]

Edward Bromley, surgeon of the *Calcutta*, was responsible for choosing 300 convicts out of a list of 400 names submitted to him as possible transportees. According to Lieutenant Tuckey he looked primarily at the health and age of the men, because he would receive £10 for every convict landed in health at his destination; it was a bonus if they happened to gain a new arrival born at sea.[4] Bromley had little knowledge of their characters and Tuckey was critical that there was no knowledge of their trades, although they should have been aware of one existing document setting out those chosen from the hulks *Prudentia* and *Stanislaus* at Woolwich, which stated ages and designated trades.[5] It would appear that before the short list reached Bromley, some care had been given to obtaining persons with a wide range of trades useful in pioneering a new colony. True, there were not many on this list who had had much agricultural experience. Of those in the Woolwich hulks more than half had been convicted in London and many more in the more heavily populated areas. But the majority of those in the Portsmouth hulks tended to come from the rural areas, while seventy-five out of eighty taken on in Langston gave village domiciles.[6] This certainly indicates that many might have been agricultural labourers, in spite of Collins' later complaint that he was short of men trained in farming methods. However, quite a number had known how to steal sheep and horses. Collins later discovered that many of his convicts worked harder and were better suited to producing supplies than any of his free settlers, although many of the latter were hampered by the scarcity of labour which existed during the first few years of settlement. William Drew had stated that he was a farmer and Joseph Pendall called himself a horse doctor and farmer. William Smith of Middlesex said he was a drover. Thirteen from the counties gave their occupation as husbandmen and thirty-two as labourers. But Collins gave the latter number as 137.[7] It is evident from the trials that most had been at some time engaged in the work-force.

Court records indicated at least 264 had trades or occupations at the time of trial. There were twelve shoemakers, eight butchers, eight blacksmiths, seven gardeners, eleven clerks. Collins listed some who would be useful in building construction: three carpenters and three cabinet makers, nine sawyers, four brickmakers and six bricklayers. There were also five bakers and two pastrycooks.[8] Others suggested a variety of callings, among which were a buttonmaker, lapidary, refiner, silversmith, ropemaker, hemp spinner, brewer, sailmaker, schoolmaster, carpet weaver, stocking weaver, brass founder, locksmith and so on. Tuckey had seen little use for gentlemen's servants, hairdressers, hackney-coachmen, silk weavers, calico printers, merchants' clerks and even gentlemen. Could a watchmaker, he queried, make 100 nails a day?[9] It would have surprised him had he learnt how some of these men adjusted. He would never have believed how, when forced to become agricultural labourers, many would, as quickly, succeed as landowners.

Lord Hobart was well aware of the need for artificers and basic materials in a new colony. Before the *Calcutta* sailed, he wrote to Governor King directing him to spare, for Port Phillip, as many carpenters, bricklayers, masons, sawyers and smiths with bricks, planks, etc. as possible, as well as a proportion of every kind of livestock, seeds and roots.[10] When the time came Collins obviously found he had a larger number of useful people than he had at first thought, because he only asked King for two men to be sent down from Sydney. In return he was able to provide King with an excellent brewer, Thomas Rushton.[11]

The *Calcutta*'s victuals were chosen from among those items best suited to withstand a long and difficult voyage. No expense was spared in ensuring that the quality and quantity were up to the standards expected in the Royal Navy. In this respect the prisoners probably fared better than the settlers in the *Ocean*, who would have received the meagre rations normally allowed by its merchant owners, even though it was chartered to carry most of the stores for the proposed colony.

Lord Hobart in his instructions to Collins prior to the departure of the ships listed the rations to be allocated to 547 persons over a period of two years. These included four pounds of pork or seven pounds of beef a week for each man; six ounces of sugar, and twelve and a half pounds of wheat, or a proportionate quantity of biscuit or flour. Wine and spirits were regularly available for the military detachment and officers. As a special indulgence a small quantity of wine and spirits, tea and sugar, might be available to all.[12] There was only one reported incidence when one convict over-indulged and was charged with drunkenness.[13] There was an assortment of medicines, three

sets of surgical instruments, furniture and other necessities for a hospital, tea, wine and vinegar for the sick.[14]

Seeds for planting on arrival included English wheat, barley and oats, green and white peas, rye, maize, turnip, potato, carrot, cucumber, cabbage, onion, lettuce, celery, and red and white clover. Articles for bartering were to be sold at fifty per cent over the prime cost as an encouragement for the populace to earn enough to supplement the regular issue.[15]

Ironmongery, tools and other implements had the markings of the King's Broad Arrow on the letters N.S.W. and included everything one could imagine necessary for a pioneering society. There were enough spades, shovels, hoes, axes and saws allocated to go around.[16] But unfortunately after unpacking them Collins would find that the quality was poor and some items were almost unfit for use. There was no twist, glue, borax, resin or a bar of steel. The four iron guns were odd and the triangle sent to weigh them had one leg rotten. Collins had no complaints about the hundreds of other items ranging from ship's bells to call the people to labour, writing slates and pencils, beeswax, timber carriages or 'Beeds [*sic*], glasses, clasps, knives and other Trifles, as presents for the Natives to the amount of £20'.[17]

The arts or artifices of war and peace were not forgotten. The Office of Ordinance at Portsmouth provided enormous amounts of arms and ammunition which might be needed to proclaim the strength of the mother country. The Church of England provided the fine silver communion service (now held in St David's Cathedral, Hobart) which might proclaim the strength of the Christian faith.[18] But at the last minute Collins found that there was neither a clock nor hour-glass among the stores. He was able to procure the latter from the naval stores at Portsmouth, and these would be watched over and changed at Port Phillip by timekeepers. He had the opportunity during the voyage, when they called at Rio, to buy a clock of Arnold's construction for fourteen guineas from the commander of an Indiaman then in port.[19]

•   •   •

Until the time that the ships arrived at Port Phillip and disembarked their passengers, the captains were in complete charge. Captain Woodriff had first served in the Royal Navy at the age of six. He was a servant to his uncle, a master gunner in H.M.S. *Ludlow Castle*, which sailed from the west coast of Africa to the West Indies, presumably engaged in the transport of slaves. A later product of Greenwich Naval College, Woodriff joined the merchant service but returned to the Royal Navy in 1775, serving in the North Sea, the West Indies, North America and off

Convicts and free shared alike the bread placed on the silver paten at communion. The photograph shows part of the communion plate belonging to St David's Cathedral, Hobart, inscribed as follows: 'This Service of Communion Plate was presented by His Majesty King George the 3rd for the use of the chapel at His Majesty's settlement at Port Phillip Bass's Streights {sic} in New South Wales, 1803'.

the Flemish coast. He had already been to New South Wales in 1792, as an agent sent by the Admiralty in the merchant transport *Kitty*, delivering a few prisoners and much needed provisions to the starving colony. He was to report that the defences at Port Jackson were totally inadequate and that the one man who could load and fire a cannon was a habitual drunkard.[20]

Like David Collins, Woodriff had married an American girl, the daughter of a loyalist from South Carolina. She had made a home on the Isle of Wight. Three sons were midshipmen in the Navy and planned to sail in the *Calcutta*, but one withdrew at the last minute.[21] Unlike two of his lieutenants, James Hingston Tuckey and Nicholas Pateshall, Woodriff had, in all his years in the Royal Navy, seen little of actual naval engagements. His expertise had been diverted to convoy and transport duties. It was not until the *Calcutta* herself became a victim of war in 1805 that he, together with Lieutenant Tuckey and many of his men, would experience the loss of a ship and serve as a prisoner of the French.[22]

No sooner was the *Calcutta* ready to leave, having taken on her final contingent of convicts from the hulks at Portsmouth, than a delay occurred. According to John Pascoe Fawkner, Hannah, the wife of Irish forger Matthew Power, sought Collins' leave to have a boat sent ashore at St Helen's to collect her pet poodle which she had left behind. Perhaps this was fictitious,

but certainly she did attract the eye of Collins at an early stage of the journey. She had been fortunate to escape conviction as her husband's accomplice in his crime. Matthew was a printer from Dublin, distinguished looking, dark and, at five feet ten inches, a tall man compared with most of his contemporaries. The twenty-three-year-old Hannah, also Irish, was petite and fair, and had lived in London before moving to Thanington, Kent, where Matthew had a labouring job. They were both committed to Newgate for uttering a forged banknote. Their trial at Maidstone on 4 August 1802 took place on the same day as the trials of six other *Calcutta* convicts. Daniel Anchor, a butcher, received a similar conviction for uttering counterfeit notes. His wife Fanny was to become one of Hannah's closest women associates. They shared reasonably comfortable quarters in the gunroom of the *Calcutta* with the woman known as Mary Whitehead. Mary had boarded the ship as the wife of Andrew Whitehead, the London clerk who had embezzled £40 from his employers and was apprehended when actually boarding an American ship, *Industry*, bound for New York.[23]

Two other women whose acknowledged status kept them somewhat aloof from the other women were Susannah Grove and Hannah Fawkner, whose husbands were James Grove from Birmingham, the engraver of Bank of England notes, and John Fawkner, also born in Birmingham but living in London, who had received a large supply of valuable jewellery, gold and silver. The families became friendly during the voyage when sharing berths in the fore cockpit and, unlike the women already mentioned, they had children. Most married couples had to endure accommodation on the starboard side, between the fore and main masts and in between decks, with some partitioning for a little privacy.

Mrs Grove had received her dowry of £3 000, which Grove anticipated would yield £150 annually. Mrs Fawkner came from the Pascoe family of Cornwall, of whom her son John later wrote with some pride. He had lived for some years with the Pascoe grandparents in Cock Lane who had sent him to a dame's school. Later he attended an academy in Cheyne Row, Chelsea, run by a man named Edwards who boarded seventy boys. Young John was a diligent pupil who responded well to the teachings of a priest who had fled from France at the time of the Revolution. The untimely arrest of his father and the imminent removal of the family to New South Wales stopped short a career in which some sparks of interest in learning and the betterment of his position in society were already manifest.[24]

Even before they set out there is evidence that Susannah Grove and Hannah Fawkner could command some respect. The missionaries, the Reverend

William Crook and his wife, had actually come to the *Calcutta* just before it sailed (he was leaving in the *Ocean*) to dine with the Grove family.[25] Hannah Fawkner had had the nous to get an interview with a Mr Capper at the Home Office to make her family's own arrangements for joining the ship. She organised the children and as many of their possessions as possible on to a mail-coach, receiving an inside seat for the cost of a guinea. She headed for Portsmouth on a tiresome night ride which her son described in detail many years later.[26]

The Fawkners were at first upset that they had had to sell their feather beds as these were not allowed on board and flock beds were substituted. But John Fawkner and James Grove were able to pay for the use of the boatswain's and carpenter's quarters on the orlop deck at twenty guineas apiece for the comfort of their wives and families.[27] They had a comparatively comfortable journey to the Antipodes, in spite of the seasickness that beset Susannah Grove and her son Daniel in the first few days when strong gales occurred in the Bay of Biscay. Writing to his friend Thomas Bensley from Tenerife, James Grove indicated that his wife had 'found but one female [Mrs Fawkner?] with whom she can exchange a word. The one who called on her in London — whose husband is on board — turns out a disgrace to her sex'.[28] The pious Grove, who was indulging in new-found religious fervour that was making him 'a humble follower of CHRIST', was probably referring to the behaviour of Hannah Power whom we might assume would have remained in London to be close to her husband in Newgate. If she were the woman visitor, Grove reverts to double standards of behaviour when he praises Governor Collins for the latter's attention to his wife, whom he received

very politely, and always speaks to her of me in the most friendly way. Also to my boy when they meet on the poop . . . Dr Nopwood [*sic*], the chaplain, and magistrate of the settlement comes down to our cabin, and converses with us in the most affable and friendly manner; hopes we shall bear up against this tide of misfortune, . . . the captain is very merry, notices his namesake [i.e. Daniel] . . . I do not think there is one who would not render us any service which could be needed.[29]

As they took farewell of England, the feelings of those who set sail were as varied as one might expect. Lieutenant Tuckey noted that on the whole the sentiment seemed to be one of indifference. Obviously those leaving of their own free will would not have been unduly saddened, while many whose situation had been forced upon them had some hopes for a better future. Tuckey wrote that a few women 'whose birth and education had promised them a different fate, were affected by this heart-rending, though vol-untary exile'. Some of these women had married their prodigal partners

in the sunshine of prosperity, when the world smiled deceitfully, and their path of life appeared strewed with unfading flowers; in the season of adversity they would not be separated, but reposed their heads upon the same thorny pillow; and as they had shared with them the cup of joy, they refused not that of sorrow. Those alone who know the miserable and degraded situation of a transported felon can appretiate [*sic*] the degree of connubial love, that could induce these women to accompany their guilty husbands in their exile . . . To these helpless females, all the attentions that humanity dictated . . . were extended, but still it was impossible to separate their situations entirely from their guilty husbands, they were consequently far, very far, from being comfortable . . .[30]

Lieutenant Pateshall reported that many relations of the convicts came on board to take their last farewell. He observed that if the 'keen affliction of leaving friends brought tears to the eyes of the oldest seaman, what must have been the feelings of the unhappy Convicts, banished for ever from their homes'.[31]

Captain Woodriff had received instructions to sail as swiftly as possible to Port Phillip, calling only at such places as might be convenient to obtain fresh supplies. Tuckey found that many of the men were prepared to forego their daily supply of meat in order to try and hook the shark, the hereditary foe of sailors, but that when sucessful and the

deluded victim is dragged on board, no pack of hungry fox-hounds can be more restless, till they receive the reward of their labours, than the sailors to tear out the bowels, and examine the stomach of the shark. Here they often recover the pieces of meat used to bait the hooks . . .[32]

Pateshall thought the shark was as tasty as the conger or sea eel. In the Bay of Biscay they sent boats out to catch turtles, which they made into soup for the sick and convalescent. But there were relatively few chances to procure fresh food and by the time they arrived at Santa Cruz, where they took on supplies of water and food, signs of scurvy among the prisoners were already discernible. There they procured a large quantity of lemons and fresh vegetables. John Pascoe Fawkner remembered that plums, lime juice and vinegar were provided for all on board, as well as medical attendance and wine for both bound and free.

Good hygiene was the main preventative of disease, therefore calling at various ports to make free use of fresh water was important when so many were crowded together. Sanitation and health were among the major considerations of both the government and those contracted to transport convicts halfway across the world on a journey that could last anything from three to five months. In charge of the health of the convicts and settlers were three doctors, the senior being William I'Anson, with Matthew Bowden and William Hopley as assistants.[33] They were supplied with an assortment of medicines, three complete sets of surgical instruments, furniture and other necessities for a hospital, including adequate bedding. But the surgical instruments were said to be obsolete and used previously. Most had the mark of Evans, yet Stodart had already improved on the Evans instruments.

Surgeon Bowden, who was closest to the Reverend Robert Knopwood, was to take as mistress Maria Sergeant, the wife of one of the sergeants of marines whose marriage ceremony Knopwood had performed on the day the *Calcutta* sailed from Portsmouth. She was Maria Stanfield, a camp-follower from Gosport, who had formed an attachment to the sergeant and was obviously intent on a life of adventure. Fawkner noted that soon after they sailed she was frequently in Knopwood's cabin. Bowden himself sailed in the *Ocean* and would have had little chance to be with her until their arrival at Port Phillip. From then on, they were together for the rest of their lives.

Mary, 'Mrs Whitehead', apart from an affair with Leonard Fosbrook, the Deputy Commissary, appears to have remained faithful for a time to the man she chose to follow to the ends of the earth. But when it came to light that she was merely the de facto wife of Andrew Whitehead, the embezzler from County Stirling, Collins sent her off to Sydney, neglecting to formalise the relationship between the impious couple. He would also discover when at Port Phillip, that 'Mrs Garrett', who had boarded with Richard Garrett, a spur-maker, tempted to steal cloth in Shropshire, was actually Hannah Harvey.[34] Hannah Power and Fanny Anchor openly became the mistresses of Governor Collins and Fosbrook with the knowledge and concurrence of the cuckold husbands, who obviously received special treatment in return.[35]

It was Isabella, the wife of the prisoner Thomas Riley, who appears to have sparked off an unpleasant scene. According to Fawkner she was tried before the lieutenant (Edward Lord?) in charge of the prisoners and two other officers for stealing a cap from another woman. She was sentenced to two dozen lashes which one of the boatswain's mates inflicted on her naked back. Fawkner related that the flogging took place on the fore hatch screened in between the decks and the piteous cries of the sufferer were heard throughout the *Calcutta*.[36]

The *Calcutta* sailed via Tenerife, Rio de Janeiro and Simon's Town at the Cape of Good Hope, replenishing with fresh food and water at each stop and taking on stock at the Cape. The *Ocean*, sailing direct from Rio, arrived at Port Phillip Heads on 7 October and the *Calcutta* arrived two days later. The captains of the two ships were to carry out their duties with admirable results. The mortality of the convicts during the voyage out was low and 300 arrived safely at Port Phillip.[37] Only two deaths occurred in the *Ocean*.

The unsanitary gaols and hulks had not been conducive to maintaining the health of the inmates and warding off infections, fevers and contagious diseases. Little attention had been paid to a balanced diet and the rigors of the voyage would soon eliminate those who were not in reasonably good health. Eight convicts (that is, one in thirty-eight) and the wife of a convict died on board the *Calcutta*, mostly from scurvy induced by the state of debility in which they had embarked. This speaks well for the naval discipline of Captain Woodriff and the cleanliness and hygienic standards in the ship — one of only two naval transports to bring out convicts at this time. Professor Shaw has noted in *Convicts and the Colonies* that between 1801 and 1815 the deaths were one in twenty-four.[38] Tuckey condemned those transports in which there had been many lives lost because of the lack of personal hygiene and cleanliness in the ship itself. Convicts in general were indolent and careless, unused to ship life, and severity was needed to prevent their becoming the 'most disgusting objects from vermin and dirt'. He later made recommendations that when the prison was on the orlop deck of transports it should never be wetted, that the dirt should be scraped off every morning and the deck scrubbed; that receptacles for bones or other filth should be found; that no wet clothes should be hung in the prison. Royal naval ships carried hammocks but hired transports had fixed bed-places and bedding was rarely removed to air or allowed to dry out during the wet. Tuckey advised on methods of fumigation, warned against allowing too much moisture into the sleeping quarters and suggested fires of sea-coal to clear the prisons of foul air. In the warmer climates convicts should bathe twice weekly. At all times they should receive a wholesome diet, sufficient exercise and proper attention to cleanliness.[39]

Even so, the *Calcutta* convicts were herded together with relatively little room to move below the Plimsoll line. There most of them lived and tried to breathe in extremes of temperature for several months without stepping on terra firma. The stench of those bodies, dripping with perspiration in the tropics, combined with the tainted and stuffy air produced by a mixture of vomit, infant faeces and menstruating women, was all too much for Ann Stocker, the daughter of Captain Pemberton, R.N., whose death during her pregnancy, Pateshall believed, was due to a broken heart. Knopwood dutifully committed her body to the deep, an unpleasant duty he had to perform twice in the next three days.[40]

What Pateshall apparently did not know was that Ann Stocker had also been charged with her husband

Dimensions of H.M. Ship Calcutta	F.	I.
Poop Deck long	48	6
Breadth fore end from out side to Out Side	32	9½
After End	22	1
Main Deck Inside	169	5
Gun Deck Inside	162	5½
" " out side	166	"
height from Deck to Beam	5	7
Orlop Deck from the fore side the Stem to the afterside the Stern Post at the height of Wing Transom	161	4
Breadth Extreme	41	7½
Orlop Deck to Gun Deck Beams	5	5

upper D.P. 2.3 + d own 2.6 fore & aft.
lower DP 2.5 .   2.11½

	Masts		Yards	
	Length Yds In	Clementon In	Length Yds In	In
Main Mast	31..12	32	27.12	14
" Top Mast	18..0	17½	18.24	13½
" " Gallant Mast	9..0	9	12..0	8½
Fore Mast	29..0	30½	25.12	17½
" Top Mast	18..0	17½	18.24	13½
" " Gallant Mast	8..24	9	11..12	8
Mizen Mast	22..24	21	15.12	11½
" Top Mast	13..24	12	16..0	9½
" " Gallant Mast	6..24	6½	8..24	6
Bowsprit	20..24	30	18..24	12½
Jib Boom	14..0	13	11..12	8
Cross Jack	"	"	18..24	12½
Flying Jib	12..6	7	..	..

Captain Woodriff's memo-book shows that H.M.S. Calcutta was not only the tallest of the tall ships transporting convicts to Australia, but was more than twice the tonnage of any of the First Fleet transports.

of being in possession of counterfeit notes and that both pleaded guilty and were committed to Newgate in April 1802, although the charges against Ann were dropped. Perhaps it was through her death that Stocker, a resourceful and educated man, was soon noticed by Collins and Knopwood. He was to become a long-standing friend and associate of both men, together with those whose wives received certain privileges.

The ports of call were not always conducive to the improvement of one's health. In spite of the fresh water and fresh supplies, one could be in danger of contracting some of the local diseases which could be derived from the filth and squalor of local conditions. Tuckey described the unhealthy settlement of St Sebastian and the dirty customs of its inhabitants: diseases most prevalent were fevers, dysentery and hydrocele, the fevers multiplied by the noxious effluvia arising from the filthy streets.[41] At Rio the surgeon's health report indicated that eight men were suffering from debility, four had slight complaints of cold, and fifteen had a scorbutic appearance and were on an antiseptic diet. He found a different situation in Cape Town, where the cleanliness and industry of the Dutch were in striking contrast to the dirt and indo-

lence of the Portuguese.[42] And in any port there was always the chance of any person going ashore contracting, or passing on, what they called the 'Frenchman's disease'. At least one of the marines would later die of such association.

Collins attributed some of the illnesses to want of suitable clothing. Some convicts had come aboard almost naked and in rags. He gave these persons first priority in the distribution of some sixty suits made up in the *Calcutta*. Others who benefited were those working on deck who were frequently exposed to the vicissitudes of all weathers. But he was loath to replace the wretched clothing in which they had embarked until they reached their destination.[43] Sadly, he found that many of the materials provided were bad and much of the thread rotten. He found as much employment as possible during the voyage for those trustworthy convicts who had a trade. Woollen cloth, leather and hemp were among the articles which might produce work for the men. Women received worsted for knitting, along with needles, thimbles, buttons and bustles. Those who were tailors crafted extra jackets and trousers from serge for the cooler climate, although broadcloth and brown and white checked linen had been issued for the tropics.

Others had a certain amount of freedom through Captain Woodriff's need for further deck hands. Convicts acted as servants to the officers, three boys became messengers, nineteen became sailors, and twenty were employed variously on deck as part of the carpenter's crew, cooks, butcher, baker and poulterers. Samuel Warriner as schoolmaster instructed the children. Woodriff allowed others to cast off their leg irons.[44] Pateshall wrote that upwards of 100 were released from irons and that 'in this indulgence I did not forget some Herefordshire friends on board'.[45]

At Rio the water casks were in need of repair. Female members of the company gathered together the filthy garments and washed them at a dilapidated monastery.[46] James Grove, confined to the ship as all convicts were, occupied some time sketching the view and had hoped to write something of the people, but found that particulars escaped him. He earned a little money there by 'piercing some plates from trades-men's cards. I could have gained much more by making some crosses, etc — here conscience interfered, and would not suffer me to act the part of an idol-maker'.[47]

Knopwood listed stock taken on at Rio, including thirty-six turkeys at 6s each, thirteen dozen fine capons and fowls (4s a couple), sixty-eight ducks at 4s a couple, four very good geese at 6s a couple, thirteen pigs at 4d a pound, as well as a great quantity of fruit and vegetables.[48] Collins bought indigenous plants and seed. While in port he supplied the convicts and settlers with a pound of fresh meat daily, procured at 2d a pound, and four to six oranges each. He also procured some hay, two tons of beef and mutton and a ton of biscuit. He deferred additions to the larger livestock until they reached the Cape of Good Hope. There were too many problems stowing cattle on the decks during the wintry months of the voyage.[49] However, several of the Ocean settlers and officers chose to take on stock at Rio since the ship would bypass the Cape. One of the Rio cows was to give birth to a calf at Port Phillip and two fine bulls survived the journey. Three heifers, which men from the Calcutta bought at the Cape, succumbed to the cold in the Roaring Forties and died. Pateshall considered that, after all the stock taken on at Cape Town, the ship began to resemble Noah's Ark. He found the Cape sheep remarkable in that they were covered with hair rather than wool, had amazingly long tails of solid fat and weighed from ten to fourteen pounds. However, he found their flesh far from good.[50]

From reports of the behaviour of the intemperate and difficult John Hartley, intending settlers in the Ocean appear to have been more trouble than the convicts. Captain Mertho reported to Collins when at Rio, that they were continually in a state of riot, although the scrappy Ocean log itself ignores the problems.[51] Collins appointed a Court of Enquiry and placed a corporal and six privates of the marines under Lieutenant William Sladden to keep order aboard the Ocean for the rest of the journey.[52]

Captain Woodriff maintained fairly strict discipline aboard his ship but this was not to imply that he could control all his men, especially when they went ashore. The officers had a wild time at each port and the young midshipmen were particularly high-spirited, even though they included his two sons and a future admiral, the young Vernon-Harcourt, son of the Bishop of Carlisle (later Archbishop of York). All the civil officers, except Knopwood and Surgeon William I'Anson, travelled in the Ocean. Collins had hardly had a chance to get to know his colleagues when the surveyor George Prideaux Harris wrote to his brother from Rio that Collins had 'behaved extremely odd to all his officers civil and military . . . we have never been invited on board the Calcutta since we left England though a week in harbour in Tenerife and a fortnight here'. Harris soon discovered the reason at the opera in Rio, where he found the box presented to his party already occupied by some of the officers from the Calcutta with some convict wives 'whom they keep', the box having been sold to the ship's master and party for £6 by an employee of the Viceroy.[53]

Although Knopwood attended the opera 'Neinha' (which must have been the French comic opera Nina by Nicolas Dalayrac) he was more interested in dallying at the convent of Adjuda. There he 'frequently visited' and 'conversed with a very beautiful young lady named Antonia Januaria. Her polite attention I shall not easily forget'. He thought better of filling in the blank page opposite this entry, but refers several times to the 'beautiful girl . . . from her I received fruits, etc.' and 'the charming girl Antonia'. She was, it seems, one who boarded at the convent, having lost her parents, and would remain there until such time as she married. He 'visited D. Adjuda for the last time' and saw 'Antonia this eve at 5, and we took leave of each other with Regret. Vale!'[54]

Such young ladies were supposed to converse with strangers only from behind iron bars but Tuckey, himself enamoured with the enchantment of the 'silvery tones of a secluded damsel', found the iron bars not quite as hard nor the walls so high and that the 'watchful eye of the dragon, who guards the Hesperian fruit, has more than once been deluded by British ingenuity or lulled to sleep by Brasilian gold'.[55] One cannot help but question whether the charming Antonia was subject to spitting or tearing her tresses to rid herself of the 'inhabitants' that Tuckey also noted in the hair of most of the women.

Such pleasures were not as readily available at Cape Town, or were not recorded in detail if they were. There was not the time. The social highlight was a bucks' dinner at Hudson's Hotel. In the wild country beyond Cape Town, Knopwood and Pateshall joined Dutch officers to hunt wild deer. They saw the print of a tiger's paw, the dens of three wolves, and killed a brace of partridge. Tuckey diligently took note of the landscape and the customs of the local people. In a veiled reference he did infer that his countrymen took advantage of the 'Batavian fair ones' partiality for the 'gay, attentive, and well-dressed English officer' rather than the 'grumbling, coarse, and phlegmatic Dutchman'.[56]

By this time the *Ocean* was entering the most difficult part of its voyage. For those on board, conditions had at all times been considerably inferior to those in His Majesty's ship. They had quickly run out of provisions taken on at Rio. Some of the livestock was lost, or perished in the cold and squally weather encountered beyond Tristan da Cunha. The wild seas entered some of the cabins and most of the crockery was broken. Harris and Humphrey would have echoed the distressed feelings of all when they wrote of the condition of their food supplies and other vicissitudes. Rather than starve, they had to eat beef 'smelling like the steam from a tallow-chandler's copper'. The wet and mouldy bread attracted insects and in desperation Humphrey lived on water gruel for fourteen days, even though the water was stinking.[57] Gloom descended upon everyone. Harris thought he had never been so melancholy, but he did find some solace in pouring out his troubles to a willing listener, the young Ann Jane Hobbs who in her short life, as will be seen, had had enough of her own.[58] In a less innocent relationship the settler John Ingle had begun an affair with Rebecca Hobbs (of which the Reverend William Crook would not have approved).[59] Throughout the voyage Crook prayed that all their souls might be saved, and doubtless during those dangerous weeks in the Roaring Forties prayed even more piously for those in peril on the sea.

On the whole the convicts appear to have created little trouble during the *Calcutta*'s voyage. Captain Woodriff's son Daniel, one of the midshipmen, kept a record of some petty offences. William Smith was double ironed and sent into the lower prison room for 'breach of trust'. William Bryant was also confined to the lower prison room for drunkenness, Michael Crener for theft, Henry Pizzey, Thomas Pritchard and Charles Shore all punished for insolence, the last double-ironed. The boy John Gwynn committed two offences, theft and stabbing a man in the hand with a pen-knife. Likewise, Irishman Patrick Plunkett received punishments for insolence and fighting. John Cole had to be discharged as Knopwood's servant and double-ironed for 'inattention and on strong suspicion of robbing a chest in the wardroom steward's berth'.[60]

As captain of a ship of the Royal Navy, Captain Woodriff would have been responsible for the punishments, and except for those specifically noted, these would undoubtedly have meant floggings up to 500 lashes with the cat-o'-nine tails. Lashings in convict ships normally took place on the bulkhead, administered by the drummer and fifer, and attended by the surgeon and chaplain. But compared with most transports, the treatment of these prisoners appears to have been much less harsh. Perhaps the discipline in a naval ship, the better conditions and a captain who displayed some humanity combined to make the voyage of the *Calcutta* a more successful one than most.

One sad incident occurred at Simon's Town when John Cashman, a sixteen-year-old London forger employed as a servant to Richard Wright, master of the *Calcutta*, stole a watch from Surgeon Bromley. Collins, who thought him a 'fine youth', reported that he had tried to escape from the ship, although some believed he could not face further disgrace and committed suicide by drowning.[61] Fawkner described his death:

Coleman [*sic*], whilst dipping up some sea water, in a great pot, tumbled, or threw himself, overboard. The cry of man overboard caused the ship to be put about, a boat lowered, and pulled to where his head was seen above water; the boat on arrival found his cap, and the tin pot, but Coleman was never more seen by us. It was commonly thought that he had committed suicide for the drag of a quart of water could not have pulled him overboard — Some said it was a presentiment that caused him to ask his messmates to report his death some days before that death took place.[62]

But the Scotsman Robert Stewart, who claimed to have been an officer in the Royal Navy and would ultimately be the person who seized the brig *Harrington* in Sydney Cove, was in trouble from the beginning. He was probably one of the prisoners who tried to seize a boat at Woolwich while confined to the hulks. Fawkner related an incident on board the *Calcutta* in which Stewart was involved, except that Fawkner seemed to have confused Stewart as the victim rather than the culprit. It appears that at some time between Rio and the Cape one of the prisoners reported that there was a plan to capture the *Calcutta* and leave the crew and officers on an uninhabited island. They hoped to sail to North America, but if detained by a French vessel they would give up the ship conditional on their being landed in a French or American port. According to Fawkner the ringleaders were arrested, confined separately and ultimately tried by court martial. Captain Woodriff did not believe the plan could possibly succeed because the *Calcutta* was fully armed and his marines were always on guard at every hatchway. Fawkner recorded that after a

toilsome examination it became apparent that the informer had hatched the story to injure a prisoner, by name Stewart, a Scotchman, who had formerly been a sea-going officer. Some quarrel arose between them and Stewart struck *the informer* down, he fell against a ringbolt, and cut his head. In revenge he attempted Stewart's life, for he would most likely have been hung at the yard arm for attempt at piracy. This was clearly made out, and Captain

Stewart was fully acquitted. *This same man* [here Fawkner must mean Stewart] twice attempted to escape from the colonies. The last time he and his associates seized the brig *Harrington*.[63]

But Fawkner got some of his facts wrong, as related in a later chapter.

• • •

Britain declared war against France only a fortnight after the *Calcutta*'s voyage began, although even before they sailed the renewal of war between England and its enemies seemed imminent. It would be eight months before Collins and Woodriff heard the news that hostilities had resumed. It is doubtful whether any reliable reports of the outbreak of war had reached the Cape of Good Hope at the time the ship arrived. But there were at least some rumours abroad when the *Calcutta* anchored off Cape Town. Precautions were taken. The *Calcutta* log recorded on 12 August: 'Beat to Quarters and cleared ship for action should the Dutch squadron attempt to be hostile'.

They saw the Dutch colours flying on the hill over the anchorage at Simon's Town. There were three ships in the bay, two flying the Dutch flag, including a former British ship, the *Prince William Henry*, renamed the *Johana Magdalena*. Both these ships were laden with coffee and sugar from Batavia for Amsterdam. The third ship was a British whaler, the *Thomas*, from London.[64]

The port officers came aboard and one of the *Calcutta* officers went ashore to visit the Commandant of the Garrison to clarify if the *Calcutta*'s salutes would be returned with an equal number of guns. All seemed in order. The *Calcutta* gave the salute with eleven guns and the Dutch retaliated. The convicts, including Fawkner senior, might have overheard fragments of the discussion and did not understand why the saluting took place. Fawkner junior wrote spiritedly that during the stay at the Cape a small armed vessel arrived from Holland bringing the news that war had broken out in May. The Dutch commodore had sent his representative on board the *Calcutta* to demand the surrender of the ship and its contents. Woodriff tried to detain the officer while Tuckey was ordering the guns to be sent up from the hold. They formed a council of war, committing the Dutchman to a cabin where he might overhear their voices occasionally, but not their words. They pretended to argue for two hours before Woodriff, in a 'true Jack Tar's answer' told the Dutchman to return to his commodore and tell him that 'if he wants this ship he must come and take her if he can'. He conducted the envoy around the ship so that he could see the

arrangements made in those valuable two hours. Men, sailors and marines were at quarter, the guns and munitions as well as the men were ready. When the Dutchman returned to shore, the commodore, after consultation with his own officers, sent word that if the *Calcutta* did not leave the port within twenty-four hours he would sink her but 'did not wish to capture such a large number of thieves'. The master's mate, William Gammon, came to the prison room to ask if any of the convicts would volunteer to fight and work the ship. The affirmative replies were unanimous from every able young man, while old soldiers and sailors offered to hoist the guns and pass up the powder and shot. Surprised at the change in the ship and apparently at the willingness of so many displays of patriotism from a subjugated class of society, the Dutch advised peaceful consultation and allowed Woodriff time to take on supplies and secure his ship. Fawkner believed Woodriff was worried that more Dutch men-of-war might arrive and hurried the departure, leaving behind much useful cargo.[65]

Fawkner's account has a ring of truth in it. One cannot help but believe that by then the Dutch could easily have heard unofficial reports that England and France were at war. The Cape was important strategically to both England and Holland in times of hostility. Yet official records ignored the incident, which a young boy remembered, one supposes, from stories told over and over again by his parents and others who sailed in the *Calcutta*. Woodriff recorded no such incident and followed orders to deliver his cargo of felons and pick up a cargo of timber.

In his conversation with the Dutch and others, Pateshall discerned that most inhabitants sincerely regretted the departure of the English. He was certain that if the British attacked again 'the mob would join us'.[66] Great jealousy existed between the civil and military of what had been little more than a pleasant trading post used largely by the Dutch East India Company rather than as a colony for the Dutch. Tuckey similarly had found the people more partial to the English because the Dutch government at the Cape was so much under the influence of the 'Corsican usurper'. Napoleon considered the Cape 'as one of the steps by which he intends to mount the Asiatic thrones' but he was to lose the colony to the British after the Battle of Trafalgar. Tuckey also believed that money was 'the supreme divinity of a Dutchman, for which he would renounce his religion, sell his wife, or betray his friend'.[67]

From the ship to which they were bound, convicts had a different view. James Grove could only picture Simon's Town as 'a little mean, contemptible place, almost unworthy of the name of town'. But he and others with money were able to organise some purchases there, including some livestock and an amount of tallow which would help to set them up in business.[68]

As they left the Cape, one might imagine Collins' feelings as he had written them down many years before, now copied down almost word for word by Knopwood, who was experiencing the same uncertainties. They are Collins' words, but Knopwood felt them too:

It was natural[y for us (K.)] to indulge at this moment a melancholy reflection which obtruded itself upon the mind [minds of those who were settlers at Port Phillip (K.)] The land behind us was the abode of a civilized people; that before us was the residence of savages. When, if ever we might again enjoy the commerce of the world, was doubtful and uncertain. The refreshments and the pleasures of what we had so liberally partaken at the Cape, [and Simon's Bay (K.)] were to be exchanged for coarse fare and hard labour at New South Wales. [Port Phillip. — and we may truly say — (K.)] All communication with families and friends now cut off, we were leaving the world behind us, to enter on a state unknown.[69]

11 WATER, WATER EVERYWHERE

THE *OCEAN* ARRIVED at Port Phillip two days before the *Calcutta*. Strong winds and roaring surf at the mouth of the harbour alarmed Captain Mertho. The settler, William Collins, and mineralogist, A. W. H. Humphrey, volunteered, with six others, to examine the opening. Humphrey reported that '. . . it would be impossible for any Ship to go in . . . on hearing which, I thought the Captain, though a brave Man, would have sunk on the Deck, and he exclaimed, My God, what shall I do!'[1] But with every sail set, a strong current flowing and a heavy gale, the ship drew twelve miles off-shore. They were lucky not to have been wrecked on the rocky shelf deceptively guarding the narrow entrance. During the high drama the baby daughter, born the previous July at sea to the wife of settler Anthony Fletcher, died as they entered the heads, thereby becoming the first known European to die at Port Phillip.

It was not until the following afternoon, in calmer seas and with a strong breeze, that they were able to cast anchor off Point King and survey what, a year earlier, Murray's first mate Bowen had declared 'a most noble sheet of water'.[2] Humphrey claimed to be the first of the civil officers to set foot on terra firma. 'I take possession of this Country in the Name of the King of England', he cried with jubilance as he sprang from the boat ahead of Surveyor Harris, Commissary Fosbrook and surgeons Bowden and Hopley.[3] They set out on a ten-mile walk, hugging the coastline. They discovered the sands coloured with the charcoal of native fires. There seemed to be no fresh water, the soil was poor and the trees small.

During their absence the *Calcutta*, having experienced two months of severe gales and thunder storms, reached Port Phillip on the morning of Sunday 9 October with damaged rigging. Captain Woodriff had battled the previous night, tacking and sounding in squally conditions until he was sure that they had arrived at the dangerous entrance described by Murray, where he found a ten fathom bar 'stretches itself a good way across, and, with a strong tide out and wind

in, the ripple is such as to cause a stranger to suspect rock or shoals ahead'.[4] Captain Woodriff recognised the headland on the larboard shaped like a whale head and knew that they had reached their destination. Entry to the harbour would be a challenge to his navigational skill. He called for the decks to be cleared for anchoring, cables ranged, soundings checked and made ready to sail in at full tide.[5]

It must have startled everyone when a shout from the masthead alerted the company with the cry 'Ahoy, ship ahoy!'. For a moment the party might well have feared that the French had arrived to take possession ahead of the British. Perhaps Woodriff was already preparing to show the colours. It might be *another* scientific expedition! What a shock the French would get when they sighted a British man-of-war! They probably would not even know about the peace. It might be necessary to use a bit of bluff, by calling for volunteers among the prisoners, a ploy which, Fawkner reported, had been successful with the Dutch at the Cape.

Shock turned to incredulity when they realised that the ship was the old *Ocean*. They had secretly doubted that the 'old tub' would survive the squalls which they had encountered in the Roaring Forties. When they last sighted her she had seemed to be in serious trouble. That was some two months earlier, in the vicinity of Tristan da Cunha. She must have been the strange sail they later tried to signal in the Indian Ocean, but the seas were high and they had soon lost sight of her.[6] Obviously she had sailed further south and missed the gales they had passed through.

A fair wind and flood tide carried the *Calcutta* safely through the narrow entrance, dodging the treacherous rocks that in later years would deceive many unfortunate mariners. One might expect that Knopwood might dutifully have closed at least one eye and offered a prayer for their safe arrival. He would have wasted little time in thanksgiving. There were new experiences ahead, new friends to greet when they caught up with the *Ocean*. He had already noticed the abundant bird-life as the ship sailed through calmer waters. He longed to set foot on the virgin soil that no Europeans had yet occupied. This land for him would have a future, for it was his philosophy that life, wherever you live, is what you make of it and he would be next in importance to the Governor. He might not have much time to minister to the religious needs of the convicts. Still less would he be bothered trying to convert a lot of heathen blacks. Unlike the Reverend William Crook, he had no missionary zeal at all. He would build up from nothing a social life with a new flavour. There would be no one to bother him provided he called them all together for a few prayers on Sunday, weather and his health permitting, and performed the odd baptismal or marriage service, entering them, together with any reported death, on a register, if he remembered.

Captain Mertho boarded the *Calcutta* and reported how the strong winds and roaring surf at the mouth of the harbour had alarmed him also. Humphrey and his companions returned with their unfavourable report and Captain Woodriff, with Collins, was to spend the next four days searching for a place to land the impatient people and the stores.[7]

Among the fortunate convicts allowed to disembark immediately were those who accompanied their masters during the several days it took to search for water. Collins might have taken young William Keep who had waited on him in the *Calcutta*, John Buckley, Tuckey's servant (later bequeathed to Collins), and Thomas Williams, also known as Long, who served William Gammon, then acting as master of the *Calcutta*. The ship's carpenter was allowed ashore to search unsuccessfully for wood to secure the head and knees of the ship that had suffered badly during the voyage.

The rest of the company waited impatiently on board until their return. It all proved too much for Lieutenant Donovan. The curving white sands beckoned him ashore, after which Captain Woodriff confined him to his cabin. How much more frustrating for all those who had not set foot on land since leaving England! The land was so near yet so far, the decision-making delayed for days that seemed like weeks, until they found some sort of landing-place. Had they only had Surveyor-General Charles Grimes' map showing the Yarra it would have simplified the whole situation.[8]

The disappointment and disillusionment Collins felt is easy to understand when one recalls Murray's and Bowen's descriptions of Port Phillip. Murray had seen resemblances to both Greenwich Park and a walk on Blackheath: 'The hills and valleys rise and fall with inexpressible elegance', he wrote. Although he was there in the height of summer, there must have been enough rain that year for new grass to shoot, for he had found the land green. The number of natives' huts

indicated there should be fresh water and abundant wild-life for food. Murray's party had discovered suitable water in the present Chinamans Creek, a channel which they had sounded between ten and fourteen fathoms extending from the Heads to Arthur's Seat, and 'many fine coves and entrances . . . the appearance and probability of rivers'. Yet, as stated previously, his survey was quite superficial considering the lengthy period of time he spent there.[9]

With hindsight it is easy to criticise Murray's report but it was unfortunate that neither Flinders' nor Grimes' reports and charts were then available to Collins.[10] It also appears likely that the summer of Collins' occupation had followed months of less than average rainfall because they had trouble finding fresh drinking water. Collins was mortified because it was becoming urgent to boost the morale of the people and to land them after such a lengthy voyage. But the best he could do was to encamp some four or five miles east of the Heads where they had discovered a sheltered bay. The masters of the ships directed their vessels to the chosen landing-place, sounding the depths and sailing as close as they could to the bay. Because of the shallows they had to cast anchor a mile and a half offshore. A party of marines and convicts led by Lieutenant J. M. Johnson rowed ahead in a jolly-boat to pitch some tents, carrying some livestock and various items of equipment. They grabbed some sturdy casks that had held their salted provisions and sank them in the sand to form wells that could hold some brackish water at high tide. Collins named the little bay after the Under-Secretary for War and the Colonies, John Sullivan. He gave 'Sullivan' as the parole word for the day and 'Woodriff' as the countersign.[11]

Collins reported to King on 5 November 1803 that he had sunk several water casks in the sand. He wrote 'The water certainly is good — at least my sick List does not indicate that it is otherwise'. This cask is one of the few tangible remains of the Collins settlement.

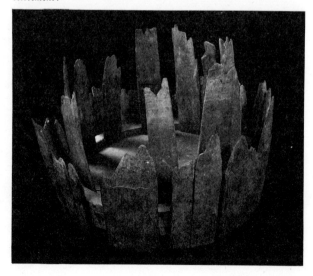

On 16 October Collins ordered the landing of the convicts and their baggage. It took five hours. Then he delegated a party of convicts to unload the stores, wading waist deep through the shoals. They staggered under the weight of the heavy cargo, some naked under the heat of the sun, but with the utmost cheerfulness and much excitement, to Collins' total satisfaction.

One can imagine the scene as they stumbled groggily ashore on that pleasant spring day, a motley crowd of prisoners and scarlet-coated marines, some keeping a watchful eye on wives and children, some guarding the precious stock they had managed to buy during the voyage. James Grove had bought a ewe, and Fawkner, Manby, Ronaldson and Mrs Anchor struggled ashore with sows. Fowls had been a popular purchase, Michaels acquired a baker's dozen. Mrs Anchor had also invested in fowls, as had Mrs Power, Mrs Piroelle and Mrs Peters.[12]

After they had waded through the water, even those whose feet were gripped in irons, must have thrilled to feel the solid earth under them after six to eight months' close confinement on board ship. It would have been a scene of varied emotions: to Collins, the great relief of having landed them all safely and the joy that his old tub of a store ship, the *Ocean*, had not let them down; to the prisoners with families, the chance to live together once more with some possibility of privacy; to Mrs Hobbs, the naval widow who came with her five children, the thought that they all might have a fresh chance in life; and the thoughts in the minds of some prisoners that here was a place from which they might escape — and at least twenty-seven of them did.

Tuckey admitted that at first he was deluded into dreams of fruitfulness and plenty because he found:

The face of the country bordering on the port is beautifully picturesque, swelling into gentle elevations of the brightest verdure, and dotted with trees, as if planted by the hand of taste, while the ground is covered with a profusion of flowers of every colour.[13]

Pateshall was enthusiastic because he found that 'the beautiful green plains with lofty trees . . . appeared more like pleasure grounds than a wild Savage continent'.[14] Such descriptions, including those of William Crook, who noted the grassland and lack of undergrowth, confirm the present belief that the Aborigines were in the habit of seasonally burning off the grass to control fire danger as well as the fragile ecology. There were traces of natives every few yards and Crook found many trees partly burnt.[15]

Tuckey, Harris, William Collins and Gammon then took a launch and spent ten days charting the bay. Apart from their servants they took other convicts experienced in seamanship. Woodriff's son Daniel and the boatswain's mate of the *Calcutta*, Samuel Innis, were also in the party. Harris probably took Francis Shipman (embezzler), whom he had acquired as an assistant surveyor. They found no water in Chinamans Creek. Tuckey noted

a deep bay, which is the northern extremity of Port Phillip . . . a break in the land, which had the appearance of a river mouth was seen here in passing but the badness of the weather at the time, this being then a dead lee shore with a heavy surf beating on it, prevented a more minute examination.[16]

From his chart it is evident that he crossed from the present Point Ormond to Gellibrand Point. Knopwood noted that they discovered 'an apparent passage towards the sea . . . intended to have explored but was driven southward during the night by a tide of current from the apparent straight'.[17] Woodriff's entry supposed that because of the

swell of the westward that an opening must certainly be in that neighbourhood into the ocean on the west side of the land, possibly about Cape Bridgewater . . . but the swell and a strong current or tide setting from the N.W. drove the boats as far to leeward as to prevent their getting up again.[18]

Pateshall concluded that several fresh water rivers were too distant from the ship; that navigation was too difficult, and that it 'would be impossible for a colony to flourish there, as the soil was little better than sand'.[19] Tuckey tried once more to investigate the bay to the north, discovering the Kananook Creek. He thought it could be the tributary of a larger river, but time and inclement weather prevented proper examination. This little excursion had its bright moments when they thought they had discovered gold. The bed of the stream, covered with foliaceous mica, had the appearance of gold dust. Some fifty years later Victorian soil would produce one third of the world's gold.[20]

Tuckey's party ultimately reached present-day Corio Bay. The crew of one of his boats turned to shore to prepare a meal and procure water. When the other boat was out of sight the natives surrounded the party, which included Gammon, Harris and Daniel Woodriff, junior, who had sunk a shaft to look for water in the vicinity of what became known as Limeburners' Point. This confrontation, examined in more detail in a later chapter, may be connected also with one of the most intriguing discoveries in Victorian history.[21] It almost certainly explains the mystery of the Geelong keys, which some lime-burners discovered in September 1847 while digging at this point on Corio Bay.[22]

(The Well)

George Gordon McCrae's sketch of Sullivan Bay, 1804, depicting the Royal Marines on the parade ground while others collected water from a well. McCrae's illustration was made during a visit to Sullivan Bay in the 1840s.

Harris as Deputy Surveyor was officially responsible to the Surveyor-General, at Port Jackson. Although he described enthusiastically the variety of wild life and botany in letters to his mother,[23] Harris' unflattering report to Governor Collins found that the land generally carried a 'deceitful appearance', that the soil was mostly sandy and 'very thinly wooded'. He did, however, believe that 'Good water is found in many parts of the Eastern Coast of the Harbour . . . The Northern Shore is more numerously inhabited than any other parts, from which it is likely that Water is to be found . . . Good Clay and Stone is found in abundance . . .'[24]

What black mould he found on the heights and in the valleys was insufficient in grade and amount for agricultural purposes, except for some found in the western bay. He did note that good water was available in many parts of the eastern coast and that the northern shore had more numerous inhabitants, suggesting water must be there. He found abundant good clay and stone on the eastern shore that would be fit for building.

Tuckey expanded on these scanty observations and included a realistic assessment that although many watercourses were visible they were often dry. He believed that the rainy season would be 'by no means annually regular', an astute prophecy which Port Phillip's later settlers have learned to live with.[25] Tuckey later complained that ten days employed on his survey was 'so short a time that it was impossible to accomplish a minutely correct survey of so extensive a place. Many parts of the shore were inaccessible to the boats, and in others straightness of the coastline would not admit of measurement by triangles on shore . . .'[26]

Collins had to find ways and means to inform Governor King of the quandary he was in, but how to go about it was the rub.

12 'A COALITION OF BANDITTI'

A FEW SKETCHES which Harris made remain almost the only illustrative evidence of the appearance of the settlement. They show the plan of the camp and indicate where the people pitched their tents or built their huts, and where the public offices stood.[1] Most of the convicts camped on an area of flat land below the Western Sister, close to the shoreline, surrounded by marines. The surgeons and a hospital tent, which Collins appointed Samuel Lightfoot to supervise, were in the grassland beyond the marines. Between the two headlands was a parade ground. On the edge of this were the Commissariat stores. Some of the other civil officers and the settlers were allowed a little land for cultivation in a pleasant valley which, at the time of their arrival, might have been carpeted with the scarlet *Kennedya prostrata* ('running postman') and clad with the trailing clematis and the Swainson pea.[2] Casuarinas and banksias provided the shade which they would welcome as the temperature increased during a warmer summer than most had ever experienced. Collins at first had to store the bread, flour and salt provisions in piles in the open air, while goods held in bales, such as wine, spirits and valuables, occupied the precious space in tents closely guarded by sentinels.

Within the settlement, not only the convicts and settlers but also the marines had to be strictly controlled to ensure cleanliness. Collins threatened to take away their tents if they could not keep them clean. No dirt or rubbish was to be left in the streets of the camp. He continually had to exhort all those under his direct control to create some sort of discipline.[3] He abhorred lack of hygiene and slovenliness, and was determined to retain standards that could all too easily deteriorate in a land so close to a state of nature. One of the first jobs after landing had been the erection of a copper for washing purposes, for which Collins appointed several women as laundresses.

Collins found the timber for building purposes disappointing, while Woodriff found the wood at Arthur's Seat less suitable for naval purposes than he

had hoped.[4] Nevertheless, Collins did allocate a number of the convicts to chop down trees as a means of keeping them occupied. Augustus Morris was one; he had used force and arms to steal from his master, and according to Fawkner he was the tallest and most stalwart of the *Calcutta* convicts allocated to the gang to select and cut timber. When the logs were sawn they would pile them on a carriage. This became onerous and difficult work, particularly on the occasions when it had to be drawn downhill. Often the carriages became bogged in the sand. It was Morris' responsibility to guide the wheels, together with any other active young man he cared to choose. In spite of all precautions, they could not help the wheels coming up against a stump or two as they descended. It was quite common for some men to be struck down and severely cut by the stakes fastened to the ropes by which they dragged the heavy loads. This had slowed up the process of building a secure timber storehouse for the Commissariat, resulting in continual robberies from the store huts.

Collins had nine sawyers to choose from. These included James Waltham, who had stolen cheese, and a watch stealer William Fletcher. The four convict carpenters were also thieves: James Riley, a pickpocket; Thomas Haywood, who stole kitchen utensils; Samuel Cross, cloth; and Joseph Bradley, a cart. There was also the carpenter settler William Nicholls. The sound of felling and sawing of timber and the burning of the local lime to mix into mortar were signs of the first huts being built, some of which the favoured convicts acquired, such as the forger James Grove and receivers John Fawkner and William Buckley.

Most of the huts had chimneys and fireplaces with bricks made by those convicts whose trade was brickmaking. One of these, the horse-stealer Thomas Croft, happily bragged that he could make bricks for Collins as 'red as your Honour's red coat', which is an apt description of the rich red soil found at present-day Red Hill near Arthur's Seat.[5] The forger and utterer Michael Michaels, the highway robber James North, and Edward Deacon, whose crime is unknown, were also brickmakers by trade. William Buckley was one of three bricklayers, the others being William Roberts, a highway robber, and George Jones, who had stolen clothes. There was plentiful lime stone which the only known stonemason, the settler Anthony Fletcher, would have used. Any plastering could have been done by Thomas Tit, convicted for stealing clothes, Charles Clarke, who had embezzled money while acting as a waiter at Covent Garden, or the sheep stealer William Cormack. Buckley helped build a bomb-proof magazine of stone, cemented with lime to contain the ammunition; the remains of Buckley's work now form the pathway to a private home. Collins also had a battery constructed on the Western Sister towards the end of his occupation in Port Phillip.[6] Some of Fletcher's work remained until relatively recent years: a tombstone he erected at what became the quarantine cemetery commemorated the loss of his baby daughter.[7]

Mechanics were allowed to occupy huts outside the line of sentinels, but the labourers were placed under more careful control, mainly because lime-burners, brickmakers and sawyers were working in all directions and at some distance from the camp itself. There were also those convicts who were more favoured than the mechanics whose wives, such as Mrs Power and the woman known as Mrs Whitehead, had sleeping quarters close to David Collins and Leonard Fosbrook.

Fawkner junior described the small sod hut about twelve feet by ten which his family had built among those of other prisoners. The sides were only three feet high. Light poles made from the local timber served as rafters, covered over with canvas, bed ticks and bed covers, and were just high enough in the centre for a man to stand upright. They were lucky to have it for their own use, undisturbed by the chatter of others or of intruders. They probably had a chimney built from limestone, as did several of the other settlers who were allowed to construct their own huts as they wished. They began to grow a garden on the surrounding plot of land. Collins saw little prospect of the land being useful for agriculture, but settlers also began gardens, mostly from seeds and plants bought at Rio de Janeiro. Bulbous plants like the gladioli from South Africa have multiplied over the whole peninsula.

Collins himself lived in a simple wooden house, brought from England and set up on the Eastern Sister. Before leaving Port Phillip he had it dismantled and later rebuilt at Hobart Town. Knopwood soon arranged for a marquee near the Governor's, from which he could survey the world around him in a little more style than his fellow officers, most of whom remained in tents.

Unlike William Caw, the other missionary who transferred directly from the *Ocean* to live aboard the *Calcutta* before going on to Sydney, Crook took the advice of Captain Woodriff that his wife would not be comfortable among the wild midshipmen who had been accustomed to loose women on their passage from England. The Crooks went ashore and were happier in a tent, appreciating the chance of getting a few fresh vegetables and shellfish, and sustained by their belief that a good God reigneth to help them bear the pain of being left there for an unknown period of detention. At times they felt very cold, but they contrived a canopy with some flannel and a curtain in their tent to keep them warmer, and drier as the rain beat down. They found the extremes of temperature uncomfortable — as low as 50°F and sometimes as high as 96°F, which was hot for the beginning of November; it was to rise much higher when summer arrived. But temperature variation was not the only discomfort; insects and snakes also made life rather unbearable, ordinary ants getting into everything and bull ants stinging with great pain.[8]

One settler, John Hartley, later threatened action against the government for the loss of his house at Sullivan Bay. One cannot entirely accept that such a house as he described existed, although he and his family had expected to remain at Port Phillip, hoping to establish a whaling base there. The family consisted of his wife Hezekiah and son Joseph. Accompanying them were his German servant John Joachim Gravie, a cutler and armourer by trade, and Edward Ford Hamilton, the young son of Sir Charles Hamilton, Bart, emigrating to Port Jackson under Hartley's protection.[9] They lived in a good bell tent covering an area of eighteen feet in diameter. But they might well have improved their life-style more than Collins realised before they moved to Van Diemen's Land.

Hartley eventually claimed to have built a 'comfortable house, kitchen garden and well, with considerable materials to build a vessel', as well as a blacksmith's shop, boat-house and saw-pit. He later asked Governor King for compensation of £500 for the loss of his house and livelihood there. Collins, whom he needled continuously, explained that the family had only lived in a tent but understood that after his (Collins') departure he moved to a 'covered place that he had erected for a storeroom, the sides of which were wattled but not plaistered [sic]; and the man who made his kitchen assures me it was nothing more than an open circular hole dug in the ground, lined with stone, and raised a foot or two above it'.[10] A large hollow still visible may mark the actual spot. This man informed Collins that when breaking the stone for this purpose they found water and, after sinking to ten feet, stopped.

Collins admitted that Hartley might have had an acre of garden but he took his vegetables and plants away in the *Lady Nelson*. Collins also affirmed that he had more baggage with him than the Transport Board allowed for a settler, including much iron-work packed in small cases which he had smuggled aboard the *Ocean*. Collins had allowed him to sell some articles on condition of his not demanding more than fifty per cent profit. Hartley said this was not enough to cover his losses and expenses and at first refused to sell any. But he retailed some privately, asking up to 400 per cent profit.[11] These might have included such articles as he advertised for sale in the *Sydney Gazette* in January 1805 when he planned to leave the colony: gold and silver watches, a German clock, books, pistols, a musket and fowling piece, various tools, wire and brass articles, farming equipment, fishing gear, and a fire engine, 'very easy to work and capable of throwing water to a considerable height'. Among their possessions was a 'compleat [*sic*] set of books on midwifery by Smyth'. A copper stove he made there was one of Port Phillip's first manufactures.[12]

Fawkner recorded that his parents had a chest made in 1803 at Port Phillip from boxwood cut at Arthur's Seat. In 1865 it was still sound and serviceable and is treasured today by descendants of his sister. Perhaps the carpenter Bradley, who was also skilled as a trunk maker, made it, or James Riley, also known as a cabinet maker. Thomas Bowman, who stole blankets, described his occupation as a chairmaker. He might also have experimented with using boxwood to make chairs and tables, which would have been among the early necessities of life. It is certain that Collins tried to occupy everyone, even if it meant putting the men to work at tasks in which he could see little future. If their work were not up to standard, they had every good reason to complain of the quality of the tools. A few items of ironmongery were quite unfit for use. It is doubtful whether they even bothered to unpack any of the crates which held other building materials such as 1 000 sheets of tin for roofing. The pickpocket Charles Williams and the nailer John Pearsall, who had stolen valuable livestock, were adept at cutting files, which they put to better use in the colony than at the time of their crimes.[13]

The men worked from sunrise to sunset. They turned out for work at the ringing of a bell at 6 a.m. They had half-hour breaks between 8.00 and 8.30 a.m. and 4.00 and 4.30 p.m., with an hour's break for their midday meal at 12.00 p.m. The quarter drum beat the retreat at 6.30 in the evening, when they had to return their tools to the superintendents and overseers. A bell at 8.00 p.m. was their curfew.[14] The strictest rules concerned access to the stores, over which the sentinels were ever vigilant. Prisoners were forbidden to leave their tents for any reason after 9.00 p.m. Collins admitted that the hardest labour had been discharging the stores, but had rewarded the group so employed

by issuing them with supplies of spirits and water each Saturday night.[15] But Tuckey described his own emotions of pity, astonishment and sometimes laughter as he watched the hapless men so degraded by their crimes: '*naked*, wading to their shoulders in water to unlade [*sic*] the boats, while a burning sun struck its meridian rays upon their uncovered heads'. He expressed his feelings of sadness for those who, (like Augustus Morris), were 'yoked to and sweating under a timber carriage, the wheels of which were sunk up to the axle in sand'. He never ceased to wonder at the ridiculous dilemmas in which the women found themselves 'by the novelty of their situations . . . What once seemed more valuable than life itself, even female virtue, grows weaker by degrees, and at last falls sacrifice to present circumstances'.[16]

Each male convict received new clothing to replace the wretched apparel in which he had landed, worn out during the sweaty and uncomfortable voyage. Rations included a jacket, a waistcoat, two check shirts, one pair of breeches or drawers, three pairs of duck trousers, three pairs of socks, one pair of shoes and one hat.[17] Collins had to give frequent reminders that shoes had to be kept mended before they got to the stage where repair was impossible. It is significant that among the convicts were a dozen shoemakers, the largest number representing one trade. They would be kept busy; one wonders at the ingenuity which had to be displayed in altering shoes and boots, of which only one size was provided, to fit those whose feet were too big or too small. Arthur Connelly, a highway robber, was a skinner and leather draper who might have used kangaroo or possum skins to enlarge the footwear. Among the shoemakers were four convicted for stealing: John Wade had stolen butter, John Davis had stolen bacon, John Wilkinson had stolen a pocket-book, and John Willis, who specialised in making women's shoes, had stolen woollen cloth.

Another who had stolen woollen cloth was Daniel Crawley, a tailor. Together with Samuel Jacobs, who had stolen leather shoes, and three unnamed tailors, he would be busy making up and altering clothes for the women and children. Collins also employed his detachment tailor to alter the scarlet jackets provided for the marines, made up according to the pattern established by the Admiralty.[18]

The only known weaver was James Alexander, who had forged bills. But he could not have contributed much because he was suffering from severe scurvy and eventually died in early spring at the Derwent. Another cheese stealer, James Roberts, was a button maker who would be occupied at the finishing stage of garment making. Did he try to use some imagination and produce buttons made from the local wood? Together with the lapidary, James Duff who had stolen bread, he might have wandered along the shore during the spring high tides which produce many beautiful shells, some of which he might substitute for the bone of buttons or make necklaces for the women. The sheep stealer John Lawrence might have joined them. He was a jeweller by trade but it is likely that the new trade he had learnt in Dorset gaol when employed making hats would have been more useful.

Richard Dukes was a pattern maker who designed coaches. His taste in jewellery, silver, gold and ivory was expensive and rather choosy when he decided to burgle the house of a baronet. Among the convicts there was one who could have driven a coach — the sheep stealing coachman, Joseph Powell. But who was likely to need such a vehicle or its driver on the sands of Port Phillip?

Most of the settlers were men with some training, although few practised their trade in the colony, becoming instead small, and mostly unsuccessful, farmers. Some had commercial interests at stake. William Collins and John Hartley, both of whom had been masters in the Navy, had emigrated with the express purpose of entering the fisheries industry.[19]

Many of the convicts themselves had been experienced sailors, convicted for petty crimes while in port in England. When they had served their sentences, or received early pardons, they were among those who joined whaling and sealing vessels and sailed the seas as far south as Kerguelen, as far east as Otaheite and the Galapagos Islands.

Among the convicts, Collins listed eight mariners, six watermen and five fishermen (but there were others known to have been sailors), most of whom were interested in becoming whalers and sealers. Because of the urgency of breaking into the trade, in which the Americans were already engaged in the south seas, several of those convicts were later trusted to join Captain William Collins' crews before they had served their full sentence. But only those who were the servants of officers, and six who volunteered to go to Port Jackson with William Collins, were allowed near boats at Port Phillip.[20] Those known to be fishermen were David Wakefield, who had stolen clothes from a boat, and one William Smith and his friend Thomas Davies, who had stolen barley from a barge. John Whitehead was a waterman who had stolen clothes but soon fell a victim to scurvy.

Those who were sailors, apart from those who claimed to have served in the Royal Navy, were Christopher Forsha who had stolen copper; John Williams, alias Johnson, who had stolen clothing; a horse stealer James Price who drowned after arrival in Hobart Town; Stephen Byrne, who had stolen a pocket-book but died during the voyage out; John Curtis, who had stolen clothes and died the following year in Hobart Town; Joseph Fernandez, who had stolen gum and

became a bushranger; George Scholer, who had stolen a money box; James Brown, who had stolen clothes while serving on an East India Company ship the *Warley* (coincidentally the original name of the *Calcutta*); Richard Wall, who had blackened his face before he committed assault and robbery at Exeter; and Thomas Tombs, a highway robber whose name would long be remembered in Van Diemen's Land. William Vasey, who had stolen a pocket-book, John Blackmore who had stolen £7 and William Thomas who had stolen sugar, all committed their crimes while employed on ships.

Knopwood's servant Daniel McAllenan had claimed to be a sailor when acquitted of horse stealing, only later to be convicted of stealing silverware. Samuel Gunn, who had served as a shipwright in the Navy and in the carpenter's crew of the *Calcutta*, was a useful assistant when huts were being built.

Collins made the most of the educated and literate prisoners, who included the embezzlers Thomas Fitzgerald, Samuel Warriner and John Clark, all experienced clerks. Warriner took on minor secretarial work and Fitzgerald, who claimed to have been an army captain during the war, taught some of the young people. Of the three printers, Robert Walsh who had stolen clothing, was suspect because he had been an Irish rebel. Collins had found a place under a shady tree for the little printing press he had brought with him. The printer Francis Barnes, who had also been a soldier and wounded in battle, could have been the person who printed the General and Garrison Orders. But it is more likely that Collins gave this attractive job to Matthew Power, who had uttered counterfeit money and to whom he already owed many favours. Collins was to find the press one of his most useful pieces of equipment, although more type and paper were badly needed. The first printed news appeared on 16 October, soon after they landed. The General Orders of that day were concerned with the rations allowed to the civil, military and free settlers. The Garrison Orders explained the duties of the guard.

The activity and the lively transformation of the camp had amazed Tuckey. Although he held out little hope for its future as a permanent settlement, he indulged in a little fantasy when he contemplated the possibilities. He beheld 'a second Rome, rising from a coalition of banditti. I beheld it giving laws to the world, and superlative in arms and in the arts, looking down with proud superiority upon the barbarous nations of the northern hemisphere . . .'[21]

The need to improvise produced some splendid results. Several of the convicts, using a little ingenuity and skill, will be remembered in the history of Victoria as the 'first' in a particular industry. Thomas Rushton, one of the oldest convicts transported, a tanner and hemp spinner by trade, actually began to manufacture cloth from the flax at Port Phillip.[22] He appeared to understand enough of the process to declare that the resulting product was equal to any in Europe and he was well able to prepare the flax for making linen. Under his supervision the men collected, according to Fawkner, tons of flax growing wild on the sandy peninsula. It had be thrown away when the order came for removal to Van Diemen's Land.

But the most intelligent manufacturer was Victoria's first industrial chemist James Grove, whose forgeries had already brought him fame. He first set foot on shore at Port Phillip anticipating pleasure, but was immediately disappointed by the barrenness of the land. He seemed surprised that during the time there Collins had even bothered to have a garden and had allowed huts to be built, when it seemed obvious that the settlement would be temporary.

Yet Grove was to prove that nature itself was already providing useful vegetable substances at Sullivan Bay. Collins had allowed him and his family to remain there until May 1804, because he had become partly incapacitated after a fall. From the local woods he made a large tea chest, some three hundred-weight in weight. This was to contain the tea he had made ('equal to any of the common black teas sold in England') from one of the native tea-trees, so called because of its slight oriental flavour.[23]

He was delighted to find a luxuriant natural substance which produced a marine alkali, or soda, then only in its infancy as a compound element for domestic and industrial use, especially in the manufacture of soap. Collins wrote to Banks about the 'ingenious' person who had extracted it from the *Atriplex halimifolia*, a species of kelp which grew in the sands close to the high-water mark.[24] Grove had burnt leaves and branches of the plant in a large iron pot heated to redness over a fire; when the ashes were lixiviated the solution evaporated. Each 100 pounds of the plant yielded three and a half pounds of marine alkali. Five men cut, burned and purified nearly two tons of the alkali in forty days. With some tallow he had bought at the Cape of Good Hope, believing it would be useful to set himself up in trade, Grove was then able to manufacture soap while at Port Phillip 'equal to any of the Windsor you pay so dear for in London'.[25] When he later arrived in Hobart Town he was astounded to find that common yellow soap from Sydney sold at 2s 6d per pound and that from his outlay of ten guineas he would be able to make £100, although somewhat conscience-stricken because he felt it both a duty to his family and a favour to his customers. He sent a sample of soap to Mrs King in Sydney and thirteen casks were sent to London.[26]

• • • •

From the time of their arrival at Port Phillip until the end of December 1804, prisoners as well as settlers, civil officers and military, and all dependents were wholly or partly victualled from the public stores. The food rations for prisoners included flour, beef, pork, sugar, molasses, oatmeal, rice, raisins, suet, wheat and maize. Many were able to eke out their ration with what they were able to hunt on the land or fish from the sea.[27]

In contrast, the original inhabitants, who had lived in harmony with the land and its offerings for thousands of years, thrived on possums, snakes and all manner of vegetation, as well as shellfish and other varieties of marine life. Food was plentiful and their diet well balanced, although not to Tuckey's taste. He abhorred their partiality for lizards and grubs, and believed that the kangaroo was out of reach of their ingenuity and weapons because he saw no use of kangaroo skin.[28]

Listing the plants found at Port Phillip, Tuckey found several which he believed were 'potable', including wild celery, wild parsnip, scurvy grass and several species of samphire which Crook found very good to eat. They ate the acid cone of the she-oak, wild raspberries and the Port Jackson cherry.[29] Knopwood reported in detail the measurement of a sixty-eight-pound kangaroo which officers from the *Calcutta* relished.[30] Convicts who served as boats' crews brought in 500 pounds of crayfish one evening, as well as good rock cod, mullet, kingfish, parrot fish, leatherjacket and stingrays. But the catch was barely sufficient to feed the civil officers, settlers and marines. There was only one seine fit for use, although they were well supplied with fishing lines and hooks.

The scarcity of small fish was more likely due to the large number of voracious sharks and stingrays which

'Lieutenant Pateshall kill a kangaroo . . . What officers could be spared from H.M. ship Calcutta *came and dind {sic} at the camp of the kangaroo, and very excellent it was . . .' (Knopwood, Diaries, 13, 14 November 1803, ML). Artist George Gordon McCrae later captured the scene, which was described to him by the settler James Hobbs.*

abounded in the bay. They found the meat of shark coarse but it became a luxury when fried. Knopwood and others seemed to have little trouble collecting quantities of fine crayfish from the rocks on the ocean side across the narrow neck of land separating Bass Strait from the calm of Port Phillip. He probably improvised traps in the manner of those used by the natives. Some who ventured across to fish from the rocks misjudged the creeping tides and were swept mercilessly into the dangerous currents that have since claimed many lives, including that of a Prime Minister in December 1967.[31] Collins warned the people that fishing could be a hazard as well as bathing, even in front of the encampment. Apart from the scurvy which had been evident from the time the expedition set sail, and accounted for most of the deaths during the voyage, illness at Port Phillip appears to have been minimal. Diarrhoea was the main complaint, largely the result of drinking water they had not been accustomed to, although from the beginning the surgeons had reported that what water there was appeared to be good.[32] Fawkner was later critical of Collins for not taking notice of the runaway David Gibson, who returned to camp to alert him about the fine freshwater river at the head of the bay.[33]

The people on the whole were healthy and well behaved. The only death since their arrival was from 'debility', but there were never less than thirty under medical treatment. Those needing care were largely suffering from ailments caused by contusions, some of which occurred during the unloading of the boats. Grove injured his hip quite badly when he fell headlong down a cliff on to the rocks. After a year of salt food, some were unable to withstand the crippling effects. Their limbs became soft and Fawkner likened their fingers to pieces of dough. Any exertion caused intense pain when the sinews in their legs became contorted. Those most afflicted were fed on kangaroo or other fresh meat and fish. Many prisoners cut the wild parsley and added it to the meat to make soup. They carefully rationed the lime juice, and occasionally port wine was allowed for the worst cases of scurvy. Mrs Hartley, however, wrote to her sister how much she liked the climate, which all records indicate was as changeable then as now. During her time at Port Phillip — four months — she had never had an ache or pain. One can only wonder how she survived the psychological pain if her husband were really as cantankerous as others depicted him.[34]

Many of the convicts were usefully employed in feeding the hungry population, and preparing and apportioning the food in the best possible manner to counteract disease. David Wakefield, the fisherman who had been mate to Woodriff's cook, probably cooked at Port Phillip before rowing to Port Jackson with William Collins. Several other convicts had helped with the provision of meals in the Calcutta. The horse stealer Joseph Pendridge, who had baked bread during the voyage, might have had the assistance of the baker John Edwards who had stolen a pocket book and silver case, or the burglar, John Manning who eventually became a successful baker in Hobart Town. The forger, Daniel Anchor was a good butcher. Others known to have worked as butchers included John Manby, a horse stealer, and Richard Grover, a highway robber. John Thomas, who was also a butcher, had died at sea.

Two sheep stealers, Richard Godwin and Jonathan Spencer, had both served as poulterers in the Calcutta.[35] They would have needed little encouragement to serve up the ducks, parrots, cockatoos, quail, swan and pelicans which Pateshall and Knopwood reported in abundance and enjoyed shooting. Harris found swans in flocks of 100 and killed up to twelve in one morning, but found they were coarse to eat. Soon after arrival Harris tasted a goose which would have been thrown away on a dunghill in England.[36] So starved were they for fresh meat, they welcomed it, even if only as a change from the tough alternative fare salted long before in England. Even Lieutenant Sladden's delicate wife actually relished the taste of the questionable goose meat. The two poulterers, however, were among the earliest deaths. The fresh meat readily available to them, if not to all the convicts, was too late to prevent the dreaded scurvy from which they were suffering. Both died in March 1804, Godwin at Port Phillip and Spencer at Risdon. Thomas Stokes was a stocking trimmer, and his crime unknown, but Captain Woodriff had co-opted him together with Thomas Bowman, the chairmaker, as wardroom cooks, while John Margetts, a silversmith who had stolen blankets, William Constable, a sailor from Bengal who had stolen gloves, and James Brown, the sailor from the Warley, had been assisting the convicts' cooks during the voyage.[37] Stokes and Bowman had also trained as pastrycooks.

Nicholas Piroelle, the Frenchman, was a confectioner who had stolen apricots and sugar; one might imagine that he would have enjoyed the opportunity, had it been available, to produce crystallised apricots or petits fours, or embellish his confections with ingredients that had no place at Sullivan Bay. He too would fall an early victim in Hobart Town to a disease that warranted Dr Bowden's conducting an autopsy.

13 OFFICERS, 'GENTLEMEN' AND A LADY

COLLINS DID NOT have much time for relaxation but he continued his association with Mrs Power and her obliging husband, and occasionally dined with Knopwood and the civil and military officers. Dr Bowden had formed what was to be a lifelong alliance with Maria Sergeant, wife of one of the marines, and Leonard Fosbrook took time off from his duties as commissary to be with 'Mrs Whitehead', who appears to have abandoned her Scottish embezzler. The officers had a mess hut built in which they had regulations that no member could have more than one pint of wine a day, except when the Governor dined there or if an officer invited a friend. Then he was allowed, at his own expense, an extra pint. Contrary to his original assessment of Collins, Harris informed his mother that they had much in common and that Collins 'is one of the pleasantest men I ever met with at his own table and in every other respect I have found him polite and affable'.[1]

A. W. H. Humphrey, the mineralogist and George Harris, the surveyor, and Lieutenants Lord and Johnson of the marines were among those with whom Knopwood frequently associated. But Knopwood's particularly gregarious nature allowed him to enjoy the company of any who would accompany him fishing or shooting or smoke a pipe with him. He more than anyone helped create new strata of society with the polyglot human material at hand. Officers and some of the chosen convicts appreciated sharing with him a repast concocted from the fresh catch of the day, together with what he harvested from his vegetable garden and could spare from his ration of wine.

Although he was at the centre of social life at both Port Phillip and Hobart Town, Knopwood received only the basic liquor allowance — one pint of wine a day — which to him was a deprivation, but he made sure that more was available to him from other sources. He and his fellow officers enjoyed the hospitality meted out on board the *Calcutta* and the *Ocean* while they were in port. Knopwood in particular also fraternised with the captains and crews of the *Lady*

Nelson and other vessels when they called. Frequently he would sleep overnight in the ships. This often occurred on a Saturday evening and the ensuing Sunday diary entries are illuminating. By a remarkable coincidence he often reported that he was too ill to conduct divine service following the overindulgences of a convivial evening.

Knopwood also formed close friendships with the surgeons Bowden and I'Anson, while Harris and Humphrey became his associates on the Bench of Magistrates.[2] But of all the civil officers he was the only one who really accepted convicts into his society from the beginning. Those he could not tolerate, whether convict or free, became his worst enemies. He was, in his own way, a snob and he found it easy to forget the reasons for the emigration of some of the more educated or superior men who became his friends, especially if they had money or had fallen from some rank of society which he could accept. He was extraordinarily adept at manipulating people and situations to suit himself. One of his convict friends was James Grove, who wrote from Port Phillip that he was 'looking around to see if there is any opening, in any way, to establish a little society among us: of which at present there appears but little probability'.[3] Grove really meant some sort of society for the propagation of religious teaching. Grove had remained friendly with the Crooks and had his tent pitched near theirs. There was no love lost between the Crooks and Knopwood and it was not until after the Crooks left Port Phillip that the Groves and Knopwood became friends.

Dr William Hopley was the only married officer. He needed to keep a watchful eye on his extended family and rarely socialised with the other officers. The matriarch of the family, his mother-in-law Jane, was a forty-two-year-old widow, an American loyalist who was born in New York and about 1780 had married Lieutenant William Hobbs of the Royal Navy, a Cornishman serving on the American station. Their daughter, later Judith Hopley, was also

American-born. Lieutenant Hobbs had died at Portsmouth of severe internal injuries after a fall while in command of H.M. brig *Bounder* in the Jersey roads in 1799. He had served in twenty-one confrontations with the enemy. Soon afterwards their sons William, already a lieutenant, and the boy James saw service in Egypt, where William was killed. Hopley himself had been a naval surgeon. He had an excellent record but ill health (and some influence from Admiral Nugent) had caused him to apply for his discharge with the request that he should be considered for appointment to New South Wales and that the whole family should accompany him as settlers.[4]

Mrs Hobbs must have been a strong character to have sailed in the *Ocean* to make a new life with her remaining son, still only eleven (he was nine when in Egypt), her four daughters, son-in-law, and granddaughter Julia. During the voyage both Judith Hopley and the sixteen-year-old Rebecca Hobbs became pregnant. Rebecca's baby was born at Port Phillip and Knopwood married her to its father, the settler John Ingle, shortly after their arrival in Hobart Town.[5]

Fawkner wrote with more admiration of Judith Hopley, whose son Richard was the first European born in Hobart, than perhaps of any other woman apart from his own mother. Mrs Hopley was to him a lady, 'an attentive kind wife, a tender mother, and a thorough English matron: her conduct was exemplary and had some weight in counteracting the gross immorality in high places'.[6]

The same might well have been written about the two younger sisters, Ann Jane and Charity, who would later marry George Harris and William Collins.[7] Even during the voyage Harris was attracted to the young fifteen-year-old, from whom he became inseparable. He was then escaping from a disappointment in love, bewailing the 'fickleness of the sex', and feeling 'like a solitary exile wandering on the expanse of the ocean without a friend to confide in'. He informed his brother Henry that he and Ann Jane used 'to sit or walk together for hours by moonlight on the quarter deck' with no thought other than that of friendship. He assured his mother of his 'perfect happiness' when he married the young blue-eyed girl: 'My sweet little girl is one of the most amenable disposition I ever met with and her affectionate attachment to me is such as must render my life devoted to her happiness in return . . .'[8]

But most of the settlers could hardly be classed as any better than, if as good as, the convicts.[9] Apart from Henry Hayes, who has already been referred to as Fawkner's friend and accomplice and was acquitted, while his wife had to pay the price of transportation, there were others with dubious records.

One such person was Samuel Lightfoot, who had been a First Fleet convict, served his time, returned to England and decided he wished to settle at Port Phillip. He had originally been tried at the Devon Assizes held at Exeter in March 1785 for burglary and sentenced to transportation to New South Wales for seven years. He sailed in the *Charlotte*.[10] There is little evidence of how he was employed in the colony. But the report of a summons before the Bench of Magistrates of a man named Coffin, charged with stealing liquor from the hospital and supplying Lightfoot and others, suggests Lightfoot might then have been a hospital assistant. He received a 30-acre land grant in 1794 (probably when free by servitude) north of Sydney, but sold it to Thomas Muir, one of the Scottish Martyrs, presumably when he decided to return to England.[11]

Lightfoot must have produced favourable witnesses to his character to be able to return in the *Ocean*. He had a wife planning to sail with him. She did not arrive; it is possible that she died on the voyage. Although there was no provision on the civilian establishment for a hospital attendant, Collins would have believed it important to create the position.[12] He would need to rely on someone to take charge of the stores and direct convicts detailed for duty. He would have remembered Lightfoot from earlier days and knew he would be useful in such work.

The Reverend William Crook and William Caw had both received appointments as missionaries from the Society for Propagating the Gospel. Originally they were expected to stay for a while at Port Jackson to work among the Aborigines.[13] Crook (or Croc) was said to be the son of a French count, an émigré, influenced by the teachings of Dr Waugh. He liked to refer to himself as the Lord's servant, which caused some historians to believe his occupation had been that of a gentleman's servant. He was actually trained as a tin maker at Tottenham Court Chapel during his course in missionary work. He first sailed in the *Duff* in 1797 to the Marquesas Group. There he had gained the respect and affection of the people simply by living as they did. He learned their language and later became the first person to translate the Bible into Polynesian. On his return to London he became an itinerant preacher until the chance came to obtain a passage to New South Wales. He had hoped eventually to reach Otaheite. He married his wife Mary just two days before they sailed.[14]

Crook would probably have conducted some sort of burial service over the body of John Skelthorn, a butler, and the baby Fletcher, who were the first to die at Port Phillip. The Fletchers had also lost a baby at Tenerife. As they were passengers in the *Ocean*, he would have been their pastor. Knopwood mentioned neither death in his journal and recorded only Skelthorn in the register. Another unregistered death was that of Michael McCarty, the *Calcutta*'s cook, whom they buried on shore while anchored off Sullivan Bay.[15]

Collins tried to instil into his marines a sense of pride in which they should hold the honour entrusted them, that of helping establish a new outpost for Britain. He berated them for their alcoholic excesses and their gambling. He demanded strict obedience from them, hoping to hold them up as examples to others who might join them at a future date. Within a day or so of these orders, Lieutenant Sladden as adjutant had to confine Sergeant Richard Sergeant for drunkenness and misconduct. His lapse had undoubtedly been provoked by the actions of his wife, Maria. After a court martial Sergeant was demoted to the rank of private, but on account of his previous good conduct the Governor reinstated him soon afterwards, probably because Collins realised that his contingent was too small for the job it had to do and he could ill afford to lose one of Sergeant's rank.[16] He had to ask Captain Woodriff, who willingly obliged, for the loan of a company of his marines under Lieutenant Charles Menzies to serve on shore and assist with the execution of many unexpected duties.[17]

Several other wives and families of the marines had accompanied their husbands. To occupy their time Collins directed three of the wives of privates to do the laundry for forty-four persons, so that the marines would have no excuse for appearing in a dirty and unsoldierlike manner.

One of the happiest occasions for the contingent would have been on 25 November when Ann, the wife of Sergeant Samuel Thorne, gave birth to their son, the first born of European parents. Knopwood was 'very unwell' the next day.[18] On Christmas morning the Governor, Lieutenant Johnson, Mrs Power and the supposed Mrs Whitehead stood as sponsors at the baptismal ceremony of William James Port Phillip Thorne, who was to live to a great age in Tasmania. Mercifully, they later changed his name to William James Hobart Thorne.[19]

A sadder occasion was when Susannah Wiggins, who had given birth to a son during the *Calcutta*'s

'I publickly {sic} baptised Sarjent Thorn's {sic} child. The Governor, Lieut. Johnson, Mrs Powers and Mrs Whitehead stood for the child, the first birth in the colony' (Knopwood, Diaries, Christmas Day 1803, ML). George Gordon McCrae's impressions of one of the highlights at Sullivan Bay in 1803.

voyage, and her husband Samuel, a private in the marines, lost their three-year-old daughter Ann. Her grave could be among those at the Collins' Settlement Historic Site. Tradition holds that one of the graves is that of a child and hers is the only known child's death after the actual landing at Sullivan Bay.[20]

14 IN BLACK AND WHITE

ONE DOES NOT know for sure when the two cultures, black and white, met for the first time within the confines of Port Phillip Bay. It might have been long before Lieutenant John Murray sailed warily through the narrow heads. It might have been much earlier, if some scanty evidence can ever prove that a legendary Portuguese caravel charted the indentures of the bay. Or some survivors of the *Sydney Cove*, wrecked off Preservation Island in February 1797, may have reached the mainland. There was also the record of escapes from Port Jackson itself. Bass came across some fourteen Port Jackson men stranded on one of the Glennies Islands off Wilson's Promontory. They were mostly Irish and their seven mates had, a few months earlier, treacherously left them on the island, too cut off from the mainland to consider braving the tempestuous strait. Bass had had to deliver five of them on the mainland, leaving them with as many provisions as he could spare and the necessary directions to make their way north. He could only manage to return with two who were ill in his small craft.[1] The fate of the others was never discovered. During the *Lady Nelson*'s voyage south in March 1801 Ensign Francis Barrallier discovered the charred remains of a skeleton at Jervis Bay whom the local natives indicated was that of a white man who had come from the south in a canoe after his ship had 'tumbled down'. They believed that the bush tribe had killed and eaten him. Lieutenant James Grant was more interested in this discovery than he was in nautical surveying. He had the bones sent to an English surgeon who was unable to classify them.[2]

It may not be that all escapees from Port Jackson perished. William Buckley later afforded living proof that a strong and astute person could come to terms with a different civilisation if life, liberty and hunger were at stake.[3] Others might well have fallen in with friendly natives in the south. Among certain Aboriginal tribes early visitors noticed distinct evidence of a paler pigmentation and softening of features that suggest Aboriginal and European blood had mingled in

Victoria by the end of the eighteenth century.[4] Black skin ranged from the hue as seen in darkest Africa to a light brown, just as the skin of the newcomers who arrived with Governor Collins might range from that of the pallid Celt, changing to lobster red as the summer sun penetrated with its rays, to the olive of the Portuguese Fernandez and the darkness of the Jewish complexions.

On the Mornington Peninsula itself it is doubtful whether the native population ever exceeded more than 500 at any one time. One can only speculate that occupation was seasonal. Middens occur between Mount Martha and Moorooduc, along the sandy coastline between Coolart Creek and Flinders, from Frankston to Mount Martha and at the Sorrento and Portsea ocean beaches. Sullivan Bay is an area in which a small archaeological survey has lately produced enough evidence to show that Aborigines had made regular visits there over a period of several thousand years.[5] They had camped on the slopes of the Eastern Sister when collecting shellfish and they returned there after the abandonment of the 1803 settlement. They belonged to the Bunerong tribe which wandered seasonally between the east coast of Port Phillip, and beyond Western Port to an area between Warragul and Cape Liptrap.[6] During the French exploration Captain Emmanuel Hamelin of the French corvette *Naturaliste*, spent eight days in Western Port and his botanical assistant Senior Officer Pierre Milius actually described one small Aboriginal as so ugly that he doubted whether he was even a human being![7]

The Aborigines were already aware that intruders who sailed the sea in strange large crafts and covered their bodies with unknown fabrics had access to dangerous and magical weapons. If escapees or wrecked or deserted seamen were not their first contacts with Europeans, it is possible that some sealers had strayed in and out of Port Phillip before the acknowledged discoverers from the *Lady Nelson*. It was not far from Sullivan Bay that Murray's party had seen numerous native huts and had encountered members of the tribe. The mate Bowen dressed them in white shirts and in exchange received a neatly made straw basket. Murray tried to barter with bread, looking glasses, a tomahawk and a picture of their spears and opossum skin clothes. After the first friendly meeting, the natives became suspicious of the strangers. According to Murray, they began to throw spears, narrowly missing his men. And so the first sound of gunfire was unleashed on the bewildered inhabitants of Port Phillip, probably killing at least one whose blood spattered his native soil for some distance.[8]

The following April had seen the arrival of the *Investigator* captained by Matthew Flinders in Port Phillip. He reported sighting many signs of native occupancy, including deserted fire places and heaps of oyster shells in the vicinity of Arthur's Seat. He and his men saw smoke rising in the southern part of the peninsula but at first no natives.[9] The botanist Robert Brown and gardener Peter Good, as they wandered around the Nepean Peninsula, observed only the remains of native fires. The botanical artist Ferdinand Bauer found a native waddy decorated with circles of zig-zags. William Westall refrained from including any image of *homo sapiens* in the topographical sketch he made.[10]

Then they reached Indented Head. There Flinders bestowed presents on a group who were not a bit surprised when he shot at a bird. Some had perhaps experienced first hand the deadly use of gun-shot, having been fired on by Murray's party. Flinders was to conjecture that if a settlement were made at Port Phillip 'it would not be difficult to establish a friendly intercourse with the natives, for they are acquainted with the effect of firearms, and desirous of possessing many of our conveniences'.[11]

The great potential of gunpowder was barely grasped, but they recognised it could kill. Spears could kill, too, and if necessary they would be sharp and ready for use. This Aboriginal tribe was not prepared to succumb without putting up a fight.

When the *Cumberland* entered Port Phillip in January 1803, after Charles Robbins and his party had dealt with the intruding French at King Island, the surveyor, Charles Grimes, was able to carry out his survey.[12] The party stepped off the boat at Rye and traversed the countryside. They appear to have crossed the land from Dromana to the mangroves beyond Sandy Point at Western Port. There is evidence of huts which they thought might have been built by Europeans. The natives disappeared when they approached. It was the dry season and it is likely they did not normally frequent the area at that time. Perhaps they had become wary of intruders and kept out of sight. Natives whom the party encountered along the Kananook Creek and on the Bellarine Peninsula showed neither fear nor hostility. They proudly showed their spears, ate bread and accepted

gifts. Two showed marks of the smallpox which must have been spread by Europeans.[13]

But visitors from the *Lady Nelson*, the *Investigator* and the *Cumberland* were few in number. When the natives first realised that a larger ship — the *Ocean*, containing women and children as well as adult men — had arrived, they were ill-prepared for their first encounter with the invaders. One of the natives approached the strangers, brandishing a shield and spear, fearing the consequences if they landed. Captain Mertho's party fired a musket over his head and followed the man and his kinsfolk into a primitive hut where they stole one of his bark baskets. This family in the vicinity of Swan Bay had lit a little fire, as was the native custom, probably for cooking an indoor meal. Their hut was made from a few branches of trees set against a reclining tree or a piece of wood. Crook expressed horror that some of his countrymen scattered the fire in such a manner that it burnt the dwelling.[14]

Their fears must have been horrendous when they heard the first shots and saw the devastating results. To prove their superior marksmanship, one of the invading party shot down a bird. No tribal disputes would have been quite as fearsome. At first they would have thought, among themselves, that either side had a fair chance of winning. But the white magic was invincible. They repeatedly exclaimed: "Warree! Warree! Mallo! Mallo!" in stunned tones that were not harsh, later described by Pateshall as expressions of astonishment.[15]

Three persons shot at another native and killed him after which the sailors stripped him and brought away his ornaments and weapons. 'What impression this first visit made on the natives', wrote Crook, 'I leave to you . . .'[16]

When hundreds more arrived in the *Calcutta* the native population must have experienced traumas inconceivable to us today, realising that here was a party planning a more permanent occupancy of the place to which they themselves came regularly. They were to watch the strangers gather the mussels and limpets that clung to the rocks and the oysters that washed ashore in plenty; catch their birds, their fish, their kangaroos, the food that had kept them, until then, a proud and strong race. They learned that the white man could hunt with more sophisticated weapons than the spear and the fish traps they had devised. They knew that warfare among their own tribes resulted in bloodshed and death; consequently any altercation between the two civilisations could mean a bloodbath. But protection of one's people and one's land and its resources is instinctively universal and the Aboriginal people of Australia believe that they are part of the land itself. What happened during the Collins invasion is not at all surprising.

Tuckey's sketch is the first known portrayal of Port Phillip Aborigines. 'The huts merely serve the purpose of temporary shelter from the weather . . .' (Tuckey, Voyage, *p. 181).*

The Aborigines would have noted with a curiosity turning to terror that ships off-loaded boats in which small parties of men went in search of what they might have guessed was water. Even so, while searching for a landing place Tuckey received a friendly greeting from three natives who presented him with a spear. Woodriff and Collins as well as Tuckey tried to communicate with him and his friends, giving them blankets and biscuit. They appeared friendly during further visits and other gifts were exchanged, thereby creating an atmosphere at first of some trust.[17] Among the products the natives produced was some rice, indicating previous contact with Europeans, perhaps given to them by Murray's men, perhaps some of the harvest of Grant's crop planted on Churchill Island, or, earlier still, perhaps even rice Bass had provided for some of the escapees he landed at Wilson's Promontory.

Then they prepared to watch in silence, in wonderment, as the human chain of prisoners lined up in the shallows for those first few weeks unloading the stores from the *Ocean*. They would have seen every arrival on the clean white sand stagger ashore after the long voyage. They would have wondered why many could barely walk at all, why some had single irons that impeded their gait and some were encumbered with double irons that even more severely slowed them down. Many of the strangers would have been bearded, like themselves, but other persons like Humphrey, the mineralogist, might have chosen to clean shave in celebration of their arrival on dry land. Women in dresses with high waistlines and bonnets, marines in scarlet uniforms, and prisoners in blue duck trousers and check shirts must have been a sight as strange to behold as we today might perceive an invasion from outer space.

The sounds of Europe were in sharp contrast to the monotones of the native population heard at some distance. Mingling with the cries of the gulls on the water's edge as they fought over any scraps the people cast away, and the warbling of the magpies from the banksias and she-oaks, strange sounds came from the roll of drums at the flag-raising ceremony when the company lustily begged God to save their gracious King. The three volleys fired by the Royal Marines to honour the anniversary of His Majesty's accession to the throne and the *Calcutta*'s response of twenty-one guns produced a noise not unlike the thunder that had inspired the legends of their dreamtime. But instinctively they knew that this had evil and unnatural connotations and was the prologue of a tragedy that, for them, was still to be performed.

Drummers and fifers had other duties when they were delegated to carry out the floggings which were sure to produce less pleasing sounds made by the human voice. How could the natives have understood any provocation that allowed two human beings to deliver 200 lashes on the bare back of another until blood appeared and the flesh fell apart? In a happier vein, there were occasions when the young Sergeant Thorne or Lieutenant Pateshall might produce mellifluous sounds from their flutes. An American negro — and the only known American convict was William Thomas — had entertained the party with a viol, perhaps accompanying those who sang boisterous songs and hymns with melodies from another world. Exotic aromas from the salted beef and pork had been unknown to them and they would barely have understood how the white man could lapse into a stupor after a session of debauchery and alcohol. And what were bits of paper on which a press had printed the orders of the day meant to be? The 'mooing' of a cow, the neigh of a horse, the 'baas' of sheep, the grunt of a pig, suddenly introduced to them a world beyond their comprehension. And what would have been their reaction when awakened at dawn by the call of a rooster?

All these and many more customs and curiosities of the usurpers would have mystified the original occupants of the coastal areas of Port Phillip. As they watched the erection of canvas tents and makeshift huts on the territory that was their birthright, did they realise that time was running out for them, that people with superior weapons had come to destroy all that they had in the past cherished as their own? They abandoned their own huts and silently watched the small boats set off to survey the bay with Tuckey in charge. They must have wondered what George Harris was doing as he took the soundings at regular intervals, and when on shore, examined the soil, taking notes on the minerals and vegetation.

The newcomers found the area in the north-west corner of Corio Bay to be more promising than anywhere else. Tuckey's party returned after a few days to check out the fresh water which appeared in a number of ponds.[18] Here was good rich soil and luxuriant grass near a 'snug cove', deep and secure enough for ships. They crossed over to the area now known as Limeburner's Point where they found building materials right on the spot. Here they were met by natives who belonged to the Kurunji tribe who appeared as if in friendship and received some further gifts.[19] Tuckey himself left in one of the boats during the preparation of dinner. It was the sign for 200 odd natives to swarm forward menacingly in all directions, carrying their chiefs in ceremonial fashion, singing

war songs and brandishing their spears. They crowded around the boat and stole a tomahawk, an axe and a saw. They invaded the tent and the safety of Harris and two of the boat's crew was at stake. A native grabbed the mate Gammon from one of the boats, and there was a general cry of 'Fire, sir; for God's sake, fire!' as Tuckey arrived back on the scene.[20]

There was general panic. The natives dropped their cloaks and retreated, only to return with reinforcements and all armed with spears. Tuckey placed his gun on the ground and courageously approached the chief to return the cloaks, necklaces and spears they had left on the ground. Some showed more anger than fear, and as they advanced, Tuckey ordered Boatswain Innis to fire three muskets at fifty yards' distance aimed at the most vociferous member of the tribe. He fell dead on the spot and his colleagues turned and fled, leaving his body behind.[21]

Tuckey noticed among them certain apparent ranks. The chief's figure was 'masculine and well proportioned, and his air bold and commanding'. He wore a necklace of reeds and strings of human hair over his breast. The beautiful wing feathers of a swan formed a coronet or turban of feathers, as Pateshall later described the feathered plumes as worn by one chief.[22] Tuckey found that in painting their faces the 'savage' takes as much trouble 'bedaubing his face with clays, or anointing his skin with the blubber of a whale' as the refined courtier of Europe, the Parisian beau who cares for his hair and perfumes himself with the odours of the East. Red, white and yellow clay formed patterns on the faces, while a bone up to two feet long pierced the septum of the nose. Scars and punctures marked the bodies which they covered in the colder weather with their cloaks of opossum skin, neatly sewn together forming squares or lozenges.[23]

As far as the convicts could judge from the limited knowledge they could have had of the natives, few would have wished to leave the relative security of their position to take a chance among the unknown. Those who had accompanied their masters around the bay and had come in contact with the inhabitants would have passed on frightening stories of their savagery and their filth as they saw it. Those who were with Tuckey had seen how eager they were to acquire food to eat and blankets and clothing to keep warm. These items appeared to have a higher priority than even tomahawks and other offerings. Tuckey had observed the extremities to which the scarcity of food had reduced them, even in the more luxuriant parts in Corio Bay. It horrified him to find they were feeding on lizards, even though this might have been their choice rather than necessity. Tuckey also found sods of every swamp turned up, as if in search of worms, for there were no roots that might serve as food. There were some crude traps in which they tried to catch water fowl, but it was a bad season and the traps were decayed through lack of use. Tuckey reported a scarcity of fish although the Grimes party had reported there were plenty. There was certainly no lack of shellfish.[24]

Tuckey's meeting with the natives at Corio was obviously more than the 'skirmish' that official reports suggest. Tuckey's Memoir of his Chart of Port Phillip describes the event in much more detail than his published book.

Crook had, as we have seen, been deeply shocked by the earlier affray soon after the *Ocean* arrived. His comments on the later more serious confrontation are scanty, as if he knew little of what had happened or had learnt to live with a situation he had little chance of controlling. 'It was thought necessary to show them the effect of firearms', he wrote; and also noted that the sailors stripped the native and carried off his weapons and ornaments.[25]

Knopwood did not share Crook's more sympathetic understanding of Aboriginal attitudes. Crook's mission was to Christianize the savages, a completely different function from that of Knopwood, who as chaplain to a largely convict congregation, had to go along with officialdom. Occupation and defence of the land, if necessary by force, was the purpose of the exercise. His commission from Lord Hobart held only that he would carefully and diligently discharge his duties and observe and follow orders and direction from the Governor of New South Wales or other superior officer without specifying what those duties might be.[26] There was no mention at all of Abo-

rigines, nor was there any reference to them in the instructions given to Collins himself.

Collins was probably relieved that he had no responsibility to report the matter in despatches to either Governor King or Lord Hobart. Knopwood's 'Private Remark' given him by Harris and Tuckey tells even less than Tuckey's versions, except that he named the boatswain Innis as the person who shot the native and adds the quaint remark that 'Had not Mr Tuckey fortunately came up with the boat, no doubt they would have killd [*sic*] Mr Gammon and Mr Harris and the two men, and have eat them'.[27]

Collins issued a general order on 20 November informing his company that Woodriff supposed that large numbers of natives were gathering close to the settlement. He warned convicts and others against going in the direction of Arthur's Seat in their leisure hours. But Collins was wary of an unwritten duty towards the native population. According to records, Collins was more humane than most officers in his previous dealings with them in earlier days at Botany Bay.

Rather belatedly, on 12 January 1804, Collins delivered his only orders relating to the inhabitants of Port Phillip. Anyone removing 'spears, fishgigs, gum, or any other articles from the natives, or out of their huts, or from the beach where it is their custom to leave these articles' would be punished for robbery and 'if any of the natives are wantonly or inconsiderably killed or wounded or if any violence is offered to a woman, the offender will be tried for his life'.[28]

15 THE ROYAL MAIL GETS THROUGH

AN UNEXPECTED OPPORTUNITY arose for six of the convicts with seafaring experience to gain a few weeks of relative freedom. Collins had to inform Governor King somehow of his safe arrival, give an account of Port Phillip and at the same time obtain his agreement (he did not need his permission) to move to a better site than any he had found within the extensive bay.[1]

William Collins, whose exact relationship to David Collins has not been proved satisfactorily (he might have been an illegitimate cousin or nephew — he was certainly very close to the Governor) offered to take Collins' reports to King in a small colonial cutter, well armed and provisioned for a month.[2]

Of the six convicts chosen from among those who volunteered for the hazardous journey, four had seven-year sentences for minor thefts mostly carried out on board ships. Urias Allender, James Price, William Thomas and John Ronaldson had already served successfully as sailors in the *Calcutta*. Another, David Wakefield, served as cook's mate on deck. The sixth, Christopher Forsha, was a caulker whose knowledge might have been useful in an emergency.

William Collins was confident of success, although it was with much anxiety that the Lieutenant-Governor let him go. But he had no option. He dared not send the official despatches from England with the adventurers, admitting that he believed the mission to be a precarious one. By now he had expected that King might have anticipated his arrival and probably hoped for some form of communication from him.

Even before unloading the ships, Collins might have contemplated further investigation of the upper part of the harbour, where Tuckey had reported the possibility of a river. But he wrote to King that the disadvantages of Port Phillip, *held in a commercial light*, were immense. He was adamant that they should move elsewhere.[3]

Apart from the lack of water, it was unsatisfactory as a source of naval timber.[4] But the worst feature was the deep and dangerous bight between Cape Albany Otway and Cape Schanck in which the entrance to Port Phillip was situated. A ship could only enter if it were well manned and well found, with a leading wind and at a certain time of tide. At ebb tide the rate of flow was from five to seven knots. Collins could not forget that the *Calcutta* herself had experienced a dangerous situation on her arrival in a gale of wind. The risks were much too great to create a regular port of call for whalers to refit and replenish there.[5]

Collins was full of praise for his people and asked King to contemplate that at that moment he had between 300 and 400 persons sitting down cheerfully with no other or more certain supply of water than what was filtered daily through the perforated sides of six or eight casks sunk in the sand. Captain Woodriff had also obligingly furnished him with all the necessary aid, including the loan of some marines to strengthen his own force. But these would need replacements from Sydney when the *Calcutta* had to leave. This would depend on King's reply and he warned him that the north was full of natives — he would need four times the present strength of marines to guard a settlement there.[6]

The brave little party rowed away from Sullivan Bay on Saturday 6 November 1803, a cloudy day with south-west winds. On the way they picked up mail from the *Calcutta* and, unknown to the authorities, one convict was carrying a telltale letter written by the Irish rebel Robert Walsh to 'General' Holt, his former colleague serving a sentence at Port Jackson. Squalls and rain had developed and they lost time waiting for the weather to clear before they could risk rowing through the Heads.

Divine service was to take place on the following day. Much had been made about the service on the previous evening when Collins had ordered a parade of marines and the overseers to muster the convicts, who had to be suitably dressed. The weather was 78°F at noon, the winds south-westerly, and it was cloudy. Knopwood visited the Governor in the morning and reported that 'the day was so unfavourable I could not

*William Collins, a hero of early Port Phillip. He commended the
'meritorious conduct' of six* Calcutta *convicts who sailed with him
carrying despatches for Governor King.*

do duty'. Was the cancellation anything to do with
the cavortings the night before? Knopwood had left
the *Calcutta* to go on shore with Harris and two of the
officers. His friends on board the *Calcutta* 'would feign
have kept me longer'.[7]

The celebrations, perhaps a farewell to William
Collins when he arrived to collect the ship's mail,
went on all day Sunday. Lieutenant Donovan was put
under arrest. Knopwood dined with Governor Collins
and 'all the officers on board were very merry'. The
signs for the day were 'Sydney Cove' and 'Expedition'.
Perhaps William Collins was also too affected when
on the following day he could not get out of the
harbour's mouth. Perhaps he, too, had been as touched
by the farewells as by the vicious currents of Port
Phillip's rip. The next day Knopwood and Bowden,
believing the party had set sail, crossed the peninsula
to watch from the windy sand dunes hoping to see the
boat appear after it rounded Point Nepean. Knopwood, well used to the mountainous seas of the Atlantic, was shocked to 'see the most dreadful surge I ever
beheld'.[8] Here, on the south-west coast, probably at
St Paul's, the highest point, they set up a watch. They
must have believed that the cutter could never survive
such treacherous waters. Actually it did not leave
until the following Thursday.

The long-awaited service of thanksgiving for their
arrival at Port Phillip took place on Sunday 13 November. From the slope of the Western Sister which Harris
labelled Church Hill, Knopwood delivered his historic
words as a return of thanks to Almighty God for their
safe arrival after a long voyage. The congregation
assembled below in the barracks square.

Knopwood took as his text words from the 139th
Psalm: 'If I take the wings of the morning; and remain
in the uttermost parts of the sea; even there also shall
Thy hand lead me, and Thy right hand shall hold
me'.[9] In the course of his sermon Knopwood invoked
not only the words of the Psalmist but those of David
from the Book of Samuel, the narrator of the flood in
Genesis VII, the wisdom of Solomon and the prophet
Isaiah, of Nahum who decreed that God is jealous, is
'slow to anger . . . He will not acquit the wicked' but
that 'His way is in the whirlwind, and in the storm,
and the clouds are the dust of His feet'.

He blessed God's name for having 'protected us and
preserved us from many perils and dangers in our
voyage across that immense track of ocean . . . Thou
has been our defender both by night and day, in every
place where we have been, and hast at last brought us
in peace and safety to our appointed destination'.

Nor did Knopwood forget his friend William
Collins and the little party somewhere in the wild seas
of Bass Strait. He blessed those who needed God's
fatherly protection from the perils of the sea and
beseeched Him to conduct them in safety to their
desired haven. He reminded his congregation of several
instances where the power of the Almighty had succoured men in distress and delivered them from destruction, as in the remarkable escape of Captain Bligh
and his *Bounty* companions; and of the people saved
from the *Guardian* which had struck an iceberg during its voyage to Botany Bay.[10] He ended his sermon
with the wish that God might give unto all 'an eternal
haven of bliss'.

One person who did not approve of Knopwood's
preaching was the missionary, Crook. He was probably responsible for delivering the first sermon at Port
Phillip from the deck of the *Ocean*. He had preached to
the settlers regularly, even though he felt the effects
might be 'like the morning cloud and like the early
dew'. He had hoped to conduct further services at
Port Phillip but Collins politely refused him as Knopwood was the official chaplain. Crook expected to see
little encouragement to the Gospel as his (Collins')life
was 'immoral'. On reflection he decided that he would
have few attentive listeners if people were coerced into
attending his services. He preferred to carry on his
teachings in private. Unfortunately, Crook found that
his fellow preacher, Caw, was a very quarrelsome
man. He was a most improper person, diametrically
opposing all that the London Missionary Society and

Christianity stood for. Crook had advised him to study the character of Christ when he happily threatened some respectable people with a flogging, wished others dead, and threatened to knock down anyone approaching his place. Crook had tried to calm him down, but he did nothing but oppose his preaching because the people were so wicked no good could come of it.[11] Grove also condemned Caw as a most unmannerly person whom a foremost man of the London Missionary Society had recommended, for what reason nobody knew.[12]

Nine days after William Collins had left Port Phillip, the *Ocean*, having discharged stores, got ready to leave for China where she hoped to pick up a cargo. Captain Mertho gave a dinner on board the *Ocean*. Knopwood chose to stay overnight. Mertho had not expected to call at Port Jackson but Collins had settlers who were impatient to reach their destination, including the Crooks. The captain agreed to take them aboard and hoped to pick up a cargo of sealskins to repay his trouble.[13] Henry Hayes, the settler, who had been one of John Fawkner's partners in crime, left at the last minute in the *Ocean*. He was not victualled at Sullivan Bay after 13 November.[14] He would have been more than anxious to rejoin his convicted wife as well as his daughter at Port Jackson. The settler, Robert Miller, whom John Palmer the Commissary at Port Jackson had engaged as a shipwright, departed at the same time.

The *Ocean* had trouble getting out of the bay. Woodriff sent one of his officers to the ship to search for possible deserters from the *Calcutta* or prisoners from the camp. Winds were variable and he sent the Master and boat's crew to assist the *Ocean* down to the rip. It took a further twenty-four hours before the winds had moderated and Captain Mertho dared sail.[15] Some sixty miles south of Port Jackson he encountered William Collins and his party, who had experienced tempestuous weather ever since they had left. Captain Mertho towed the cutter the rest of the way to Port Jackson.[16] Somehow, some time, the mail had to go through.[17]

First impressions of the harbour at Port Jackson must have been at least as exciting to the visitors in 1803 as to one seeing it today for the first time. It was cloudy and there was a moderate breeze as the ship anchored off Sydney Cove not far from the rotting hulk of H.M.S. *Supply*, in which Governor Phillip had sailed with the First Fleet. There were a few ships in the Cove and many small craft ready to transport any merchandise ashore. The settlement looked prosperous, with rows of neat public buildings. Houses of some substance already dotted the surrounding hillside, here and there were some tents, a windmill, a church tower, a flagstaff, and lots of trees already in the line of the axe and the plough.

Captain Mertho had little cargo to unload apart from two tons of porter, ten boxes of soap and a small quantity of butter and cheese.[18] The wonder is that even this amount found space among the large consignment of stores he had delivered to Port Phillip. No one was allowed to board the ship until she was properly secured in the Cove, an order which was directed to try and control those who might buy up entire cargoes and create monopolies. This had been the root of the corruption that had undermined the Governor's authority in the colony as the power of the officers of the New South Wales Corps increased. Soldiers trying to draw on their salaries found that they were forced to receive goods in lieu of pay. Joseph Holt remembered that Captain Anthony Fenn Kemp would threaten soldiers with a flogging if they demanded money rather than tobacco at 10s a pound or tea at 8s, goods for which they could get only half that price if re-selling. Thus it was, wrote Holt, that so many old 'tailors, and shoemakers, staymakers, man milliners, tobacconists, and pedlars, that were called captains and lieutenants, made their fortunes; by the extortion and the oppression of the soldier, the settler, and the poor'.[19]

It was a situation that Governor King had inherited and it was to get worse before it got better. The ex-staymaker's apprentice John Macarthur, then in exile, was already one of the most powerful men with interests in the colony. His friends and supporters had been leading the campaign against the Governor with a series of anonymous lampoons. King's attempt to establish a government store that would provide fairly for all was not in their interests. Nothing was sacred in their condemnation of King and the barbs were piercing and largely unjustified as they touched all those whom King had tried to help:

The convicts I'd starve, and sell all their rations,
As well as their slops, for my private occasion.
The salaries of superintendents are mine
If e'er they neglect to secure them in time.
From the orphan collection I take what I dare,
Of whaler's investments I own I've a share.
Tythes, taxes, and quit-rents unto me belong,
And duties on spirits I claim as my own.
Such pickings are surely beyond all resistance,
And such as I covet for future subsistence . . .[20]

Captain Mertho had to go ashore before anyone else could land, report to Governor King and receive port orders. He probably just missed meeting Captain Gibbs West and his men from the brig *Wertha Ann* which had left the same day after calling in from New York to replenish wood and water. William Thomas, the American convict who had sailed with William Collins, would have felt particularly saddened that he had lost an opportunity to meet some compatriots.

They had off-loaded some welcome supplies of butter and cheese, a barrel of rum, a barrel of tar and twenty boxes of mould candles.[21] More importantly, the ship had brought the devastating but not surprising news that hostilities had again broken out between England and France some six months earlier.[22] Governor King had hardly expected to hear that the *Calcutta* had arrived at Port Phillip, believing that it would be well occupied on active service. However, he had carried out orders to supply the large amount of timber to return in the *Calcutta* and would await its arrival.

Another ship, the *Patterson* from Providence, had also arrived in port, bearing rum, port wine, and tobacco and a Boston newspaper reporting news from the other side of the world. But George Howe, an 'ingenious man' who edited and printed the newly established *Sydney Gazette and New South Wales Advertiser*, Australia's first newspaper, recognised the priorities of news-gathering. Local news took precedence over international news. Under the allegorical masthead of Hope indicating the signs of Peace and Prosperity in the new colony at Port Jackson, his *Ship News* of 27 November led with a column and a half's coverage of the safe arrival of David Collins and his party before printing the lengthy story from Boston.[23]

At least King must have been relieved to know that his plans had come to some sort of fruition. The *Gazette* gave a brief outline of the epic journey, the failure of Surveyor Grimes' report on Port Phillip to reach England before the *Calcutta* sailed, the dangerous voyage of William Collins to bring the letters, and Captain Mertho's humane action in bringing the party on board the *Ocean*.

As Captains West of the *Wertha Ann* and J. Aborn of the *Patterson* had left Port Jackson with all available cargoes of 1 000 and 400 seal skins respectively,[24] Mertho was probably quite happy to accept Governor King's charter to return to Port Phillip and remove the party within four months to another area of Collins' choice.[25] It could be weeks before more skins arrived. The *Lady Nelson*, His Majesty's armed tender, also in port and loaded with supplies for Norfolk Island, was immediately cleared. King ordered it to sail for Port Phillip with the *Ocean* to help in the removal. They left on 29 November, just four days after the *Ocean*'s arrival.[26]

What prompted King to move so quickly was undoubtedly the fear that had beset him when he had first dreamed that British interests should extend to Bass Strait. He had already despatched a small party under Lieutenant John Bowen to the Derwent, having learnt from Grimes' survey that apart from the freshwater river (the Yarra), Port Phillip had little to commend it as a place for settlement.[27]

The straits were obviously becoming increasingly important strategically and were to be protected from possible seizure by England's arch enemy. The reports that the United States of America was enjoying a 'perfect tranquillity, which is not at present likely to be interrupted', was also little consolation to King, well aware that American sealing and whaling interests were likely to encroach on territory claimed by Britain. The ominous reports of orders despatched from the Admiralty to the commanding officers of all His Majesty's ships-of-war, heightened his insecurity when he realised that Collins would soon be deprived of the services of the *Calcutta*. His Majesty's ships were authorised to CAPTURE, SINK, BURN and DESTROY ships and vessels belonging to the Republic of France.[28] He would expect France to reciprocate. Perhaps he spared a thought for Matthew Flinders, who had sailed for England in the *Cumberland* only a few weeks earlier, hoping that if he called at Ile de France as intended the French would respect him as a non-combatant. That was not to be.[29]

One joyous occasion during the *Ocean*'s sojourn at Port Jackson must have been the reunion of the Hayes family. Henry would have heard from his convict wife Mary about the tempestuous voyage of the *Glatton*, which called at Madeira and Rio on the way and took 169 days, one longer that the *Calcutta*.[30] During the voyage Captain Colnett's relationship with a convict, Mary Serjeant, and his unsuccessful efforts to gain her free pardon from Governor King on their arrival at Port Jackson so that she could accompany him on the return journey, made the philanderings of David Collins almost puritanical by comparison. 'No man left a Colony so Universally despised as Captain Colnet [*sic*]' wrote King in censuring him for this and other matters which had caused disputes between Colnett and other officers during his stay at Port Jackson.[31]

The example set by this Captain during the voyage did little to promote the glory of the Royal Navy or encourage chastity among the female convicts and settlers on board. Nothing is known of Mary Hayes' behaviour but the young Lieutenant Bowen certainly noticed her daughter, Martha, and their relationship grew in intensity after the *Glatton*'s arrival at Port Jackson on 11 March 1803. Perhaps through his intervention the mother might have received some immediate privileges. Within a month she was conducting a business as a milliner and mantua-maker, respectfully informing ladies through the *Sydney Gazette* that 'such Commands as they may be pleased to honour her with . . . shall be executed in a Style of fashionable taste and neatness, with the utmost punctuality . . .' She also flattered herself that she would be able to make up child-bed linen with satisfaction.[32]

By then Governor King had sent Bowen in charge of the party to establish the settlement at Risdon Cove, taking the young, pregnant Martha with him.[33]

16 WAR CLOUDS

URING THE ABSENCE of the *Ocean*, a period of five weeks, one can barely imagine the traumas of David Collins and his people left behind at Port Phillip, knowing how much depended upon the success of the mail getting through. The *Calcutta* moved to a position off Arthur's Seat to take on timber for the Navy.[1] Members of the carpenter's crew examined the she-oak which Tuckey thought only fit for cabinet wood, and blue gum, stringybark and honeysuckle, all growing to a size which could be useful for shipbuilding. Honeysuckle growing there would probably be acceptable as compass timber for line-of-battle ships.[2] Further to the north-west there was timber suitable for building wharves on the spot. Tuckey reported the use of some timbers from which they might procure knees but he was extremely disappointed that what he perceived was the main purpose of the *Calcutta's* voyage was to date almost fruitless.[3] Pateshall, however, wrote glowingly of the general appearance of the 'forest of amazingly large trees, different from any ever yet known in other parts of the Globe, which produce a succession of leaves in all seasons, and yield vast quantities of gum'.[4] But he was referring here to the tall timbers hugging the coastline of the south-eastern part of the Continent.

The ship's log does indicate the enormous amount of timber cut, especially that prepared as compass timber. Captain Woodriff meticulously recorded in a separate notebook the lengths of timber, mainly honeysuckle and black gum, the longest being forty-eight feet. In all, he loaded 185 pieces of timber from Port Phillip.[5] But there is no record that the flax found there was sufficiently useful either in quality or quantity for naval supplies.[6] They took on fifty-five tons of fresh water from the Kananook Creek but thunderous squalls hampered their passage, stirring up the surf so that the salt infiltrated the freshwater creek. A puncheon of rum began to leak and a cask of molasses and a keg of essences of malt stored in the after-hold suffered severe damage.

The sojourn at Arthur's Seat was an anxious time.

About four hundred natives foregathered close to the carpenters' huts on shore. The men had to return to the ship to pick up ammunition. Back at the main camp a party pitched a tent near the Governor's garden as a safeguard against possible attacks. Aborigines, unaccustomed to using much wood themselves, must have been astonished to find so much desecration of their land in such a short period of time.

After three weeks the *Calcutta* returned to the anchorage off Sullivan Bay. Carpenters continued to fell some of the timber. There was still no news from Port Jackson. Tuckey decided to organise a short exploration inland. Accompanied by Dr Bowden, Lieutenants Johnson and McCulloch of the marines, and the purser from the *Calcutta*, Edward White, they took three soldiers and seven men to carry enough provisions for four days, and crossed to Western Port.[7]

Murray, Flinders and Grimes had all climbed Arthur's Seat, and Grimes' party had spent another day exploring the area to the north-east of Arthur's Seat as far as Hastings and Sandy Point. Grant, who had earlier explored the northern parts of Western Port, had seen rich soils which he thought better adapted to agriculture than the land around Sydney or Parramatta, while the great harbour itself was 'capable of containing several hundred sail of ships with perfect security from storms'.[8]

Tuckey was the first to record any observations of significance while exploring the terrain of the Mornington Peninsula through to Western Port.[9] The party followed the ridge from Arthur's Seat, catching glimpses of the sea. They built a little shelter resembling a native hut for an overnight stay just inland from Cape Schanck. The following day they crossed over deep ravines carved in an age long before the Oligocene, when even the smooth lavas failed to stop the flow of water from the wooded hills. A pocket compass guided them to the entrance of Western Port, which Tuckey mistakenly believed Flinders had discovered. They found it to be more extensive than they had expected. Already they were a man short, and low in provisions, for this man had absconded with their bread. They all carried supplies of fresh water as a precaution, but they discovered several fresh runs of water when they journeyed along the western shore. They crossed the luxuriant hills and valleys, thick with lofty gum trees, such as may be seen at Shoreham today. Tuckey watched the strong surf dangerously breaking along the beach at the present Point Leo. They walked some twelve miles from Flinders Head, probably as far as the present-day Coles Beach, when they turned back. Tuckey remarked on the 'black-plate rock' alternating with the flat sands which indicates that he did journey some distance beyond the old basalt outcrops that form geometrical patterns along the picturesque coastline. He referred to three runs of fresh water falling from the hills and creating little pools ending in sand bars where there were teals of beautiful plumage, and 'what was to us of much more importance, a beautiful flavour'. There are just three creeks creating sandbars beyond the entrance to Western Port, thereby tallying closely with Tuckey's assessment that they travelled near the shore for twelve miles.

They had heard that Western Port had abundant coal deposits and did observe patches of black peaty earth, but nothing remarkable.[10] Apparently, after turning back, they camped inland from Point Leo. The following day they found the journey quite mountainous, with small runs of water trickling through a 'near impenetrable jungle of prickly shrubs bound together with creeping plants'. It took four hours to cross eight deep chasms in six miles before they headed once more towards Cape Schanck, where they spent the third night.[11]

Tuckey found it a disappointing expedition. They found no coal and the several projections of land did not provide safe anchorage but only an attraction for violent seas. They met up with herds of kangaroos and several large wolves which might have been related to the Tasmanian tiger. They sowed seeds from Rio de Janeiro and the Cape, including oranges, limes, melons, pumpkin, Indian corn and other garden seeds in places they thought best adapted for their survival. Tuckey concluded that, as only two huts were found on their track and not a native seen, the 'kangaroo seems to reign undisturbed lord of the soil, a dominion which, by the evacuation of Port Philip [sic] he is likely to retain for ages'.[12]

Tuckey had left on his journey at a time when anxiety for the fate of the *Ocean* and the party led by William Collins was beginning to create tensions at Sullivan Bay. David Collins would have felt some personal fears for the fate of his kinsman as well as anxiety for members of the whole party, which included some of his most resourceful men. The thirteen-year-old Charity Hobbs, a daughter of the widowed settler, might well have tossed and turned to shake off the nightmares that conjured up a vision of her loved hero floating in the ocean depths. She would pray for his safe return, and one day she would be old enough for him to ask her mother if, in spite of their age difference, they might marry.[13] John Hartley was more likely to have thoughts that he might have to face a future in the whaling industry without the expert seamanship of his proposed partner.

Knopwood walked to the watching post on the south-west coast to see whether there might be a sail coming from the direction of Port Jackson, 'being in great expectation of one every day'.[14] Three days later a signal came from the post that a ship was in sight. Within six hours the reliable old *Ocean*, to their surprise, entered the Heads, bringing not only the long-awaited despatches and some extra stock for the colony, but also those who had volunteered to journey forth in the open boat. Her usually skimpy and uninformative log-book gives a detailed nautical account of the rough and squally return voyage. Some of her crew were sea-sick. Captain Mertho was probably glad of the assistance provided by the convict volunteers.

On 12 December he navigated the entrance to Port Phillip with considerable ease and anchored close to the *Calcutta*. There was much to report to Governor Collins and Captain Woodriff. The outbreak of war would, to the latter, be news of highest priority but Knopwood never mentioned it in his diary, where entries referred to matters of the moment and probably reflected the feelings of those who were there to form a permanent settlement: the welcome return of the *Ocean* and its charter for the next four months; the return of the crew which had taken the despatches; the information that since September a young Lieutenant Bowen had been in command of a small settlement at Risdon Cove on the Derwent; that the *Ocean* and the *Lady Nelson* would remove the people of Port Phillip there 'or where the Lieutenant-Governor should think proper'; and that Lee and another convict (Gibson) had escaped that morning. Setting his white hen on twenty-one eggs and soon afterwards setting his spotted hen, later producing seven 'chickings', were truly satisfying events.[15]

Why did Knopwood not mention either then or later that England and France were at war? He himself had served in the Royal Navy on active service. But time and distance can readily dismiss the problems of a world left behind. Knopwood's new life revolved around the somewhat idyllic existence he was creating with its accent on fishing and hunting; drinking and eating, ordered only by occasional admonitions when he sat as a magistrate or pontificated from his improvised pulpit on Church Hill. The news in the *Sydney Gazette* would have meant little to most of the convicts, although a surprising number of them could read. Naturally, they were more concerned about their present and future condition. One might expect that for the first time some would have been thankful that they were far from Europe, particularly those who had seen service in the Army, the Gibraltar mutineers and others who might have been pressed into the Navy.

To Captain Woodriff and his men it was a different story. Pateshall's comments re-echoed the feeling of his fellows when he wrote that 'I need not say how mortified we all were at being so great a distance from the seat of War'.[16] They had one duty, which was to complete their present assignment and return to England to await Admiralty orders as quickly as possible. They would pick up the timber awaiting them at Port Jackson and delay no further. This was contrary to King's expectation that Woodriff would give all possible assistance to Collins. But the naval disciplinarian, Captain Woodriff, was adamant that he must leave at once.[17] Collins later wrote of his 'mortification' to learn that Woodriff 'did not think it advisable to risk the King's ship in exploring a new harbour'.[18] He admitted he felt slighted and hurt to be left to move the company with inadequate help. On reflection, he admitted that Woodriff had weighty reasons to return and began to organise the arduous task ahead of him.

Woodriff would have been more than disturbed by the final report in the *Sydney Gazette*. He would have been aware that the French would also have decreed that ships must be captured, sunk, burned and destroyed. He feared for the *Calcutta* and his men. He was not then to know that the ship of which he was so proud would suffer destruction at the hands of the French, that many of his men would lose their lives and that he and Tuckey would become prisoners.[19] The edict, issued on the outbreak of war, seems to have been ignored when historians have questioned the imprisonment of Matthew Flinders. War is war and makes its own rules, new rules supplanting all others.[20] Flinders had been an alien in an alien vessel. That Baudin and his colleagues were well received and provided with much hospitality at Port Jackson during the peace was irrelevant. The irrationalities of war at any time magnify the human tragedy.

Literate convicts who might have had access to copies of the *Sydney Gazette* would almost certainly have included James Grove, Samuel Warriner, Francis Barnes, William Stocker and Matthew Power. They would have passed on news they had gathered, including useful instructions to those who might be farming in the colony or managing a dairy. The more optimistic would be pleased to note that, as soon as they had

served their sentence, they would be 'wanted' men, for there was work to be had for the able and willing, the sober and the steady. The women would have heard with envy of the articles available in the warehouse of J. Driver or the house of Ann Grant in Pitt's Row (later Pitt Street) and wondered how long it might be before ships filled with merchandise from China, America, India, Spain and South America as well as England might call to supply their needs. Sergeant Packer was advertising goods from India at reduced prices, including gurrahs and blue ginghams as well as coral pendants, punjums and silver shoe-buckles. The laces and muslins, Leghorn hats and hair ribbons, gilded buttons and Bengal dimity, the Spanish leather shoes and Persian silks must have conjured up the vision of something out of the Arabian Nights. Everyone would have been interested to learn that the convict wife of Henry Hayes had established, it appeared, a reasonably successful business.[21]

Several of the settlers and convicts at Sullivan Bay had money burning holes in their pockets. But the rather sturdy British clothing and goods they could purchase at astronomical prices from settlers John Hartley and John Blinkworth, who had received licences to sell goods from their tents, would have hardly created much of a sensation.[22]

Not least of the interest which some convicts might have taken in the *Sydney Gazette* was that the editor himself, George Howe, was a convict. Even the few issues that might have arrived at Port Phillip in the *Ocean*, and later in the *Lady Nelson*, the whaler *Edwin*, the colonial schooner *Francis*, and the *Nancy* as well as the *Integrity*, which called on 4 February 1804, were enough to indicate the opportunities available for those who were prepared to grasp them, as well as the fate that might befall those who lapsed back into waywardness.[23] There was hope for a future. None seemed better placed than the selected few whom Collins appointed members of the night watch, the organisation he created to give some of the more responsible convicts duties they could hardly have conceived possible a few weeks before.

•   •   •

Collins received King's agreement that he should move, the survey report by Grimes confirmed that Port Phillip was 'unfit in every point of view . . . the prospect of the soil not being equal to raise anything for the support of the settlement'.[24] However, King did presume that the 'Upper part of the bay at the head of the river may not have escaped your notice, as that is the only part Mr Grimes . . . Speak[s] the least [most] favourably of . . .'. Collins carefully studied King's summary of the advantages and disadvantages of moving either to Port Dalrymple or the Derwent.[25]

Yet why did he not take another look at the north of Port Phillip and follow the course of the fresh water river that Grimes had surveyed as far as the present suburb of Kew? That expedition had found not only fresh water but tracts of good land and excellent pasture, fine clay for bricks, abundance of stone, what appeared fine timber further up-country, and plenty of fish in the bay.

Lord Hobart had made it quite clear to Collins in his original instructions that although Port Phillip was favoured as the site for the settlement, it was Collins' prerogative to move to 'any other part of the Southern coast of New South Wales, or any of the islands in Bass's Streight's [sic]'. He had drawn his attention to the possibility that King Island (then known as King's Island) might be an advantageous choice.[26] The support of King gave Collins an additional impetus to move south rather than north. Collins was a person of wide experience. He would well have remembered that Sydney Cove was not the original site at which they settled in New South Wales. There had been hesitation and speculation then. The first choice had been Botany Bay, which had proved quite inhospitable. While King, then a lieutenant, had set off to examine that bay a little

further, Collins himself had accompanied Governor Phillip and a small party of marines northwards, knowing that Port Jackson and Broken Bay were possible alternatives. Captain Cook had seen these only from a distance.[27] There was no doubt in their minds (nor has there been since) that they made the right decision to quit-Botany Bay. On their return there they met a surprised French exploration party under La Perouse, who admitted that until he had looked around Botany Bay 'he could not divine the cause of our quitting it'.[28]

Forced to accept Woodriff's determination to return to Europe as soon as possible, Collins awaited the arrival of the *Lady Nelson* and other craft which might usefully assist him. Tuckey had returned from his Western Port excursion and stayed overnight in Knopwood's marquee. For several days there were farewells to the officers of the *Calcutta* as they prepared to leave. There were breakfasts on shore, pipes in the evening, and fine catches of crayfish for the final wining and dining. Collins, still shocked that Woodriff would desert him, reluctantly returned the detachment of marines who belonged to the ship, and linked them together with the six convicts who had rowed to Port Jackson in a general order expressing much satisfaction at their meritorious conduct. Of the convicts, he added that he would not lose sight of the service which they had performed with credit. They would be among the first to receive conditional emancipations.[29]

G. P. Harris sketched the jetty, built to assist the withdrawal from Port Phillip. It was still visible at low tide until early this century.

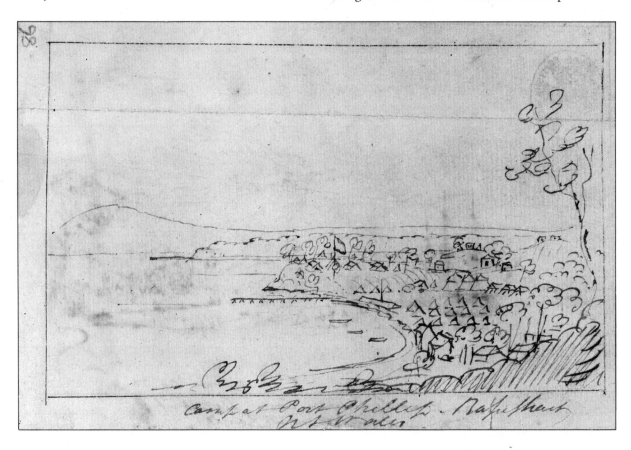

Collins passed over the despatches and private letters to Woodriff for delivery at Port Jackson. He informed King that he would have Port Dalrymple examined before making a final decision on their destination. At least Woodriff had left him with six surplus sheep and six hogs. Woodriff also returned fifteen convicts he had borrowed, probably those used during the timber-cutting exercise.

Collins gave the settlers the option of going on to Port Jackson or remaining with him. William Caw, the missionary, got ready to sail in the *Calcutta*. Anthony Fletcher the stonemason, with his wife and child, also decided to go. But after a few weeks' experience of life at Port Jackson the Hayes and Fletchers were to receive King's permission to board

H.M. schooner *Integrity* and settle in Van Diemen's Land.[30]

Some settlers decided to remain at Sullivan Bay until after the first batch of convicts had been removed. One settler, Edward Miller, and his family agreed to stay and salvage as much of the seed as possible. Collins directed that all those preparing for the departure would work on Sundays and promised to reward them at a later date for their extra labour. He wrote to King complaining that the thought of accomplishing the move with only one ship would be difficult, especially if the *Lady Nelson* did not arrive. By Sunday 18 December the *Calcutta* left on a fair breeze. The people continued to load the stores in the *Ocean*. Divine service did not take place.

17 LAW AND OUTLAW

THE APPOINTED DEPUTY Judge Advocate for the new settlement, Benjamin Barbauld, did not sail with the Collins' party. He had married Collins' sister Ann and had taken extended leave.[1] It was to be three years before the new colony welcomed Samuel Bate in his place, and until that time justice had to be dispensed by a Bench of Magistrates consisting variously of Knopwood, Harris, Humphrey and Sladden.[2] When he did arrive, Bate proved to be not only incompetent but dissolute, and his authority did not carry much weight.

The first civil action recorded at Port Phillip occurred on 2 November when Collins apparently informed Knopwood that his (Collins') servant Buckley (John, not William Buckley) had claimed a waistcoat promised him by Robert Kennedy, Humphrey's servant. Kennedy had served Sir Gregory Page-Turner and Sir John Dryden in England, and had fallen by the wayside when he bought a stolen watch. According to Humphrey, he had become 'the best servant in the place'.[3] The Bench, then comprising Knopwood and Harris, found that Kennedy had promised Buckley the waistcoat for a pair of shoes, which Kennedy had actually worn.[4] As a description of John Buckley indicates that he had large feet, the issue of shoes on 30 October, all the same size, had given him some bargaining power to gain a waistcoat. He was ordered to give up the waistcoat. This John Buckley, whose services Collins had acquired from Tuckey after they landed, had like Kennedy previously shown some interest in procuring a time-keeper, having stolen a silver watch, for which he was convicted at Taunton in Somerset.

But the convicts were not the only offenders. In actual fact the first court to assemble at Port Phillip was the garrison court martial held on 20 October at Lieutenant Johnson's marquee, with Lieutenants Menzies and Lord assisting Johnson. This was the occasion when Sergeant Sergeant of the Royal Marines had been confined the previous evening for drunkeness and misconduct, but was later reinstated.[5] Fawkner had the idea, and he was probably right, that the authorities were trying to humiliate him because Sergeant naturally objected to Bowden's attention to his wife. Fawkner believed Collins warned him not to interrupt the 'seducer of his wife and the robber of his watch . . . the mean doctor kept the Sergeant's watch and his wife too; and a large family was the consequence', which was true.[6]

Collins proclaimed the punishable offences which the prisoners (or settlers and anyone else for that matter) might commit at Port Phillip in his Garrison Orders. He issued many orders relating to the duties of sentinels, on livestock and cleanliness. The crime of gambling was rampant among the marines and convicts alike ('so big in itself with their certain ruin, it is his duty by every means in his power . . . he will most certainly punish every man that is guilty of it in opposition to this order').[7] There was little he could do but charge them to appear before the Bench of Magistrates. Confinement or floggings were the usual punishments meted out to those proved guilty.

Collins, acutely aware of the need to conserve what natural resources were available, was the first conservationist in the European settlement of Victoria. Several orders relate to his fear that fires indiscriminately lit might get out of control. One order forbade the needless felling of timber and another warned against persons who are 'bringing birds' nests into the Encampment containing either eggs, or young and unfledged birds . . . a practice at once so cruel and destructive'.[8]

Another order discloses that two of the convicts and one of the wives had acquired articles from Thomas Hodgeman, a private of the marines. The military had nothing of their own to dispose of and the purchasers of such articles would be regarded as greater offenders than the sellers.[9] Naturally enough, when he was expecting likely ships to enter the harbour, Collins anticipated there could well be a liquor problem. It was bad enough among his own civil and military officers. He warned against the clandestine introduction of spirits into the settlement, ordering that any spirits landed must be at the official landing place under the scrutiny of the sentinel and with the knowledge of the Officer of the Guard.[10] He declared drunkenness a crime, but must have often turned a blind eye to the rule that was flouted so frequently.

Punishments available also took the form of restricted food allowances (two-thirds of provisions for one month) for those who failed to attend divine service on Sundays. As the Reverend Robert Knopwood also occasionally absented himself for reasons already noted, it is doubtful whether anyone incurred this form of punishment which, at least on equitable grounds, should have also applied to the reverend gentleman himself.

When prisoners were to receive floggings, the magistrates fixed the number of lashes. Fawkner believed that Knopwood seldom gave fewer than one hundred and frequently as many as five hundred and Collins was more disposed to clemency, at times reducing the sentence by half or even a quarter. But when the overseer of blacksmiths, Anthony Lowe, was to receive only twenty-five lashes by Collins' order for drunkenness, Collins heard him remark to the drummer and fifer of the marines, who were the floggers, 'Oh, that is hardly worth pulling off my shirt for', with the result that Collins ordered fifty lashes minimum from then on. Humphrey often allowed the prisoner to give his own explanation. He was much more lenient than Knopwood, who rarely let the accused give evidence. To Fawkner, Knopwood was revengeful and Humphrey merciful.[11]

James Calder, who interviewed several of Collins' contemporaries in later years, came to different conclusions. He was assured that Collins himself regularly witnessed punishments, especially when they involved such a spectacle as he quoted, when there was severe torturing of an old man 'in which indeed he seems to have taken much the same sort of pleasure that Caligula is said to have felt in signing death warrants'.[12] This, however, does not tally with what many others have recorded. Collins probably *did* attend most floggings in the course of duty, as he had in the early days at Port Jackson. Once the magistrates had passed sentence, he would rarely interfere. By most reports he was a humane man with more compassion for convicts or other wrong-doers than most of his contemporaries. Harris found that he never let merit go unrewarded and showed 'every possible kindness and attention even to the meanest of his convicts if his conduct is good'.[13] Joseph Holt, the Irish rebel, also wrote in the most kindly terms of the compassion Collins showed towards the convicts.[14]

The worst case of punishment reported at Port Phillip was not that of a convict but of a marine, Private Robert Andrews. He had shown some skill as a carpenter and had made some boxes for the use of Hannah Power. Lieutenant Sladden's wife, Susannah, was envious and wanted some too. Andrews refused, protesting that there was no more suitable timber left. Sladden ordered him to make some, apparently from the local timber, because 'he had made them for the Governor's Madam; if you do not make them it will be the worse for you'.[15] It was. Sladden waited for a plausible opportunity to discipline him.

Over the Christmas period, when certain relaxations were allowed and several convicts had escaped, Andrews was one whose indulgence in liquor at this time not only exceeded the bounds of prudence but was to coincide with his performance of sentry duty. He fell asleep when Sladden as duty officer passed by and challenged him. Collins ordered a garrison court martial to be presided over by Sladden, concerned at the shameful conduct of several of the soldiers. 'Drunkenness is a crime that he will not pass over', he declared, and directed that in future their spirits would be watered and mixed in the presence of the officer of the day.[16] He significantly chose the words 'Vigilance' and 'Attention' for the pass-words of 27 December.

Collins made it clear when writing to Governor King six weeks later that he had been motivated to set an example to others in his military force, which was becoming increasingly lax and discontented with disciplinary measures such as daily drill. He reported that he had ordered Andrews and a fellow marine, James Ray, to receive 900 lashes apiece, of which one received 700 and the other 500.[17] There is no reason to doubt Fawkner, who stated that one flogger was left-handed and the other right-handed. After 530 lashes, the doctor ordered that Andrews could receive no more without endangering his life. Collins ordered that he be released from the halberts, but Fawkner reported that the brutal Lieutenant Sladden, as soon as the doctor reported Andrews recovered, ordered him again to be taken out. Later the floggers inflicted the balance of the 800 lashes on the newly-made skin. Fawkner, who was probably giving his father's version of the story, told that Andrews was never able to do a day's work again. He became doubled up, 'a victim of court martial law, where the accuser has very often the power of causing whatever sentence he pleases to be passed on the sufferer'.[18] There is no similar occasion related at Port Phillip in which the severity of the punishment administered to Andrews and Ray was dealt out to other miscreants, convict or free.

There were other offences. One unknown person kicked to death a precious female goat. Collins offered a reward of £5 for information leading to the discovery of the culprit. Collins tried to warn prospective escapees of the dangers if they strayed far along the beach in their leisure hours, including the danger of meeting up with the natives. The unwary might well be taken by surprise as a reprisal for the killing of the native at Corio Bay.

From the very first, plans for stealing a boat or taking command of any water craft by force were contingencies against which Collins had to guard. He had experienced many such occurrences as Judge Advocate in New South Wales. In a summary of the original 'Instructions to be given the Chief Officer in the Direction of the New Settlement at Port Phillip', attached to the memorandum of late 1802, the fifteenth item concerned the prohibition of building vessels or boats, the reason given that they might interfere with the East India Company's exclusive right of trading with India.[19] Lord Hobart, in his instructions to Collins of 7 February 1803, confirmed the need to prevent the escape of any convicts who might communicate clandestinely with any possessions of the East India Company, the coast of China and any other islands where European nations had established intercourse.[20]

Collins had more trouble with convicts absconding to the woods than he had with any trying to pirate a boat. No one attempted to escape by sea, although it would become a common means of escape from Van Diemen's Land. Boats were few and boat-building materials even fewer. He allowed the most trustworthy convicts to accompany officers on the exploration of the bay and on fishing expeditions. Surprisingly, Knopwood allowed the future pirate, Robert Stewart, to take his boat fishing. The settler Hartley claimed to have built a boat while there, although Lord Hobart had warned Collins not to allow craft of any sort to be built for the use of private individuals without the written consent of the Governor of New South Wales.[21]

There were also strict orders that permission must be granted before anyone could board a vessel arriving at the settlement. Masters were bound by charter to the government and would be heavily penalised if they took on board anyone without a permit. Collins had to issue warnings to prospective escapees reminding them of the hazards of travelling thousands of miles as they rounded the headlands of many harbours before they might reach Port Jackson. They would be more likely to die of hunger, fatigue or attack by the natives before reaching their destination alive, or, if they did, would in any case be apprehended there and duly punished. He knew only too well the great barriers that the mountains of New South Wales were to the people at Port Jackson.[22]

This did not deter at least twenty-seven from absconding at Port Phillip by land. Of these, twenty returned before the *Ocean* sailed in May 1804 on its final journey to Van Diemen's Land, leaving behind on the mainland six who ultimately perished there,

'Having known what might be done by courageous men when combating for life and liberty, I determined on braving everything, and, if possible, making my escape . . . one of the sentinels challenged . . . immediately fired, shooting the last man of the four of us . . .' (William Buckley to his biographer, John Morgan). George Gordon McCrae's portrayal of Buckley's escape.

and William Buckley.[23] The latter survived and lived among the natives for nearly thirty-two years before meeting John Helder Wedge and his party at Indented Head in 1835.[24]

If Buckley (a much more intelligent person than early historians represented) were housed beyond the sentinels, as he told his biographer, John Morgan, he was certainly in a better position than most to evaluate the possibilities of escaping and succeeding. He was not the first but among the last and certainly the best known to leave the security of the camp for the great unknown. Knopwood reported the first three escapes on 9 November and five more within two days. Collins had already reported that twelve had deserted within a week. Five returned after a few days of freedom.

Desperately short of marines who might apprehend the others, Collins sent out a search party which included some convicts on whom he could depend. They discovered five of the escapees sixty miles away and returned with them on 16 November. To set an example, he ordered that they receive punishment of one hundred lashes each on the following day. It marred an otherwise joyous ceremony at which Collins' commission was read by the Reverend Robert Knopwood and the military fired three volleys. According to Knopwood all the convicts lined up, were clean-dressed and all gave three cheers.[25]

Collins was aware that some convicts believed that China, for which Captain Mertho was preparing to sail the *Ocean*, was just a short distance from Port Jackson and beyond British jurisdiction. But warnings of the hopelessness of survival, of the slim chances of reaching either destination and of the savagery of the natives did not deter some of the more desperate among the convicts from attempting escape. Some of the deserters were intelligent men whose yearning for freedom far outweighed reason. Fawkner believed some Connaught men had seriously thought of reaching China. The only escapees believed to have been Irishmen, McAllenan and Lee, would have known that China was thousands of miles away. More ignorant men had gone off with a piece of paper on which a compass had been sketched and expected to be able to steer their course by it.

Collins intercepted five more who planned to desert, chained them to each other, and placed them on two-thirds of their allowance of provisions until such time as they informed on the plans of their fellows. He addressed the convicts, reminding them of the comforts they enjoyed. A day later three others returned. Collins felt some compassion on seeing their haggard appearance and believed they had been punished enough by the obvious hardships they had borne. He begged others to observe the wretched appearance of Hangan and his two associates, who had discovered that they could not trust even their colleagues who, while these three were procuring water for the whole party, treacherously escaped with all the provisions in their care.[26] Collins wanted as few invalids as possible. These men needed immediate medical care and he hoped that others might henceforward be deterred from absconding.

The captives did not take long to turn informers. Collins discovered that the twelve expected to reach a bay on the south coast which they had heard was a seasonal resort for South Sea whalers. At that stage little would have been known about any possible whaling stations on Victoria's southern coastline. Snippets of conversation between William Collins and John Hartley could have led them to believe they might fall in with one of Enderby's or Campbell's ships or even one of the American vessels already entering the trade off the Australian and New Zealand coasts. It was more likely that they had heard of Sealers' Cove at Wilson's Promontory where survivors from the wreck of the *Sydney Cove* had taken refuge when placed there in 1797. They might also have had some conversation with sailors of the *Britannia*, one of Enderby's whalers, which was in port at Rio at the same time as the *Calcutta*.

One of the more determined and most intelligent escapees at Port Phillip was George Lee, a person with leadership qualities, who might have had a good future in the colony. He had fallen from a status in society in which he had been well equipped by education and family position to have acquired a commission in the Army. According to Tuckey he was 'A character well known to persons of respectability in England'.[27] The settler John Ingle, who had begun a little trading, employed him as his clerk at Port Phillip. Collins confirmed that he was a person of capabilities and education, superior to the rest. He had excused Lee from hard labour and allowed him to construct his own small hut, but he had abused these privileges by creating dissatisfaction among other prisoners and casting illiberal reflections upon the officers.[28] Harris described Lee as a 'well-looking young man but quite a pedant, eternally quoting passages from the Greek and Latin authors.'

He had for some time been writing scurrilous verses against Collins and had a grudge against him and other officers. He had had opportunities to make something of his life and was prepared to throw them away for the uncertainty of freedom.[29] There was to have been a court of enquiry into the circulation of the malicious verses, but first Knopwood had to investigate charges that Lee had accused Superintendents Clark and Ingle of infamous conduct, for which he had no supporting evidence. He had also maliciously accused the convict John Manning of coining.[30]

Fawkner's version of the story described Lee as an Irishman condemned for what was called rebellion. He believed that Ingle had abused and ill-treated him. When brought before Collins, the latter threatened him with a warning, and, if brought before him again, with a 'damn good flogging'. Lee said he would 'rather take to the bush and perish sooner than submit to the torture to please the tyrant, the ignorant brute placed over him as a slave driver'.[31] It is likely that Lee, who would have known more about Ingle's movements than anyone, was aware of Ingle's relations with the young Rebecca Hobbs, then about three months pregnant by Ingle. Collins disgraced Lee by removing his privileges and ordered him to a gang.[32]

Lee's esteem among some convicts was considerable. They believed he was resourceful and perhaps able to live independently of public stores. Several were prepared to join him if he planned to escape. He managed to acquire a gun and ammunition from William Keep, then in charge of Collins' garden, convincing him that he had orders to receive it. On 12 December, the day he escaped, everyone was excited at the unexpected return of the *Ocean* from Port Jackson. David Gibson, the young Scotsman with whom Lee had been friendly since they were together in the hulks at Langston, accompanied him.[33]

It should have been a sobering thought for other potential escapees to contemplate such folly when the *Ocean* arrived with copies of the newly published *Sydney Gazette*. One report in particular related the experience of the only survivor of a group possibly known to *Calcutta* convicts. He had served in the hulks at the same time and had arrived in the colony in the sister ship H.M.S. *Glatton*. He and his mates had absconded from labour some six months earlier from Castle Hill. They attempted to cross the distant mountains, which no one at that time had traversed. Although expecting to be able to reach China, their rashness produced only misery and ultimately death from hunger and exposure, having after some twenty days travelled not much beyond Richmond Hill. A kangaroo hunter and some natives had discovered the survivor despairing of life and led him to the hospital at Parramatta.[34]

The melancholy account did not, however, deter those who had already planned their escape during the Christmas festivities. They rightly guessed that there would be some laxity among the establishment, in spite of Collins' public caution two days before Christmas. Before escaping, it was customary to commit a robbery. Several robberies took place while Knopwood, pleased with having produced the first green peas and delighted with his catch of the day (eight fine crayfish, a mullet and two dotterel), called on Collins and the 'gentlemen of the mess' with his gifts.[35] Escapees raided the hospital tent and the Commissariat marquee for supplies. One of the men, Daniel McAllenan, dared to steal a gun and a pair of boots from beside Commissary Fosbrook's bed while he was asleep. The sentry ignored him, perhaps because he knew McAllenan was one of Knopwood's servants. Other convicts entered the hospital tent and stole provisions.[36]

Collins immediately proclaimed that he would procure conditional emancipation for any convict who could assist with the conviction of those guilty of such outrages. Thomas Page and Daniel Anchor had been at large for some time. After apprehension Page, who was in a very weak state, turned informer.[37] He confided to Collins that five others had been planning to escape that night to join him and Anchor, who had probably helped plan the escape. Anchor well knew of Fosbrook's movements and had good reason to disappear: Fosbrook's roving eye had been diverted from 'Mrs Whitehead' to Anchor's buxom wife, Fanny.

Rather than apprehend the suspects immediately, Collins decided to catch them in the act. He posted some armed men at a point they would have to pass. At 1 a.m. some of the party apprehended the deserters, firing and wounding one, Charles Shore, a trouble-maker during the voyage who had been put in double irons for insolence. Shaw was dangerously wounded. Dr Bowden took a cart and went to attend him; a slug had lodged in his stomach. Yet even in his pain he refused to make further disclosures about his associates.[38]

Page died on 27 January aged thirty-one, with a few pathetic and tragic notes against his name to show that he had ever inhabited this earth: the 'bastard child' of a woman named Sarah Offyflow of Littleover, Melbourne, in Derby; several charges of poaching with a gun; a framework knitter who had committed highway robbery and been sentenced to death.[39] Foolishly, he had thought he had little to lose by trying to escape. Ultimately he lost everything.

The departure of the *Calcutta* a week before Christmas, with the loss of the sixteen marines he had borrowed from Captain Woodriff to help control the more intrepid convicts and to guard the settlement from possible attacks by the Aborigines, had been a heavy blow to Collins. His own marines were also restless and likely to cause trouble. Among the convicts he recognised that he had a number of persons trained in the armed forces, accustomed to discipline and only too happy to begin their rehabilitation. He appointed William Thomas Stocker, widowed during the voyage, as principal of the night watch and patrol, with four of the mutineers from Gibraltar to assist him.[40] He forbade prisoners from going to the seashore for crayfish between sunset and sunrise. He threatened punishment to any prisoner absenting himself from his tent during a regular muster he was to institute. Because of the abuse by prisoners such as Lee and William Buckley, who had their own huts outside the camp, Collins ordered these huts to be pulled down and such transferred to tents. They had to report each morning to Knopwood. There was fear that the more desperate would watch for an opportunity to quit before the party moved on to Van Diemen's Land.[41]

Over dinner Collins and Knopwood, expecting an insurrection over the New Year period, planned the formation of an association of the civil officers. Two of the officers would patrol each night together with subordinates to watch for any suspicious circumstances such as convicts selling or bartering their clothing or provisions, gambling and robbery. The officers would be armed and their convict subordinates provided with a short staff. John Ingle was the only settler named as a subordinate. Collins was wary about involving the settlers and preferred to rely on trusted convicts. He included six of the Gibraltar mutineers, Crute, Haynes, McCarthy, Sculler, Taylor and van Straten, as well as Stocker, Andrew Whitehead, John Boothman, Matthew Power, James Grove and Francis Shipman, who was assistant to Harris. Within days Collins decided to arm these convicts.[42] For Knopwood it was the beginning of a strong friendship with those he henceforth referred to as *Mr* Grove, *Mr* Power, *Mr* Whitehead and *Mr* Stocker. George Harris described some of the qualities of these better types:

Stocker — for his good conduct has the greatest confidence placed in him and commands men of the night watch and of all parties out in search of deserters . . . a very useful man and behaves with great civility to everyone . . .

Among the men six soldiers from the Gibraltar mutiny — fine fellows whom you might trust your life with and behave extremely well form part of the night association.[43]

For several days the patrollers went searching for the escapees, one of whom had dared to shoot at a soldier guarding the signal tent. On New Year's Eve Knopwood thought that the deserters must be responsible for the great fires seen in the distance. He named those missing from the camp: his own servant McAllenan, Pye, Pritchard, Marmon, Buckley, Lee and Gibson.[44] As the year closed Collins brooded over the fate of the missing men, deluded though they might be that they could exist without the aid of government: 'Their madness will be manifest to themselves when they shall feel, too late, that they have wrought their own ruin'.[45] He decided to make no further search because he believed they would soon return or perish by famine. He refused to issue any more shoes, in spite of daily requests, and urged his people to take care of those they already had.[46] Good strong shoes were almost as important as food when one was planning to escape.

New Year's Day 1804 was a cold and rainy day. Collins served duck and green peas with fresh beans. One doubts whether any convicts except the most favoured enjoyed such a splendid repast. They had to work, because of the imminent departure from Port Phillip, on that day as on any other. Knopwood and I'Anson had dined with Collins in a somewhat temperate fashion, for they were responsible for keeping-watch for any who had said their farewells to society. They set out for the harbour's mouth in company with Stocker. During their searches they found several places where escapees had been and abandoned some of their belongings. Gibson returned early in the New Year, leaving Lee to his own devices after they discovered a fresh water river (the Yarra River). Gibson doubtless hoped that such a discovery might interest Collins and that perhaps he might receive some reward or at least a pardon. There is no record that he was either commended or punished.[47] William Keep, who was Collins' servant at the time, told James Bonwick years later that he saw Gibson on his return. He was taken to hospital, a 'mere skeleton from his privations in the bush' and so altered that he could scarcely recognise him.[48] In 1835 Fawkner found the falls in the river just as Gibson had described them and an old iron pot one of the escapees might have left nearby.

By mid-January McAllenan had arrived back in camp unexpectedly, returning Fosbrook's gun and surrendering himself. He said he had walked some one hundred miles around Port Phillip and subsisted mainly on gum and shellfish. His companions had decided to continue in the direction of the mountains west of Port Phillip. Knopwood took McAllenan's deposition. He was among those who had escaped when Shore was shot and he returned in a miserable condition. He believed those whom he had left behind were by now too far away to recall. Their provisions were few and they lived in constant fear of the natives. They might have returned but had dreaded punishment.[49] Collins decided against harassing his marines any further by sending them on what would assuredly be a futile mission.

Shore was soon well enough for Knopwood to take his deposition just as H.M. brig *Lady Nelson* (Acting Lieutenant Symonds) came in sight to assist the *Ocean* with the removal from Sullivan Bay. The schooner *Edwin* (William Stewart, master) appeared from King Island. Three days later half the convicts embarked with their baggage on board the *Ocean*. One who had been absent for a long time, an older convict, John Jones, limped into the camp in such a weak state that he was to stay at Port Phillip. He died three weeks later.

Collins later reported that twenty-one (a miscalculation — there were six more) convicts deserted at Port Phillip, stating that seven had perished in the woods including James Taylor, William Brown, George Lee, Jeremiah [*sic*] Buckley and William Vosper.[50] He intimated that he knew of the fate of the last three by the return of Gibson. Six others returned to camp after a month's absence. These would have been Marmon, Anchor and McAllenan as well as Page and Jones. Five others were pursued, taken and flogged. Collins refrained from reporting Gibson's discovery of good fresh water in the river at the head of the bay. The boats were already loading. Collins had made up his mind to move for other reasons and he was not going to waste any further time in exploration.[51]

William Buckley survived his ordeal and lived for thirty-two years with the Aborigines. Apart from James Grove, he was the only *Calcutta* convict who left any authentic account of his trials. John Morgan set down his story, published in Hobart in 1852. In retrospect Buckley believed the attempt was

little short of madness, for there was before me the chances of being retaken, and probable death, or other dreadful punishment; or again, starvation in an unknown country inhabited by savages, with whose language and habits, I was totally unacquainted . . .[52]

But Buckley admitted he had great personal strength, a good constitution and the knowledge of men's courage when fighting for life and liberty as he had done during the war in Holland. His party of four, which had included McAllenan, had Fosbrook's gun to shoot kangaroos and possums as well as many provisions and utensils. They had chosen a dark night to escape and the sentry on duty, receiving no answer to his challenge, shot one of the party (Shore). They

William Buckley, the wild white man, as seen by the French forger, Charles Constantini. 'Had he {Buckley} not been at Port Phillip when the first settlers arrived, they would, most probably, have encountered dangers' (John Morgan, 1852).

and reached the You Yangs, where they finished the last bread and meat they had stolen from the stores. They arrived at Corio Bay where they gathered shellfish and found fresh water, probably at the ponds on which Tuckey had reported. They were already exhausted and lit fires at night to try and signal to the *Calcutta* (he meant the *Ocean*) which they could see anchored at the other side of the bay. (Knopwood noted the fires.) A boat appeared as if to cross the bay to rescue them but turned back in spite of other signals they were making with shirts hoisted on trees and poles.[55]

Buckley's mates despaired and decided to retrace their steps, taking the gun with them and hoping to make the camp. Some time later he learned from the Aborigines that they had succoured the escapees for a time but when one 'made too free with their women' they killed him. Buckley did not realise that McAllenan would survive and reach the camp. When they parted Buckley was

overwhelmed with the various feelings which oppressed me . . . I thought of the friends of my youth, the scenes of my boyhood, and early manhood, of the slavery of my punishment, of the liberty I had panted for, and which although now realised, after a fashion, made the heart sick, even at its enjoyment . . . the most severe mental sufferings for several hours, and then pursued my solitary journey.[56]

He found it hard to explain how he had deceived himself into believing he could ever reach Sydney. The whole affair seemed to be a 'species of madness'. He kept alive by eating berries and collecting fresh fish. Ultimately the Aboriginal tribe which was to befriend him taught him the ways of the black man. He survived. He thought the others either starved to death or were killed by natives, perhaps eaten. Knopwood wrote that they had every reason to believe the natives were cannibals. However, there is no other evidence that the natives of Port Phillip were. It is just as likely that one of the starving white escapees might have succumbed to eating the flesh of one of his own. It certainly happened later in Van Diemen's Land.

ran for the first few hours and rested at a stream the natives called Darkee Barwin (the Mordialloc Creek). They met up with a large party of natives but dispersed them by firing a shot.[53] Surprisingly his old partner in crime, William Marmon, from whom he had received burgled goods in 1802,[54] deserted him early in the escape. Marmon returned to camp with scurvy but recovered to live peacefully in Hobart for many years.

Buckley and his remaining companions (probably James Taylor and William Vosper) crossed the Yarra

18 ABANDONMENT

LEFT WITHOUT THE support of Woodriff and the security of the *Calcutta*, Collins weighed King's suggestions and awaited the arrival of other boats he hoped were on the way. Certainly the Derwent offered many attractions. To King its primary importance was the depth and accessibility of its harbour, a port at which either ships en route to China or whalers seeking water and supplies might readily call. Bass and Flinders had both reported on the excellent facilities for shipping and the fine soil found there. It had already been settled and stocked on a small scale. But less knowledge of Port Dalrymple's soil was available for there had been some difficulty gaining access at the entrance. The approaches were intermittently gale-swept, a factor making the (reportedly) more sheltered Derwent the more attractive alternative. Colqnial vessels would be needed ever increasingly to patrol the coast, protecting potential fisheries at King and Cape Barren Islands upon which the Americans were now encroaching. They were likely to give King as much trouble and anxiety as the French, even more especially if, as was feared at the time, they were to enter a war on the side of the French.

There was anxiety for the fate of H.M. brig *Lady Nelson* captained by Acting Lieutenant James Symonds, who had been a midshipman in the *Glatton*. He had left Port Jackson twenty-four hours before the *Ocean*, and must have struck the strong gales reported along the east coast. Two other ships, the whaler *Edwin* (William Stewart), and the colonial schooner *Francis* (Robert Rushworth), were also on their way to assist Collins. The *Lady Nelson* struck some frightening south-westerlies in the strait. She sought refuge in the Kent group where Robert Brown, the eminent botanist who had accompanied Flinders in the *Investigator*, usefully occupied himself by identifying twelve new plants.[1] In the meantime the *Francis* arrived at Port Phillip after Rushworth reported having observed smoke arising from the vicinity of the Kent Group. When the *Edwin* arrived at Sullivan Bay Captain Stewart was able to add to Collins' contingent of con-

victs. He had picked up John Harris, an escapee from Van Diemen's Land, at Cape Barren.[2]

The little *Francis* was nine years old and already in disrepair. She had faithfully served the colony and Flinders had used her when he discovered the Furneaux group in 1798. She was the only vessel available to go in search of the *Lady Nelson* and explore the Van Diemen's Land port but Collins first had to get the carpenters to improve her leaky condition, which took several days. Samuel Gunn, experienced in boat building, was one whom he must have employed. Soon afterwards Collins announced Gunn's official appointment as director of the department of ship-wrights.[3] At the same time he appointed a settler, William Nicholls, as superintendent of convicts, a carpenter by trade who had originally sought Sir Joseph Banks' recommendation that he try 'his fortune in the distant regions of Botoney [sic] Bay'.[4] John Benjamin Fell, a former London clerk and embezzler, was proclaimed assistant to Fosbrook in the issue of stores and provisions.[5]

Before making the final decision on whether to move to Port Dalrymple or the Derwent, Collins accepted William Collins' offer to lead the search for the *Lady Nelson* and explore the northern river.[6] His party included Thomas Clark, one of the superintendents of convicts, who years before had sailed in the ill-fated *Guardian* and been injured when it struck an iceberg south of the Cape of Good Hope, leaving him permanently lame. Humphrey also joined the party as mineralogist and was accompanied by either Robert Kennedy or John Smith, his two servants. William Collins would surely have taken one or two who served him well during the voyage to Port Jackson. They sailed on Christmas Day, coinciding with the unrest in the camp and the prisoner escapes.

After a distressful three days out, during which they had to pump water continuously from the frail vessel, they arrived at the Kent Group to find the *Lady Nelson* had negotiated the treacherous rocks and was waiting for a fair wind before setting sail. The party in the *Francis* joined the more seaworthy brig to continue the voyage of exploration. The *Francis* returned to Port Jackson for further repairs. Humphrey in particular was delighted to meet Robert Brown, who was glad of the opportunity to return to Port Phillip and collect some more botanical specimens to replace those he had despatched with Flinders. These had been lost when the *Porpoise* was wrecked on Wreck Reef the previous August. Brown was not the only person aboard the *Lady Nelson* who would have excited the interest of an explorer. The mate John Johnson, in reality the Danish seaman-adventurer Jorgen Jorgensen, had joined the brig in Cape Town on its maiden voyage. He had been with Murray when he first sailed through the entrance of Port Phillip and claimed to have sailed in the *Investigator* with Flinders as far as the Northumberland Islands.[7]

The *Lady Nelson* arrived at Port Dalrymple on New Year's Day. The party landed on the sandy eastern shore somewhere north of George Town. While Brown gathered plants, the others walked about seven miles along the harbour. Their journey was to be fraught with danger. At one stage they found themselves almost surrounded by a bushfire. They had to scurry for the water, delayed somewhat by Clark's lameness.

Soon afterwards they met up with a frightened native who 'screamed in a dreadful manner', as one might imagine, and ran away. He returned with his colleagues, one of whom threw a spear. The Englishmen did not retaliate with their guns. Instead, they tried to make friendly signs before being joined by others from the ship.[8]

Two days later they decided to explore the river from the brig. About three miles inland they tried communicating with natives who were not as friendly. When one almost speared Brown they began to use their guns on them and the natives disappeared.[9]

Ultimately the party passed the point which Bass and Flinders had explored in November 1798. Being short of fresh water, they started a search which resulted in the discovery of the beautiful Cataract Gorge.[10] On their return journey the natives seemed friendlier than before and called out to them, but when they approached the shore large stones were thrown as if to oppose any landing. The boat party fired over their heads to ward them off.[11]

They collected specimens of timber and remarked on its availability. Clark, in particular, was quite specific about the size and quality, mentioning the timber discovered each day in the diary he kept; he also mentioned that they found flax five feet high.[12] Timber and flax and their uses appear to have been uppermost in their minds as well as the availability of water and good soil.

Back at the camp David Collins resolved, without waiting for any further reports, to move to the Derwent.[13] Had he been able to retain the supernumeraries he had borrowed from Captain Woodriff, he might have decided differently. He might even have felt tempted to explore the fresh water river at the head of Port Phillip.

Tuckey's advice as an experienced naval officer must have already persuaded him that Port Phillip itself was a completely unsatisfactory base for use as a safe port for any ship, and particularly as a refuge for whalers. For the same reason it would not therefore have appealed to the French or Americans if they were to show some initial interest in it. Tuckey was aware of the dangers of the violent surf breaking across the difficult egress of the bay, with no apparent channel, while the ebb tide was running at about six knots and meeting southerly winds. Most of those entering and leaving the port in 1803-04 had trouble. Tuckey was adamant that ships entering the bay would find difficulty clearing either Point (Cape) Schanck on the south-east approach or Cape Otway on the south-west.[14] Between Point Nepean and Cape Schanck he had found the remains of one large boat built partly of teak and partly of she-oak obviously made some years before in Port Jackson. This must have been the *Eliza* which had been lost after relieving those wrecked from the *Sydney Cove* in 1797.[15]

The many wrecks of sailing ships in later years within this area bear witness to Tuckey's nautical knowledge and advice. Tuckey believed in particular that

this circumstance will certainly prevent Whalers from ever making it a place of rendezvous; to this may also be added the danger of the Coast between Port Phillip and Western Port, a tremendous surf breaking even in the calmest weather at a mile or two distant from the shore.[16]

This in itself was sufficient reason for wishing to leave Port Phillip. Lack of water was a simple excuse easily explained to the convicts and settlers, rather than several other more complex reasons for the abandonment.

Collins could sense the dangers of remaining where he was. He had previous experience of lonely, hungry years in a colonial outpost left entirely dependent on its own meagre resources, forgotten while Britain was engaged in a long drawn out war. This time he had seemingly even fewer resources and a most inadequate military attachment to face an enemy. Suspicions that the French scientific explorers were nothing more than crafty spies were renewed. Collins panicked. The appearance of a French ship would not have surprised him and in that event he knew he would be without adequate defences.

It was true that Collins was virtually defenceless against those he regarded as potential enemies. These included not only the French but also the Aborigines. As early as 8 November the missionary Crook wrote that 'The objection against settling here is the number of the natives and the small number of marines we have; so that it is probable the colony will be removed to Port Dalrymple . . .'[17]

Large numbers were gathering in the north and sounds which the Europeans feared to be war cries, drifted across the water. It was thought that they might well wreak vengeance on those who had earlier slaughtered some of their race. They were an ever-increasing cause for alarm. The continual flickering of their fires at night, growing closer, kindled a fear that the invaders might be taken unawares in the dark and completely obliterated. Collins had been distressed at incidents in earlier days at Port Jackson and he believed the fires were danger signs, not understanding that such fires were associated with environmental control.

It was not only the French and the Aborigines who had driven both the fear of God and the Devil into Collins. He found he could not even trust some of his marines who fell asleep while on duty, often drunk. Then there were the convicts who were escaping, and others among them, particularly the Irish, who had no great cause to love the English, and who might well join forces with the French if they happened to appear. Even the settlers were becoming disgruntled because they could see little return for the cultivation of their crops. The quarrelsome John Hartley was continually encouraging their discontent, although there was little they could do about it but wait patiently. Collins in desperation was pinning his faith on those trustworthy convicts to alert the military and civil officers of any unusual happenings. He was a frightened man and the attraction of taking charge, as King had decreed, of Bowen's little establishment at Risdon Cove appealed to him more and more.[18]

To facilitate the loading of the *Ocean*, Collins had a temporary jetty and wharf constructed in the shallow bay. He chose two of the convicts, Joseph Myers and John Whitehead, to work as overseers of two gangs of fifteen each, to be selected by Superintendent Clark, while Superintendent Patterson was to direct a gang supervising the stores. John Ingle took his stand on the beach to make sure that the precious cargo remained free from water damage during the loading.[19] It took more than a month to transfer all the stores in the much warmer weather and probably with less heart than when they unloaded them. When they began construction of the jetty the temperature was 92°F one day, with a late change and rain, then extreme cold and gales from the south-west. The unpredictable weather continued with several hot days in the nineties and one as high as 102°F. One day thunder and lightning preceded a violent tempest in the direction of Swan Island when a boat from the *Ocean* was upset and three men drowned.[20]

Collins had no time to waste. King had chartered the *Ocean* for only four months and Collins was more than anxious to 'leave this unpromising and unproductive country . . . to reap the benefits and enjoy the comforts of a more fertile spot . . .'[21] He was aware that they would have to erect more comfortable dwellings than canvas tents before the winter set in. Collins planned to send half of the detachment with those to embark for Van Diemen's Land, together with half of the stores.

Knopwood and other civil officers were kept busy during their nightly duties, watching both for escapees and native fires. On one of his rounds of the camp Knopwood sprained his ankle badly. Collins had to warn prisoners against escaping on any ships that might appear in port. The natives must have gazed with some interest on the activities. It would not have surprised them to see the white people move on as if just going walkabout, as they themselves might. But the speed with which the interlopers worked under the hot sun's rays, the amount of stores they had to move, must have caused some wonder. At least the natives would have realised that their territory was being abandoned and that their food supplies and well-being would be inviolable for the time being.

By mid-January members of the military were able to parade in new uniforms which had been specially made for them. They held a celebration on the hottest day since their arrival by firing three volleys to honour the King's birthday. The temperature rose, according to Knopwood, to 102°F in the shade — 120°F in the sun. A fire in the camp burnt the huts of Lieutenants Johnson and Lord and almost set the marquees ablaze. Fire was also raging on Arthur's Seat until a heavy thunderstorm appeared to have doused the flames.

The colonial sloop *Nancy* (Knopwood called it the *Ann*) appeared from Port Jackson a few days before Collins was to leave for the Derwent. Governor King had sent it with a despatch for Collins, notifying him of the safe arrival of the *Calcutta*. He also informed him that a schooner (Kable and Co.'s *Governor King*) had arrived from Port Dalrymple after an inimical encounter with natives and a poor report on its facilities as a port. He told Collins that to date no settlement had been made on King's Island, although whalers and sealers frequented it to procure oil and skins. Americans on the ship *Charles*, from Boston, had lately molested the crew. However, he advised against any thought of it as a venue because of the likelihood of driving away the sea-elephants. He agreed the Derwent would be the most suitable place at which to settle.[22]

Collins learned from King that, although there were two Port Jackson men whom he had hoped would join him to oversee some of the building, there

99

was already at the Derwent a very good stonemason. King could not spare any more mechanics. He strongly recommended building in stone rather than brick.

The *Lady Nelson* at last arrived on 21 January together with the *Edwin* on its return from King Island. Although William Collins believed that the great waterfall presented a beautiful scene 'probably not surpassed in the world' and that Port Dalrymple possessed a number of local advantages which might merit attention for a settlement, David Collins' plans to move to the Derwent were too far advanced. Together with the *Nancy*, the two ships anchored opposite the camp near the end of the jetty, the construction of which the convicts had managed to complete in record time.

The last recorded divine service took place on 22 January during a further heat wave. The fire from Arthur's Seat, which had flared up again, had reached the Yellow Bluff (White Cliffs) not far from the camp. Knopwood's sprained ankle was getting better. Together with Sladden and Harris he heard another civil court action. Hartley's German servant, John Joachim Gravie, a sailor from Hamburg who had been pressed into the Navy, had lodged a successful claim against his master for the balance of wages not paid him. The Bench of Magistrates ordered Hartley to pay

Gravie £2 7d after the deduction of costs and other charges.[23]

The detachment of Royal Marines who were to sail in the *Ocean* embarked with their baggage, followed by half of the convicts. Most of the settlers joined the *Lady Nelson*. Knopwood gave a farewell dinner in the mess with Lieutenant Johnson and smoked a pipe with Dr I'Anson, with whom he dined the following night after he had sent his marquee on board. These friends were to remain at Sullivan Bay together with Sladden, who was to take charge of the establishment remaining at Port Phillip. On 26 January, just sixteen years since he had unfurled the old British flag in Sydney Cove, Collins went on board the *Ocean* together with Knopwood, Lieutenant Lord, Harris, Humphrey and Bowden.

Captain Mertho logged little apart from the necessary weather and nautical information to indicate that a large party of Europeans was vacating the bay named in honour of the first Governor of New South Wales. When a light breeze sprang up from the south-west, Mertho weighed and ran down to the harbour's mouth, anchoring in ten fathoms of water. He hoisted in a cutter and made clear for the sea, but they were still unable to get out of the harbour. The next day they were anxious to find out what was happening in the camp because they saw a great fire approaching. Captain Mertho, Humphrey and Knopwood went ashore the next day for another farewell dinner. They heard that natives had surrounded the camp, probably

Resting in peace — some twenty graves at Sullivan Bay, as painted by the grandson of Samuel Gunn in 1864.

curious to know what was going on, and perhaps waiting to acquire what they could of any abandoned items. They heard that one native was actually in the camp.

From the *Ocean* Collins wrote to King, delivering the letter to William Stewart of the *Edwin*. He brought King up to date on his movements and enclosed the reports of both William Collins and Thomas Clark on the survey of Port Dalrymple, as well as a return of those embarking in the *Ocean* for the Derwent. He had ordered that prisoners would be deployed into three divisions, with one division at a time on deck, as for watches at sea. During the morning watch they would wash and cleanse themselves. Three of the Gibraltar mutineers would each be attached to a watch and entrusted with the same duties as at Sullivan Bay.[24]

All who were to sail were aboard again when, at dawn on 30 January, the *Ocean* at last departed from Port Phillip with the *Lady Nelson* and settlers in company. Knopwood and Collins, not unduly affected by the usual heavy swell and ripplings as the ebb tide flowed fast through the rip, dined together as they sailed into the wind, still in sight of the land at Port Phillip which they were destined never to see again.

•   •   •

By deserting Port Phillip Collins did *not* fail in his mission.[25] He was sent to found a new settlement in the area of Bass Strait. By abandoning his first choice, he succeeded in founding Hobart Town. The more

positive results of his few months on the mainland site were to come long afterwards. From the decks of the *Ocean* he could then scarcely envisage that among those whose dreams of the future had temporarily been thwarted was the son of the convict Fawkner, a lad who had spent his eleventh birthday on the shores of Sullivan Bay, who would return to settle on the banks of the rejected river to the north and help found a great city.[26] Nor would Collins have conceived that the toddling daughter of the convict Peters would die as the wealthy matriarch of a long line of distinguished Victorians at The Hermitage, the great mansion which her husband, George Armytage, would build on the western arm of Port Phillip not far from the shore where Aborigines had defended themselves so tragically against the invaders.[27] One of her sons chose later to be buried nearer Sullivan Bay itself. Close to Point Nepean he built a replica of a large Norman style castle and from its turrets he could watch the ships buffetted about in the Strait as they tried to enter or leave Port Phillip through the heads that have remained a danger even to large modern vessels.[28]

Harris and Pateshall could never have foreseen what the future held for their servants, the two cousins James Austin and John Earle from Somerset. Pateshall returned to the wars and died in 1854, a retired Rear-Admiral.[29] Harris would die in relative poverty in Hobart, while Austin's nephews and their descendants would inherit immense riches which they ploughed back into the great grazing lands of the Western District of Victoria.

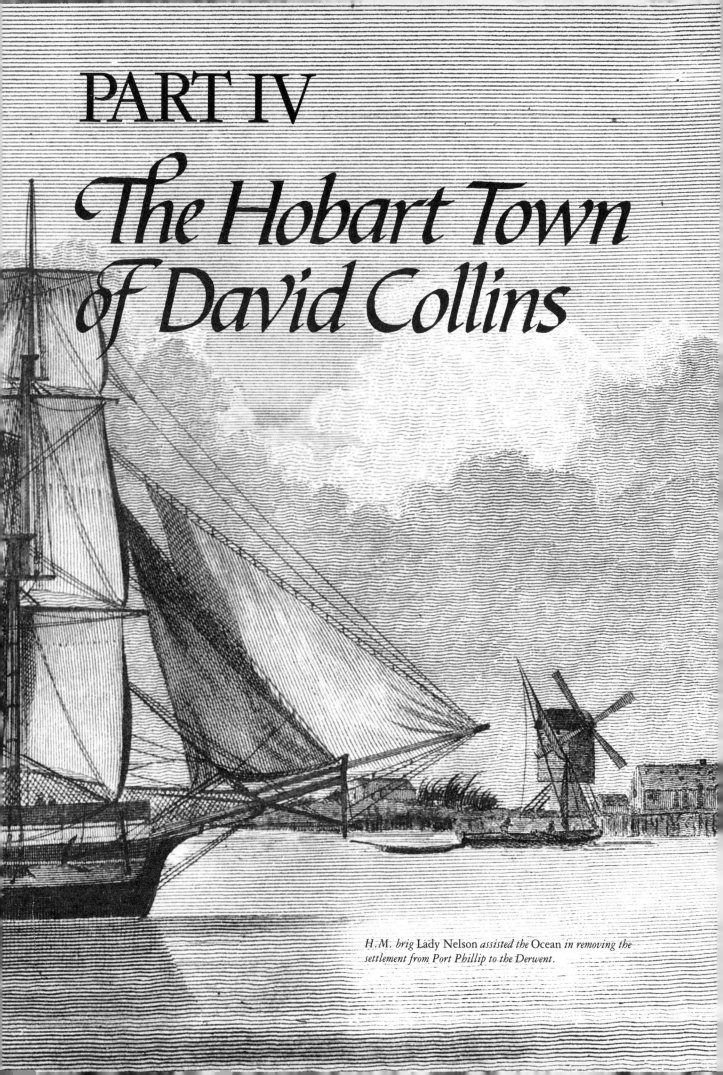

PART IV
The Hobart Town of David Collins

H.M. brig Lady Nelson *assisted the* Ocean *in removing the settlement from Port Phillip to the Derwent.*

19 JOURNEY'S END

URING ONE OF the strongest gales Humphrey had ever witnessed, the *Ocean* arrived at Frederick Henry Bay on 11 February 1804. He and Lieutenant Edward Lord, accompanied by two trusted men and four body servants (who probably included Humphrey's servants Joshua Thatcher, Robert Kennedy and John Smith, and Lord's man John Lawrence) walked some twenty-odd miles from present day Lauderdale off which the *Ocean* had cast anchor.[1] Harris, who was suffering from ophthalmia, was disappointed at being unable to be among the first ashore. He had to remain quietly aboard the ship.[2] Once the winds subsided the sun became warmer. Those who had gone ashore became thirstier and lack of fresh water caused them to dehydrate. One of Humphrey's men became quite ill and had to be left behind. The party had Flinders' map of the Derwent estuary to guide them around the hilly country in order to find Bowen's camp at Risdon Cove.

Bowen himself was not there. He had taken the opportunity, when the American whaler *Ferret* had called for water, to sail in her to Port Jackson.[3] A lieutenant in the Royal Navy, Bowen might have been motivated by some patriotic desire, as Captain Woodriff and the men of the *Calcutta* had been, to sort out where his priorities lay when he heard about the outbreak of war. He had as a pretext the need for someone to take his sergeant to stand trial in Sydney along with some convicts who had robbed his stores. It was almost certainly his desire to make some arrangements for the future of Martha Hayes and their expected child.[4]

Captain Mertho, Dr Bowden, William Collins and Knopwood, arming themselves in case of a confrontation with the original inhabitants, went ashore the following day. They were delighted to find a variety of birds that might provide good food: wild fowl, emus, pigeons, quails, ducks and teal. They gathered a large number of oysters. The size of the trees and the abundance of flax confirmed that the decision to leave Port Phillip was a wise one if they were to pursue the search for naval supplies. Mertho took three days inspecting the estuary. When the *Lady Nelson* arrived, Collins decided that the two ships should move up the river to Risdon, which they discovered had already been referred to as Hobart.[5]

In the absence of Bowen, Lieutenant William Moore of the New South Wales Corps received David Collins with some formality, while Mertho ordered an eleven-gun salute. Collins, aware of the sensitivity of his position, had to tread carefully when he realised that the site was far from being the ideal place to situate a town. The camp as it existed was nothing more than a watching post, consisting of the commandant, a surgeon, storekeeper, eighteen marines, a few settlers and assigned servants — amounting in all to about one hundred persons.

Knopwood immediately befriended the surgeon Mountgarret, dining with him on the first night. The plentiful oysters and other fresh fish, as well as vegetables from the cultivated gardens, would have been a rare treat. the day after baptising Catherine Potaski, daughter of John and Catherine, who had been born aboard the *Ocean* shortly before arrival, Knopwood went exploring with Governor Collins and William Collins. They examined the extensive plain at the foot of the mountain, which brought back memories of the Table Mountain at the Cape of Good Hope. There they found a stream of good water, obviously always available, even in the dry season. They decided to move the ships and company from Risdon. There was a small island named after Governor Hunter jutting into the deep waters of the bay. A narrow spit attached it to the land. They anchored alongside and were able to land the stores and people with much greater ease than at Port Phillip. Collins named the place Sullivan Cove but soon began to call it Hobart's Town or Hobart Town and frequently the Derwent.[6]

Knopwood was pleased to have his marquee pitched near the Governor's, as it had been at Sullivan Bay and, one assumes, cheek-by-jowl with the tent occupied by Matthew and Hannah Power. Other tents and marquees soon transformed the coastline in the area between Battery Point and the rivulet. Within weeks of the landing William Fletcher had organised his fellow sawyers, one of whom was James Waltham, to cut down trees for building purposes as well as to erect a bridge across the rivulet.

The Reverend Robert Knopwood preached on the first Sunday after the landing. This time he took as his text a verse from Psalm 107: 'Whoso is wise and considereth these things, even they shall understand the kindness of the Lord'. He reminded his congregation of the advantages they would all enjoy and the goodness of God for establishing them in a land of plenty. He gave thanks to God for the appearance of prosperity and prayed for a blessing that it might increase still further. Officers from Risdon Cove came across to attend their first church service in months. Knopwood then went to Risdon to perform his duty to the convicts stationed there.[7]

It did not take the reverend gentleman long to settle into his usual social routine together with his cronies and the officers of the two ships in port. He was also anxious to explore the beautiful countryside around Sullivan Cove as quickly as possible. All officers had the services of convict servants and one who accompanied Knopwood in the early days was Thomas Salmon. With his two scientific colleagues, Humphrey and Robert Brown, Knopwood took two days travelling as far as the present New Norfolk. They found it useful to have Dr Mountgarret as their guide. A few days later Knopwood again went with Humphrey, as well as William Collins and Harris, to the Coal River area.[8] During further exploration, Humphrey and Brown, taking provisions for four days for themselves and three men, including Humphrey's servants, ascended the Table Mountain, finding some of the largest trees in the world. They slept in the hollow of one which was eleven feet in diameter but Brown ('a gentleman in whom the utmost confidence may be placed', according to Humphrey) informed him that he had actually seen a fallen tree, large enough for a coach and six to be driven along it, measuring seventy feet in circumference. He made one observation which was significant in light of the naval interest in the availability of timber in the Antipodes: 'The Trees in this Country are all streight [sic], and not branched out till near the Top; so that a first rate Man of War might have Masts all of one piece'. William Collins was later to report on its extent and usage: 'fine Timber for all purposes of Building, and good Spars to answer for Masts and Yards, etc.' Even though it was still February and the height of summer, it was snowing at the top of the mount, but the party collected as many botanical and geological specimens as they could carry.[9]

They saw numerous native huts during their jour-

ney, but little sign of the natives by day. At night their fires flickered and Knopwood remarked that 'no doubt but they see us'. Both races viewed each other with some caution, and at a distance. As yet there was no realisation that the newcomers might endanger the hunting grounds of the indigenous population or that they might ultimately destroy their way of life. Food appeared plentiful enough to provide for all for the time being.

The situation at Risdon was difficult. During Bowen's absence Collins was happy to let the settlement there carry on as before. Lieutenant Moore had received no direct instructions from Port Jackson that Collins was to be in supreme command at the Derwent. Most of his people had been more troublesome than those in Collins' care. He had ruffians among his soldiers, as well as the Irish convicts whom King had been glad to send south. Collins found that John Duce and his companions who had escaped in a boat loaded with guns, ammunition and food to join sealers at Cape Barren Island, were 'more hardened and atrocious than those who may be imported from the Jails in England'. He begged King not to make the new settlement a place of confinement for such characters.[10]

Bowen was expected back any day, but the armed cutter in which he sailed from Port Jackson, H.M. Integrity, had to call first at Port Phillip. Thomas Rushworth, the master, was then to sail to Port Dalrymple or the Derwent if he found Collins had left for either place. Bowen carried with him instructions to return to Port Jackson after giving up his command to Collins.[11] This formality was more to satisfy Bowen and not intended as an affront to Collins, as the latter would have realised. Collins had no need to receive any instructions concerning his command from King. The commission accredited him by Lord Hobart was enough. But Collins and King were old friends who understood the nuances of diplomacy.

There would have been some interesting reunions when the Integrity arrived at Port Phillip. She had several passengers on board, including Anthony Fletcher, the stonemason, and his wife who would surely have paid a visit to the grave of the child they had buried there. Henry Hayes, returning after reunion with his wife, would introduce her to his colleagues. Bowen had successfully arranged for the family's transfer to the Derwent to rejoin their daughter. At Sullivan Bay they would all have been amazed at the changed situation where Lieutenant Sladden was in charge of a much smaller settlement. They would have observed how James Grove and his assistants were busily engaged in filling casks with the alkali they had produced from the marine vegetation. They would have been saddened to hear of the many deaths that had occurred at Port Phillip since they had left there, especially that of the three-year-old Ann

Wiggins. Edward Miller and his family were trying to harvest any of the seeds that might germinate in Van Diemen's Land.

The *Integrity* was already in trouble at Port Phillip, with a rudder problem. As there was no other way in which he could solicit help, Rushworth had to sail on. In sight of Cape Barren Island the rudder fastenings broke, stranding the cutter. Distress signals alerted the American schooner *Pilgrim* and a brig from Boston, the *Perseverance*, both fortunately at hand on sealing expeditions. The wily and opportunistic Captain Amaso Delano of the *Pilgrim* saw his chance and offered to transfer the party to his vessel. After a verbal agreement, he landed them in Hobart Town on 10 March to enjoy some shore leave before organising the salvage of the *Integrity*. He later presented the surprised Governor King with an extortionate account for £400. King had no option but to pay.[12]

Knopwood immediately attached himself to the Hayes family after their arrival. He always had an eye for a pretty young woman. Joseph Holt later described Martha as the 'prettiest violet I saw growing on the banks of the Derwent' and the mother as 'very pleasant, as my friend and I carried a bottle of good wine with us'.[13] Mary Hayes long before had proved that she enjoyed a good drop and would later make a small fortune out of the convivial hostelry that she would rule over in Hobart Town. They at first joined the other settlers beyond the rivulet at New Town. There the soil of the virgin forest was rich and the water plentiful. They received, along with other settlers, the 100-acre blocks they had been promised, and must have believed they were in Paradise. Martha's daughter was born at the end of March. Bowen arranged that she be granted settler status and receive the same considerations as male settlers.[14]

There at New Town, Martha was to be much better off than if she had stayed at Risdon, which was beset with problems. Little seed in the beginning had produced a sparse amount of grain for the people there. Their huts were miserable and they were so short of food that Collins had to eke out his own party's rations to feed them. He took over their starving stock, but adamantly refused to have anything to do with their mutinous soldiers and convicts. In the course of time he sent all but one of them back to Governor King, again demonstrating his concern that his own comparatively well-disciplined company would remain uncontaminated.[15]

The sloop *Nancy* arrived in Hobart Town in May 1804 bringing news of the *Calcutta*'s delay at Port Jackson. Just as she was set to sail for England, having loaded some 600 logs of naval timber which were awaiting her, alarm bells and guns firing on shore alerted the naval vessel to the outbreak of an insurrection of Irish convicts at Castle Hill. Captain Woodriff

landed his marines. They joined the men of the New South Wales Corps under Major George Johnston and marched to Parramatta. Governor King proclaimed martial law. More than two hundred rebels, mostly serving sentences for sedition, had forgathered after the pre-arranged signal of setting a house ablaze and ringing a bell. The cries of 'Death or Liberty' resounded as the insurgents raided the houses of settlers for arms and ammunition. They hoped to gather more than a thousand others when they marched on Government House, and to proceed to Sydney before embarking on the ships in the harbour. Elizabeth Macarthur described her family's flight from Elizabeth Farm and the sight of the *Calcutta* 'beautifully lit up. Most of the officers were on shore and kindly received us poor fugitives at the wharf'.[16]

Although his friend Joseph Holt was not actively associated with the uprising on that occasion, Robert Walsh, who had written him the letter from Port Phillip, would have heard the devastating news that his former colleague Phil Cunningham was the principal rebel leader. He had been wounded and soon afterwards executed together with eight others. Nine were flogged and fifty were to be sent to Coal Harbour, the new establishment Governor King had planned on the Hunter River for secondary punishments. He had been happy to appoint First Lieutenant Charles Menzies, R.N., who had arrived in the *Calcutta*, to command and superintend the northern settlement. Lieutenant John Houston likewise left the *Calcutta* to accept the Governor's appointment as Lieutenant Governor of Norfolk Island.[17]

King gave much credit to the presence of Captain Woodriff and his men for their timely assistance in guarding Government House and generally helping to quell the troubles which he knew had been simmering for some time. He had been inadequately prepared for such an uprising and had the *Calcutta* sailed earlier the result could well have been a blood bath.[18]

Pateshall thought that King needed not only a large military force but also a man-of-war at hand. He had heard rumours that 'Men of Rank and respectability were at the head of the Rebellion and like Cowards waited the fate of a parcel of ignorant wretches sent before to sound the way'.[19] King himself had suspected that Maurice Margarot, one of the Scottish Martyrs, had urged the men on, together with the wealthy Sir Henry Brown Hayes, who had been a sheriff in Cork convicted for the abduction of a wealthy heiress.[20]

During the *Calcutta*'s sojourn at Port Jackson, Tuckey had occupied himself studying every aspect of the colony for a comprehensive report which he later submitted to the First Lord of the Admiralty, Viscount Melville.[21] He had almost completed his observations on the present state of the colony when

The Irish convict rebellion at Castle Hill in 1804. 'Prisoners at Public Labour at Castle Hill and the settlers men, were in a state of Insurrection, and had already committed many daring Outrages . . . The Captain, officers, marines and ship's Company of His Majesty's ship Calcutta *came on shore {to assist} . . .' (Sydney Gazette, 11 March 1804).*

the insurrection took place. He had written that to date there had not been the slightest attempt to protect New South Wales against the 'probable revolt of the disaffected convicts or the hostile attacks of a foreign enemy'.[22] He strongly recommended a small naval force, which was in any case necessary to protect the fisheries from foreign interlopers as well as the 'wild Irish'.[23]

The presence of the French had worried him and he tried to discover what had really occurred when the Baudin expedition was at Port Jackson. His comments, preserved in a little-known document, may throw further light on their motives:

that this remote colony had not escaped the thoughts of our enemy is clearly demonstrated by two French frigates . . . remaining at Port Jackson two or three months, during which the officers minutely surveyed the harbour, and also made scientific excursions into the interior by which they acquired a more extensive knowledge of the nature of the country than the colonists themselves possess.[24]

Tuckey's thoughts on another race were most enlightened. He held the Chinese in great respect and hoped that Britain would encourage them to settle in New South Wales — several thousand of them — as they

had done in the Malay Islands. That he was able to express such thoughts, as Matra had done some twenty years earlier, again suggests that the trading possibilities of the new colony were at least as important as its use as a penitentiary. But he warned that:

should such an event be brought about it must be remembered that their customs both religious and domestic are engrafted into the very essence of their being, and that although they quietly submit to the general laws of the government they live under, they must be gratified by the free use of their own internal regulations, and must also be efficiently protected from every species of insult and injury.[25]

He believed China would be a good market for the sealskins in exchange for cotton, that coal might be exported to the Cape of Good Hope, and that the trade in oil and skins could be most productive and should be directed to India, China and the numerous

107

islands which the East India Company's charter disallowed, which was injurious to the colony. Flax and tobacco could grow luxuriantly, much of the timber was adaptable, and knowledge of navigation had vastly improved since Flinders had charted the seas. The passage to China was through seas which he believed were virtually stormless.[26]

Meanwhile, Woodriff himself had seen at first hand the importance of Port Jackson and the need to protect it from both the enemy within and without. When he returned to England he prepared a memorandum for the Admiralty not only on the timber and naval supplies available in New South Wales, but also with recommendations on how to preserve and protect what they had, the need for proper moorings, and the need to staff the colony with proper officers. He saw an immense need for much more craft — a schooner, a river barge, a pilot boat, a gun brig for a collector of customs to control the smuggling, and, above all, a small British naval force. He thought that the French might attack from Mauritius. He believed that Baudin, when he took correct plans of Port Jackson and purchased a vessel there, was on a reconnaissance when he sailed through Bass Strait. Woodriff was certain that only Baudin's death in 1803 prevented him from visiting the colony again for the purpose of annihilating the settlement.[27]

Woodriff was also appalled at American insults to His Majesty's subjects, who had actually been taken from a colonial vessel and 'Confined in Irons' by a 'power almost without a Navy'. He had heard at first hand from Captain William Moody about an event that had occurred a few weeks earlier in the Kent Group. Moody's ship, the *Governor King*, and the *Calcutta* had both arrived at Port Jackson the day after Christmas Day. As Woodriff would have interpreted it, the incident was an example of what might readily recur between conceivable enemies when the spoils of trade and commerce were at stake. The news of such a confrontation relatively close to his own domain would have alarmed David Collins.[28]

It was still only the beginnings of the fishing industry, and at that time the rewards appeared great. The American whaler *Charles* from Boston, which had sailed from Mauritius bringing news of the outbreak of war, had put in to the Kent Group to refit. In November 1803 the *Governor King* met up with the captain of the *Charles*, Charles Percival, and his crew

of thirty-two men who had collected 300 tons of oil. They threatened Moody and his nine men. It was Percival's intention to enlist more men to work in sealing gangs. Some were seized and bound, receiving severe blows. Several were placed on one of the smaller islands without water. When Moody remonstrated, Percival accused the British of denying him his rights by allowing a 'lot of predators' to be let loose on his fishing grounds. Moody managed to gather together his crew, returning to home base with thirty-seven tons of oil, seven hundred sealskins and one man with a head so violently beaten up that splinters still remained.[29]

King was running his own head against a stone when he proclaimed that Americans were not only incommoding His Majesty's subjects in the islands of Bass Strait but also building vessels 'in violation of the Laws of Nations'. For what it was worth, he forbade any foreigner to continue the practice of ship building, unless a ship be wrecked, without authority. He threatened that any such vessels would be seized and confiscated. The same ruling would apply in Van Diemen's Land.[30]

The *Calcutta* sailed away from Port Jackson on 16 March. Pateshall's thoughts turned to the pleasant ten weeks they had spent in the infant colony. He felt he had 'never left a place with greater reluctance or ever experienced more hospitality: the Gentlemen found amusements for us by day and the Ladies never failed to make themselves agreeable in the evenings.'[31]

Those in Hobart Town who read the *Sydney Gazette* must have envied them their few weeks there. How Knopwood would have sighed as he envisaged the 'elegant entertainment', in the style he knew well, that the *Calcutta* officers would have given the officers of the colony, both civil and military,

at which many Ladies were present. In the evening a Ball commenced which continued till an early hour; and the day following the festivities were renewed with equal spirit and taste, and continued till the pale-fac'd moon gave earnest of approaching day.[32]

It was reminiscent of those wonderful nights they had enjoyed together at Rio and Cape Town, where the locals had added to their pleasures in a manner almost unknown at Port Phillip and early Hobart Town.

20 THE RETURN OF THE *OCEAN*

B Y THE TIME the *Ocean* returned to the Derwent on 25 June, together with Sladden's party of ninety-nine convicts and others from Port Phillip, members of the pioneering party were reasonably well housed in preparation for the winter. Those already established offered to share their little huts with the newcomers, who must have received a fine welcome as reinforcements for the establishment. They were excused labour for the first days because their voyage had been a perilous one and they took some time to recover from it.[1]

While still at Port Phillip Captain Mertho discovered that rats had destroyed many of the ship's provisions which caused some delay while the ship had to be smoked to get rid of them — more than two hundred. Before they sailed, one of the convicts who was acting as a seaman, John Newland, was stupidly smoking in the lower prison room and almost set fire to the *Ocean*, whereupon Mertho ordered fifty lashes. Two days later he received a further fifty lashes for the same offence. The Scotsman, Robert Hay had to face up to eighty lashes for theft. Edward Biddle Smith received fifty lashes for contempt of the sentinel. It would appear that Mertho, who had previously had trouble with the settlers, was unable to gain the same sort of respect that Woodriff obviously enjoyed.

Expecting the journey to take even less than the eleven days it had taken on the first trip south, the ship set sail on 18 May. It was to take five weeks in appalling conditions keeping even the most unruly passengers in check. Strong gales soon created more panic on the ship than any convict behaviour. By the time they were nearing Cape Pillar, Mertho realised that he was heading into a hurricane which took them completely off course. For three weeks without sail he had to battle with the elements in unknown seas. The *Ocean* was swept so far to the south-east of Van Diemen's Land that at one stage it reached longitude 149.5E and latitude 44.36S, placing the ship at least 150 miles off course. It was already winter and they were ill-prepared to face the freezing temperatures.

Compass readings were impossible to observe for many of the days. Mertho had to reduce the water allowance twice. They dropped to three pints a day. Most of the people were seasick or suffering from scurvy. Only eight men of the ship's company were available for deck duties. Mertho had to rely on some of the convicts. Mountainous seas crashed over the ship, masts were damaged and sails stripped. Rather than try to fight his way into the aptly named Storm Bay, the exhausted captain guided the ship back towards Oyster Bay, where they were able to anchor and take on some fresh water, aided by friendly natives who took them to a swamp where they filled casks with two tons of good water.

Two of the seamen who could not tolerate the nightmare any longer disappeared into the woods, but turned up in Hobart Town a few weeks later in the whaler *Alexander*.[2] James Grove reported that the animals on board were dying fast and stock still alive had to be fed on grass acquired at Oyster Bay. They had been living on flour for days. All private stock had to be killed so that they were not a drain on the public stores. Grove was lucky to save his sheep by feeding them the tea he had manufactured at Port Phillip, but he lost one old hen that flew overboard. In all, eighteen sheep, seventeen hogs, ten ducks, a male goat and six fowls were lost during the voyage. Mertho admitted to Grove that he and all his men had never before experienced such severe gales. Grove had found much consolation in going on deck 'to search the foundation of my hope, during the perils of the sea . . . I had a humble hope that, whatsoever the event might be, I was safe . . .[3] The Groves might well have wished themselves back in the sturdy *Calcutta*, even in the prison quarters of which they had complained before bargaining with the carpenter for his better cabin.

The people at Hobart Town were relieved when their friends on board the *Ocean* arrived at last, having almost given up hope for their safety. They were also distressed to find how much of the livestock had been lost in the storms and how many of the stores had been damaged by the rats. They feared that unless Governor King could keep up a constant food supply from Port Jackson they would run short of rations.

Knopwood was soon renewing his social life with the newcomers. Captain Mertho, Lieutenants Sladden and Johnson and Dr I'Anson spent most of their first day ashore with Knopwood. Fosbrook was able to continue his affair with Fanny Anchor. As there had been no-one to marry them at Port Phillip, Knopwood performed an urgent ceremony to unite the settlers John Ingle and Rebecca Hobbs in the presence of William Hopley and George Harris. The newly arrived convicts received the same rations of new and warm clothing which must have been even more acceptable to them than to those who had arrived earlier at the settlement.

There were other ceremonies of interest to the people at the Derwent. Tongues must have wagged when Ann Skelthorn, whose settler husband was the first adult to die at Port Phillip, married the marine Corporal William Gangell some five months later in Hobart Town. The widow Jane Heels, whose husband John had also died at Port Phillip, married the ex-thief John Hangan, whose escape at Port Phillip had caused Collins to feel much compassion for his miserable appearance.[4]

The settler John Blinkworth had originally been transported to Botany Bay, but after serving his sentence he had returned to England. He had good references, not only from Governor Hunter but from Collins himself, allowing him to settle at Port Phillip. Elizabeth Cummings, then free by servitude, with a child known as Robert Blinkworth, arrived from Port Jackson, probably in the *Lady Nelson*. John Blinkworth married her soon afterwards. The child was nine years old and was perhaps his son by a wife in England who had died. Francis Barnes, now a government clerk, and Edward Lord witnessed the marriage on 21 March 1804. Barnes was to witness many similar ceremonies when *Calcutta* convicts and others married during the next decade. His constant appearance at what passed as a church and the supplications of his reverend patron to forgive them all their trespasses were a far cry from Barnes' former happy hunting ground at the Drury Lane Theatre.

Grove had become friendly with a young man who had served with the Royal Navy and had been present at the Battle of Copenhagen. This was Samuel Gunn. He was a widower when he arrived at Sullivan Bay with a young child and a seven-year sentence for stealing a saddle and bridle at Fordham, Norfolk. Gunn, whom Collins had chosen to direct shipwrights at Port Phillip, had remained there with the settlers as well as the Groves until May.[5]

During those months, when a few convicts had

considerable freedom, the young Janet Patterson, daughter of the superintendent of convicts William Patterson, found herself 'in the family way.' In July the Reverend Knopwood married Janet to Samuel Gunn in the presence of her settler father and George Harris. Their first daughter was born before the year ended. A few days later Knopwood baptised Elizabeth, the child born to John and Rebecca Ingle after their hasty marriage.

When they first arrived the Gunns shared a house with the Groves. Gunn was the only person in the *Captivity* hulk with Grove who would have been capable of building the three-roomed house consisting of a kitchen and two bedrooms — 'the best built of any in the camp'. It was erected on land in Bridge Street close to a rivulet and the port. It was, with the Collins Street land of William Patterson, Gunn's father-in-law, to be the subject of boundary disputes in later years when the streets were realigned.[6]

Sladden had only good reports on the behaviour of the Port Phillip people entrusted to his care, especially the detachment of marines, who appeared healthy and soldierlike. They would be much needed to help guard the camp from the robberies that had begun to occur and to keep watch at night for unusual incidents such as a strange boat coming up the river.

While in port the *Ocean* had to be safely guarded in case any stowaways boarded. Lieutenant Bowen and the botanist Robert Brown were among the passengers to sail in her. Bowen had made further domestic arrangements for Martha Hayes, their daughter Henrietta having been born in April, but without actually committing himself to marriage. He built her a farmhouse on the fifty acres of land granted her at Swamp Lagoon near her parents, who were at Stainsforth's Cove. According to Knopwood he slept at her house just before they sailed. Their second daughter, Martha Charlotte, whom Bowen would never see, was born nine months later.[7]

It was most unlikely that Bowen would have married Martha Hayes, the daughter of a convicted woman and a shady character of a man. As the son of a rear-admiral, he himself had great ambitions. He saw in the war an opportunity to further these ambitions. Rising to the rank of captain, he sought appointment as lieutenant-governor of Van Diemen's Land on two occasions without success. In 1819 he also tried to accompany Commissioner J. T. Bigge to New South Wales. Perhaps he had hoped to return to Martha and the daughters he had provided for. But he never saw them again. Two years before he died in 1827 he married the niece of a countess, but they had no children. He had many worthy and well-known descendants by Martha Hayes.[8]

21 SETTLING IN

*F*ROM THE MOMENT they arrived there was full employment for all the artisans: the sawyers, carpenters, bricklayers, lime and charcoal burners, blacksmiths and stonemasons. One in three of the whole company was engaged in the building industry. Those without a trade were soon absorbed as builders' labourers. Thomas Croft took charge of the brickmakers, as at Port Phillip, and Anthony Lowe of the blacksmiths, assisted by James Lord who kept the charcoal fires burning. Augustus Morris continued to guide the gang of men drawing the logs from the sawpit, one of the more dangerous undertakings. Charles Williams and John Pearsall produced some of the earliest ironmongery in the colony. When the carpenters and cabinet makers discovered the durability and beauty of Huon pine they began to fashion simple furniture that would last.[1]

But for the first few months Hobart Town was nothing more than a camp, referred to as such even in some official correspondence. Gradually the frames of huts began to appear and later houses replaced the canvas town which had dotted the coastline, crossed the rivulet and rose along the leafy slopes of Mount Wellington. But most were little more than skillings. Fawkner described the first huts as generally formed by posts of about four inches in diameter, sunk in up to two feet of earth and some were as high as ten feet above the ground. Lathe and wattle, worked in and plastered, filled the interstices, and round poles formed rafters for the roof which were crossed with wattles and thatched with grass. Patched canvas took the place of glass for doors and windows. Some used oiled paper or thin cloth and for protection built wooden shutters and boards as timber became available.[2]

The superintendent of convicts was Richard Clark, a settler who had arrived with Bowen and was the only man of that party whom Collins allowed to remain.[3] He was a stonemason who began training others in his trade. It is likely that Anthony Fletcher assisted him in the construction of the earliest public buildings in Hobart Town. Collins believed that most of the public buildings should be built of stone. One of the first priorities was the structure of a storehouse on Hunter's Island. It was to hold all the dry goods and most of the provisions. There the ships could readily unload their cargoes and would be well protected by members of the night watch. After completion of the storehouse Collins ordered the construction of two rooms of a magazine to hold the powder.

But in spite of the need for good building materials, Collins frequently showed that he was keen to conserve natural resources, by adopting measures such as forbidding indiscriminate chopping down of trees and the removal of too much stone from the one quarry.[4] He also showed concern for animal species when he noted the harassment caused to swans in the river at a time when the females were known to be full of eggs.[5] He had to issue warnings against the destruction and disturbance of these same birds during the week of their first Christmas when one might expect they would make good festive eating.[6] Knopwood did not set a very good example. Only a few weeks before his men had collected a bag of seventy-eight swans at the Huon and he frequently referred to the collection of swans' eggs, young swans and swanskins. Two years later Collins would have to put aside his noble principles in order that the colony might survive.

In October 1804 the Commissary issued each prisoner with a further set of wearing apparel, which was expected to last six months. Supplies were short, but bolts of duck and flannel were available and there were enough tailors who, with the assistance of some of the women, were able to make up extra clothes. Wives of prisoners received a shift, a jacket, petticoat, a pair of shoes, stockings and a cap.[7] Three years later Collins had to warn those who received shoes, woollen socks and woollen nightcaps that if they were known to sell any of these items, which were in particularly short supply, they would be severely punished and excluded from the next ration.[8] There was plenty of white thread to repair clothes, check cloth, linen, canvas, leather and metal buttons, needles and thimbles.

As replacements were slow to arrive in the colony, many of the convicts took to wearing jackets, trousers and sometimes caps made from kangaroo skins. These provided much-needed warmth during the colder months. The American captain, Delano, saw how easy the innocent animals were to snare. He had watched them eat flowers or berries out of a person's hand on the same day that they were caught. Dogs would hold them fast until a huntsman arrived on the scene. They were then slain without mutilation. They were very sweet and delicately flavoured and Delano commended their use as the 'handsomest leather for boots and shoes that can be found and very durable'.[9]

The process of tanning, using the bark of the blue gum and black wattle, produced good results when applied to the kangaroo skins for upper leather. There was difficulty finding enough suitable leather for soles. They saved skins which had arrived as packing for meal and the skins of Bengal cattle that died, enabling Collins to issue a pair of locally made shoes to each of the prisoners.[10]

Four men were trusted to engage in boat-building and twenty-one used in boat crews. Others became overseers and there was work for the clerks, a printer, a bellringer, a barber, cooks, bakers, wheelwrights, millwrights and gardeners, all occupations represented by the *Calcutta* convicts. Thirty-two acted as servants to the military and civil officers.

Prevention of disease was essential from the beginning. One of Collins' earliest orders was to caution persons 'against polluting the stream by any means whatsoever' and would arrange for a proper place for them to bathe. He showed some anxiety about the proper care for the hair of his people and issued two combs and a brush to all those who applied for them. Overseers had to report those who did not keep their heads clean. He wanted no lice-infested persons in his community.[11]

As principal of the night watch, Stocker and his fellow members, mostly those who had been the mutineers at Gibraltar, were to inspect the huts regularly. Not only were they to see they were kept clean but also that the bedding and clothing were frequently aired, weather permitting. Collins appointed Robert Stewart an overseer to keep 'the camp clean and the stream pure from filth', and to point out a proper place for a privy.[12] This was the same Robert Stewart who had shown himself to be troublesome in the *Calcutta*, but by some devious means had at one stage enveigled Collins into allowing him to visit Port Jackson. He appears to have sailed in the *Calcutta* and tried to see Governor King, who was then preoccu-

pied with the troubles brewing at Castle hill. This however did not deter Stewart. He managed to falsify documents when he returned, presumably in the *Francis*, to Collins at Port Phillip with a recommendation that he be given some special consideration. It was not long before Stewart abused the trust placed in him.[13]

•   •   •

An early return of occupations in Hobart showed that by July 1804, 265 convicts had jobs out of the 279 landed in Van Diemen's Land. The balance were sick or convalescent. Of the original 308 who had embarked in the *Calcutta* eight had died during the voyage, fifteen were buried at Port Phillip and seven were presumed to have perished there.[14]

I'Anson's medical return of November 1804 showed that there were three marines, five free persons and twenty-eight convicts sick: twenty-one still affected by scurvy and five by diarrhoea. For the first time he noted one with consumption. There were several accident cases accounting for lameness, a contused knee, a dislocated toe and a sore head.[15] To combat the scurvy, Fosbrook offered sixpence a pound to anyone able to bring kangaroo meat to the stores.[16] At the hospital building the surgeons kept two boilers producing meat boiled with rice and whatever wild greens were available for those afflicted. Towards the end of 1804 one person had been suffering from lues for 420 days, that is, from about the time of arrival at Port Phillip.[17]

Eighteen more were to die before the New Year. By then the sick rate had dwindled and the payment for kangaroo meat stopped. Only six more died during the following three years. The causes of death were often loosely described as 'debility' and sometimes 'cough' and 'catarrh' when they were probably pneumonia or consumption.[18] The vagaries of an unknown climate were unkind. Everyone suffered while under canvas from both unaccustomed heat in the summer and howling gales and rain in the colder weather. Even Humphrey, relatively well housed, sometimes slept with water up to six inches in depth under his bed. During the wet season it was almost impossible to get fires to burn and even when one could, the steam would rise from a person's wet clothes.[19]

Deaths and illness had also affected the marines. One had been ill since leaving England and died of the unmentionable 'French' disease brought with him. Collins reported that one sergeant suffered from severe rheumatism and he expected little duty from him again. This must have been Andrews whose excessive punishment received at the halberds at Port Phillip had crippled him for life. Collins also discharged Corporal John Jubal Sutton, not for neglect of duty but to promote him as a superintendent of convicts. Samuel Lightfoot, the ex-convict turned settler, remained for many years in his job as hospital assistant, conscientiously guarding the stores from runaway convicts whose need to steal medical supplies when going bush was just as important as food.[20]

But in spite of short rations and the low stock of medical supplies, most people remained quite healthy. Collins feared the onset of winter because they were mostly without rugs and blankets. It was not long before they recognised the value of sealskins, when they could get them, and possum rugs such as the Aborigines used in the cold Tasmanian winters. The sudden death of the Frenchman, Piroelle, in May 1804, leaving a wife Sarah and a son Henry, was at first a mystery. Collins ordered Bowden to hold the first inquest, as a rumour spread around that he had been poisoned. Bowden reported that

Upon opening the thorax, the pericardium and both sides of the chest contained a large quantity of water, which had stopped the action of the lungs. The heart was unusually large, but not otherwise diseased. In the abdomen I examined the stomach and intestines particularly, which were perfectly healthy, and contained a small quantity of half digested food, in which there was nothing remarkable. The liver was also much enlarged from some former disease.[21]

Perhaps his earlier occupation as confectioner and pastrycook had something to do with the liverish condition, but the quantity of water affecting the lungs suggests that Piroelle had drowned. During the next few years one of the most frequent causes of death was by drowning. Altogether, from the time Cashman drowned at Simon's Bay, nine *Calcutta* convicts met their death in this manner, and probably many more who were later shipwrecked and whose fate has been difficult to trace.

I'Anson had shown particular interest in Dr Edward Jenner's controversial research into smallpox before leaving England. When the first vaccine arrived at Port Jackson in the *Coromandel*, the Surgeon, Dr John Jamison sent a supply to Hobart Town. The controversy continued in the colony. The inoculation of Bowden's son John by Maria Sergeant and Dr Hopley's son Richard, as well as the two children of Samuel Thorne, were the first inoculations in Van Diemen's Land.[22]

The effects of scurvy and the attempts to prevent it were to continue for a long time. William Dregg, at one time captain of the whaler *Santa Anna*, told of a custom practised in Hobart Town in 1811 as a cure for scurvy: 'Two holes were dug in a garden for me to put my legs in, and when they began to feel cold I was ordered to take them out . . . my legs soon got well'.[23]

Bowden's sick list for the first two years included many scorbutic patients. To counteract this the doctors found it desirable to give most patients a daily allowance of wine. Excessive diarrhoea affected twelve men during the winter and caused several deaths. I'Anson begged for more medical stores including large quantities of olive oil, lime juice, portable soup, digitalis, flannel for chest complaints, calico for bandages, lancets and bougies as well as the much needed rugs and blankets.[24]

But there were also diseases too anti-social in character to appear in the records, and probably much more common than officialdom would have one believe. One Hobart citizen, William Allison, kept a notebook in 1811 in which he recorded recipes for curing the 'Venerial', as well as some of the more common ailments. For that, the mention of which should be eschewed, he recommended mixing 'Two pennyworth of Pelicotia, 3d of Gum Booge, 2d of bitter apple, 3d of Calomels, one of jalap mint, into 30 pills, one at night and two in the morning'. For a mere headache he mixed a scruple of aloes, one of calomel, one of rhubarb and a dram and a half of castile soap, making twenty pills in all. He included a recipe for the making of sherry wine which he believed was an excellent cure for rheumatism.[25]

•   •   •

After the expiration of six months from their landing, all officials had to pay for their servants except the magistrates and superintendents. Settlers also were subject to pay for what labour they needed and could afford under set charges for piece work, such as £1 10s per acre for the felling and burning of timber or £4 per acre for grubbing and burning. For the less arduous jobs, threepence a bushel was the rate for threshing wheat or delivering a bushel of oyster shells, and for sixpence one might have labour for digging a rood of garden or gathering a bundle of thatch. For a general day's work of ten hours, mechanics would charge three shillings and sixpence and labourers two shillings and sixpence. Payments could be made in kind, equations for salted beef being ninepence per pound, pork and flour one shilling, kangaroo eightpence and wheat meal sixpence.[26]

Stocker's responsibilities as principal of the night watch began to increase. He and his men had to keep guard over the public store on Hunter's Island during opening hours, three days a week. Orders were to shoot anyone who came near the store. Members of the night watch were also responsible for preventing maurauding animals such as hogs from attacking the stores during the night. They had to keep a vigilant eye on the farms as well as the huts to prevent petty robberies. Watches, which had always had an attraction for thieves, had been disappearing. Perhaps some were optimistic enough to think that they could do some trading with visitors from the ships that called.[27]

In July 1804 the first recorded crime was the theft of a lamb from Dr Bowden. Collins offered a conditional pardon for anyone producing information on the theft. He named Knopwood, Sladden and Harris as magistrates.[28] Knopwood's diary from the time of the appointment of the magistrates is tantalisingly brief about most of the misdemeanours in the colony. Over many years his remarks are rarely more than that he and Harris or Sladden, and later Humphrey or others, 'met on business' in the morning.

The Bench of Magistrates' first case was that of the rebellious Stewart, who received fifty lashes and was placed in a gang.[29] He had lost his chance, as an overseer, to make some worthwhile contribution to the new society. There is no record of his crime but the case of the stolen lamb three days earlier suggests that he might have been the culprit, even though this was inconsistent with his normal crimes.

Francis Shipman was the first of the *Calcutta* convicts to receive an official position on the civil establishment when he became clerk to Collins in March 1804 and public storekeeper to Fosbrook six months later. He had done a good job directing the loading of stores at Port Phillip. Until then some of the settlers had served as superintendents. Collins recommended that Shipman receive a free pardon together with Matthew Power. Governor King agreed and by January 1805 the two men had joined the class of free persons.[30] The following year Power and John Fawkner became the first *Calcutta* convicts to receive grants of land, although wives had received some considerations.[31] The wife of Thomas Peters already had a grant of forty acres in her own name and the favoured Mrs Anchor and Mrs Power, as well as the widow of Nicolas Piroelle, had accumulated stock. Prisoners who owned stock included Grove, Margetts, Fawkner, Peters, Michaels, Ronaldson, Jacobs, Pendridge, Carmichael, Manby, Pope and Thomas Riley.[32] All these men had probably had some money to make purchases while the *Calcutta* was at Rio de Janeiro and the Cape.

The first return of livestock and land which Collins sent from the Derwent shows that some of the women held stock and land in their own names. It has been noted that Bowen intervened to have Martha Hayes declared a free settler in her own right and provided her with some stock. Sarah Piroelle was on the first return as the possessor of two fowls, while Fanny Anchor had six fowls and a sow and Hannah Power six fowls. By October 1806 Martha Hayes had received her land grant of fifty acres and had increased her stock considerably. Matthew Power's name began to

appear in place of his wife's, when he became free. Elizabeth Peters was again named a female proprietor occupying a forty-acre grant, together with her two children, and the convict assigned to her as a servant was her husband. The wives of other favoured *Calcutta* men who had servants (their husbands) were Hannah Fawkner, Hannah Power and Jane Hangan. In time these husbands were classed as settlers even before receiving their formal pardons.

Janet Gunn, the daughter of Superintendent Patterson, had thirty acres at Hangan's Point in her own name. She grew wheat and barley while her husband, still a convict, was occupied as a shipwright. This land later became the test-case in a dispute in which Governor Macquarie held that Collins had no right to make land grants.[33]

The policy of allowing some women and children to accompany their breadwinner to a distant land therefore had significant results. Most wives of convicts immediately became recognised settlers, themselves employing labour, rather than becoming servants to their husband or anyone else. To be a female in the early days had both distinct social advantages and bargaining power, especially if a wife became a favourite of one of the officers. They assuredly formed the nucleus of a 'respectable' society, proving that a family-like structure had a special role to play in the development of a community which would benefit greatly from the calibre of most of its founding mothers. In a quiet way they portrayed a strength of purpose and character that was rare at other times in the history of Australia's earliest colonies.

John Pascoe Fawkner paid tribute to the women who came in the *Calcutta* and criticised the Reverend John West for his uncharitable remarks that the 'morals of the officers, or of the women, were not superior either to the service or the times'. Fawkner thought the sneer undeserved for the sobriety, chastity and prudent and moral conduct, which he thought irreproachable, of the far greater proportion of them. Some, he thought, were bad and debased, but by far the greater number behaved well and proved themselves to be 'good wives, tender mothers, and guides to the rising generation'. The children of loose liaisons in particular were well behaved and he resisted mentioning their names because of their contribution to the colony.[34]

The elder Fawkner was to have three wives in his time and only one surviving daughter, as well as his famous son, by his resourceful first wife Hannah. They had lost two babies in infancy. The young Elizabeth was a capable girl whom Hannah was able to leave in charge of her father and brother during a three-year visit to England in 1806. Hannah had come into an inheritance from her father. An opportune moment came for her to accompany Mrs Bate, wife of the Deputy Judge Advocate, who had not long arrived in the colony and wished to return. She needed a maid and Hannah seized her opportunity, leaving in the whaler *Ocean* and returning in June 1809 on the *Aeolus* with a small fortune. She must have been glad of the break away from a husband who had begun to drink very heavily whenever he could lay his hands on a bottle of rum. It was enough to turn his son off drinking alcohol forever, but he was not averse to making money from it. At least Fawkner senior held on to his land. Young Fawkner welcomed his mother's return with great joy. To Johnny she was the 'best of mothers . . . holy, divine, amiable, truthful'. They had had a tough time with the father's excessive drinking while she was absent.[35]

There was further joy in the family when Elizabeth married Thomas Green, one of the young *Calcutta* convicts who had tried to escape in the *Myrtle* but whom Collins had believed a fitting person to receive a pardon by 1807. Within three years the Fawkners had a grandson and granddaughter. Elizabeth would lose both her husband and baby girl within four months. She was another woman settler faced with running a small farm, which adjoined the farms of her father and brother at Glenorchy.[36]

Thomas Fitzgerald, an embezzler, was the first to be officially recognised as a schoolteacher. He and Samuel Warriner had conducted lessons among the children during the voyage of the *Calcutta*. He began evening classes in Hobart Town at least as early as 1807, two years before he would have been free of his seven-year sentence. He was also a clerk in the Lieutenant Governor's office, responsible for the payment of salaries and serving the Bench of Magistrates. Warriner became Collins' chief clerk, a superintendent, and before his premature death in 1813 rose to the position of postmaster. His signature appears on many of the early official documents.[37]

The Groves were among the first to be regarded rather as settlers than as convict class. They lived well and happily, encouraged by the close friendships they had formed with Collins and Knopwood. Grove believed that 'God has made this thorny bed a bed of roses — this bitter cup the sweetest draught that ever I took in life . . . there is not a place on earth I would, at this moment wish to be in preference to the present'.[38]

Knopwood regularly reported the social activities of the Grove family and their special relationship with Collins. He celebrated his forty-third birthday with them with a seven-pound crayfish he had caught and they tried unsuccessfully to bargain for some sheep from a whaler, the *Richard and Mary*. Knopwood always referred to them as 'Mr and Mrs Groves' with a deference he reserved only at that time for two other convicts, Matthew Power and William Thomas Stocker.

Susannah Grove was flattered by the attentions of Knopwood and his respect for her and her small boy Daniel, whom he treated like a son. During a visit to Bruny Island he marked a tree with the initials 'D.G.' to honour the young Daniel. Governor King allowed a conditional emancipation for Grove when Collins recommended it because of Grove's ingenuity, usefulness and good behaviour which might leave him 'a few steps of the ladder higher than where he is now', King could not allow a full pardon for one who had been capitally reprieved, nor could Governor Macquarie when Edward Lord made further approaches in 1810. His crime of forgery on the Bank of England was too serious to extend the royal mercy.[39] He would die an unofficially free person.

By the end of the first year there were many durable and reasonably comfortable huts which industrious prisoners had constructed. Many of the early houses probably looked like the one occupied by George Harris in a sketch he made in 1804. He wrote to his mother that, although formerly living in a rented canvas house, he now had a miserable thatched hovel of two rooms, with two windows, one door, and one chimney and no garden or land. He paid £50 annually in rent while the Governor had 'built *elegant houses* for *convicts* where the wife was a favourite'. He found he could not visit the houses of other officers who had made female companions of these and other women, especially after his marriage to Ann Jane Hobbs.[40]

Humphrey proudly described the small house, which Collins named 'the house in the woods', the first in Hobart Town, which he and Lieutenant Lord had built. He acknowledged how much assistance they had received from the Governor who had given them nails, locks, glass, paint, a fire stove, pitch and tar for the top, and men to help. They had an acre of ground. The house itself consisted of four rooms in which he was able to keep his apparatus. The Sladdens occupied a second room after their later arrival from Port Phillip. Lord occupied the third room and the fourth served as a sitting room. The total cost was £50. Although offered more for it, Humphrey acknowledged that within a year it would be worth five times as much.

He was disappointed that the length of chimney he had ordered to be sent from England with the stores did not arrive. He had to ask a favour from Collins to add to the unsatisfactory three feet he had, but he was aware that he would be impoverishing the store of its tin. Some of his equipment was not as he had ordered and the quality poor. The crucibles were of the one size and without covers.[41]

Knopwood was able to get Forsha, one of William Collins' oarsmen, and George Munday to build his cottage at Battery Point. They collected rushes to thatch the roof, but before they could put them up,

The 'miserable hovel' of surveyor George Harris and his wife Ann Jane. It was the prototype of the first mean dwellings.

the kitchen caught fire, destroying the stove as well as spreading to the garden where the fruit trees suffered. For many years the high-spirited chaplain would extend his customary hospitality from Cottage Green. Knopwood lent his man Thomas Salmon to help James Grove cut rails and rafters for his new house, perhaps under Gunn's supervision. It appears to have been a substantial construction surrounded by a good garden and built on the corner of Collins and Harrington Streets in 1805. Fosbrook chose to have his own cottage on the far side of the rivulet. There he might more privately woo the wife of Daniel Anchor and utilise the services of his assigned man Robert Waring.[42]

Yet for all the activity Collins himself did not choose to live in any sort of abode that might be in keeping with his office. He remained in the prefabricated dwelling he had brought from England, in much less style than some of his colleagues. He did recognise that his limited resources had to be used in the best possible way. His men could not work well unless they were well fed. In the early years many workers had to be diverted to hunt for food to keep them fit, rather than to construct unnecessarily elaborate buildings.

By April 1805 the people were all occupying huts but could not move from one to another. Their names were listed on the boards outside each one, the person whose name was on the top being responsible for cleanliness and good order, as well as for taking all precautions against the possibility of fire, which was a perennial risk. During the next years fires did occur, often with tragic results. Cooking within the huts was always a danger, while carelessness and occasionally arson caused loss of life and stock as well as loss of property. Michael Michaels was one of the first to lose his house by fire.[43]

King did his best to supply the new establishment with extra women, when they were available. In January 1805 he managed to send in William Collins' whaler, the *Sophia*, thirty female convicts who had arrived at Port Jackson in the *Experiment*. Among these were some useful and well behaved women. But Collins did not think highly of them all. He had hoped that he would receive female convicts direct from England, before they had been tainted by life at Port Jackson. He was concerned that one in particular, whom he remembered from earlier days, Elizabeth Leonard alias Kellyhorn, was a 'Veteran in Infamy'. She was already in her fifties when she arrived in Hobart Town. She would be no use at all as a breeder of good young colonists, but was seemingly good at spreading her evil practices.[44]

On the other hand, Collins himself attracted no such complaints for his efforts. Rather, the male population welcomed any women who arrived and even those females whose characters had not been very good in the past, improved after marriage and the establishment of a family in a new environment — that is, those who married *Calcutta* convicts. It was the invasion of secondary offenders, both male and female, the scum of Port Jackson, who came in later times to fill the penitentiaries at Macquarie Harbour, Port Arthur and Maria Island, who proved that transportation was not necessarily a deterrent to crime.

Knopwood continued to enjoy the vivacious company of the Hayes women. Mary, with her experience as a milliner, occupied herself plaiting straw from the local grasses as well as breeding dogs, which were in great demand. She could sell the puppies for £10 each. When Joseph Holt, who probably knew Mary at Port Jackson, visited them he took a bottle of good rum, which contributed to a very pleasant visit.

Gradually other women arrived in Hobart Town. Officers who were without wives or mistresses went to Port Jackson to select a female companion. Lieutenants Johnson and Lord both brought back women, Mildred Rose alias Harrison and Maria Riseley, with whom they cohabited for some time. Johnson had acquired some stock and, wishing to extend it, had applied for a land grant of five hundred acres. This was not granted. Collins informed Governor King that 'a Female has arrived here under the Protection of Lieut. Johnson, but I have not received any Intimation of this circumstance from your Excellency'. When Sladden, now a captain, and his wife returned to England, Collins acquired their house Cottage Farm, at Sandy Bay at the cost of £800 for the Commissariat, intending to turn it into a school. Instead he leased it to Johnson for one year for £60, where Knopwood enjoyed the Johnsons' company from time to time.[45]

It was made of lath and plaster, whitewashed and floored throughout, with a thatched roof, and probably not unlike but certainly larger than the one occupied by George and Ann Harris. It had two sitting rooms, thirteen by twelve feet, a hall eight by nine feet, a study eight by eight feet, and a bedroom and kitchen, each fourteen by twelve feet. There was a weatherboard barn, a sheep pen, a garden well paled in and about ten acres of land in cultivation.[46]

Mildred appears to have had a son who, soon afterwards, nearly lost his life when his clothes caught fire. The following year Mildred gave birth to Johnson's daughter, baptised Maria on 1 August, shortly before the father, by then a captain, returned to England leaving his family behind.[47]

Edward Lord and Maria Riseley then occupied the house. Knopwood's observations over the next three years occasionally mentioned 'Mr Lord's friend' with some discretion. Lord and Maria Riseley had a child before the end of 1807. Knopwood christened it on New Year's Day 1808 and soon afterwards married the parents.[48]

It would be about this time that William Williams, free by servitude, was working for or caring for Mildred Harrison. Knopwood continued to entertain her at dinner. In September 1809 James Belbin served on a jury at the inquest on the body of a female child, stillborn to Mildred Harrison. On 6 November Knopwood married her to Williams, with Stocker as a witness. Johnson had apparently left Mildred and her child provided for, with a long-term lease of valuable land in Macquarie Street adjoining trader T. W. Birch, and, one assumes, the stock in hand which was the basic stock from which Williams built up his own holdings. Williams worked as a clerk and receiver of money for the Police Fund, which had control of all public monies.[49]

Likewise Humphrey became attached to a young woman, Harriet Sutton, daughter of a convict storekeeper at Newcastle. Her father took action against Humphrey in the Court of Civil Jurisdiction after Humphrey had ignored Governor King's command forbidding all persons against 'harbouring or illegally secreting the said Harriet Sutton'. Five guineas had been offered as a reward for her return. But somehow she arrived at the Derwent and Knopwood put the seal of approval on 'Mr Humphrey's friend' when he entertained her, although it was six years after their meeting that he married them. There were continuous moves to have her returned to her father.[50]

One cannot help but query the father's motives in trying so desperately to prevent his daughter from associating herself with a man in Humphrey's position, one of the least profligate and most honest of all the civil officers in the colony. If William Sutton had been a widower he might have felt he was losing a housekeeper. He obviously regarded his daughter as his personal property. Such an interpretation even suggests a more sinister reason for keeping her under his roof. Incest as well as rape were among the many vices perpetrated upon women at Port Jackson. Life in Hobart Town with Humphrey, whether married or not, was obviously preferable to the young girl to living in semi-slavery with her father.

Dr Bowden brought up a family of two children

who were left, according to his tombstone at St David's Park in Hobart, 'with a disconsolate mother to lament the loss of their dear protector who *fulfilled* [my italics] the duties of an affectionate husband a tender father and a faitful [*sic*] friend'. This was Maria Sergeant, who had married her soldier-husband just before the *Calcutta* sailed and deserted him during the voyage.[51]

Collins knew that if he were to attract more free settlers they would need to trade their surplus produce after they had supplied the Commissariat. He remembered that the plans for a settlement at Botany Bay insisted that the public stores receive the products of all labour so there was little incentive for private enterprise. Many of the early settlers, particularly those on Norfolk Island, had given up their farms to join the ranks of corruption in the New South Wales Corps. The situation in Van Diemen's Land should have been different. Even though he had brought out free settlers, who expected to receive large land grants, Collins found they were mostly of a calibre that did not match the quality of many of the convicts. He decided to establish a government farm at New Town, not far from the land allocated to the settlers at Stainsforth Cove. He had wheat, oats and rye in cultivation and erected a barn, hoping for favourable results from the reaping of grain. He found his purchases of seed from the Cape were rewarding. None of the English seed germinated because it did not survive the heat of the passage.[52]

Thirty-five persons were put to work on agricultural production and care of the government stock which, together with that in private hands, amounted to 334 animals. There would have been more but for the losses during the second voyage of the *Ocean* from Port Phillip. Several pigs which managed to survive soon died after feeding on a species of grass that poisoned them. It took some twenty years before the colony had enough free persons, including many ex-convicts, capable of providing sufficient grain with which they could trade profitably without having to sell at the fixed price to the public stores. To supplement rations they gathered the plentiful mesembry-anthemum which climbed along the beaches, finding it a good substitute for traditional green vegetables which were scarce.

Governor King had rapidly put into force arrangements for replenishing stock at the Derwent. He contracted with merchant Robert Campbell to deliver Bengal breeding cattle and other animals to stock the government farm. Two hundred and fifty-six arrived in the *Lady Barlow* in August 1804 and by the following February Collins was able to inform Lord Hobart of a significant increase in the livestock by some 419 animals. Before the end of the year the cattle had produced eighty-five calves. Unfortunately the rest of the cargo in the *Lady Barlow* consisted of weevilly flour and rancid pork. The quality of the casks was so poor that the pickle had run out.[53]

There was no guarantee that supplies would be regular. News from England was disquieting and infrequent. It seemed they were a forgotten people. Settlers and convicts or their wives with any currency or means of barter were encouraged to purchase stock from American whalers or any other incoming ships. Coinage from ships was grasped whenever possible, the countermarked or overstruck Spanish dollars being particularly sought after because of their international appeal. English copper coins which had appeared at Port Jackson in 1799 became inflated in value with the result that visiting sea captains, who preferred the silver Spanish dollar, placed extortionate prices on goods they knew the people in the colonies needed. Bank notes were in common usage among the colonists who had them, but those with only their labour to offer relied heavily on promissory notes, often signed with a cross. When Michael Michaels, who had obviously come to the colony with money other than the counterfeit notes found in his possession, left for England in 1812 he had £2256 7s 4d owing to him. Most of this would have been for goods obtained from his store. Surprisingly, through his agents and Knopwood who held his power of attorney, Michaels appears to have received most of this back in the course of time from customers who had established good credit with him.[54]

22 THE HUNGRY YEARS

*T*HE ORIGINAL STORES brought in the *Ocean* had been enough for two years. The settlement remained at full rations for a while, but the effects of the war in Europe began to be felt by the end of 1805. Supplies from England to Port Jackson were diminishing. Wheat for harvesting was still scarce so that flour, and also sugar, were the first items to be severely rationed. Collins found history repeating itself. He remembered the famine when they had settled at Sydney Cove, the isolated years when they had watched on the headlands for any ship that might bring supplies to alleviate their hunger. He despaired when those which sailed into the Derwent did not bring enough food to ameliorate their condition, the more so when their cargo consisted of more mouths to feed. Had it not been for the hunting of the kangaroo and emu and the availability of fish in the warmer weather, supplies of meat would have been extremely short well before rationing had to be introduced in May 1805.[1] They all felt they had been forgotten and forsaken.

The Commissary, anxious to obtain as much fresh meat as possible, offered payment for any game taken, unwittingly giving the impetus, on their being freed to hunt, for prisoners to abscond. For some it was worth a taste of freedom and some additional payment for their booty. In many cases punishments were not carried out. The eye of authority could feign blindness if men returned with meat.

To help alleviate the lack of meat supplies, Knopwood spent much time in his boat fishing, often with little success. He and other officers despatched their more trustworthy servants with dogs and guns to hunt kangaroos. Knopwood was always losing or changing servants.[2] Humphrey was satisfied with his men, Thatcher and Robert Kennedy. He found it sensible to be in partnership with Edward Lord, who could mind his stock during his absences. They purchased five dogs at £25 each which would kill 1 000 pounds of kangaroo a week. They also formed a barter system, providing the captains of ships with fresh meat in

exchange for flour. They found the skins would sell at four shillings each to make shoes for the women. They had in stock twenty fowls, a goat and kid, two sows, pigs and a goose, and bought a cow and a calf for £45 and eight sheep at £5 a head. They also had in store a large stock of Indian corn which they obtained from the *Lady Barlow*.[3]

The near-famine was to last for years. This included the most terrible, tragic situation of all — a shortage of spirits. 'Not a glass of spirits in the colony to be had', lamented Knopwood in August 1805 when even shorter rations of meat and flour had to be introduced. 'You may see distress in everyone's countenance', he wrote in October. His men, who included John Gain and Thomas Salmon, combined to bring in one kangaroo which, when skinned and cleaned, weighed 105 pounds. In just over two months they killed sixty-six, producing 2 153 pounds of meat valued at £107.[4]

The kangaroo was the main supply of food for the native population. The more dangerous escapees, becoming bushrangers and living off the land in their desperation to gain freedom, were not the most desirable persons to confront a native race. Not only were the Aborigines forced to attack and spear those who were depriving them of their traditional food, but they also found some of the interlopers were seducing their womenfolk. Such a distressing situation was to have disastrous social effects on the relationship between the Aboriginal and white cultures. In time it would be the survival of the fittest.

During the shortages Harris, on his miserable annual salary of £91 5s, mourned that he could not afford some nice feminine attire for his new wife. He wrote home for ribbons, a straw bonnet, stockings and some beaver hats. He found that cloth sold locally for a pair of pantaloons cost seven guineas, hats were three guineas, boots three to five, and shoes twenty-five a pair. More importantly there was no tea, sugar, coffee, soap, candles, oil, wine, spirits, beer, porter, cheese or butter available in February 1806 and even the coinage to buy what might have been available

The abundant wild life supplemented the meagre rations of the Europeans at the expense of the natives.

was lacking. But he was collecting furs and feathers to send home for muffs and tippets.[5]

The following October he wrote that his dear Anne Jane had not tasted bread for a fortnight because of the famine. Crops had failed. There was no flour from England. In 1807 they were living on coffee made from bran, without sugar, and kangaroo fried in rancid pork fat. The arrival of a ship from India brought some tea and rice but rations were down to two pounds of salt pork each week per person. A second-grade piece of cloth for a pair of pantaloons cost him £23. Paper was scarcer than ever which prevented him from accomplishing any work. He asked for more newspapers, drawing paper, black lead and camel-hair pencils, explaining that he had made a vast number of rough drawings of natural history but could not finish them for want of more paper. His servants had stolen all that he had in one night.[6] Harris complained for years that he was hampered in his work, of which only a few sketches survive, because he had so little paper on which to draw. Other painting and sketching materials had either not been sent or had been lost. He has often been described as indolent but one must

spare some sympathy for him, recognising his frustrations and the effect of the increasing attacks of epilepsy which would cause his premature death in 1810.[7]

Bowden, writing to his attorney in London in October 1805, confirmed that a whaler brought a scanty supply when there were only three weeks' provisions in the stores. He complained that not only had they been treated with great inattention by Governor King, but that any comfort received from Port Jackson had been sold at an enormous rate.[8] Robert Jones, known as 'Buckey', formerly a gaoler on Norfolk Island, reminisced that they often had to eat seaweed as a vegetable.[9] Matters were so serious by May 1806 that Collins convened his Bench of Magistrates to consider the present state of the settlement. They discussed the best way of regulating the high price of provisions and examined the position of bakers as well as how best they might defend the stores. They decided there should be no more than four bakers, who were to include two of the *Calcutta* convicts. One of these was Thomas Riley, whose earlier avocations as stocking weaver and soldier in the Royal Artillery were far removed from the baking of a loaf. The other was John Edwards, who had once been a clerk in London. Sarah Piroelle, the widow of the French confectioner, and Richard Coleman were the other bakers. Between them they became responsible for the entire production of the settlement's bread supply during the next six months at regulated prices for each loaf. Eightpence a pound was the charge for the best bread and fourpence halfpenny for inferior, with penalties up to £10 for persons offering or giving more.[10]

'It is truly lamentable to see the distress that the people are in' wrote Knopwood in October. 'Not a man able to do any work . . . All our poultry are dying having nothing to give them. The poor piggs [sic] . . . are all dying and at this season we should have young ducks and chickings [sic]. My poor pigeons are all most dead for want of provisions — only 4 remaining out of 16'.[11] As they scanned the horizon for ships during the years of famine many were hopeful that some of the supplies would be liquid. But some relief had arrived when the whaler *King George* sailed into port with a supply of salt provisions and enough spirits for Knopwood to collect fifteen gallons of rum. The following day his men brought in a large haul of fish, a fitting repast to celebrate the first anniversary of the Battle of Trafalgar.[12]

Collins' attitude towards spirits was evident over and over again. He refused to condone drunkenness but had little chance of preventing it. He found that some employers providing convicts with raw spirits in exchange for their labour created the problem of increased absenteeism from duty. He punished two and directed that no more than half a pint of spirits — a liberal enough allowance — should ever be paid to a prisoner in one day.[13] This was the amount allowed on special occasions, such as the King's birthday or for rewarding a prisoner for extra labour or other consideration. It gave every man a chance to drown his sorrows.

Unless they were servants to officers who had access to liquor, the early years were very abstemious ones for the ordinary convict. It was necessary to caution those who might forgo the odd reward by selling their ration to others. Sergeant Thorne discovered William Marsh had obtained an extra bottle of spirits in March 1807 and was supplying convicts who were creating a disturbance among the military patrol. They were confined to the guardhouse, tried and punished with either 200 or 100 lashes: 'All but Salmon', noted Knopwood of his servant, 'who was drunk'.[14] Knopwood probably did not care to incapacitate him for any longer period than his recovery after a hangover.

For the first few years the production of liquor was barely thought of while rations of rum and porter arrived in the colony at uncertain intervals. When Collins sent the brewer Thomas Rushton to Port Jackson, he could not foresee that some fifteen years later Lieutenant Jeffreys would state that all India 'might be supplied with malt liquor from the barley and hops

which V. D.'s L. is capable of producing'.[15] On one occasion when a quantity of barley arrived, Collins discovered some of the people were using their ration for brewing. He had to threaten a penalty of £20 for any settler who did not obey his orders countermanding this practice, and other serious punishments for defiant convicts.[16]

There were also restrictions on what the officers themselves could obtain. Collins reminded them of the well-known evils resulting from the illicit trade in spirits at Port Jackson. He was determined to clamp down on any such practice his officers might engage in. He prohibited their trading with ships entering the harbour, an order that contributed to antagonism between him and the rapacious Lieutenant Lord. Later at the northern settlement established by Governor King at Port Dalrymple, Lieutenant-Governor William Paterson threatened to withdraw spirits from his detachment because he found his officers were frequently drunk.[17] In 1806 some of his prisoners disappeared forever with the brig *Venus*, which had on board gallons of spirits and a barrel of porter consigned to Hobart Town.[18]

Collins assured King that he would however allow liquor to be landed at fixed prices. The masters of ships intent on selling spirits must have the approval of His Excellency. But this did not prevent a certain amount of trafficking with the captains of American or other ships who were not subject to rules made in Sydney. The social comings and goings of those whose survival appeared to be largely dependent on alcohol is well documented in Knopwood's diary. The interminable number of occasions when he and his cronies accepted hospitality on board almost every visiting ship bears witness to that. The colony had been running dry for some time when the brig *Duchess of York* arrived from India in March 1807 with a cargo of rum. All the inhabitants appear to have gone on a spree, in spite of Governor Bligh's order and Collins' efforts to prevent the bartering of all commodities, as well as labour, in exchange for spirits. The Captain entertained Collins and Mrs Power on board as well as Knopwood, who reported that they took tiffin and 'a quantity of spirits was landed and almost everyone was drunk'. The chaplain alone bought 228 gallons and nearly every day for the next fortnight he was unwell.[19]

During this period of laxity the slaying of a bullock and arson on the house of Mrs Peters were among the crimes committed. Soldiers and servants caused disturbances and received floggings up to 200 lashes.[20] Matthew Power had to appear before the magistrates after obtaining bills of credit the previous October for spirits and other provisions to the value of £538 11s. These he had received on behalf of Fosbrook from Captain Moody of the whaler *King George*. After examination, Knopwood reported that the Judge Advocate's Court had 'sat late upon the business' and after a further sitting the next morning the magistrates sent the proceedings to the Lieutenant-Governor. 'He was dissatisfied with them and requested that the magistrates would alter their opinion in sendin [*sic*] Mr Power to Sydney, but we would not', commented Knopwood. Collins informed Judge Bate that it was unnecessary to send Power to Sydney, as no fraud (criminal offence) had been established. One cannot help but wonder at the strange and accommodating relationship between Collins and the Powers.[21]

By April 1808 Collins, at last accepting the inevitable, allowed the landing and bonding of a large quantity of spirits from the brig *Perseverance* belonging to Campbell & Co. in Sydney. He allocated issues ranging from two gallons each for male and female prisoners to forty gallons for civil and military officers.[22]

By this time several houses were disposing of liquor, inspected nightly by the military patrol until the beating of the tattoo, after which it was illegal to drink in public. There would be severe punishments, including ironing, for convicts incapable of attending government work.

It was a bacchanalian occasion when the civil and military officers celebrated the opening of the first recorded public house, the Sign of the Whale Fishery on 25 July 1807. One of Collins' servants, Thomas (Alexander?) Hopkins, was the licensee. While all were delighting in the merriment of the occasion, William Collins had his house robbed. Soon afterwards the printer, Francis Barnes, became licensee of the Hope Inn, which he conducted from George's Square.[23]

With the distribution of further land grants, mainly to convicts who had families, came convict servants, a practice that was a constant irritation to Norfolk Islanders, who had arrived free in 1807 and had found labour scarce and expensive.[24] Although most had been convicts or were the offspring of convicts, they resented the distinction, especially when they found some wives had land in their own right and their husbands assigned to them.

Two simple words give an indication to one famous convict's entirely different attitude to women. James Lord, forty-four years of age when sentenced at Halifax, Yorkshire, for stealing three bushels of oats, rose from burning charcoal for the blacksmiths to being a rich farmer, grazier and inn-keeper. He had left his wife Grace and children behind, yet his son David, when he sent for him in 1815, soon became the richest man in the colony. But the two simple words, pencilled in a great-grandson's copy of *Historical Records of Australia*, III, i, alongside one paragraph in a letter from Collins to Bligh in October 1806 relating

to the arrival of some females on the *King George*, were 'more Vimmen!'[25] Surely this refers to a little bit of oral history in the Lord family. They tell us a lot about the man. Not unexpectedly, he had a north country accent, pronouncing w's as v's. They also suggest that he was a bit of a misogynist who resented the arrival of any more women in the male environment. He made no attempt to bring his wife to Van Diemen's Land. There is no suggestion of any women in his life in the colony. He was probably too intent on adding to his wealth, selling spirits without a licence. He himself remained a model of sobriety but took advantage of those who had mortgaged their farms to him for a bottle of rum an acre. Yet in later years a contemporary described him to J. E. Calder as 'a remarkably civil person and a general favourite'. He dressed peculiarly to the last and quite with the style of the previous century, with knee breeches and with large buckles on his shoes.[26]

Nevertheless, sex was a form of currency alive and well in the community. It was, to those who had it for disposal, worth more than any silver dollars or stock. Sex could buy almost anything. John Pascoe Fawkner summed the situation up in a nutshell when he wrote that Matthew Power, when still a convict, 'had no property except it was his good-looking wife'. He was able to barter her (and she was very willing to oblige) for a lease, a pardon by 1805, and then a fifty-acre grant of land adjoining Collins' garden. He also had a job as printer and confidant of the Governor. Her position as first lady remained unchallenged for years. Fawkner remains on record as criticising Collins for what he believed was unforgiveable conduct, 'most injurious to the colonists and is yet felt in Tasmania'.[27]

Collins had expected to be relieved of duty in 1807 and hoped to recommend more deserving convicts for pardons before he left. Yet he remained in Hobart for reasons unknown, perhaps because he believed his wife Maria would arrive. He had been faithful to her, in his fashion. He wrote to his brother in September: 'Maria informed me that I might shortly expect her here . . . She will be a great comfort to me . . . yet I can hardly think she will leave her mother . . .'[28]

By this time the Powers were planning to return to England. If Maria had joined her husband there would have been no real embarrassments. She had known long before of her husband's children by Ann Yeates, for in 1793 she had written to him while he was still at Port Jackson about gossip spread in England by Major Roger Ross whom Maria found 'very bitter in his mention of you . . . ' She also wrote that he had been very delicate in her presence but she knew from David's mother that he had spoken disrespectfully of his conduct. Her husband's letter received that day had filled 'her heart with anxiety, it wants the tenderness I have been used to meet from you; but yet I will hope and often that . . . I am with truth of heart your ever affectionate wife.'[29] Ann Yeates had long since faded from Collins' life although she was still alive at Port Jackson at the time of Collins' death in 1810.[30] He had, however, welcomed their children, George and Mariamne Laetitia, during their several visits to Hobart. Knopwood frequently enjoyed their company and that of Mariamne's husband, the American-born Captain Samuel Rodman Chase, whose trading activities had begun when sealing in Bass Strait in 1798. He was a partner with William Campbell in the ill-fated brig *Harrington*.[31]

The free settlers on the whole proved to be unequal to the task of pioneering a new land and most made little effort to rise much beyond the class of peasant proprietor. They had had to face up to more problems than they had anticipated. They were, like the convicts, civil officers and the military, on public stores for two years from the time they had left England. They had then received small grants of land, mostly at Stainsforth Cove which became New Town. There they expected to be self-sufficient and well established within a short time. There were many obstacles, which Collins appreciated when he assigned them each an extra servant as long as they provided suitable accommodation in return. They were unable to exchange their convicts or hire them out. They were issued with grain, seeds and stock but were not allowed to dispose of ewes and their first lamb.[32]

One of the more useful settlers, William Nicholls, who had arrived with his wife Frances and three children, continued the work he had been given at Port Phillip as superintendent in charge of the carpenters. No one was to cut down any timber without his knowledge and Collins had to remind people that no one could interrupt Nicholls in the course of his duty. He was responsible to Collins alone. Maria Nicholls, one of his offspring, married the blacksmith John Pearsall, whose subsequent activities as a successful farmer at Clarence Plains were far removed from the County Court at Stafford.[33] When his son-in-law died, Nicholls' daughter and granddaughters would be known as 'land proprietors, merchants, bankers and professional persons'.[34] Nicholls was a more industrious farmer than most other early settlers. He also held a grazing licence between York Plains and Blackman's River.

If any had expected that, because they were free persons, they would receive large grants of lands, their hopes were soon dashed. They were not the types to form a society of colonial gentry. Only Richard Pitt, said to be a kinsman of William Pitt, became reasonably prosperous and even he, in later years, would not be too proud to follow the ex-convict John Wade as chief constable.[35] Pitt's wife did not accompany him to the colony, but the three children who

did married well and had numerous descendants. The trouble-maker John Hartley had good connections. The young settler Edward Ford Hamilton, son of a Scottish baronet, had been placed in the charge of Hartley, who not only had brought out his wife and child but also a German servant. Hartley, the best equipped of the settlers, and one who might have succeeded in the fisheries had he not behaved so objectionably, had left with his family soon after their arrival and Hamilton joined the whaler *King George*, later returning to England. Before leaving, Collins had to pay extortionate prices for the stock Hartley had for sale — an English sow and her offspring and £20 alone for a boar he had bought in Rio and which the settlement could not afford to lose.[36]

Some settlers were physically disadvantaged. Robert Littlejohn was, according to Fawkner, a poor broken-backed cripple, yet a first-rate water colour painter whose work does not appear to have survived. He was educated and tried to teach but could get no scholars. When he tried to farm he failed.[37] The superintendent Thomas Clark had, as already noted, only one leg after his injury in the *Guardian* in 1789. Tom Issell was 'a dirty slothful fellow — a slothful encumberer of the earth' in Fawkner's eyes. He failed and left the colony. Thomas Preston was lazy and Thomas Hayes 'middling'.[38] Henry Hayes' greatest strength was his wife, who had borne the punishment for the crime for which he had been declared not guilty. The careers of the convict mother and her daughter were to prove far more successful than that of the settler Henry.

Those who had families such as the Pitts, Cockerills and Millers fared better than most, while the American widow, Jane Hobbs, provided the settlement with its most desirable commodity — four daughters without a 'convict stain' to 'taint' the next generation, as well as an explorer son. Two of the Cockerill daughters married a pair of the less successful *Ocean* settlers, Thomas Littlefield and John Dacres, and Mrs Cockerill's niece, Sophia Chilvers, married the pilot, Michael Mansfield whom she had met as a crew member of the *Ocean*. It was probably one of the Pitt daughters whom James Backhouse, the Quaker missionary, met in 1832 and who described those first years in Hobart Town as she remembered them from childhood:

. . . on landing was lodged with some others under a blanket supported by sticks, near the place where the Commissariat Office now stands . . . After spending a night there, they were removed to the spot where the village of New Town now stands, and lodged in a hollow tree. Here they were first visited by the Aborigines, with whom the children were often left, and who treated them kindly. Provisions becoming scarce, the people often cooked maritime plants collected on the sea shore . . . Sometimes they collected for food the crap or refuse of the blubber of whales, out of which the oil had been taken by whaling vessels and which was washed up on the shores . . .[39]

One of the great advantages for those who received land grants was the proximity to great rivers. Even before the building of roads, navigable rivers played a vital role in the development of Hobart Town. Boats and ferries began to operate and were a cheap form of transport, enabling timber and other industries to emerge. The harnessing of water power was important to farmers who had no distance to send their grain to flour mills. Even so, settlers were anxious to establish better communication with the centre of activities and met together to submit to the Lieutenant-Governor a plan for a convenient road and a bridge across the town rivulet that separated the farms. They would contribute towards the cost of the road and elected Thomas Hayes, who was a millwright by trade, as their representative. He was to execute the plan in co-operation with the lame superintendent, Thomas Clark, who had agreed to provide the bullocks.[40]

By 1807 Collins was recommending for pardon several of his more useful convicts who had behaved well. In the case of the capable and shrewd Andrew Whitehead who managed the government farm, the pardon was absolute. His printer, Francis Barnes, and the newly appointed overseer John Avery were to receive conditional remissions along with Prestage, Manby, Richard Brown and, surprisingly, Thomas Green, whose attempt to escape in the *Myrtle* must have been forgiven. He was a literate young man and perhaps already attached to the well regarded Fawkner family.[41]

The horse-stealer Manby was one who had already begun to speculate in the building trade. He had actually been a butcher and had brought his family in the *Calcutta*. Although he had a sentence for life, Collins had made him one of his earliest stock-keepers. Fosbrook's assistant William Maum, from Norfolk Island, described him as a 'very decent man' who had built a shell of a good house by January 1808, with two front rooms and a skilling. Maum, acting as agent, offered it for sale to a Norfolk Island settler, Robert Nash, for £150.[42] Ten years later Manby was offering the same house, or a similar one, for sale as a 'tyled' [*sic*] dwelling house near the government garden at the upper end of Macquarie Street, consisting of a parlour, bedroom and kitchen with outhouses and ground nearby adjoining Davey Street.[43]

There was a general feeling in 1807-08, when some 554 Norfolk Islanders arrived to settle in Van Diemen's Land, that they would be a useful and hard-working group, bringing fresh skills and benefits. They were mostly free by servitude, mostly Irish, mostly troublesome and very demanding. They did not relish the thought of immediate hard work, having presumed they would receive assigned servants and other benefits. There was no easy solution because there were relatively few labourers available. The majority of the *Calcutta* convicts were either already employed on government works or were assigned to other settlers, officers or wives of convicts. Apart from the few who had already received pardons, many had almost served their seven-year sentences and were well on the way to receiving indulgences for good behaviour and good work or preparing to leave the colony. A few would always be delinquents who absented themselves from duty over and over again. The Norfolk Islanders created a bad impression of Van Diemen's Land among those who would arrive in the later removal from Norfolk Island. Some would, according to Robert 'Buckey' Jones, injure themselves in order that they might not have to go and others ate sand or drank large quantities of salt water to make themselves ill.[44] As free settlers they had expected to become immediate landowners and employers of labour themselves. They did have a grievance. Some had been First Fleeters and free for a long time, with adult families who had been born free. Already some of the best jobs had gone to *Calcutta* convicts. Those from Norfolk Island with farming experience were ultimately settled largely at New Norfolk, where Denis McCarty became the acknowledged and irascible leader of the group while others of a highly volatile nature, such as James Belbin, settled in the town.[45]

A very uneasy situation soon developed with the unexpected and controversial appearance of Governor Bligh after his deposition in Sydney.[46] It is no wonder that many convicts, having served their sentences, left the colony at this time. One Norfolk Islander in particular gained the favour of Governor Collins, replacing Hannah Power even before the latter left with her husband for England. William Collins described the young Margaret Eddington as 'most beautiful'; Fawkner thought she was 'good-looking'; but Bligh referred to her in scathing terms.[47]

23 CHASING THE WHALE

GOVERNOR COLLINS MADE one important new appointment, as his instructions allowed, that of William Collins as harbour master at fifteen shillings a day.[1] He was obviously the most capable man for the position. From the age of eight, when William entered Greenwich Naval College, the sea had been his life. He had served as master in the Merchant Navy and as Acting Lieutenant in the R.N. flagship in the Jamaica station.[2] His appointment gave the temperamental John Hartley a further chance to complain of the Governor's prejudice, whereupon he packed up his family in a fit of pique and left for Port Jackson where he fared no better. But William Collins had shown initiative and bravery in the two boat expeditions he had made from Port Phillip. He had wisely judged the right men among those who had volunteered to sail with him in the cutter to Port Jackson. David Collins could not afford to lose his services to any questionable private enterprise, although he knew William's heart was set on developing a private whale fishery. Regrettably, he remained harbour master for only four months from April 1804. During that time he explored both the Derwent and Huon Rivers. He superintended the construction of a wharf and stone store-house to replace the wooden hut on Hunter's Island. He also projected a magazine on the foreshore near the corner of the present Brooke and Morrison Streets. He, together with Dr Bowden and Captain McAskill, supervised the unloading of the cargo from the *Lady Barlow* and was aghast at the rottenness of the stores.[3]

Knopwood mentioned the presence of whales in the Derwent in their first winter, so close that boats had to keep in-shore to avoid collisions. The English whaler *Alexander* (Captain Rhodes), called at Hobart in July and stayed for several weeks. Jorgen Jorgensen, the adventurous Dane who had sailed as mate in the *Lady Nelson*, was aboard and claimed to have taken the first whale in the river. When Rhodes arrived at Port Jackson the following December he had a cargo of 210 tons of oil and seventy tons of bone. Fourteen thousand skins, which included kangaroos as well as seal, formed part of the cargo when the *Alexander* finally left Australian waters.[4]

In August, prior to his resignation, William Collins submitted an account of the prospects of whaling at the Derwent, which Governor Collins sent on to Lord Hobart. He had found many advantages to support the establishment of a South Sea whaling fishery, having observed considerable numbers of black whales in the months of July, August and September close to shore and in the shoals of the river. There was splendid timber for building boats and good spars for masts and yards. He envisaged that two or three ships not exceeding 250 tons each, supplied with provisions for three or four years and casks to hold 800 tons of oil, together with forty or fifty try-pots, would be enough to equip the industry.[5]

The skin trade with China was becoming temporarily depressed because of the competition from the Americans, who operated between the Siberian waters and the South Pacific. The best that the British could hope for was to provide a good market in England for the making of felt hats. By June 1804 Governor King was aware of the presence in the Straits of at least three American ships, the *Perseverance*, the *Pilgrim* and the *Charles* procuring sealskins for the China market. He had sent William Paterson as Lieutenant-Governor to form a settlement at Port Dalrymple.[6] King had heard that the Americans were actually building a vessel from the remains of the wreck of the *Sydney Cove* and had erected a semi-permanent abode on Cape Barren Island. This was contrary to a treaty signed in 1795 between England and the United States which prohibited any such action concerning the amity, commerce and navigation conducted between the two countries. There was bound to be trouble.

The best documented occasion was at Cape Barren in October 1804 when the American Captain Amaso Delano, master of the ship *Perseverance* and saviour of Lieutenant Bowen and his party of the *Integrity*, later picked a quarrel with Joseph Murrell, master of the

Surprise, a sloop belonging to Kable and Underwood. The outcome was a cruel and bloody fight. Both Murrell's and Delano's lengthy reports to Governor King and the published narrative of Delano are at variance. Any judgement as to which party was the more guilty or more provoked is still difficult to decipher. It probably represented a reasonably common situation when two rival parties met on sealing grounds which they regarded as their own domain. There is little wonder that King was anxious to see more settlement to protect British interests. The French had behaved in a civilised way compared with these ruffians. King realised they would be a greater threat if they continued to molest the people in the Strait.[7]

But this flagrant abuse of His Majesty's subjects, whom Delano had arraigned as only a 'convict-caste' of men, found King helpless to deal with the immediate situation. Delano had even persuaded some of the men employed by Robert Campbell and Kable and Underwood, as well as an escaped convict, to join his crew. They took with them sails, rigging and other implements for the procurement of skins and oil. Rewards offered for their apprehension brought no luck. Fortunately for the British, Delano and his men, satisfied with a valuable cargo, departed from Bass Strait and directed their future activities between Peru and Canton. They had not ventured far enough to understand how great a treasure trove in sealskins was still available for exploitation in the south seas.

William Collins sailed for Port Jackson towards the end of 1804, probably in the *Lady Barlow*, which he assisted in salvaging after its near wreckage in a severe storm in the harbour there. While there he discussed his plans with Governor King, who granted him rights to set up a bay whaling station. He became master of the *Sophia*, a 250-ton vessel acquired by Robert Campbell as the *Swift*, a Dutch prize captured near Amboyna. It had brought a welcome cargo of beef, clothing, wine and arrack intended for the Dutch garrison at Batavia. The ship had been an embarrassment to Campbell. Weighing more than 100 tons it exceeded the regulations allowed for trading spirits in the colony. Governor King was in a quandary, especially when he had chartered the ship from Campbell for six months for sealing purposes. The idea of using it at a whaling station seemed a good compromise.[8]

William Collins set out for Hobart, soon discovering that the *Sophia* was leaky. He had to put in to Botany Bay for repairs when carrying some thirty female convicts to Hobart. Also on board was the Governor's daughter, whom David Collins had not seen since infancy.

Governor Collins allocated a position at Ralph's Bay for William Collins to establish the first,

although unsuccessful, station in March 1806. Knopwood was not at all happy to have one of the stonemasons taken away from building his oven to work for William Collins. Observing through glasses what luck the latter might be having in his new venture proved to be too tempting for the inquisitive parson, who watched the boats chase three whales, killing one in Farm Bay and towing it down to the try-works.[9] Could this be the answer to the economic problems of New South Wales? The Derwent would be an ideal harbour for whalers from all over the world to call and trade. Its own inhabitants must get a local industry started to compete with those already in the Pacific trade. Experienced men from Nantucket and the London and Sydney-based shipowners who already knew the south seas had cornered most of the markets.

William Collins had employed Philip Strickland as his personal servant. It is likely that he also engaged the services of the experienced seamen who had accompanied him from Port Phillip to Port Jackson. Five of the six had received conditional pardons in December 1805 for their meritorious conduct. The sixth, James Price, had drowned while attempting escape in the *Myrtle* the previous February.[10]

Knopwood employed Christopher Forsha, another of Collin's emancipated men. He paid him a guinea a quarter to care for his boat but, according to Knopwood, the temptation was too much. Forsha planned with a group of convicts to seize one of the new whale boats and escape to New Zealand. Although questioned, there was not enough evidence to convict them. Forsha probably left the colony soon afterwards, a free man.[11]

William Collins bought 1500 gallons of spirits from the *Myrtle* while it was in port. This, added to 15000 gallons of rum that Campbell had smuggled from Bengal, caused King to inform Earl Camden of the daring contempt of His Majesty's instructions. He also referred to his own orders of 11 October 1801 that 'whenever Spirits, Wine, or any other Strong Drink are taken out of a ship on any account without the Governor's and Naval Officer's Permit, they become seizable wherever found'. He found it necessary to obtain Judge Advocate Atkins's interpretation of the regulations, who believed that neither Campbell nor William Collins could be charged with smuggling under statutory laws that could not apply to New South Wales, where there was neither a Customs House nor Revenue Officer.[12]

During one of its early voyages between Sydney and Hobart the *Sophia* left eight of Collins' men sealing at Oyster Bay. There they built a little hut but natives set fire to it and robbed them of their provisions. They had collected some 2000 skins and while absent on a visit to Maria Island the natives destroyed the skins. The *Nancy*, which had been sealing in the Straits, called by and discovered their plight, taking them aboard before returning northwards. The *Nancy* sank just south of Jervis Bay but most of the crew escaped. Captain Demaria reported that their survival and arrival in Sydney was due to the 'civility from the natives which would do credit to a more polished race of man, as it even extended to the liberal partition of their scanty fare among his little party when they were much exhausted', although a Sydney native who had accompanied them on the voyage unfortunately stole articles from the wreckage, including a useful axe, and abandoned them.[13]

Several *Calcutta* convicts were among the eight men rescued at Oyster Bay. These included Richard Wall, a sailor from Exeter, who later lost his life in the wreck of the *Nancy*; Henry Robinson from Kent who had been a sailor and William Smith a London fisherman; James Brown, a sailor from an East Indiaman and the Scotsman James or Archibald Campbell as well as the sailor-settler from the *Ocean*, Michael Mansfield.[14] During May they had announced their intention of leaving Port Jackson and appear to have sailed for Hobart Town in either the *Richard and Mary* or *Sophia*. This journey of the *Sophia* proved a difficult one for William Collins, who struck extremely rough seas. The desperate situation must have alarmed those who had already survived one shipwreck. He had to jettison much of the cargo of salted pork that was badly needed in Van Diemen's Land.[15]

The growing number of small whaling and sealing vessels continued to increase. The sealing captains would collect the skins from the gangs left in remote parts, return with them to Port Jackson, load up with a cargo of supplies for Hobart Town, and return once more to their gangs. At first the whalers operated close to the two ports, according to the number of whales they could tow to the try-works. Once established near the colonial shipyards they compensated for the loss of friendly ports in South America.[16]

The whalers were a hardy lot who lived for the day. It was dangerous and difficult work to steer the boat alongside the whale. Much precision was necessary to throw the harpoon high in the air at an angle and speed which would drive the barbed end most deeply into the target. Then they would tow the whale for some distance, allowing it to tire before the slaughter. Surely there is no smell on earth stronger or more unpleasant than the rendering of whale blubber! One can scarcely believe the tales of the old whaling days when men could chew the raw flesh, swilled down with endless rum. Old salts befuddled with booze told how they kept a permanent hole in their huts to hold the rum. When they could no longer stand up they might lie on the floor and lap it up. One would wish there had been many more tales recorded of the whale that got away. Did not Melville ascribe any honour or glory he might have attained to his whaling days? For to him 'a whaleship was my Yale College and my Harvard', and how many who set out on such journeys

The marine artist, William Duke, captured a lively scene at the rounding of a whale.

were suppressing, in their subconscious mind, the maniacal obsession to search for the great white whale?[17]

William Atkinson, together with John Green, one of the John Williams, Henry Robinson, John Davis, William Jones, Robert Kennedy, Charles Smith, James Byrne, Robert Barwise, Samuel Gray and Thomas Arnott were among the earliest of the *Calcutta* convicts who joined the scarred and tattooed seamen who sailed the South Pacific. That so many with previous seafaring experience were given the freedom to leave the colony even before their sentences had expired confirms the urgency with which the government encouraged the growth of the industry. Such privileges were normally extended only to men serving seven-year sentences and whose conduct in the colony had been good. After Governor Macquarie had pardoned most of the other living *Calcutta* convicts, several others whose sentences had been for longer periods were allowed to join those who sought adventure on the high seas.[18]

Captains had little trouble replenishing their crews as convicts regained their freedom. They were obliged to advertise their names in the *Sydney Gazette* if they planned to sail. All claims and demands had to be presented at the office of the Governor's Secretary. Some sailed for years in the same colonial vessel with the fervent belief that their Saviour would guide them, sometimes in a craft too small to withstand the gales and hurricanes of tropical monsoons or the Roaring Forties. It had been written in ancient times that they who go down to the sea in ships, who mount up to the heaven and go down again to the depths, 'cry unto the Lord in their trouble and he bringeth them out of their distress'. One learns of many losses among those who went to sea in little more than a sieve. How many more persons perished, in tragedies unrecorded, in Antipodean waters?

Some of the *Calcutta* convicts who left never returned to Van Diemen's Land. Names of some who were absent during the muster of 1811 reappear on the musters of 1818 or 1819, after their seafaring days were over, some settling to married life, domesticity and a land grant. Others who escaped the shackles of the law by sea were often never heard of again.

Of those belonging to William Collins' original crew, Ronaldson had a wife (and a mother-in-law) to return to in England. He appears to have left before the 1811 muster. The American William Thomas went to Port Jackson in 1808. He returned to Hobart with a wife and family some ten years later. Allender merits special attention later as one of the more colourful figures of early Tasmanian history when he became a ferryman between Kangaroo Point and Hobart. David Wakefield went into partnership for a while with William Collins. He foolishly sold his small farm to Major Andrew Geils for £50 in 1812, after which he managed one of Geils' farms and continued to farm in the area.[19]

Most of the small ships were filthy and disease-ridden, crawling with every small member of the animal kingdom that could squeeze through the wooden framework, or hop, fly or jump on to the decks. The *Cumberland,* as described by Matthew Flinders in a letter to Governor King, was probably typical of most of those which traded around the south seas in the early part of the nineteenth century. Flinders found the schooner full of bugs, lice, fleas, weevils, mosquitoes, cockroaches large and small, and mice rising superior to them all.

We have almost got the better of the fleas, lice and mosquites [*sic*] but in spite of boiling water and daily destruction amongst them, the bugs still kept their ground . . . I have at least a hundred lumps upon my body and arms; and before the vile bug-like smell will leave me, must, I believe, as well as my clothes, undergo a good boiling in the large kettle.[20]

As each little ship would tear itself away from the slender ropes which bound it to the shore, so the ties of the sailor with his earth-bound loves receded into the background, enabling him to devote his time and energies and thoughts to the love of his life, the sea. For him, the mysteries and the perpetual struggle against the elements, the ever-present sense of the supernatural, the superstitions engendered by tales of the Sargossa, the sight of an albatross, or St Elmo's fire, drove him on through perpetual dangers, his restless spirit defying all rational explanations.

24 COLONIAL CRIME

AT FIRST THERE was no prison as such because, until they might receive a pardon, all convicts were regarded as prisoners of the Crown under the discretion of the Lieutenant-Governor, although technically they were no longer prisoners. Collins reminded the people that the laws of England would protect their persons and property from natives, but the Aboriginal inhabitants were to be equally entitled to protection under the law.

The earliest crimes committed in the new colony were not very different from many of the crimes committed in the Old Country. The instinct for survival in the face of near starvation caused the robbing of stores for food. Absconders to the bush sought not only freedom but more food to stay alive. Sometimes they would take arms and dogs belonging to their masters. Depredations regularly occurring in the Commissariat might well have been due to the laxity either of some members of the night watch or of those in charge of the stores. Any persons apprehended for an offence during the night would remain in the custody of the night watch until the morning. They would then come before the court but the magistrates could do little more than punish the offenders with floggings.[1]

There was enough opportunity for corruption, as was later provided. The position became serious enough for Collins to doubt the integrity of some members of his night watch. In September 1806 he appointed in its place a military patrol from among the marines, and ordered a beating of retreat in the evening and reveille in the morning. All convicts except servants on lawful business had to remain in their huts between beats. Sergeant Macauley was in charge of the patrol, assisted by a corporal and six privates.[2]

A really large number of lashes was not necessarily a deterrent to crime because tough 'characters' could endure the fiercest attacks across their bare shoulders from a cat-o'-nine-tails. Joseph Holt, the United Irishman, described a flogging which the Reverend Marsden had ordered in Sydney in 1800 on a young Irish lad who received 300 lashes without a whimper or flinch. After the first 100, when he was cut to the bone between the shoulder blade, the doctor ordered the next to be lower down which 'reduced his flesh to such a jelly that the doctor ordered him to have the remaining hundred on the calves of his legs'.[3]

Holt thought highly of Collins when he visited Hobart Town in 1805, praising him for compassionate treatment of runaway convicts. He thought Collins was extraordinarily merciful to those who returned from the woods half-dead with cold and hunger, dropping on their knees before him and imploring his pardon:

'Well', he would say to them, 'now that you have lived in the bush, do you think the change you made was for the better? Are you sorry for what you have done?'

'Yes, sir.'

'And will you promise me never to go away again?'

'Never, sir!'

'Go to the storekeeper, then', the benevolent Collins would say 'and get a suit of slops and your week's rations, and then go to the overseer and attend to your work. I will give you my pardon, but remember, that I expect you will keep your promise to me.'[4]

It greatly surprised Holt because he had never heard of any governor or commandant acting in such a manner. Nor had he witnessed such leniency, believing that there was less crime and fewer faults committed under Collins than in any other settlement, being the 'surest proof that mercy and humanity are the best policy'. John Pascoe Fawkner agreed with this assessment.

Escapes from custody were to continue for many years, the *Calcutta* men contributing their fair share to the numbers. In all at least sixty-eight of these would abscond at some time, some more than once. Stewart made at least three unsuccessful attempts at piracy

1. Gov? House
2. Chaplains
3. D? Surveyor gen?
4. Surgeon
5. Commissary
6. Printing Office
7. Guard House
8. Hospital
9. Assistant Surgeon
10. Commissary Cottage
11. Blacksmiths &c
12. Hunters Island Storehouse
13. Jetty
14. Magazine
15. Barrack
16. Capt Haddens Cottage
17. G.P.H. Cottage
18. Table Mount
19. Rivulet

Harris sketched Hobart Town as it developed. The ship at anchor may be the Sophia, *one of the few of its size in port during the winter of 1806.*

before succeeding. Gibson, Morris, Salmon, Campbell and Plunkett escaped three times, the latter never to be heard of again.

Lieutenant-Governor Paterson at Port Dalrymple had taken the first serious step to alleviate the robbing of his stores when he sent one convict, James Keating, for trial at the Court of Criminal Jurisdiction in Sydney. The Court returned him for execution in Hobart Town in April 1806. Knopwood attended him with the sacrament before the whole community witnessed his tragic ending.[5]

Knopwood usually attended the executions as well as the floggings, presumably to give some sort of spiritual succour to the victims. When in 1815 he was to be hanged for the murder of the settler Carlisle, Hugh Burn received the usual recommendatory prayer from Knopwood before he left the courthouse. Knopwood respected his wish not to attend him at the gallows because he was a Catholic, and Michael Lawler witnessed the sorry event on Knopwood's behalf.[6]

The stressful years of famine, the laxity of discipline and the knowledge gained that it was possible to live off the land, encouraged the desperate convicts to become bushrangers. Armed with stolen guns and dogs, they raided the homes of settlers in outlying districts, intimidating families, stealing and slaugh-

tering their animals for food and barter. If apprehended they were sent to the Court of Criminal Jurisdiction at Port Jackson for trial. Rewards were offered to anyone able to give information about bushrangers or robberies, but it was rare for any of those serving sentences themselves to inform on their mates, except when the more serious crimes such as murder had occurred. One instance gives credence to this view. Knopwood reported that on 25 July 1807 William Collins was robbed in his own house of £250–£300. This was the day that Hopkins opened his public house.

After William Collins reported the robbery and some prisoners including his own servants were questioned, Governor Collins offered the reward of a free pardon and passage to England to any male or female who had information leading to a conviction. Philip Strickland, one of William Collins' servants, confessed to Knopwood and implicated Stocker, P. Nowland and Maria Gardner. In fear of his life, Strickland remained most of the day with Knopwood and the following day he was taken and put aboard the whaler *Albion* then due to leave for Sydney.[7]

Strickland's arrival in Sydney was apparently not too well received by Governor Bligh who wrote to Collins with some admonishment and in no uncertain terms about his attitude to an informer.

I stand on no ceremony with Persons in this Predicament here, by which means they become bold and the threats of their adversaries insignificant. Two men, who informed against our late conspirators, I gave a pardon to; and every person said they would be murdered, but they are living without any dread or apprehension and their Enemies have more regard for their own lives than to do them an injury.

Ironically Bligh was about to flee from his own adversaries in complete terror, while Strickland soon gained his full pardon, a grant of land, a wife and a family. He remained at Port Jackson.[8]

There was a tendency to try to settle the cases in Hobart because of the mounting costs of sending offenders, together with over-willing witnesses, to the higher court. In many cases it appeared that some of the crimes had been committed just for a change of scene, perhaps even in conspiracy with those who were to act as witnesses. In October 1806 Thomas Jones, a horse stealer from Sussex, who had stolen and slaughtered a cow valued at £25, was fortuitously acquitted at Port Jackson because of the evidence given by a fellow prisoner, Francis Cobb.[9]

Two months later Sylvester Lush, transported for life for sheep stealing in Dorset, had not learnt his lesson and had to be tried for stealing a wether sheep valued at £2 10s 0d. He managed to escape and records do not reveal the outcome of the charges.[10] Perhaps he had a good defence because sheep stealing was still on the books as a capital offence. Execution was quite frequently carried out as an example to others at a time when every animal was a precious component of the colonial economy. Lush was able to return to Hobart Town and farmed at Glenorchy with his wife-to-be, Ann Burrows from Norfolk Island, whom he married in 1812 when she was only twelve years old.[11]

Knopwood's diary entries indicate that local court business tended to be on an *ad hoc* basis. There were probably many minor crimes and perhaps many accused were discharged leaving no record. Thomas Fitzgerald kept some records when he was clerk of courts. Some of these survived in scattered and sometimes unexpected places. There is also some belief that others were stored in the roof and were lost when Fitzgerald's house was later destroyed.[12]

Some *Calcutta* convicts turned out to be incurable offenders and had long lists of petty crimes. One of these was John Gwynn. At the age of twelve he had been sentenced to seven years for stealing clothes from a dwelling house in Bloomsbury (having previously incurred a whipping for stealing a stewpan).[13] He appeared regularly before the magistrates for misdemeanors, none severe enough, however, to lose his freedom once he had served out his time by 1809. For his first offence in the colony he received twenty-five lashes for stealing cabbages from the garden of William Bean in 1806. In June the following year Knopwood ordered 200 lashes when he absented himself from duty. Three months later his back could

hardly have healed when he received 200 further lashes for stealing blankets. When he purloined a cask containing spirits from Lieutenant Wright, the sentence was government labour for three years. He was employed as a boatman, whereupon he was frequently in trouble for taking prisoners on boats and was either fined or received more floggings. He retailed spirits without a licence, slaughtered a sheep without being licensed, and enticed an assigned female servant away from service. He had to be reprimanded for assaulting and beating his wife and, on another occasion, a constable. He stole whale oil and whale bone from Captain James Kelly. The later charges, mostly when drunk and disorderly, occurred after he had a thirty-acre land grant on the Carlton River (1812) and came to little more than 5s fines or discharges. Perhaps even Knopwood finally came to accept Gwynn's irredeemability. He died at Forcett in 1859, aged 72, and his occupation then was given as fisherman.[14]

One sad case related to charges brought against John Wilkinson, one of the shoemakers, in 1807. He had a wife and four small children in England and was almost free to return home. He had already appeared as prosecutor before the court after a free man had broken into his house. Soon afterwards his original sentence of seven years for stealing a pocket-book had expired. He then perpetrated an unforgivable crime. In a two-hour examination at Cottage Green Knopwood questioned Wilkinson regarding 'Loui's child of 5 years and 3 months old'. This took place at the time they were all getting ready for the opening of The Sign of the Whale Fishery. A few days later Knopwood and Harris sat in judgement on Wilkinson. It took five more days to pronounce some sort of sentence. Part of Knopwood's entry for the date is missing, but enough remains to discover the outcome: '. . . pillory one hour according to the order of the magistrate for having committed an assault on the body of Sarah Lewis a child of 5 years old'. Surely this was an ironic and dreadful miscarriage of justice, when one considers that hanging was the penalty for stealing a sheep. Ironic too that the father, James Lewis, was overseer of the gaol gang.[15]

Anchor the butcher had more reason than most for misbehaviour in the colony because his wife, Fanny, remained the faithful partner of Leonard Fosbrook. Anchor made many appearances before the Bench of Magistrates in Hobart on charges relating to stealing wheat from the government stores, killing sheep without having them inspected, frequent absences from muster for church, enticing away the wife of John Coward and various other misdemeanours which delayed the grant of a full pardon until 1838. He was one of the last of the *Calcutta* men to remain a convict. For stealing wheat Knopwood ordered his punishment of 200 lashes, at other times he received fines ranging

131

from 5s to £20, but when Humphrey was on the bench he frequently discharged the old offender after a mild reprimand.[16]

Fosbrook's job was one of the most responsible in the civil office and one of the most difficult. Collins trusted him entirely. He employed a staff of the most worthy ex-convicts, including Francis Shipman, the first *Calcutta* convict whom Collins used as a clerk. Shipman, the recipient of one of the earliest pardons, was well aware that corrupt practices were the order of the day as far as the stores were concerned when he became public storekeeper.[17] Robberies were associated with excessive corruption within the Commissariat itself. Not only robberies of goods, but the issue of vouchers for non-existent kangaroo meat seemingly taken in to the stores was always a temptation to ex-forgers who had found little difficulty getting jobs as clerks in the civil establishment.

Suspicions were raised about the security of the stores and the issue of receipts. But it was difficult to pin down those responsible for any malpractices when Matthew Power was exonerated of charges of forging Fosbrook's signature on bills and had been acquitted through Collins' intervention.[18] Shipman would stir up a hornet's nest when, during a visit to Port Jackson in 1810 on his way home to England, he spread rumours that Fosbrook had issued forged receipts between 1807 and 1809. The accusations would have unexpected results several years later, when Fosbrook returned to England, accompanied by the faithful Fanny, after his disgrace for defrauding the government in 1813, thereby proving that not all those who stood trial on criminal charges came to Australia as convicts.[19]

· · ·

Calcutta convicts were sometimes the victims of crime. Old Thomas Croft and his wife Mary lived in Elizabeth Street and occasionally visited a property at New Norfolk where they grazed with moderate success. Croft was a busy man in the early years as overseer of the brickmakers, carrying out his earlier promise to Collins that he would make good bricks. Other prisoners resented their success when, in August 1807, three men with bags over their faces broke into their house. They may have included the bushrangers Samuel Tomlin and William Russell who broke into Clark's stockyard on the same night. They were probably looking for food.

More serious was the occasion in October 1809 when Job Stokes, formerly one of the marines who had arrived in the *Calcutta*, attempted a burglary at the Crofts' house. Mary had been anxious about her husband who was out drinking with a friend. At midnight she left her empty house to look for him, as she was afraid. She returned alone and, hearing a noise and seeing a light in the kitchen and the bedroom window open, called for the night watch. Private Alan Young, R.M. (also a *Calcutta* arrival) appeared. Stokes grabbed his pistol and jumped through the window, leaving behind a chisel and file, with which he had forced open the window, a sugar bag, and wearing apparel belonging to the Crofts.

They reported the robbery to Private John Downs of the Royal Marines who was patrolling the streets. Downes caught up with Stokes at Henry Hacking's and with the assistance of Private John Taylor, another on patrol, forced Stokes to give himself up. Knopwood arrived with several others of the patrol and they confined Stokes to the guardhouse. It seems that half the population was out on the town, but there is no record as to whether Thomas Croft himself arrived home that night.[20]

The outcome was that Stokes was sent on his second trip to Port Jackson to appear before the Court of Criminal Jurisdiction. Judge Advocate Bent sentenced him to death and he was returned to Hobart for execution.[21] He was one of several who, having arrived free, turned criminal.

25 THE PIRATES WERE NOT PENITENTS

*P*IRACY WAS ONE of the most hazardous under-takings as well as one of the worst crimes that a convict might commit in his search for freedom. Whatever one's love of the sea or experience in time past, the unknown waters of the southern ocean invited only the most desperate and adventurous to lead and some of the more stupid to follow. Some time in Van Diemen's Land one of the local bards proclaimed the sentiments of those who illegally had sailed before the mast:

We'll crest the white waves gallantly,
    That rage and hiss below:—
Comrades, huzza! we're free — we're free —
    We own no master now!

. . .

Huzza! She sweeps her gallant way,
    Cheer comrades, at my call!—
The wide world is our enemy,
    But we will dare it all![1]

Piratical seizures or attempted seizures of craft were often a temptation to ex-seamen, but escapees were usually caught before they got very far. Collins frequently had to remind his people about the strict regulations relating to the building and use of boats, and the consequences of people leaving illegally in them or trying to escape in ships leaving the harbour.

At least fourteen *Calcutta* men did succeed in capturing vessels while others escaped in visiting ships. Most of these were apprehended without the loss of the craft, but it was an ever-present hazard when many of the convicts themselves had some understanding of seamanship and were impatient at remaining on the far side of the world when all the action was taking place in the Atlantic. They too would have to appear at Port Jackson, where they would be tried before the Vice-Admiralty Court.

Two young horse-stealers, James Price from Surrey and Thomas Green from Warwick, together with Richard Wright, were among the first stowaways. They planned to escape in the *Myrtle* in February 1805. Price was one of the sailors who had rowed from Port Phillip with William Collins when he took despatches to Governor King. He drowned while swimming out to the *Myrtle*.[2] Thomas Green and Richard Wright got aboard, expecting to hide in the ship, which was engaged in the fur trade on the north-west coast of America. But Captain Barber, on their discovery, off-loaded them at Port Jackson. Governor King returned them in confinement to the Derwent but there is no record of any punishment.[3] Indeed Green, who was then only twenty-one became, together with William Trim, a government gamekeeper. During the following years there were many more attempts, some of which were successful and had surprising results.

When the sloop *Venus* was captured at Port Dalrymple in June 1806, none of the *Calcutta* convicts were involved. However David Evans, who had been a gunner's mate in the *Calcutta* and convicted for desertion, was among those who knocked down the second mate and sailed away in the *Venus*.[4] It was full of much-needed provisions for the people of Van Diemen's Land who had suffered from the scarcity of supplies for so long. The ship's captain, Samuel Rodman Chase, was taken unawares; at the time he was courting the daughter of David Collins.

The ultimate fate of the *Venus* has never been confirmed. Yet when *Calcutta* ex-convicts William Cooper, William Mansfield and John Hunter joined the crew of the *Active* taking members of the Church Missionary Society headed by the Reverend Samuel Marsden to New Zealand in October 1814 'to commence the benign labour of opening the minds of the natives to those benevolent and just conceptions which adorn the Christian religion . . . in a region of cannibals', they heard a strange story. Marsden enquired from the natives whether any ship had previously been at Bream Cove. He heard that the *Venus* from Port Jackson had visited long ago, pulling in also at the North Cape. Members of the crew had taken two native women, one from the Bay of Islands and one from Bream Cove, after which the ship was to have sailed to the River Thames. The crew also seized the Chief Houpa and one of his daughters, but Houpa's canoe followed them down the river and he jumped overboard. None of the women had been heard of since. 'Such', moralised the reverend gentleman who himself was not entirely beyond reproach where women were concerned, 'are the horrid crimes which Europeans, who bear the Christian name, commit upon the savage nations.'[5]

Dr Hopley's servant, David Gibson, the young Scotsman who had escaped at Port Phillip and told Collins about the fresh water river, also received severe punishment for his absence during the Christmas–New Year period, 1805–06. Knopwood sentenced him and his companions (who included *Calcutta* men Morris, Cocksworth, Carmichael, Campbell and William Woolley) to 300 lashes.[6] They were to work in irons for a year. As soon as the year ended, Gibson escaped again. This time two of his fellow escapees were Knopwood's servants, James Taylor (one of the Gibraltar mutineers) and John Williams along with Thomas Bray, as well as Richard Wright and Thomas Hayward, whose previous attempts to escape in a whale boat had failed. Most had had some seafaring experience and their plan was to head north and join one of the sealing gangs. On the way they fell in with John Morey, the unwilling accomplice of two notorious bushrangers from Port Dalrymple, John Brown and Richard Lemon. They joined forces at Oyster Bay but the *Calcutta* men, appalled by their atrocities, combined to leave them bound to a tree, an action which assisted with their capture, later related, before continuing their own journey to Bass Strait.[7] There they seized the colonial schooner *Marcia,* owned by Kable and Underwood. It was only a small vessel of twenty-six tons with a crew of five, engaged in the sealing industry in Bass Strait. They were apprehended and appeared on a charge of piracy before a Vice-Admiralty Court at Port Jackson in February 1808.

The outcome was unexpected, because certain events of the time overshadowed even the course of justice. Governor Bligh had been arrested on 26 January and Major George Johnston had taken control of the administration. The Court sentenced the pirates to death but Johnston notified Collins that he had extended the royal mercy on condition of their serving as prisoners for the remainder of their lives. He had received a petition from the owners of the *Marcia* to spare their lives on proof that the offenders had shown humanity towards the master and crew.[8]

In May the trial of John Brown took place at the Court of Criminal Jurisdiction. Brown had survived his partner in crime, Richard Lemon, and was executed. But the part which the *Calcutta* convicts played in his capture was revealed during the trial and might

well have contributed to their early release and rehabilitation.[9]

Of those pirates, one succeeded while at Port Jackson to gain immediate favour with the merchant Robert Campbell. This was David Gibson. Campbell, in some unknown manner, managed to get Collins' permission to allow Gibson to settle in the north of Van Diemen's Land where he might care for his stock, which he did with amazing results.[10]

Gibson's success story, yet to be told, was very different from that of the swashbuckling pirate Stewart who succeeded in an entirely different manner. Soon after their arrival in Van Diemen's Land Collins appointed Robert Stewart, although he had been suspected of previous trouble, an overseer. Among his duties was to set aside a proper place for a privy and erect a copper for cooking. By July Knopwood noted that he and Harris, acting as magistrates, sat upon 'some business respecting Robert Stewart, who we ordered fifty lashes and to be sent into a gang'.[11] Stewart's credibility had, it seems, impressed Captain Woodriff or Collins while the party was still at Port Phillip. He had been one of Knopwood's fishing companions and had been allowed to sail on to Port Jackson in the *Calcutta* for reasons unknown. Or did he stow away? Whatever happened he was then returned to Hobart Town.

But the following year, in June 1805, Stewart had begun to plan his escape with several other *Calcutta* men, including the Portuguese sailor Joseph Fernandez, James Wright, Augustus Morris who had claimed he was a soldier, and two fellow-Scotsmen, ex-soldier Adam Carmichael and Archibald (James) Campbell, an experienced seaman. Campbell and Fernandez appeared to have taken Knopwood's boat after stealing some stores and having hidden them at Sandy Point, whereupon the others deserted and joined them. It seemed they intended to seize the *Governor Hunter* on her passage to Schouten Island. Collins sent after them with Henry Hacking, the pilot, and four marines, who captured the escapees. Harris and Knopwood met to receive the prisoners but from Knopwood's scanty references to the affair they waited all the morning of 16 July without their appearance.[12]

In September Stewart, together with Morris and Thomas Tombs, who was a good sailor and bushman, escaped with dogs stolen from Harris and Sergeant Thorne. Stewart and Morris returned after three days in the woods. They were probably attempting to join those who had managed to disappear in Knopwood's boat at Schouten Island, but within days Knopwood reported his great joy that four of the escapees, having exhausted their provisions, had returned from the island.[13]

Stewart's determination knew no bounds. Collins reported to King on 2 November that

that truly vaurien [sic] Stewart has made another attempt to escape . . . he says now he has seen his error, assured me I may trust him; but unfortunately I know exactly how far. I have in my possession the paper containing the forgery of your initials, which, as he never betrayed anyone by it, I have promised him not to bring forward against him. No possible evil can accrue from it now, so it shall be destroyed when I hear from you, that you have not a will to see it.[14]

In February 1806 Stewart along with Fernandez, his only remaining loyal colleague, persuaded the so-far unblemished sailor James Carrett to ask the pilot, Henry Hacking, for the loan of the black cutter *Flinders* to go to Sandy Point to fetch a load of grass.[15] Carrett was trusted to use the boat until the next morning. Stewart had in the meantime loaded settler John Blinkworth's boat with stores and set out to join the cutter with George Harris (not the surveyor), Wisdom, Cowlan (Coward?) and James Brown who had been a sailor in an East Indiaman. This time they planned to lie in wait for the colonial schooner *Estramina,* a former Spanish vessel which William Campbell's brig, *Harrington,* had salvaged off the coast of Peru. But the *Estramina's* acting commander, John Oxley (later to explore the Riverina), was alert to the likelihood of seizure by prisoners. He arrived at the Derwent after overcoming Stewart and two of his friends, which Collins hoped 'must convince the prisoners of the extravagant folly of endeavouring to effect their escape hence, even in a boat . . .'[16]

When the *Estramina* left Hobart Town for Port Jackson, she took on board Stewart and James Brown as well as the pilot, Henry Hacking, who was to give evidence when they appeared before the Court of Criminal Jurisdiction. Stewart was in gaol there by 25 May 1806 under the heading 'examination' before his committal for trial on 8 June.[17] What records are available indicate that the evidence against Stewart was rather slight. In August Collins had to explain why he had to send Hacking from his post and the good reasons for his displeasure with the plausible Stewart. He was

unwilling that such an offender as Stewart should by his being detained here escape the justice that is due to him . . . I trust that if conviction ensues, the example to be made of him and his associates, together with the punishment inflicted on them . . . may have proper effect.[18]

Stewart's luck held when Bligh took office as Governor and extended a general amnesty to all criminals in gaol awaiting trial. He returned to Hobart Town with Hacking in the *King George* in October 1806. Collins must have had many misgivings about accepting him back.[19]

Twelve months later Stewart might well have been one of the unnamed convicts who attempted escape in the Boston-based ship *Topaz.* Captain Mayhew Folger, on a sealing mission, had managed to steer his ship safely through a violent snowstorm to seek refuge in Adventure Bay. Then in company with the *Porpoise,* Folger sailed into the Derwent, where he landed some welcome supplies of rum and gin. He invited some of the natives on board to see over the ship, but there were others more eager to seek an opportunity to go aboard. Several deserters in a small boat pulled out towards the *Topaz* when it was about to depart from the more remote Adventure Bay. Folger would not risk shortening sail and appeared to have left them behind. The *Topaz* left for Pitcairn Island, where Folger discovered the last of the *Bounty* mutineers and heard the story of their fate.[20]

The *Sydney Gazette* of 22 May 1808 announced that for six days Robert Stewart and several others had not joined their government groups for work, which indicates that he was back in gaol at Port Jackson. The same issue reported the startling news that the brig then owned by Chase, Chinnery and Co., the *Harrington* (Captain William Campbell) of 182 tons, coppered, armed with thirteen guns, with substantial stores loaded in preparation for a voyage to Otaheite, had been missing from her moorings at Farm Cove.[21]

Major Johnston ordered a search to be made to discover the government gangs who might be missing. As Stewart had not reported for duty, it seemed obvious that he must be the leader of this desperate escapade involving as many as fifty men. The darkness of night had allowed them to cut the cables without attracting attention and, with cat-like tread, they had boarded the vessel. When out to sea they placed the mate and crew of twenty-three in boats. Johnston ordered the small vessel *Halcyon* with a sergeant and ten privates in pursuit. During its absence of one month there was no sighting of the *Harrington.* A further unsuccessful search in the Bay of Islands area by the *Pegasus* (Captain Symonds) lasted nine weeks at a cost to the government of £1 000. Captains Eber Bunker and Graham Campbell, part of the *Harrington's* crew, twenty privates, two corporals and two sergeants of the N.S.W. Corps accompanied them.

When Chief Officer Fisk returned with his boat crew, he reported that the ship's crew had been awakened and held at gunpoint; that Stewart was the leader; and that they had towed the vessel out, having cut away both anchors. They were presumably hoping to capture the American brig *Eliza* and the cargo it had lately picked up at Port Jackson. The pirates had sailed without anchors, boat or time-piece on board. Early in June there was an unsubstantiated report of the sighting of the *Harrington* at the Bay of Islands.

Then there was silence until the *Sydney Gazette* reported that Captain William Campbell had had some information of its arrival in London, together with the capture of most of the offenders.[22] Again this was a rumour. However, by the *Lady Barlow* (Captain McAskill), arriving from Calcutta in August 1809, came the true story of the *Harrington*'s fate. While on her way to Manila she fell in with the frigate *Phoenix*, which took Stewart and some of the convicts out of the ship, leaving others on board in custody. The *Harrington* went on shore, breaking up on the coast of Luconia. The pirates still on board managed to escape.[23]

But that was not the end of the story of Robert Stewart. Within a week of this report the *Sydney Gazette* carried the further astounding news from Calcutta that in April 1809 a young convict from New South Wales, Robert Bruce Keith Stewart, was brought ashore from the *Phaeton* (the *Phoenix*?) frigate and lodged in gaol. The report refers to his capture of the *Harrington* before reaching Manila when the frigate *Dédaigneuse* took possession of it, transferring Stewart to the *Phaeton* when at Prince of Wales Island.[24] Two of Stewart's accomplices were returned to Hobart Town in the *Venus* whose captain, Eber Bunker, had earlier searched for the pirates in the *Pegasus*. They were Terence Flynn, alias Peter Hay, and Thomas Dawson. Well trained by Stewart, they managed to escape from custody in the *Venus*.[25] Dawson submitted a deposition before Knopwood to the effect that when Flynn believed fifty soldiers to be in pursuit he was determined to shoot some of them. Dawson had replied, 'For God's sake do not do anything of the kind, there is plenty of time for us to get away'. Flynn had then shot him. Dawson lived for a fortnight after the shooting. After trial for murder in

June 1810 at the Court of Criminal Jurisdiction, at which Captain Bunker gave him a good character, Flynn returned to Hobart Town for execution at the same time as Job Stokes, the man who had burgled the house of Mrs Mary Croft. Flynn's body was delivered to the surgeons for dissection.[26]

One doubts that a gaol in India would have held Robert Stewart for long. Fawkner believed he had arrived back at Port Jackson from India but had escaped as the ship entered the Heads with the help of the captain, a fellow Scotsman. There would have been no trouble getting a passage because ships belonging to Robert Campbell, John Palmer, William Collins and others were in and out of Calcutta frequently. The brig *Cyclops* (Captain Bruce) had arrived in Sydney in Februry 1810 from Calcutta.[27] In the same ship another Scottish captain returned to Sydney. This was the same William Campbell who had a half-share in the *Harrington* and who sailed the next year to London to claim more than £4 000 insurance for the loss of the *Harrington*.[28] Coincidence? Collusion? We know not. But we do know that Stewart was a person of extraordinary enterprise and courage, with some education and considerable navigational knowledge. These qualities might have been useful to a trader who might have turned a blind eye to a man's past. This was not unusual at that time and place. It makes one think that there really were good reasons for asking questions about the mystery surrounding the brig's real ownership: why was she lying a little within the cove, fully equipped and ready for sea, but without a guard or watch? And why was her absence not reported earlier?

26 THE ENEMIES WITHIN

COLLINS' UNEASINESS WITH his deputy Edward Lord and the antagonism which developed between Collins and Governor Bligh have both defied rational explanation. Of the latter problem, some documentation has survived among official papers. But there is evidence which, on examination, shows some interrelationship between the two problems. Records of individual convicts, as well as of civil officers, hint at something rather rotten in the land of Van Diemen during the period prior to Collins' untimely death.

From the very beginning there had been discord between Collins and the devious Edward Lord. Even Knopwood had become wary of Lord, whom a descendant has described as the John Macarthur of Van Diemen's Land.[1] Lord had powerful friends in England and, unlike Macarthur, a family pedigree that provided him with a 'born to rule' disposition.[2] He was haughty and ambitious to the point of ruthlessness, believing that his success in the colony was more likely to be in the pursuit of commercial interests than through advancement in the course of his duty as a marine officer. Hopefully he might combine both, because he believed that when Sladden and Johnson ultimately returned to England he would be second-in-command to Collins, only one heartbeat from the lieutenant-governorship.

Knopwood removed from his diary some entries as early as October 1804 which might have thrown some light on affairs that prudence dictated were better left unrecorded. The entries, discovered 110 years later, confirm that Collins, who knew success in the colonies depended largely on some trust placed in the convict population, accepted men for what they were worth, whatever their backgrounds.[3] Knopwood noted that he, accompanied by Grove, went sixteen miles down the river to catch fish and sent his servant Salmon with dogs to catch kangaroos, an action of which Collins disapproved, ordering confinement of Salmon. In the evening Knopwood released him. In the meantime some words arose between the Lt. Governor and Lt. Lord (of the Royal Marines) respecting Powers [sic] (a convict), and Powers [sic] came forward & the Lt. Governor defended him and pushed Lt. Lord back. Mr Lord said to the Governor that if it was not for his situation which he held & the two epaulettes he would knock him down and kick him for falling. Lt. Lord likewise mentioned to him that the Governor kept Powers [sic] a pimp for him. The Lt. Governor said to Mr Lord: 'Sir, you may one day see me in a plain coat.' Lt. Lord replied: 'Sir, I believe you will stay here (in Sullivan's Cove) too long.' The Govr. on their parting said 'his insult I shall never forget.' Lt. Lord replied: 'Then I hope you will always keep it in memory.'[4]

A few days previously Knopwood recorded that 'N.B. The Lieut. Gov. and Lt. Col. of the Royal Marines . . . had breakfasted with a convict and his wife by name of Mathew Powers [sic] — she always lives at the Col. table'.[5] The day before the missing entry Collins had taken Mrs Power to the farm in his boat. The affair had probably begun, as has been related, soon after the *Calcutta* had sailed from Portsmouth and during the time at Port Phillip. It would last until some time in 1808.

At this stage Lord, as far as we know, had no woman for himself and was either jealous of or outraged by his superior officer's behaviour. In either case, during the ensuing years tensions increased between the two men. The complexities of life in the settlement did not encourage lasting loyalties and expediency was more likely to control the daily life of the players. Hence, Knopwood in retrospect chose to expunge his comments from the record.

Obviously afraid that he might be stabbed in the back if he journeyed too far from Hobart, Lord went briefly to Port Jackson in 1805, partly to find a woman for himself. He might have improved his social status had he then gone to England. However he chose to ally himself with Maria Riseley who was as tough and ambitious as himself. Lord made the first of many return visits to England four months later, mostly to be with another woman and the four children he later had by her.[6]

At this time a serious situation was developing at Port Jackson. Governor Bligh's arrest and imprisonment in January 1808, manipulated by his arch-enemy John Macarthur and carried out by Major George Johnston, then acting Commander of the New South Wales Corps, constituted an act of rebellion against the legal government.[7] From his command at Port Dalrymple William Paterson, actually their superior officer, heard the news. He notified Collins who wrote to Bligh of his shock and support. He knew from his days as Judge Advocate that the scheming Macarthur and wretchedly weak Johnston, whatever the faults of Bligh, would create a far worse situation in the rum-ridden colony. He was also aware that Edward Lord had, during several visits to Port Jackson, become one of their cronies and had wheedled an extra land grant for himself during the short administration of Lieutenant Colonel Joseph Foveaux. The latter, formerly commandant at Norfolk Island, returned from England, where he had been ingratiating himself with the powers that be such as James Chapman, Under-Secretary for War and the Colonies. He had attacked Collins, probably hoping that the latter might be recalled and that he himself would be appointed lieutenant-governor in Hobart Town. During this time Foveaux became friendly with Edward Lord who, while supposed to be finding out what was going on, made the most of his opportunity to get not only his grant of 500 acres, but an appointment as a magistrate and a pardon for Maria Riseley. This Governor Bligh later countermanded, having found her a 'convict woman of infamous character'.[8]

Lord was tempted to use his high-handed authority and hopefully embarrass Collins, while temporarily in command of the settlement when Collins was absent in the country. He had just replaced George Harris as one of the magistrates. Harris, reputed to be indolent, had been in ill-health for some time, suffering from epilepsy. He had complained in a letter to his sister that he had very heavy duties in his work. He fearlessly questioned Lord's punishment of a convict woman, Martha Hudson (later married to William Roberts of Muddy Plains, a *Calcutta* convict), for what was said to be nothing more than abusive language.[9] The Norfolk Island troublemaker James Belbin related that a dispute arose when the victim called at the store run by Lord's wife (he had married Maria Riseley on 8 October 1808), of whose reputation at Port Jackson Martha was probably aware, and

Mrs R. had a devilish nasty practice of ripping up old stories and of telling more unpalatable truths than an ordinary woman could be expected to bear and kept up such a fusillade over the counter that the shop-keeping lady was at last fain to take cover in some distant recess . . .[10]

A *bird's-eye view of Hunter's Island and the original store house at the Derwent settlement, as G. P. Harris viewed the scene in 1806, from Hospital Hill.*

According to Harris, Lord pronounced without even a trial that the woman be flogged on the parade ground. He saw the flogging take place at the tail of a cart as she hung fainting, with no surgeon in attendance. Belbin wrote that she was stripped to the waist, enduring the merciless affliction of a public flogging by the drummer of the settlement. Harris believed he had the right to protest against the outrage, whereupon Lord said, 'Do you know who I am — I am now Governor and Commanding Officer, and will do as I like without your enquiry'.[11]

Lord was hell-bent on revenge. He declared it was a mutiny, ordered drums to be beaten to arms and an armed party of marines to search Harris' house and garden. But there was no appearance of insurrection in any part of the town. Harris gave himself up rather than frighten his pregnant wife with further questioning at the house. He insisted that in five years of his service he had 'seen no precedent for the public punishment of a woman without an enquiry' and would take up the matter at headquarters in Sydney.[12]

It was all some of the settlers and convicts needed to protest against Lord's behaviour to them. Belbin could not keep quiet. He found his blood was up and cried, 'Can this be a land of Christians, or is it one of savages where such an exhibition is permitted?' He believed that Harris was 'marked out for official persecution'.[13] Collins on his return was in a dilemma. Justice of the times, undefined as to the responsibilities of the civil and military officers, did not necessarily have to be seen to be done. Although Harris was his friend, Collins decided, whatever his private feelings might have been, that the person in command was the only person with authority. Knopwood and Fosbrook tried to mediate but to no avail. Collins consulted with the ailing and alcoholic Paterson, then in command at Port Jackson, to get an unbiased opinion. He wondered whether Harris, who was a civil and not a military officer, should be sent up for court martial. Paterson thought it unlikely under the terms of his commission. Harris unsuccessfully urged Paterson, with whom he had spent five happy weeks at Port Dalrymple, to intervene further. Collins thought this a gross insult to himself and countermanded his original request that he be sent for court martial. He kept Harris confined for several months.[14]

·   ·   ·

The desperate Bligh, after his own confinement for a year, had the chance to return direct to England in H.M.S. *Porpoise* and so set sail with his recently widowed daughter, Mary Putland. He remembered that Collins had indicated some support for him and decided to call at the Derwent. Among his men he had two young boys who, up till that time, would doubtless have supported him to the hilt. He knew they had influence with Collins. James Hobbs, the son of the widow Hobbs who had travelled with her young family in the *Ocean*, was a brother-in-law of four prominent Hobartians: William Collins, George Harris, William Hopley and John Ingle. The other boy was George Collins, the son of the Lieutenant-Governor.[15]

But before arrival in Hobart Town trouble was brewing aboard the *Porpoise*. There was tension between Bligh and the ship's captain, John Porteous, and Acting Lieutenant William George Kent. The last had served in the *Lady Nelson* when it helped remove the settlers from Norfolk Island to the Derwent. He had persuaded Paterson to come to Sydney (as he preferred to call Port Jackson). Bligh thought Kent had failed to rally support for him at a time when it was desperately needed, and abused him. Kent later thought it was 'impossible to describe in adequate terms his Language, Tone and Manner'. Bligh had expected, with early support from Paterson, that they could have 'blown down the town of Sydney about the ears of the Inhabitants'. He did not realise that when Paterson did arrive he would bow to the inevitable and give some reluctant support to the rebels. Captain Porteous, newly arrived from England to take command of the *Porpoise*, had arrested Kent at

Bligh's command; several of the crew deserted ship in Sydney and six others had been arrested.[16]

On 31 March 1809 Collins stepped aboard the vessel when it anchored off Hobart Town, in the company of Lieutenant Edward Lord, Captain William Collins and the Reverend Robert Knopwood. The salute of nineteen guns reverberated around the settlement, while young George Collins no doubt greeted his father and filled him in with some details of the unhappy ship. The six arrested seamen managed to escape and, although two were later captured and flogged, the others disappeared without trace. At the same time an unnamed midshipman received twenty-four lashes for drunkenness and neglect of duty. James Hobbs, when an old man, recalled that this midshipman was actually the son of the Lieutenant-Governor.[17] Such action could well have been the beginning of Collins' rejection of Bligh.

Collins had moved from his humble Government House to allow Bligh and his daughter some change from shipboard living. Bligh's report on the accommodation and on Collins' personal life was scathingly critical, and he himself preferred to sleep on board the ship. He wrote to the Secretary of State for War and the Colonies, Viscount Castlereagh, that the so-called Government House was a 'poor miserable shell, with three rooms, the Walls a brick thick, and neither wind nor water proof, lately built and without conveniences . . .'[18] He was shocked to find that Collins walked about the town arm-in-arm with his 'kept Woman (a poor, low creature) . . . bringing her almost daily to his Office'.[19] This was the young Margaret Eddington, who had arrived with her ex-convict father and brother from Norfolk Island and replaced Hannah Power as the Governor's paramour.[20]

Bligh described, perhaps with some exaggeration, other facets of the small township which he looked on with marked disapproval. He found the shell of a building called an Orphan School which alternated as a shelter for both cattle and men. There was a blacksmith's shop and an old storehouse remaining together with the beginnings of a new brick store, a 'deplorable House in the Lumber Yard, under the shed of which Divine Service is performed', and some two hundred huts of two or three rooms.[21] Likewise John Oxley, the Surveyor-General, who had accompanied Bligh from Sydney, found the houses of the very lowest quality. He thought the officers scarcely better lodged. Settlers at New Town, however, lived in comfortable white cottages and their 'tolerable good Gardens afford a pleasing Contrast to the Wilderness of the surrounding Scenery'.[22] It was Lord who accompanied Bligh on his excursion around the town and their distrust of each other was mutual. Bligh probably knew of Lord's friendship with Foveaux as well as the feeling in the community

In January 1810 the kangaroo also 'reigned' beside Government House, which was still 'a poor miserable shell' — as Bligh had described it to Viscount Castlereagh in June 1809.

against Lord, particularly from the Irish-born Norfolk Islanders, who were anti-Foveaux; moreover, he wholeheartedly disapproved of Lord's wife.

Rather from the convenience of necessity than through friendship, Lord had gone into partnership with William Collins in a store. As Naval officer and superintendent of public works Collins was already receiving a government salary which prohibited officers from engaging in trade. Perhaps Bligh also wrongly suspected that David Collins, in contracting Campbell & Co. to deliver first three hundred and then five hundred Bengal cows to Hobart Town without reference to the Governor-in-Chief in Sydney, was dealing privately for his own gain. Foveaux had been only too ready to criticise Collins, who had acted to short-cut delays in importing supplies to alleviate the constant threat of famine. He had sometimes notified Sydney of his arrangements after the event.[23]

When Paterson suspected or learned that Bligh was sheltering at Hobart Town with some token ac-

knowledgement from Collins that Bligh was still the Governor-in-Chief, he sent a proclamation forbidding all forms of communication with Bligh.[24] Collins felt he could do no more at that stage than inform his officers of the rebel's stance at Port Jackson. Lord, of course, did not agree with him. After all, he had still more to gain by supporting the friends to whom he already owed so much. Collins was gradually weakening under Lord's autocratic behaviour.

Some local forces, particularly the Norfolk Islanders, rallied in support of Bligh. They saw in him a possible saviour from the tired rule of David Collins. Influenced by James Belbin, they expressed their loyalty in a memorial which alluded to Bligh as the 'true and only Representative of our August Sovereign in his Colonys [*sic*], and our determined abhorrence of those measures which have been taken by a set of Disloyal and Unprincipled men . . .'[25] Belbin spent the day surreptitiously collecting signatures.

But there were reports that there was a *spy* in the camp keeping Collins informed of the memorial. Belbin always believed that Anchor, the butcher, had disclosed the plot to the police. The Belbins shared a house in Collins Street with Daniel and Fanny Anchor (when she was not with Fosbrook) and Fanny had been close to Hannah Power since their husbands had been gaoled and sentenced together at Maidstone for a similar crime. Collins reluctantly allowed Lord to take action. The latter had long been waiting for the moment to catch Belbin unawares after his outburst at the arrest of Harris. Lord appeared before Belbin in full dress, discarding the dilapidated and mudstained suit he usually wore in camp, and marched through heavy rainfall to the Belbin household.

Belbin described how he was forcibly taken from his children and dwelling house and the address to Bligh snatched from him. He was kicked and thrown in the mud and ill-treated by Lord on the road to the guardhouse. The latter delivered him to the patrols and gave him in charge as a mutineer to Sergeant William Gangell and Lord declared that he would hang for mutiny.[26]

The next night Collins dined with Bligh and his daughter for the last time, after which it was obvious that relations had deteriorated between the two men. Mrs Putland returned to the *Porpoise*. Two days later, Belbin appeared before the Bench of Magistrates, still declaring his loyalty to Bligh, but he gave credit to Knopwood for acting like a gentleman with candour and impartiality, while Lord was 'turbulent and prejudiced against me upbraided me with once being a convict . . .'[27]

Bligh, in condemning Paterson's proclamation, had retaliated by demanding that Collins issue a further proclamation that he was still legally in command of the government of New South Wales. But Matthew Power, who was in charge of printing Government and Garrison Orders, made sure that the ink to print such a proclamation disappeared overnight.[28]

A further correspondence received from Paterson in May assured Collins that the rebels were firmly established at Port Jackson. Collins was forced to weaken and have his clerk Samuel Warriner call together the settlers and convicts to hear the proclamation read while Knopwood delivered it in church as well.[29]

Eighteen of the Norfolk Islanders again rose in protest and sent a loyal address to Bligh. The military patrol discovered Belbin breaking curfew and on such a trumped-up charge turned him over to Knopwood as magistrate, but Collins released him the next day.[30]

Bligh was now virtually a prisoner. Rather than sail for England immediately, he spent the next few months hoping for news from England which might reinstate him and desperately trying to buy in what supplies he might need to withstand the siege.

Bligh had the ship weigh anchor first off Sandy Bay and later near Bruny Island. For six months dedicated supporters such as Norfolk Islander George Guest and opportunist traders risked smuggling supplies aboard. John Ingle, related by marriage to some of the factions

in the small community, managed to escape censure and traded openly without criticism.

However, the ordinary person could be severely punished. Belbin reported the case of the unnecessary flogging of an old man who hawked vegetables around the town. He was nearly seventy and probably did not know that he was forbidden to visit the *Porpoise* to sell his wares when Bligh was aboard. There was no hearing and two stalwart drummers carried out the penalty and, according to Belbin, Collins himself viewed the event with some kind of pleasure. Belbin protested because he thought it a despotic action and was heartily sick of the military domination.

Bligh intercepted ships to take on further supplies. He resisted the impulse to refuse payment for the 500-odd gallons of rum he seized from the *Mary Ann*, which would have constituted an act of piracy. Bligh (and those who went) took a great risk when he sent men ashore to procure wood and water. At first they were threatened with gunfire, but later proceeded without further challenge.[31]

Meanwhile Harris, who was still imprisoned, sent copies of Bligh's proclamation and all the correspondence to his brother in England, together with a memorial to Viscount Castlereagh and a character reference from his fellow officers, testifying that during the six years they had known Harris they had

never seen anything in his conduct that could for a moment induce us to believe he would be guilty of being an abettor of sedition or mutiny — on the contrary . . . he is a loyal subject and one who has always conducted himself peaceably and quietly and as an officer and gentleman.[32]

The signatories were I'Anson, Fosbrook, Humphrey, Knopwood and Bowden. This may have influenced Collins to release Harris from confinement and appoint him Deputy Commissary in August 1809, when Fosbrook resigned in protest at the whole affair. But Harris had become frailer and was unable to fight any further injustices.

In September Belbin decided to risk all and meet up with Bligh for the first time. Although awaiting a further opportunity to discredit him, the officers had no proof of Belbin's visit and waited until November when, on a charge of insolence, Harris imprisoned him and bail was refused. He appeared before the Magistrates' Court and it was a foregone conclusion that he would be judged guilty; Knopwood, Lord and William Collins ordered 500 lashes. It was ten weeks before David Collins allowed the sentence to be carried out, with doctors I'Anson and Bowden in attendance. They found Belbin's pulse feeble when a tenth of the sentence had been inflicted. Uncharacteristically Collins was said to have ordered the drummers to go on and one of the doctors cried, 'At your peril, sir. You have done too much already.' Collins muttered that 'he shall have the rest another time'.[33]

Through the intercession of the enterprising Michael Michaels, Belbin had the chance to see one daughter well installed at Government House to nurse Eliza, Collins' infant daughter by Margaret Eddington. Belbin at first had forbidden her going. As a result he believed his confinement would be prolonged but he was released after ten weeks. Belbin, a widower, and his five daughters and one son, had to survive for a time without rations. He had been a thorn in Collins' side but was likely to be of greater danger while imprisoned as a martyr. While he was in gaol, one of the Norfolk Island men, William Sherrard, raped one of Belbin's younger daughters. Belbin's only son, who was injured in an accident, was allowed to stay with him in gaol.[34]

At the time of Belbin's confinement, the *Union* and its self-seeking master R.W. Loane, a successful merchant from India, sailed into port with a large cargo. Bligh was able to intercept it and buy all he needed to depart from the Derwent. William Collins took Loane into partnership almost immediately.[35] The whaler *Albion* arrived with news that Colonel Lachlan Macquarie and the 73rd Regiment had sailed to replace the New South Wales Corps.[36] The celebrations on Christmas Day, which followed three days after the news, must have created mixed feelings in the hearts of all those at the southern settlement. Bligh at least knew there was nothing further he could do until he reached England. Collins was only able to throw off one enemy, whom he had just held in control, by courtesy of Edward Lord, and only by compromising his own situation as well as some of his ideals. Now he had to watch constantly for Lord's next move, knowing full well that Foveaux, too, would still be awaiting any chance to take control if the opportunity arose.

There is still much to unravel about the seriousness of the episodes related. The paucity of records for such a turbulent time is frustrating. There can be little doubt that Collins knew he had an explosive situation on hand, with the potential to give way to insurrection at any moment. He could not afford to be openly hostile to Lord, and had reluctantly sacrificed both Harris and Belbin until the troubles subsided. In any case his own future looked doomed.

•   •   •

There was however at least one *Calcutta* convict who knew a great deal more of the events of 1809–10 than has been disclosed. This was Richard Kidman, the clock-mender from Cambridge, whose penchant for college silver had earned him a life sentence. He was one of five *Calcutta* 'lifers', mostly known to have worked closely with Collins, who surprisingly received an absolute pardon in 1810.[37]

Only in extremely unusual circumstances could an early pardon be given to a convict who had been capitally reprieved and transported for life. Matthew Power had served only three of his fourteen years when fully pardoned, no doubt as a gesture to his wife. Those who rowed to Port Jackson from Port Phillip, with sentences of seven to fourteen years, had received conditional pardons in 1806. John Buckley, faithful servant to Collins, was the first 'lifer' to receive a full pardon in 1810. But some time before this date Collins had recommended the pardon of four who should have served for the term of their natural lives. These were Michael Michaels, David Belton, William Trim and Richard Kidman.[38] Michaels, who had independent means, and had returned to England, was an industrious man from the beginning and Collins had appointed him an overseer. William Trim was Collins' gamekeeper, unfortunately later to impose on his privileges and be executed for sheep stealing. Belton's lesser crime of stealing ribbons at New Windsor appears to have been committed solely for an unknown domestic reason that had something to do with his wife, who accompanied him to rejoin two children who were at Port Jackson. In 1806 Elizabeth Belton had received permission to bring them to Hobart Town. She died in June 1810 and the recommendation for his pardon might well have been a compassionate one to allow him to return to England with the children, which he did.[39] There was also some evidence that Grove might receive a pardon to allow him and his family to return to England. He had earned a conditional pardon by 1806. According to the fictionalised story of Grove, the convict 'Lagged' had unhappily found that:

The brand of degradation was on him. The iron had entered his soul. The scar of the wound was indelible. He burned now, at the close of his life, to expiate the crime he had long since repented of. Strong as were his ties, both of love and interest in the new colony, he determined to break them all and go and die where he was launched — at home.[40]

One suspects that Dickens was the author who asserted that Collins, 'now known in history as the "good governor"', was loth to part with 'so useful a coadjutor', who was preparing to give up his house and garden as well as a well-stocked farm and 'manufactory'.[41] But Grove's pardon had not yet arrived to allow him to sail.

The name of Richard Kidman is the one whose pardon causes surprise. He was not possessed of substance, education or influence such as might wangle an early pardon for the serious burglaries he had committed in the Cambridge colleges. He was not known as the faithful servant of any officer. He had even escaped at one time together with four other prisoners and some dogs, spending three months in the bush, during which time the party saw the elusive Tasmanian tiger (*Thylacinus cynocephalus*).[42]

Years later, the publication referring to the trial of Kidman, contained a tantalisingly brief report on Kidman's life in Van Diemen's Land. It does imply that Collins was in danger of his life. One learns that:

> After an exile of several years he [Kidman] received a free pardon from the governor, in return for revealing a plot which had been laid by his fellow-convicts to murder the governor, and effect their own liberation. Through the agency of Kidman, the chief conspirators were taken into custody and severely punished; while Kidman, to the astonishment of the good folks of Cambridge, again appeared within the precincts of the town.[43]

That there was contemplation of murder and that the conspirators were taken into custody has some credence when one examines the loose pieces of information available in James Belbin's diary, George Harris' letters, Bligh's papers and the address from the 'loyal' settlers at the Derwent to Bligh in 1809. Some person or persons wished to murder 'the Governor' and through the intercession of Richard Kidman plans were thwarted, and as much evidence as possible destroyed. Was he the person rather than Daniel Anchor who was the spy to whom Belbin referred? Or was there more than one spy? Kidman was obviously involved to the extent that Collins believed he and perhaps others, had earned full pardons. There the man from Cambridge was, probably seeing and hearing a great deal, managing not to be caught unawares, and from past experience would have had enough dexterity to evade the military patrol. Somewhere in the settlement he and the other pardoned men had unearthed a conspiracy. Some warning must have protected Collins, at least for the time being.

27 THE FRIEND AND FATHER OF THEM ALL

LIFE FOR MOST of the *Calcutta* men had gone on in relative peace and quiet during the last year of Collins' life, as far as one can tell from the scanty records of the time. The death rate had declined dramatically because those less resistant to disease and hardship had already died. Joseph Edwards, James Fawcett, Michael Crener and a baby son of the Ingles died during the year, but the Wades, Thomas and Frances Williams, the Briscoes and Hangans all added to their families. Knopwood performed marriage ceremonies for William Horne, John Birchall, Thomas Green, William Williams, William Mansfield and John Hoberman. He baptised Eliza and John Eddington, the children of David Collins and Margaret Eddington.[1] The Powers had settled all claims and returned to England.[2] By now the health of many who had previously never known three meals a day had improved. The cool, damp climate had proved to be not very different from the climate of their homeland. Once food, warmth and shelter, however humble, were available to everyone, conditions were better than most had experienced in the mother country.

There were no real warnings nor were any comets seen when David Collins died suddenly on 24 April 1810. He was only fifty-four. Fifteen years of his life had been spent in the colony, a longer period than that of any other senior official. The dampness of an early autumn and the cold winds off Mount Wellington's snowy peak had aggravated a slight cold, but nothing to create anxiety. He had worked in his office with Samuel Warriner during the afternoon and Dr Bowden had called to see him when he slumped in his chair and was gone.[3]

Edward Lord rushed to Government House when he heard the news. William Maum, an assistant to the Commissariat (and who had arrived in the *Porpoise* with Bligh), informed the Land Commissioners years later that 'Mr — and Mrs — went over to Government House, and in the Governor's office, for purposes best known to themselves, destroyed by fire all the official documents'.[4] The incendiarists, believed to have been the Lords, with the probable collusion of Bowden, must have acted from mixed motives. Some documents were said to have been unfavourable regarding land they had hoped to acquire. Government orders, correspondence and the records of the newly established newspaper edited by George Harris went up in flames. Even copies of despatches have never been found nor, coincidentally, have Knopwood's diaries of the time. Something was surely amiss when even the gossip from Cottage Green was unfit for the eyes of posterity.

Young Margaret Eddington was grieving with her children when William Collins visited, just after his ship, the *Union* berthed. He was bringing news that Governor Macquarie had at last arrived at Port Jackson. He expressed astonishment at finding a beautiful young mother in the kitchen, changing her three-month-old baby. He had until then been unaware of her relationship with the Governor.[5]

Although it seems likely that the cause of death was a massive coronary brought on by years of work-strain, family responsibilities and financial insecurity, the problems that Bligh and Lord had created had obviously been an added burden. Some believed that suicide was the cause of death. Collins was insolvent because he was incorruptible, with not even an acre of land to his name. When he wrote to his brother George in August 1808 he swore that he had 'never appropriated a sixpence of the Government money to my own use'.[6] But other rumours spread that Collins had been murdered, a theory that reason dictates one should dismiss except for the deliberate attempts to destroy records and the discovery of the intriguing publication which recorded the story of Richard Kidman. The question is, was another plot other than that unearthed by Kidman successful and was Collins, as some believed, murdered?

•   •   •

The next four days saw a grieving society frantically

Norfolk Island was the birthplace of several wives of Calcutta *convicts.*

preparing for the lavish funeral that Lord, as administrator, ordered. The resting place of David Collins would be on the spot planned for the altar of the church, yet to be erected. Macquarie, the architect of a new society at Port Jackson, would have no objection to supporting the need for a church, but would strongly object to the account which Lord sent for the funeral expenses. Costs amounted to £507 8s 3d. George Harris as Deputy Commissary and in charge of arrangements, went on a buying spree and must have purchased most of John Ingle's stock in order to fit out the mourners. And what John Ingle could not provide, John Fawkner did, making his own little profit from the sale of black breeches, stockings and black hat ribbands. Even a pound of pins and two gallons of best vinegar were not forgotten.[7]

Because many of the clothes needed to be made specially, tailors and their assistants had to work long hours to have the results of their labours ready for the solemn occasion. Pall bearers all received a complete set of black clothing, even to muslin handkerchiefs and gloves. Taffeta silk draped the coffin itself. Six persons gained fine new hats. The sergeants of the Royal marines paraded in new pantaloons, while eleven wives of the marines and their four servants preened themselves in new black gowns, petticoats, stockings, European shoes, silk and leather gloves, bonnets and even handkerchiefs.[8]

They covered the body with black cloth and a silver plate which James Grove engraved with Collins' name and date of death. Then they placed his earthly

remains in a shell of Huon pine (noting that it would be impenetrable to the worm!), enclosing it in a leaden coffin within another coffin made from Huon pine. Poor Grove, who was allowed to screw down the coffin, was dreadfully affected by the loss of his friend and mentor. Even Edward Lord remembered, many years later, that Grove's 'eyes were suffused with tears the whole time, and the shock had such an effect on him that he never rallied'.[9] He had been preparing to leave for England at the time. Perhaps his feelings were those of 'Lagged' as expressed in *All the Year Round*:

Now his strongest tie was broken by the stern black hand, he had less to restrain him, but he must stay to shed a few tears over the closing grave . . . how soon he, too, would cross the black sea and go where the sun is not.[10]

All spirits shops had to close, by order, during the funeral. The colours were flown from Hunter's Island while the *Union* and the *Cyclops*, the only two ships in port, hoisted their flags at half-mast. Lieutenant Breedon and the detachment of Royal Marines headed the procession. Knopwood and Bowden were at the head of the bier while William Collins, Fosbrook and I'Anson were among the pall-bearers. As chief mourner Lord followed next, flanked by Harris and Deputy Judge Advocate Samuel Bate. Officers' wives, domestics and wives of the military, superintendents, overseers and constables 'with silk hatbands' were followed, in the pecking order of the day, by 600 settlers with their wives and families and a 'numerous attendance of Male and Female prisoners'. They wended their way from the long room at Government House and across the barrack square to the final resting place, a deep vault, accompanied by drummers and fifers playing the Dead March from *Saul*. During the parade guns fired every minute, fifty-seven times. No more melancholy occasion had yet been witnessed in Van Diemen's Land.[11]

Few would have been more affected at the death of Collins than Knopwood, who took the text for an 'appropriate and pathetic' sermon from Revelations:

And I heard a voice from heaven saying unto me, Write, Blessed *are* the dead which die in the Lord from henceforth: Yea, saith the Spirit, that they may rest from their labours; and their works do follow them.[12]

George Harris too felt the death deeply, in spite of the difficulties of the previous year. He wrote an obituary for the newspaper, describing Collins' 'graceful and commanding' person. 'His manners were affable and kind. He had read much — and his conversation was equally instructive and amusing.'[13]

He referred to Collins' humanity towards convicts as 'most conspicuous, being even more ready to pardon than to punish the offender'. He did not wish to use the voice of adulation: 'he is now equally insensible to the blandishments of flattery and the shaft of censure', and challenged those who might be 'so despicable, so devoid of humanity, as to wish to "rake up the ashes of the honoured dead", and cast reflections on the memory of him who is now unable to refute their calumnies'. With equal rhetoric he recommended such hypocrites to 'first cast the beam out of thine own eye'.[14]

But of course there was hypocrisy abroad. Lord's own orders regarding arrangements for the funeral had referred to Collins as 'their late beloved Governor — one who has ever had their real Interests at heart, who was a FATHER to all, and whose loss must and will be universally felt and deplored'. He re-echoed these sentiments when writing to Macquarie, informing him that it was not his 'single voice, but of every department whatsoever in the Settlement, who with the most heartfelt regret universally acknowledge him to have been the Father and Friend of all'.[15]

Bowden wasted no time in notifying Collins' brother George of the Governor's death. He wrote two days after the funeral.[16] Harris informed his own mother that 'Poor Collins was snatched from us in a moment and whatever his failings may have been they are buried in oblivion with him . . . he had virtues infinitely surpassing them and his loss has been truly and sincerely felt and deplored.'[17] One of his greatest

virtues had been his lack of corruption. Macquarie was shocked to find that he had little personal property, barely enough to cover his debts. Maria Collins as sole heir to his estate would gain nothing but a pittance.[18]

Meanwhile William Collins engaged Captain John Nichols of the brig *Cyclops* to take the *Union* on to Cape Town. He did not want to be absent while so many changes might take place. Others could not get to Port Jackson quickly enough and probably left in the *Cyclops* a few days after the funeral. Harris, Hopley and Fosbrook were some known to have been there at the one time, returning in June. Lord arrived in Sydney in September. Macquarie must have been at his wits' end to try and sort out what was happening at the Derwent. He reinstated Fosbrook as Deputy Commissary and seemed convinced that Harris was quite hopeless, not realising that severe illness was draining his life away. Lord had already written to the Secretary of State for the Colonies applying for the lieutenant governorship, but Macquarie was unimpressed and chose to appoint Captain John Murray as commandant until a suitable person might be found to govern. Macquarie granted Edward Lord leave for twelve months so that he might go to England, at the same time instructing Captain Murray to treat Lord 'with all due attention and delicacy'.[19] It took three years to replace Collins. Lieutenant-Colonel Thomas Davey who, as it turned out, was a poor choice,[20] arrived in Hobart Town in February 1813.

•   •   •

When the *King George* sailed into Hobart Town in July 1810 it brought Captain Murray and members of the 73rd Regiment, as well as the officers and others who had been at Port Jackson, it was said, to give 'evidence'.[21] Perhaps there was an inquest on Collins' death, of which there was no record.

James Grove's death occurred suddenly some three months after Collins. He had been nervous, depressed, heart-broken. They buried him beside the Governor.[22] Mrs Grove decided to return to England. She sold her fine house near the rivulet to Captain Murray for £135, to be used as temporary barracks for officers of the government. Later Murray occupied it himself and over a period of years evaded repayment of the purchase sum to the government.[23]

As soon as Kidman received his pardon he arranged his passage home in the *New Zealand*. Also travelling in the same ship were Susannah Grove and her son, as well as Edward Lord, anxious to pursue his claims to the governorship and use the influence of his brother, then a member of parliament, who had by then inherited the wealthy Orielton estates near Pembroke.[24] James Belbin hurriedly left for a brief visit in November 1811. Some persons were obviously anxious to clear the air in England as soon as possible.

On arrival in England, Kidman was restless and dissatisfied. There is no further mention of Sarah Kidman and it would appear that, after ten years' separation from her husband, she had either died or made a new life for herself. Kidman left for America, determined to try his fortune in the New World.[25]

Benjamin Bensley, then a boy, and his father, the London printer, welcomed the Groves home. But they do not seem to have remained in England. Where else? According to Bensley 'the widow removed to a distance'. He kept in touch for fifty years and knew the son was still alive in 1859 'and that his worldly career has been moderately prosperous'.[26]

Susannah's financial position was such that she might also have emigrated to America, perhaps with Kidman. But this is pure speculation which might provide a tidy end to the story. Kidman himself soon entered another phase of his life. He was not successful in America. To take up the narrative of his life once more:

after an absence of twelve months, he returned to the scenes of his early depredations, declaring the Americans to be greater rogues than the English. He now settled down at Cambridge, following his old vocation of a repairer and cleaner of clocks, in which he continued for several years, until January 1832, when he died, and was buried in the churchyard of St Giles.[27]

•   •   •

The settlement at Hobart Town had witnessed the end of an era. Harris, who had previously complained bitterly of the morals of his fellow officers and had written home that there was hardly a female with whom his young wife might associate (except for the wife of Captain Sladden and her own relatives), lived only a short time to enjoy some pleasant entertainments that Captain Murray ('a pleasant gentlemanlike man') and Mrs Murray ('a most accomplished woman') gave at Government House.[28] Hopley wrote of his brother-in-law's death in October 1810: 'his abilities were an ornament [sic] to human nature and his virtues were felt and respected by all ranks in this colony'.[29] He also was buried in a vault beside Collins. I'Anson died a year later. By 1813 Mrs Hobbs and her daugh-

The Collins' memorial in St David's Park was erected by Sir John Franklin in 1838. It was presumed to be on the site of his grave, formerly beneath the altar of old St David's.

ter Judith Hopley had died, as well as Collins' clerk Samuel Warriner. Matthew Bowden died the following year.[30] Others had set out for England, including Fosbrook, Fanny Anchor, Francis Shipman and John Benjamin Fell, all of whom were in touch with the Powers, who had led the exodus homewards.[31]

As Lord's application for advancement was unacceptable he resigned from the Royal Marines. He returned to Hobart Town in the *James Hay*, his newly acquired brig, as a free settler with the order of a land grant of 3 000 acres. It was the beginning of estates comprising 30 000 acres, which would earn him a reputation as 'one of the greatest destroyers of the prosperity of this Colony . . . Corruption was the order of the day', according to the Land Commissioners.[32] Maria Lord would continue to ply her trade as a storekeeper and kept sending to the Reverend Robert Knopwood the gallons of porter that he demanded in the grubby little notes his messengers regularly brought to her.[33]

PART V
From Camp to Colony

Hobart, as Macquarie saw it in 1821, a contrast to his visit of
1811: 'the wretched Huts and Cottages . . . being now converted
into regular Substantial Buildings, and the whole laid out in
regular Streets, Several of the Houses being two Stories high,
spacious and not deficient in architectural Taste . . .'
(Government and General Orders, 16 July 1821).

28 THE FAMILY WAY

THE FIRST VISIT of Governor and Mrs Macquarie to Van Diemen's Land brought some recognition in Sydney that a settlement of some consequence was emerging, albeit in a haphazard manner. No one seemed to know what the population was and who had rights to certain lands. Macquarie ordered a muster in 1811 at which all convicts and free persons in the counties of Buckinghamshire in the south and Cornwall in the north had to attend. The names of ninety-nine *Calcutta* convicts were not on this muster. Some appeared on later ones but the rest had either died, or returned to England or had gone elsewhere. For several years from 1817, musters took place more regularly, providing useful information relating to the population, including dependents of the listed proprietor.

Contemporary returns of livestock also showed in detail the number of horses, bulls, cows, calves, rams, ewes, wethers, lambs, geese, ducks, he-goats, she-goats, kids, boars, pigs, fowls and turkeys held by each owner, as well as the amounts and species of grain held in store. A hut had become a home and a furrow had become a farm. Poverty had turned into property, and property would signify power.

By this time George Phipps, as government gardener, had discovered the excellence of the soil and climate for the production of fruit and vegetables, and was able to offer a wide variety of produce to customers. For Captain Murray he began an excellent orchard producing fine apples, pears, peaches, plums, almonds, currants, grapes and a variety of pines and other small European trees (113 in all), as well as rows of asparagus, artichokes, herbs and other annual roots. Murray's successor, Major Andrew Geils, placed a large order repeating most of these varieties and including the first strawberries. Altogether Geils bought 172 trees in June 1812, plus 150 small fruit trees, from which numerous trees around Risdon and other localities were propagated. Thus from such humble origins sprang the great fruit industry of Tasmania.[1]

The first of many ships to disembark convicts direct from England was the *Indefatigable*, which arrived at Hobart Town in 1812 and landed 199 male prisoners, including Michael Howe and other undesirables.[2] It was the first influx of any size since the arrival of the Norfolk Islanders, making it necessary to replan the burgeoning town, inducing government purchases of some of the buildings and allotments already occupied by the earliest settlers. In 1813 Arthur Connelly received £15 for his house in Argyle Street, Daniel Anchor £11 4s for a house in Collins Street, Francis Barnes £12 for a house in George's Square and Hannah, widow of Richard Garrett whom she had married at Port Phillip, £7 for a skilling in Liverpool Street.[3] Hannah Garrett, presumably with her two children, was fortunate to become housekeeper to James Austin and live in the fine house which he built at Austin's Ferry. There the Macquaries stayed during their second visit to Van Diemen's Land in 1821, naming the house Roseneath. Hannah inherited a life interest in the property when Austin died in 1832 — an inheritance which was attractive to her new husband, Constable George Madden, a much younger ex-convict.[4]

Some of the established town-dwellers among the *Calcutta* convicts would not have been very happy with the rearrangement of streets, although those who lost their houses were also provided with other building lots. By 1818 John Newland received £10 for a hut in Collins Street and the following year Oliver Smith and John Manby each received £20 for houses. Andrew Whitehead was forced to sacrifice a much more valuable property in 1817 when he had to settle for the payment of £1 300 for his house, outhouse and 1 105 acres of land at New Town to complete a track to the rivulet there. James Lord surrendered a house in Davey Street worth £50 and boatman John Gwynn a skilling worth £30 near the water.[5]

In September 1815 James Lord found himself in a position to provide for his family and hoped to bring them to Hobart (as the town became more popularly known during Davey's governorship). Lord petitioned Davey, explaining that his son David, daughter-in-law and five children wished to come as settlers to the colony. There was no mention of his wife, who had probably died. He was then fifty-seven and his position, increasing in substance every day, must have been an attraction to his son and heir. He entered into a bond to erect a first-class dwelling house costing £2 000 on the corner of Macquarie and Elizabeth Streets, for many years known as Lord's Corner until its demolition in 1900 when the present post office arose in its place.[6]

The Peters' weatherboard town house had good stables and garden and was at the foot of the Wellington Bridge by the sign of the old Duke of York, which was probably the origin of the Armytage family's belief that their ancestor Peters had served as an officer in the Duke of York's regiment. Peters had partly completed the building of a new brick house, two storeys high, adjoining the bridge, when his wife Ann died. He later moved to Bagdad.[7]

The highly regarded William Stocker had been in no hurry to remarry after the death of his wife during the voyage of the *Calcutta,* even though he must have been one of the most eligible men: a man of substance and a plausible, educated character. But the convict taint was there and the available women, apart from convicts, few. When Henry Hayes, who became reasonably successful as a landed settler, died, his widow, Mary, was already a nimble-tongued business woman running the Derwent Hotel. She had married off Martha to Andrew Whitehead, then considered another respectable person. In spite of being several years older, Mary obviously made up her mind that Stocker was to be her new husband. They married, as the *Hobart Town Gazette* quaintly reported, 'after a tedious courtship of *two* years'.[8] At forty-six she was beyond the likelihood of bearing children, but her three granddaughters, the two Bowen girls and Mary Whitehead, were to bring long periods of joy to the household when they came to live with her while attending Stone's school. Stocker's butcher shop in Collins Street advertised a 'constant supply of prime fresh meat and other provisions at the lowest market prices'. Captains and supercargoes were among his most lucrative customers.[9]

Mary Stocker continued as a publican for many years and retained the farm which Henry Hayes had provided, but Stocker saw to it that she transferred everything to his name. He made many improvements to the hotel, including a six-stall stable, while they themselves lived in a two-storey brick house. He gave his wife full credit for her business acumen when he wrote to Governor Arthur's secretary, Captain Montagu, in 1825, stating that Mrs Stocker had 'always managed the Derwent Hotel in Macquarie St,

from its first erection and for several years while [still] Mrs Hayes without interference from myself since marriage. . .'[10]

A further interesting sidelight on the ability of these early pioneer women is that Thomas Preston who, like Mary Stocker's first husband, had arrived in the *Ocean* as a settler, appointed her and Martha Whitehead executrices of his will. When he died after a fall from a horse they attended to mortgages on his farms, warned trespassers against his property and ultimately sold his estate by auction.[11] One has only to read the many references in the Knopwood diary to recognise how large a part the Hayes, Stockers and Whiteheads played in the social and business life of Hobart Town.[12]

In 1828 Stocker advertised that he was moving his old-established butcher shop from Collins Street to Elizabeth Street adjoining the Derwent Hotel. He assured his numerous friends that he would provide an uninterrupted supply of beef and mutton 'as will not be excelled . . . families and shipping supplied on the most liberal terms. . .' Two years later he decided to retire from the butcher shop. He and his wife continued to run the hotel, while he had more time to concentrate on his interests out of town. Advising his intention to let the shop and meat stores, he described his

most extensive business, connection and custom of the first respectability; the buildings of which are new and consist of a large commodious and well arranged sale shop, with office and clerk's bedroom attached, a large sitting-room and two bedrooms on the upper floor and a convenient salting-house and slaughter-house for sheep detached, with a well of fine water on the premises . . .[13]

The stock-hut he had kept near Ross for many years was the scene of many confrontations with bushrangers and Aborigines, but he was notorious as a double-dealer and the hut served the interests of one who might have been a party, disguised by his accepted respectability, to the activities of some of the more nefarious bushrangers.[14]

Thomas Fitzgerald, when he was clerk to the magistrates, lived in a small thatched cottage in Davey Street in 1807. It was from there he conducted school lessons, but the place was damp and inadequate. When Governor Macquarie ordered that stone and brick buildings in the area of the public square were to replace the paltry and mean houses, Fitzgerald was loath to move until threatened with having his place pulled down without compensation. This was the house in which dampness had affected some of the court records which he had kept in a loft and they were lost forever. But it was 1818 before he agreed to give up these premises which Edward Lord, who had recently acquired John Ingle's house next door, needed for

151

expansion. Fitzgerald wrote to Lord that he only agreed because the Governor-in-Chief wished that he should do so and that he should receive full remuneration for his privation. He acquired and improved new premises in Campbell Street, on to which he built a proper schoolroom, enabling him to accommodate more pupils than in the past.[15]

Fitzgerald had married a widow Mary Agnes Martin, on a 'remarkably fine day', according to Knopwood, who performed the ceremony on 14 August 1815. She had also been a convict who, on the recommendation of the Reverend Samuel Marsden, had arrived from Sydney. She was a person of some education and the widow of a surgeon in the Royal Navy. James Bonwick paid her much credit: 'highly honourable to the gentle sex that a woman was the earliest teacher of the young in . . . Hobart Town'.[16] Although the Fitzgeralds both gave their ages as thirty-seven at the time of their marriage, they were to have at least four children, the last born in 1825 after the death of his father.

Lieutenant-Governor William Sorell, who had replaced Davey in April 1816, was anxious that Governor Macquarie should provide Fitzgerald with an adequate supply of books for his scholars, and specified the need for Bibles, prayer books and spelling books. Reading, writing, spelling, 'figures', grammar, geography and perhaps a little history appear to have been the subjects taught to boys, while girls had additional instruction in sewing and needlework. The following year Mary Fitzgerald received some financial recognition for her role as schoolmistress on the recommendation of Sorell, because she 'pays much attention to the female scholars'. Indeed, she was at the time having trouble getting some payment for the tuition of Susan Nash, whose well-to-do father, Robert Nash, had died, owing her seven quarters at 18s per quarter and the cost of two copy books and writing paper. Mary complained to Mrs Maria Lord by letter that although other debts had been settled, the money owing to her was overdue by three years. Part of the arrangement in conducting the school was that the public purse would pay for some basic costs and that the Fitzgeralds would charge reasonable fees for those requiring education.[17]

Sorell notified Macquarie in August 1818 of the need for a school for poor free people and the children of convicts. The schools kept by Mr Fitzgerald and one by a Mrs Jones were not sufficient for those classes. He felt that the Fitzgeralds kept the best and most expensive school in their own house and they educated several children free of charge. Commissioner Bigge found that sums paid from the parents of children were from 1s to 1s 6d weekly and that Mr & Mrs Fitzgerald both received money from the Colonial Fund, as well as two government men on rations.[18]

Knopwood provided Bigge with a summary of the return of schools and scholars in Van Diemen's Land, finding that in April 1820 Thomas Fitzgerald had thirty-five and Mary Fitzgerald twenty-four scholars. The following October Peter Mulgrave was appointed superintendent of schools in Van Diemen's Land after attending the national system of education as introduced by Dr Bell. In providing Sorell with a return of the state education, Mulgrave expressed some surprise and satisfaction that in regard to former education 'the foundation . . . considering the nature of the Colony, been so admirably well laid and widely extended'.

He discovered that of 236 children aged between four and seventeen years in Hobart, the Fitzgeralds had partially educated or were in the course of educating 200; thirty-six were uneducated, but of the latter thirty-two were uneducated but would be prepared to attend public school. Sixty-one males and, surprisingly, sixty-two females would be attending the public school in the course of the next year. Mulgrave also found that the Fitzgeralds, in addition to their government funding, received about £3 8s weekly from parents.[19]

There were of course other teachers in the outlying areas. Tuition was available at Clarence Plains, Sorell, Coal River, the Black Snake, New Norfolk, Black Brush, Launceston and George Town. Other children of *Calcutta* convicts whose names appear on an 1820 return of the juvenile population requiring education and not then attending Fitzgeralds', were able to read and knew their cyphers. It was arranged that in future they would attend, paying 1s a week. The eleven-year-old son of William Williams, the eight-year-old daughter of Andrew Whitehead, and five of James Lord's grandchildren were among those attending the more expensive establishment which Thomas Stone began for the education of young ladies and gentlemen at his cottage on Hospital Hill.[20]

In 1824 Thomas Fitzgerald received superannuation from the colonial revenue in consideration of his long service to government, but he died soon afterwards on 2 September, aged forty-nine. He had obviously worked hard but the alcoholic excesses of earlier days had probably caught up with him. Mrs Fitzgerald, then pregnant, moved to Campbell Street, near the new bridge. In 1826 she announced the opening of a new day school for children, stating that she was the widow of a respectable schoolmaster and left to struggle with difficulty to maintain a large family.[21]

Numerous misfortunes had oppressed her, not least of which had been an occasion when she had need to write to James Scott Esq., complaining about the conduct of a Mr Kirby and appealing for her protection. She stated that she was continually in danger from his molesting her during visits to her house, and she stated her own 'conduct will allow complete scrutiny'.[22]

She continued to conduct her school in Campbell Street during 1827 as an Academy for Young Ladies but had moved to Goulburn Street by the end of the year when it was noted in a return of children that Mary Ann Fitzgerald's mother was a woman of good character and Protestant.[23]

In 1829 Knopwood married Mary Agnes Fitzgerald to William Nicholls, also widowed. He had arrived as a settler in the *Ocean*, was a carpenter by trade, and had acquired a good farm at Clarence Plains. One of his daughters had married John Pearsall. Sad to say, Mary Agnes enjoyed only twenty months of her new marriage. Knopwood buried her in 1831.[24]

Mildred, wife of William Williams of Macquarie Street had, when she first came to Hobart Town, lived with Lieutenant (later Captain) Johnson in the finest house built in the early years, as already described. The Williams had four children but one had been stillborn.[25] Mildred had previously lost her child by Johnson in a fire. She was shockingly burnt when removing an iron pot off the kitchen fire and a spark caught her clothes. She would have died immediately had not help arrived. She lay in a deplorable state for nearly three months before she died on 3 September 1817, aged thirty-nine. The *Hobart Town Gazette* warned that several such accidents had occurred in the colony and advised anyone caught in such a situation to lie down if their clothes were on fire as tests with printed cotton had shown that the volume of flame and length of burning were considerably lessened when the body was prone. The *Gazette* reported that she had borne her lingering and painful illness with 'exemplary fortitude . . . may her lamentable sufferings give the females of this colony an obliterated lesson of the strictest precaution'.[26]

William Williams would have had no time to get over the tragedy of his wife's death when Michael Howe murdered his shepherd, William Drew, who cared for Williams' stock grazing in the Macquarie district. But worse was to come when Thomas Peters, on his return to Bagdad from Hobart in February 1818, took an overloaded cart on the ferry at the Black Snake, causing the ferry to overturn and twelve persons to drown, including Isabella, the fine six-year-old little girl of William and Mildred Williams.[27]

There is no record that Williams, left with only two of the children, remarried. He remained in Hobart, at least until the lease of Captain Johnson's house expired. Sorell appears to have thought him unworthy by character of an indulgence without giving any further information. He joined the Auxiliary Bible Society and donated £2 to the Wesleyan Methodist Chapel for Sunday School for his children. In the education return of 1821 he had one son of eleven, Robert, whom he was educating at Stone's, and a daughter of six, Mary, who knew her letters. It appears likely that he went to live on the sixty acre farm he acquired beyond New Norfolk, where he was living at the time of his death on 24 April 1853.[28]

Tragedy struck in 1814 for the Fawkner family when John junior's foolhardy assistance to some absconders attempting, as he later described it, 'to escape from slavery', ended with a term of three years' hard labour at the Coal River, Newcastle.[29] During his absence Elizabeth remarried. Her new husband, Richard Lucas, was a constable. He had come with his First Fleeter parents from Norfolk Island, where his father had been a corporal in the Royal Marines. They had a large family from which there are hundreds of descendants, some of whom settled in the Port Phillip district after their uncle had made his name as the father of Melbourne.

Troubles in the family did not cease with the return of John junior from Newcastle, for in 1819 his father received two hundred lashes and a sentence at the Coal River for stealing more flour than he was allowed as a baker from His Majesty's Stores.[30] Hannah Fawkner had truly had her fill of sorrows. This time she did not accompany her husband in his exile, although he only served part of the time, during which he would have caught up with the questionable activities of a former *Calcutta* colleague, Joseph Raphael. Late in 1825, after Hannah's death in January of that year, the Reverend William Bedford performed Fawkner's marriage to a widow, Ann Archer.

Thomas Peters and his wife Ann, née Hughes, already had a two-year-old daughter when he was on trial at York for having taken part in the theft of ten valuable old silver pint cups, for which he received a life sentence after a capital reprieve. A second daughter was born at Port Phillip and six more girls and one son were born in Van Diemen's Land. Ann would not live to see the happy times, because she died of a throat infection at her house in Elizabeth Street when only thirty-nine years of age, a short time after her daughter Elizabeth's marriage to the promising young farmer, George Armytage. Nor would she live to see the sad times, when the two youngest daughters she left behind were speared by Aborigines.[31]

She had, as already noted, been one of the first women farmers, with her husband assigned to her. By 1807 she had increased her stock to two cows, two bull calves, two ewes and a female goat and was growing wheat and barley. Other prisoners may have been jealous of the family's quick rise to prosperity, for at this time a convict servant, Ann Allen, was sent to Sydney for trial on a charge of arson in the dwelling house of Mrs Peters, while Sylvester Lush, William Jones and James Wright were also sent north for stealing her bullock.[32]

The Fawkner family's home in Macquarie St, Hobart, built in 1817.

Ann Peters was one of the few wives of convicts whose death notice appeared in the early *Hobart Town Gazette*. It referred to her as the wife of Thomas Peters, 'an inhabitant much respected', leaving four or five of her eight children 'at a time they most need a mother's care'.[33]

One of the earliest marriages of *Calcutta* convicts in Hobart took place in December 1809 when William Mansfield married the fourteen-year-old Maria Nicholls, half sister of Ann Lush, daughter of Norfolk Islanders. It was just two years after their marriage that Mansfield had to appear at Port Jackson on a charge of sheep stealing, but was acquitted. In her husband's absence Maria must have established a secure position for the family, probably with some assistance from her family.[34] The first of the Mansfields' seventeen children had already arrived, and they kept on arriving, even though Mansfield spent a few years at sea. By the time William had given up his wanderings about 1816–17, he had taken out a licence for a good grazing run from the first river to the Black Snake run at Glenorchy. They acquired a small acreage and inherited another from a friend, splendid pastures where sheep might safely graze. But in 1828 Mansfield claimed that the sixty

acres of land he held at Glenorchy were scarcely worth the improvements he had made. These included a two-storey house, boarded and shingled, twenty-four feet by twelve feet, with a skilling along the back, to the value of £300; shingled out-houses thirty-four by twelve feet with a granary worth £60; and another log shingled building twelve by twelve feet with a granary worth £20. There were also a thatched log-built barn thirty by twelve feet, a thatched dwelling house twenty by twelve feet and other buildings such as pigsties and fowl houses worth £40. The family owned 350 sheep, twenty head of cattle and three horses.[35]

Although the parents could not even sign their names at the time of their marriage, they were keen to contribute towards education for their large family. The Mansfields declared their religion to be Independent and records indicate the family was of good character.[36] Most of the children survived to adulthood (there were two sets of twins) and through their numerous marriages hundreds of Australians descended from this hardy, successful partnership.

Several of the women who were prematurely widowed have become the unsung heroines of early Van Diemen's Land. They carried on the farms and often reared and educated young, large families, generally filling the role of two parents. It was not an easy job when teenagers of both sexes were surrounded by persons with far worse records in the colony than those of the *Calcutta* convicts.

One outstanding woman, whose background is worth relating, was Catherine Wade, wife of one of the most successful of all the *Calcutta* men. The Wades had five daughters and three sons. The oldest boy was only fifteen when his father died and barely old enough to take control of a large and successful farm. But his mother, born Catherine Morgan, was an indomitable woman, a currency lass born on Norfolk Island about 1790 to a couple who were among those who married soon after the First Fleeters arrived at Port Jackson.

Her mother was Elizabeth Lock who had arrived in the *Lady Penrhyn* and her father was Richard Morgan who came in the *Alexander*. Richard had been tried at the Gloucestershire Lent Assizes held at Gloucester on 23 March 1785 for assaulting John Trevillian and stealing from him a metal watch valued at three guineas; also threatening to murder him and by force unlawfully obtaining from him a promissory note for the payment to him of £500. Elizabeth Lock, of the parish of Woodchester, spinster, was also tried at Gloucester just two years earlier and her crime was burglariously breaking open the dwelling house of Samuel Hillier at Woodchester and stealing a black silk hat valued at 6d, a scarlet cloth coat (7s), a linen cap (3s) and a silk ribbon (4d). Both were sentenced to transportation for seven years after Elizabeth was capitally reprieved. They were both gaoled at Gloucester county gaol and Morgan at one stage seemed destined to be sent to West Africa.[37]

Their marriage took place at Port Jackson on 30 March 1788. The following January a man named John Russel caused a disturbance in one of the huts apparently occupied by Elizabeth Morgan and others. He was taken under guard and charged with violently assaulting, beating and kicking Elizabeth Morgan and Mary Love. He claimed that he meant no harm and that he was only defending himself from them, but he was found guilty after the women gave evidence and received three hundred lashes. David Collins as Judge Advocate sat upon the bench.[38]

Soon afterwards the Morgans must have left for Norfolk Island where their daughter was born as well as a son, Richard junior. The father arrived in Hobart Town as a free settler in the *King George* on 21 September 1806 with his son and two convict servants. But there was no mention of his wife and daughter. We know, however, that the names of women were frequently left off the lists sent from the Commissariat's office. In this particular ship Elizabeth Belton was one who, with her two children, was not listed on her voyage south to rejoin her husband David with whom she had originally sailed in the *Calcutta*. Morgan received a land grant of 175 acres just after arrival at

Pitt Water and soon had a few acres sown with wheat and barley and had sheep, cattle and swine. He still had his two servants and two children in 1807 but no wife. He might have remarried because Knopwood, with whom he was on friendly terms, reported the accidental death of a son when he fell from a cart in 1815. Morgan as one of the racing fraternity became acceptable in all society. When he sold his farm in 1831 the purchaser was Joseph Hone, Attorney-General. Catherine, who had had some education and could read and write, married John Wade the following summer. Her father and brother continued as successful farmers with further land grants and grazing rights at Prosser's Plains east of Pitt Water.[39]

The Morgans and Wades had gone from strength to strength. As chief constable John Wade would have greeted Governor Macquarie when he landed near the Wade farm and noted that he met several of the most respectable settlers. The children were all attending school regularly and could all read. Catherine Wade was used to her husband being away. If he were not on dangerous missions hunting down bushrangers he was attending committee meetings of the Auxiliary Branch Bible Society or racing horses. Her own responsibilities must have been considerable, even though they employed eleven labourers on the farm.[40]

When Wade attended Lieutenant-Colonel Andrew Geils' auction he bought mostly practical utensils and implements for the farm and the horses which were his passion. But he did buy two lots of blue chintz, fifty-one yards in all. One wonders whether Catherine Wade was happy with what must have draped the windows of her farm house, or whether she might have envied Mrs Peters and Mrs Maum the gilt china tea sets they received when her own household purchases were nineteen pieces of earthenware and two kettles. Still, she did get one hundred pounds of coffee, enough to last quite a long time.[41]

According to his obituary in the *Colonial Times* when he died in 1829, Wade had himself a great deal of original wit and humour and his company was much coveted. He was known as

. . . a good neighbour, an affectionate husband and an indulgent parent. He leaves a large family, who severely regret the loss of so good a husband and parent; and his death will be much lamented by all who had the pleasure of his acquaintance.[42]

Soon afterwards the doughty Catherine applied for extra land, stating she owned three hundred acres by grant and six hundred by purchase. Her capital then was £1656 15s and she had spent £1931 on improvements to the property. She made a careful inventory of all her implements, buildings and fences. She had an overseer of the land for her eldest son was only fourteen. The Land Board recommended a grant to

Governor Arthur who acceded to her request. She obviously became a power in her own right.[43]

When John Wade junior came of age he inherited part of the farm which had not been cultivated. There were harsh exchanges between him and the Board of Assignment when he tried to obtain more servants to develop the farm. When it was pointed out that he had inherited a well-developed farm, he made it clear in no uncertain terms that Mother ran the cultivated part.[44]

Not only that, but Catherine Wade extended her interests north and owned or leased land in Prosser's Plains, probably some of the rich lands inherited from her father. One of her employees had been transported for burglary, and after several convictions and transportation to Macquarie Harbour she recommended him for a ticket of leave. She was tough when he showed disrespectful conduct and insolence to her daughter 'Miss Ann' and she saw he was punished with fifty lashes.[45]

Her sons John and George, perhaps tired of submitting to their mother's domination, as well as three older sisters, migrated to Kaikoura County in New Zealand. They were among the earliest to bring cattle and horses from Tasmania as well as six sets of whaling gear. They took part in race meetings there and financed the beginnings of a whaling industry. But George was drowned when his ship was wrecked near Pari-Pari. John settled for a time in Wellington where he must have gained some legal knowledge. In 1849 he left for California and, as one of the Fortyniners, remained there to become a pioneer of San Francisco. When he died in 1885 an obituary in the *San Francisco Call* referred to him as a lawyer by profession.[46]

Mother Catherine, as one would expect, lived to the great age of eighty-six and she died at the home she made in her retirement in Balfour Street, Launceston, on 5 July 1876. She had probably gone there to be near her eldest daughter who had married Brereton Rolls Ross Porter Pemberton Watson, a former officer of the East India Company who had settled at Scottsdale. He claimed relationship with several families of the nobility. One direct descendant is, not surprisingly, an internationally known feminist in the entertainment world.[47]

·   ·   ·

But some of the wives of the *Calcutta* convicts had had a bad start, and would not have much opportunity to rise in society. Others were damned by association before they disembarked. Ann Burn was one Irish woman who had arrived at Port Jackson in the *Marquis Cornwallis* from Cork as early as 1796. At the age of about sixteen she had been sentenced at Dublin in April 1790 to transportation for seven years, and had already served most of her confinement in a Dublin gaol.[48] Her voyage to Australia, one of the most eventful in the history of transportation, indicated something of the dangers women might experience.

Even before the ship sailed from Portsmouth to pick up 163 men and seventy women in Cork, men of the New South Wales Corps on board had proved to be of a mutinous nature. By the time they were in the vicinity of the Cape Verde Islands, some of the prisoners disclosed to the master, Michael Hogan, that soldiers under the leadership of Sergeant Ellis, were conspiring to seize the ship with the help of willing prisoners whom they would release from their irons and arm with knives. Ensign John Brabyn feared Ellis and refused to take action. In the meantime some of the female convicts were carrying knives to the male prisoners. Those employed in the galleys were pounding glass into the crew's food. Prisoners planned to seize the master while Ellis and his colleagues on deck were to attack the officers, gain their arms, and issue them to those below.

Brabyn continued to dodge the issue, although as commander of the guard it was his responsibility. Instead John Hogan, the ship's doctor, aware of the plan, ordered the immediate flogging of forty-two men and six women while Ellis himself had his head shaven. He was then confined with handcuffs, thumb-screwed and leg-bolted to one of his supporters, but not before one of the informers had been strangled. After the insurrection seven men died of gunshot wounds as a result of Captain Hogan's order to fire and Ellis himself, probably wounded, died nine days after being ironed.[49]

Ann Burn spent some time at Norfolk Island and, after arriving in Hobart Town, Knopwood married her to a *Calcutta* convict, Denis Kennedy (a sheep stealer who hailed from Ernly in Tipperary, a literate man) in January 1811, in the presence of Stocker and Sergeant McCauley. Kennedy carried on his calling as a tailor and lived in a good house. They appear to have had one child, Jane, described as an orphan living at New Norfolk by 1827. Her mother had died three years earlier, aged fifty.[50]

Ann Burn was only one of many who arrived from Ireland with equally alarming experiences, which hardened their hearts and toughened their skins. Some who were subjected to contempt and castigation became strong and resourceful, not at all bad characters. They often survived their partners, continuing to manage farms and businesses. One hardy character was Mary Deal, who hailed from Cork, arriving in the infamous transport *Janus* in 1820. Commissioner Bigge took its captain Thomas Mowat severely to task because of the extremely lax morality on board. By the time they arrived in Sydney many of the women were

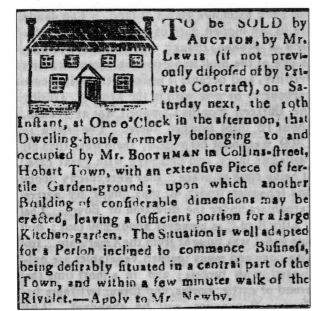

The first illustrated advertisement in the Hobart Town Gazette
was for Boothman's house in Launceston.

pregnant. The colonial brig *Princess Charlotte* (Edward Devine, master) delivered most of the others to Van Diemen's Land. Devine landed half at George Town. They were placed in the hospital and in a house opposite John Boothman's. As superintendent Boothman had the job of disciplining the newcomers. Bigge specially examined the treatment of these female convicts. One notorious case was that of Alice Blackstone, who was forced to walk from George Town to Launceston, a distance of twenty-five miles, suckling her child, with an iron collar weighing more than five pounds around her neck for some minor offence. Surgeon R. W. Owen from Launceston certified that the punishments of the women at George Town were not too severe. In fact, they were 'too mild. The men frequently laugh when they go away'.[51]

Mary Deal arrived some time afterwards in Hobart where her fortunes changed in the traditional manner when she married Kemp, a man old enough to be her father, in 1823. She was twenty-four and he was fifty, but she was to have as good a life as she could expect after a bad start in life. Kemp was free, literate, and had once worked as a servant to Knopwood. He had learnt how to live in a pioneering land and had his own small farm at Green Hills, by Pitt Water. He lived long enough (until 1847) for the two to enjoy their family of one son and six daughters. Mary probably carried on the management of the farm for a while before her death at the age of eighty-five. They too, had some fine descendants.[52]

The Crofts who came to the colony together had been childless for many years until about 1812, when their daughter Elizabeth arrived. At the age of forty-two Mary Croft was approaching middle age with a baby daughter, living in fear as many others did of a sudden attack by bushrangers. The child was an invalid by 1819 and died accidentally in July 1822, a year after her sixty-year-old mother.[53]

There were others who seemed to have had everything before them such as Augustus Morris, who had a young family, a prosperous inn and ferry service and good land and stock, when both he and his wife died within weeks of each other. During his dying hours perhaps he still dreamed that he had been educated at a military college in England and as a cadet had fought at the Battle of Alexandria on Aboukir Hill in 1801. He had married Constantia Hibbins, the daughter of Thomas Hibbins by his first marriage, said to have been a member of an old Shropshire family of Hibbins of Rowton and Weco. Hibbins had come to Australia in 1795 to be Judge Advocate of Norfolk Island on the recommendation of the Earl of Morton. But a series of domestic misfortunes had caused his downfall. His first wife died leaving him with three young babies. He subsequently married the Ann Clark who had incestuously borne a child to her own father, the Deputy Commissary Zachariah Clark. Hibbins' addiction to alcohol, which ruined his life at Norfolk Island, was already beyond his control when he arrived in Van Diemen's Land in 1807. Instead of his lost hopes of one day becoming governor of New South Wales, he settled at New Norfolk, gradually drinking himself to death by 1816 and leaving his wife and five children on charity.

When his daughter Constantia married Morris, then a free man, her station in life as the wife of an ex-convict rising fast in the world was preferable to being the daughter of an ex-Etonian, ex-deputy judge advocate on the verge of delirium tremens. Yet for several generations their very successful descendants did not view it in that light and created a vast and more respectable family tree, ignoring what they did not wish to acknowledge on a scale only surpassed by many descendants of Thomas Peters.[54]

Unlike Pearsall, Allender, Thomas Williams and others, who had married the free offspring of Norfolk Island families, most of the *Calcutta* ex-convicts eagerly awaited ships arriving with female convicts. But they needed to obtain the Governor's permission before marriage. In later years John Fawkner's famous son left a vivid description of how he himself obtained a bride in 1822. After discovering when a ship was due in Launceston with single girls aboard, he addressed himself to Master David Smith of the colonial brig *Elizabeth Henrietta*. The young Fawkner was able to interest the most attractive of the thirty-odd females who lined the deck. While walking with her along the street to arrange their marriage, a friend lured her away, whereupon Fawkner returned to the ship to select the plainest looking of them all, Eliza Cobb, whom he always declared had been 'a good wife to him ever since'. Sadly, the Fawkners would have no children, although her crime had been that of abducting a young child because she had yearned for one of her own.[55]

A number of other *Calcutta* men who married did not have a peaceful and happy domestic life, although there is little evidence to suggest whether the wives or the men themselves were the defaulters. In a society where men far outnumbered women it was usual for some of the women to take their affections elsewhere. This was the most common cause of dissension, although it rarely seemed to happen when there were children involved. The men would advertise that they were not responsible for the debts their wives might incur, and as in the case of James Ballance warned that credit should not be extended to them.

The marriage of Joseph Williams to Ann Bennett lasted only two months. James Ballance, in spite of his success as a farmer and innkeeper, lost his wife Hannah after six years of marriage, apparently childless. Theirs was a reasonably civilised mutual separation for the times, in which Ballance at first allowed her a weekly sum for support and maintenance. But two years later he reported in the *Hobart Town Gazette* that although her character remained morally good he had to discontinue the weekly allowance because improper conduct (whatever he meant by that) deprived her of it. She took civil action in the Lieutenant-Governor's Court for recovery. Ballance obtained a verdict in his favour and he cautioned persons against granting her any credit.[56]

A few years after Mary Croft died, her aged husband, then settled on the South Esk River, met a convict woman, Sarah Skelton, whom he wished to marry. In August 1831 the two petitioned Governor Arthur to allow her marriage. Sarah was married but had no children at the time of her sentence, 10 September 1829 (place unknown) to transportation for seven years for stealing paint from a shop. She had arrived in the *Eliza* in Van Diemen's Land in February 1830. On 26 May she appeared drunk and disorderly and absent from service without leave, whereupon she was confined to the House of Correction and placed on bread and water for five days before returning to service. Her bad conduct continued. When she was discovered teaching her master's child to blaspheme she spent a further ten days confined and on a diet of bread and water, after which she was assigned to the interior. Ultimately she became an assigned servant to a man named Reece of Patterson's Plains who certified her conduct to be good and that she was a sober, honest and industrious woman, in every way worthy of the indulgence prayed for — that was, marriage to Thomas Croft. E. D. Wedge found that Croft had conducted himself with propriety and sobriety during a period at Snake Banks as his tenant. Croft stated that the two had formed a mutual attachment. He was well able to support a wife, and most humbly prayed that His Excellency would consent to their marriage, which he did approve on 29 August 1831. But there is no evidence that the marriage took place. Croft died just three weeks after Governor Arthur had given his consent and was buried at Launceston.[57]

29 CRIME MARCHES ON

THE INVESTIGATION OF charges laid against Commissary Leonard Fosbrook did not take place until September 1813, when he had to appear before a court martial in Sydney. By that time the Earl of Liverpool had sent papers from London which included the examination of Shipman, and also implicated one of Governor Collins' clerks, John Broadhurst Boothman.[1] Like Shipman, Boothman had been one of the trusted subordinates of the night watch at Port Phillip and the early days in Hobart Town. He, according to Shipman, had forged receipts for grain and animal food. Knopwood gave the only indication that any kind of enquiry into these activities had taken place in an entry of 25 April 1808: 'Engaged all the morn upon the bench respecting Boothman', after which he called on Fosbrook and took a pipe with Grove. Just six months earlier Knopwood had noted that 'Mr Shipman the storekeeper was discharged *ex officio*' and twelve months prior to that the Bench had enquired into Fosbrook's unorthodox method of making out bills in favour of Matthew Power, as related earlier.[2]

No correspondence from Collins or any other source throws much light upon the frauds until Macquarie received Shipman's formal accusations in 1813. But Shipman indicated that Boothman confessed before Knopwood after a reward was paid for his apprehension. Boothman was gaoled for twenty months until after Collins' death.[3] Shortage of paper, extreme as it was at the time, could hardly have been sufficient excuse for Collins to ignore reporting the situation, although shortage of paper in Sydney for the first five months of 1807 prevented publication of the *Sydney Gazette* which sometimes carried news of the troubles in Hobart Town.

Collins was unwillingly providing refuge to Bligh, with whom Fosbrook had openly taken sides. In August Fosbrook had to resign as Deputy Commissary but Macquarie reinstated him when he went to Sydney and also appointed him as a magistrate. At the same time Macquarie released Boothman and replaced him in his former situation.[4]

From London Shipman charged Fosbrook with other fraudulent conduct concerned with deficiencies of large amounts of spirits in the stores, and with bribery by the commander of a trading vessel and other malpractices regarding the receipt of kangaroo meat at the stores. He cited two persons then living in London who were cognisant of Fosbrook's corruption and could corroborate his statements — John Benjamin Fell, who had completed his sentence, relinquished his position of storekeeper in Hobart Town and returned to London, and Matthew Power, whose signature Fosbrook was known to have forged on a voucher. They all appeared to be implicated one way or another in shady dealings. It is not surprising that so many persons attached to the Commissariat had left the colony when they had the opportunity.[5]

In a strange twist of judicial fate, Shipman's charges were disregarded, yet other charges against Fosbrook for embezzlement emerged. The court martial which took place in Sydney in February 1814 found him guilty of both fraudulent conduct and of gross and criminal neglect of duty. He was dismissed and had to make good damages to the amount of £553 8s 4d. He left for England soon afterwards with the ever-faithful Fanny Anchor. It must have given him some satisfaction to find that Shipman had been forced to admit that he had disclosed the frauds in expectation of a monetary reward and had already been executed in London on charges unknown.[6]

Boothman's future was reasonably good, although not entirely unscathed. He became chief district constable in Launceston in 1818. Although involved in various disputes and insubordination due to clashes of temperament, nothing of a criminal nature was ever proved.[7]

A very different case which came before Humphrey and his magisterial colleagues in 1813–14 concerns the relationship of several of the *Calcutta* convicts with Denis McCarty. They were ready to condemn him for the short weight he was giving as a storekeeper. He was ready to vent his ire and accused others of killing government stock, which he had actually killed for his own purpose and for which he was ultimately sent to trial in Sydney.

The story is quite Gilbertian and the length of the trial, only recently discovered, portrays a cameo of life in early Van Diemen's Land where squabbles, lies and innuendoes were the order of the day. It also shows how serious the slaughter of a cow was during a period when stock was in short supply.[8] Sander van Straten, one of the Gibraltar mutineers who had accompanied William Collins on the hazardous boat voyage to Port Jackson in 1803, had received not only his pardon in 1806 but also a farm at New Norfolk in July 1807. There he resided happily with his 'woman' as a settler. Captain Murray put them on public stores and they sold their provisions, £14 for his and £9 for the woman's, for twelve months to McCarty. As they were working for settlers at New Norfolk it did not pay to collect the provisions at Hobart. McCarty was giving short weight and, together with others similarly situated, van Straten complained. He had also signed for a cow which was never delivered. George King, employed as a government stock-keeper since the *Lady Barlow* first arrived in Hobart in 1804 with a cargo of Bengal cattle, was one of those who protested against McCarty after he became storekeeper. McCarty had denied delivering him a three-year-old cow in place of a one-year-old heifer, whereupon he had knocked King down, tied his hands and feet, and beaten him. A young girl of eleven, Elizabeth Gay, had untied him and he absconded into the bush.

When McCarty was taken to court, Captain Murray himself presided but adjourned the case until December when Knopwood and Humphrey sat on the bench. McCarty was charged with killing cattle for his own use and obtaining the signatures of settlers at New Norfolk for vouchers. McCarty reiterated that James Davis, also a *Calcutta* man, was an informer with malicious intentions and that he had perjured himself. Davis kept interrupting and Humphrey ordered him to hold his tongue. Another *Calcutta* convict, Robert Hay, by then the district constable at New Norfolk, summoned other witnesses who swore that Hay had offered them no inducement, in the execution of his duty as a constable, to appear.

McCarty cross-examined van Straten, reminding him that when Captain Murray had taken the muster at the Falls, he (van Straten) had spoken highly of McCarty to Murray, which van Straten denied. McCarty questioned James Clesshold who had been overseer of government stock when Collins was alive. Clesshold informed the court that George King was not, at that stage, a stock-keeper as he was bushranging. Andrew Whitehead as superintendent of government herds had ordered Clesshold to keep King to his duty and away from the settlers. McCarty considered King a fool and infamous character long before

the Norfolk settlers arrived to be swindled. He admitted he had been a good servant to Richard Clark, the sole survivor of Bowen's men at Risdon.

Simon Adams in evidence said that three years previously he had been stock-keeper with King at the Falls and had never known him to be punished for any misdemeanour. Although he had twice been bushranging, he had not heard that he went bush because he had killed a government cow. They looked after the same crossbreed herd for some weeks up on the River Styx.

McCarty called on Whitehead, the perennially shrewd opportunist, who agreed that King had committed faults in his job as stock-keeper. He had always considered him a bad character but he could not recollect whether the *Lady Barlow* had carried any bullocks. John Gibson, however, remembered that while in New Norfolk at Captain Murray's command, Thomas Williams and Anchor were there for several days during which time a small Bengal cow was delivered by the stock-keeper to Anchor on his property. Anchor killed it in the yard in the presence of George King whom McCarty threw in the river. He remembered little else because he was drunk at the time.

Joseph Myers recollected that Anchor and Williams were at McCarty's house. He had no recollection of King, who could not swim, being thrown from a boat into the river. Another *Calcutta* man, Charles Everitt, was the government stock-keeper at New Norfolk. He was present at the slaughtering of cattle. He killed a Bengal cow and a steer for McCarty.

Anchor said Collins had sent him to work as stockkeeper at the Falls. He had left there when King killed a cow after throwing a stone at it. He went up to the Falls with Williams, Gibson and others to draw the cattle. The cow he killed was his own property. He did not remember King being there and did not know that the cow was with calf. He had killed it for the troops and others in attendance at the muster. The situation was serious. The loss of a cow at any time was a tragedy.

Thomas Fitzgerald, as clerk to the Bench of Magistrates, presented a letter in which Governor Davey ordered McCarty to lay before the Bench the public stock book containing receipts and issue of stock belonging to the Crown. After examining the book and considering its verdict, the court reassembled on 12 January 1814 and charged McCarty with killing government cattle and acting under false pretences. From the Bench, Knopwood expressed an opinion that the charges were not sufficient to commit McCarty for trial from the particulars brought forward by George King and James Davis. (He had, not surprisingly, dined several times during the case with the McCartys and the Whiteheads.) The court ordered that McCarty take trial at the Court of Criminal Jurisdiction.[9] Governor Macquarie thought all proceedings against McCarty were 'useless and unavailing', wrongly believing that the examinations Humphrey took '*in secret*' were in an 'illegal and very improper manner'. Soon afterwards McCarty did have to appear in Sydney on a charge of smuggling, but this did not prevent his appointment later in the year as deputy to Provost-Marshal Gore.

· · ·

One of the sheep stealers who received no mercy was Robert Holdham. His original crime was unique among the *Calcutta* convicts. He had received a sentence of seven years' transportation for bigamy and should have had every opportunity to make good in the colony. He was a twenty-four-year-old gardener from Lincolnshire.[10] He was among the witnesses sent to Sydney in the *Estramina* in 1806 to attend trials of Van Diemen's Land prisoners at the Court of Criminal Jurisdiction. He gave evidence against the woman accused of committing arson in the dwelling house of Thomas Peters and his family. He had purchased eighty acres of land at Elizabeth Town (New Norfolk) and by 1812 he was in debt to Michael Michaels for £3 17s. As this same debt appears against his name in 1819, it seems likely that he had defaulted on his payments. According to Knopwood, he squandered everything away through keeping bad company.[11]

On 7 February and 5 March 1823 he was tried at a specially convened Criminal Court in Hobart before Judge Wylde for sheep stealing, and convicted and sentenced to death. Governor Brisbane signed the death warrant 'acting on the advice of the Court of Criminal Jurisdiction in and for the dependency of Van Diemen's Land'. During his confinement at His Majesty's Gaol with other prisoners awaiting execution, one James Smith hanged himself by a silk handkerchief on the eve of execution. Knopwood stayed with the prisoners to perform divine service and read the condemned sermon. He attended the unhappy men the following morning, noted that they were very penitent and that the Reverend William Bedford attended them at the place of execution because he himself was very unwell. The execution took place in Hobart on 14 April 1823. Holdham was fifty years of age.[12]

Perhaps his whole career in Van Diemen's Land might have taken a different course had he been able to bring out one of his women or had married in the colony. It was generally a different story when a man had a stable relationship with a female, especially if he had a large family, as in the case of the former highway robber, William Mansfield. His is a good example of one whose criminal instincts showed up early in the colony, but he overcame them.

Soon after arriving in Van Diemen's Land he had become an employee of Dr Bowden, together with his friend from Somerset days, John Dinham, who had been charged on the same day as Mansfield for sheep stealing (together with Robert Lawrence) from the Countess Dowager of Chatham, widow of William Pitt. Mansfield, Dinham and Lawrence were capitally reprieved and transported for life.[13]

They were probably labourers. The receiver of the Countess' stolen sheep, Thomas Baker, was a young farmer of property who was judged guilty of the lesser crime of receiving and sentenced to transportation for fourteen years. It was likely, according to the justice of the times, that influential connections in Ilminster who petitioned on his behalf got Baker off more lightly.

In Van Diemen's Land Mansfield worked as an agricultural labourer and Dinham was stock-keeper, while Lawrence appears to have been a model of good behaviour. Mansfield saved enough of his earnings to purchase goods such as 'sceins of thread' and a shirt valued at 16s from Bowden's store as well as the odd pound of tobacco and bottle of rum.[14] But in 1811 he and Dinham were both in trouble. Bowden charged them, together with Samuel Levy, with stealing eight ewes valued at £20, using force and arms. They and four witnesses, including Bowden and Richard Burrows, who was Mansfield's stepfather-in-law, were sent for trial in Sydney. Mansfield made a very respectful address before Judge Ellis Bent: 'Gentlemen, standing in the awful predicament . . . begs liberty to explain his conduct. . .' He claimed to have no control over Bowden's stock and that Joseph Heatley had received the sheep on behalf of the crown from John Dinham. Dinham corroborated this testimony, asserting that he had worked as Bowden's shepherd for seven years and that he had taken the sheep to Heatley for the purpose of curing them because they had been inflicted with scab.

The verdict was favourable to Mansfield, in the form of an acquittal, but Dinham and Levy were sentenced to death. However a capital reprieve allowed Dinham to receive a life sentence and transfer to Newcastle. He was still at Newcastle during the muster of 1817.[15]

Several of the original sheep stealers continued their activities in the colony. Not all paid the supreme penalty. They knew a good sheep when they saw one, but instead of stealing one sheep they sometimes stole in hundreds, as the settler Robert Dixon noted with horror in 1824.[16]

Just as unscrupulous as those caught stealing were some who should have become pillars of society but who, on seeing a few odd sheep straying across fenceless properties away from their home-base, led them to their own pens and re-branded them. In one famous case, Joseph Trimby and his two sons were tried for stealing some 200 sheep. In this case the person who laid the charges was David Gibson, once the perpetrator of an outrageous burglary, notorious for his attempts to escape, and now the model of propriety as Robert Campbell's successful manager and the father figure of an increasing family. He attended the court in Sydney to declare on oath that the sheep belonged not only to Robert Campbell, but also to himself and to Edward Lord. They worked their flocks jointly. Others he knew belonged to Mr Skelton of Launceston. Witnesses who gave evidence were able to prove that the Trimbys were guilty of altering the brand signs on the sheep. The three prisoners received sentences of fourteen years at Newcastle for receiving sheep, knowing them to have been stolen. Shortly afterwards, Gibson received a land grant of thirty acres — the first of many which would make him a wealthy farmer within the next few years.[17]

For eight years John Wade held the position of Chief Constable at Hobart Town, from the administration of Collins to that of Sorell. General approbation of the manner in which he discharged his duties with firmness, justice and without any suspicion of corruption mark him as a model of righteousness and diplomacy. It is significant that when he resigned from office in 1818, the well-respected settler Richard Pitt replaced him.[18]

This was a job that nearly broke Wade's spirit on several occasions. When under examination by Commissioner Bigge in 1820, he admitted that the habits and employment of the convict labourers were very different from what they had been in the past. The early convicts worked hard all day and remained at home in the evenings, causing little trouble, so that when their sentences expired they became, with few exceptions, settlers or workmen who reverted to an honest livelihood and gained respectability. He believed that the Superintendent of Convicts in Sydney selected bad characters from the gaol gang to come to Hobart. These were often 'idling about and mostly unemployed', demanding high wages for the short time they worked. He found in particular that these people, many of whom became bushrangers, were sometimes in league with settlers in parts where there was a sparse population.[19]

•   •   •

More and more settlers were migrating to the colonies, but their friends in England were sceptical of their successes and could hardly comprehend that a new nation was emerging from its dubious beginnings. Even an educated person like Charles Lamb, with little understanding of the situation in New South Wales, had written to his friend Barron Field,

who had become a judge there in 1816, querying the manners of the inhabitants:

how does the land of thieves use you? and how do you pass your time, in your extra-judicial intervals? Going about the streets with a lantern, like Diogenes, looking for an honest man? . . . They don't thieve all day long do they? . . . And what do they do when they an't stealing . . . I would not trust an idea, or a pocket-handkerchief of mine, among 'em. You are almost competent to answer Lord Bacon's problem, whether a nation of atheists can subsist together. You are practically in one:
So thievish 'tis, that the eight commandment itself
Scarce seemeth there to be.[20]

It worried Sydney Smith too, when he read J. T. Bigge's report. He had never changed his opinion that transportation would necessarily deter crime when a fellow might soon possess a thousand-acre farm, distant from those just and necessary wars, which deprived Englishmen so rapidly of their comforts, and made England scarcely worth living in. Years earlier when reviewing David Collins' book he had queried: 'Are we to spend another hundred millions of money in discovering its strength and to humble ourselves again before a fresh set of Washingtons and Franklins?'[21]

To Smith, Bigge's report on Van Diemen's Land was 'striking and picturesque'. Bigge had described the Van Demonian convicts, garbed in kangaroo skin, labouring as shepherds and stock-keepers sometimes thirty or forty miles off the road between Hobart and Launceston, and supplied with wheat, tea and sugar during monthly visits from their employers.

They were allowed the use of arms to guard against the natives, dogs to hunt the kangaroo which supplied their food, and skins with which to barter for other goods from passing travellers. They cultivated vegetables, lived in huts made of turf and thatched, and enjoyed a life and freedom far from their old haunts in London or the English countryside.

A London thief, clothed in kangaroo skins, lodged under the bark of the dwarf eucalyptus, and keeping sheep, fourteen thousand miles from Piccadilly, with a crook in the shape of a picklock, is not an uninteresting picture; and an engraving of it might have a very salutary effect — provided no engraving were made of his convict master, to whom the sheep belong.[22]

Smith found from reading Bigge that to use the colonies as places of punishment at such enormous expense was a mockery of law and justice. The wicked little tailor who might arrive and be of little use to the architectural projects of Governor Macquarie would be turned over to a settler for 5s a week, stealing and snipping where he could. He might write home that he was as comfortable as a finger in a thimble,. . . he has several wives, and is filled every day with rum and kangaroo . . . what is true of tailors, is true of tinkers and all other trades. The chances of escape from labour . . . are accurately reported, and perfectly understood, in the flash-houses of St Giles.[23]

What these men, from the libraries of their comfortable homes in England, did not know was that Bigge ignored the opinions of many worthy people in the colony. He lacked the historical perspective to realize the amazing transformation of New South Wales from a rum-sodden and corrupt settlement into an organized and relatively peaceful society. Many of his assessments lacked balance because he relied too much on Macarthur and his ilk and was only too ready to listen to condemnations of the Governor and his achievements.

But some of Bigge's recommendations were to have wide effects in Van Diemen's Land. The passing of an Act to provide for the 'better *permanent* Administration of Justice in New South Wales and Van Diemen's Land' took place in England on 19 July 1823. It granted Charters of Justice to the two colonies and allowed for the institution of criminal courts in any new colony; an order-in-council could extend trial by jury; and Van Diemen's Land was to become a separate colony with separate jurisdiction. It was the most important Act in the first fifty years of the colonies, ensuring that the courts would be modelled on the Westminster system and that the government would be essentially English.[24]

. . .

The sins of the fathers had rarely fallen upon the children of *Calcutta* convicts. The worst instance concerned the Potaskis. Fawkner called Catherine Potaski, the mother, a 'lowbred dirty idle Connaught woman' whose Polish husband was an 'incorrigibly bad man'.[25] Other records neither confirm nor deny this less than flattering description. Catherine had a thirty-acre land grant which she worked in her own name, and John Potaski worked some of the most productive farms in the colony. Fawkner added that they brought up their children in 'filth and ignorance' and 'evil practices', without elaboration. They certainly had their share of troubles. Their daughter Catherine, the first white child born in Van Diemen's Land (the birth took place as the *Ocean* berthed at Risdon Cove on 17 February 1804) was obviously a worry, according to the flimsy pieces of evidence relating to her early years. In 1818 she was in court on a charge of stealing a hat from the house of R. W. Loane, but she was discharged. In May 1820 she gave birth to an illegitimate son William, father unknown.

William died two years later. She herself survived to enjoy happier times when Father Conolly married her on 29 June 1824 to Edward McDonald (McDonnell) at St Virgil's poor little chapel described as a 'poor scarecrow of a church with loose floor boards, unceiled and unplastered'. They had three daughters and two sons, one son Joseph perhaps called after her brother who had caused the family its greatest tragedy. Yet they had worthy descendants.[26]

Joseph, born in England, was probably the main reason for Fawkner's vindictiveness against the family as a whole. One can barely imagine the grief this son created when he attacked the wife of Alfred Thrupp, agent for the Geilston property which the Potaskis had leased.

On charges of robbery and rape, he was sent to the Court of Criminal Jurisdiction in Sydney in March 1821 where he was convicted and returned to Hobart for execution. Governor Macquarie was in Hobart at the time and signed the writs of execution of Joseph [sic] Potaski and nine others. The noose fell on John Potaski on 28 April 1821 during a week of celebrations, a levée, illuminations and a heavy snowfall on Mount Wellington. He was buried at St David's by the Reverend Robert Knopwood, whose diary of the year 1821 is missing, so that his reaction to the sad end of a young man he had known as a baby is not available.[27]

Colonel George Arthur arrived in Hobart on 14 May 1824, with the full powers of Governor although he retained the title of Lieutenant-Governor. Van Diemen's Land was now officially a colony in its own right.[28] Governor Arthur, determined to rid the community of its worst offenders, particularly bushrangers who had been such a menace to society and signed orders for the execution without remissions for mercy of no fewer than 103 persons during 1825 and 1826.[29]

Knopwood was shocked at the severity of the sentences of the Supreme Court. It appeared that the new Governor was determined to impart a savagely retributive regime to a community whose members had grown somewhat lax in recent years. Knopwood experienced

One of the most lamentable sights which can be exhibited in any country . . . Seventy-one human beings to receive their sentences for crimes of every degree of terpitude [sic] committed in a country where the population is so comparitively [sic] small and where the inducements are so few.[30]

Several of them had been associated with the bushranger James McCabe, who received the death sentence at the same sitting as the more fortunate *Calcutta* men, Joseph Williams, formerly assistant to the printer Francis Barnes, and ex-constable George Bagley, who were sentenced to transportation for seven years.[31]

Francis Barnes was a victim of these outrages when one of McCabe's associates, a young Dubliner named John Johnson (not the *Calcutta* John Johnson) committed an 'atrocious' burglary when he entered the Hope Inn, conducted by the reformed and respected Barnes. The barking of a dog had disturbed Barnes. Johnson assaulted him by striking several blows to his head. Together with a brother-in-law, Barnes managed to secure him and delivered him up to the police.[32] Johnson was one of the twenty-five unhappy men under sentence of death to whom Knopwood preached in His Majesty's Gaol on Christmas Day 1825. Knopwood's diary for those weeks shows that he had many meetings with Father Conolly who, perhaps, was interceding for some of the miscreants of his faith. Johnson was, however, executed and buried at St Virgil's on 6 January 1826.[33]

Knopwood felt a more personal tragedy when he heard that Edward Hangan had received the death sentence, along with ten others, in May 1828, a time when Arthur was determined to show no mercy.[34] The youth Hangan was one of the first children born at Sullivan Cove, the son of John Hangan and his wife, Jane, who both came out in the *Calcutta*. Knopwood had read the burial service over the mother's first husband, John Heels, when he had died at Port Phillip. He had performed the marriage ceremony when she had wed John Hangan at Sullivan Cove. He had officiated at the baptism of their first baby, the condemned young man whom he remembered from almost the beginnings of settlement. He appeared gravely distressed about the fate of the prisoners, although the Reverend William Bedford was now senior chaplain. Knopwood called almost daily on the Sheriff over a period of weeks, performing divine service for the prisoners and visiting the gaol. As in the case some years earlier, when he had administered to the need of Robert Holdham, he could only understate his feelings in his diary by recording that he was 'very unwell'.

As was the custom, the hapless men heard the 'condemned sermon' in their cells and the chant of hymns and prayers was heard during the night as the men prepared themselves for death. Holy Communion was available early the next morning before the hooded men, arms pinioned, nooses placed around their necks, would make their earthly farewell from the gallows. Bedford's words 'In the midst of life we are in death' were the last they would ever hear before the hangman performed his ghastly duty.

The venerable Archdeacon Thomas Scott was in Hobart at the time of these executions. Knopwood referred to many meetings he had with him and Father Conolly. One has the feeling that Knopwood had tried to intervene. He sorrowfully entered the event in his diary with special reference to the youth Hangan. But the next day was a 'very delightful day'. The Sheriff and Conolly called again and the Lieutenant-Governor and the Archdeacon went horse-riding. And life went on.

Of the Gibraltar mutineers Crute was the only one to leave a notorious record of his life in the colony. He was sentenced before the Supreme Court and executed on 19 September 1826 on a charge of sheep stealing from David Lord. The *Colonial Times* reported that John Cruitt [*sic*] was a notorious character 'who had long infested the settlement at Pitt Water'. Chief Justice Pedder, on passing the death sentence, reminded the jury that 'we live here by this species of property and the extensive habits of depredation were such as to effect not merely individual property but the whole community.' Crute confessed that he was the culprit and was an old and hardened offender who had never been previously detected. He acknowledged that he had committed more sins than anyone on the island and hoped that 'Jesus Christ would forgive him'.[35]

Executions lessened after the year 1830, in which there were thirty. Most of those guilty of capital crimes were transported to other penal settlements where they might remain in solitary confinement for months or be put to hard labour in chains. Often a settler would try to minimise the punishment for his assigned servant hoping that flagellation (but not too severe) would ensure that he would not be deprived of a useful labourer.

Punishment for crimes which did not carry the death sentence was transportation to a place of secondary punishment, such as the notorious Macquarie Harbour which Sorell had established in 1822. In 1825 Arthur had created a penal station at Maria Island for lesser offenders and closed Macquarie Harbour in 1832 after creating a model prison at Port Arthur two years earlier. Relatively minor offenders continued to be punished with floggings which were still extremely harsh. Prisoners with a knowledge of the language used at Botany Bay had their own slang for them: a *tester*, according to John Dunmore Lang, being for twenty-five lashes; a *bob*, fifty lashes; a *bull*, seventy-five lashes; and a *canary*, one hundred lashes. The names were taken from that of the slang for coins of the time, that is, the sixpence, shilling, crown and guinea.[36]

One *Calcutta* man who had to spend some time at Macquarie Harbour was Sylvester Lush who seems to have escaped punishment when sent to Sydney many years before for sheep stealing. After his marriage all appeared to go well for him. He had received a conditional pardon in 1814 and acquired a thirty-acre

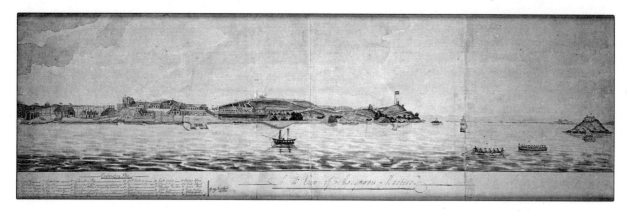

Macquarie Harbour: the isolated penitentiary for several of the Calcutta*'s secondary offenders.*

land grant at Glenorchy. He was able to provide the Commissariat with wheat and also grazed sheep. With his neighbours, Austin and Earle, he had to caution trespassers against grazing sheep and cattle on their farms. He had two daughters and in 1820 was prepared to pay £20 towards education expenses for the elder one but thought the school too far away to send the younger one. He regularly subscribed to the Auxiliary Bible Society. As a good and lawful man he gave evidence at the inquests on Hugh Gourlay in 1822 and on John Street in 1824. However, in February 1822 Lush was charged with assault and beating up his wife. He was ordered to keep the peace with bonds amounting to £100. Later in the year he took action before Humphrey when the hapless Ann Lush 'absconded without provocation' taking with her their six-year-old daughter, to live with John Vale, an assigned servant to George Evans, deputy surveyor. Vale 'hath harboured, succoured and maintained his wife and child contrary to his wishes, to his affections and to his great injury and loss in his domestic concerns and family treatment . . .'[37]

It was therefore no surprise to learn that Lush went to pieces and returned to crime. This time he received thirty-six ewes valued at £36 knowing them to have been stolen from William Walkingshaw. In June 1824 the Supreme Court of Criminal Jurisdiction found him guilty in one of its earliest trials in Hobart. He received a sentence of transportation for fourteen years at Macquarie Harbour. A penitent Ann Lush petitioned the Governor for release of the property from mortgage: 'words cannot utter, tongue cannot express a wife without a husband, children without a protector exposed to the utmost calamity . . .'[38]

She claimed that the government had seized farms at the Black Snake and sold them for less than they were worth — £155 5s for the property and produce. The Crown insisted that the amount paid was to cover the mortgage and that Mrs Lush was aware of all the circumstances. The new owner agreed she could have the property on payment of the mortgage, but by 1832 she was still petitioning Governor Arthur who noted that 'the property of her husband was not seized by the Crown but sold by the Sheriff under an Execution at suit of an individual named Vale — Government cannot interfere'.[39]

Lush arrived at Macquarie Harbour soon after the escape from there of the notorious bushrangers led by Matthew Brady. He would have borne terrible tidings to those who were to become his fellow prisoners. While Lush was awaiting his own sentence Alexander Pearce, the cannibal escapee from Macquarie Harbour, was executed in Hobart.[40] The prospect of entering the remote gaol in the western wilderness must have filled Lush, a literate person who had almost reformed, with horror.

Yet the fate of those who had escaped with Pearce and who had ended their tragic days satisfying his hunger, did not deter other prisoners at the distant penitentiary from trying to escape through the near impenetrable rain forests. While Lush was gaoled there, fellow prisoners Edward Broughton and Matthew Maccavoy, faced the hangman's noose in Hobart for the wilful axing of three of their colleagues who had attempted escape. They had cut into pieces and greedily roasted the flesh all at once, later explaining in court that it was 'lighter to carry and would keep longer, and would not be so easily discovered'.[41] These together with the murders commited by Pearce and his companions were surely the most barbarous and cold-blooded murders to occur in Tasmania.

Lush served at Macquarie Harbour for five years during which he was 'very well conducted', twice seeking indulgence for restoration of his ticket-of-leave. He was eventually assigned to his wife and it was granted in 1832.[42] Soon afterwards he received a full pardon, although a newly born daughter who died the following year, was described as 'a convict's child — from the factory'. Another daughter, Sarah, gave birth to an illegitimate child at New Norfolk also in the same year. Lush himself died at Hobart in 1839. He was buried at St David's on 17 July, aged 74, and died a free man, described as a settler.[43]

Others on their way to Macquarie Harbour in 1829 seized the brig *Cyprus*, landing passengers and crew on a remote part of the coast. They abandoned the vessel when nearing the China coast, but those who survived were later apprehended in Canton, sent to England and received sentences there for execution and re-transportation to Van Diemen's Land.[44]

John Avery, who had lived a model life as a good family man for some twenty years, succumbed to temptation in 1824. He was another *Calcutta* man to appear before the new Supreme Court in Hobart, receiving a sentence of fourteen years transportation to Macquarie Harbour for stealing several sheep.[45] While held in Hobart Town gaol before embarking on H.M.'s schooner *Waterloo* for the grim gaol on the rugged western harbour, Avery petitioned Governor Arthur for assistance. His wife was in a forward state of pregnancy and five children would be destitute. An official noted 'send for Mrs Avery [*sic*] and let us speak to her'. Avery further petitioned the Governor stating that he had been a free man married to a free woman now with 'an infant three weeks old at the breast', and other young children in the greatest distress and unprovided for. He had never appeared before a magistrate for any offence.

Avery did not dispute the verdict of the jury and admitted the justice of the trial but stated that the principal evidence against him was from an approver and a principal in several most extensive robberies. The trial is not available. Mary Avery confirmed that the family was without support. The Attorney-General ruled that Avery's house in Hobart, together with his farm, cattle and all the articles on the farm were to be given to his wife but these had already been seized for debt and she had nothing to find for herself or her children. An official noted that she had 'no prospect of support from the Government but there would be persons enough connected with her and her husband, who had no doubt recommended this application'.[46]

There is no record of how the family fared during the next six years. When Avery returned from Macquarie Harbour he became the assigned servant of an old mate from *Calcutta* days, Henry Robinson, who was farming at Carlton, after which he received a ticket-of-leave. At this time Avery and Daniel Anchor were the only remaining *Calcutta* convicts in Van Diemen's Land who had not received their full pardon. Anchor, who had continued to be a nuisance gained his full pardon in July 1838 and Avery in 1842.[47]

30 THE LEISURE HOURS

*T*HERE HAD, FOR the first fifteen years, been little time for recreation and even less for any cultural pursuits. Drinking in the public house and worshipping in the church were almost the only activities in which the people might socialise outside the long working hours. Those who could read might look forward to the spasmodic arrival of the *Sydney Gazette* and any other newspapers or reading matter that might arrive in a visiting ship. The public house was to become the centre of activity and entertainment for the ordinary person. As was the case in England, it was always known as the 'house' whereas a person's home was signified as a 'dwelling house'.

Captain William Dregg of the whaler *Santa Anna* had to wait two months in Hobart Town during 1811 but he enjoyed passing many days in a barn-like building — probably one of the inns — listening to the tales told by convicts of the crimes committed in old England, Scotland and Ireland.[1] Down at the Whale Fishery alone there would have been plenty about the whale that got away. Dominoes, darts and card-playing at the inns were always popular, combined with the inevitable gambling. When wives and children were present someone might organise charades, but this was an activity more likely to be conducted in the home than in a public house.

The whole community celebrated Samuel Gunn's early success as a shipbuilder when he built a substantial brig of 133 tons for the merchant R. W. Loane. At the launching of the *Campbell Macquarie* on 17 January 1813 Loane gave 'an elegant entertainment . . . to the gentlemen of the colony'. There was 'good cheer and conviviality' and he did not forget to see that 'his artificers and labourers also participated in a similar repast under the superintendence of the master builder Mr Samuel Gunn', giving him much credit for the 'well built, strong and handsomely moulded vessel'.[2] Gunn had built it with little help in nine months. The ship's first voyage was to Otaheite and the Pearl Islands. She appeared to have been used mainly as a coastal vessel, often confused with another

Campbell Macquarie built in Calcutta about the same time.

The primitive press Collins had used at Port Phillip and during the early days in Hobart to print his General and Garrison orders became useful with the advent of the first newspaper. George Clark and Francis Barnes (Fawkner referred to him as a 'printer's devil') produced the first issues of the *Derwent Star and Van Diemen's Land Intelligencer* in 1810 under the editorship of George Harris and with strict supervision from the Lieutenant-Governor. It was issued fortnightly at two shillings a copy. The only surviving number among the many believed to have been printed reported the demise of David Collins, otherwise it seemed to be little more than official news and orders with an occasional advertisement and news of ships as they sailed in and out of harbour.

There were three attempts at producing a newspaper before the third one, the *Hobart Town Gazette and Southern Reporter* succeeded. The pages of the *Gazette* indicate that a few spent a little of their time writing verse. One wonders who 'L.G.' might have been, who wrote feelingly of Liberty and Love in his 'Sonnet to the lark on the Derwent'. And who was the unknown writer of the tender verses — ten in all — called simply 'WOMAN'?[3]

Other contributors had quite a sense of humour, seen in the 'Lines exhibited in the window of an Irish barber' and another 'Addressed to a person who complained of his candles being stolen', with the inevitable ending that of course 'They all will come to light'.[4]

The Printers' 'HOUR OF PEACE' informed us that it was not when his page was full or work was done, not even when long advertisements met his eye or numerous names appeared:

No . . . reader, no — the Printer's hour,
  His hour of *real* sweet repose,
Is not when by some magic pow'r
  His list of patrons daily grows:

But O! 'tis when stern Winter, drear,
 Comes rob'd in snow, and rain and vapor,
He hears, in whispers soft and clear,
 We've come to PAY you for the PAPER.'[5]

As the colony became a little more settled, some of those who had begun to improve their station in life returned to school in their leisure time. In 1818 Fitzgerald announced that in response to the requests of several young men in the colony, he would re-open classes in the evening so that they could take advantage of improving their education while working during the day. Hours would be from 6 pm till 9 pm. It was quite common for many who had obviously had no education and who at first signed their names with crosses to learn reading and writing skills, or make at least sufficient progress to be able to sign their own name.[6]

But books were few and Harris continued to complain in letters written on criss-cross lines to his family of the problems of getting paper or paints and the scarcity of books — 'those here read over and over again.' He listed books needed: Burns' works; Shaw's *Genera Zoology*; Pinkerton's *Modern Geography*; Chatterton's works; Miss Bentham's memoirs of celebrated women; *Tom Jones*; *Amelia*; *Humphrey Clinker*; *The Arabian Nights*; and good magazines. Humphrey reported that his books had arrived in good condition and he hoped to continue his subscription to *Nicholson's Journal*. He badly needed geological works such as a translation of Abraham Gottlob Werner's works (not then available, however) and asked for good reading on pottery and the art of glass-making.[7]

The scarcity of paper was one of the vexations when one remembers the lost opportunities for the several persons in the colony with some artistic merit. There were very few early sketches of the times. Harris himself tried but was always frustrated when the equipment ordered failed to arrive. John Lewin later used several of his sketches and paintings of birds as a basis for his work — *Birds of New Holland with their Natural History*.[8] Harris was probably the artist of the painting of the landing of stores at Hunter's Island (see cover illustration), obviously done in 1804 before the building of the storehouse, and sometimes attributed to James Grove.[9] There was alternatively another artist Robert Littlejohn, one of the settlers, whose work is unknown but was a noted limner according to Bowden.[10] Fawkner thought Littlejohn a 'man of good understanding and a first-rate water colour painter.' But he was unable to get enough scholars to support his work and took up farming somewhat unsuccessfully. He was a cripple and his 'learning availed him little among the founders of a new country where everyone's time was occupied providing food.'[11]

There must have been some music in the colony's early days but it was rarely mentioned. We know that Sergeant Thorne could play the flute, and that an unknown American negro had a viol and Captain Kelly played the accordion. The drummer and fifer in the Marine Corps doubtless used their talents when they weren't engaged in producing the anguished tones that would have produced a different kind of sound as they wielded the cat o' nine tails made from the sturdy sinews of the kangaroo. Perhaps Robert Holdham and James Waltham, who had come from Lincolnshire, might have sung 'The Lincolnshire Poacher' and David Gibson, noted for his rich Caledonian voice, might have contributed 'The Fair Maid of Perth'. Perhaps there were also fiddles and after a while an odd piano in the community. Before he died in 1822 in Sydney, Thomas Rushton would acquire a chamber organ, which was perhaps a rarity.

Church services, conducted at first under the marquee as at Port Phillip, provided another occasion for regular meetings of the community, whether for willing communicants or captive unbelievers, of which there were many. Attendance at divine service was a pre-requisite to obtaining rations. The first chapel was not much more than a room with a thatched roof and earth floor. Early in the settlement at Hobart there were celebrations for St David's Day, first noted by Knopwood on 1 March 1806. Whether they then anticipated that the Anglican Church would later be known as St David's is doubtful. St George had received some recognition the previous year. On such occasions flags were flown on Hunter's Island. Later St Patrick and St Andrew were remembered.

The site of the cemetery was originally set aside as the site for a church. For a time a wooden chapel had served as a place of worship there, built over the grave of David Collins. The new church was built during Governor Davey's administration. Knopwood reported the ceremony of the laying of the foundation stone and the naming of St David's to honour the first Governor. All the officers and company attended Government House in their new clothes and the Freemasons in full dress. Knopwood who had been ill for weeks, preached from 1 Corinthians, 3 Chapter, Verse 11: 'For other foundation, can no man lay than that is laid, which is Christ Jesus'.[12] He usually celebrated after a church service, as well as the night before. One wonders whether he ever took the text of the day from Isaiah 22:13, 'Let us eat and drink; for tomorrow we die'.

On 5 December 1819 the new church, although not quite completed, opened its doors for the first full service. Knopwood gave the first sermon but the church was not consecrated until the Reverend Samuel Marsden came in February 1823. The *Sydney Gazette* had praised its beauty and convenience 'which cannot be excelled by any in the Australasian hemisphere,' and noted that it was better attended than in days of yore.[13]

When Andrew Bent, the printer of the *Hobart Town Gazette*, heard that an Auxiliary Bible Society had formed in Sydney under Macquarie's patronage, he (an ex-burglar from London) was inspired to take on the role of preacher himself in a purple passage of rhetoric hardly representative of the thoughts of the more hardened persons who were arriving in Hobart in 1817. He believed that there was no place on earth that needed the assistance of such a benevolent institution. He regarded the need for a religious education as necessary for juvenile minds. He believed that contemplation of what he saw as the 'ignorance' of the natives of the island must make people ardently wish for 'diffusion of that knowledge so admirably calculated to bring glory to God and happiness to Mankind'.[14]

Nothing he believed,

breathes a purer fragrance or bears a more heavenly aspect than education. It is a companion which no misfortune can depress — no clime destroy — no enemy alienate — no despotism enslave; at home a friend — abroad an introduction — in fortitude a solace — in society an ornament. It chastens vice — it guides virtue — it gives at once a grace and ornament to genius; without it, what is man? A splendid slave; a maligning savage; vacillating between the intelligence derived from God and the degradation of passions participated with brutes and in the accident their alternative ascendancy shuddering at the terror of a hereafter or hugging the horrid hope of reconciliation.[15]

Bent considered this world

A mighty maze and all without a plan; a dark, desolate and dreary cavern, without wealth, or ornament, or order; but light up within the torch of knowledge and see how wondrous the transition; the seasons change — the atmosphere breathes — the landscape lives — earth unfolds its fruits — ocean rolls in its magnificence — the heavens display their constelled canopy — and the grand animated spectacle of nature revealed before him; its varieties regulated and its mysteries resolved; the Phenomena which bewilder — the prejudices which debate — the superstitions which enslave vanish before education.[16]

And so what happened in Sydney, Hobart had to follow. Knopwood received a number of Bibles and Testaments from the Auxiliary Bible Society in Sydney, to distribute either by sale or gift to persons at Hobart and Port Dalrymple.[17] In April 1819, Governor Sorell sanctioned those wishing to meet and form an Auxiliary Branch Bible Society. He invited the Deputy Judge Advocate Abbott, Major Thomas Bell and Knopwood to Government House to frame the rules. They were all in mourning for the death of Queen Charlotte, 'after a tedious illness, which Her Majesty bore with the most pious fortitude and resig-

nation,' as orders from Government House proclaimed it. But that week the committee, while all the shops and even the court and public houses closed, checked on those who owned Bibles and Testaments. A memorial service for the Queen took place in the new church, its first service, and the church was very full. There were prayers but no sermon because there were, as yet, no windows in the church. Sorell, moreover, did not wish a funeral sermon to be the first sermon in the church.[18]

Benefactions to the Society came in rapidly. James Lord, together with his son David, was the only ex-*Calcutta* convict able to equal the amount of five guineas donated to the Society by Governor Sorell, Edward Lord and T. W. Birch. But other *Calcutta* men who joined were John Wade (two guineas), Urias Allender (£2), John Earle and James Austin (£1 each) and Oliver Smith (10s). Of the settlers who had left England in the *Ocean*, William Cockerill and Richard Pitt were able to afford a guinea each. Subsequently at a meeting held at Port Dalrymple, David Gibson provided two guineas, and further members in Hobart were William and Mary Stocker (one guinea each), William Cooper (£1) and William Williams (10s). Others who paid annual subscriptions to join included Michael Lawler, James Ballance, William Roberts and Sylvester Lush, whose membership did not prevent him from falling by the wayside soon afterwards.[19]

Not surprisingly, one learns little of the activities of the Bible Society from Knopwood, apart from the bare fact that he attended an odd annual meeting when the Governor was in the chair. In 1829 he came across from Clarence Plains to find they had a very full meeting in the Quarter Sessions room, after a good dinner provided by Governor Arthur, which to Knopwood was probably more memorable.[20]

Little is known of the activities of the Society, apart from its function to educate and propagate the Christian religion; but even less is known of the Freemasons, who were operating in Hobart at least as early as 1815. Knopwood conducted the burial service on Elizabeth Fawkner's father-in-law, Thomas Lucas, who had been a marine at Norfolk Island. He was buried by the Brothers in Masonic form. It was Sir Henry Browne Hayes, abductor of a Quaker heiress and a suspect at the time of the Castle Hill rising, who had founded the first Masonic Lodge in Sydney in 1803. Freemasons who had appeared at the laying of the foundation stone of St David's presumably paraded at all official ceremonies, which would have included the King's birthday, the anniversary of the King's accession to the throne, and any others decreed by the Governor.

Books had a low priority on the cargoes of goods which store-keepers advertised for sale in the earliest

Hobart Town Gazette, but as the literacy of the population increased more publications began to appear. Those which were available to the Fitzgeralds by 1822, and suitable for teaching purposes, included Dilworth's *Schoolmaster*, Carpenter's *Spelling Assistant*, Murray's *Exercises*, William Guthrie's *Grammar and Geography*, Brady's *Classical Poetry*, Bradley's *Geography*, Smith's *Writing Master*, Hill's *Improved Penmanship*, Enfield's *English Grammar*, Blair's *Dictionary*, Walkinghome's *Tutor's Assistant*, Clark's *Atlas*, Enfield's *Speaker*, and Hume's and Smollett's *History of England*. Some other books had won the approval not only of George III but also of Dr Johnson: Hugh Blair's *Sermons*, James Hervey's *Meditations*, sundry prayer books, John Wesley's *Commentaries on the Old and New Testaments*, and two volumes of Stackhouse's *History of the Bible*. There was also *Robinson Crusoe* which had been delighting young and old alike for more than a century, Madame de Genlis' *Dialogues in Six Languages*, a complete set (26 volumes) of the *Evangelical Magazine*, and Atmore's *Sermons on the Lord's Prayer*. There was a new edition available of the *Encyclopedia Britannica*, four volumes of Burns' poems, several histories of France, Rome and Greece, works in French and German, Nicholson's *Encyclopedia of the Arts and Sciences*, seven volumes of Moor's Works, Goldsmith's *Rome*, books on agriculture, medicine, law and travel. The works advertised were more secular than one might have imagined.[21]

Times had changed since George Harris had complained bitterly about the shortage of paper. Quills, pens and black-lead pencils, only a recent discovery, were available, as well as slates and all manner of stationery.

Spectator sport would have developed at a very early date in Van Diemen's Land. The privileged participants were rarely convicts or ex-convicts, but no one could prevent a good many 'government men' from forming an audience, even though those who were still ironed could hardly have been very competitive. Yet there were a few *Calcutta* men who made significant contributions to the entertainment of their fellows as the years rolled by and priorities began to change.

Hunting and fishing and shooting had formed part of the necessary means of survival in the early years of the settlement and were not considered recreational sports, although officers from the *Calcutta* had enjoyed such sportive activity while at the Cape of Good Hope. At Port Phillip, Knopwood and others had occupied many days shooting not so much as a sport, which they had enjoyed in the past, as to obtain fresh meat. Again at Sullivan Cove many of the convicts would have regarded the relaxed discipline, which

'Knoppy' on his favourite pony — a posthumous likeness by an unknown artist. The original painting, formerly attributed to T. G. Gregson, belongs to the Diocese of Tasmania.

almost encouraged them to escape on account of the near-famine, as an occasion to exercise their skills at marksmanship.

Horses were an indispensable means of personal transport. What tales of riotous living and occasional tender pastoral care that most famous white pony, which Knopwood rode for thirty years, must have harboured! When a man had a horse he became anxious to display its speed.[22] As a result horse-racing was one of the earliest sports introduced to the colony. The first racing of any account was at Cornelian Bay. In June 1813 James Meehan surveyed Andrew Whitehead's land at the Government Farm and marked off a section at the half-mile post for the racecourse.[23] Some of the *Calcutta* men were among the earliest to contribute to the development of this sport.

When there was a suggestion that a forthcoming race meeting might be moved from New Town, the *Hobart Town Gazette* thought it would cause considerable disappointment to the sporting fraternity and the public in general. New Town had attracted 'all the fashion in the colony'. In October, however, it reported that races at Orielton Park (Edward Lord's estate) attracted a number of gentlemen and settlers who were 'highly delighted with the Beautiful and Picturesque scene, on which the favourite Animals were to exhibit their speed'.[24]

When James Mitchell and Thomas McNeeland raced their horses in May 1814 for a £5 bet over the best of three two-mile heats (won by McNeeland) Knopwood was there to report the event attended by all the ladies, civil and military officers and 'other gents', presumably meaning those who had been pardoned and served their sentences as well as the free settlers.[25]

Andrew Geils, during the time of his command in Hobart, had bred a number of horses which might have performed reasonably well in a race. Several *Calcutta* men, including Daniel Anchor, John Wade and Thomas Peters acquired some of these horses when they were auctioned at Restdown after Geils left Geilston. The Norfolk Island man William Maum bought Beauty, together with a filly foal which became a fine mare, described as much larger than her mother and which would beat anything in the country. Maum matched her with a mare belonging to James Stynes and Richard Troy, so they could race at the following Michaelmas races at Orielton Park. In the meantime the mares were put to stud and each produced young foals.[26]

Wade bought a bay filly, described as 'one of the sweetest things in the country', for £80 which came out of a mare that Geils had exchanged for the horse Countess. She, too, proved with foal and could not race on the turf although she was considered very fast.[27]

Anchor, who was a good horseman, bought a dark brown pony for £36 and a chestnut pony for £80. Mann paid £100 for a black filly, daughter to Gipsy and aged eighteen months. Thomas Peters was racing horses as early as September 1814 when he won against John Ingle's mare Diana over the best of three four-mile heats. Lieutenant-Governor Davey set the vice-regal seal on the event. Peters' grey horse and a horse owned by William Stocker were among the regular challengers. The St Patrick's Day races of 1815 had to be cancelled, the reason given being that there were many bushrangers abroad and the Governor's apprehensions that the confusion and drunkenness created at the races would be against the public interest. One of Stocker's horses, Ross, which had won several races over two miles weight-for-age, was put to stud at three guineas.[28]

The following July, Knopwood referred to the first trotting race. At the meeting in August 1815 Governor Davey celebrated the event with a dinner to all the civil and military officers and gentlemen of the colony followed by a ball and supper at Government house. One wonders whether the Whiteheads and Stockers, who had entertained Davey often in their capacity as members of the racing fraternity, had yet achieved the right to attend Government House functions.

Maum employed one of the true characters among the *Calcutta* graduates, Thomas Tombs, to ride Beauty. He claimed to have been the former jockey of Lord Barrymore. Tombs won easily on Beauty in October 1816 at Orielton when the stake was £300, but lost when he rode Captain Blyth's horse Jacky there the following week. John Ingle, retaining faith in his mare Diana, put her in a challenge against any horse in the colony to race against her at Orielton Park provided the loser paid £500. But some of the owners who entered their horses disputed this and the race was cancelled.[29]

Peters, when living in Liverpool Street, kept stables which he let to persons who wished to breed. In 1816 James Gordon stood the celebrated stallion St Andrew, that he had bought from the Geils' estate, at Peters' stables for the fee of seven guineas and one shilling for the groom.[30] Through his daughter Elizabeth, succeeding generations of Peters' descendants have been among the best-known members of the racing and horse-breeding fraternity.

The auction of Geils' belongings had been a great social occasion for a number of *Calcutta* convicts who had begun to prosper within ten years of their arrival in Van Diemen's Land. Apart from Peters, Wade and Mann, Thomas Williams and Andrew Whitehead also made purchases. They were for once able to compete on equal terms with officers and those who had come free to the colony. Peters, then employed as a blacksmith at Restdown, spent £45 19s 6d. He paid eleven guineas for seven cedar cane-bottom chairs and £9 for a gilded china teaset which might have been Dr Wall's Worcester or Derby.

Peters, having also acquired a 'set of body cloaths' for seven guineas (presumably the clothes of the acting Lieutenant-Governor) was already well on the way to respectability. He and Wade bought 100 pounds of coffee each, while Williams obtained a nine-piece china dessert set for £2 5s. Wade settled for nineteen pieces of earthenware for which he paid £2 18s, twenty yards of blue chintz (£7) and another twenty-eight yards of chintz (£5 15s). Williams got a bargain with twelve mahogany stuffed cotton chairs at £27 6s and a Huon pine bedstead for £5.[31]

These were some of the little luxuries these successful convicts acquired, as well as more practical objects such as saddles, bridles, agricultural equipment, candles and the brass drawer locks and cupboard locks which took Andrew Whitehead's fancy. One would suspect that Whitehead's shady dealings had already provided him with enough comforts and necessities and that the locks would adorn some fine Huon pine furnishings made, perhaps, by the cabinet maker, James Riley.

Peters was again to the fore in October 1815 when a boat race between his boat and naval officer, James Gordon's boat competed to win fifty guineas, but Peters lost. He had by then presumably received a free pardon, having petitioned Governor Macquarie in 1812.[32] Boat races became popular and challenges frequent, but none more dangerous in the Derwent waters than the occasions when Urias Allender, fearless in his cups, and other ferrymen tried to race each other. Boats were still strongly discouraged, and few convicts were entrusted with command of even the smallest craft.

During the Christmas holidays at the end of 1815 and 1816, Knopwood mentioned that the people were playing cricket and other games at Sandy Bay, but cricket must have also been played earlier given the report that *Calcutta* men played at Port Phillip. Martha Whitehead and Lieutenant Bowen were ancestors of a test cricketer as well as one of Australia's most prominent woman educationalists.[33]

The Vandemonians didn't need much encouragement to patronise boxing tournaments. Unscheduled ones occurred every day in the taverns or on the waterfront. It is not surprising that boxing was one of the earliest organised sports and that Allender must have been the star turn, whether drunk or sober. In March 1818 the grand *milling* matches fought on a private field a mile from the town, which they called the 'Waterloo of the fisty-cuffs', provided four contests. The set-to between Richard Herring and Allender (named as a rough customer in the ring) took only a few rounds but the *Gazette* reported that 'a numerous concourse of spectators attended, all apparently much delighted with their afternoon's entertainment'.[34]

Foot-racing, with or without irons, would have occurred on the sands at Sullivan Bay, but the first organised athletics meeting was a race on the road to New Town on the King's birthday holiday in June 1816. Twelve gentlemen started at the top of the hill near the potteries and ran two miles to the house of George Gunning, recently married to Ann Jane Harris (née Hobbs), the widow of George Harris. The populace had to be content, as usual, with the firing of the royal salute and hoisting of the royal standard to mark the occasion. An American schooner, the *Ontario*, was in town and it was a remarkably fine day. That evening the Governor gave an elegant dinner for thirty-four persons, including the athletes. None but the military officers and gentlemen were eligible to attend. In Macquarie's Sydney it might have been different. The Peters, Whiteheads and Stockers had apparently still no access to Government House on official occasions. Even so, they had already come a long way.[35]

31 PUTTING DOWN ROOTS

MOST OF THOSE who took up the land prospered, some more than others. This was especially the case if the man had a woman in his life. Marriage or cohabitation usually brought children who, from the tenderest years, would be trained to till the soil, to sow the seeds, to tend the crops, to gather the harvest. They helped milk the cows, feed the poultry and the dogs, harness or tether the horses, chase up the straying sheep and, in between times, amuse the newest baby. In the outlying areas there were no schools for a long time. Some of the children remained as illiterate as their parents. Others had parents able to teach them. In 1829 the population of the settled districts of Tasmania was 13 000. Twelve hundred children were at school, and of these 120 were receiving a classical education.[1]

But children generally were not a liability. They were the unpaid servants, often working side by side with a ticket-of-leave man assigned to the family on government rations. Apart from the Mansfields' seventeen children, the Pearsalls and Mundays each had eleven; the Peters and the Welsh Thomas Williams had ten; the Hays, Hangans, Birchalls and Allenders produced nine in each family; the Richardsons had eight and the Wades seven. In the north John Boothman had eight, James Davey had seven and David Gibson brought up twelve children, including the two love-children of his wife Elizabeth (by Captain Piper and John Holmes), both born at Norfolk Island. All the *Calcutta* convicts who remained in the towns had much smaller families.

It was no surprise to find that many of the early landowners grew rich. Their expenses were minimal and their rewards great. But they worked day and night for what they got. They worked until their sinews stood out, hard like the veins of iron deposits interstratified with limestone. Their women grew old and bowed with years of child-bearing, old and cowed with years of drudgery and fear.

Yet they too, like those who went down to the sea in ships, were happy with their lot, for different reasons. They constituted a society which they knew would bring great benefits to their descendants — or their heirs, as James Austin and Joseph Johnson sensed when, childless, they brought out their nephews from England. How often they must have paused to contemplate their turn of fortune, comparing their condition with that of earlier times. In England, had they been lucky enough to get even a lowly job, they could never have risen above the labouring class from which most of them had sprung in the first place. But there were a few who could philosophise and make themselves believe that, after all their vicissitudes, the cultivation of their own garden and the work that would preserve them from those evils of weariness, vice and want, should have made them the most content of human beings. At least their children had a future. However, greed became the order of the day for most and the acquisition of more and more land, more and more stock, created a wealthy ex-convict class bound to the virgin soil of Van Diemen's Land.

Peace at long last on the other side of the world had brought new problems in its train. Unemployment and the population both increased rapidly. At the same time Britain saw a new world arising; sea lanes would be safe for her ships, new markets for traders on the make, new lands to colonise. Young men and their families received encouragement to emigrate. Small farmers and tradesmen with families could find opportunities for a future that they could never experience in the class-conscious land of their birth. Within a few years of the Battle of Waterloo more and more settlers began to arrive. Many would rise to a status in society that helped diminish the military control that had dominated a largely convict colony.

They had strong prejudices. Persons like Roderic O'Connor, who helped prepare the report of the Land Commissioners, vehemently opposed the system by which ex-convicts had received grants of good ground. Even worse was the system by which, after emancipation and a free land grant, some of the unwary had lost all they had to a rapacious creditor or land-hungry shark in exchange for little more than that popular currency, a bottle of rum. David Gibson, James Lord and William Thomas Stocker in particular were singled out as occupying immense tracts of land on which they did not support one stock-keeper. They owned large numbers of flocks and herds, impossible to remove, and turned a blind eye when ruffians on the make marked and branded as their own the stock of the small settler, who was saddled with so many restrictions.[2] The Land Commissioners especially criticised the quit rent system by which James Lord's son David, for instance, the richest man in the colony, paid about 40s a year quit rent for 2 100 acres at York Plains on which he grazed about 1 500 head of cattle and 4 500 sheep, his only improvement on the whole property being a 'miserable log hut . . . He does not cut one Tree, he makes no Fences . . . he employs no more Men than suffice to keep his Sheep together, the Cattle being allowed to roam a distance of eighteen or twenty Miles'.[3]

The determination of the new type of settler to quell the influence of the convict class almost succeeded. Van Diemen's Land was already becoming a repository for the worst types of convicts and the aspiring rich supported the system of transportation to the hilt. For them it meant a continuing supply of cheap labour and great profits which could only increase their pastoral dominance.

The virgin soil of Van Diemen's Land yielded some remarkable products that astounded the newcomers with their size. In 1819 the *Gazette* reported that Oliver Smith dug out a horseradish from his garden in Collins Street which measured two feet eight inches, while one single potato root produced 113 fine kidney-shaped potatoes, most weighing up to one pound each. By 1826 James Austin announced that his prize ox weighed 1 228 pounds without the offal. The suet alone weighed 130 pounds.[4]

Some of the better farmers, anxious to increase their crops or reap a good harvest to beat any inclement weather, would advertise incentives to workers. One was Augustus Morris who offered encouragement to his fifteen to twenty reapers in the form of a suit of new wearing apparel to be given to the best reaper.[5]

Those who failed to make good mainly frittered away their money in the ever-present temptation of alcohol. They could not meet their creditors and lost their land and other possessions, including a wife if they had one. Opportunity once lost, rarely returned to those whose weaknesses led them along the paths of licentiousness and dissipation.

By the year 1824 they had spread out in many directions. Changes in the political and judicial systems meant little to the men and women on the land. Their immediate interests were to provide a better world for their children. When James Lord died in

1824 of 'a painful illness which he bore with Christian fortitude' he left an estate worth at least £50 000 which helped his son David increase his own capital at a great rate. James had been 'one of the oldest and most respected inhabitants, and his eccentric style of dressing in old fashioned knee breeches and large buckled shoes would be missed.[6] During the same year Augustus Morris, already widowed, had died and the orphaned children inherited an estate which Adolarius Humphrey wisely administered.[7]

Some of the townsfolk had managed to acquire runs in the country either by lease or grant from which they could derive great benefits at low labour costs. By 1826 Stocker had advertised a 400-acre property on the Macquarie River (at present-day Ross) and his team of bullocks to let or to lease to any industrious person or persons. There were two farmhouses. The land had been cultivated and enclosed. It was lightly covered with small timber, chiefly mimosa.

In the Oatlands area there were stock huts belonging to David Lord and John Earle, who was pound keeper at the Eastern Marshes, while Henry Rice, the explorer, lived in a little mud hut at the Coal River. In contrast James Austin's Roseneath and David Lord's Richmond Park, built on his father's land at Richmond, were fine solid two-storey houses, still standing until burnt down during the 1967 bushfires.

John Clark's house Rosewood at the Tea Tree Brush stands to this day in a sound state of preservation and is cherished by the Gangell family, descendants of Corporal William Gangell, one of the marines who arrived with Governor Collins. Clark built the original house and outbuildings soon after receiving his land grant in 1817. Clark's great-great-great-grandson has provided the writer with a detailed description of the property as he saw it in 1983. It is a farmhouse probably typical of those belonging to the more successful convicts who took up life on the land:

The present 'Rosewood' is originally a two-storey handcut stone dwelling which would have had a shingle roof as did all the other buildings. The bakehouse is a wonderfully constructed room external to the main building . . . Another external room is the 'smoke room' where all meat was hung and smoked so as to preserve it. The timber used was pit sawn slab lain over hand cut joists and close lain (no cracks) from the ceilings, the walls being constructed in similar ways. Nails if used would have been hand-made. Marks from the pit saw, broad axe and adze are clearly discernible on the smoke stained timber . . .

The stables are built of free stone and have flagstone floors . . . The cow-bails are built of hand split slab as are the stables for the work horses and the feed troughs and mangers are all still quite functional. There is a hay rack above the mangers in the work horse stalls . . . The shearing shed is still much the same as when it was built, hand cut and sawn timber much in evidence. It has a high roof

John Clark's house Rosewood at Tea Tree Brush before alterations. It is the present home of Gangell descendants.

and light wells in the roof to allow for as much sunlight to get through as possible . . . there is a ten-metre-deep well which still supplies water when required. A rather rusty windmill sits astride the opening. Adjacent is a stone fence built from loose stones gathered up when the fields were ploughed. The stones now are covered in moss and lichens, some of which would no doubt predate 'Rosewood' . . .

The hawthorn tree seedlings now grow through this rock wall which at its end joins up with a hand-made post and rail fence which has withstood the ravages of time.

On the front of the building the right hand half of the upper and lower verandas has been built in by the addition of two delightful rooms with bay windows and the front entrance is now on the right of the entrance steps, the original door and architraves being used.

The interior of the house has been restored to original splendour with magnificent embossed period type wallpaper. There are burgundy coloured carpets on the floor and the narrow staircase has been restored . . .
Furnishings of the period are gradually being added to the house and rooms are taking on the appearance which only tender loving care, time, patience and money can acquire.[8]

At Green Ponds there was a prosperous community and good camaraderie among the ex-*Calcutta* convicts. It was to this area, many years later, that William Buckley came to rendezvous with his old shipmates and regale them with the stories of his thirty-two years among the natives at Port Phillip.[9] George Ashton, Joseph Johnson and Thomas Poole had taken up land grants at Green Ponds. Before any inns were built in the locality, travellers received a fine welcome

at what James Ross called 'Ashton's neat little cottage, a feature of hospitality characteristic of settlers in the remote and less populated parts of Van Diemen's Land'.[10] Peter Murdoch and Roderic O'Connor, as Land Commissioners, visited Green Ponds in 1826, discovering that Constable Ashton's place Glenfern was 'neat and comfortable', with much tillage on his 160 acres where 500 sheep grazed.[11] The Commissioners also visited several others who had arrived in 1804: Thomas Poole, who had 'a good farm', James Waltham, 'a poor man who had lost his sight', and the prosperous Richard Pitt, the most respected of the settlers who had sailed in the *Ocean*.[12] One unfortunate incident occurred in 1827 when a fierce hailstorm caused £200 worth of damage to Ashton's corn crop and devastated his excellent garden.[13]

Joseph Johnson named his property Tissington after the charming village in Derbyshire, venerated by its inhabitants since the fourteenth century when the purity of the water in its wells spared them from the ravages of the Black Death. The brick house of two storeys and a freestone barn had the date A.D. 1827 incised into the keystone above the entrance. Just one hundred years later a newer and bigger house was built between the original house and barn.[14]

Murdoch and O'Connor had also called at Tissington where they discovered an abundance of wheat

Joseph Johnson of Tissington, Green Ponds, 'an elderly man by whom we were courteously received and invited to lodge' (James Backhouse, March 1834).

stored in the barn and a delightful stream running at the back of the house. They found the wealthy Johnson a 'fine, sensible old Man, of great integrity', an 'excellent character' who had fenced in many of his 350 acres with heavy logs expected to last for some forty or fifty years. He had fifty acres in cultivation and ran 1200 sheep, 100 head of cattle and about fifty goats.[15]

In March 1834 James Backhouse spent a night at Johnson's house where the elderly man received him courteously. He had 'prospered greatly and now possessed of 5000 acres — 2000 sheep, some horned cattle. He has taught himself to read and write, and his Bible has the appearance of being well read'. His wife who was formerly a prisoner 'prepared us tea and waited on us very kindly.' This was Jane Hadden whose 'marriage' to Johnson, as it turned out, was a bigamous one.[16]

John (known also as Thomas) Prestage seemed one of the least likely of all the convicts to have succeeded in anything that required hard work. He had come from a family of ne'er-do-wells in Northampton, the father and most of the children, including himself (aged thirty-eight at the time of conviction) on poor relief. Yet he was one of the first pardoned and became among the most industrious farmers at Pitt Water. There he had a good house with three rooms for him-

self and an outhouse for the four men he employed on his sixty acres. He had installed an *oven*, which indicates it was probably as important a feature then as a dishwasher might be today. There was a weatherboard barn containing 600 bushels of wheat and a good outhouse and stable for men, a garden orchard of two acres and farmer's utensils. He lost extensive grain crops in March 1820 when they were set alight by an incendiarist. The government and local settlers offered £100 reward for information relating to the fire and everyone lamented the loss. Thomas Riley was at first suspected of lighting one of the stacks in which a firestick had been found, and Thomas Welsh and Francis Gallagher spread what appeared to be a false rumour that Riley was the culprit after Prestage took legal action before the Bench of Magistrates against the accusers. Gallagher was a ticket-of-leave man working for Riley and Welsh was a convict servant. It appeared to have been a dry season and a week before Riley had been advised of the danger of lighting fires. Accusations flew around the court. Prestage began to suspect his own brother-in-law, a man named Heatley, and Magistrate James Gordon suggested it was an Oyster Bay black who went under the stacks with his wife and children for shelter, and who lit the fire and ran away. The court found Gallagher and Welsh were the guilty ones. Gallagher lost his ticket-of-leave and the two received 100 lashes each and transportation to Newcastle for three years.[17]

John Birchall's place at Pitt Water, near the Sorell rivulet and formerly part of Humphrey's land, was known as Marsh Farm. He had a spacious dwelling house which he advertised to let in 1825, consisting of seven good rooms in excellent repair, with several allotments in cultivation and houses on each, all in the most fertile land in the district. He had farmed there since 1809, the first in the district, where he had been granted 155 acres and purchased at least 833 further acres by 1831. By 1827 two of his sons had left the local school, but he still had five other children as pupils there. John Wade, in the same area, had his two eldest at the school but the four younger ones were taught at home.[18] It seems that those living in urban areas such as Hobart and Launceston had greater educational opportunities than those in rural areas, where families were often larger and more likely to become agricultural workers on the family property.

John Pearsall had by 1825 installed his family in a large commodious weatherboard house at Clarence Plains, where he had a farm of seventy acres including a five-acre garden. His house had six good rooms together with barns and outhouses.[19]

The 1828 census showed William Richardson's house, situated on fifty acres of land purchased from William Hoskins at Muddy Plains, was built of timber and consisted of a house twenty-four feet long valued at £20, a barn £30, stock yards and pigsties £5. This would have been the typical abode of the small-time farmers.

The rise of David Gibson had been phenomenal after his second escape from the hangman's noose. A change of company and life style when he became one of Robert Campbell's stock-keepers and later overseer of Edward Lord's great estates gave him some responsibility and an opportunity to open up vast agricultural lands to become the acknowledged pioneer of Tasmania's north. Within the space of a few years he was able to acquire his own vast estates in the island's richest area and to become one of the wealthiest men in the colony.

In February 1814 Knopwood took a trip by chaise from Hobart to Launceston. Gibson, visiting Hobart from Port Dalrymple, was to take charge of a bullock cart, assisted by three men hired to carry the baggage. They stopped at Mrs Hayes' at Bagdad for refreshments and, while Knopwood (being unwell afterwards) decided to sleep at John Ingle's stock-hut, Gibson took the cart on to Green Ponds. The next night they all stayed at Macquarie Springs, having killed several kangaroos along the way. They killed more the next day before arriving that evening at the Duck Ponds. The following evening they reached the Black Snake on the final stage of their journey before arrival at Port Dalrymple. The guard of the 73rd Regiment checked their passes and the list of goods they carried in the cart so that no contraband might be brought into the northern settlement. [20]

During his visit to the north Knopwood baptised many children and performed marriage ceremonies for several couples whose unions had received some sort of recognition by a magistrate. Five years would pass before the Reverend John Youl arrived as the recognised clergyman at Port Dalrymple. He would then marry David Gibson and Elizabeth Nicholls, the ex-mistress of Captain John Piper, Commandant at Norfolk Island, and on the same day baptise two of her children, the first of many by Gibson. They had farmed neighbouring lands, Elizabeth having received fifty acres and valuable stock in her own right after she arrived in 1813. [21]

In the meantime Gibson had been the victim of robberies in which bushrangers stole muslin, silver, bed-linen, clothing, a pistol and a musket.

Probably as a result of this and the theft of 1 000 sheep by that incorrigible family of sheep stealers, the Trimbys, Gibson signed a petition from the settlers at Launceston to Deputy Judge Advocate Abbott asking for a regular court session at Launceston, but the petition was refused. [22] He was also aware that his business arrangements with the Lords would not enhance his own reputation in the higher circles which he hoped to cultivate. Governor Macquarie had thought Lord

David Gibson, of Pleasant Banks, Evandale, rose from piracy to riches. In March 1828 Governor Arthur observed that 'his prosperity is now enormous'.

'vindictive and implacable'. Lord was currently in trouble, suspected of smuggling from the *Kangaroo*, whose master, Charles Jeffreys, formerly a Royal Naval lieutenant, had probably met Gibson during an earlier visit to the colony and had found him an 'opulent and industrious grazier'. [23]

An absolute pardon gave Gibson the confidence to go his own way. He then wrote to Maria Lord from Launceston (in big, black, bold handwriting) asking her to send someone to kill off some of her sheep, as the stock was becoming too numerous to keep within any limits of ground. He advised that some of her bullocks had strayed as far as seventy miles from the Black Snake area. He was too often away from home and had servants' wages to pay. He was anxious to manage only his own affairs. [24]

The break with Lord paid off. By 1820 Gibson had a grant of 1 000 extra acres from Governor Macquarie and, in addition to an original thirty acres, had purchased 760 acres. [25] The Macquaries, with their son Lachlan, were his guests at Pleasant Banks, his home on the South Esk River at present-day Evandale. It was a two-storeyed house made of pit sawn boards, and stood until demolished about 1915. The viceregal visit was the imprimatur that Gibson had needed for his acceptance in the community. But his success would inflame jealousy among the free settlers for a long time to come.

177

Governor Macquarie found his house 'a most comfortable one indeed; and where we found abundance of everything that was good'. On their return from Launceston they crossed the river 'in Mr Gibson's boat immediately under his house . . . Mr Gibson attended at the ferry . . . was most civil and useful in rendering us every assistance . . . We had a good dinner of beef steakes [sic] and went early to bed'.[26]

The following day Macquarie wrote enthusiastically that he 'returned home to dinner after a most beautiful and interesting ride through a very rich tract of country'. The next day he decided to stay one day longer and sent his baggage on ahead. He went down the river, convinced that the locals needed a public ferry, and fixed on the place, also on the site of a township for 'the part of the country adjoining the ferry on a very rich point of land, which I have named Perth; Mr Gibson who is a native of that town having promised to build a good inn there directly'. Two days later they set out from Gibson's on their journey south.[27]

Godwin's *Emigrant's Guide* (of 1823) directed visitors to the property of the 'industrious grazier, at whose house the traveller may always ensure a friendly reception and accommodation'. He was echoing sentiments expressed by surveyor G. W. Evans.[28] Many took this advice and called on David Gibson at Pleasant Banks and had good words to say of him, from James Fenton to Richard Howitt, Henry Widowson and Henry Melville. John Helder Wedge surveyed his surrounding land and fell into the river with his horse, and was roused by Gibson's laughter, but assurance in his Scottish accent that 'it was no laughing matter when ye were floundering aboot in the River . . . ye may go in here — it is quite foordable.' Wedge stayed the night in Gibson's hut but was bitten by fleas.[29] Widowson remarked that 'the house and premises are pleasantly situated, although there is nothing very elegant in their construction'.[30] Surveyor Thomas Scott, who accompanied Lieutenant-Governor Arthur on his northern tour in 1829, remarked on the 'very extensive plain of beautiful grazing land claimed by Mr Gibson who has built a stock-hut there. This plain is 12 miles across in one direction and well-watered . . . We named these plains the Dairy Plains'.[31] Gibson had now extended his territory beyond the future Deloraine!

In 1829 James Ross described the situations of Gibson's farms and stockyards 'passing through a tract of the richest land in the island'. His *Almanack* informed readers that the fourth Post Office messenger received his load at 'Mr Willis's at Wanstead and arrives at Mr Gibson's on the South Esk about five in the afternoon. Here he deposits all the letters addressed to persons in that neighbourhood . . .'[32]

G. A. Robinson passed through this area in September 1830 but did not call. He noted that Gibson's stock-keeper had helped to massacre a party of natives. 'On one occasion he ripped up a man's belly with his knife.'[33] This was at a time when the blacks were spearing women and children and went hunting with wild dogs, the time when Governor Arthur formed his famous Black Line to try to drive the hostile natives towards the Tasman Peninsula. But Gibson's own attitude to the blacks was said to be sensible and kindly and he occasionally killed a sheep or a bullock, hanging it on a tree for the blacks to come and help themselves so that they would leave his stock alone.[34]

Newspapers frequently reported his activities and those of his family. According to the *Hobart Town Gazette*'s list of tenders for meat for September 1820, Gibson was providing as much as 6 000 pounds for the Commissariat. In 1826 the same paper reported 'Mr Gibson of the South Esk has, we learn, fed an ox which will weigh little short of 2 000 lb'.[35]

Gibson applied to Lieutenant-Governor Arthur for more land in March 1828 but his request was refused. Arthur could 'not lose sight of the circumstances under which Mr Gibson came to this colony . . . His prosperity is now enormous . . .'[36] He had bought to date 6 500 acres in addition to his previous grants. He owned 1 500 head of cattle, 4 000 sheep, twenty-seven horses and was employing eleven Crown servants. He had spent £2200 in improvements on his property. Apparently in 1839 he failed to pay £48 7s 5d interest to the Crown on 868 acres purchased in 1828 and government notices in the *Hobart Town Gazette* and *Courier* threatened action against him. Two years later the *Courier* gave notice that claims for grants would be ready for examination. Gibson was claiming a further 467 acres in Cleveland.[37]

The *Colonial Times* disclosed in November 1840 that he had 1 000 acres under the plough 'without the intervention of a single stump'. He averaged thirty bushels of wheat per acre in 1839 at ten shillings per bushel. Five hundred acres were under wheat. He produced many turnips weighing up to '50 lb [each!] without tops or roots . . . seven fat oxen, fed upon turnips, which will average 1 200 lb each . . .'. He paid £500 each for two bulls of the pure Durham breed imported from England. He showed at the cattle show in Launceston and sent wheat to the Paris Exhibition of 1855.[38]

By 1840 he had built on to Pleasant Banks, which the *Colonial Times* described as this 'splendid mansion cannot cost less than £10 000, and in point of situation, accommodation, materials and workmanship, even that sum would be almost inadequate'.[39] The style was mock-Georgian with cast-iron balustrades. At the time of the 1842 census thirty-one lived on the property. Thirteen were free persons.

The house was almost destroyed by fire a few years later. The fire occurred on Christmas morning during the preparation of a festive dinner. The Gibsons sat down sadly to eat all that was left of their meal — the Christmas pudding. The house was rebuilt and life returned to normal.[40]

The Gibson family headed the petition to the government for the establishment of a Presbyterian Church at Evandale.[41] During its construction in 1839 and before his own cottage was ready to live in, the Reverend Robert Russell, the first clergyman of the delightful St Andrew's, lived at Pleasant Banks. The Governor, Sir John Franklin, came to lay the foundation stone and, according to the clergyman, 'paid us Scotchmen a very high compliment because of the efficiency of our church at home. I trusted that the same important results would follow its establishment here'.[42]

Here it was that David Gibson came to rest. He died of 'debility' on 15 April 1858 in his eighty-second year and all who knew him mourned his passing. His old friend, the Reverend Russell, eulogised: 'Like a shock fully ripe, he has gone down from among us, accompanied by the regrets of almost every man in the colony whose good opinion is worth having. My little church did not nearly hold those who were assembled at the funeral'.[43]

In appearance we know that David Gibson was of medium height and that he had red hair. As an old man, a portrait by an anonymous artist shows him as a still somewhat tough, indomitable character, which he must have been to have survived those early years; he had a determined mouth but rather sad eyes. But they had been far-seeing eyes and the prudence which came instinctively to him, even when he had to decide to return and take the consequences after his three dangerous escapades, certainly brought him and his descendants handsome rewards.

The Gibsons for several generations have provided Tasmania with some of its leading citizens. One son, William Gibson, alone gave away more than £40 000, mostly for the establishment of Baptist churches. Other descendants entered the judiciary, parliament and other leading professions and their contribution to public life has been immense. The stud merinos developed by James Gibson, David's sixth son who became an MLC, were known throughout the world. Some of his fine properties are still in the hands of the family today. One branch still lives at the beautiful Native Point. Pleasant Banks remained in the Gibson family until 1929 when Mr and Mrs R. J. Foster bought the property, later opening it up as a pleasant venue for paying guests.

32 DROWNING THEIR SORROWS

ON ALL EVIDENCE available, the record of the *Calcutta* convicts provides a picture of a fairly well behaved and abstemious group. Many were described as sober upright men during the course of their lives. Had they been anything else the achievements of the pioneering days, the sheer survival of the fittest, would have been very different. But they had their moments and many were not averse to providing the occasion and the venue for conviviality or ribaldry, sometimes causing loss of land, sometimes causing loss of life.

Governor Macquarie, after his first visit to Van Diemen's Land in 1811, instituted a series of regulations which allowed an annual quota of spirits to officers and publicans. In February 1812 he notified Commandant Geils that 1 500 gallons of good Bengal rum would arrive at the Derwent. In any future arrangements made with the contractors the intake of a 2 000 gallon limit would be imposed on any one trader at the one time.[1]

Bengal and Jamaican rum were fixed at 7s 6d a gallon to the importer plus 3s duty to go to the Police Fund. All civil and military officers were allowed fifty gallons annually, with diminishing amounts for subordinate ranks in the public service. The Irish who came free from Norfolk Island were particularly dependent on alcohol as the mainstay of their social life. As at Port Jackson, rum was also a very useful commodity as a recognised form of currency.

There could be nothing more frustrating to those who were trying to keep law and order than the antics of Andrew Whitehead who had conspired with the ex-Norfolk Islander Denis McCarty to smuggle spirits in 1814. It hadn't helped that Macquarie himself and his wife had been impressed by the comfortable hospitality they had received in 1811 from McCarty at Birch Grove, his farm at New Norfolk which lent an air of respectability to the ex-convict from Norfolk Island. Most of the locals had objected to his methods, accusing him of giving them short measure and lying. Even when he lost his official job it was only

temporary. The gift of the blarney had managed to inveigle Whitehead, Stocker and others of substance and influence into his circle. He was never out of trouble, even though he suffered little from his misdemeanours and malpractices.[2]

Since October 1807, soon after receiving an absolute pardon, Whitehead had been overseer in the care and management of the government farm at Cornelian Bay, New Town, whereupon he became a neighbour to most of those who had arrived as free settlers in the *Ocean*, including the two Hayes families. He was, together with McCarty, R. W. Loane and T. W. Birch, among the four signatories to a salutory address to the Macquaries when they first arrived in Hobart Town. The vice-regal visitors had inspected his farm at New Town and referred to him as a 'respectable farmer'. His recent marriage to Martha Hayes Quinn, the mother of Lieutenant Bowen's children, had granted him some status.[3] By 1814 Knopwood was referring to the Whiteheads as among the gentlemen and ladies of the colony. Sometimes he attended, in their company, the frequent meetings at the racecourse which was on their property. On other occasions he called with the little orphan girl he had adopted, taking gifts of spring peas and strawberries grown in his garden at Cottage Green.[4]

But Whitehead was drawn towards the shady speculative deals which Denis McCarty plotted. Whitehead was one of the few who gave witness on his behalf before the Bench of Magistrates in December 1813 when settlers brought charges against McCarty, as superintendent of stock, for trafficking in cattle and provisions. Because of his private commitments, Macquarie advised against McCarty's continuance as a government employee. But McCarty was a survivor. He was by far the ablest person in the district.

During this period the association of McCarty and Whitehead became closer and the visits of Knopwood more frequent. In fact, between January 1814 and May 1814 when the *Argo* reached port, Knopwood visited the Whiteheads at least twenty times. In addi-

180

tion, he recorded hurried meetings between himself, Captain Carr of the schooner *Derwent,* Captain John Poore Dixon of the *Argo,* the trader R. W. Loane, as well as McCarty and Whitehead.

In spite of his friendship with the last and the probability that he himself was to some extent implicated, Knopwood as a magistrate had to record on 11 June that he had 'seised [*sic*] Mr Whitehead's spirits and brought it to the stores.' On 26 June the Bench of Magistrates confirmed that Governor Davey's overbearing secretary, Lieutenant Thomas Lascelles, had seized 2 800 gallons of spirits smuggled from the *Argo* by McCarty and Whitehead.[5] They received sentences of twelve months gaol in Sydney, but Whitehead remained at Hobart Town under house arrest.[6]

Macquarie expressed his 'very great surprise that so invidious a distinction should have been made' between the two settlers. On examining the evidence he had thought there had been a 'glaring partiality,' inconsistent with justice, believing Whitehead was involved to a much greater degree, being one 'whose guilt does not admit of a shadow of doubt . . .'[7]

The winners were the wily Edward and Maria Lord who appear for once to have kept out of the dealings. But Lord was around at the right time when the spirits were put up for sale at a public auction. He paid 16s a gallon for half the quantity and 16s 6d for the other half. That evening Knopwood entertained Whitehead, McCarty and Captain Carr as well as Loane and Madame D'Hotsman, a Mauritius-born woman whom Loane had brought from Calcutta, at what must have seemed like a wake.[8] The dreams of riches and even greater opportunities to wallow in alcohol (or rather, make money from others who did) had passed for the time being.

Captain Dixon himself got away in the *Argo* by an act of piracy, no doubt afraid that his own collusion would lead him to trial. He illegally departed, taking on some convicts, including Dr Hopley's servant, Michael Doyle, a highway robber before his transportation in the *Calcutta.* Governor Davey armed the schooner *Estramina* to pursue the *Argo* but it escaped capture. Dixon, aware of the consequences of harbouring one with a life sentence, callously off-loaded Doyle in a leaky boat in Storm Bay soon after they set sail. Nothing more was heard of Doyle.[9]

Macquarie was fast losing patience with these shady subjects at the Derwent about whom he had been warned by Governor Davey, not least of the schemers being Knopwood himself. Macquarie continued his blasting:

The Piratical escape and illegal departure of the Ship *Argo* from the Derwent is much to be lamented, and is of so atrocious and daring a nature, when coupled with the other circumstances attending that Transaction, as to call for the most severe and exemplary Punishment being inflicted on the Perpetrators, whenever they can be found or apprehended.[10]

He sent a statement of the incident to the government of Bengal where the *Argo* belonged, asking that Captain Dixon be returned for trial for piracy and seducing convicts. He also expressed a belief that Loane and Carr were also deeply involved in 'this atrocious transaction' as well as in the smuggling of the spirits but he could not detain them on mere suspicion.[11] The government of Bengal appears to have ignored Macquarie. The latter also upbraided Governor Davey for having used Lascelles to seize the smuggled spirits at Whitehead's in preference to the constabulary as it placed Lascelles in the position of having acted from 'sordid selfish motives'. As it transpired, Lascelles was as corrupt as any of them and within months was fighting a duel, for reasons unknown, with James Gordon, who as naval officer had the difficult task of trying to control the smugglers of spirits. The two men exchanged shot but neither was hurt and Knopwood gave no information on the outcome when magistrates met the following morning.[12] By 1816 the *Sydney Gazette* presumed that Captain Dixon and his Argonauts had been lost at sea.

Bushrangers moved in on the McCarty property during his absence enabling Macquarie to use this as an excuse to remit his sentence. All on the Knopwood-Whitehead front appeared beyond reproach. Knopwood's visits became even more regular to New Town. It was a joyous day in April 1815 when Knopwood was able to report that 'Mr Whitehead was liberated from confinement to his farm' and the merry-making could continue.[13]

In spite of the examples Macquarie made of McCarty and Whitehead, it was common knowledge that others in the community were engaging in similar activities, although not always smuggling from ships. James Lord was one known to have traded his liquor allowance without a licence.[14] By 1818 persons wishing to conduct inns and receive licences to sell wine, beer and spirits had to apply annually with memorials to the Lieutenant-Governor who, in consultation with the Deputy Judge Advocate, would decide on those eligible among the more worthy applicants.

Francis Barnes continued to run the Hope Inn, at the same time printing infrequent newspaper issues and appearing as a witness at the numerous marriages of his old *Calcutta* friends. He carried on business at St George's Square until the rearrangement of streets in Hobart in 1815. Forced to move, he accepted £12 compensation for the compulsory acquisition of his little tavern and by 1818 had built a more substantial inn in Macquarie Street. Unfortunately for him there was need to surrender some ground again. He received a further indemnity, and, forever the optimist, renamed it the Hope and Anchor at 9 Macquarie Street, adjoining the market place, opposite the Commissariat. It is the earliest inn still standing on the site, but has been rebuilt and is now known as the Alexandra. Barnes acted as mine host for many years at this well-frequented hostelry. There he provided good fare and reading matter which included *Lloyd's List, London News Price Current, London Mercantile Price Current, London Shipping and Commercial list, The Customs, Imports and Exports of London, The Times,* the *Courier,* the *Sun,* the *Morning Chronicle* and *St James Chronicle.* He kept a white female kangaroo puppy with a black spot over each eye and offered £1 as a reward when it was lost. He described it as showing 'much of the greyhound and answers to the name of Lady'.[15]

Thomas Fitzgerald as clerk of magistrates was responsible for calling meetings of justices of the peace to grant licences to innkeepers and retailers of spirituous liquors and beers in the county of Buckingham. This association became an occupational hazard, for by June 1817 Governor Sorell saw fit to dismiss him from the Bench of Magistrates because there had been 'repeated complaints of his drunkenness and neglect . . . business was placed at a stand, his absence continuing for several days.'[16] Governor Macquarie expressed sorrow that he had turned out such a drunkard, agreeing that it was right to dismiss him from the Bench. But he also agreed with Governor Sorell that he was well qualified to remain a schoolmaster 'for which he is very fit if he could be kept sober . . . If he reforms and proves himself worthy, make a small increase in his salary . . .', suggested Macquarie.[17]

In one instance Fitzgerald was present during a rowdy session at the Great Wharf when Bartholomew Reardon and other Irish from Norfolk Island had got together in July 1818, perhaps aided and abetted by Robert Nash. Thomas Peters put down £40 for Reardon to keep the peace.[18] This was not an unusual occurrence in old Hobart Town when most evenings were charged with the noise of rowdy inebriates who had little else in the way of entertainment but that provided by comradeship in and around the public houses.

Apart from Knopwood's testimony before Mr Justice Bigge in 1820 that 'Fitzgerald's conduct has been pretty good although he is sometimes guilty of excess in liquor' there is no further evidence that Fitzgerald was anything but hard-working and conscientious.[19] By 1817, in addition to his educational duties he was leasing land in the area on which he ran a considerable amount of stock and employed two government servants. He was under contract to the Commissariat for supplying regularly up to 1 000 pounds of meat, and

although it dropped at one stage to 500, he had increased it to the optimum quota by 1820.[20]

Calcutta men were among the first to take out the new licences to sell wine and spirits and some established prosperous inns in conjunction with their ferrying activities. Andrew Whitehead held a licence at Herdsman's Cove House before relinquishing it to Augustus Morris, who had begun his ferry service there.[21]

James Austin conducted the Roseneath Inn and John Earle the Compton Arms in conjunction with their ferry services.[22] Governor Macquarie had given the name Roseneath to this place when he and his wife stayed overnight with the ex-convict in 1821. Macquarie wrote that the great beauty and picturesque scenery reminded him of Roseneath, the seat of the Duke of Argyle on the River Clyde.[23] The boys who had stolen honey from their uncle's bee-hives had come a long way to receive such an accolade.

Stocker took over the licence of the remunerative Derwent Hotel, which the Hayes family had established.[24] The efficient Mrs Hayes-Stocker continued to preside over the bar for many years. The hotel had four parlours and a sitting room, twelve bedrooms and huge cellars. Alongside this extensive two-storeyed building there was a fine fruit garden. On many occasions Knopwood referred to his visits to the Hayes and later the Stockers, partaking of fruit as well as liquid refreshments. There the locals spent almost everything they had, while the captains, officers and crews of ships in port made a beeline for the Derwent soon after their ships had berthed. Some of the inns provided amenities such as a billiard room as well as newspapers. The Derwent was the site of many riproaring celebrations and commiserations, reunions and brawls. The clink of Spanish dollars and American coins, with the IOUs from Hobartians, must have made Madame Mary forever grateful to the British law that banished her from the Bell Inn at the Red Lion market to become the grand dame of a flourishing inn at the other end of the earth.

Other *Calcutta* men who participated in the liquor trade in Hobart Town were James Lord and John Clarke (the Dusty Miller), Thomas Peters (the Plough and the Duke of York) and John Manby (the Crooked Billet New Inn).[25] James Ballance advertised the Freemasons' Arms at Kangaroo Point as a 'well-known and much resorted establishment. Good accommodation in stabling and lodging'. He charged moderately; meals, lodging and stabling each cost one shilling, but he did not advertise the hidden charges of his supplies of porter, rum, wine and spirits. He held the licence from 1818 until his death in 1825, taking in boarders on a regular basis, including a James Johnson (not the *Calcutta* one) who in 1824 reported on the missing plasterer, Matthew Keane, whom he had sup-

A view of Austin's Ferry. Governor Macquarie wrote 'Mrs Macquarie and myself (after obtaining the sanction of Austin and his partner Earle) named their place Roseneath (the seat of the Duke of Argyle on the River Clyde) on account of the great beauty and very picturesque scenery of this place' (Macquarie, Journals, 9 June 1821).

posed to be murdered in the Launceston area. Keane had worked and boarded at Ballance's for about twelve months in 1820. Ballance swore on oath that he had neither seen nor heard of Keane, after making many enquiries, for four years.[26]

Maria Sergeant probably gathered in far more money pulling beer at the Sign of the Calcutta than the father of her children acquired from his surgery (he had found the need to run a store on the side and acquire some livestock).[27] The young settler George Armytage took over the Plough for a short time as part of a marriage settlement when he wed Thomas Peters' daughter Elizabeth.[28] Arthur Connelly's brother Charles, a settler, capitalised on his relationship to acquire some of the custom from the *Calcutta* convicts when in 1816 at his hostelry, the Bricklayers' Arms in Elizabeth Street, he called together those persons who had first arrived in the *Calcutta* to form themselves into a Friendly Society with the purpose of supporting each other in old age or infirmity.[29]

When they got together, some coming by ferry from as far as the Coal River and Pitt Water, Clarence Plains and Kangaroo Point all from across the Derwent, and from New Norfolk and other settlements fringing the river, one can imagine the gammon and banter as they all caught up on news of their families and their fortunes. By then almost all sentenced to transportation for life had received pardons, the latest batch coming through in May 1816. Within the past few months several of them had added to their fami-

lies and only one, John Mellows, had died. The Mansfields had had their third child, a second son, and the Averys their first, also a son. Thomas and Ann Peters needed all the money their hotel could produce, in addition to their farming products, to provide for their ninth and newly arrived child. Their children were mostly daughters who would be more useful serving behind the bar than working the land! The Hangans' sixth child and fifth son, and the four sons of Thomas and Frances Williams, would be considered lucky assets for a farmer, while the Connellys would surely have shouted drinks on the house for the Briscoes' new arrival, the third son of four children, another bounty for their little farm.

John Manby, who had his cottage up for sale, could now report that one of his geese had hatched four times in spite of the severe winter and had *twenty-seven* goslings alive, 'the last are just a month old, and the mother is now laying eggs for *another* brood! — an instance of such fruitfulness we have rarely ever heard of'.[30] But one is not surprised when one compares the fecundity of the human beings.

183

Two of those Belbin girls, daughters of that hot-headed Irishman from Norfolk Island (considerably quieter as a prosperous farmer), had just been married. Elizabeth Fawkner, widowed by one of their own crowd, Thomas Green, had remarried Richard Lucas, the son of a First Fleeter corporal. There had been a great chase when the *Alexander* arrived with women convicts. That little boy whom the *Calcutta* had taken from the *Prudentia* hulk, William Jones formerly one of Knopwood's servants, and had just sailed with Captain James Kelly in his recent exploration of Macquarie Harbour, had been the first to find an *Alexander* wife, followed by George Phipps, Thomas Smith and John Dawson, while James Waltham was just about to tie the knot. Poor Joseph Williams, an assistant government printer, had married one of them. He was fifty and she was only thirty, and he had just refused responsibility for her debts. She had left home after only a few weeks of marriage 'without any provocation'.[31]

One guesses that these would be among the gossipy items of interest to all, but anxiety about Michael Howe and his bushranging colleagues, who were at large, must have provoked much discussion as to where they might attack next. Stock-keepers were alarmed at the murders already committed and at the theft and loss of their straying animals. Farmers would have suffered through the severe winter. Business in the town appeared to be thriving, but townsfolk would be anxious about the replanning of the streets and inadequate compensation. Some would have good reason to complain about the extortionate charges of Edward and Maria Lord. That week of the reunion they would have relished the piratical seizure of his brig, *Trial*, and all its cargo. But Edward Lord would not suffer much by it, having just tendered 150 000 pounds of meat for the stores, while James Lord and John Birchall were managing quite well for ex-convicts tendering 4 000 and 2 000 pounds of meat respectively.[32]

Anecdotes were still coming in about the Battle of Waterloo and there was news that Captain James Tuckey, no longer a prisoner of the French, would lead a British expedition to Africa to explore the mouth of the river Zaïre (Congo).[33] At long last it seemed that there would be peace within their time. Well, not so much peace at home, when the women might drive their husbands mad for all the fripperies available at Reibey's store. The men would mostly prefer to spend their hard-earned money at the races at Orielton Park or in the taverns. But for the more provident members of the *Calcutta* fraternity, the meetings at the Bricklayers' Arms must have been worthwhile occasions to air some thoughts about what the future might hold.

• • •

There can be little doubt that alcohol then, as since, contributed a great deal to life's more miserable moments in the colony, proving that where the drink goes in the wit goes out. In the early years of Hobart's history, Humphrey had the unpleasant duty of sitting as coroner when an inquest had to be held. It is not surprising to find that excessive drinking and sudden death often went hand-in-hand, as in the case of Private Samuel Wiggins, who died suddenly in July 1811, a man whose baby daughter was one of those who died in earlier years at Port Phillip. Several free men who had been *Calcutta* convicts gave evidence that Wiggins was found dead on his bed from excessive drinking. The witnesses were all *Calcutta* men — John Prestage, David Belton, John Clark, Samuel Gunn and James Harfield. Again in December 1816, William Stocker, Thomas Williams, Anthony Lowe, John Willis and others attended at Hospital Hill to bear witness that Richard Francis had died in a state of insensibility by voluntarily imbibing a large volume of spirits.[34]

Another time there was a serious brawl at Andrew Whitehead's public house at Herdsman's Cove between Private Thomas Williams of the 46th Regiment and a free man Alexander Seaton. The soldier had been among those present at the surrender of the Frenchman, John Brown, an accomplice of Michael Howe. There was much ribaldry, and after much drinking, a violent quarrel over a female. As a result, Williams, with force and arms and 'in the fury of his mind', struck and 'pierced' Alexander Seaton. The verdict was manslaughter after provocation, the result of musket fire, and the sentence two months gaol. A statement from the *Hobart Town Gazette* that intoxication was the cause of the 'melancholy catastrophe' cautioned 'every rational mind against being hurried into ETERNITY by that dreadful propensity'.[35]

Michael Lawler, one of the Irish *Calcutta* men, who had received a land grant at Muddy Plains, was assigned a servant from the *Admiral Cockburn* in September 1819. Within days the man, Christopher Keegan, went on a heavy drinking bout at the Sign of the Chequers. He lost his way home in the woods on a dark rainy night and perished before any help could reach him. There were many similar cases.[36] James Wright lost his life in 1820 when he was walking along Bridge Street, Hobart, one night and staggered into a quarry after a drunken session.

Authorities encouraged the establishment of an inn in conjunction with a ferry terminal. Although open to criticism that this practice might constitute a monopoly, there was some justification. An inn was good business, which acted as some form of security for a public service. Expenses for providing ferries, most necessary in the Derwent River estuary, were heavy. Ferry owners needed continuous capital for boats, horses and stables, as well as labour. Bad weather or the need to wait for the turning of the tide, with variable and unpredictable currents, frequently delayed travellers. Known as 'floating bridges', ferries were essential to transport persons, carts and livestock in large numbers. They had flat bottoms and strong railings around the decks to withstand the impact of wild cattle that might be buffetted from side to side with the pitching of the vessel. They were never really safe and were always top-heavy. The frequent use of stone as ballast was also troublesome and dangerous. Boatmen, notorious for their insobriety and negligence, took many chances, resulting in frequent accidents and numerous drownings. When one of James Austin's overloaded ferries capsized on the Derwent in February 1818 twelve persons perished. Charles Clark, the only survivor, was in an exhausted state when saved.[37]

Urias Allender of Kangaroo Point became one of the most hard-drinking and rumbunctious ferry proprietors. Yet he was successful enough to employ several men while he and his large family worked their adjacent farm. His original grant was for his 'meritorious conduct' when he accompanied William Collins from Port Phillip to Port Jackson. In September 1819 the Derwent was swollen and had risen some thirty feet. Gale forces from the Antarctic brought boisterous and stormy weather, washing away the new bridge at Argyle Street. Two boatmen whom Allender employed were returning his ferry-boat from Hobart with Benjamin Briscoe aboard, on his way home to Clarence Plains. The boat overturned and the three men drowned. All at Hobart Town were saddened by the melancholy incident. Briscoe had been one of the earliest *Calcutta* convicts to marry. He had a large family who could have been destitute but for the generosity of many friends who rallied to support the widow and enabled her not only to keep her little property ('her all') but also to purchase an extra twenty acres to add to the fifty-acre farm.[38]

Charles Goodridge, who had been a castaway on an island in the Crozet group (Indian Ocean) for two years had arrived in Hobart in 1824 and worked as a ferryman for John Earle. Goodwin found him and his cousin, Austin, to be men of respectability and sobriety who shared their good fortune and provided good service and accommodation. Earle's Compton ferry service was more profitable than Austin's Roseneath ferry because Earle had slaughtering facilities for cattle arriving from the outer runs.[39]

Goodridge, before purchasing one of Earle's ferries, joined Archibald Campbell on the more dangerous crossing from Hobart to Kangaroo Point. There was much competition for custom. One day Goodridge was transporting Catherine, wife of John Wade, the constable from Pitt Water, across the mouth of the Derwent. This ferry had previously been upset and three persons drowned, possibly on the occasion when Briscoe lost his life. When Mrs Wade stepped in, one of the other ferrymen, highly intoxicated, tried to inveigle her into his boat and warned her that she was in 'the drowning boat'. She soon let him know that there was more safety in a drowning boat with a sober man than a safe boat with a drunkard! She was lucky as well as wise. A sudden squall upset the other boat and the drunken ferryman drowned.[40]

Stocker had owned a ferry at Stony Point and Augustus Morris was a very successful proprieter of the service at Cove Point, also on the Derwent, where his inn (formerly Andrew Whitehead's) became another popular stopover. By 1824 Morris was charging persons sixpence to cross by his ferry from the Black Snake to Cove Point, one shilling and sixpence for each horse or head of cattle with a concession of sixpence if they were under one year old, a pig, dog or goat twopence apiece, a cart two shillings and sixpence, a chaise three shillings, one shilling and eightpence per score of sheep, and twopence for each bushel of grain. For those wishing to use the ferry between Herdsman's Cove, Cove Point, Green Point and Hobart, the fare was two shillings, half price for children and sixpence per hogshead of wine or spirits and other prices accordingly.[41]

That same year Morris and his wife Constantia died. Their profitable business passed to their young children, held in trust by the former mineralogist A. W. H. Humphrey, then Chief Police Magistrate, and his clerk. It had been the humble beginnings of a wealthy and influential dynasty.[42]

Commissioner Bigge's lengthy enquiry had a profound effect on the abuses rising from alcohol. Several persons bore witness that hops and barley were capable of producing abundant crops and that the people's health would benefit from the production of a good beer rather than continually drinking the spirits and porter that produced 'grog fever' and were the staple liquid of the times.[43] Bigge was responsible for encouraging George Gatehouse to establish a brewery in Hobart. He bought the land at New Town on which in 1822 he set up as a maltster and brewer. At first he was not very successful because he had found, in spite of high expectations, that the hops grown there were unsuitable. He and others began to import from England. They extended their crops along the Derwent valley, finding fertile river flats around and beyond New Norfolk that were perfect for cultivation.[44]

The beginning of the Cascade Brewery in Hobart in 1824 was a turning point in the drinking habits of Tasmanians. The licences to sell ale as well as spirits increased. In Hobart alone there were forty-seven inns and taverns by 1830 and 121 throughout the colony.[45]

Of course it was not the end of drunkenness. Even

though beer was less damaging to one's health than spirits, warnings against the evils of intoxication continued to appear in print. In 1824 Andrew Bent quoted Old Parr's maxims of health in his Van Diemen's Land Pocket Almanack: '*Keep* your *feet* warm by *exercise*, your *head* cool through *temperance*; never eat till you are hungry, nor drink but when Nature requires it.'[46]

James Ross found that drunkenness continued to be the cause of many tragedies. It impaired the health and system, unfitting the person for performance of the common ways of life and inducing premature death by apoplexy, suffocation and other sudden or accidental death or by crimes resulting in murders and execution. Ross stated that half of those dying in the colony perished either directly or indirectly through drunkenness.[47]

The annual licence to retail wine or spirits by 1829 was two shillings and sixpence, while it cost ten shillings and sixpence for a licence to brew beer for sale. A distiller's licence cost £25 and duty on brandy and Geneva or Hollands was ten shillings and on rum seven shillings and sixpence. By comparison, bakers also had to pay five shillings for a licence to bake bread, hawkers and pedlars £20, and ferry or passage-boat owners ten shillings and sixpence.[48]

Although it is tempting to believe that drunkenness was a major problem in the early days, William Molesworth found that the convictions for drunkenness in 1824 were only $3^{57}/_{126}$ to 100 of the whole population, but had risen to $9^{231}/_{290}$ to 100 by 1832.

The Sign of the Black Snake Inn (right) on the Derwent faced Green Point (left) where Augustus Morris conducted a ferry service.

One noteworthy remark was the relatively low proportion of drunkenness among the convicts, compared with the free population. Molesworth's report also produced evidence supported by the Chief Police Magistrate, the principal superintendent of convicts, and the director-general of roads and bridges that

One-fourth of the convicts have never been brought before a magistrate for misconduct, one-half are tolerably well conducted, one-eighth are ill-conducted and the remaining one-eighth are very bad indeed.[49]

The 'thirties and 'forties recorded a number of deaths for which inquest reports are available. These were usually violent deaths and again it is not surprising to find that alcohol was often involved. They included some of the *Calcutta* convicts who had settled in the north.

John Coward lived on the George Town Road with John Bolden. In April 1845 they had a pint of wine at the house of William Jones junior, by the sign of the East Bank Inn at Launceston. On the way home Coward complained of pains in the chest. There was evidence that he had received injuries as if the wheel of a cart had passed over him, leaving bruises between his eighth and ninth ribs as well as on his forehead. He appears to have walked some distance after the injury which caused his death on the East Tamar, aged sixty-eight.[50]

Thomas Bray died during the same month from natural causes at Launceston. He had actually been committed to the town gaol the week before for an unknown crime which one suspects might have been connected with a drunken spree. While in gaol Surgeon Murdoch attended him daily for fever and removed him to the Colonial Hospital. He managed to find his way to the Scottish Chief, a hostelry kept by John McKenzie, at which he died aged fifty-eight.[51]

But an inquest held on 23 January 1846 on James Davey, a well respected citizen of Launceston, showed that he died 'by the visitation of God' from natural causes without the help of alcohol. Death came suddenly to his house in Brisbane Street. The doctor who attended found no marks of violence but believed he died painlessly of apoplexy after a 'great veinous congestion of the brain'. Mrs Davey gave evidence that they had retired for the night. Their son Samuel said his father had come to get a candle to go to bed. His mother awakened him at half-past ten to tell him his father, who was sixty-five and in better health than for some time, was dead.[52]

The former baker who became a painter and glazier, Robert Armstrong, was seventy-nine when he was painting the Mogul Tavern in Argyle Street, Hobart, for William Sims. On 2 October 1851 he fell off a ladder on to the stone pavement while 'greatly intoxicated' and fractured his spine. He died soon afterwards at the General Hospital. He was one who probably drank away the two land grants he had received.[53]

William Roberts of Brighton died more peacefully in 1867 at William Sharp's Crown Inn, County of Monmouth, and the coroner declared that he 'came by his death . . . by the visitation of God from natural causes'. He was ninety-seven.[54]

There is a particularly strong connection between one innkeeper of Tasmania and the mainland. The son of John Fawkner would provide the continuing link between H.M.S. *Calcutta*'s arrival in 1803 to form a settlement at Sullivan Bay and the foundation of the permanent settlement on the site where the city of Melbourne now stands. The abstemious John Fawkner junior, hoping to shake off some of the smears attached to the family disgrace, had gone to Launceston but even there could not escape his own foolish past. Partly with money borrowed from Maria Lord, he built the thirteen-roomed Cornwall Arms for £2 500.[55] One historic evening John Batman, a regular drinker there, sidled up to him in the parlour while Fawkner's friends, Samuel Jackson, an architect, and his miserly brother, William, listened to their chatter over a game of cribbage during which the exodus to the mainland was planned.

'Johnny', says Batman, 'when a boy, you were with the party under Governor Collins . . . did you see any land where sheep and cattle might live?'

Fawkner: 'A poor looking country, Bat, as seen from where we were located. Bobby Knopwood, the parson, said he saw something to the eastward that might feed a flock of geese.'[56]

Batman and Fawkner, according to Samuel, discussed the likelihood of crossing Bass Strait and making their fortunes. It was Fawkner's experience as a publican that urged him to provide some comforts and social life in the early days of Melbourne, when he established his first hotel complete with his extensive 'Table Hotty', fine library and newspapers. Within four years as Father of Melbourne he had accumulated £20 000 and begun a newspaper, the *Port Phillip Patriot and Melbourne Advertiser* and a bookselling and stationery business. Another city had begun.[57]

In the meantime, the old ex-convict father, when his second wife died, was not ready to deprive himself of female company. At the age of seventy-four he found himself another wife, Eliza Carr, with whom he spent most of his remaining twelve years in Melbourne. This wife kept up a newsy correspondence with her stepson when he and his wife were spending some of their time in Sydney due to John junior's health. The elderly father was 'inactive as ever but I let him have his own way', she wrote, giving the news of the day, the weather and comments on their neighbours.[58] In actual fact he was the nominal proprietor of his son's newspaper which his son assigned to him during the depression of the 'forties'.[59] Others commented on the old man himself: 'the finest man of his years, without exception, in this hemisphere', wrote John J. Walsh, the solicitor who married John Pascoe Fawkner's widow.[60] James Fenton reported a visit to Fawkner senior at Pascoe Vale, renewing his acquaintanceship of days when he lived in Macquarie Street, Hobart. 'He was a man of very slender build', wrote Fenton, 'with a pair of black silk stockings over a pair of calfless legs, black tights, and a tall beaver, which made him look more slender still'.[61] He had only one eye, had had quite serious convictions, and was said to have been a heavy drinker. Yet he must have had something, in days when females were scarce, to have attracted three good women to share his life.

187

33 VIOLENCE ON THE FRONTIER

*T*HE FIRST FEW years of settlement were relatively free from atrocities. The most violent acts were arguably those in which the authorities punished those who had offended against the law. There was some confrontation with the Aboriginal population with some unfortunate results, mostly when the natives were trying to protect their own food supply from the guns and dogs of the invader. But after a few years those who took to the bush, whether bushrangers or stockmen, became their enemies for other reasons. Others who sought adventure beyond the bush and entered the sealing fraternity exhibited some of the more brutalising aspects of man's inhumanity, especially towards females. The women were an economic asset to the sealers and sexually desirable to both sealers and the men of the bush.

Bushranging was a direct result of leniency extended to convicts, many of whom found they could learn to live with the Aborigines on their terms, which included bartering dogs for women. The frontier in Van Diemen's Land, as well as New South Wales, engendered relatively few fears compared with the American colonies where the deadly use of the arrow and the more hostile indigines readily and understandably let slip the dogs of war. Such a situation in America had dictated the distance men might stray from the settled areas. From Hobart the freedom of life in the bush beckoned the malcontents and the adventurous. A few dogs and some muskets were all they needed to survive.

Collins had, in common with Governors King and Hunter, some respect for the native population and the long cherished hope that the two civilisations could learn to live side by side.[1] In 1799 when there were depredations at Port Jackson and Hunter had found it necessary to arraign five men for the wanton murder of two natives, the Court of Criminal Jurisdiction found the men guilty. They received the royal pardon but with advice from Lord Hobart that it should be 'clearly understood . . . any instance of injustice or wanton cruelty towards the natives will be punished with the utmost severity of the law'.[2]

At the beginning of his administration in Hobart Town Collins had to suffer the effects of a confrontation at Risdon. During a drunken bout some of Bowen's men shot at a party of Aborigines about to perform a corroboree, culminating in the slaughter of several, including a couple whose orphaned child Knopwood took for christening.[3]

Except for this occasion, what intercourse the Collins party had with the native population was minimal and friendly for some time. When the time arose Collins would declare that the Aborigines were as much under the protection of the British law as any of the people.[4] But turning a blind eye towards escapees, or even trusting men to go unattended to hunt in the woods for food, was to create a source of danger to other inhabitants. These men learnt the ways of scavenging and of living off the land as the Aborigines had for thousands of years. Bushrangers they were and the term bushranging became an indelible feature of the Australian language.

They fanned out from the civilised areas to the outlying districts where the lonesome keeper, often no more law-abiding than themselves, might have to guard stock spread out over a large area. Their former experiences as sheep stealers or marauders on the English countryside stood them in good stead. Sometimes they took liberties when allowed the use of their master's boat. This was the case with John Brown, one of the brothers from Reading who had stolen food and clothing. He was a servant of Captain Johnson. With two others in Johnson's employ, he tried to escape in the government cutter *Flinders* in February 1806. They caught several kangaroos at Pitt Water, whereupon the Aborigines speared Brown, killed two of the dogs, wounded another and took three of the kangaroos which the original inhabitants rightly deemed were theirs. Brown recovered from his wound and supplied several of his bushranging mates with food.

Later he joined them. These included several with whom he had previously tried to escape, including Carrett and Fernandez, as well as Samuel Tomlins and George Watts. They were all armed and had a number of dogs. Although Sergeant McCauley and some marines made some token effort to pursue them, the episode took place at a time when Collins was almost relieved to have fewer on his rations. They all survived for a while off the land and most probably returned during the six years' gap in Knopwood's diary. Brown didn't live much longer. He died in February 1811 and was buried at St David's.[5]

James Duff and John Jones joined forces with settler Michael Mansfield, a former crew member from the *Ocean*, forming the party that discovered two of the earliest and most notorious bushrangers who had terrorised some of the isolated settlers. Richard Lemon and another John Brown, escapees from Port Dalrymple, had committed robberies and murders over a period of twenty months. In November 1807 they reached Oyster Bay where the eight escapees from Hobart, including David Gibson, left clues which led to their capture by Duff and Jones.[6] George Prideaux Harris believed the bushrangers had stolen four dogs valued at £25 each and were responsible for killing about twenty natives and free settlers in cold blood, plundering poor people of clothes and provisions and making them carry their plunder a certain distance before shooting them. When the murderers disagreed, two of them contrived to shoot the third. Lemon, the more hardened of the two, was shot and the other brought in a prisoner. In addition to killing settlers, they were responsible for the wanton murder of the Aborigines who had dared retaliate when they had stolen their women. Harris expressed horror at the dilemma the white man was in. Naturally, in revenge, the Aborigines began to kill some of the servants out hunting so that it became more dangerous to go out into the bush.[7] The consequences for some *Calcutta* convicts who met up with natives were tragic.

Robert Waring was one of Fosbrook's men who hunted regularly during the years when food supplies were short. In February 1807 Lieutenant Laycock had just arrived from Port Dalrymple on the first overland journey made by a European to Hobart Town. People in the northern settlement were starving and he had hoped to procure some relief, but the distress in the south was just as great. At this time Waring was one of many allowed a gun to defend himself and to procure what kangaroo meat could be obtained, either by using dogs to catch the 'roos or bartering with the natives. Waring kept his own hut above New Norfolk. Just after Laycock's arrival Knopwood himself took a gun but could not find anything to kill. The next day the natives came to Waring's hut. According

to Knopwood they forced him from it, throwing a spear which entered his side. He was able to pull out the spear and as the natives tried again to spear him he shot one and killed him. They dispersed. With great difficulty he made his way to the river. A boat brought him back to Hobart Town, but he died of wounds soon afterwards.[8]

There seems to be some confusion about the fate of Devonshire man George Munday. H. W. Parker and later H. Ling Roth and others, acknowledged that he was the first white man to be murdered by Aborigines in Van Diemen's Land. This appears to have arisen from Knopwood's statement presented to the House of Commons in 1831 describing the murder: 'the native had a spear concealed and held by his toes, and, as Monday [*sic*] turned from him, he caught up his spear and threw it at him'. The event occurred in 1807. The alleged killer had just received food from Munday who observed no signs of enmity. Knopwood failed to register Munday's death. It was likely that he was wounded and recovered. His name as a *Calcutta* convict, arrived 1804, appeared in the musters for 1811, 1819 and 1823.[9]

No one seemed to employ more *Calcutta* men as servants than Knopwood. He gave work to about a dozen within the first few years. Several, such as John Earle, William Richardson, John Gain, Thomas Stokes and Thomas Salmon were allowed to take guns and dogs into the bush. A fortnight after Waring's death some of Knopwood's and Bowden's men, and others employed by Fosbrook and Shipman to procure fresh supplies for the Commissariat, were cut off by some sixty natives. Bowden's man George Brewer was speared and left to die while Richardson, with eighty hundredweight of kangaroo, returned to relate the story of the affray. With Earle and Kemp he was in the bush when the natives threw stones with remarkable accuracy and shook their spears. Their tactics were to try and keep the men and dogs in the valleys so that they could attack with greater effect. They almost speared both Earle and Richardson. The latter shot two of the offending natives. The others built a fire to burn the dead.[10]

Within days the starving settlement was to some extent relieved when the *Duchess of York* arrived with supplies and enough spirits to create alcoholic chaos for the next fortnight. Knopwood did not forget to share with his men. What the Aboriginal reaction was to the lull in activities is not recorded. It was, however, little more than a truce.

On another occasion in 1807 Richardson, armed with dogs, was absent for nineteen days. Natives were about to kill him when some of Collins' men arrived in time and killed a native. Knopwood remarked that they had become so hardened that they didn't mind being shot.[11] It had become very dangerous to be out alone. Many years later Richardson became an overseer of Aborigines at Bruny Island where he was in charge of rations until George Robinson succeeded him in 1829.[12]

Augustus Morris, known as 'The Don', learnt how to live off the land when he made at least three escapes from the settlement. He had dogs which he would well have known were the frontierman's chief survival kit. Long before 1814, whether during one of his escapades or at a slightly later date when he was free and grazing in the Macquarie River area, he was waylaid by a number of natives. He managed to race up a small dome-shaped outcrop rising out of the salt pan plains formed like a rampart, in the vicinity of Grimes' Sugarloaf and Mona Vale. He fiercely resisted his adversaries, but it took him all of one afternoon. He had only a broken musket and no powder left but he used sticks and stones, bruising and battering the blacks until they disappeared after dark. Ever afterwards the hill was called Don's Battery.[13]

Collins was well aware that the natives had cause for redress and were irritated, to say the least, by those who had invaded their hunting grounds. He warned newly arrived settlers from Norfolk Island in particular to be on their guard against the natives. But at the same time he foreshadowed that anyone who was known to 'offer wantonly any violence to a Native, or in any way injure or molest them or their Women and Children, will be criminally prosecuted for such Offence'.[14] But there is little evidence that punishments of such a nature took place. James Carrett, for instance, openly claimed to have committed one of the most bloodthirsty violations. He acquired a native woman when hiding out at Oyster Bay, having killed her husband and tortured her by suspending her man's head upon a string around her neck.[15]

Carrett, with the happy-go-lucky Thomas Tombs, proved to be useful in tracking down bushrangers. They were instrumental in capturing the desperadoes James McCabe (an *Indefatigable* transportee), Townshend and Geary, at their hideaway at Oyster Bay. McCabe had threatened to kill William Parish and his family just before Christmas 1812 at New Norfolk. He had wounded Parish in the breast and Mrs Parish lost three to four pints of blood during the attack.[16]

When he had met up with Tombs and Carrett at Oyster Bay, McCabe told them he had 'killed and slaughtered and beat him [Parish] with an old musket til he bent like an old iron hoop'. While Townshend remained in charge of their hut and pups, Carrett and Tombs went in one direction and William Thompson went with McCabe. They arranged to meet up when the latter was asleep and removed his gun. They made strong strings from kangaroo hide and secured him fast. While Carrett held on to McCabe the others secured and bound Townshend. They appeared before

Thomas Scott's gnome-like servant James Carrett prepares breakfast in the bush.

the Court of Criminal Jurisdiction in Sydney as witnesses for the prosecution, and recognised the prisoners as those they disturbed stealing ducks and fowls. Mrs Parish identified thirty-seven stolen muslin and chintz gowns, as well as thirteen petticoats and twenty balls of cotton. The Parish's servant Charles Clark, also a *Calcutta* man, was a witness to the ghastly outrage. The three notorious bushrangers were executed and Tombs and Carrett, both transported for life, received conditional pardons from Governor Macquarie and land grants of thirty acres each.[17]

These two rascals should have been set for life, but both were too adventurous to endure the security of life on a farm. Apart from becoming a jockey of some note, Tombs sailed with Captain Kelly on his exploration of the west coast, after which he was fully pardoned.[18] James Carrett was a sealer for a while, explored part of the west coast with James Hobbs, and accompanied Thomas Scott on his explorations. He was also fully pardoned. Both, as was inevitable, lost their land, Tombs being one who did actually exchange his for the proverbial bottle of rum.[19]

Tombs was only too happy to get back to the bush when he volunteered to join Denis McCarty's party in the search for the bushrangers led by John Whitehead in 1815. Whitehead (no relation to the two Whiteheads who sailed in the *Calcutta*) had robbed and murdered the settlers James O'Byrne and Thomas Carlisle and threatened George King at New Norfolk. Armed with fowling pieces and pistols, Tombs and his party ambushed the robbers and forced them to surrender their arms. This was the gang that was to increase its power under Michael Howe, the selfstyled 'Lieutenant-Governor of the Woods'! Members had armed themselves well and intimidated many of the settlers who provided them with supplies. Lieutenant-Governor Davey declared martial law but Macquarie abolished it a few months later.[20]

Tombs had seemed anxious to rejoin a wife and family in England. He wrote after his pardon in 1816 that he intended to return. He was his own master, owning a quantity of horned cattle and sheep and had sufficient to make them all comfortable. The wife herself had been ill and unable to make the long journey to join him. But he did not return; the call of the bush was too great. The bottle and the bush continued to be his downfall. Sadly, his son Lewis, a labourer of Great Marlow, County Bucks, had aspirations of great wealth left by his father, believed to be dead, and claimed his inheritance in 1834.[21] Tombs was still alive, in the service of Thomas Anstey. He replied that he had no property whatsoever except some kangaroo dogs. He resided at Michael Howe's Marsh (where he had previously held his own land) and was the person who discovered the lake between Mahoney's Sugar Loaf and the Eastern Coast (still known as Lake Tooms). He gained a living by hunting kangaroos and selling the skins. J. C. Calder was the last person to record seeing him when he met the old character in 1837 on Table Mountain.[22]

Michael Howe, who had arrived in the *Indefatigible*, crossed the paths of several old *Calcutta* men. He was one bushranger whom settlers feared to the extent that they were more inclined to protect him than to inform on him, and perhaps even succumbed to the payment of 'hush money'. Howe was cunning enough to claim that even Knopwood was an accomplice and he hounded Humphrey, who as magistrate was after his blood. His gang burned part of the Humphrey property at Pitt Water.[23]

Stocker might well have been a party to one incident which took place at the height of his raids. During regular journeys between Hobart and his properties on the Macquarie River — as mail contractor he and his men journeyed at least fortnightly — Stocker had been subject to attacks from both bushrangers and natives. He usually broke the journey to stay at Bagdad with Thomas Hayes. With his wife, Mary, and the Whitehead family, he was present when Michael Howe and eight of his associates appeared. On this occasion the Stockers and Hayes were delivering a valuable load to Port Dalrymple.

The variety of goods then available throws some light on the society of 1816. It also raises the question of how Michael Howe would have off-loaded the goods. Were they actually receivers of fine silks and linens, and to whom might Howe have disposed of them? It is not difficult to imagine what might happen to the two cases of rum and two gallons of gin, although one of the rum casks was the victim of gun-

fire and all the rum in it was lost. The bushrangers might have been thankful to receive forty-five cakes of soap, two sacks of sugar and a chest of green tea. But thirty pounds of pepper would go a long way and fancy ribbons would be rather useless. There were five red shirts, six striped cotton shirts, three waistcoats, twelve Irish linen shirts, three pairs of shoes, three black silk handkerchiefs, twenty-eight yards of cotton print, three yards of dark corduroy for pantaloons, twenty shawls, four yards of black silk, twenty-four yards of cambric muslin, as well as sewing silk, tape, a watch with two gold seals and a gold key. This was Stocker's own property, for which he offered a £5 reward. Because they had given themselves up voluntarily, three of the bushrangers who were apprehended escaped capital punishment. Instead they received 200 lashes each and labour at the Coal River, in irons, for two years.[24]

Another *Calcutta* convict met his death at the hands of Michael Howe. William Drew, known as 'Slambo', was a very small person, not much taller than a dwarf. In 1817 he was caring for the flocks of William Williams at New Norfolk when he became involved with Howe. Drew appears to have been at first a willing party to the depredations. But he then conspired with George Watts, whose bushranging activities had also caused concern, to capture Howe. During a scuffle Watts was able to tie Howe but dropped his gun, which Howe seized, killing Drew and wounding Watts. The coroner's inquest showed that death was due to a musket ball passing through the thorax, whereupon 105 guineas were offered for capture of the murderer. Watts, a runaway from Newcastle, had surprisingly been a successor to the affections of Governor Collins' young mistress, Margaret Eddington. They were married and had a baby daughter when he died of his wounds while awaiting trial in Sydney.[25]

In earlier times Stocker had a mud hut, thatched with grass, on the Macquarie River. When natives burned it he rebuilt it in time for the escapees from Macquarie Harbour headed by Matthew Brady to rob and occupy it. They robbed him of stores and spirits, wine and tobacco in July 1824. Brady and his gang played cards there all night while a sentry kept watch. But Lieutenant Henry Edward Robinson and men from the 48th Regiment intercepted three of the bushrangers and took them prisoner, finding in their possession silver plate.[26] George Robinson reported that they were well-dressed and cheerful, except one who appeared dejected and wept. They also admitted that when huts got burnt by accident the men usually reported that it was the natives. He thought Stocker's hut was a miserable dwelling. Perhaps after such troubles Stocker was not prepared to invest much capital in providing anything more than a shelter for his

William Stocker's hut on the Macquarie River was well known to travellers, who included bushrangers and Aborigines.

men. His own country dwelling was Ross Bridge House, equipped with a large kitchen, stables and other farm buildings. He had fenced in fifty acres beside the Macquarie River. Even there he was still subject to trespassers and robberies, although the place had housed officers for years without any charge before becoming tenanted. The remains of his early inn near Ross (Man o'Ross) were visible until recent years.[27]

•   •   •

Most of the frontier troubles had their origin in the early days when rations were scarce. The Aborigines saw justice in killing the domesticated animals after witnessing the wholesale slaughter of native animals upon which they relied for their own sustenance. If necessary they might kill the stock-keepers who stood in their way. They had also grown to like the foreign meat, but the intrusion of stock on their traditional hunting grounds, the felling of trees and the destruction of their native herbage were accelerating at a pace that understandably inflamed their fear and hatred.

In 1819 a large number of natives attacked Stocker's flock, spearing one of the stockmen, Robert Jones, and a servant named McCandless. It was said that they had maltreated the wife of the chief and that

she had escaped. Two hundred of the tribe, their naked bodies smothered in red ochre, had returned to retaliate. They attacked with spears, waddies and stones, hemming the men in a gully. The stockmen's guns at first would not fire and Jones received three spears. After seven hours' struggle they managed to shoot the chief dead and the tribe hurriedly disappeared.[28]

It was not unusual for the lonely stockman to take an Aboriginal woman for his mate but it was unusual for him to tie the legal knot. Stocker, whose own record with the natives was not such a bad one, encouraged mixed marriages, as was the case in 1831 when he recommended that Governor Arthur grant his stock-keeper at Meander River, Thomas Johnson, permission to marry Dalrymple Briggs, an Aboriginal who was the mother of Johnson's child and with whom he had cohabited on the property. She already had a child by one Baker, overseer to David Gibson on the South Esk, and was herself a daughter of George Briggs, who arrived free in 1806 in Van Diemen's Land.[29] Briggs had cohabited from time to time with numerous Aboriginal women and had several half-caste children whom he had abandoned. He was in James Kelly's crew, together with Thomas Tombs and William Jones, when they circumnavigated Van Diemen's Land in 1815.

In January 1826 natives attacked James Cupid, one of Stocker's stockmen, near the Western Creek. They ran away after he fired, but not before a spear had lodged between his neck and shoulder leaving a four-inch deep wound. For weeks his recovery was doubtful. Later he guided George Robinson around the Eastern Marshes. Cupid believed the natives in the area had been very peaceable at first but were driven to commit atrocities because of the outrages inflicted on them. When he had asked why they attempted to kill white men, one who understood English had said, 'If black man came and took away his lubra and killed his piccaninnies, would he not kill black man for it?' This man lived amicably with his own half-caste woman and they had two children, one with very fair hair.[30]

Robinson passed on to David Gibson's hut but did not call. He discovered that there had been many massacres in the area and that Gibson's stock-keeper was as bad as any. He had once taken a knife and ripped open the belly of a native who had called at his hut when he was taken unawares and without a gun. One native threw a spear at him but missed. Gibson's man got to Stocker's hut and with the latter's stock-keeper went out to shoot up nine natives.[31]

The Gibraltar mutineer, Patrick McCarthy, was one Irishman who was never in any trouble in the colony, although he had chosen to live alongside the discontented Irish from Norfolk Island. In November 1823, while out checking on stock that he kept at Sorell Plains, McCarthy was speared by the Oyster Bay native Black Jack.[32] The latter had already faced trial and been acquitted of aiding and abetting the Sydney Aboriginal known as Musquito, who had tracked Michael Howe. But Musquito had murdered two persons at Grindstone Bay. The trials and executions of these two natives created a precedent in Van Diemen's Land, accelerating the extermination of the indigenous race.[33]

But how could the Aborigines understand the laws of a people who they saw as plunderers, rapists and murderers? They knew that they had inhabited the country long before the arrival of Europeans. When Governor Arthur had proclaimed martial law (hoping to drive all Aborigines to the Tasman Peninsula), Black Tom whom Arthur had hoped to use as a conciliator, ridiculed Arthur's suggestion that Maria Island might be an alternative:

Riah Island!! I like to hear you talk dat b . . . y foolish — ha! ha! ha! A'nt he go dere himself come back again . . . I tell you dat, him own Wallaby ground — he mak't catamaran, come back . . . Put him in gaol, Mata Guburna!! You take it him own country, take it him black woman, kill't right out, all him litta child — den you put him in your gaol . . . 'pose all same black un. I nebber like dat way. You better kill it right out.[34]

Battery Point (then known as Mulgrave Battery) was the terminal for Urias Allender's ferry, serviced from the distant Kangaroo Point. The painting by Augustus Earle shows part of the panorama of Hobart, c. 1826, with H.M.S. Rainbow *in the Derwent Estuary and one of the semaphores forming a communication service with Port Arthur to alert authorities of escaping convicts. The semaphores were later used during the Black War.*

Thomas Peters suffered at the time of the Black War when three natives plundered his house at Bagdad in November 1830 and attacked two of his youngest daughters, Ann aged fourteen and Sophia aged sixteen. One of the natives was about six feet in height and resembled the local chieftain, Montpeleter. To them he was a frightening sight with his face and hair ornamented with red ochre. Peters arrived with a musket in time to ward them off, but he was afraid to fire in case they speared him. They had already penetrated Ann's stays with a spear which had lodged in her chest, and Dr T. F. Gorringe, the surgeon at Green Ponds, could not save her life. She died soon afterwards. Not far from there Aborigines speared a son of Dr Hopley during the same week.[35]

The local inhabitants spent the next few days searching for the murderers. Peters' dogs who accompanied them returned with their mouths covered in blood, presumably having severely bitten some of them. George Robinson believed that the two girls had been slain, but Sophia was wounded in the palm of the hand and recovered later to marry James Pillinger of Antill Ponds.

Although 5 000 men took part in the Black War, which cost £30 000, only two Aborigines were captured. George Robinson spent the next frustrating years in attempts at reconciliation.[36] The race was fast dying out. Governor Arthur's war against the natives was to have the effect of completely annihilating all the full blooded Tasmanian Aborigines. But much of their culture and traditions would be passed on through the descendants of those women who formed unions with ex-convict sealers.[37]

34 SEALERS AND SAILORS

SEVERAL *CALCUTTA* CONVICTS, when free, were among the first to join the sealing gangs in Bass Strait and there is enough evidence to show that some formed alliances with particular native women which might have meant something more than using the women for economic gain. Sealers, unlike other invaders, had no interest in acquiring land. So that in spite of horrors perpetrated from time to time, the sealers and natives were able to achieve some sort of economic interdependence with the natives.

Sealers also, however rough and often brutal, did pay their way, providing flour, dogs and sometimes the products of the deal in exchange for the use of the young native woman whom they took around the age of puberty. It was customary for every sealer in the Straits to have from two to five native women for his own use or benefit. From these he would select the most suitable to cohabit with as a wife. Captain James Kelly found the children born of such unions to be a 'fine, active and hardy race. The males were good boatmen, kangaroo hunters and sealers; the women extraordinarily clever assistants to them. They were generally very good-looking and of a light copper colour'.[1] The white men, mostly ex-convicts, enjoyed the free life. They asked for little more than to live in a rough and lawless society, out of which grew an island community that did not become extinct when the rest of the Tasmanian race died out.[2]

Equipped with special knives and clubs, muskets and ammunition, dogs for hunting kangaroos and enough provisions to last several months, they remained on the rocky islands. They had roughly built huts and some small boats, but life was uncertain and they never really knew when relief would come. Meanwhile they collected the skins, hundreds, sometimes thousands at a time.[3] Sealers at first had little fear of and some co-operation from the natives, but there was the ever-present anxiety that some foreign vessel might call and overpower them.

One of Knopwood's young boatmen, William Jones, undeterred by experiences (later recorded) when strand-ed for four years in the Foveaux Straits, had served in numerous ships before deserting the *Baring*, which he had joined as it set sail for England.[4] He returned to Hobart Town in company with a fellow deserter, the Glaswegian Archibald (or James) Campbell, by which time Jones was a fresh-complexioned youth of five feet two-and-a-half inches and aged twenty-six years. He had been one of the youngest *Calcutta* boys, only twelve when sentenced and only three feet eleven inches in height.[5] Together with his old friend Thomas Tombs — the two had once tried to escape by boat from Hobart — Jones joined Captain James Kelly's crew in a five-oared whaleboat, the *Elizabeth*. Another member of Kelly's crew was George Briggs who had spent a few years with the natives in the north-east and learnt some of their language. He had at this time at least two wives and several children on the islands, although he was not able to communicate with the tribe they would meet on the west coast.[6] The purpose of the voyage was to explore the west coast of Van Diemen's Land on behalf of the trader and ex-surgeon, T. W. Birch. The party was, as it transpired, to learn much about the strange relationship established between the two peoples engaged in sealing operations.

Kelly and his sailors set out in December 1815 and, after discovering and naming Port Davey after the Lieutenant-Governor, they made friends with some alarmed Aborigines by presenting them with some of the numerous swans they had shot along the coast. These natives were about six feet tall. Their arms and legs were very thin and their stomachs large. Although the natives had piled up some three tons of crayfish, which could be found in abundance at the water's edge, it seemed that they were nearly starving. At one small bay the explorers stopped off to roast a black swan and make a three-decker pie for a first-rate Christmas dinner, throwing a glass of brandy into 'Christmas Cove' and giving three hearty cheers.[7]

The next day they entered, through a screen of smoke from bushfires that were raging all along the

Protection from the icy blasts — Charles Goodridge in typical sealer's garb.

western coast, the narrow passage that later became known as Hell's Gates. They sailed into the extensive harbour to which Kelly gave Governor Macquarie's name. They spent several days exploring the inlet and river where they discovered large quantities of Huon pine which would ensure the success of the commercial aspects of the voyage. One can imagine the exhilaration they experienced on seeing the towering peak of Frenchman's Cap from their boat as they sailed the silent clear waters of the Gordon River — here surely was Eden. How could Jones and Tombs, or any of the others, even contemplate that within a few years the name of Macquarie Harbour would become synonymous with hell, a place of confinement at which four of their *Calcutta* colleagues would serve time? It would become a natural prison from which few would dare escape; and if and when they did, there were to be among them those who would lose all sense of human dignity, so that even the killing of their mates

to assuage their hunger would no longer seem a crime.

Heavy seas and tide-rips made the passage northwards extremely hazardous. They met some less friendly natives but found, according to Kelly, that 'fortune favours the brave', when they delighted them with further gifts of swans. One old man was about six feet seven and although there was little flesh on his bones he danced and sang for them, pulling ugly faces, but during a skirmish with others who tried to take more swans from Briggs, Kelly fired a pistol to frighten them away. These natives had probably never before seen any white persons.

Ultimately they reached Launceston where they only just survived the interrogations of Major James Stewart, who arrested them because they were in an open boat. Stewart mistook them for associates of Michael Howe for whom he had been searching and had heard the bushrangers were waiting to seize a boat to take them across the Straits.[8]

Briggs met up with one native chief whom he called his 'Lamanbunganah', or Laman, that is his 'father-in-law', who received daily smokes from his daughter at Cape Barren that she and the children were safe. Laman wanted the party to join him and attack another tribe led by his brother Tolobunganah, who it seemed was with Michael Howe's party. The situation was sticky but they managed to get away to King George's Island. There they joined the rival party led by Tolo who greeted Briggs warmly and assured him that the bushrangers were bad men. They all appeared to get along well and stayed on the island for nine days, procuring 122 seal skins and 246 kangaroo skins.[9]

Kelly described how the lithe naked body of a young woman could shoot through the waves, cunningly imitating the flapping of the seals, which she could attract and then club more adeptly than any man could:

They went to the water's edge and wet themselves all over their heads and bodies . . . [to] keep the seals from smelling them as they walked along the rocks . . . Two women went to each rock with their clubs in hand, crept closely up to a seal each, and lay down with their clubs alongside. Some of the seals lifted their heads up to inspect their new visitors and smell them. The seals scratched themselves . . .

The women went through the same motions as the seal, holding up their left elbow and scratching themselves . . . the women still imitating every movement . . . After they had lain upon the rocks for nearly an hour . . . the women rose up in their seats, their clubs lifted up at arm's length, each struck the seals on the nose and killed him; in an instant they all jumped up as if by magic and killed one more each. After giving the seals several blows on the head, and securing them, they commenced laughing aloud and began dancing. They each dragged the seal into the water, and swam with it to the rock upon which we were standing . . .[10]

After such an exercise the women then cooked a supper of the shoulder flesh from young seals, throwing it on a fire, and while eating rubbed the oil on their skins and remarked that they had had 'a glorious meal'. Before sailing from the island Kelly's men witnessed an extraordinary dance and mock warfare display.[11] It was a happier meeting than many other encounters between the two cultures recorded in the history of Van Diemen's Land.

For Kelly the results of the voyage were gratifying. Birch was anxious to exploit the Huon pines which Kelly had discovered growing profusely at Macquarie Harbour. Kelly received a land grant on Bruny Island and with his family made Hobart his headquarters. He continued to engage in other dangerous voyages, later becoming Pilot Harbour Master at the Derwent and a person of considerable influence and respectability.[12] Jones returned to the Pacific trade and Tombs went on his merry way, living by his wits.

But Birch later claimed that he himself had discovered Port Davey with the rapscallion Denis McCarty in the schooner *Geordy*, before James Kelly sailed in and out of the west coast harbours.[13] There was then some rivalry between the Kelly and McCarty parties, but there is little doubt that Kelly and his men preceded McCarty to Macquarie Harbour and probably also to Port Davey, although some of the dates in various reports do not coincide.

McCarty employed one ex-*Calcutta* convict, Thomas Jones. On one of the *Geordy*'s voyages down from Sydney in March 1815, with a cargo of wheat and potatoes for the Derwent, a storm blew them along Bass Strait and they were driven to the entrance of Port Phillip.[14] Later that year James Carrett together with Charles Shore, who had tried to escape at Port Phillip and received a shotgun wound, joined the *Geordy* crew to explore the south-west coast. The ship struck heavy gales and parted both her cables off the South Cape in December 1815. McCarty ran her on shore and arrived back in Hobart in his boat. Shore appears to have drowned at the time but others survived.[15]

The best-known of the *Calcutta* men among the sealers who had a firm relationship with a native woman was Samuel Tomlins. One of the earliest bushrangers, he had learnt something of the harsh life and could barely wait for his freedom, which he gained in 1809.[16] Soon after the 1811 muster he left Hobart legally, probably joining the crew of a sealing vessel. He took up with Bulra, one of the native women whose history can be traced.

George Robinson gave Bulra's tribal name as POOL.RER.RE.RER. and her rendezvous in 1830 as Hunter's Island, but she was on Cape Barren Island when her son Edward by Samuel Tomlins was born in 1813.[17] During the Reverend John Youl's visit to

Port Dalrymple in January 1819 he baptised sixty-seven children, including the young half-caste Tomlins. At this time Samuel was a crew member of the *Jupiter* which had been in the area for several weeks. Probably both parents were present when the numerous children of 'marriage' without the benefit of clergy attended the historic ceremony.[18] David Gibson was one well-known example who took this opportunity of having his union with Elizabeth Nicholls blessed by the church and her four children baptised.

Sadly, it was the last pleasant occasion that Tomlins and Bulra might have had together. Captain B. Ainsworth and his crew departed for Kangaroo Island. When they returned to the Derwent in April 1819 with 3 200 seals, 2 400 kangaroo skins and thirty tons of salt, they brought the news that Chief Officer C. Feen and Samuel Tomlins, one of the island men, were drowned while the brig lay in the Bay of Shoals at Kangaroo Island.[19]

Bulra appears to have remained on the island for several years, living with one known as 'Young Scott'. They brought up her son who was to become one of the more famous sealers, a stocky young man about five feet eight in height. He was excellent with the harpoon and was an associate of William Dutton in the early days at Portland. He made Hunter's Island his headquarters and petitioned Governor Darling for the return of his mother in 1832.[20] Darling wrote to George Robinson for information and the reply indicated that Tomlins' apparent filial affection was but a crafty design. However, Bulra arrived in Launceston and joined her son at Hunter's Island where he abandoned her while he set off on a whaling voyage to the west coast of New Holland. She was a woman of marvellous dexterity in the water, still able to perform the same motions as the seals in the manner that Kelly had described.[21]

It is likely that young Tomlins sold or bartered his mother to the Europeans who were on the island. She was co-habiting with John Dodson in 1832 and later Robert Rew, both ex-convicts. Rew had been coxswain on J. H. Wedge's boat when he surveyed the west coast in 1828. When harshly treated, Bulra approached Robinson when he was visiting Hunter's Island. Rew was forced to sign a certificate that, of her own free will and consent, she was leaving him to join the established settlement. Robinson declared that her own son was wholly under the influence of the other sealers and addicted to drunkenness and immorality. At that time Robinson judged her to be thirty-five to forty years old. She was sent to the Aboriginal Settlement where she died sometime before September 1835. Ned Tomlins followed in his father's footsteps and lived with a young native from Ben Lomond known as Little Mary (NICK.ER. EM

POW. ER.RER.TER) but she died before October 1835.[22]

There was one union which suggests that a happier situation and some understanding between the two cultures could exist. Archibald Campbell, who had tried to escape with Stewart early in his career, had learnt to live off the land without much trouble. In his time he had acquired scars on his eyebrows and a gunshot wound on his ankle, had received 300 lashes ordered by Knopwood, and by 1814 had been outlawed at the same time as the bushranger Peter Mills. He became part of the sealing fraternity in the Straits, making his headquarters at Gun Carriage Island. He discovered a crystal mine in a small bight opposite Woody Island. It became known as Jemmy Campbell's mine.[23] He must have heard of Governor Macquarie's proclamation of May 1814 to those outlawed in Van Diemen's Land offering an amnesty on their return within a certain time. Campbell gathered as much of the crystal as he could, together with other curiosities, and returned to Hobart with William Jones to offer himself up to Lieutenant-Governor Davey who arranged for his free pardon.[24]

Probably during his sealing days, Campbell had formed an attachment to one of the native women, her name unknown, who accompanied him everywhere. They do not appear to have had any children. His woman appeared quite happy with town life and encouraged her old friends to visit the town. Governor Davey had sent clothing to some who were living on the South Arm collected from various persons in the settlement. Archibald Campbell brought his more curious friends in but others were suspicious of the white man's motives and moved to Betsey Island. Campbell and his woman (and friends who were clothed) took a boat to look for them. The reaction of the natives, crouched miserably around a fire on a cold winter's day, must have been extraordinary as they saw children warmly clad, and wanted to feel their clothes. They all rushed for the boat and nearly sank it in their eagerness to visit the strange parts which Campbell's woman had described.[25]

Campbell arrived back in Hobart with thirteen natives whom the Governor clothed. They indicated their desire to go to Bruny Island which he arranged. Campbell must have treated his woman with some humanity as he had formed some trust among her people. With various degrees of trepidation they began to come into the settled areas. Knopwood had several visits from his 'sable' friends whom he allowed into his kitchen and provided with bread, meat and potatoes which they roasted. He showed them a doll which his adopted orphan girl Betsey Mack had dressed. They thought it was a dead baby. One of the old Aboriginal women took it and kept it because it was their custom to carry a dead babe about with them. The following morning, after another good meal, they wandered down to the bottom of Cottage Green where they lit a fire to roast oysters and mussels. The townsfolk drifted in and out all day in wonderment.[26] Those who had had contact with natives in the past had not usually met them within the environs of the town.

But some white men continued to offend the docile blacks and were censured by Governor Davey. Some had taken children from the natives by force. On one occasion the natives decided to take action when a hundred of them alarmed a household at South Arm. They refused to eat the food offered. An older Aboriginal tried to line up the householder so other natives might spear him. Fortunately for the white man, one of the natives turned out to be one of Archibald Campbell's acquaintances who had visited Hobart. He talked his fellows out of murder because of the humanity that some whites had shown.[27] But all members of the party, on retreating to their habitat on Bruny Island, drowned except one woman.

Campbell had probably learned some of the language and was able to communicate with some tribes. That would be one good reason for his accompanying *Calcutta* man Henry Rice on exploration of the east coast in 1820. Ever loyal to his woman, he took her with him but there was a sad ending: 'We came to the Main Ocean to a place call'd the Stoney Boat Harbour, where we buried Campbell's black woman'.[28] Three years later, the Reverend William Bedford, newly arrived in Hobart, married Campbell to Jane Jarvis, a forty-year-old convict woman who had arrived in the *Mary Ann*. His sealing and roving days over, he became a ferry man, working for Goodridge from Kangaroo Point. He died and was buried at St Andrew's, Hobart, in June 1829.[29]

Sealing as an economic proposition had not been viable off the coast of Van Diemen's Land for many years, but the descendants lived on, and there are today among the islanders some proud descendants of the two cultures whose forebears had co-habited some eighteen decades ago and included, so it would seem, some *Calcutta* convicts.

35 MACQUARIE LAND AND BEYOND

SEVERAL OF THE *Calcutta* convicts moved on to Port Jackson, where they found life more varied and stimulating than in the smaller settlement. Some of these contributed in varying degrees to the multi-faceted society which was well established there under the benevolent governorship of Lachlan Macquarie.

Some also came as visitors, after they were free by servitude, to look at the older establishment before returning to England. Others were there to appear before the courts, whether in the dock or as witnesses. As has been noted, some of the wrongdoers, when proven guilty, were removed to penitentiaries or hanged. Others, like the *Marcia* pirates, were lucky and were reprieved. Of these James Taylor, one of the Gibraltar mutineers, remained at Port Jackson. Reported to be a good-looking man with sandy hair, he served for a while as a constable but was dismissed for 'gross neglect of duty'. After receiving a condition-al pardon in 1815, he seems to have had a somewhat uneventful future as a carpenter.[1]

Two convicts who benefited from the move to Port Jackson had come from established county families — Thomas Rushton from Macclesfield in Cheshire and Philip Strickland from Corfe Mullen in Dorset. The former had been a forger and the latter had stolen gold coins and other articles.[2] Strickland had hoped to obtain a free pardon when he informed against his fellow-convicts in 1807, then fled from Hobart Town in fear of his life (and with the consent of Governor Collins) to become a successful landowner in the Windsor district, with a wife and several children.[3]

King reluctantly had to remove one of his few skilled linen manufacturers, an unruly Irishman, to Norfolk Island and Rushton was to be his replace-ment. As early as May 1802 King had begged the Duke of Portland to send someone acquainted with the growth and manufacture of flax.[4] Rushton, whose given trade was tanner and hemp-spinner, also had considerable knowledge of brewing. It appears that Rushton and William Oram (a sheep stealer from Leicester) left Hobart Town in the *Lady Nelson* soon

after their arrival there.[5] Little is known about Oram's life, but Rushton was a great bonus to the people of Port Jackson. Although he did not enter the flax-producing industry he was soon able to produce a good ale many years before the southerners would open their Cascade Brewery.

The government leased a brewery at Parramatta to Rushton for two years from 1806, together with brewing utensils and cooperage. He agreed to supply table beer at sixpence and strong beer at one shilling per gallon to the Commissariat, and provided a security of £250.[6] His contract prevented him from dispensing to any individuals for the purpose of monopolising its sale by retail. Somehow the mo-nopoly on the rum trade had to be broken. Distribu-tion was to be as general as possible. After two years Rushton advertised that he was brewing good strong beer at two shillings a gallon and fine table beer for private families at eightpence a gallon, bittered with hops only, at the Brickfields, Sydney. There he had rented premises owned by James Wilshire, the Depu-ty Commissary, who had also established the largest tannery in the colony. Rushton purchased all the hops available in the brig *Fox* which arrived from the Cape of Good Hope and he contracted for further supplies.[7]

After a dispute between Rushton and Wilshire, heard before the Court of Civil Judicature in June 1809, Wilshire had to choose between his private industry and public service. The Commissary depart-ment in England finally forbade civil officers to engage in private business. Wilshire chose to concen-trate on his private activities, while Rushton con-tinued to have his licence renewed as a public brewer.[8] Others were entering the field as the consumption of beer, encouraged by Macquarie as the preferred alter-native to rum, increased.

Rushton became agent for Absolom West, who had opened a brewery at Dawes' Point in 1809. He him-self was operating his business from a house on the corner of Hunter and Clarence Streets which he adver-tised for sale in 1811–12 as a 'neat, substantial and commodious dwelling-house with out-houses' which would make a suitable residence for a family. It also had an excellent flock-yard, an extensive and well-cultivated garden and a constant supply of pure water, a somewhat rare commodity at the time.[9]

By 1813 he was cultivating his own hops at Parramatta and the following year contracted for 6000 bushels of barley at 7s a bushel. He supplied large quantities of yeast to the prisoners' barracks. A son Charles, who appears to have been born in England, arrived to join his successful and ever-industrious but elderly father.[10]

Another whose more colourful career created some interest was Joseph Raphael. Whatever he did seemed to generate discord, unlike his other Jewish colleagues. While still at the Derwent he had tried to board the whaler *Sarah* in October 1807. He had arrived at Port Jackson by some means and without a pardon (his was a life sentence). He soon managed to open up an extensive business supplying the government stores with shoes, hoop-iron and other sundries.[11]

Some time before 1817 Raphael was sentenced to a term at Newcastle for an unknown crime. He wrote to Macquarie that he was 'so unfortunate as to involve himself in a dilemma he shall ever deplore before he had the benefit of that emancipation . . .' He was a contemporary at Newcastle of the artist, Joseph Lycett, and James Hardy Vaux, who wrote of his own early life as a convict.[12]

In July 1818 Macquarie arrived at Newcastle in the brig *Elizabeth Henrietta* with his wife and child. There was a great fanfare, with a band playing and the *Lady Nelson* (then in port) saluting, followed by a quick exploration of the mosquito-ridden Hunter River. Macquarie returned to name the newly built Christ Church. There, on 3 August, the Reverend William Cowper married Raphael to Ann Clements, a young Protestant woman who had received a ticket of leave, and James Vaux married an Irish convict washerwoman, his second wife. The soldiers received rum to celebrate the occasion and the convicts had a holiday and an issue of fresh meat.

Soon afterwards the Raphaels were allowed to return to Port Jackson but Joseph was in court again when he faced an action relating to the seizure of six chests of tea, a cart, a mare and harness. Together with a fellow Jew, Solomon Davis, he managed to confuse the Supreme Court bench so much that Mr Justice Barron Field, in awarding the defendants a general verdict, summed up (with some suggestion of anti-Semitism) by saying that the case was a 'mere juggle between two Jews to save as much as possible of Davis's property from the hands of the creditors . . .'[13] However, as a result of a petition to Macquarie, a conditional pardon followed soon afterwards.[14]

Raphael was the subject of one of the exchanges between Macquarie and Hannibal Macarthur in 1819. The latter had convicted Raphael for exposing to sale by public auction a quantity of merchandise and contravening acts relating to hawkers and pedlars. Raphael had occupied a stall in the Sydney market as well as conducting a business from 11 Pitt Street, where he advertised English and Bengal goods, sugar, wholesale and retail, and tobacco by the basket. His wife probably cared for the business while he was hawking around the countryside. The court fined him £40. The Bench of Magistrates, consisting of D'Arcy Wentworth, Simeon Lord, Richard Brooks and John Harris, upheld an appeal. Macarthur was furious and wrote to Macquarie criticising those who had taken it upon themselves to reconsider his verdict and his character as a magistrate. The case became part of the evidence brought forward before Commissioner Bigge when he was examining Macquarie's lenient attitude towards the emancipists. Raphael was later to donate £4 towards the Macquarie monument. During this time he was also a regular subscriber to the Benevolent Society.[15]

For a short time Raphael was in partnership with a man named Solomon (probably Solomon Solomons) who had served three years at Newcastle between 1816 and 1819 and was later listed as a dealer in Pitt Street. He had been deprived of a publican's licence for keeping a disorderly house. Raphael was in further trouble by June 1820 when he was forced into liquidation. His creditors had him detained in prison for debt. He took legal action against those who had circulated rumours that he owed £500 and owned more cash than he had offered his creditors. In December he appeared before the Judge Advocate in the Criminal Court and was sentenced to prison for three months and fined £10 for assaulting Captain Brabyn and a magistrate in the course of duty. His effects had to be sold the following year to pay his creditors.[16]

Raphael opened new stores in 1822, first at 26 and then at 16 Pitt Street. He was then supplying wheat to the government stores and was also among the well-known Jews of Sydney who were rich enough to keep a tilbury.[17] In 1824 he charged Henry Lamb for assaulting him on the racecourse, after which Lamb served six months in prison. Raphael advertised his premises in Pitt Street, consisting of a cellar, storehouse and stable, to let with immediate possession. His wife received a conditional pardon in 1825 and the following year he received a licence to act as an auctioneer.[18]

But it seemed that he could not keep out of trouble, although one is inclined to believe that he was often provoked at a time when waves of anti-Semitism spread throughout the colony. He was acquitted of using bad language in the Sydney market but one incident indicates how strong local prejudices could be.

About the time of the birth of their daughter Jane in 1819, the Raphaels had adopted two children, one an orphan boy. They enrolled him at the Parramatta Commercial Academy in 1826. The headmaster, B. Thurston, for some reason found need to explain that Raphael had brought the boy as a boarder to his seminary, had paid £7 17s 6d in advance, and provided him with every other requisite equal to every other child. Thurston wrote that he was warned he would lose all his other scholars if the boy were allowed to stay. He was himself surprised at such ill-feeling, telling the critics that they should not take a dislike to a child because of the father. He would publish the names of the uncharitable persons which, strangely enough, included the name of a Mr Aarons, who would have been none other than an ex-convict at one time assigned to Raphael and now a dealer in George Street in a 'sort of moveable shop'. Unfortunately the outcome of the incident has not been recorded. Raphael himself addressed the readers of the *Sydney Gazette* in touching words that echo the sentiments of many Jews through the ages:

though a humble individual I yet feel it my duty to assist the friendless as far as it lies in my power . . . presented them for the benefits of a good school . . . certain ladies including the wife of Mr Harpher the butcher and Mrs Josephson felt aggrieved . . .[19]

Raphael doubtless had a grievance too against Mrs Josephson, the wife of a Pitt Street jeweller who had become an official of the Society for the Propagation of Christianity to the Jews. She was active in the Methodist Church. Her stepdaughter had just made a splendid marriage to Barnett Levey who was the first male Jewish free settler in Australia and the promoter of many grandiose schemes, including the tallest building in Sydney and later the building of the Theatre Royal. Levey charged Raphael with assault on his person but Raphael was declared to be not guilty.[20]

Over the years Raphael continually applied for and received assigned servants, but none remained with him for long. For many years he had tried to get the Governor to assign him Samuel Levy, an elderly convict who had served thirteen years at Newcastle and one at Port Macquarie for sheep stealing in Van Diemen's Land. Soon after Raphael's request was granted, Levy repaid his benefactor with 'gross insolence and disobedience' and Raphael had him sent to a chain gang.[21]

Raphael received a licence to open the Manchester Arms Hotel in George Street in 1830. These mansion-like premises had been built by Daniel Cooper, partner of Solomon Levey (the emancipist brother of Barnett)

who had an extensive export trading and shipping business. Described as an alderman and philanthropist, J. G. Raphael of lower George Street, was at this time manager of the 'Old established Seaman's Shipping and Registry Office', perhaps a concern that came with the acquisition of Cooper's interests.[22]

By 1835 he was known as 'of facetious notoriety' when a female stall holder at the market charged him with indecently exposing his person.[23] There were numerous reported arguments and assaults, receiving stolen goods, in all of which he appears to have escaped convictions other than fines. He was an incorrigible and his life, from the time of his original crime in London, was a continuous struggle against those with whom he came in contact. He obviously had many good qualities and there are many instances of his generosity as a subscriber to relief funds, other organisations and charities, which indicates he had acquired wealth in spite of the fact that he was declared insolvent in 1832, 1835 and 1843. But he was perhaps over-sensitive and reacted aggressively and unwisely in a society that was not known for its tolerance of his ilk. It does appear that he received considerable leniency compared with other Jews who received harsher punishments for lesser misdemeanours in the colony than did Raphael.

On the recommendation of Governor Gipps he received, at long last, an absolute pardon in 1843, the last of the *Calcutta* convicts to be allowed the freedom, if he wished, to return to England.[24] There is no record that he even made a return visit. He died in Sydney on 26 September 1853 aged 68, and surprisingly was buried (perhaps at his widow's instigation) by the Reverend J. Eggleston, a Methodist minister, although he was listed in 1845 as a seat-holder in the Sydney synagogue.[25]

•   •   •

Of all those *Calcutta* convicts who had found their way to Port Jackson, no single group had a more adventurous future than those who had originally arrived in the colony as ex-sailors or had shown some sea-faring prowess. Some who sailed before the mast contributed much to the sea lore of early Pacific trading days. This is not surprising when one recalls that they had been specifically selected from the hulks as potential employees in the infant fishing industry. Previously there had been fears that men with such experience would too readily escape, but because they were needed urgently, some received premature pardons and several were permitted to join boat crews under supervision. Competitive and indiscriminate slaughter was already exhausting many of the sealing grounds in Bass Strait; only those who had settled comfortably into their free life with the Bass Strait Islanders remained to eke out a meagre living off the Van Diemen's Land coast. For others the islands off the south coast of New Zealand and Macquarie Island indicated better prospects.

Some of those who had rowed from Port Phillip to Port Jackson with William Collins had been among the first to leave Hobart Town after receiving their pardons.[26] Others were more adventurous, lured by the greed and opportunism of Sydney merchants who were trading across the Pacific and in the southern seas. Masters of colonial vessels were allowed to trade in competition with other British merchants without infringing the rights of the East India Company. The *Sydney Gazette* advertised the crews joining the ships and reported many of the voyages in some detail.

Colonial ships were arriving with supplies of breadfruit, palm oil, pearl shells, sandalwood and rice from the islands, including Fiji, Samoa, the Society and the Friendly Islands, and the Tuomotos. Merchant ships from overseas were departing with sperm oil, sealskins, cedar and other timber already bartered by middlemen such as Campbell & Co. Salt pork from Otaheite in particular was one of the more important items in any ship's cargo. Many times it helped to alleviate distress when the colonies were running short of meat and, indeed, was deemed equal to the product derived from Paddy's pigs.

Charles Smith, a former shoemaker, arrived at Port Jackson from Hobart Town in 1808, and signed on as a crew member for Campbell & Co. For several years he engaged in some of the more exciting voyages in the South Seas. His introduction to the Pacific Ocean was to be a memorable one, enough to quench the adventurous spirit of most of his kin. He sailed in the American brig *Favourite* with Captain William Campbell, formerly of the *Harrington*, to the Fiji Islands with the intention of going on to China.[27] They called at Tongataboo in the Friendly Islands in quest of sandalwood. The Captain sent three boats ashore before learning that the chieftain Bullendam was about to make war upon the inhabitants of another island, Taffeia. One hundred and forty canoes cut off the path of two of the three boats from the *Favourite* and took prisoner the second officer and a former chief officer of the American ship *Jenny*, together with six of the crew. The natives hoped for some co-operation and promised help to obtain sandalwood when they had subjugated the Taffeians.

Clubs and spears were the weapons used in a horrifying scene in which Bullendam's men massacred mostly women and children, whose menfolk had fled in fright. In a beautiful valley shaded with coconut and breadfruit trees, the British prisoners were forced to witness the burning of some hundred village houses. The bodies of forty-two dead were piled in a canoe and taken back to Tongataboo with much acclamation. After dismemberment, the limbs were suspended from the boughs of trees and roasted. Charles Smith rejected with abhorrence the offer of a succulent human leg. He had not eaten for days and was afraid of the consequences. The cannibalistic festival merrily continued, while every minute the prisoners expected that they too would be victims of a ritual they could not condone. To their surprise, release came suddenly. They received traces of unexpected kindness from Bullendam and his people, whose enemies they began to realise were not the British but people of their own race. The *Favourite* appears to have sailed on to China and returned to Port Jackson in February 1809.[28]

The Polynesian run was popular. Apart from the obvious feminine attractions, the weather was much warmer and more stable than that in the temperate zone and the Roaring Forties. The cargoes were cleaner and life generally more pleasant. But there must have been times when, becalmed in the doldrums, the sailor born to the sea might even wish to exchange the calm of the blue Pacific for the excitement of a hurricane in more southerly latitudes. Sealing and whaling were dangerous occupations at any time and in wintry conditions life was a gamble. Monsoons and typhoons of the tropics were less recurrent.

But there were always some perils to be faced, as when Robert Barwise and Thomas Williams (believed to be Thomas Williams alias Long) joined the crew of the *Mercury* in October 1808 and sailed on a Pacific voyage.[29] At Vavoo (Vava'u), the most beautiful of the Tongan group of islands, natives planned to surprise the crew and take the vessel. An Englishman, Nicholas Blake, who lived in the group, and one of the sub-chiefs who could speak a little English, warned Captain Siddons of the *Mercury* that the people were treacherous and not to deal with them. Blake was a former crew member of the *Port au Prince*, a privateer which the natives had captured in November 1806, murdering the captain and thirty or forty of the crew.[30] Blake and some twenty-four who had gone ashore dispersed among the islands, where there were more hidden inlets than almost anywhere in the Pacific. He was able to supply the *Mercury* with water, although the inhabitants were ready to take the ship. Siddons had to force a passage through sixty or seventy canoes, astonishing and enraging the natives, who unsuccessfully pursued the ship until darkness in their war canoes.[31] Barwise, after a few less eventful months in the brig *Star* on a sealing expedition, then joined the crew in the colonial brig *Trial*. Her captain, Matthew Folger, was the man who had discovered the fate of the *Bounty* mutineers. As nothing more has been recorded about Barwise, one must assume that he was among the four persons Folger left on the Palliser Islands with several natives to gather pearls and shells. In an unguarded moment these natives killed three of the men and wounded the fourth, after challenging them as aggressors who had already killed one of their own men.[32]

Life in a sealing gang, too, was hazardous and unpredictable. Ship's masters often left their men for about six months with provisions, but there were times when the ships never returned and the fate of those stranded defies imagination. On at least two occasions in 1809 *Calcutta* men were left in gangs that survived for several years before rescue. John Davis and Robert Kennedy, formerly one of Humphrey's servants, had joined Campbell & Co.'s brig *Fox* (Captain Cox) a vessel notorious for virulent outbreaks of scurvy among the crew.[33] Kennedy was one of those left on Solander's Island in Foveaux Strait. The *Fox* was then wrecked off Amsterdam Island in the Indian Ocean and, although passing ships picked up the crew and cargo, no one appeared to remember the men left in New Zealand waters.[34] At much the same time, William Jones, with Thomas Williams, answered Captain John Bader's persuasive advertisement in the *Sydney Gazette* for active seamen 'to proceed on a pleasant and highly promising voyage'. They sailed out of Port Jackson in the London-based brig *Active* and, along with eight others, were also left with limited provisions in Foveaux Strait.[35] The mother ship was never heard of again.

Four years passed before one of Campbell & Co.'s brigs, the *Perseverance*, discovered the men on Solander's Island, and Master Grono, of the colonial schooner *Governor Bligh*, rescued the ten left by the *Active*.[36] Solander's Island was mostly barren rock some four or five miles in circumference. It yielded little to succour the forgotten men but they survived on a few birds, seal flesh and fish. Sealskins provided some protection from the Antarctic gales but the perpetual seaspray over their rugged habitation had ruined attempts to grow potatoes and cabbages from the seed left them. They had to leave behind a large quantity of dried and salted skins which they sold to the Sydney merchant Simeon Lord, warning others not to meddle or take them away. One of the men was a Sydney native who had, according to the *Sydney Gazette*, 'lived in perfect amity and good understanding with the others'.[37]

The men left by the *Active* survived on seal, a fern root resembling a yam, and a species of fern. They had a whaleboat in which they explored other sealing grounds. But the boat was unseaworthy and, on finding an abandoned boat, they had just finished construction of a safer vessel when a hurricane destroyed it and all their hopes of relief. Undaunted, they then made up a sealskin canoe to return to their original depot, finding the weather had severely injured their sealskins. They were at starving point but were per-

severing with the building of a further boat when the *Governor Bligh* arrived and returned a 'joyful gang' to Port Jackson.[38] William Jones must have found serving under James Kelly something of a holiday by comparison.

Charles Smith continued to work regularly for Campbell & Co. He joined the crew of the *Perseverance* and in it made several further voyages to the Fiji Islands, with Captain Hasselbourg in command, before the ship ventured into the waters south of New Zealand searching for new fisheries. In 1810 they discovered Campbell and Macquarie Islands.[39] For Campbell & Co. it was a chance to exploit new and lucrative fields and regain some of their losses, as the sealing trade nearer home had diminished. Campbells tried to keep their new fisheries a secret and left sealing gangs, which included Charles Smith, on the islands. But others, including Americans in the *Aurora* and Kable and Underwood's vessel the *Sydney Cove*, soon arrived on the scene. The *Aurora* returned to Port Jackson to report the drowning of Captain Hasselbourg at Campbell Island with three of his crew when a boat capsized. Within a few months gangs managed to collect fine quality skins from 80 000 seals. But the company found the collection of oil from the immense number of elephant-seals yielded a more profitable return on their investment.[40]

Urias Allender was one of the first to venture on a sealing voyage to Macquarie Island. He joined the brig *Concord* which left him in a gang employed by Campbell & Co. on the island in April 1811. When the ship returned to pick them up five months later, they found the men in a deplorable condition after the severe winter. They had only barely survived hurricanes and unbearable cold on an island completely covered with ice. No ships had called and they were near starvation.[41] It was enough to finish Allender's career as a sealer although his career as a ferryman also had its dangers.

After several years in the southern fisheries Charles Smith served in coastal vessels operating between Newcastle and Shoalhaven, before joining the brig *Active* in March 1814 together with three other *Calcutta* men: John Hunter, Samuel Tomlins and William Mansfield who appears to have become somewhat restless after his early marriage and two young children.[42] For some years the activities of the London Missionary Society had, through the intercession of the Reverend Samuel Marsden, worked with Campbell & Co. in its efforts to secure Christian converts from among the natives of the South Seas. Campbell was the Society's banker and occasionally traded with Pacific islands on its behalf, bringing among other goods coconut oil and pork from Otaheite for a commission of two and a half per cent. This particular voyage of the *Active*, by then Marsden's personal property, was to test the attitude of the New Zealand Maoris towards establishing more friendly intercourse. According to Marsden's belief, 'commerce promotes industry — industry civilization, and civilization opens up the way for the Gospel'.[43]

Opportunities for trading in the islands of the Pacific were just as attractive to Marsden as trying to convert the Awabakal tribe in the environs of Sydney and Newcastle. In addition New Zealand could supply spars for naval supplies, flax and perhaps minerals. Also available were erotic artefacts to titillate the merchants and traders of Sydney Town as well as the reverend gentleman, who was no prude in such matters. Commerce could add a supplement to Marsden's stipend and help pay for his flocks of imported merinos. The terrible massacre of those who had sailed in the *Boyd* a few years earlier might have pricked Marsden's conscience when he sent two missionaries on the voyage, Thomas Kendall and William Hall.[44] At the Bay of Islands they received very hospitable treatment from the natives. They took aboard three of the chiefs who wished to visit Port Jackson and meet the Governor. Macquarie's own instincts were more favourable to the Australian Aboriginal and averse to the activities of those prepared to sell their souls for a mess of pottage.

The Maori chiefs brought gifts for His Excellency, and members of the Church Missionary Society and their wives, led by Marsden, left in the *Active* for New Zealand in October 1814. Hunter and William Cooper signed on again as crew but Mansfield returned temporarily to domestic life to greet a new child. Tomlins and Charles Smith appear to have remained for a while at the Bay of Islands. Members of the Missionary Society were to 'commence the benign labour of opening the minds of the natives to those benevolent and just conceptions which adorn the Christian religion . . . in a region of cannibals'.[45]

Four *Calcutta* men, therefore, witnessed the beginnings of the colonisation of New Zealand. As they watched the British flag flying and listened to Marsden's Christmas Day sermon, 'Behold, I bring you tidings of great joy', they must have pondered during the reading of the Hundredth Psalm on the previous occasions when they had been present at the establishment of settlements at Port Phillip and the Derwent. They would have remembered moments of grave danger when confronting the people of another race. But how to convince those cannibals that they should know 'that the Lord he is God: it is he that hath made us, and not we ourselves; we are his people, and the sheep of his pasture'?[46]

The natives made a joyful noise unto the Lord they did not understand and began a war dance which fortunately did not end in a shedding of blood. The gifts which the strangers had brought and the thoughts of bartering goods for goods seemed for the time being a sounder way of conducting relations than risking even an eye or a tooth. But it must have been difficult for them to comprehend the behaviour of other white men whom they had encountered — those who had abducted some of their women years before and disappeared.[47] One cannot help but reflect, because there was no George Robinson to report on the treatment of these native women, that the idyllic life as imagined in the Polynesian world was often just as brutal for women as it was in Bass Strait and on the Tasmanian mainland.

John Hunter stayed for several years with the *Active*. On one occasion the brig sailed to Otaheite for pork in exchange for several thousand (!) books printed in the Tahitian tongue for 'furtherance of the benevolent views of the Mission'. The Reverend William Crook, who had kept his distance from Marsden, gave up his boarding school in Sydney and with his wife and several children went on board to join the missionaries at Otaheite in 'their pious labours'.[48]

The *Active* procured twenty-seven tons of sandalwood in the Society Islands and called at the Bay of Islands for spars on the return voyage from New Zealand. It would appear that Smith rejoined the ship at this stage. After returning to Port Jackson he advertised that he was joining the brig *Queen Charlotte*, which was on the Marquesas and Otaheite run. It had just arrived with sandalwood, a kind of pea known in the Caribbean Islands as 'pigeon pea', and the seed of a fruit growing in many of the tropical islands known as 'papah apple'. Both species, Powell, the captain of the ship believed, would be suitable for vegetation in New South Wales and would be a pleasant addition to 'varieties that already decorate the colonial gardens and orchards'.[49]

At the last minute Smith joined the brig *Daphne*, of which William Campbell was the owner-master. By this time he had become *Mr* Charles Smith and perhaps sailed as chief officer. The *Daphne* sailed on to the Marquesas and then to China.[50] As its home base was Calcutta, Smith must have taken the opportunity to seek his fortune in other parts. There is no record that this Charles Smith returned to New South Wales. He had seen much of the world since he was a young London shoemaker.

The Calcutta-built *Campbell Macquarie* carried several *Calcutta* convicts as crew from time to time. John Tagg sailed on a voyage through Torres Strait to Calcutta in July 1815 with a cargo of spars and oil. William Jones had left James Kelly to sail in her to Batavia in 1817 taking a cargo of coal and does not appear to have returned to the colony. She arrived back in Sydney, her hold full of tar and pitch, ten bales of piece goods, arrack, tea and sugar.[51] John Cole, who had been Knopwood's servant in the

Calcutta, joined her on a sealing voyage to Macquarie Island. They returned with seals weighing fifty-two tons and thirty gallons of elephant-seal oil. Later he drowned at Auckland Island.

Samuel Gray and Thomas Arnott had been among other early *Calcutta* men to join the Pacific traders. Gray was in Campbell & Co.'s brig *Perseverance* with William Jones when it sailed to Fiji for sandalwood in 1808. He transferred to the colonial schooner *Halcyon* with Thomas Arnott when it sailed to Otaheite for pork the following year. Then he and Arnott joined James Kelly on a sealing expedition in *The Brothers* to Bass Strait, when they acquired a cargo of 7 000 seal-skins.[52] Arnott left the sea to become a chair-maker in Hobart. Gray finally sailed for London in June 1815 in the *Sydney Packet* which had brought a cargo of 107 barrels of tar and pitch, fifty-six bundles of spades and shovels, thirty-six boxes of copper, 2 811 iron pots, 148 axle boxes, ten tons of iron, three bundles of steel, and sundries to Port Jackson. It returned to London with 188 casks and bales of wool, ninety-nine casks and 542 sealskins, fourteen casks of oil and 276 bullock hides.[53] At long last there was some indication that colonial products were occupying some of the cargo holds.

But to the ship-owners, lives were expendable as long as the cargo was saved. There was far greater loss of life than one might realise. Many sailors drowned and relatively few were killed by natives, who were usually quite friendly if there was anything to trade. A contemporary verse spells out the sentiments of the time:

From Otaheite and dependencies adjacent,
Pork is so cheap, and natives so complacent;
Two pounds for threepence, all expence [*sic*] attending,
Save paying seamen, wear and tear, but mending.
One vessel lost — mere nothing out of two,
As all the cargo's saved and saved are all the crew.[54]

The pork and breadfruit had been among the more important acquisitions to save the colonies from near starvation. Except for a few occasions, the natives *were* complacent. Almost anything could be traded for an empty bottle or any object made of iron, such as a few nails or a fish-hook, which one missionary had found more effective than a sermon. The sandalwood trade, mainly for the China market, did not last long. There was little left by 1816. Discovery of the timber in the Marquesas took the ships further afield, as did the seal fisheries. Traders became even more competitive, more ruthless, and not at all interested in conserving supplies for the future. They cut down trees that were too young just as the sealers had slaughtered pups, and wondered why their supplies were running out. They lived for the present. It would be many years before the Polynesian Islands would recover from the early invasions. But after the end of the Napoleonic war and later relaxation of the regulations of the East India Company, there would be further extensions of trade which took the adventurous to Melanesia and the islands of the East Indies, where the sandal tree grew in abundance. All the exotica of the East could be had by those who had the money to pay or the goods to trade.

36 CONVICTS UNBOUND

ABOUT THE TIME when Van Diemen's Land separated from New South Wales and became an independent colony (1825), the majority of *Calcutta* convicts who remained had married.[1] A forlorn poet, who signed himself W. W., lamented in the *Hobart Town Gazette*:

'Tis *Woman* alone, with a firmer heart,
Can see all these idols of life depart,
And love the more; and soothe and bless
Man in his utter wretchedness.[2]

Here he was echoing the sentiments of those who for a long time had yearned for something more than the loneliness enforced upon so many in their degraded state.

In earlier times some of those who became the partners of *Calcutta* men had arrived free, having been born on Norfolk Island. But there were never enough women and almost all those available in later years were or had been convicts themselves. Marriage produced not only children and stable relationships within a community, but also reduced crime and supposedly sexual perversions; the latter probably occurred far more than one can prove.

By 1822 many well-to-do ex-convicts and their wives no longer had the need to buy cast-off clothing such as that sold at the Geils auction. A wide choice of articles was available among the many imported goods brought in by those traders on the high seas. The male could dress in fine kerseymeres and cambric shirts, French neckcloths, Wellington boots, corbo coats and Valencia waistcoats. He could carry a silk umbrella and beaver gloves from Norway, and check the time with a musical watch.

His wife could wear clothes made of silk, satin, velvet, plaid or Irish linen. She had a large variety of stays to choose from. She could trim her garments with laces, furs, ribbons, spangles and wear fine kid gloves or satin gloves from Denmark. She could carry a silk or gingham parasol, wear a French gold watch, false curls, gauze veils, and a rich silk or cotton scarf or shawl. She might cover her locks with a lace cap, straw hat or Highland bonnet, or really let her head go and buy a Turkish or Spanish silk net turban — incongruous attire, surely, where muddy roads, open drains and primitive transport would normally dictate one's wearing apparel.

Those who could afford it could smoke tobacco from America or Brazil for 5s 6d a pound and sniff Violet de Strasbourg snuff, drink rum from Jamaica, English cider, madeira, real Irish whiskey. They could wash from blue and white ewers and basins which had matching soap dishes and chamber ware. They could buy English mottled and yellow soap at 15d per pound or 11d by the box. They could light their rooms with English candles at 15d per pound.

The medicine chest would contain purified Epsom salts, magnesia, essence of peppermint, Turkey rhubarb, arrowroot, American starch and spices from the Indies, the best vinegar, walnut and mushroom ketchup, anchovies, and hyson tea at 6s per pound. Hams from Westphalia and imported cheeses would all add to a more varied diet. Curtains might be made from chintz or dimity and a marcella quilt might cover the bed. Vandiemonians could furnish their houses with an

elegant and curious mahogany cabinet, with solid curls; a pair of beautiful Pembroke tables, with pillar, block, and claws; a set of elegant mahogany chairs, with satin hair bottoms . . . made of fine Spanish mahogany, and by one of the first workmen in London. A good mahogany 4-post bedstead with furniture complete, nearly new; also paper hangings of several patterns.[3]

They could buy English china tea and coffee sets, richly cut crystal bottles, goblets and wine glasses, or a very rich lady's cabinet and toilet, curios, formerly the property of the celebrated Marshal Davoust. They could adorn their walls with religious paintings drawn from a lottery held in London, or *A View of the Thames* and *A View of Athens* by Aldridge, or 'a few water paints by a lady'. They could rest on a sofa with pillows and two covers complete or an elegant pair of ottomans.

There was a wide selection of books available and bookcases to hold them. Telescopes and globes showing the latest discoveries were among other luxuries well-advertised. A prosperous farmer with musical tastes might be able to afford a grand piano forte which would cost him thirty-five guineas or the equivalent in stock or wheat. One storekeeper was able to provide a 'very neat and useful family one-horse chaise, very strongly made, and capable of accommodating six persons, with two patent lamps, a complete set of new harness, extra collars, whips, etc.'.[4]

For a lengthy journey one could buy a caboose, consisting of a tea kettle, stew pan, saucepan, salad dish, lamp with burners 'admirably adapted for all parties going in to the country, as at any place they can strike fire and boil a kettle in a few minutes'.[5] Thomas Scott during his explorations, attended by the *Calcutta* man James Carrett, had such equipment, as his sketches show.

For the less privileged there were enormous supplies of calico, flannel, Indian cotton and duck, haberdashery items, cheap working clothes such as nankeens from China, jeans and slops, strong laced boots suitable for stock-keepers, worsted pantaloons, and all the tools needed for the major trades and agricultural implements, ironmongery hardware, turners, fowling pieces, brushes, earthenware and utensils that one would need.[6]

By November 1825 the population of the whole island was 13 604. Of these 4 049 came free or were born in the colony; 2 316 had become free by pardon, servitude or emancipation. There were 7 239 convicts and their children. Among the free persons more than half were female but among the convicts the males outnumbered the females by roughly nine to one.[7] Once granted freedom, persons enjoyed the same economic and legal rights as those who had arrived free in the colony.[8]

But *Calcutta* men were still not on the invitation lists for levées and other functions at Government House, a situation reversed from the time when Collins sought the company of men like Stocker and Grove, with whom he might have an intelligent conversation. Even Governor Davey in his time had not been averse to seeking the company of ex-convicts when, in a fit of pique, he was known to march out of Government House declaring that he could always get a meal at Stocker's!

The churches, together with the inns, remained the chief meeting place for persons at all levels of society. There were many changes in religious observation in the early twenties. Father Philip Conolly, the Reverend Archibald Macarthur, the Reverend William Horton and the Reverend William Bedford had all arrived within months of each other. In the north the Reverend John Youl was already established as the Church of England minister, first at George Town and later at Launceston. Bedford was to replace the ageing Knopwood, with whom he had little in common. Conolly, who had travelled out in the disreputable *Janus*, was the first priest appointed to attend to the spiritual needs of a growing Catholic population and became one of Knopwood's closest friends.[9]

Francis Barnes and James Lord's son David assisted Horton in establishing a Wesleyan chapel and a Sunday School for children when an appeal for funds began in 1822.[10] New churches began to rise, creating their own means of social intercourse. Stocker, Wade, Peters, Whitehead, Barnes and Arthur Connelly were among those named in a list submitted to Commissioner Bigge in 1820 as occupants of pews at St David's. They were seated according to their rank in society, which was behind all the officers and gentlemen and just ahead of the unnamed troops and servants.[11]

Stocker, together with James Austin and David, the son of James Lord, was however, named as a proprietor in the charter of the newly established Bank of Van Diemen's Land in 1823.[12] (There appear to be no *Calcutta* connections with the beginnings of the Van Diemen's Land Company in 1825.) By the early twenties a new type of colonist had begun to arrive, some with considerable financial backing who were ready to invest in a colony that had weathered the pioneering days and showed some promise. There were also some unusual arrivals. One can imagine Knopwood's pleasure at receiving those whose removal as far away as possible from the Royal Family had much deeper significance than his own exile.[13]

The social pattern of Knopwood's life had changed very little. Visitors arrived regularly from across the estuary and he kept in touch with the Stockers and Whiteheads, Ann Jane Gunning (the widow of George Prideaux Harris), the Ingles, the Macauleys, and the Edward Lords who continued to keep up his spirits in more ways than one. A. W. H. Humphrey, who had become a member of the first Legislative Council of Tasmania, lived with his wife Harriet on a fine property on the Plenty River and they frequently visited him. But few persons meant more to him than the young people he gathered around him to make some pleasant social life for Betsey Mack. Among the young people he encouraged were the daughters of David Collins by Ann Yeates and Margaret Eddington. Mariamne Chase and her children, and Martha Garrett, daughter of Martha Hayes and Lieutenant Bowen, were close to him in his old age. But Betsey's premature death, after a short marriage to Henry Morrisby, was hard to accept. She had brought more joy into his life than anyone else.[14]

The ships that called continued to provide contact with the outside world and Knopwood continued to entertain or accept hospitality from the officers on board. Some brought welcome letters from overseas and most left Hobart with letters for home. Knopwood himself was a voluminous correspondent.[15]

The *Commodore Hayes* arrived in Hobart in 1823 amid great excitement. The Headquarters and staff of the 3rd Regiment (the Buffs) were on board. Although a Sunday, the band of the Buffs paraded and played after they landed and marched down the town to St David's.[16] Other regiments, such as the 63rd, continued to entertain the townsfolk when they arrived in Hobart. It was customary to play on a Wednesday afternoon in Knopwood's field where the ladies and gentlemen arrived to enjoy an afternoon's outdoor entertainment.

By the time Governor Arthur had arrived, the new Court House became the venue for concerts, and the band of His Majesty's 40th Regiment played there in October 1826. Governor and Mrs Arthur attended with all the first officers and gentlemen in Hobart Town.[17] One presumes these included some of the *Calcutta* men, now raised to the status of gentlemen. The ladies attended too, for the regimental band was a popular one. There was much singing and enjoyment, the evening going off very well in spite of a frightfully wet night which did not hinder the enthusiasm. Perhaps some wore those exotic silk turbans.

Stocker revived his interest in horse-racing, if it had ever been dampened, when there were suggestions that it should become a respectable organised sport. Influential men like Thomas Gregson, later Premier of Tasmania, and wealthy pastoralist Thomas Anstey had large interests in Jericho where there was considerable support for establishing a race course. Stocker argued that Salt Pan Plains would provide a much more suitable venue. He offered land to form a two-mile circular course adjacent to Ross Bridge as well as separate stabling for racehorses and any 'other accommodation for those who wished to attend'.[18] For a time, picnic races continued at Jericho and Ross as well as at Frederick Henry Bay beach. Michael Lackey, a settler at Clarence Plains, had a well-known horse named Favourite which had beaten Stocker's best black horse at both the Jericho and Frederick Henry Bay races in 1826.[19]

Gregson helped to organise the first real race-meeting in 1827 which was an incentive for those with the money to import better breeds. James Lord's grandson, James, and the squire of Clarendon, James Cox, imported a splendid Arab horse Hadjo Baba which became a great asset.[20] At much the same time

Cox married the young Eliza, daughter of David Collins and Margaret Eddington. The popular picnic races of yester-year in which a couple of old hacks raced in challenges several times in the one afternoon began to be a thing of the past. Stocker's own prize horse in 1830 was a Suffolk breed, Sam, and he made his services available for a limited season for five guineas including groomage. He was a powerful and much admired horse, the sire of some of the best stock in the colony. The previous year Austin announced that his horse, young Aladdin, the only horse sired in the colony by the English thoroughbred Aladdin, had already stood for twenty mares and was available all the season for the same fee.[21]

Gregson and Thomas Lowes established a proper racecourse at New Town, attended by 5 000 in 1832.[22] Governor Arthur had refused to allow prisoners to attend. There was a near riot as Arthur drove back to Government House amid hoots and insults from the populace in general. Horse-racing had come to stay for free and convict alike.

Over the years dogs hunting for food ultimately became hounds. When Gregson's hounds, imported from England, went hunting kangaroos, as one might hunt a fox, Knopwood was among those who welcomed the new sport and the establishment of the Risdon Hounds with Gregson as Master.[23] By the winter of 1836 they were well established as those participating thoroughly enjoyed meeting, sometimes several times a week, to run a kangaroo into the river or into the sea. However, membership of the Gregson set was somewhat exclusive and it is doubtful whether any of the *Calcutta* men became part of the fraternity, although James Lord's son, David, was naturally acceptable. But there was nothing to prevent the locals from watching the blood sports because the tally-hos would waken the dead, or the 'roo from his lair in the morning.[24]

Knopwood first mentioned boat-racing as early as 1815 when James Gordon, the naval officer, defeated Thomas Peters, who presumably had received a free pardon when he petitioned Governor Macquarie in March 1812. Gordon won an award of fifty guineas in the race which took place on the same day that he had fought the duel against Thomas Lascelles. But the use of boats was still strongly discouraged and few convicts were entrusted with command of even the smallest craft, although some racing appears to have continued in an unorganised fashion. By 1828 the gentlemen were challenging the native lads (that is, Europeans born in the colony) and the whalers to races and the young natives appeared superior to all others. Some had almost been born in their boats and had long since learnt the vagaries of the winds and the currents.

The first Sandy Bay Regatta was not held until

William Strutt saw John Pascoe Fawkner, M.P., as a man of elegance and culture whose spacious library contained fine pictures, including Piranesi's splendid engravings of Rome.

1848 but there had been unofficial races. Knopwood described the regatta of February 1831, starting from Mulgrave Battery to round a boat at Kangaroo Bay and another anchored off Cray Fish Point. The weather was unfavourable but he enjoyed it just the same as he watched the beautiful sight with his old friends, the widowed Mariamne Chase and her young daughter.[25]

By 1837 when the curtain went up for the first performance at the Royal Victoria Theatre, *Calcutta* convicts who might have attended, or their children, had long been established in the community and might enjoy the experience of live theatre, even though the backless stools and chilled auditorium were not conducive to comfort. Nor was the general atmosphere. The wife of Governor Franklin noted they were 'half-poisoned by the smell of stale tobacco smoke, foul breath and unwashed frowsy bodies, proceeding from a dense mass of vulgar spirit-and-beer drinking oily-haired knaves'.[26] One wonders whether

Francis Barnes was present to compare the performance with what he had once seen at an auspicious moment of his life at Drury Lane.

It had not been easy to try to graft some of the niceties of western culture on to a convict community which had largely rejected or had never known the benefits of a humane and just society. Lady Franklin was partially successful in trying to foster an interest in science and the arts. But the horrors of transportation, the atrocities committed by the invaders both towards the indigenous population and among themselves, were to remain in sharp contrast to the beautiful environment in which they were to live and in which many would prosper economically. Nor is it easy to relate the events of Tasmania's early history without questioning what happened to those Christian ideals which were supposed to bind both convicts and settlers. In his own way Knopwood had tried, even though he enjoyed the company of the more privileged. His cultivation of the Gregsons and others who could dispense wealth, patronage and power, was in character, but his financial situation could not keep up with theirs and he was always in debt, as in his youth.

Yet as the years passed there was a mellowness and

Augustus Morris junior, the son of a Calcutta *convict, became a member of Parliament, acquired extensive pastoral properties on the mainland, and pioneered refrigeration.*

compassion for his fellow creatures not visible in earlier times. Towards the end of his life it appears that his conscience worried him. Feelings of guilt towards the girl and the child he had never seen preyed on his mind. With some poignancy he wrote to a friend in England that he was still expected to provide a passage to America for a grandson he had not seen.[27] One might surmise that his devotion to Betsey Mack, and later to her family who had given him much affection, was some attempt to quell the disquiet he experienced when he reflected on his past.[28] In spite of the many veiled peccadilloes which crept into his journal, his adaptability to life in a different world made his appointment as a colonial chaplain a reasonable choice. He became the one continuous thread linking more than a generation of people whose lives had remained on the course directed from as far back as 1803.

By the time Queen Victoria had ascended the throne of Great Britain, Tasmania had a population of 42 698 persons. Between 1824 and 1836 more than 1 500 000 acres had been granted to settlers. After the Ripon regulations of 1831 there were no free grants and all land was sold for 5s an acre. Customs was the only form of tax and filled the government coffers with three-quarters of its revenue from the excise on spirits. There was no public debt. Bushranging was no longer a problem and the last of the full-blooded natives were on Flinders Island.[29]

37 A CONVICT IN THE CUPBOARD

*I*T HAD TAKEN just twenty years for Van Diemen's Land to come of age, confirming Francis Bacon's view that 'planting of colonies is like planting in woods; for you must make account to lose almost twenty years' profit, and expect your recompense in the end'.[1]

If British expansion to the South Seas were purely for profit, the planting of both convicts and settlers, together with their families, at the Derwent was ultimately a brilliant and economically sound enterprise.

Well might the British rejoice that they would never, never, never be slaves, but they had had no qualms about filling two idle warships, H.M.S. *Calcutta* and H.M.S. *Glatton*, with slaves of a kind who might usefully expedite Britannia's avowed intention to rule the waves and make the world free for the exploits of traders such as the British East India Company until its dissolution in 1858. However, it did not take these slaves long to throw off their fetters. For most, if they remained bound to anything, it was to the land they acquired for their stock, or tilled, planted and harvested, the soil that nourished them and the property that brought them comfort and often wealth.

But to meet the demands of a mercantilist policy, the employment of naval vessels during peacetime appears to have been a resourceful and neat subterfuge which might also have solved the threefold problem of timber supplies, defence strategy and the transportation of unwanted felons to provide a workforce. The naval men of the *Calcutta* never set eyes on the tall straight timbers of Van Diemen's Land that could have supplied all the navies in the world. War had prevented the effectual completion of their mission and they had to return, as did the *Glatton*, with inferior timber and no flax. But the timber they would have wished for was there in the southern forests in abundance, still to prove its value in more peaceful times. Nowadays ruthless exploitation has stunted the growth of trees in existing afforestation areas and threatened the virgin forests.

In that respect the whole operation was of less immediate success than that of raising the new Union Jack as a warning to the French and providing, for a time, some sense of security to Governor King and his successors and the strengthening of the fisheries trade. There would be further fears of French hegemony as well as American, Dutch, Russian, and an obsession about a Yellow Peril for more than a century after the Battle of Waterloo, but all were either ill-founded or forestalled until 1942 when the Japanese made the only direct attacks on the land that had once been known as Terra Australis Incognita.

An added bonus during the temporary stopover at Sullivan Bay had been the advice tendered by men of the calibre of Woodriff and Tuckey, who quickly foresaw the problem of establishing a port for whalers and passing vessels because of the difficulties involved in negotiating the narrow heads of Port Phillip. In confirming what Collins himself already believed, they were able to provide professional reasons for abandonment. Bearing in mind the state of affairs in 1803–04, one can only applaud the wisdom and vision of those who chose the final locations of settling Bass Strait. The Derwent and the Tamar were more navigable and strategically more appropriately situated, had the potential to provide better timber for the navy, and more plentiful supplies of water than any part of Port Phillip, which would have to wait for another time and other circumstances to prove its worth.

Within a short time the ports became busy havens for whalers, as Governor King had anticipated, although the sealing trade had few lasting benefits for Van Diemen's Land itself. Other ships brought trade, called for fresh supplies and frequently provided the means for many of the former *Calcutta* men with seafaring experience to engage in occupations for which they had originally been chosen. Trade enabled the island to become almost self-sufficient. The fruit trees which George Phipps had carefully tended were the forerunners of a huge industry. Former sheep stealers proved acquisitive enough to help produce fine stock and were ever ready to ward off marauding bushrangers who were much more dangerous than they themselves had been in the mother country. Nor could anyone have foreseen that the remote west, traversed by the lawless escapees, would yield immense mineral wealth and that its wild rivers would unleash some of the world's cheapest hydroelectric power.

But in spite of all the evidence that mercantilism was the underlying reason for settlements in Bass Strait, one cannot get away from the fact that the earlier loss of the American colonies led to the development of a penal society in New South Wales. At first the British government had expected to provide a new home for those loyalists who chose to leave the New World of America for the New World in the southern hemisphere. But the revolutionary wars had diverted the government's interest in settling Port Jackson with refugees who might be more useful in England itself, having proved their loyalty, than the more readily dispensable creatures overcrowding the prisons and hulks. At the time of the Peace of Amiens, American loyalists who had made their homes in England, including the wife of David Collins, were reluctant to leave after some fourteen years' residence, resulting in a much narrower choice of desirable free settlers and the adoption of Governor King's sensible recommendation to give opportunities to selected convicts and their families.

An examination of this particular shipload of convicts cannot pretend to answer any general questions on transportation. Other historians have come to different conclusions from the present writer when examining the system as a whole or by sampling, thereby being in a different position to examine the abuses and shortcomings. Professor A. G. L. Shaw believed that it failed through misunderstanding that it would be a deterrent to crime.[2] The later delegation of authority to persons who misused their power was a damning indictment of a system that was fast losing its effectiveness. But the case histories of the *Calcutta* convicts up until the time when most received pardons at least prove that the horrors and abuses were considerably less than, perhaps, at any other time in the history of transportation. They were special people and it is right that they should have been examined as an entity rather than as part of a sampling or even in a generalised study of transportation to Van Diemen's Land, which did not cease until the end of 1852.[3]

Dr Lloyd Robson believed that the convicts he sampled were 'neither simply "Village Hampdens" nor merely ne'er-do-wells from the city slums' and that the latter outweighed the Village Hampdens.[4] The present writer has found that the large majority of *Calcutta* convicts committed quite serious crimes, although there were no murderers and few perpetra-

tors of really vicious crimes among them. Many of them were clever people; property rather than person had fallen victim to their transgressions. Curiously, the greater their crime against property, the greater their reward. There were enough among them to recognise that hard work and achievement would bring security, salvation, and the consequent social acceptance of their descendants. The acquisition of property was to be their quintessential goal. It was the colonial answer to the type of 'civil society' that had been moulded many long years before by English political philosophers.

That the majority of these convicts proved an economic asset in helping to establish the new settlement cannot be denied. If some ne'er-do-wells succumbed to temptations and lost their land, it proves that there were others ready to grasp any opportunity for capital gain, often with a rapacity that might shock even present-day opportunists.

Those stalwart wives who in earlier times had received land grants and stock in their own right became bound when their husbands became unbound, so that after a few years both wives and children were no more than extra property, namelessly recorded among the returns of the landholder, after the acreage under cultivation and the amount of stock held had been taken into account. Only strong widows like Catherine Wade and Mary Fitzgerald seemed to rise above the system. Work on the land was labour-intensive and it is significant that farmers had many more children than the townsfolk, because labour was always scarce yet necessary for their survival.

The native-born would put their own stamp on the society that would evolve. Although based on British tradition and opportunities, there would be, as Dr Portia Robinson has shown in her study of the currency lads and lasses, a wide gulf between them and their counterparts in England and Ireland.[5] Yet the colonies themselves remained British to the bootstraps, even, for a century or more, largely ignoring the contributions made to the nation by those of other ethnic origins as well as those with convict birth-stains.

The study of the *Calcutta* convicts points to many other conclusions. Those convicted of the worst crimes became the most prosperous settlers. By any standards Gibson, Peters, Stocker, Whitehead, Grove, Fawkner and Barnes had committed serious felonies. Lord, Morris, and Mansfield had used force and arms to procure lesser loot and, together with the less violent Johnson, Earle and Austin, all these men (in spite of the further convictions or craftiness of some) ultimately became solid citizens. The perpetrator of the most serious burglary, Richard Kidman, somehow rose in esteem quickly enough to gain a full pardon and return to England, as did several of those who had committed the quite serious crimes of forgery, embezzlement, uttering counterfeit money and receiving. Of these Power, Michaels, Fell and Shipman had all been useful to Collins. (Shipman's later execution was for another conviction in England.) One of the forgers, Rushton, had an excellent record of service at Port Jackson. Scott Smith, Cashman, Lee and Stewart were four men who might have been valuable assets had not the first two named, ashamed of their plight, suicided before reaching their destination and the other two escaped. Here one might well include the receiver William Buckley, whose useful services as a bricklayer were lost to the community. He takes his place in history as arguably a more intelligent man than some more educated explorers who died rather than allow the Aborigines to befriend them.

Other literate criminals Boothman, John Clarke (of London), Warriner, Allender, Fitzgerald, as well as Grove, Stocker and Whitehead, all rendered service of varying merit, in most cases more satisfactorily than most of the settlers might have done. The latter two, in spite of their more spectacular deals and shady activities, came to be regarded as 'respectable gentlemen', and survived because of whom they knew. They have their parallels in modern society.

Another interesting fact emerges. Stocker, Lee, Fitzgerald and possibly Stewart and Allender were among those who held office in the services, indicating that an acceptably superior background offered temptations to commit their type of crime. But in the ranks, where one would not usually find men who were literate enough to forge or have the opportunity to embezzle, they were all larcenists except for the mutineering privates of the 25th Regiment. Other ordinary soldiers such as Reynolds and Pendridge contributed nothing to the colony and Richardson, Patrick Duff and Thomas Riley were never more than useful, law-abiding, small farmers. Nor, after their first taste of power and commendations for their good conduct, did any of the Gibraltar boys achieve much, two of whom were distinct failures. But they were not petty criminals, rather they were victims of circumstance.

Only five (Power, Whitehead, Stewart, McCarthy and Michaels) of the forty-eight convicts whose origin was not Anglo-Saxon committed crimes other than larceny. If one excepts David Gibson, whose robbery was much greater than the others, the remaining forty-two had little or no more than moderate success as convicts. Yet Gibson, even after further convictions, ultimately justified the faith that Collins and Robert Campbell had in him.

Of others who committed crimes in the colony, few were really bad although one might well argue that the lenience shown towards rapists was inconsistent when others were executed for sheep stealing. Only nine *Calcutta* convicts warranted sentences at penitentiaries: four at Newcastle, four at Macquarie Harbour and one at Moreton Bay.[6] Many of the reported escapes were made with an unofficial nod from the authorities during a time of famine, and the occasional heavy hand with the lash usually proved a deterrent. There were other minor misdemeanours, and alcoholic abuse and its consequences were often a problem. But the large majority of *Calcutta* convicts received early pardons and proved by their rehabilitation that transportation and the chance to begin life afresh had deterred them from carving out a career in crime.

In spite of their rugged life and often intemperate habits, quite a number lived to a great age. Seventy-four appear to have left the colony, but of those remaining, 194 deaths have been traced, of which thirty-three passed their seventieth year. Thirteen of these died in their seventies, sixteen in their eighties and four in their nineties. Richardson's age at death was more likely eighty-two than the 102 years claimed, and George Munday's was more likely ninety-one than 101. William Roberts (Gloucester) at ninety-seven probably lived longer than any when an inquest showed he had 'died by the visitation of God'. Some obviously perished in an unknown manner when escaping by sea or in the woods as they sought their freedom. There were at least nine known drownings and eight died accidentally. Other than the six executed some suffered violent deaths, including two after bouts of fighting and four by Aboriginal spears. But most deaths were from natural causes and many of the older people died 'by decay of Nature'.

Names of *Calcutta* convicts live on in Hangan's Point (now the Botanic Gardens), Lake Tooms (Tombs), Stocker's Bottom, Stocker's Sugarloaf, Cobb's Hill, Dowsing's Point, Don's Battery and Mount Augustus (after Morris), and Austin's Ferry. Buckley's Cave, Buckley's Well, Buckley's Falls and several other place names remind Victorians of the Wild White Man. The Austin Hospital in Melbourne is one of many memorials to the Austin family. The name Fawkner appears more than most and is a reminder that the father followed his more famous son, ending his days as a respected gentleman in Melbourne.

Tombstones throughout Tasmania commemorate the founding parents of many Australian families. Stocker conveniently shared his last resting place with his wife and her first husband, Henry Hayes, their daughter Martha and the Whitehead and Bowen families. Although several of the memorials are most impressive and others have quite amusing inscriptions, few are more interesting than the grand monument to David Collins placed in St David's Park in 1838 and the touching obelisk that Elizabeth Stanfield, daughter of the Reverend Knopwood's adopted Betsey, erected in the churchyard at Rokeby. If Collins were the 'friend and father of them all', Knopwood was to his beloved adopted family 'a man of strict Intergity [*sic*] and Active Benevolence, ever ready to relieve the distress and to ameliorate the Condition of the Afflicted'.[7] Until the time of his death in 1838 he had continued to administer the pastoral needs of the people at Clarence Plains in conjunction with his social activities. Of the families around him, several small farmers were among those who had arrived with him in the *Calcutta*: Richardson, Munday, Pearsall, Roberts, Arnott, Allender and Thomas Williams from Brecon.

One might end the story of the *Calcutta* convicts with the death on 18 September 1838 of their chaplain who had, in his own way, served them and shepherded them through the bad as well as the good times. He barely lived to hear that the shores of Port Phillip on which they had first set foot in the new land were already the subject of much speculation. There were some remarkable developments within a few years of his death. He could hardly have believed that young men, hungry for land on which they could graze their fast multiplying sheep, would cross the Strait to what had appeared a most inhospitable place. Port Phillip was to embrace the sons and daughters and other family members of many of those delinquents who had arrived in H.M.S. *Calcutta* and would help establish it with the wealth they had inherited from the sweat of their forebears and from the soil of their island home.[8]

The influence of nineteenth-century historians, who were so gratified that the state of Victoria had been spared the 'convict taint', has rested like a dead hand on a chapter of history that has assumed increasing interest and importance.[9] During that century incredible steps were taken to try to obliterate the origins of some families. Yet had those particular persons not been chosen to sail in the *Calcutta* and the *Ocean* in 1803, many men and women who have made significant contributions to the history of Victoria as well as Tasmania would never have been born. The offspring of Thomas Peters multiplied quickly and soon spread throughout the two states. Together with Augustus Morris junior, who first came to Colac and later took up some of the finest grazing land in the Riverina and Queensland, they slanted the family history to accommodate their dynastic ambitions.[10]

The Austin nephews created another wealthy dynasty with the aid of the riches they had inherited and ploughed back into the great grazing lands of the Western District of Port Phillip. They also introduced the rabbit into Australia. Some descendants have romantically embroidered their family's history, although never failing at least to acknowledge the convict origin.[11] The earlier Gibsons, living remotely in the north of Van Diemen's Land, may never have

known that their father's crime was a major one, believing instead the story of a minor injustice and an agricultural background in Scotland. Likewise the Lords for a long time believed James had sheltered political prisoners, even though his crime was relatively petty for one who was so successful.[12] Some Whitehead and Bowen descendants have been loath to talk about their connection. But the passing of time has created a sense of pride in the subsequent achievements and good records of most of the families who recognise their ancestry, such as the Wades who have shown interest from several parts of the world. All these families have made their presence felt, not only in pastoral, but also in political, judicial and commercial circles.

John Pascoe Fawkner in his writings tried to hide his origins but of course he could not.[13] Like his adversary John Batman, his convict background was too well known. In addition, his own youthful indiscretion which caused his transportation to Newcastle was also on a par with Batman, who managed to erase his own crime from most of the records. In passing one might mention that it is not well known that Batman was transported to Tasmania in 1821, gained a ticket of leave, and became the assigned servant of John Hart at Oyster Bay.[14]

These families who first came to Port Phillip were land-hungry or, as in Fawkner's case, hoped to profit from those who were squatting. They certainly pioneered thousands of acres for those who came afterwards and made possible much of the prosperity enjoyed by present-day Victorians. But they also laid claim to land that members of another race had long venerated as both their provider and part of their being, yet who had hardly disturbed the soil in thousands of years and who understood how to control the vagaries of a climate that could produce successive years of drought, fires and floods.

At first the newcomers spread out over the rich basalt plains from Geelong so they might graze their foreign stock. They prospered by their riches and in the more wealthy Western District built great mansions from the local bluestone, replaced many of the native trees with English ones, and cultivated English manners. They sent their sons to English schools and universities and married off their daughters to cousins or friends within the comfortable circle of what an earlier writer termed a 'bunyip aristocracy'.[15] Some of their descendants have since received the highest honours in the land and until recent years few would have admitted that they had a convict in their cupboard.

The final liberation came when these people of Port Phillip and the pastoral districts were able to cast off the shackles that had bound them to the infamy that was New South Wales and Van Diemen's Land. But

Looking towards a prosperous future.

when they celebrated the news of their separation on 15 November 1850, did any of those born into a convict family think of their humble beginnings? From her handsome home in the Western District, Elizabeth Armytage might have just remembered the day her father, dragging his feet in irons, carried her ashore.[16] Fawkner junior kept writing of that early settlement all his life, thereby giving considerable strength to his claims as the Father of Melbourne, as he tenaciously campaigned with the Anti-Transportation League. On that eventful day of separation his own ex-convict father might well have been helping to scatter the flysheets from the press (of which Fawkner senior was the nominal proprietor) that proclaimed separation. Here indeed was the symbol of freedom at last.[17]

By then some 77 000 persons already populated the state of Victoria, officially proclaimed in July 1851. They ran 6 000 000-odd sheep, which would certainly have amazed those like Tuckey who expected that the kangaroo would remain lord of the soil.[18] To the end of his days the younger Fawkner would fight against what he believed an injustice, namely the actions of those who had locked up the lands of the colony for their own gain. It was surely some proof that those in authority in the land of hope and glory had in 1802 every intention of expanding the Empire on an economic basis. But could any have foreseen an Empire made mightier, yet, ruled by a Queen who would leave her name in many places, that same Victoria who might never have existed but for a handful of Gibraltar mutineers, long since dead, who had disembarked from H.M.S. *Calcutta* in 1803 and spent one summer in the 'cradle of the state' at Sullivan Bay?

ABBREVIATIONS

ADB	*Australian Dictionary of Biography*	*H.T.C.*	*Hobart Town Courier*
ADM	Admiralty Records, PRO, London	*H.T.G.*	*Hobart Town Gazette*
AONSW	Archives Office of New South Wales	*JRAHS*	*Journal of the Royal Australian*
BL	British Library		*Historical Society*
BT	Board of Trade records, PRO, London	LaT.	La Trobe Collection, State Library of Victoria
CO	Colonial Office records, PRO, London	L.C.	Legislative Council
CON	Convict records, Tasmanian State Archives	LSD	Land Board records, Tasmanian State Archives
CSO	Colonial Secretary's Office	ML	Mitchell Library, State Library of New South Wales
DG	Dixson Gallery, State Library of New South Wales	*OBSP*	*Old Bailey Sessions Papers*
		pa.	parish
DL	Dixson Library, State Library of New South Wales	PRO	Public Records Office, London
		Q.S.	Quarter Sessions
EMLR	*European Magazine and London Review*	*RSTPP*	*Royal Society of Tasmania, Papers and Proceedings*
Gar. O.	Garrison Orders		
G.D.	Gaol delivery	*S.G.*	*Sydney Gazette*
Gen. O.	General Orders	S. of P.	Sessions of Peace
G.M.	*Gentleman's Magazine*	SLT	State Library of Tasmania
GO	Governor's Office	*THRAPP*	*Tasmanian Historical Research Association, Papers and Proceedings*
G.S.	Great Sessions		
HS	*Historical Studies*	TSA	Tasmanian State Archives
HO	Home Office records, PRO, London	V.D.L.	Van Diemen's land
H. of C.	House of Commons	*V.H.M.*	*Victorian Historical Magazine*
HRA	*Historical Records of Australia*, Series I, III, IV	Uni. of Tas.	University of Tasmania
		WO	War Office records, PRO, London
HRNSW	*Historical Records of New South Wales*, vols 1–7		

NOTES ON THE CHAPTERS

INTRODUCTION

1 Victor Hugo, *Les Misérables*, tr. Charles Wilbour, ed. F. M. Cooper, New York, n.d., p. 188.

2 Ibid., pp. 160–63.

3 Collins to Hobart 4 March 1804, in *HRA* III, i, p. 230: 'a collection of old, worn out, useless Men, or Children equally as useless'.

4 Collins' list of trades and occupations of the convicts landed at Port Phillip 5 Nov. 1803, in *HRA* III, i, p. 32. See also hulk records CO 201/28; records of the clerks of the Assize and other court records as listed in Bibliography.

5 Phillip to Rt Hon. W. W. Grenville, Home Secretary, 17 July 1790, in *HRA* I, i, p. 195.

6 Francis Bacon, 'Of Plantations', *Essays*, London, 1909, p. 95.

7 Plans for settlement at Bass Strait were far removed from the idea of a Gulag as portrayed by Robert Hughes, *The Fatal Shore*, London, 1987. However, arguments for and against the thesis that transportation as a method of punishment was a major element in British colonial policy have continued to engage historians in controversy. A symposium held in London in 1982 brought together several of the protagonists, including A. G. L. Shaw, Alan Frost and David Mackay, whose more recent book *A Place of Exile: the European Settlement of New South Wales*, Melbourne, 1985, is more supportive of the orthodox views held by Eris O'Brien, C. M. H. Clark and Shaw himself than those expounding the K. M. Dallas theory, as represented in the work edited by Ged Martin, *The Founding of Australia: the Argument about Australia's Origins*, Sydney, 1978. Culled partly from already published sources, this book includes major articles by Frost, Geoffrey Blainey, Clark, Geoffrey Bolton, Michael Roe, Alan Atkinson, H. T. Fry and E. C. K. Gonner as well as Dallas. The present writer would hope that her interpretation at least might be regarded as a positive approach in seeking, like Portia Robinson who has examined the first generation of convicts' children, to re-create a society which the transportation system produced. 'More often than not', J. B. Hirst wrote in *Convict Society and its Enemies*, Sydney, 1983, 'our understanding of convict society is still based on the assumption of its enemies'. Robert Hughes' recent and eminently readable account of convict society (published as this work goes to press and therefore not fully digested) appears to this author to overstate the oppressive aspects and ignore many of the positive results of Australia's beginnings.

8 James Hingston Tuckey, *An Account of a Voyage to Establish a Colony at Port Philip* [sic] *in Bass's Strait*, London, 1805, pp. 3, 4, 224–30; Tuckey, Memoir of his chart of Port Philip (sic), *in HRA* III, i, pp. 113, 117; Tuckey, Sketch of the Present State of N.S.W., MS A2001, pp. 6, 7, 31–33, ML; Woodriff papers, MS A 3006, ML. See also report of ex-Gov. John Hunter to Under Secretary John King on colonial timbers, 22 March 1802, in *HRNSW* IV, pp. 728–33.

9 G. Barton (ed.), *History of New South Wales from the Records 1789–94*, Sydney, 1889, pp. 1–11, 423–29.

10 Ibid., pp. 429–32.

11 Ibid., p. 430.

CHAPTER 1 THE 'LUXURY' OF PEACE

1 Patrick Colquhoun, *Treatise on the Police of the Metropolis*, London, 1806, ch. 13.

2 Pelham to the Lords Commissioners of the Admiralty and reply, in *HRA* I, iii, p. 570.

3 Serle to Marsden, 22 Feb. 1803, Marsden papers A1992/1/10, ML.

4 Hunter to Under Secretary King, in *HRNSW* IV, p. 728 and *passim*.

5 See instructions to Capt. James Colnett of H.M.S. *Glatton*, in *HRNSW* IV, p. 836; and to Capt. Daniel Woodriff, in *HRA* III, i, p. 13.

6 *EMLR*, 29 Apr. 1802, p. 33.

7 *Weekly Political Register*, Apr. 1802.

8 *Aris' Birmingham Gazette*, 5, 12 Apr. 1802.

9 *Dictionary of the Vulgar Tongue*, London, 1811.

10 John Gay, *The Beggar's Opera*, Oxberry, London, 1818, p. 728.

11 *G.M.*, May 1799, p. 431.

12 Sydney Smith, 'The Suppression of Vice', *Essays, Social and Political*, London, n.d., p. 26.

13 Sydney Smith, 'An Account of the Proceedings of the Society for Superseding the Necessity of Climbing Boys', in *Edinburgh Review* XXXII, Oct. 1819, p. 309.

14 Ibid.

15 Peter Quennell (ed.), *Mayhew's Characters*, London, n.d., p. 169.

16 HO 42/61, cited in E. P. Thompson, 'The Crime of Anonymity', in Douglas Hay and others (eds), *Albion's Fatal Tree: Crime and Society in Eighteenth-century England*, London, 1975, p. 333.

17 *The London Gazette*, May 1790, p. 299, cited in Thompson, op.cit., p. 337.

18 *The Farmers' Magazine* III, London, 1802, p. 136.

19 John Britton, *The Beauties of Wiltshire*, 2 vols, London, 1801.

20 *EMLR*, Sept. 1800, p. 234.

21 Ibid., Oct. 1800, p. 298.

22 Ibid.

23 Ibid., Jan. 1801, p. 23.

24 Ibid., Jan. 1801, p. 29.

25 Charles Lamb, 'On the Decay of Beggars', *The Essays of Elia*, Everyman, London, 1913, p. 136.

26 Peter Quennell (ed.), *London's Underworld*, London, n.d., p. 403.

CHAPTER 2   THE INEQUALITY OF MERCY

1 C. Beccaria, *Dei Delitti e delle Pene* (1764), tr. J. A. Farran, London, 1880, pp. 244–45. The important consideration was to 'present crimes, then see that enlightenment accompanies liberty'.

2 9 Geo. I, c. 22. Parliament continually added clauses to this act during the 18th century.

3 Gilbert White, *The Natural History of Selborne*, Everyman, London, 1909, pp. 20–21.

4 Ibid.

5 William Blackstone, *Commentaries on the Laws of England*, London, 1865–69, which netted him the sum of £14 000.

6 Jeremy Bentham, *Discourses on Civil and Penal Legislation*, London, 1802. His Panopticon scheme to relieve the hulks as an alternative to transportation was first suggested in 1787 and gained considerable support for the ingenious circular design of a prison enabling inspectors to view prisoners more easily. See L. J. Hume, 'Bentham's Panopticon: an Administrative History', in *HS* XV, 61, Oct. 1973 and XVI, 62, Apr. 1974. Among those whom Bentham tried to interest in his scheme was David Collins prior to the latter's departure in the *Calcutta* for Port Phillip, Bentham papers, Add. MSS 33544, folios 20–21, 41–42, 57–58, BL. Bentham, however, to suit his own case, ignored the more optimistic view of the future of the colony of New South Wales expressed in Collins' *An Account of the English Colony in New South Wales*, 2 vols, London, 1798–1802. Bentham preferred to use as evidence Collins' meticulously presented record of the further crimes and misery of the convicts. See J. B. Hirst, *Convict Society and its Enemies*, Sydney, 1983.

7 L. Radzinowicz, *A History of the English Criminal Law and its Administration from 1730*, vol. 1, London, 1948, p. 76.

8 Colquhoun published *Police of the Metropolis* in 1795, in London. Among *Calcutta* convicts whom he committed for trial at the Old Bailey were James Blake, James Byrne, Thomas Davies, George Reeves, William Richardson and William Smith (convicted 1801).

9 Eris O'Brien, *The Foundation of Australia*, Sydney, 1950, app. A, pp. 277–79, gives an excellent precis of crimes and punishments under the criminal law in the 17th, 18th and 19th centuries, compiled from Colquhoun and Barton.

10 Romilly and others spent many years working on the mitigation of sentences. He persevered even after his bills were rejected again and again by a stubborn Parliament. It was not until 1823 that Sir Robert Peel repealed clauses of the Black Act relating to capital offences, except those of maliciously shooting at a person or setting fire to property. 4 Geo. IV, c. 54.

11 John Locke, *Of Civil Government*, London, 1936, ch. V 'Of Property' and ch. VII 'Of Political or Civil Society'.

12 Despard was tried at the Q.S., Newington, Surrey, 7 Feb. 1803. His execution took place near Horsemonger Lane Gaol on 21 Feb., *The Times*, 22 Feb. 1803.

13 John Howard, *The State of Prisons in England and Wales, with an Account of Some Foreign Prisons*, London, 1790. The work first appeared in 1777. Howard himself had known something of prison life at first hand when, in 1756, while sailing to Lisbon, he had been captured by a French privateer and imprisoned at Brest for a brief period.

14 Elizabeth Fry was horrified when, as a young woman, she saw the inhumanities at Newgate on her first visit there in 1813 and made it her life work to alleviate the appalling conditions. See *Memoir of the Life of Elizabeth Fry, with Extracts from her Journals and Letters*, ed. by two of her daughters, London, 1848, vol. I, pp. 201–3.

15 *Hampshire Chronicle*, 27 Dec. 1800.

16 *G.M.*, 16 May 1802, p. 466.

17 Ibid., Feb. 1799, p. 160.

18 *EMLR*, Dec. 1800, p. 476.

19 HO 26/7, Criminal registers in Newgate Gaol.

20 Cited in Walter Thornbury, *Old and New London: a Narrative of its History, its People and its Places*, London, 1872–78, vol. II, p. 452. See also *EMLR*, Jan. 1802, pp. 74, 154–55.

21 The privilege of benefit of clergy originated in the 12th century but radical changes had taken place over the centuries. By 1576 persons convicted of petty or clergyable larceny were normally condemned to transportation for seven years. Major crimes were non-clergyable. The benefit was abolished in 1827. See Theodore Plucknett, *A Concise History of the Common Law*, London, 1956, pp. 439–41.

22 W. J. V. Windeyer, *Lectures in Legal History*, Sydney, 1957, pp. 66, 67, 132–35; Harold Potter, *An Historical Introduction to English Law*, London, 1932, pp. 208–9; Plucknett, op. cit., pt 2, ch. 6.

23 J. H. Plumb, *England in the Eighteenth Century 1714–1815*, London, 1861, p. 85 cites Lancashire in particular as one county where the aristocracy felt threatened by the wealthy industrialists and vowed that manufacturers would not be tolerated as colleagues on the Bench.

24 *Oyer et terminer* commissioners were to 'hear and determine' serious crimes where there appeared to be a prima facie case, with a grand jury to assist. Among *Calcutta* convicts tried by this commission were Arthur Connelly, Michael Lawler and Joseph Richards.

25 Sessions Rolls, Apr. 1801, County Museum, Truro.

26 As late as 1833 a schoolmaster imprisoned at Newgate judged the Old Bailey trials to last, on average, eight and a half minutes, and reported that so many became nervous 'seeing their fellow prisoners return, tried and found guilty in a minute or two — fully two thirds of the prisoners, on their return from their trials, cannot

tell of anything which has passed in the court . . . it is not, indeed, uncommon for a man to come back, after receiving his sentence on the day appointed for that purpose, saying, "It can't be me they mean; I have not been tried yet"; conceiving, from the celerity with which the business was performed, that he had been up to plead', anon., *An Old Bailey Experience*, London, 1833, p. 59.

27 *EMLR*, Oct. 1800, p. 316.

28 *OBSP*, IV Sessions 1801, trial 342.

29 Ibid., VII Sessions 1801, trial 638.

30 Ibid., VI Sessions 1802, trial 506 (listed as Wacy).

31 Act of 1799, 39 Geo. III, c. 85.

32 Kent assize records Maidstone, Aug. 1802, 35/242, PRO.

33 *Hampshire Chronicle*, 1 May, 24, 31 July, 7, 14 Aug. 1802.

34 Gaoler's bill, Bedford, 27 March 1800, p. 127.

35 Gaoler's account book, Warwick, 1802, p. 307.

36 *Aris' Birmingham Gazette*, 5 Apr. 1802. See also Chapter 7.

37 *Hampshire Chronicle*, 2 March 1801.

38 Lee to Mildmay 24 Jan. 1803, Bentham papers, Add. MSS 33544, folio 14, BL.

39 *G.M.*, 5 Aug. 1802, p. 74; *EMLR*, 5 Aug. 1802, p. 155.

40 See Chapter 25.

CHAPTER 3 LAND THIEVES AND WATER THIEVES

1 Tuckey, *Voyage*, op. cit., p. 187.

2 *EMLR*, Oct. 1801, p. 289.

3 *OBSP*, III Sessions 1801, trials 286, 287; HO 26/6/34 and HO 26/7/94.

4 *York Herald*, 13 March 1802.

5 *OBSP*, VI Sessions 1801, trial 606; HO 26/6/1 and HO 26/6.

6 Westminster Q.S. roll, Summer 1801; HO 26/6 Apr. 1795 and HO 26/8/64.

7 Lloyd Robson, *The Convict Settlers of Australia*, Melbourne, 1965, p. 11. In an earlier sampling C. M. H. Clark found no support for the theory that convicts had been mainly agricultural labourers. Most had come from towns. See 'Origins of Convicts Transported to Eastern Australia 1787–1852', in *HS*, May 1956. See also Marjorie Tipping, 'The *Calcutta* Convicts', in *THRAPP* XXII, i, March 1975.

8 Exeter gaol calendar, Midsummer 1802; *Exeter Flying Post*, 12, 19, 21 Aug. 1802.

9 Gay, op. cit.

10 *OBSP*, IV Sessions 1802, trial 360; HO 26/8/66.

11 *OBSP*, III Sessions 1802, trial 255; HO 26/8/29.

12 Summer Assizes, 35/242, South Eastern Circuit, 1802; HO 10/8/108 and HO 10/8/109; *Maidstone Journal*, 4 Aug. 1802.

13 See Chapter 7.

14 Summer Assizes, Norfolk Circuit Aug. 1800; *Norwich Chronicle*, 9 Aug. 1800.

15 South Circuit (Scotland) minute book, 1799, JC/12/23.

16 Cited in Henry B. Wheatley, *London: Past and Present: History, Associations, and Traditions . . .*, London, n.d., vol. I, p. 472.

17 Summer Assizes, 35/242, South Eastern Circuit 1802; Gaol calendar East Kent Q.S., Midsummer 1802; *Maidstone Journal*, 4 Aug. 1802.

18 *OBSP*, III Sessions 1802, trials 178, 234; HO 26/8/19.

19 Spring Assizes, Western Circuit Apr. 1802; Calendar of prisoners, Taunton, Apr. 1802; *Bath Chronicle*, 15 Apr. 1802.

20 Westminster Q.S., Summer 1800, WJ/SR 3657/15 and WJ/SBB 1545/47; HO 26/7.

21 Both Austin and Earle appeared on Q.S. rolls and minute books, 13 Jan. 1802. Neither appeared on HO 11/1, PRO, but were added to the indents 4/4004 and convict transportation register, AONSW.

22 Lent Assizes, Oxford Circuit 1801; *Reading Mercury*, 2, 9, and 11 March 1801. For Richard Brown see Spring Assizes, Oxford Circuit 1802; *Reading Mercury*, 31 Aug. 1801 and 1, 8, March 1802. The three other Browns were unlikely to be connected.

23 *OBSP*, VIII Sessions 1801, trial 796; HO 26/8/18. For John Everitt see Spring Assizes, Western Circuit, 25/1, March 1801. James Everitt appeared in the sampling in Robson, op. cit., p. 44.

24 Bradford Q.S. rolls, 16 July 1801, p. 321; *York Herald*, 13 Feb. 1802.

25 Summer Assizes, 42/11, 44/117, 45/41, North Eastern Circuit 1802; *York Herald*, 7, 14 Aug. 1802.

26 Spring Assizes, 14/17, 42/1, 42/11, 44/117 and 45/41, North Eastern Circuit 1802; *York Herald*, 20 Feb., 6, 13, 23 March, 29 May 1802. See also A. G. L. Shaw, *Convicts and the Colonies: a Study of Penal Transportation*, London, 1966, pp. 21–22, *re* the Scottish custom of banishment.

27 Summer Assizes, 25/1, Western Circuit 1802; *Salisbury and Winchester Journal*, 9 Aug. 1802. For James Hughes see WO 12/1249–1250, muster rolls of 16th Light Dragoons, 1801–03.

28 HO 26/8/26; *EMLR*, 15 Sept. 1801, p. 236 and 22 Oct. 1801, p. 395. See also Nicholas Pateshall, *A Short Account of a Voyage round the Globe in H.M.S.* Calcutta *1803–04*, ed. Marjorie Tipping, Melbourne, 1980, p. 39.

29 *OBSP*, III Sessions, trial 192; HO 26/8/27; Collins to Hobart 22 Aug. 1803, in *HRA* III, i, p. 25.

30 *OBSP*, VIII Sessions, trials 785, 786; HO 26/8/20.

31 *OBSP*, III Sessions, trial 253; HO 26/8/5.

32 *OBSP*, IV Sessions, trial 360; HO 26/8/66.

33 *OBSP*, IV Sessions, trial 419; HO 26/7/115, 26/8/115.

34 *OBSP*, VI Sessions, trial 620; HO 26/6/54, 26/7/54, 26/8/23. For Henry and Mary Hayes see *OBSP*, V Sessions, trial 486; HO 26/6/69. Further papers on Fawkner at London Guild Hall, Old Bailey G.D., Sept. 1800–04.

35 *OBSP*, V Sessions 1801, trial 486.

36 Ibid., VI Sessions 1801, trial 620.

37 H.M.S. *Glatton*, Indents 4/4004, AONSW, arrived at Port Jackson 11 March 1803. Shipping list, in *HRA* I, iv, p. 525.

38 *HRA*, I, iv, p. 66.

CHAPTER 4 EXILES AND EX-SERVICE

1 When it was found that 36 Geo. III, c. 8, 'An Act for the more effectually preventing seditious meetings and assemblies', only protected the monarch for three years, it was later extended to the statute 39 Geo. III, c. 79.

2 36 Geo. III, c. 7; 36 Geo. III, c. 8; 37 Geo. III, c. 70; 37 Geo. III, c. 123; 39 Geo. III, c. 79.

3 21 June 1798.

4 Many of the early records of transportation from Ireland were destroyed. See T. J. Kiernan, *Irish Exiles in Australia*, Dublin, 1954. See also George Rudé, 'Early Irish Rebels in Australia', in *HS* XVI, Apr. 1974. However, most of the papers relating to the Rebellion itself have survived in the State Paper Office in Dublin.

5 Holt (known as 'General') was a Protestant farmer who joined the United Irishmen late in the campaign. He surrendered in November 1798 and arranged to exile himself to N.S.W., arriving in January 1800. See *ADB*, vol. I.

6 The letter from Sullivan Bay dated 5 Nov. 1803 read:

Dear Joe,

You will, I dare say, be surprised to hear that your unfortunate Friend is a convict at this horrid desolated place.

I was Tried last December twelvemonths for Sedition, in London, and sentenced to be transported for seven years, so that I have five years still to continue in this wretched situation. Would to God, my dear Holt, I was at Port Jackson, Sidney [*sic*], or any place where I could enjoy the company of some of you, my fellow-sufferers and friends. I have no particular news to inform you of, only that our friend John Neil has turned out a Villain! — he resides at the *Castle*, with the bloodhounds, and is a most notorious common informer. Harry Downs, Antrim Jack, Conway, Moore, Whitty, Billy Byrne, and many others, have suffered death, but to the last behaved like men. I have had the pleasure of seeing Mick Reynolds in London; he was perfectly well, and beyond everyone's expectations recovered of his wound.

If you are acquainted with Phill [*sic*] Cunningham, Bill Leonard, John Bowen, or any of them who were transported from Clonmell in the year '99, remember me most kindly to them, and let them know I expect to hear from them per return of Bearer . . . None of my relations know of my present misfortunes, not even my old uncle . . .

Your sincere friend, Robt. Walsh.

N.B. Do not neglect writing per return of Bearer and let me know everything worth relating. Adieu.

Quoted in G. W. Rusden, *Discovery, Survey and Settlement of Port Phillip*, Melbourne, 1871, p. 19. This letter was seized from among Holt's papers after the uprising at Castle Hill, N.S.W., in 1804, after which Cunningham, one of the leaders, was hanged.

7 *OBSP*, I Sessions 1800, trial 40; HO 26/8/45.

8 Walter Besant, *London in the Eighteenth Century*, London, 1925, pp. 262 ff.

9 Cited in J. S. Levi and G. F. J. Bergman, *Australian Genesis: Jewish Convicts and Settlers 1788–1850*, Adelaide, 1974, pp. 6–7.

10 Ibid., pp. 7–8.

11 J. S. Levi, *A Dictionary of Biography of the Jews of Australia 1788–1830*, Melbourne, 1976, p. 7.

12 Ibid., p. 3.

13 *OBSP*, IV Sessions 1802, trial 317; HO 26/8/30. His name was not on HO 11/1.

14 *OBSP*, VII Sessions 1801, trial 737; HO 26/6/34, 26/7/34, 26/8/34.

15 Levi, op. cit., p. 8; Robson, op. cit., p. 14.

16 *OBSP*, III Sessions 1802, trial 262; HO 26/8/3; *EMLR*, June 1802, p. 501.

17 *OBSP*, IV Sessions 1802, trial 373; HO 26/8/142.

18 *OBSP*, VII Sessions 1800, trial 710; HO 26/6/42 and 26/7/42.

19 Information from Rabbi Levi, although my own evidence would contest this.

20 Summer Assizes, Western Circuit 1802; *Hampshire Chronicle*, 1 May and 31 July 1802.

21 Assize records for Leicester are missing. See *Leicester Journal*, March 1802.

22 Myers' name does not appear on any official list until the victualling list of those at Port Phillip. CON 22, TSA, notes that he arrived as a convict in the *Calcutta* and was tried March 1802 and sentenced to seven years.

23 Boyes to his wife 16 Jan. 1824, G. T. W. B. Boyes papers, Uni. of Tas.

24 Spring Assizes, South Eastern Circuit 1802; Gaoler's account, Horsham, 16 Jan.–30 Apr. 1802; *Sussex Weekly Advertiser*, 29 March and 5 Aug. 1802; J. P. Fawkner, Reminiscences, Box 67/1, LaT., ch. 5.

25 Information from Lech Paszkowski, Melbourne.

26 *OBSP*, IV Sessions 1802, trial 288; HO 26/8/24.

27 *OBSP*, I Sessions 1801, trial 51; HO 26/8/2.

28 *OBSP*, I Sessions 1801, trial 14; HO 26/8/2.

29 See Chapter 5.

30 *OBSP*, VI Sessions 1802, trial 581; HO 26/8/35.

31 Summer Assizes, Western Circuit, 1802; Calendar of prisoners and gaol register, Dorchester, Aug. 1802; *Western Flying Post*, 9 Aug. 1802; J. P. Fawkner, Reminiscences, ch. 2, LaT.

32 *OBSP*, IV Sessions 1802, trial 391; HO 26/8/131 and 132; Harris to his brother 29 Jan. 1804, G. P. Harris letters, maps and papers, vol. 1, Add. MSS 45156, BL.

33 Pateshall, op. cit., pp. 39–40.

34 Spring Assizes, Oxford Circuit 1802; *Berrow's Worcester Journal*, 1 March 1804; *Worcester Herald*, 13 March 1804; Harris to his brother 29 Jan. 1804, Add. MSS 45156, BL.

35 *OBSP*, III Sessions 1802, trial 255; HO 26/8/29; Harris to his brother 29 Jan. 1804, Add. MSS 45156, BL.

36 Northern Circuit (Scotland), Assize records and minute book, 1801, JC 11/48.

37 *OBSP*, III Sessions 1802, trial 205; HO 26/8/67.

38 *OBSP*, III Sessions 1802, trial 161; HO 26/8/90.

39 Summer Assizes, North Eastern Circuit 1801; *Newcastle Chronicle*, 18 March, 1, 8 Aug. 1801; *Newcastle Courant*, 1, 8 Aug. 1801.

40 Summer Assizes, Northern Circuit 1801; *York Herald*, 25 July, 1, 22 Aug. 1801.

41 Summer Assizes, South Eastern Circuit 1802; *Sussex Weekly Advertiser*, 2, 8 Aug. 1802; John Morgan, *The Life and Adventures of William Buckley*, Hobart, 1852, ch. 1 and app., pp. 149–52.

42 *OBSP*, IV Sessions 1801, trial 361; HO 26/6/37, 26/7/37.

43 Q.S. rolls 1799–1800, including gaol calendar and

gaoler's bills; *Northampton Mercury*, 16 March 1799.

44 *OBSP*, V Sessions 1801, trial 489; HO 26/7/61, 26/8/61; Woodriff, Memo book, C 269, ML.

45 Summer Assizes, Norfolk Circuit 1802; *Norfolk Chronicle*, 14 Aug. 1802.

46 See Chapter 3, n. 17. Allender would have been thirteen in 1782 when Rodney's flagship was H.M.S. *Formidable*. His name does not appear in the muster books of the *Formidable*, ADM 36/9118–9120 covering 1782–83. See, however, his memorial to Gov. Arthur 22 May 1826, CSO 1/289/6929.

CHAPTER 5 THE MUTINY AT GIBRALTAR

1 See Chapter 4, nn. 41 and 42.

2 See Rex and Thea Rienits, 'Some Notes on the Ancestry and Life of the Rev. Robert Knopwood', in *THRAPP* XII, 2 Apr. 1965.

3 See Lytton Strachey, *Queen Victoria*, London, 1921, for a racy account of the Queen's antecedents and the Duke's relationship with Madame St Laurent.

4 Ibid., 1933 edn, p. 8.

5 See J.W. Fortescue, *A History of the British Army*, London, 1889, vol. IV, p. 856.

6 Ibid., p. 927.

7 Ibid., p. 924.

8 See *Dictionary of National Biography*, vol. VII.

9 Fortescue, op. cit., pp. 856, 918.

10 See *Dictionary of National Biography*, vol. XI. A major biography of the Duke by Erskine Neale was probably encouraged by Queen Victoria. See Erskine Neale, *Life of Field-Marshal H.R.H., Edward, the Duke of Kent*, London, 1850.

11 Capt. Sayer, *The History of Gibraltar and of its Political Relation to Events in Europe*, London, 1862, p. 428.

12 WO 1/701, p. 27, *re* mutiny of British troops at Gibraltar 1803; *The Times* first reported the mutiny 25 Jan. 1803. *The Times* continued to report developments during January and February, underplaying the events. A leader of 26 Jan., p. 2, col. 1, criticised the *Moniteur* and the *Argus* for magnifying 'this unfortunate affair into a Mutiny — reasonable for soldiers to be sick of garrison duty, as sailors on a cruise'. However, *The Times* did rely on the French correspondents to provide some of the news, the most colourful report as quoted appearing 5 Feb.

13 *The Times*, 16 Jan. 1803.

14 The Dutchmen Pastoret and Teighman and the Irishman O'Reilly.

15 *The Times*, loc. cit.

16 A list of soldiers received for mutiny, Woodriff, C 269, ML.

17 Thomas Hague, a close friend of the Duke's private secretary who had access to private papers, published letters in pamphlet form between 1809 and 1831. Some exposed the conduct of the Royal Dukes, their expense, services, and pretensions but he was more sympathetic to the Duke of Kent. In 1862 Sayer wrote of the injustice of Kent's removal from Gibraltar 'aggravated by the conduct of the government who ever after refused to allow any investigation to be made into the circumstances', Sayer, op. cit., pp. 428 ff.

18 Neale, op. cit., p. 107, quoting from Hague who interviewed Salisbury. This information further questions how much had been erased from or not entered into the records.

19 CO 201/7/2, 1802–03 (Gibraltar) should have recorded any courts martial held during this period. The nearest date entered in the book is 8 Jan. 1803 when Pte Richard Murray 8th Rgt was acquitted of murder. Two other privates were acquitted of rape on 14 Jan.

20 HO 11/1 omits these names and those of thirteen others who joined the *Calcutta* shortly before the ship sailed.

21 The shipping indent 4/4004, AONSW, adds the seven names but no further information.

22 CON 22, TSA.

23 See n. 16.

24 Harris to his brother Henry 15 Nov. 1803, Add. MSS 45156, BL. Collins' Gar. O., 26 Dec. 1803 and Plan of Association listing six of the men (excluding Cronbury who died 14 Nov. 1805) as subordinates of the night watch, in *HRA* III, i, p. 87. Knopwood, Diaries, ML, copied the entry (4 Jan.) adding a line that of 'the 6 soldiers mutiners [*sic*] from Gibralter [*sic*] Crombe [*sic*] died at Port Phillip'. It was not unusual for Knopwood to confuse names and dates.

Collins' Gen. O., 27 Jan. 1804, *HRA* III, i, on board the *Ocean*, referred to three men on board 'late belonging to the 25th foot, [who] will be classed at each watch and will perform the same duty which they were entrusted with at Sullivan Bay'. It would appear that the other three were left behind to sail to V.D.L. with the second contingent.

25 *S.G.*, 23 June 1805.

26 The musters appear to be the only other official sources available indicating that soldiers were transported for mutiny at Gibraltar. Against the names of Haynes and Crute a clerk had noted that they were tried by court martial at Gibraltar. In 1811 the length of sentence is not given but the 1817 and 1819 musters indicate that those who were, by then, free, had received life sentences at Gibraltar: Van Straten, Crute and McCarthy in 1802 and Haynes in 1803. The 1811 Sydney muster is a little more specific about James Taylor and indicates that he was sentenced to transportation for life at Gibraltar in January 1803, and the Sydney muster of 1817 adds 'court martial January 1802 [*sic*]'. Sculler's name disappeared from records after mention that he captured a bushranger in 1808. See Knopwood, Diaries, 12 Apr. 1808, Uni. of Tas. When these convicts received pardons from Gov. Macquarie, no mention was made of their time or place of sentence.

Only one remained a convict. CON 23, TSA, confirms that the unhappy John Cruitt (*sic*), later executed, was tried at Gibraltar 1802, sentenced to transportation for life and was a member of the 25th Foot Rgt. He had the mark of a gunshot wound on his right thigh and a scar on his left cheek, probably received while on active service.

27 They should be examined alongside similar protesters such as those included by George Rudé, *Protest and Punishment*, Oxford, 1978.

28 Duke of Sussex to Angus Hugh McIntyre who proposed

to write the history of the mutiny. Quoted in Neale, op. cit., Preface, p. vi.

29 Ibid., pp. vi, viii.

30 Ibid., pp. 110 ff.

31 Ibid., p. 116. See also *The Times*, 8 Feb. 1803, noting the Hospital Return from Gibraltar, 'convincing proof of the beneficial effects of the system introduced by His Royal Highness the Duke of Kent'. It notes also that since he assumed command deaths had been reduced from 146 annually (an average taken over six years) to only 13 in six months.

CHAPTER 6 CAMBRIDGE CAPERS

1 Cambridge Assizes held at Cambridge, 11 March 1801. See *The Trials of W. Grimshaw and R. Kidman for Burglary (with a Sketch of their Lives) and of H. Cohen as an Accessory before and after the Fact*, W. Rowton, Cambridge, 1850. No first edition of *The Trials of W. Grimshaw and R. Kidman* has ever been traced, but the case was so unusual that Rowton must have decided to re-publish it as an 85-page book.

2 Ibid., pp. 14–15.

3 Ibid., 'A short narrative of the life of Richard Kidman', pp. 74–79.

4 Ibid., p. 75. See also 'The voluntary examination and confession of Richard Kidman', pp. 79–83 and 'The dying words and confession of William Grimshaw', pp. 84–85.

5 Ibid., p. 75.

6 Ibid.

7 Ibid., p. 76.

8 Ibid., pp. 18–20, 76–77.

9 *G.M.*, 6 May 1800, p. 679.

10 *The Trials of W. Grimshaw and R. Kidman*, op. cit., p. 79.

11 Ibid., pp. 35–44.

12 Ibid., p. 40.

13 Ibid., p. 35.

14 Ibid., pp. 42, 44.

15 Ibid., p. 61–64.

16 Ibid., p. 66–73.

17 Ibid., p. 70–73.

18 Ibid., p. 73.

19 Ibid., p. 85.

20 CO 201/28.

CHAPTER 7 A THREAD OF THREADNEEDLE STREET

1 R. K. Dent, *Old and New Birmingham*, Birmingham, 1880, p. 187.

2 Grove's story became the subject of an article 'A Piece of Blood Money' in the periodical *All the Year Round*, ed. Charles Dickens, 20 Aug. 1859. The article referred to the experiences of one 'Lagged' who was at Port Phillip and the Derwent in 1803–04. Historian John Earnshaw traced the character to the person who figured as the author of letters published in a rare work, Benjamin Bensley (ed.), *Lost and Found: or Light in the Prison*, London, 1859. Thomas Bensley, d. 1833, was the latter's father. See *Dictionary of National Biography*, vol. II, which refers to his friendship with Grove. Earnshaw found that between 1789 and 1805 one J. Grove

exhibited 20 landscapes at the Royal Academy and that between 1814 and 1820 a Mrs J. Groves exhibited sixteen times at the Academy and the Old Water Colour Society. (See also John Earnshaw, 'Select Letters of James Grove, Convict: Port Phillip and the Derwent', in *THRAPP* VIII, i, Aug. and ii, Oct. 1959.) However, according to the *Dictionary of National Biography*, John Thomas Groves, d. 1811, architect of the G.P.O., was the artist exhibiting.

3 *The Times* adopted certain mechanical adjustments which Bensley recommended in 1814. They might well have been inspired by the ingenious Grove.

4 Bensley was dedicated to good causes. In 1809 he published a work *Of the Education of the Poor*. Sydney Smith reviewed his *Report of the Society for Bettering the Condition of Prisons*, London, 1820. See Smith, *Essays*, op. cit., pp. 223 ff. Interestingly, Bensley published a rare and beautiful book, *Birds of New Holland* by John W. Lewin in 1808. Lewin copied some of the bird drawings and landscapes from sketches made in Hobart by G. P. Harris.

5 HO 11/1 and 26/8/4 Jan. 1802; Shipping indents, 4/4004, AONSW; *Aris' Birmingham Gazette*, 4 Apr. 1802 and 3 May 1802.

6 Benjamin Bensley (ed.), *Lost and Found: or Light in the Prison*, London, 1859, Letter from Warwick Gaol, 28 March 1802.

7 Ibid.

8 Ibid., 10 Apr. 1802.

9 Ibid., 28 Apr. 1802.

10 Ibid., 4 June 1802.

11 Ibid., 4 July 1802.

12 Ibid., Letter from the *Captivity* hulk at Portsmouth, 28 Sept. 1802.

13 Ibid., 22 Oct. 1802.

14 Ibid., Letter from the *Calcutta*, 5 Apr. 1803. See also Fawkner, Reminiscences, ch. 2, LaT.

15 See *ADB*, vol. I. See also William Pascoe Crook, *An Account of the Settlement at Sullivan Bay Port Phillip*, ed. John Currey, Melbourne, 1983.

16 See Chapter 4, n. 45. In a later letter from Hobart Town, n.d., Grove referred to his family living in a house 'belonging to a man that came from the "Captivity", whom there and ever since I have esteem'.

17 In later years Benjamin Bensley kept in touch with Daniel Grove who became moderately prosperous after returning to England with his widowed mother. Young Grove told Bensley that his father tried to procure leave to go without his irons in order to hide some of his shame from his son. He was permitted to go single-ironed, saying, 'Now, my dear Boy, thou shalt never see thy Father's fetters', Bensley, op. cit., pp. 139 ff.

CHAPTER 8 A FISHY STORY

1 M. H. Ellis believed King had more than a little at stake and that he traded through an agent, although this is doubtful. When Gov. Bligh took office he granted Mrs King 790 acres in the district of Evan where she had formerly received 2 350 acres granted illegally by King and transferred to the names of her four children. King had also granted his daughter 600 acres, but these

amounts are relatively small compared with what many other officials received. See M. H. Ellis, *John Macarthur*, Sydney, 1955, p. 261.

2 Melville to Messrs Samuel Enderby and Sons, 29 Nov. 1791, cited in John Hunter, *An Historical Journal of the Transactions at Port Jackson and Norfolk Island*, London, 1793, pp. 558–59. The youthful Arthur Phillip had also become familiar with sperm whaling when he served in Brazilian waters with the Portuguese Navy 1774–78.

3 Gov. Phillip's instructions prohibited intercourse with foreign ports and the building of any craft for the use of private individuals, *HRA* I, i, p. 15. King believed the East India Co. by statute had exclusive rights between the Cape of Good Hope and Straits of Magellan. King to Portland 28 Sept. 1800, in *HRA* I, ii, p. 613.

4 American whalers first invaded the Pacific in 1792.

5 BT Minute 26 Dec. 1797, in *HRNSW* III, p. 335.

6 Collins, *Account*, op. cit., vol. II, 6 June 1799, p. 153.

7 This was the *Nostra Senora de Bethlehem*, captured off the coast of Peru, Collins, op. cit., vol. II, Apr. 1799, p. 147. See also Hunter to Portland 15 Nov. 1799, in *HRA* I, ii, p. 399, explaining the need to build boats for fishing along the coast, yet showing awareness of infringement of the Charter.

8 George Bass named Western Port, but the name was contracted for many years to Westernport. The official *Register of Place Names in Victoria*, Melbourne, 1983, p. 205, registers the name as Western Port. See also Bass's Journal in the whaleboat, in *HRNSW* III, pp. 312–33.

9 They entered these rivers during their voyage in the sloop *Norfolk*. The Tamar was then known as Port Dalrymple. See Matthew Flinders, *Observations on the Coasts of Van Diemen's Land . . .*, London, 1801.

10 J. H. L. Cumpston, *First Visitors to Bass Strait*, Canberra, 1973, pp. 11–12.

11 Ibid., pp. 29 ff.

12 Ibid., p. 46. See also *HRNSW* V, especially pp. 519–21, in which Joseph Murrell related to Kable and Underwood the brutalities experienced in 1804 during a confrontation with Samuel Delano, captain of the American whaler *Pilgrim*.

13 King to Portland 1 March 1802, in *HRA* I, iii, pp. 437–38.

14 Phillip to Under Secretary Nepean 9 July 1788, in *HRA* I, i, p. 58.

15 James Grant, *The Narrative of a Voyage of Discovery, Performed in His Majesty's Vessel the Lady Nelson*, London, 1803; Ida Lee, *The Log-books of the Lady Nelson*, London, 1915. Port King later became Port Phillip and Point Paterson became Point King.

16 Nicolas Baudin, *The Journal of Post Captain Nicolas Baudin . . .*, ed. Christine Cornell, Adelaide, 1974, pp. 379–380; M. F. Péron, *A Voyage of Discovery to the Southern Hemisphere . . .*, London, 1809, pp. 250–51; Matthew Flinders, *A Voyage to Terra Australis*, London, 1814, vol. I, pp. 188–95, 212–20. Flinders' chart of Port Phillip shows the River Yarra as far as the present day Kew. He took the information from Charles Grimes' later survey. See chart in *Port Phillip: First Survey and Settlement of*, with a preface and notes by J. J. Shillinglaw, Melbourne, 1878.

17 Péron, op. cit., p. 306.

18 *HRNSW* V, pp. 530–31.

19 Ibid.

20 Ibid. p. 832.

21 Péron, op. cit., pp. 312–13.

22 Ibid., p. 314.

23 In the French-held St Domingue (present day Haiti), negroes taken for slavery were fighting to gain some status. In 1800 a black slave, Toussaint Louverture, who had risen to the rank of Commander-in-Chief, had fought like Spartacus to get independence for his country. The Napoleonic outcry reflected the belief common to most Europeans of the time: 'This comedy of government must cease! We must not permit military honours to be worn by apes and monkeys!'. Napoleon upbraided the French abolitionist Truguet with the words 'I am for the whites because I am a white man . . . those who want the liberty of the blacks want the slavery of the whites'. Then in 1802 a bloodbath occurred during a barbarous confrontation. The French troops also fell victim to yellow fever and other pestilences. The deaths within a few months were 50 000. Although the outbreak of hostilities with Britain curtailed Napoleon's ambitions to quell the black population of St Domingue, Louverture spent his last days imprisoned in a dark dungeon at Besançon, in the Jura Mountains, dying of cold and possibly poison in the winter of 1803.

24 An abridged version of his report to the *Institut* is in Péron, op. cit., pp. iii–vii. This report remained almost forgotten. In 1818 the French Ministry for the Interior was to resurrect his observations and suggest that France needed to expand its territories, fostering the idea of using transportation as a means to colonise King George Sound or other parts of Western Australia. This laid the ground for suspicion of the motives for French explorations of the 1820s, leading to another unsuccessful British attempt at settlement on the South Coast, at Western Port in 1826.

25 King to Portland 21 May 1802, in *HRNSW* IV, p. 766. See also King to Banks 5 June 1802, in *HRNSW* IV, pp. 783 ff.

26 King to Portland, loc. cit. Flinders reported a conversation with the French First Lieutenant, Henri de Freycinet, who remarked that 'if we had not been kept so long picking up shells and catching butterflies at Van Diemen's Land, you would not have discovered the South Coast before us'. Flinders, op. cit., p. 193. King himself had been over-eager to believe allegations of ulterior motives for the lengthy sojourn of the French in southern waters, see n. 29.

27 David Garrick had first written the verses to accompany William Hogarth's print 'The Invasion of France', 1759. See John Ireland and John Nicholls, *Hogarth's Works*, series III, London, n.d., pp. 139–140.

28 *HRNSW* V, pp. 123–27.

29 Paterson reported to King (although Baudin himself suspected that it was Anthony Fenn Kemp) that the French officers intended to go to King I. perhaps to

establish a base there, and that he could even produce a chart showing the projected settlement. See correspondence between King and Paterson, Baudin papers, in *HRNSW* IV, pp. 1006–1008. King sent Lieut. Charles Robbins in command of the *Cumberland* to follow them and establish Britain's sovereignty. Robbins, accompanied by surveyor Charles Grimes, was then to sail on a surveying expedition to Port Phillip. At King I. the British were provoked when seeing the French tricolour flying over the camp, although the French were busily engaged in the studies they had been sent out to pursue. The British hoisted the Union Jack in protest. Martin Petit, a gunner, sketched a cartoon of the scene, which Baudin tore up in disgust, and ridiculed the episode as a childish ceremony. See Baudin to King 23 Dec. 1802, in *HRNSW* V, pp. 5, 7; Robbins and Grimes to King 18 Jan. 1803, in *HRNSW* V, pp. 830 ff.

30 Hobart to King 14 Feb. 1803, in *HRA* I, iv, pp. 8–10.
31 *HRA* III, i, p. 1.
32 Ibid, pp. 2, 3.

CHAPTER 9 THE GOVERNOR AND THE CHAPLAIN

1 Muster books, Captain's log and Master's log, H.M.S. *Calcutta*, ADM 16070, 16071, 51/1425, 52/3578, PRO; *Ocean* log, L/MAR/B/222J, India Office records, London. See also Collins' commission, in *HRA* III, i, p. 4.
2 *ADB*, vol. 1.
3 Collins, *Account*, op. cit., vol. I, p. 139.
4 Ibid., p. 187.
5 Ross to Nepean 16 Nov. 1788, in *HRNSW* I, ii, p. 212.
6 Ann (Nancy) Yeates, milliner, was convicted 9 July 1785 at York and sentenced to seven years transportation. She sailed in the *Lady Penrhyn*. She was one of six well-behaved women recommended to go to Norfolk I. but presumably Collins decided she would remain at Port Jackson. See Bowes Smyth, Journal, MS 995, ML, pp. 87 ff. (This is actually a copy of an original by Arthur Bowes Smyth, surgeon in the *Lady Penrhyn*.)
7 Mariamne Laetitia Yeates, bap. 13 Sept. 1790, and George Reynold Yeates, bap. 28 June 1793, St Phillip's Register, Sydney. The daughter has invariably been called Mariamne and other derivatives. Both Mariamne and George later took the surname Collins.
8 Maria to David Collins 31 Jan. 1793, Collins family papers, vol. I, ML.
9 Collins to Banks 26 Dec. 1802, MS, ANL.
10 Collins to his mother 23 Dec. 1802, Collins family papers, Add. MSS 700, vol. I, ML.
11 Copy of Collins' will, Bonwick transcripts, vol. 1, Biography, A 2000-1, ML.
12 *Edinburgh Review*, vol. 2, Apr. 1803, pp. 30 ff.
13 Ibid.
14 Ibid.
15 Two ex-convicts, James Ruse and Charles Williams alias Christopher Magee had in 1794 been allowed to join settlers on the Hawkesbury to engage in farming

on their own behalf. Collins, *Account*, op. cit., vol. I, p. 285.
16 *Edinburgh Review*, loc. cit.
17 *ADB*, vol. II. See also Rex and Thea Rienits, 'Some notes on the Ancestry and Life of the Rev. Robert Knopwood', op. cit., pp. 114–18.
18 Rienits, loc. cit.
19 Rienits, loc. cit.
20 Rienits, loc. cit.
21 The description could well have been written about Knopwood. Bertram C. A. Windle, Introduction to White, op. cit., p. xiv.
22 See Henry Savery, *The Hermit in Van Diemen's Land*, Hobart, 1829.
23 James Bonwick, 'The First Chaplain of Van Diemen's Land', *Curious Facts of Old Colonial Days*, London, 1870, p. 231.
24 R. W. Giblin, *The Early History of Tasmania: the Geographical Era 1642–1804*, London, 1928, vol. 2, p. 31.
25 P. H. Stannard to Knopwood 12 Oct. 1830, cited in Mabel Hookey, *Bobby Knopwood and His Times*, Hobart, 1929, pp. 148 ff.
26 Knopwood, Miscellaneous papers, C 235–2, ML and ANL.
27 Knopwood, *Resolution* journal, ML.

CHAPTER 10 A LONG SEA VOYAGE

1 *EMLR*, May 1803, p. 405.
2 Hobart to Collins 7 Feb. 1803, in *HRA* I, iv, p. 10.
3 I have arrived at these figures from numerous sources but the most accurate figure has been obtained by check-listing with the victualling list in the Commissariat returns, see Appendices.
4 Tuckey, *Voyage*, op. cit., pp. 233–34.
5 CO 201/28.
6 Woodriff, Memo book, C 269, ML.
7 Collins to King 5 Nov. 1803, in *HRA* III, i, p. 32.
8 Ibid.
9 Tuckey, op. cit., p. 232.
10 Hobart to King 26 Feb. 1803, in *HRA* I, iv, pp. 45–50.
11 The two men were James Bloodsworth, who might have been a useful builder had he not refused to leave Port Jackson, and John Maguire who arrived Oct. 1806. Rushton had been sentenced at Chester for forgery. *Chester Courant*, Apr. 1802.
12 Hobart to Collins, in *HRA* I, iv, pp. 10 ff., and *HRA* III, i, pp. 7–11.
13 This was William Briant. Woodriff, C 269, ML.
14 *HRA* I, iv, pp. 3–7.
15 Ibid., pp. 7, 9.
16 Ibid., pp. 7, 8.
17 *HRA* III, i, p. 9.
18 Ibid., p. 11.
19 Collins to Under Secretary John Sullivan 16 July 1803, in *HRA* III, i, p. 23.
20 Woodriff's instructions, in *HRA* III, i, p. 13, also note, p. 785; John Marshall, *Royal Naval Biography*, London, 1830, vol. VIII, pt iv; typescript copy of

Woodriff's petition to the Duke of Clarence outlining his career, n.d., and memo of N.S.W., n.d., Woodriff papers, ML. See also D. Tilghman, 'Captain Daniel Woodriff, C.B., R.N.', in *V.H.M.* XXXII, Feb. 1962, pp. 143–61.

21 Robert Matthew Woodriff was discharged 6 Apr. 1803 but John Robert Woodriff sailed as a midshipman and Daniel James Woodriff as master's mate, H.M.S. *Calcutta* muster, ADM 16070, PRO.

22 *Naval Chronicle*, vol. 17, 1807; William James, *The Naval History of Great Britain from the Declaration of War in 1793 to the Accession of George IV*, London, 1837.

23 Fawkner, Reminiscences, ch. 2, LaT.

24 Ibid., ch. 1.

25 See Chapter 13.

26 Fawkner, loc. cit.

27 Ibid.

28 Grove to Bensley 20 May 1803, from Tenerife, cited in John Earnshaw, 'Select Letters of James Grove, Convict: Port Phillip and the Derwent', in *THRAPP* VIII, i, Aug., and ii, Oct. 1959.

29 Ibid.

30 Tuckey, op. cit., pp. 12–14.

31 Pateshall, op. cit., p. 37.

32 Tuckey, op. cit., pp. 33–34.

33 Dr Edward Bromley, R.N., was the surgeon in charge during the voyage of the *Calcutta*, and therefore senior to the three doctors. He later served on convict ships and eventually settled in Hobart, becoming a foundation shareholder in the bank of V.D.L. He misappropriated funds and died destitute in England. See *ADB*, vol. I.

34 Collins to Sullivan 3 Aug. 1804, and enclosures, in *HRA* III, i, pp. 262–63.

35 Fawkner, loc. cit. References to the relationship between Collins and Hannah Power are frequent in the Knopwood diaries over a period of years.

36 Fawkner, loc. cit.

37 Register of deaths, C 190, TSA.

38 The Transport Commissioners had issued new instructions for the transportation of felons in 1801. See Shaw, op. cit., pp. 112 ff.

39 Tuckey, op. cit., pp. 231–39.

40 Pateshall, op. cit., p. 49.

41 Tuckey, op. cit., p. 73.

42 Ibid., p. 137.

43 Collins to Hobart 14 Nov. 1803, in *HRA* III, i, p. 37.

44 Woodriff, Memo book, C 269, ML.

45 Pateshall, op. cit., p. 37.

46 Ibid., p. 45.

47 John Earnshaw, 'Select letters of James Grove, Convict: Port Phillip and the Derwent', in *THRAPP*, VIII, i, Aug., and ii, Oct. 1959, p. 31.

48 Knopwood, Diaries, 21 July 1803, ML.

49 Collins to Hobart 15 July 1803, in *HRA* III, i, p. 22.

50 Pateshall, op. cit., pp. 54–55.

51 See n. 49.

52 Collins to Sullivan 16 July 1803, in *HRA* III, i, p. 24.

53 Harris to his brother 17 July 1803, Add. MSS 45156, BL.

54 Knopwood, Diaries, 30 June–17 July 1803, ML.

55 Tuckey, op. cit., pp. 62–63.

56 Ibid., pp. 135–36.

57 Humphrey to his father 15 Nov. 1803 from Sullivan Bay, in Hamilton and Grenville papers, vol. IV, Add. MSS 42071, BL; Humphrey's letters published in T. G. Vallance, 'The Start of Government Science in Australia: A. W. H. Humphrey, His Majesty's Mineralogist in New South Wales, 1803–12', in *Proceedings of the Linnean Society of New South Wales*, 1981; Harris to his mother 11 Nov. 1803, from Port Phillip, Add. MSS 45156, BL.

58 Harris to his brother 15 Oct. 1805, Add. MSS 45156, BL.

59 Their daughter Elizabeth was born at Port Phillip 14 Apr. 1804 and their marriage took place in Hobart Town 1 July 1804. Return of births and marriages, NS 282/8/1, TSA.

60 Woodriff, C 269, ML.

61 Collins to Hobart 22 Aug. 1803, in *HRA* III, i, p. 25.

62 Fawkner, op. cit., ch. 2, p. 11.

63 Ibid.

64 *Calcutta* Captain's log, 12–13 Aug. 1803, ADM 51/1485, PRO.

65 Fawkner, loc. cit.

66 Pateshall, op. cit., p. 52.

67 Tuckey, op. cit., p. 138.

68 Cited in Earnshaw, op. cit., pp. 31–32.

69 Collins, *Account*, op. cit., vol. I, pp. lxxxv–vi; Knopwood, Diaries, 25 Aug. 1803, ML.

CHAPTER 11 WATER, WATER EVERYWHERE

1 *Ocean* log, 7 Oct. 1803, L/MAR/B/222J, India Office records; Humphrey to his father 17 Nov. 1803, in T. G. Vallance, 'The Start of Government Science in Australia: A. W. H. Humphrey, His Majesty's Mineralogist in New South Wales, 1803–12', in *Proceedings of the Linnean Society of New South Wales* 105, 2, 1981, p. 130.

2 The almost illegible writing, seen some 30 years ago on a headstone in the Quarantine Station at Portsea, Victoria, indicated that 'Sarah Fletcher, stone [mason's daughter?] aged three months died 1803 during the entrance to the Port Phillip Bay area with Captain R. [*sic*] Collins'.

3 Humphrey, loc. cit.

4 Ida Lee, op. cit., p. 134.

5 *Calcutta* Captain's and Master's logs, 9 Oct. 1803, ADM 51/1485 and ADM 52/3578, PRO.

6 Knopwood, Diaries, 5 Sept. 1803, ML.

7 Knopwood, Diaries, 10 Oct. 1803, ML, and *Calcutta* logs, 10 Oct. 1803, ADM 51/1485 and ADM 52/3578, PRO; Tuckey, *Voyage*, op. cit., pp. 154–55; Collins to King 5 Nov. 1803, in *HRA* III, i, pp. 26–27.

8 Gov. King had sent Grimes together with Lieut. Charles Robbins in the *Cumberland* to survey Port Phillip. They arrived 20 Jan. 1803 and spent more than five weeks in the harbour. See Order of the Legislative Assembly publication of report, *Port Phillip*, op. cit., pp. 13–17. They discovered the River Yarra, remarking on the suitability of a site for settlement

where the city of Melbourne now stands, but their reports and chart did not reach Collins before he sailed from England.

9 Lee, op. cit., pp. 134–36.

10 See n. 8.

11 Collins to King 5 Nov. 1803, in *HRA* III, i, pp. 26–27, Gen. O. and Gar. O. 16 Oct. 1803, LaT.

12 Return of livestock, 4 Aug. 1804, in *HRA* III, i, p. 255.

13 Tuckey, *Voyage*, op. cit., p. 57.

14 Pateshall, op. cit., p. 57.

15 Crook, op. cit., p. 35.

16 Tuckey, Memoir of his chart, in *HRA* III, p. 114.

17 Knopwood, Diaries, 21 Oct. 1803, ML.

18 *Calcutta* Master's log 21 Oct. 1803, ADM 51/1485, PRO.

19 Pateshall, op. cit., p. 19.

20 Tuckey, *Voyage*, op. cit., p. 160.

21 Ibid., pp. 167–74.

22 See Chapter 14 for events relating to the confrontation. In 1847 Charles La Trobe, then superintendent of the Port Phillip District, reported seeing the keys the day after they were found. He could not 'suppose that 50 years had elapsed since they were dropped or washed up on that beach'. Some have been anxious to believe the bunch of keys to have been of Portuguese origin, lost some 320 years earlier by Cristovão de Mendonça. Others have suggested they might have been lost when Grimes was in Port Phillip in 1803. But the men of the *Cumberland* do not appear to have gone ashore at this point. One can probably eliminate, also, the three men from the *Ocean* whose boat overturned and who were drowned during a squall off Swan I. in January 1804. Ordinary seamen would hardly have carried a bunch of keys.

The most likely explanation is that the keys were among the objects taken by the Aborigines in the area of Limeburners' Point during this skirmish with Tuckey's party. Tuckey himself, as first lieutenant of the *Calcutta*, would have had access to numerous keys. One reliable witness was Daniel Woodriff jun. In 1854 he met La Trobe's friend Jacques du Bois, whose family had bought land in Melbourne in November 1837. Du Bois described the keys as of an 'ancient pattern such as used fifty or sixty years back by seafaring people'. Woodriff told du Bois he was one of the boat's crew in Corio Bay. They had camped near Geelong and had sunk holes for water, finding some on the beach near a gully. They had wandered off in various directions to look for water. Du Bois believed that as the Bay was deeply indented there and they would be in sight of the camp, there would be no more likely spot to stop and perhaps lose the keys. The keys, discovered at a depth of 15 feet, were probably dropped down the shaft by one of the party who was stooping to dig for water. From du Bois' letter to *Australasian*, 29 July 1871.

23 Harris to his mother 11 Nov. 1803, Add. MSS 45156, BL.

24 Harris, Survey of Port Phillip, in *HRA* III, i, p. 31.

25 Tuckey, Memoir of his chart, op. cit., p. 116.

26 A note signed J.H.T., Banks papers, A 78–3, ML.

CHAPTER 12 'A COALITION OF BANDITTI'

1 See Harris, Add. MSS 45156, pp. 12, 13, 86, BL.

2 Collins to Hobart 14 Nov. 1803, in *HRA* III, i, p. 36.

3 Gen. O., 30 Oct. 1803, in *HRA* III, i, p. 70.

4 Woodriff's manifest of the timber cut at Arthur's Seat stated that much was 'of a very inferior species of timber', A 3006, ML.

5 Fawkner, Reminiscences, ch. 4, LaT.

6 George Gordon McCrae's 'Col. Collins' Bomb-proof Magazine . . .', in *Victorian Geographical Journal* XXV, 1907, pp. 86 ff., has an account of the site as he and others remembered it from 1845 onwards, but later discoveries have refuted several of the assumptions, such as the statement that because the Revd Knopwood failed to note any funeral services in his diary it was unlikely that there were deaths at Sullivan Bay.

7 See Chapter 11, n. 2.

8 Fawkner, op. cit., chs 2–5; Crook, op. cit., pp. 31, 44.

9 Return of settlers seeking Lord Hobart's permission to proceed as settlers to Port Phillip, in *HRA* III, i, p. 18. See also descriptions of settlers in George Mackaness, 'The Journal of Matthew Bowden, Surgeon of the *Ocean*', in *JRAHS* XXIV, iv, 1938, pp. 319–22.

10 Collins to King 8 Dec. 1804, in *HRNSW* V, pp. 503–8.

11 Ibid., p. 505.

12 The Hartleys would sail to England in the whaler *Ferret* in July 1805, *S.G.*, 28 July 1805, and return to Sydney as immigrants in the *Indispensable*, *S.G.*, 20 Aug. 1809, to cause more trouble.

13 Fawkner, op. cit., ch. 4 and Book 1, cancelled passages, p. 20.

14 Ibid., ch. 4; Gen. O., 8 Nov. 1803, in *HRA* III, i, p. 73.

15 Collins to Hobart, op. cit., p. 37.

16 Tuckey, *Voyage*, op. cit., pp. 188–89.

17 Gen. O., 29 Oct. 1803, in *HRA* III, i, p. 70.

18 Gen O., 13 Nov. 1803, in *HRA* III, i, p. 74.

19 See also George Mackaness, 'The Journal of Matthew Bowden, Surgeon of the *Ocean*, in *JRAHS* XXIV, iv, 1938, pp. 319–22.

20 See Chapter 15.

21 Tuckey, op. cit., p. 190. The crimes have all been traced through the Assize records of their respective counties held in the PRO, London, through some Q.S. records held in the towns or cities of their trials or from local newspapers.

22 In Book 1, a draft of his Reminiscences, Fawkner, op. cit., referred to Rushton as Rushworth, p. 18.

23 Cited in John Earnshaw, 'Select Letters of James Grove, Convict: Port Phillip and the Derwent', in *THRAPP* VIII, i, Aug., and ii, Oct. 1959, p. 33.

24 Collins to Banks 19 Apr. 1804, MS ANL.

25 Cited in Earnshaw, op. cit., pp. 32–33.

26 Ibid.

27 The civil officers, especially Knopwood, were usually accompanied by their servants who managed to eat well.

28 Tuckey, op. cit., p. 180.

29 Ibid., p. 162. See also Tuckey's list of plants found at Port Phillip, pp. 218–19.

30 Knopwood, Diaries, 14 Nov. 1803, ML. When the skin and entrails were removed it weighed 68 lb.

31 Gen. O., 19 Oct. 1803, in *HRA* III, i, p. 67.

32 Collins to King 5 Nov. 1803, in *HRA* III, i, p. 28.

33 Fawkner, op. cit., ch. 4.

34 I write this by H.M.S. *Investigator*, in which ship we should have returned to England, but we could not be comfortably accommodated, therefore must wait an arrival from England, which is daily expected. I informed you before I left England that our destined place was Port Phillip; when I arrived there in October 1803. My pen is not able to describe half the beauties of that delightful spot; we were four months there, and much to my mortification, as well as loss, we were obliged to abandon the settlement through the whim and caprice of the Lieutenant-Governor, who shewed [*sic*] no disposition to render the British government any recompense for the great expense in so liberally fitting out our expedition. Additional expense to government and additional loss to individuals were incurred by removing to Van Diemen's Land; which, there is little hope, can ever be made to answer.

Our disappointment is so great that 10,000 l. [pounds] cannot repair it. Our stay at Van Diemen's Land was five months. We left its barren mountains in August 1804 and since that time have been at this place [Sydney] waiting an opportunity to return to England. During our residence on the River Derwent in Van Diemen's Land my husband's health was so very much impaired that little hope was entertained of his recovery. But, thank God, this country agrees with both our constitutions very well. It is a most desirable climate; yet Port Phillip is my favourite and has my warmest wishes. During the time we were there, I never felt one ache or pain, and I parted from it with more regret than I did from my native land . . .

From *Geographical, Political and Commercial Essays*, Valpy, London, 1812.

35 Woodriff, C 269, ML.

36 Harris to his mother 11 Nov. 1803, Add. MSS 45156, BL.

37 Woodriff, op. cit.

CHAPTER 13 OFFICERS, 'GENTLEMEN' AND A LADY

1 Harris shared with Collins a childhood spent in Exeter. Harris to his mother 11 Nov. 1803, Add. MSS 45156, BL.

2 The first civil suit heard at Port Phillip was on 24 Jan. 1804 before Knopwood, Harris and Lieut. Sladden. John Joachim Gravie successfully sued John Hartley for wages due to him, in *HRA* III, i, p. 124. See also Knopwood, Diaries, 23, 24 Jan. 1804, ML. Prior to this, Knopwood had heard complaints and passed judgment such as in a dispute between Robert Kennedy and John Buckley, 2 Nov. 1803.

3 Grove to Bensley, n.d., cited in Earnshaw, op. cit., p. 34.

4 See Hopley's memorial to Gov. Macquarie, 12 March 1810, and references, in *HRA* III, i, pp. 503–6. See also *ADB*, vol. I.

5 It was common for naval officers to introduce their sons to the sea at an early age. James, sometimes known as William Hobbs, later sailed with Gov. Bligh in the *Porpoise*. His later years were spent in Melbourne where he died in 1880. See *ADB*, vol I.

6 See Chapter 10, n. 59.

7 Fawkner, Reminiscences, ch. 6, p. 77, LaT.

8 Ann Jane married Harris in Hobart 17 Feb. 1805 and Charity married William Collins on 8 Oct. 1808, St David's marriage registers, NS 282/8/1, TSA.

9 Harris to his mother 12 Oct. 1805 and to his brother Henry 15 Oct. 1805, Add. MSS 45156, BL.

10 HO 10/6 and 10/7; CO 201/2/245.

11 Supreme Court papers, 11/38, AONSW; Return of lands granted 30 Apr. 1794, in *HRA* I, i, p. 473; letter from Thomas Muir in Sydney, 3 Dec. 1794, to a Dr Moffatt in London *re* the purchase of a farm.

12 Information from A. J. Gray, Sydney.

13 See *ADB*, vol. I. See also Crook's letters in his *An Account of the Settlement*, op. cit.

14 In later life Crook returned to Port Phillip after his wife's death in Sydney in 1837. He died in Melbourne, where a son was living, in June 1846.

15 '. . . departed this life Mr Michael McCarty ship's cook A. M. . . . interred the deceased on shore.' *Calcutta* Master's log, 15 Nov. 1803, ADM 52/3578, PRO. Knopwood notes that he buried the *Calcutta's* cook on shore on 16 Nov. but did not enter the death in the register.

16 Gar. O., 23 Oct. 1803, in *HRA* III, i, p. 68.

17 Gar. O., 19 Oct. and 1 Nov. 1803, in *HRA* III, i, pp. 67, 71.

18 Knopwood, Diaries, 25–26 Nov. 1803, ML.

19 Ibid., 25 Dec. 1803. St David's register of baptisms, NS 282/8/1, TSA. The Royal Historical Society of Victoria has a photograph of this first-born, as a very old man.

20 See App. E.

CHAPTER 14 IN BLACK AND WHITE

1 Hunter to Portland 1 March 1798, in *HRNSW* III, pp. 363–65.

2 Grant, op. cit., pp. 113–16.

3 See Morgan, op. cit.; *ADB*, vol. I.

4 Not only escaped convicts but sealers, probably including some French and American sealers, and, even earlier, Portuguese sailors were likely persons who had co-habited or had fleeting relationships with Aboriginal women. Pateshall, op. cit., p. 63, noted that the 'King' was 'a man of two or three and twenty, remarkably handsome, well made and of a much fairer complection [*sic*] than the rest'.

5 P. J. F. Coutts, *Victoria's First Official Settlement, Sullivans* [*sic*] *Bay, Port Phillip*, Melbourne, 1981, and *An Archaeological Survey of Sullivans* [*sic*] *Bay, Sorrento*, Melbourne, 1982.

6 See Norman Tindale, *Aboriginal Tribes of Australia*, Canberra, 1974, pp. 203 ff.

7 Report of Capt. Millius (*sic*) upon his examination of Western Port, Archives Nationales, Paris, trs. in Ernest Scott, 'The Early History of Western Port', pt 1, in *V.H.M.* VI, i, Sept. 1917, p. 17.

8 *Lady Nelson* log, 17 Feb. 1802. The log books of the *Lady Nelson* are in ADM, PRO, and the charts in BL. See also Ida Lee, op. cit., pp. 138–41.

9 Flinders, *Observations on the Coasts*, op. cit., pp. 214–15.

10 Westall's were the first known sketches of the southeast coast of New Holland. See T. M. Perry and Donald H. Simpson, *Drawings by William Westall*, London, 1962. Brown made a collection of seeds and Bauer made 350 drawings of plants and 100 of animals. Brown to Banks 30 May 1802, in *HRNSW* IV, p. 777.

11 Flinders, op. cit., p. 219.

12 See Chapter 8, n. 29.

13 See *Port Phillip*, op. cit., pp. 13–16, which includes Grimes' chart.

14 Crook, op. cit., pp. 35–36.

15 Pateshall, op. cit., pp. 58, 63.

16 Crook, loc. cit.

17 Tuckey, *Voyage*, op. cit., pp. 154–55.

18 Tuckey, Memoir of his chart, in *HRA* III, i, pp. 114–16.

19 Tuckey, *Voyage*, op. cit., pp. 167 ff.; Pateshall, op. cit., pp. 61–62.

20 Tuckey, op. cit., p. 159.

21 Ibid., p. 174.

22 Ibid.; Pateshall, op. cit., p. 63.

23 Tuckey, op. cit., pp. 176–85.

24 Ibid., p. 164.

25 Crook, op. cit., pp. 36–37.

26 Knopwood's commission, in *HRA* III, i, pp. 4–5.

27 Knopwood, Diaries, 23 Oct. 1803, ML.

28 Gar. O. (Port Orders), 10 Jan. 1804, in *HRA* III, i, p. 90.

CHAPTER 15 THE ROYAL MAIL GETS THROUGH

1 Collins to King, three despatches, 5 Nov. 1803, enclosing Harris' survey of Port Phillip and list of the trades and occupations of the convicts, in *HRA* III, i, pp. 26–32; transmission of returns of civil and military officers, supernumeries from the *Calcutta*, and surgeon's return, in *HRA* III, i, pp. 32–33; and a request for instructions, in *HRA* III, i, p. 34.

2 William Collins was registered at the Royal Hospital School at Greenwich, 25 July 1768. Bonwick transcripts, vol. 2, Biography, A 2000–2, p. 448, ML. He was aged eight, an ordinary seaman, bound for seven years, and served concurrently with Daniel Woodriff. Although unproven, there can be little doubt that there was some relationship to David Collins. Geelong descendants of William possess Ham relics which have been passed down through the family. David's brother George married Mary Trelawny of Ham. Information from Dr Philip Brown. Early historians referred to them as cousins. David did have a brother William who sailed with him in the First Fleet, but he was born in 1765 and returned to England.

3 He also wrote to Lord Hobart, 14 Nov. 1803, in similar vein and added that he favoured a settlement at Port Dalrymple, in *HRA* III, i, p. 35.

4 Tuckey, *Voyage*, op. cit., p. 161, thought the timber found at Port Phillip to be good enough, perhaps, to be used in the upper works of ships, for knees etc.; they found better timber at Port Jackson, p. 227. See also Tuckey, Memoir of his chart, in *HRA* III, i, p. 117.

5 Tuckey, Memoir of his chart, in *HRA* III, i, p. 110; *Calcutta* Captain's and Master's logs 9 Oct. 1803, ADM 51/1485 and ADM 52/3578, PRO.

6 Collins to King, loc. cit.

7 Knopwood, Diaries, 5, 6 Oct. 1803, ML.

8 Ibid., 8 Oct. 1803.

9 The Church of England *Messenger* published the sermon, 14 Feb. 1878.

10 Knopwood would have had a first hand account of the December 1789 disaster from Thomas Clark, a former farmer who had sailed in the *Guardian* as a superintendent of convicts and had been one of the survivors. He occupied the same position under Collins.

11 Crook, op. cit., pp. 38–44.

12 Cited in Earnshaw, op. cit., p. 34.

13 Collins to King 14 Nov. 1803, in *HRA* III, i, p. 38; Crook, op. cit., pp. 45–46.

14 There is confusion between the two Hayes, Henry and Thomas, who were probably related. But the original victualling list clearly has Henry Hayes, settler, victualled only until 13 Nov. 1803 at Port Phillip. He had every reason to leave at the first opportunity to join his wife, who had remained at Port Jackson while their daughter had left for the Derwent with Lieut. John Bowen. He was victualled again when he arrived in Hobart Town in the *Pilgrim* in March 1804. Thomas Hayes and his family remained on Collins' victualling list, in spite of reports to the contrary that they had gone to Port Jackson. They had not the same need.

15 *Ocean* log, L/MAR/B/222J, India Office records; Knopwood, Diaries, 16, 17 Nov. 1803, ML.

16 *S.G.*, 27 Nov. 1803.

17 In 1806 Knopwood, who had never been close to William Collins, and was possibly jealous of his advancement in the new colony, wrote somewhat disparagingly and perhaps untruthfully of the boat journey. He recorded that when Collins was out some distance from Port Phillip he coasted the boat, running into every place of shelter that he could, and that 'when the boat was out and not with a strong breeze he turnd too [*sic*] and got very drunk, leaving the boat to the care of the prisoners'.

The *Ocean* must have taken many letters when she departed from Port Phillip. Every convict who could write and any others who could get another to write for him must have begged for some paper, which was in short supply from the beginning, to send word home. The mineralogist A. W. H. Humphrey sent two letters written in mid-November. Captain Mertho obviously thought it too risky to pass mail on to dubious sea captains when he discovered, while in Sydney, that he had to return to Port Phillip. It was more reliable to pass them on to Surgeon Bromley of the *Calcutta* when he returned to Port Phillip. The letters ultimately arrived with the *Calcutta* in London in September 1804 — ten months later. Other mail that Humphrey sent from Hobart took as long as thirteen months to arrive. Harris was to receive twenty-four letters all at once in Hobart — the first news he had had from home for nearly three years.

James Grove's letters to Thomas Bensley were also

written and probably delivered at much the same time. Hezekiah Hartley's letter, sent from Sydney to her sister, might have taken considerably less time if it had caught a ship returning direct to England.

18 Returns of cargo, 1 March 1804, in *HRA* I, iv, p. 527.

19 T. C. Croker (ed.), *Memoirs of Joseph Holt*, London, 1838, vol. II, p. 295.

20 *HRNSW* V, p. 126.

21 Returns of cargo, loc. cit.

22 *S.G.*, 27 Nov. 1803.

23 Ibid.

24 Returns of shipping, July–Dec. 1803, in *HRA* I, iv, p. 526.

25 King to Mertho 25 Nov. 1803, in *HRA* III, i, p. 44; for charter party see *HRA* I, v, pp. 147 ff.

26 King to Collins 26 Nov. 1803, in *HRA* III, i, p. 41; *S.G.*, 4 Dec. 1803.

27 King to Hobart 9 May 1803, in *HRA* I, iv, p. 144; King's instructions to Bowen, in *HRA* I, iv, p. 152.

28 ADM orders despatched to commanding officers of all H.M. ships of war, proclaimed *S.G.*, 27 Nov. 1803.

29 Flinders arrived at Mauritius 17 Dec. 1803. The French detained him there until 14 June 1810.

30 He found that his daughter, Martha, had already left for V.D.L.

31 King to Under Secretary John King 14 Aug. 1804, in *HRA* I, v, p. 137.

32 *S.G.*, 17 Apr. 1803.

33 Martha's daughter and son-in-law's memorial states that Martha lived with Bowen as his wife from May 1803 until Aug. 1804, CS 01/374/8531, TSA. See also Commissariat return, 27 Sept. 1803, in *HRA* III, i, p. 200, showing two women settlers *not* victualled. Presumably Martha was kept by Bowen. See Frank Bolt, 'Female Settler Martha Hayes 1786–1871', in *RSTPP* CXIII, 1979.

CHAPTER 16   WAR CLOUDS

1 *Calcutta* Captain's and Master's logs 18 Nov. 1803, ADM 51/1485 and ADM 52/3578, PRO.

2 Tuckey, Memoir of his chart, in *HRA* III, i, p. 113.

3 See Marjorie Tipping, 'The Occupation and Abandonment of Victoria's First Official British Settlement at Sullivan Bay 1803–04', in *VHJ* LIII, May–Aug. 1982, pp. 83–94.

4 Pateshall, op. cit., p. 68.

5 Woodriff, A 3006, ML.

6 Only Fawkner appeared to note that Rushworth (*sic*) collected flax and manufactured linen at Port Phillip. Fawkner, Reminiscences, cancelled passage in Book 1, p. 18, LaT.

7 Tuckey, *Voyage*, op. cit., pp. 193–202.

8 Grant, op. cit., p. 144.

9 He was searching for coal but found black stone which would burn into a strong lime. He wrote of the thick vegetation, wild life and streams ending in sand bars.

10 William Hovell was the first to discover coal in the area (actually at Cape Paterson) during a survey in the summer of 1826–27. In his report to Gov. Darling, Hovell praised Tuckey's earlier report of the country but did

not refer to Tuckey's references to coal, in *HRA* III, v, p. 858.

11 J. C. E. Campbell, a former president of the Royal Historical Society of Victoria, has made a careful unpublished study of Tuckey's track.

12 Tuckey, op. cit., p. 202.

13 The three unmarried Hobbs girls were among the most eligible in the colony (the fourth, Judith, had already married Dr Hopley). They eventually made 'suitable' marriages — Rebecca to the settler John Ingle, Ann Jane to G. P. Harris, and Charity to William Collins.

14 Knopwood, Diaries, 8 Dec. 1803, ML.

15 *Ocean* log, L/MAR/B/222J, India Office records; Knopwood, Diaries, 12 Dec. and following entries, ML.

16 Pateshall, op. cit., p. 67.

17 Correspondence between Collins and Woodriff 2, 14, 15 Nov. 1803, in *HRA* III, i, pp. 63–64.

18 Collins to Hobart 28 Feb. 1804, in *HRA* III, i, p. 60.

19 The French sank the *Calcutta* while on convoy duties in the Bay of Biscay in 1805. After an exchange of prisoners, Woodriff returned to duty but Tuckey remained in prison at Verdun until 1814. See John Goldsworth Alger, *Napoleon's British Visitors and Captives 1801–1815*, Westminster, 1904; see also Woodriff, Document relating to the engagement of H.M.S. *Calcutta* with the Rochefort Fleet, Woodriff papers, ANL; James, op. cit., vol. IV, pp. 46–49; *Naval Chronicle*, vol. XL, pp. 165–80, 245–57.

20 Baudin, in *Le Géographe*, slipped out of Mauritius the day before Flinders arrived and might well have alerted the French to Flinders' probable movements.

21 The *Sydney Gazette* from its first publication on 5 March 1803 courted advertisements from subscribers at 1s 6d for up to twelve lines. M. Haye who advertised in the *S.G.* later in 1804 was not Mary Hayes.

22 Gen. O., 29 Oct. 1803, allowed Blinkworth to sell a few articles of wearing apparel, in *HRA* III, i, p. 70; Gen. O., 8 Nov. 1803, allowed Hartley a licence to sell goods, in *HRA* III, i, p. 72.

23 There were articles on management of a dairy and instructions from *The Complete Farmer*, as well as a report that a Henry Hacken [*sic*], had been capitally reprieved and would be transported to V.D.L. for seven years. This was Hacking who would become a useful pilot.

24 At long last Collins had access to the Grimes survey and chart as well as Flinders' extensive chart and report on Port Phillip, together with his pamphlet published in 1801, *Observations on the Coasts of Van Diemen's Land, on Bass's Strait and its Islands, and on part of the Coasts of New South Wales, intended to accompany the Charts of the late Discoveries*. Collins also received on loan the precious manuscript journals of Bass and Flinders, although there were no other copies.

25 King to Collins 26 Nov. 1803, in *HRA* III, i, p. 40.

26 Hobart to Collins 7 Feb. 1803, in *HRA* I, iv, p. 15.

27 Collins, *Account*, op. cit., vol. I, pp. 2–3.

28 Ibid., p. 4.

29 By Gen. O., 21 Jan. 1806, they received conditional emancipations from Gov. King, in *HRA* III, i, p. 538.

30 The Fletchers decided to leave Port Jackson and re-join

the settlers at the Derwent. They arrived in the *Pilgrim* with Lieut. Bowen and Henry (not Thomas, as King noted) and Mary Hayes. King to Collins 4 Feb. 1804, in *HRA* III, i, p. 56. The Thomas Hayes family were still on Collins' victualling list and could not, as frequently surmised, have gone to Port Jackson.

CHAPTER 17 LAW AND OUTLAW

1 Collins family tree, Collins family papers, vol. IV, ML: Barbauld never did arrive in the colony.
2 Samuel Bate arrived in Hobart Town 14 May 1806, in *HRA* III, i, p. 365.
3 Bristol S. of P., 20 Oct. 1801; G.D. fiats Bristol 1802; Humphrey, in T. G. Vallance, 'The Start of Government Science in Australia: A. W. H Humphrey, His Majesty's Mineralogist in New South Wales, 1803–12', in *Proceedings of the Linnean Society of New South Wales* 105, 2, 1981, p. 141.
4 Knopwood, Diaries, 2 Nov. 1803, ML.
5 Court martial of Sergeant, Gar. O., 22, 23 Oct. 1803, in *HRA* III, i, p. 68.
6 Fawkner, Reminiscences, ch. 5, LaT.
7 Gen. O., 2 Nov. 1803, in *HRA* III, i, p. 71.
8 Gen. O., 30 Nov. 1803, in *HRA* III, i, p. 77.
9 Ibid., and Gar. O., 30 Nov. 1803, in *HRA* III, i, p. 78.
10 Gar. O., 23 Nov., 28 Dec. 1803, in *HRA* III, i, pp. 76, 85; Port Orders, 10 Jan. 1804, in *HRA* III, i, p. 90.
11 Fawkner, op. cit., ch. 6.
12 Calder correspondence, A 594, p. 663, ML.
13 Harris to his brother Henry 29 Jan. 1804, Add. MSS 45156, BL.
14 Croker, op. cit., vol. II, pp. 252 ff. See also Chapter 24.
15 Fawkner, op. cit., ch. 3; Gar. O., 3 Jan. 1804, in *HRA* III, i, p. 88; Gar. O., 23 Jan., in *HRA* III, i, p. 92.
16 Gar. O., 28 Dec. 1803, in *HRA* III, i, p. 85.
17 Collins to King 28 Feb. 1804, in *HRA* III, i, p. 217. He did not actually name them in the despatch.
18 Fawkner, loc. cit.
19 *HRA* III, i, p. 4.
20 Hobart to Collins 7 Feb. 1803, in *HRA* I, iv, pp. 15–16.
21 Ibid.
22 Gen. O., 10 Nov. 1803, in *HRA* III, i, p. 73; Gen. O., 21 Nov., in *HRA* III, i, pp. 75–76; a public caution 23 Dec., in *HRA* III, i, p. 82.
23 See App. E.
24 Morgan, op. cit., pp. 110 ff; J.H. Wedge papers, and Todd papers, LaT.
25 Knopwood, Diaries, 17 Nov. 1803, ML.
26 Gen. O., 21 Nov. 1803, in *HRA* III, i, pp. 75–76.
27 Tuckey, *Voyage*, op. cit., p. 203.
28 Collins to King 28 Dec. 1803, in *HRA* III, i, p. 49; Collins to Hobart 28 Feb. 1804, in *HRA* III, i, p. 58.
29 Harris to his brother Henry 29 Jan. 1804, op. cit.
30 Knopwood, Diaries, 9, 10, 12, 31 Dec. 1803, ML.
31 Fawkner, op. cit., cancelled passage in Book I, p. 19.
32 Ibid.

33 Knopwood, Diaries, 12 Dec. 1803, ML.
34 *S.G.*, 18 Dec. 1803.
35 Knopwood, Diaries, 24, 25 Dec. 1803, ML.
36 Ibid.
37 Gen. O., 26 Dec. 1803, in *HRA* III, i, p. 83.
38 Collins to Hobart 28 Feb. 1804, in *HRA* III, i, p. 59.
39 Register of deaths, Port Phillip, C 190, ML; Q.S. order book 1801–03, Shire record office, Matlock, Derbyshire.
40 Gen. O., 26 Dec. 1803, in *HRA* III, i, p. 84.
41 Gen. O., 28 Dec. 1803, in *HRA* III, i, p. 84.
42 His Plan of Association included the civil officers as principals while subordinates of the night watch included John Ingle and the twelve convicts. Gar. O., 31 Dec. 1803, in *HRA* III, i, pp. 86–87.
43 Harris to his brother Henry 29 Jan. 1804, op. cit.
44 Knopwood, Diaries, 31 Dec. 1803, ML.
45 Gen. O., 31 Dec. 1803, in *HRA* III, i, p. 86.
46 Ibid.
47 Knopwood, Diaries, 6 Jan. 1804, ML; Fawkner, op. cit., ch. 3. The fresh water river was the River Yarra.
48 Bonwick, op. cit., p. 513.
49 Knopwood, Diaries, 17 Jan. 1804, ML; Gen. O., 20 Jan. 1804, in *HRA* III, i, p. 91.
50 Gen. O., 28 July 1805, in *HRA* III, i, p. 533.
51 See Tipping, 'Occupation and Abandonment', op. cit., for an analysis of the reasons.
52 Morgan, op. cit., p. 6.
53 Ibid., op. cit., p. 8.
54 Marmon (whose name has sometimes been misread as Warner) must have been one who returned safely. He appears on later musters in 1811, 1818 and 1819.
55 Morgan, op. cit., pp. 9–10.
56 Ibid., pp. 10–11.

CHAPTER 18 ABANDONMENT

1 Unfortunately Brown's botanical specimens collected at Port Phillip while in the *Investigator* had been lost in the wreck of the *Porpoise* in Aug. 1803.
2 John Harris had escaped with John Duce and others from Bowen's settlement at Risdon Cove. See his declaration 29 Feb. 1804, in *HRA* III, i, pp. 228–30. Rushworth did a little exploration of his own to the mouth of the bay where he discovered a boat unnoticed by others. Casks with the name *Porpoise* were found on the shore. It was supposed that Duce and his associates had taken the boat. *S.G.*, 15 Jan. 1804.
3 Gen. O., 21 Jan. 1804, in *HRA* III, i, p. 92.
4 Ibid.
5 Ibid.
6 Collins to King 16 Dec. 1803, in *HRA* III, i, p. 47; reports of William Collins and Thomas Clark's survey of Port Dalrymple, in *HRA* III, i, pp. 583–87.
7 Humphrey to his father 1 Aug. 1804, in T. G. Vallance, 'The Start of Government Science in Australia: A. W. H. Humphrey, His Majesty's Mineralogist in New South Wales, 1803–12', in *Proceedings of the Linnean Society of New South Wales* 105, 2, 1981, pp. 132–35. See also J. F. Hogan, *The Convict King* [Jorgen Jorgensen], Hobart, n.d.
8 Humphrey, op. cit., p. 133.
9 Ibid.

10 Ibid. William Collins thought 'The Basin forms a fine spacious Harbour, affording many good and safe Anchorages . . .'
11 Humphrey, op. cit., p. 134.
12 *HRA* III, i, pp. 585–86.
13 Collins to King 27 Jan. 1804, in *HRA* III, i, pp. 53–54.
14 Tuckey, Memoir of his chart, in *HRA* III, i, p. 110.
15 Ibid.
16 Ibid.
17 Crook, op. cit., p. 37.
18 Among the forty-nine settlers and convicts there were eight soldiers of the N.S.W. Corps.
19 Gen. O., 18 Dec. 1803, in *HRA* III, i, p. 81.
20 *Ocean* log, 15 Jan. 1804, L/MAR/B/222J, India Office records.
21 Collins to King 16 Dec. 1803, op. cit., p. 46.
22 King to Collins 30 Dec. 1803, in *HRA* III, i, pp. 50 ff.
23 See verdict in suit of J. J. Gravey (*sic*) *v.* J. Hartley, 24 Jan. 1804, in *HRA* III, i, p. 123.
24 Gen. O., 27 Jan. 1804, in *HRA* III, i, p. 93.
25 See Tipping, 'Occupation and Abandonment', in op. cit., pp. 92–94.
26 John Pascoe Fawkner sent his agent, Captain John Lancey, in Fawkner's own schooner, the *Enterprise*, to form a settlement on the mainland. Lancey chose the present site of Melbourne on the River Yarra, and began to land horses and stores on 30 Aug. 1835. Fawkner himself arrived on 12 Oct. 1835. Fawkner's Journal, held ANL, in C. P. Billot (ed.), *Fawkner's Missing Chronicles*, Melbourne, 1982. See also Hugh Anderson, *Out of the Shadow*, Melbourne, 1962 and *ADB*, vol I.
27 The Armytage family, it seemed, liked the play on words when they acquired The Hermitage, originally a hut which they replaced with a palatial mansion.
28 This was Delgany, used for many years as a Home for the Deaf and recently bought for development as a country club.
29 See Introduction and biography by M. Tipping, in Pateshall, op. cit., pp. 13–32.

CHAPTER 19 JOURNEY'S END
1 Humphrey to his father, in T. G. Vallance, 'The Start of Government Science in Australia: A. W. H. Humphrey, His Majesty's Mineralogist in New South Wales, 1803–12', in Proceedings of the Linnean Society of New South Wales 105, 2, 1981, p. 135.
2 Harris to his brother Henry 14, 15 Feb. 1804, Add. MSS 45156, BL.
3 Humphrey to his father, loc. cit.
4 He did not then know that her father had rejoined the mother at Port Jackson.
5 Knopwood, Diaries, 12, 13 Jan. 1804, ML; *Ocean* log, L/MAR/B/222J, India Office records.
6 *Ocean* log, 19 Feb. 1804, L/MAR/B/222J, India Office records, first recorded the name Sullivan Cove. Collins, Gen. O., 20 Feb., in *HRA* III, i, recorded Sullivan Cove, Derwent River.
7 The sermon has been published in Karl von Steiglitz, *The Pioneer Church in Van Diemen's Land*, Hobart, 1954.

8 Knopwood, Diaries, 5–9 March 1804, ML; Humphrey, in Vallance, op. cit., pp. 137–39.
9 Humphrey, in T. G. Vallance, 'The Start of Government Science in Australia: A. W. H. Humphrey, His Majesty's Mineralogist in New South Wales, 1803–12', in Proceedings of the Linnean Society of New South Wales 105, 2, 1981, p. 137; William Collins' Account of Prospects of Whaling at the Derwent 4 Aug. 1804, in *HRA* III, i, p. 277.
10 Collins to King 20 Feb. 1804, in *HRA* III, i, p. 226.
11 Relative correspondence between King and Bowen, in *HRA* III, i, pp. 206–13.
12 Ibid. See also Delano to King 4 Aug. 1804, in Amaso Delano, *A Narrative of a Voyage to New Holland and Van Diemen's Land*, Boston, 1817, pt 2.
13 Croker, op. cit., vol. II, p. 249.
14 See Chapter 20, n. 7.
15 Collins to King 15 May 1804, 31 July 1804, in *HRA* III, i, pp. 238–39, 251–52.
16 *S.G.*, March 1804; Pateshall, op. cit., pp. 75–76; Elizabeth Macarthur to Capt. John Piper, n.d., Piper papers, A 256, p. 423, ML.
17 Gen. O., 9 Jan. 1804, Gen. O., 24 March 1804, in *HRA* I, v, pp. 74, 80.
18 Gen. O. relating to the insurrection are in *HRA* I, iv, pp. 570–73.
19 Pateshall, op. cit., p. 77.
20 King to Under Secretary King 14 Aug. 1804, and King to Under Secretary Sullivan 21 Aug. 1804, in *HRA* I, v, pp. 138, 142.
21 Tuckey, Sketch of the Present State of New South Wales, MS A 2001, ML.
22 Ibid., p. 40.
23 Ibid., p. 44.
24 Ibid., p. 40.
25 Ibid., p. 31.
26 Ibid., pp. 24–29.
27 Woodriff, Memorandums on New South Wales, typescript, Woodriff papers, ML.
28 Ibid.
29 *S.G.*, 1 Jan. 1804.
30 King to Hobart 14 Aug. 1804, in *HRA* I, v, p. 7; Proclamation 26 May 1804, in *HRA* I, v, p. 83.
31 Pateshall, op. cit., p. 77.
32 *S.G.*, 4 March 1804.

CHAPTER 20 THE RETURN OF THE *OCEAN*
1 The *Ocean* log is more informative about this aspect of its Antipodean journey than at any other time.
2 Abraham Moseley and Michael Mansfield.
3 Cited in John Earnshaw, 'Select Letters of James Grove, Convict: Port Phillip and the Derwent', in *THRAPP* VIII, i, Aug., and ii, Oct. 1959, pp. 32–33. In all, 18 sheep, 17 hogs, 10 ducks, a male goat, and 6 fowls were lost during the voyage.
4 Knopwood, Diaries, 1 July 1804, ML; St David's marriage register, NS 282/8/1, TSA.
5 Gen. O., 21 Jan. 1804, in *HRA* III, i, p. 92. Very little was recorded about the activities at Port Phillip during Sladden's command.

6 Gov. Sorell ultimately decided no lease of the land had ever been granted so that no one had a claim to the land. Sorell to Loane 12 Dec. 1819, Bigge, App., Bonwick transcripts 19, pp. 2960–61, ML.

7 Knopwood, Diaries, 29 March 1804, ML, noted that 'Bowen's young friend was confind [*sic*] to her bed'. Knopwood baptised the two girls 20 September 1805.

8 See *ADB*, vol. 1.

CHAPTER 21 SETTLING IN

1 The explorer John Oxley expressed surprise that the durability of the Huon pine, on which he reported in 1810, was not fully appreciated. Remarks on the Country and Settlements formed in V.D.L., in *HRA* III, i, p. 572. For comments on the convicts see Fawkner, Reminiscences, ch. 4, LaT.

2 Fawkner, loc. cit.

3 Richard Clark joined the Collins' party with his wife Maria on 2 June 1804. Commissariat return, in *HRA* III, i, pp. 108–09.

4 Gen. O., 27 Feb., 13 Sept. 1804, in *HRA* III, i, pp. 220, 525.

5 Gen. O., 10 March 1804, in *HRA* III, i, p. 264.

6 Gen. O., 22 Dec. 1804, in *HRA* III, i, p. 527.

7 Gen. O., 28 Oct. 1804, 21 Aug. 1806, in *HRA* III, i, p. 527, 546.

8 Gen. O., 11 June 1804, in *HRA* III, i, p. 556.

9 Delano, op. cit., end of pt 1.

10 Collins to Hobart 1 March 1805, in *HRA* III, i, p. 320; Collins to King 15 Oct. 1805, in *HRA* III, i, pp. 320, 331. John Henderson, in *Observations on the Colonies of New South Wales and Van Diemen's Land*, Calcutta, 1832, noted the large numbers of convicts belonging to trades such as shoe-making. One might believe that it was not so much that this particular trade invited more crime, but rather that shoe-making was a labour intensive trade and therefore the pioneer society required as many skilled shoemakers as possible.

11 Gen. O., 21 Feb., 22 Feb. 1804, in *HRA* III, i, p. 219.

12 Gen. O., 28 Feb. 1804, in *HRA* III, i, p. 220.

13 See Chapter 24.

14 St David's burial register, NS 282/8/1, TSA. Collins presumed Buckley was one who had perished at Port Phillip. See also App. E.

15 Return of sick 10 Nov. 1804, in *HRA* III, i, p. 291.

16 Collins to King 10 Nov. 1804, in *HRA* III, i, p. 290.

17 Surgeon's report Dec. 1804, in *HRA* III, i, p. 300.

18 Collins to Hobart 3 Aug. 1804 reported that scurvy, diarrhoea and catarrh were the most prevalent diseases, in *HRA* III, i, p. 257.

19 Humphrey, in T. G. Vallance, 'The Start of Government Science in Australia: A. W. H. Humphrey, His Majesty's Mineralogist in New South Wales, 1803–12', in *Proceedings of the Linnean Society of New South Wales* 105, 2, 1981, p. 141.

20 Lightfoot's position appears to have been unofficial until his name appears as an overseer in a Return of Civil and Military Employments furnished by Gov. Macquarie in 1810, in *HRNSW* VII, p. 367.

21 Surgeon's report 29 May 1804, in *HRA* III, i, p. 269.

22 *S.G.*, 12 May 1805, reported the arrival of the vaccine from the Royal Jennerian Society. King sent a supply to Collins. See William Crowther, *Some Medical Aspects of the Derwent River Settlement 1803–05*, Australian Medical Publishing Co., 1927.

23 George Miller, *A Trip to Sea 1810–15*, Boston, 1854.

24 I'Anson to Collins 8 Sept. 1804, 16 Jan. 1805, in *HRA* III, i, pp. 288, 314.

25 William Allison, Notebook, MS N5261, TSA.

26 Gen. O., 1 June 1804, in *HRA* III, i, p. 269.

27 Gen. O., 5 July 1804, in *HRA* III, i, p. 273.

28 Gen. O., 29 June 1804, 1 July 1804, in *HRA* III, i, pp. 272, 273.

29 Knopwood, Diaries, 5 July 1804, ML.

30 Gen. O., 3 Jan. 1805, in *HRA* III, i, p. 529. This unusual order announced that Gov. King had, in answer to Collins' application, directed warrants of emancipation to be made out and the Commissary to erase the names of Powers (*sic*) and Shipman and insert them in the class of free people.

31 List of lands granted by Gov. King shows that Faulkner (*sic*) and Matthew Power each received 50 acres near the rivulet and at Sullivan Cove respectively, Return of Lands, in *HRA* III, i, p. 568.

32 Return of Lands, loc. cit. See also Return of Lands, in *HRA* III, i, p. 255.

33 See Chapter 20, n. 6.

34 Fawkner, op. cit., ch. 4. See also John West, *The History of Tasmania*, Launceston, 1852, vol. I, p. 28.

35 Fawkner, op. cit., ch. 5.

36 Green who was one of Collins' gamekeepers died in 1812.

37 Woodriff, MS C269, ML; Fawkner, op. cit., ch. 6; Bigge's examination of Knopwood 3 Apr. 1820, in *HRA* III, iii, p. 367; Gar. O., 1 June 1812, Add. MSS 336, DL; Civil and military return, in *HRNSW* VII, p. 367.

38 Cited in Earnshaw, op. cit., p. 34.

39 Collins to King 19 Dec. 1805, Macquarie to Lord 16 June 1810, *HRA* III, i, pp. 345, 452. He received a conditional emancipation by Gen. O., 2 May 1806, in *HRA* III, i, p. 540.

40 Harris to his mother 12 Oct. 1805, Add. MSS 45156, BL.

41 Humphrey, op. cit., p. 140.

42 The first Cottage Green, little more than a hut, stood on Knopwood's 30 acre land grant where St David's Park now stands.

43 Gen. O., 17 Apr. 1805, in *HRA* III, i, p. 267; Knopwood, Diaries, 3 Jan. 1805, Uni. of Tas.

44 Collins to King 26 Feb. 1805, in *HRA* III, i, p. 315.

45 Collins to King 20 Apr. 1806, in *HRA* III, i, p. 359; Collins to King 2 Sept. 1806, in *HRA* III, i, p. 378.

46 Fosbrook described the house to Gov. Macquarie, 30 Nov. 1811, in *HRA* I, vii, p. 547, and see also p. 548.

47 St David's baptismal register, NS 282/8/1, 1 Aug. 1807, TSA. See also *H.T.G.*, 21 June 1817.

48 St David's marriage register, 8 Oct. 1808, NS 282/8/1, TSA.

49 Belbin diary, 23, 24 Sept. 1809, Uni. of Tas.; St David's marriage register, 6 Nov. 1809, NS 282/8/1,

TSA; Old Tas. Papers, Police Fund, 30 June 1812, ML.

50 *S.G.*, 27 Apr., 18 May, 7 June 1806.

51 *Inscriptions in Stone: St David's Burial Ground 1804–1872*, comp. Richard Lord, Hobart, 1976, p. 28, illus. p. 159.

52 Gen. O., 24 March 1804, in *HRA* III, i, p. 265; Collins to Hobart 29 Feb. 1804 and 31 July, in *HRA* III, i, pp. 220, 248.

53 Fosbrook to Collins 14 Aug. 1804, in *HRA* III, i, pp. 278–79. See also Margaret Steven, *Merchant Campbell 1769–1846*, Melbourne, 1965, pp. 72–78.

54 Knopwood legal documents, no. 6, 29 May 1816, MS Q15, DL.

CHAPTER 22 THE HUNGRY YEARS

1 Gen. O., 24 May 1805, in *HRA* III, i, p. 532.

2 There is every evidence that he treated them well, in spite of his complaints about many of them. Most of them had been *Calcutta* convicts, including Cole, McAllenan, Earl, Salmon, Gain, Charles Clark, Forsha, William Jones, Kemp, Stokes and Charles Williams.

3 Humphrey, op. cit., pp. 140–42.

4 Knopwood, Diaries, 6 Aug., 30 Oct., 5 Oct. 1805, Uni. of Tas.

5 Harris to his brother Henry 15 Oct. 1805, 1 Feb. 1806, Add. MSS 45156, BL.

6 Harris to his brother Henry 17 Oct. 1806, Add. MSS 45156, BL.

7 Harris writing to Banks 31 Aug. 1806, MS ANL (Nan Kivell collection), stated that he was preparing a work 'Illustrations of the Zoology of Van Diemen's Land', comprising 'accurate coloured drawings of descriptions from life of Birds, quadrupeds, Fish, Insects, etc.' and that he had already completed 150 drawings. He hoped to send these by the next ships (*sic*). These have not been traced and very little of his work appears to have survived.

8 Bowden to Charles Cox 17 Oct. 1805, MS ANL.

9 Robert 'Buckey' Jones, Recollections, 15 June 1823, MS Safe 1/2D, ML.

10 Gen. O., 9 June 1806, in *HRA* III, i, pp. 542–43.

11 Knopwood, Diaries, 13 Oct. 1805, Uni. of Tas.

12 Ibid., 20, 21 Oct. 1805.

13 Gen. O., 22 Sept. 1804, in *HRA* III, i, p. 525.

14 Knopwood, Diaries, 19, 20, 21 March 1806, Uni. of Tas.

15 Charles Jeffreys, *Geographical and Descriptive Delineations of the Island of Van Dieman's* [sic] *Land*, London, 1820, p. 74.

16 Gen. O., 27 May 1806, in *HRA* III, i, p. 541.

17 Gen. O. (at Port Dalrymple), 26 Nov. 1804, in *HRA* III, i, p. 610.

18 *S.G.*, 13 July 1806. Among the pirates was David Evans who had arrived as gunner's mate in the *Calcutta*. See Chapter 35 for a possible explanation.

19 Knopwood, Diaries, 7 March 1807 and following entries, Uni. of Tas.

20 Ibid., 1 April 1807.

21 Ibid., 31 March 1807; Proceedings of Bench of Magistrates 30 March 1807, in *HRA* III, i, pp. 387–89.

22 Gen. O., 25 April 1808, in *HRA* III, i, p. 565.

23 Knopwood, Diaries, 25 July 1807, Uni. of Tas.; Francis Barnes received a conditional pardon, Gen. O., 11 May 1807, in *HRA* III, i, p. 555.

24 See Chapter 26.

25 Copy in possession of the present author.

26 Calder papers, A 594, p. 204, ML.

27 Fawkner, Reminiscences, ch. 2, LaT.

28 Collins to his mother 2 Sept. 1807, Collins papers vol. I, MS 700, ML.

29 Maria Collins to David Collins 31 Jan. 1793, also one n.d., Collins papers, vol. I, MS 700, ML.

30 See letter from George Collins to his mother 14 Aug. 1810, TSA.

31 See Chapter 25.

32 Gen. O., 24 March 1804, in *HRA* III, i, p. 265; Collins to King 15 May 1804, in *HRA* III, i, p. 240.

33 Gen. O., 19 Sept. 1804, in *HRA* III, i, p. 525; St David's marriage register, 1 Jan. 1816, NS 282/8/1, TSA. Staffordshire assize records, Stafford gaol register, 23 Apr. 1801.

34 1842 Census, Richmond.

35 Pitt was one of the finest men among all the early settlers. He brought three children with him but his wife remained in England with one child. There are many descendants. See *ADB*, vol. 1.

36 Collins to King 8 Dec. 1804, in *HRNSW* V, p. 508.

37 Fawkner, op. cit., ch. 6.

38 Ibid.

39 St David's marriage register, NS 282/8/1, TSA.

40 Gen. O., 4 March 1807, in *HRA* III, i, p. 552.

41 Gen. O., 11 May 1807, in *HRA* III, i, p. 555.

42 Surrey Assizes agenda book, 31/19; Kingston gaol calendar and indictment, 1802, 35/242; Maum to Robert Nash, 28 Jan. 1808, Calder papers, LaT. The person with whom Backhouse spoke was probably Salome Bateman *née* Pitt. See James Backhouse, *A Narrative of a Visit to the Australian Colonies*, London, 1843, p. 21.

43 *H.T.G.*, 19 Oct. 1816. Manby was probably Tasmania's first 'speck' builder. Soon afterwards another house he had owned and leased to Edward Lord was for sale by auction, *H.T.G.*, 25 Jan. 1817.

44 Jones, loc. cit. 'Buckey' described V.D.L. as 'the place of murder and bloodshed where we had to live, work and fight for our own lives. The work of settlers was met with difficulties and opposition from the blacks and weather'.

45 See Chapters 26 and 29.

46 See Chapter 26.

47 Calder papers, MS 594, ML, pp. 681–82; Fawkner, op. cit.; Bligh to Castlereagh, in *HRA* I, vii, p. 128.

CHAPTER 23 CHASING THE WHALE

1 William Collins became harbour master by Gen. O., 2 Apr. 1804 and Return of overseers, 3 Aug. 1804, in *HRA* III, i, pp. 263, 266. By Gen. O., 11 May 1804, in *HRA* III, i, p. 554, he was designated Naval Officer and Inspector of Public Works. A return of officers 19 Dec. 1805, in *HRA* III, i, showed that he resigned as Harbour Master 13 Aug. 1804.

2 See Chapter 15, n. 2.

3 Gen. O., 25 Feb. 1804, Collins to King 31 July 1804, Report of survey of provisions, in *HRA* III, i, pp. 220, 252, 278–79.

4 Knopwood, Diaries, 31 July–1 Dec. 1804, ML; Hogan, op. cit., p. 58; *S.G.*, 16 Dec. 1804.

5 *HRA* III, i, pp. 276 ff. William Collins has the credit of initiating bay whaling in Australian waters. See W. J. Dakin, *Whalemen Adventurers*, Sydney, 1934, pp. 31 ff.

6 See Journal of Exploration of Port Dalrymple, during which Paterson named the Tamar River, 28 Nov. 1804, in *HRA* III, i, pp. 613–23.

7 King's instructions to Paterson, 1 June 1804, in *HRA* III, i, pp. 588 ff. See also Delano's narrative, op. cit.

8 King to David Collins 8 Jan. 1805, in *HRA* III, i, p. 305; *S.G.*, 18 Nov. 1804.

9 It was unusual to allow persons who had not completed their full time to serve as crewmen but the urgent need for experienced seamen to engage in whaling and sealing appears to have allowed some latitude. Conditionally pardoned persons could not return to England, but William Collins' men had received only seven-year sentences, would soon be free men anyway, and presumably sailed under supervision.

10 His body was found at Sandy Bay, 23 Feb. 1805, and Knopwood buried him the following day, Knopwood, Diaries, 23, 24 Feb. 1805, Uni. of Tas.

11 Knopwood, Diaries, 9 May 1805, Uni. of Tas. Forsha should have been free to leave the colony by December 1807. See *OBSP*, I Sessions, trial 60, Dec. 1800; HO 26/6/60; HO 26/7/60.

12 King to Earl Camden 30 Apr. 1805, *HRNSW* V, p. 605.

13 Knopwood, Diaries, 5 May 1805; *S.G.*, 5 May 1805, Uni. of Tas.

14 *S.G.*, 5, 12, 19 May, 2 June; Collins to Earl Camden 17 Dec. 1805, in *HRA* III, i, p. 338.

15 *S.G.*, 17 Nov. 1805.

16 Ports in the Spanish colonies had been closed to British shipping since the renewal of hostilities in 1803. This did not, however, prevent British merchant ships from intruding on seas controlled by the Spaniards. Raiders seized ships and their cargoes such as the *San Francisco y San Paulo* brig (re-named the *Elizabeth*) which the *Harrington* took off the coast of Peru and the *Santa Anna* which the privateer *Port au Prince* seized off the Mexican coast. *S.G.*, 26 May 1805, 26 Oct. 1806.

17 Herman Melville, *Moby Dick*, ch. 24. See also Thomas Dunbabin, 'Whalers, Sealers and Buccaneers', in *JRAHS* XI, 1925.

18 See Chapter 35.

19 He appears to be the William Thomas on a farm at Rushcutting (*sic*) Point at Port Jackson, *S.G.*, 16 Nov. 1816. He and his family sailed by the *Duke of Wellington* for Hobart in 1818. Macquarie to Sorell 6 Feb. 1818, in *HRA* III, ii, p. 299. For Wakefield, see Geils papers, bundles 3, iv, ix, 4, xiii, Allport Collection, SLT, *re* financial transactions and Supreme Court in Equity Proceedings, July 1812–June 1814, TSA.

20 Flinders to King 10 Dec. 1803, in *HRNSW* V, p. 241.

CHAPTER 24 COLONIAL CRIME

1 Gen. O., 7 Jan. 1805, in *HRA* III, i, p. 529; Gen. O., 5 July 1804, in *HRA* III, i, p. 273.

2 Gen. O., 15 Sept. 1806, in *HRA* III, i, p. 547; Gar. O., 16 Sept., in *HRA* III, i, p. 547.

3 Croker, *Holt*, op. cit., vol II, pp. 252 ff.

4 Ibid.

5 See Chapter 25. See also *HRA* III, i, p. 816, n. 177; Knopwood, Diaries, 13, 14 Apr. 1806, Uni. of Tas.

6 Knopwood, Diaries, 29 June 1815, ML.

7 Knopwood, Diaries, 25 July, 6, 7, 8 Aug. 1807, Uni. of Tas.

8 Bligh to Collins 1 Oct. 1807, in *HRA* III, i, p. 393; Macquarie pardon, 13 Jan. 1813, A 14, ML; CS 4/4427, ML; HO 10/8 male muster of landholders, Sydney, 1817; Government Stores ration book, Windsor 1812–18, A 803, ML; 1828 Census, N.S.W.

9 *Sussex Weekly Advertiser*, 29 March and 5 Apr. 1802; Proceedings of Court of Criminal Jurisdiction, Sydney, 'on or about' 10 Oct. 1806, 1152/117, AONSW.

10 Proceedings of the Court of Criminal Jurisdiction, Sydney, 4 Dec. 1806, 1152/117, AONSW; Calendar of prisoners, Dorset assize records, 18 Sept. 1802; see also Knopwood, Diaries, 1 Apr. 1807, Uni. of Tas., reporting Jones and Lush left for their trial in Sydney in the *Estramina*. There is a discrepancy in these dates. Collins to Judge Advocate Richard Atkins in Sydney, enclosed depositions, 31 March 1807, in *HRA* III, i, p. 387.

11 St David's marriage register, NS 282/8/1, TSA. Ann was the daughter of Elizabeth Cole or Nicholls, who arrived in the *Lady Penrhyn* and was at Norfolk I. where she lived with Richard Burrows. Their children included Ann. The *Derwent Star*, 6 March 1810, reported the marriage of Ann's parents after fourteen years cohabitation, 'better late than never'. Elizabeth's older daughter by James Tucker, Maria, married William Mansfield.

12 Many historians have referred to the loss of early court records. However, the present writer has discovered proceedings of the Judge Advocate's Court, Lieutenant-Governor's Court, and Bench of Magistrates relating to Hobart Town in numerous volumes of miscellaneous Old Tasmanian Papers held at the Mitchell Library, many filed among Supreme Court Records. Other records of the Court of Criminal Jurisdiction are in the AONSW and appear to have been overlooked because indexes do not indicate that some of the N.S.W. trials refer to persons from V.D.L.

13 *OBSP*, II Sessions, trial 546; HO 26/8/73 and HO 26/8/89.

14 CON 31/15/G1/2, TSA; Court records, Old Tas. Papers 271, ML; *H.T.G.*, 27 Sept., 25 Oct., 13 Dec. 1817; Gwynn's petitions to Gov. Arthur, 13 Aug. 1829, CSO 1/163/3899, CSO 1/56/1180; St George's burial register, Sorell, NS 229/4/5, TSA.

15 Blakeley parish registers, Northampton; *Northampton Mercury*, 19, 26 July 1800; Knopwood, Diaries, 16, 24 July, 8 Aug. 1807, Uni. of Tas.

16 CON 31/15/A3, TSA; Knopwood, Diaries, 26 Jan. 1807, Uni. of Tas.

17 See Chapter 29.

18 Collins to Judge Advocate Atkins enclosing Proceed-

ings of Bench of Magistrates 31 March 1807, in *HRA* III, i, p. 386. See also Campbell & Co.'s caution to the public against bills drawn by Fosbrook against Treasury in favour of Matthew Power, in *S.G.*, 28 Dec. 1806, 2 Jan. 1807.

19 Fosbrook was court-martialled in 1815. See Chapter 29.

20 Knopwood, Diaries, 9 Apr., 31 Aug. 1807, Uni. of Tas.; Judge Advocate's Court, depositions 24 Oct. 1809, 5/1160, AONSW.

21 Macquarie to Murray 15 June 1810, and Macquarie to Edward Lord 16 June, in *HRA* III, i, pp. 442, 451. (Note: *S.G.*, 19 May 1810, wrongly reported that Stokes committed the burglary at Port Dalrymple.) See also *S.G.*, 2 June, 1 Sept. 1810.

CHAPTER 25 THE PIRATES WERE NOT PENITENTS

1 *H.T.G.*, 11 March 1825.

2 *OBSP*, VIII Sessions, 28 Oct. 1801, trial 774; HO 26/8 (Warwick Assize records are non-existent); *Aris' Birmingham Gazette*, 5 Apr., 3 May 1802; Gen. O., 14 June, 28 July 1805, in *HRA* III, i, pp. 532, 533; Knopwood, Diaries, 13, 17, 19, 24 Feb. 1805, Uni. of Tas.

3 They returned in the whaler *Richard and Mary*, Gen. O., 14 June 1805, in *HRA* III, i, p. 532.

4 *S.G.*, 13, 20 July 1806.

5 Ibid., 5 March, 18 Oct. 1814; Public notice 18 June, in *HRNSW* VI, p. 98; King to Castlereagh 27 July 1806, in *HRA* I, v, p. 753. The story confirms what captains of the snow *Commerce* and the whaler *Elizabeth* reported, in *S.G.*, 19 Apr. 1807. Robert Campbell himself believed that the *Venus* became a Spanish prize when seized off Valparaiso. See Bigge, Appendix, vol. 140, Box 23, Bonwick transcripts, ML. The master of the whaler *La Fayette* reported seeing a white woman and child on one of the Friendly Islands in 1816, believing the woman had been from the *Venus*.

6 Knopwood, Diaries, 21, 22 Dec. 1805, Uni. of Tas.; Gen. O., 8 Jan. 1806, in *HRA* III, i, pp. 537–38. See also Chapter 33.

7 The *Marcia*, a colonial schooner, left the Derwent for Port Dalrymple. Knopwood, Diaries, 21 Jan. 1806, Uni. of Tas. The pirates must have occupied the vessel for some time before their apprehension but records of their activities are very scanty.

8 Capt. Edward Abbott, Judge Advocate of the Vice-Admiralty Court, to King 13 Feb. 1808, King papers, vol. I, p. 121j, ML; Johnston to Collins 28 March 1808, in *HRA* III, i, p. 397; Johnston to Castlereagh 11 Apr. 1808, in *HRA* I, vi, p. 275; and see also *HRA* I, vi, n. 75, p. 725.

9 *S.G.*, 5 June 1808. Taylor remained at Port Jackson, received an absolute pardon in 1810 and became a policeman. Bray completed his original seven years sentence while at Port Jackson, where he lived for a time before leaving for Port Dalrymple. McAllenan, Williams and Haywood had all had sailing experience and probably returned to England as seamen soon afterwards. Cole, also a sailor, entered the South Seas fishery

trade. Many years later he drowned off Auckland Islands.

10 See Chapter 31.

11 Gen. O., 28 Feb. 1804, in *HRA* III, i, p. 220; Knopwood, Diaries, 5 July 1804, ML.

12 Collins to King 24 June 1804, in *HRA* III, i, p. 324; *S.G.*, 21 July 1804; Knopwood, Diaries, 24, 25, 26 June, 16 July 1805, Uni. of Tas. (For Camel read Campbell.)

13 Knopwood, Diaries, 26, 29 Sept., 3, 23 Oct. 1805, Uni. of Tas.

14 Collins to King 2 Nov. 1805, in *HRA* III, i, p. 335.

15 Knopwood, Diaries, 9 Feb. 1806, Uni. of Tas.

16 Gen. O., 13 Apr. 1806, in *HRA* III, i, p. 540.

17 *S.G.*, 4 May, 8 June 1806; Sydney gaol register, 27 May 1806, King papers, vol. 9, A 1980^{-3}, ML; deposition of Henry Hacking 19 Apr. 1806, Supreme Court records, Proceedings of Bench of Magistrates, 5/1160, AONSW.

18 Collins to King 13 Aug. 1806, Colonial Secretary papers, N.S.W. (Tas.), vol. 5, MS 681, ML.

19 Collins to Bligh 18 Oct. 1806, in *HRA* III, i, p. 381.

20 *Topaz* log, Nantucket Whaling Museum.

21 *S.G.*, 22 May 1808. The company was based in Madras. See also Robert William Eastwick, *A Master Mariner. Being the Life and Adventures of Captain Robert William Eastwick*, ed. Herbert Compton, London, 1901, pp. 190–92.

22 *S.G.*, 22 May, 17, 24 July 1808.

23 Ibid., 23 Apr. 1809.

24 Ibid., 24 Aug. 1809.

25 Ibid., 27 Aug. 1809.

26 Ibid., 2, 23 June 1810; deposition of Thomas Dawson 18 Feb. 1810, Court of Criminal Jurisdiction Proceedings, 1152, p. 365, AONSW.

27 *S.G.*, 4 Feb., 10 Nov. 1810.

28 Ibid., 28 Sept. 1811. It was Gov. Bligh's belief that William Campbell had aligned himself with John Macarthur and was heavily in debt to creditors in India. Bligh to Castlereagh 30 June 1808, in *HRA* I, vi, pp. 534-35.

CHAPTER 26 THE ENEMIES WITHIN

1 E. R. Henry, 'Edward Lord: The John Macarthur of Van Diemen's Land', in *THRAPP* XX, ii, June 1973. Giblin also drew comparisons.

2 Lord belonged to a Pembroke family of substance. His maternal grandfather was Lieutenant-General John Owen, whose brother was the fourth baronet of Orielton. Lord himself was in line for the baronetcy, but an older brother with prior rights inherited it and the rich estates that went with it.

3 They must have survived in a second copy of Knopwood's diaries. These particular entries were taken from an unknown private collection in England in 1915 and published obscurely in *Notes and Queries*. See Mary Nicholls (ed.), *The Diary of the Reverend Robert Knopwood 1803–1838*, Hobart, 1977, p. 687.

4 Ibid., p. 688, app. 6 Oct. 1804.

5 Knopwood, Diaries, 1 Oct. 1804, ML.

6 As an officer of the establishment, Lord was ineligible

to become a trader but Maria Lord was a shrewd and efficient businesswoman, able to trade successfully as well as produce his legitimate family. He died in London in 1859 and Maria died soon afterwards in Bothwell, Tasmania, leaving a son and two daughters. His surviving family of three sons and one daughter by Elizabeth Storrer lived in England.

7 Much has been written about the rebellion. Many official documents are in *HRA* I, vi and vii. See also H. V. Evatt and M. H. Ellis who took opposing views. Unfortunately, the *Sydney Gazette*, during a shortage of paper, was unable to publish for several months during the period of the rebellion and Major Johnston's rule. Knopwood, Diaries, 1 March 1808, Uni. of Tas., named officers in the new government but made no comments. See also Bligh, Letters and despatches 1808–10, ML. See also unpublished correspondence with Sir Joseph Banks and a long letter from William Gore, Provost Marshal at Port Jackson, to Mrs Bligh in England advising her of the situation, 6 Oct. 1809, CY Safe 1/48, ML.

8 Collins to Bligh 4 Apr. 1808, in *HRA* I, vi, pp. 565–66. As senior officer Foveaux had assumed command when he returned from England 28 July, until William Paterson arrived from V.D.L. as Lieutenant-Governor until the appointment of Lachlan Macquarie. See also Bligh's opinion of Maria Riseley in Bligh to Castlereagh 10 June 1809, in *HRA* I, vii, p. 129.

9 Harris–Collins correspondence Dec. 1808, Add. MSS 45157, vol. II, BL.

10 Belbin diary, Royal Society Collection, Uni. of Tas. See also Calder papers, A 594, ML; Calder papers, MS 62, DL; Belbin entry *ADB*, vol. I.

11 Harris to Collins 7 Dec. 1808, Add. MSS 45157, vol. II, BL.

12 Ibid.

13 Calder papers, A 594, pp. 447 ff, ML, *re* James Belbin.

14 Collins to Paterson 18 Feb. 1809, in *HRA* III, i, pp. 412–13 and reply, 25 March 1809, p. 415.

15 There was a William Hobbs, boatswain, in the *Porpoise* in 1807 which has caused some confusion. Almost certainly they were the same person. James Hobbs, the son of a deceased naval lieutenant who had served under Bligh, had enlisted in the R.N. when only 10. He rejoined when H.M.S. *Buffalo*, captained by John Houston, formerly of the *Calcutta*, arrived in V.D.L. in Nov. 1805. See Hobbs entry *ADB*, vol. I. George Collins became a midshipman in the R.N. in 1807. Both had joined the *Porpoise* when it arrived from Norfolk I. with settlers in January 1808. See also William Maum to Robert Nash 28 Jan. 1808, Calder papers, LaT. Harris to his brother 17 Oct. 1806, Add. MSS 45156, vol. I, BL, reported that his brother-in-law was a midshipman in *Buffalo* and had nearly served time for his lieutenancy. And see also Knopwood, Diaries, 31 Oct. 1807, Uni. of Tas., and *Porpoise* log, ADM, 52/4570, PRO.

16 *Porpoise* log, ADM, 52/4570, PRO. Bligh's long letter to Castlereagh 10 June 1809, in *HRA* I, vii, pp. 114–60 (and enclosures) gives his side of the story. See also *HRA* I, vii, p. 103.

17 The sequence of events, because of the destruction of many V.D.L. records of the time, is difficult to follow. Knopwood's diary is non-existent for this period. Harris wrote to his brother 14 May 1808, Add. MSS 45 156, vol. I, BL, that Gov. Bligh was being sent home 'to be tried for tyranny and oppression . . . many varied and differing reports . . . not prudent or fair to mention them'. For a modern account see Rex and Thea Rienits 'Bligh at the Derwent', in *THRAPP* XI, iii, Apr. 1963.

18 Bligh to Castlereagh 3 June 1809, in *HRA* I, vii, p. 125.

19 Ibid., p. 128.

20 Their father, John Eddington, a Second Fleet convict, was sentenced at the Old Bailey 12 Sept. 1787 and arrived in June 1790 at Port Jackson in the *Neptune*. John Eddington jun. became a small farmer and publican of the Bird-in-Hand tavern in Hobart.

21 Bligh to Castlereagh 10 June 1809, in *HRA* I, vii, p. 129.

22 Remarks on the Country and Settlements formed in Van Diemen's Land, in *HRA* III, i, p. 573.

23 Bligh to Castlereagh 3 June 1809, and 31 July 1809, in *HRA* III, i, pp. 126, 169.

24 Originally published in *S.G.*, 19 March 1809.

25 Address of Settlers to Gov. Bligh 21 May 1809, in *HRA* I, vii, p. 159.

26 Belbin diary, 24 Apr. 1809, Uni. of Tas.

27 Ibid., 26 Apr. 1809.

28 Bligh to Collins 1 May 1809, in *HRA* I, vii, p. 153.

29 Belbin diary, 21 May 1809, Uni. of Tas.

30 Ibid., 23 May 1809.

31 Collins to Castlereagh 20 July 1809, in *HRA* III, i, p. 430. See also Bligh to Castlereagh 10 June 1809, in *HRA* III, i, pp. 425–30.

32 Harris papers, vol. 2, Enclosure E of memorial to Castlereagh, Add. MSS 45157, vol. II, BL, pp. 1-22.

33 Belbin diary, 4 Dec. 1809, Uni. of Tas.

34 Ibid., 23 Dec. 1809, 3 Jan. 1810.

35 Loane bought the *Union* from the Sydney surgeon Edward Luttrell and William Collins was master for a short time. Shipping returns, in *HRA* I, vii, pp. 320, 430.

36 Macquarie and his wife Elizabeth arrived in Sydney 31 Dec. 1809.

37 CS 4/4427, ML; Register of Free Pardons A 14 and Macquarie's despatch 27, 1 Sept. 1820, A 1192, ML.

38 Pardons of John Buckley, Michaels, Belton, Kidman and Trim, Macquarie's despatches 43, 83, 84, 85, 86, A 1192, ML. Power's pardon had come direct from Gov. King and was proclaimed in Gen. O., 3 Jan. 1805, in *HRA* III, i, p. 529.

39 Sad to relate, Belton had reason to return to V.D.L. in 1819 in the *Hibernia*, after conviction for cattle stealing, and was drowned when the ship went down just as it was reaching journey's end. He had been re-transported by the name of William Selsby, *H.T.G.*, 15 May 1819.

40 'A Piece of Blood Money', in *All the Year Round*, vol. I, p. 395.

41 Ibid.

42 Knopwood, Diaries, 25 March, 18 June 1805, Uni. of Tas.
43 See *The Trials of W. Grimshaw and R. Kidman*, op. cit., p. 79.

CHAPTER 27 THE FRIEND AND FATHER OF THEM ALL
1 Eliza and John were baptized 14 Jan. 1810, as the daughter and son of Margaret Eddington. Early registrations of baptisms, marriages and burials are in register books formerly held at St David's Cathedral and now held in the Tasmanian State Archives Office. W. T. Stocker and Francis Barnes frequently witnessed marriages.
2 They must have left hurriedly. Hannah Power's position had changed since the arrival of Margaret Eddington and Power himself was under a cloud because of his association with Fosbrook. They were certainly not in V.D.L. at the time of Collins' death and before March 1812 were living in Upper Marylebone St., London. Examination of F. Shipman by Commissioners of Audit, London, 2 May 1812, in *HRA* I, iii, p. 473. See also Power's assignment of deeds to land leased in Hobart Town to Capt. Samuel Rodman Chace (*sic*), 13 Sept. 1808, in *HRA* III, iv, p. 786.
3 *Derwent Star*, 3 Apr. 1810; *S.G.*, 21 Apr. 1810.
4 Hugh Munro Hull, *Statistical Account of Van Diemen's Land*, Hobart, 1856. See also *HRA* III, i, p. 822, quoting William Maum.
5 Notes on William Collins, Calder papers, A 594, pp. 681–82, ML.
6 Collins to his brother George Collins 30 Aug. 1808, Collins family papers, Add. MSS 700, vol. I, ML.
7 Lord to Macquarie 31 March 1810, in *HRA* I, vii, pp. 288–90; Macquarie to Lord 16 June 1810, in *HRA* III, i, p. 451.
8 Macquarie to Lord 16 June 1810, in *HRA* III, i, p. 451.
9 Bensley, op. cit., p. 139.
10 'A piece of blood-money', op. cit., pp. 395–96.
11 *Derwent Star*, 3 Apr. 1810.
12 Ibid.
13 Ibid.
14 Ibid.
15 See n. 7.
16 Bowden to George Collins 30 March 1810, Collins family papers, Add. MSS 700, vol. I, ML.
17 Harris to his mother 23 Aug. 1810, Add. MSS 45156, vol. I, p. 76, BL.
18 See Collins to Banks 26 Dec. 1802, MS ANL, outlining his pecuniary position and requesting provision for his wife in the event of his death. See also his will, Bonwick transcripts, vol. I, A 2000–1, ML. Maria ultimately received an annual allowance of £120 in 1813 and died in Apr. 1830, Collins family papers, Add. MSS 700, vol. IV, ML. See also Macquarie to Lord 16 June 1810, in *HRA* III, i, p. 451.
19 Instructions to Murray, in *HRA* III, i, pp. 443 ff.
20 Gen. O., 16 June 1810 and attached memo, in *HRA* III, i, p. 823.
21 *S.G.*, 9 June 1910.

22 He was buried 17 June 1810 aged 41, see St David's burial register, NS 282/8/1, TSA.
23 Contract of lease of land and sale of premises, in *HRA* III, i, p. 507. Interestingly, the seal on the contract shows a shield supported by an emu and kangaroo — the first recorded time when Australia's national emblems appeared. It is likely that Grove designed the seal.
24 *S.G.*, 14 and 21 Sept. 1811.
25 *The Trials of W. Grimshaw and R. Kidman*, op. cit., p. 79.
26 Bensley, op. cit., p. 139.
27 *The Trials of W. Grimshaw and R. Kidman*, op. cit., p. 79.
28 Harris to his mother 23 Aug. 1810, op. cit. Had he lived longer, however, Harris would not have approved of Mrs Murray's infidelities. See Alison Alexander, 'Governors' Wives and Mistresses in Van Diemen's Land', in *THRAPP* XXX, iii, June 1986.
29 Hopley to Thomas Harris 1 Feb. 1811, Add. MSS 45156, vol. I, BL.
30 St David's burial register, NS 282/8/1, TSA. The death also took place in May 1810 of the former Lieut. Gov. Paterson off Cape Horn during his return voyage to England. Bligh, writing to one Frank Bond 18 Dec. 1810, commented 'Col. Paterson died off Cape Horn and Col. Collins at the Derwent, being conscious a disgraceful fate awaited them . . .', Bligh papers, MS Ab 60/11, ML.
31 It was surely no coincidence that all these persons had had the confidence of Collins who had quelled suspicions regarding possible fraudulence in connection with the Commissariat. Justice would catch up with some of them.
32 *Journals of the Land Commissioners of Van Diemen's Land 1826–28*, ed. Anne McKay, Hobart, 1962, p. 12, 21 June 1826.
33 There is an extraordinary collection of these notes among the Calder papers, LaT.

CHAPTER 28 THE FAMILY WAY
1 For Phipps' theft of silverware see *Reading Mercury*, 8 Feb., 1, 8 March 1802. For Phipps' accounts, Colonial Secretary in-letters, N.S.W., pp. 335–36, ML; Knopwood letter-book and legal documents, MS Q15–6, DL.
2 The *Indefatigable*, an East India Co. vessel, arrived at the Derwent 19 Oct. 1811, CO 10/44–46; see HO 11/2 for list of those transported. See also Lloyd Robson, *A History of Tasmania*, Melbourne, 1983, vol I, pp. 544–48.
3 Return of purchases and exchanges made by government, 15 June 1813, CSO 1/112/2779, TSA; Bigge, App., Bonwick transcripts, Box 12, ML.
4 Lachlan Macquarie, *Journals of his Tours in New South Wales and Van Diemen's Land 1810–1822*, Sydney, 1956, pp. 180, 193–95; *H.T.C.*, 5 Apr. 1833; St David's marriage register 3 May 1833, NS 282/8/2, TSA; *The Van Diemen's Land Annual*, Hobart, 1836, pp. 263–66.

5 CSO 1/112/2779, TSA; *H.T.G.*, 1 Nov. 1817, 9 Jan., 18 Sept. 1819; Bigge, App., p. 155a, ML.

6 Memorial of James Lord to Gov. Davey sent to Earl Bathurst 21 Sept. 1815, in *HRA* III, ii, p. 129.

7 *H.T.G.*, 5 June 1819; St David's burial register 26 June 1819, NS 282/8/1, TSA. See also Chapter 33.

8 *H.T.G.*, 29 June 1816; St David's burial and marriage register 12 May 1813, 27 June 1816, NS 282/8/1, TSA. The register records that Martha Hayes Quinn married Andrew Whitehead 13 June 1811. There is no record of a marriage to Thomas Quinn, a *Calcutta* convict who was buried in Hobart Town 28 Dec. 1806. He was the only person with the surname Quin(n) in the colony.

9 Return of juveniles, CSO 1/240/5809, TSA. Stocker's shop opened in 1817, *H.T.G.*, 22 Nov. 1817.

10 Memorial to Gov. Arthur, and Stocker to Montagu, 18 July 1825, CSO 1/193/4756, TSA.

11 *H.T.G.*, 18 July, 8 Aug., 10 Oct. 1818, 6, 20 March 1819.

12 See also Supreme Court proceedings 1822–24, Bundle 9, no. 776 and miscellaneous, Geils papers, Allport Collection, SLT.

13 *H.T.C.*, 27 Sept. 1828; *Colonial Times*, 8 Jan. 1830.

14 See Chapter 33.

15 Bigge's examination of Knopwood, 3 Apr. 1820, in *HRA* III, iii, p. 367; Macquarie to Davey 27 May 1814, in *HRA* III, ii, p. 59.

16 Fitzgerald to Edward Lord 24 Jan. and reply 19 Feb. 1818, Calder papers, ML; Knopwood, Diaries, 14 Aug. 1815, ML; Macquarie to Davey 18 July 1815, in *HRA* III, ii, p. 117; James Bonwick, *Curious Facts of Old Colonial Days*, London, 1870, p. 284; Memorial of Mary Fitzgerald, 9 Jan. 1826, LSD 1/3/641–2–3, TSA, in which she named her first husband Abraham Martin, a surgeon in H.M. Navy. She had a son, William Joseph, by Martin, as well as two daughters Matilda and Thomas by Fitzgerald whom she married after her widowhood.

17 Sorell to Macquarie 13 Oct. 1817, 26 March 1818, in *HRA* III, ii, pp. 280, 311; Calder papers, p. 118, ML.

18 Sorell to Macquarie 10 Aug. 1818, in *HRA* III, ii, p. 345; Bigge, App., 3 Apr. 1820, p. 367, ML; Education return 10 Dec. 1821, in *HRA* III, iv, p. 40.

19 Education return, 10 Dec. 1821, in *HRA* III, iv, p. 40.

20 Return of children requiring education, 1820, CSO 1/240/5809, TSA. See also return of children, 1827–28, CSO 1/122/3073/42, TSA.

21 St David's burial register, NS 282/8/1, TSA; *Colonial Times*, 17 Nov. 1826. One cannot help but question whether Fitzgerald's alcoholic excesses were exaggerated when he appeared to have worked long hours teaching at day and night schools, as a clerk and as a primary producer with considerable stock. See Chapter 32.

22 Old Tasmanian Papers 5 Oct. 1826, A 1073, ML.

23 Return of children, 1827–28, CSO 1/122/3073/42, TSA.

24 St Matthew's marriage register, Clarence Plains, 23 Dec. 1829, NS 373/2 and St Matthew's burial register, 10 July 1831, TSA; Knopwood, Diaries, 10 July 1831, ML.

25 See Chapter 21.

26 *H.T.G.*, 21 June, 6 Sept. 1817.

27 [Thomas Wells], *Michael Howe, The Last and Worst of the Bush Rangers of Van Diemen's Land*, Hobart Town, 1818, pp. 27–29; *H.T.G.*, Supp., 28 Feb., 7 March 1818.

28 Return of children, 1827–28, op. cit. New Norfolk burial register, 28 Apr. 1853, NS 489/2, TSA.

29 *S.G.*, 16 July 1814; Knopwood, Diaries, 27 July 1814, ML; Proceedings of the Bench of Magistrates, 23 Aug. 1814, TSA.

30 St David's marriage register, 13 Aug. 1816, NS 282/8/1, TSA; *H.T.G.*, 24 July 1819. Bigge's examination of W. Holsgrove 18 May 1820, and of William Maum 27 May 1820, in *HRA* III, iii, pp. 497-98, 488. See also John Fawkner to Bigge 4 Apr. 1820, in *HRA* III, iii, p. 648.

31 St David's baptism, marriage and burial registers, NS 282/8/1, TSA. See also Chapter 33.

32 Knopwood, Diaries, 1 Apr. 1807, ML.

33 Court of Criminal Jursidiction records 31 March 1807, 1152, p. 117, AONSW.

34 St David's marriage register, 4 Dec. 1809, NS 282/8/1, TSA. W. T. Stocker and Richard Cornelius Burrows (Burroughs), who later married Maria's mother, were the witnesses. The relationships are rather obscure because the mother, Elizabeth Tucker, was also known as Nicholls.

35 *H.T.C.*, 2 Dec. 1836. See also Chapter 34.

36 Return of children, 1820, op. cit.

37 John Cobley, *The Crimes of the First Fleet Convicts*, Sydney, 1970, pp. 169, 190–91.

38 Known also as William Russell. Bench of magistrates 12 Sept. 1789, 1/296, AONSW.

39 Return of land grants, in *HRA* III, iii, p. 579; Landholders' muster 1819, 4/1235, ML.

40 Macquarie, *Journals*, op. cit., 20 June 1821, p. 196. Return of children, 1820, op. cit. For Wade's co-operation with Commissioner Bigge see Chapter 29. Wade bought horses at the Geils' auction 1814, Supreme Court in Equity proceedings, Geils papers, bundles 2, 4, Allport Collection, SLT.

41 Supreme Court in Equity proceedings, Geils papers, bundles 2, 4, Allport Collection, SLT. See also Chapter 30.

42 *Colonial Times*, 8 May 1829.

43 CSO 1/407/9204; LSD 1/109/1256, TSA.

44 Wade jun.–Colonial Secretary correspondence 1837, CSO 5/28/582, TSA. Before Wade jun. left for New Zealand he engaged in other disputes about land and private quarrels. See CSO 1/878/18582; LSD 1/26/1368, TSA.

45 William Molesworth, *Report from the Select Committee of the House of Commons on Transportation*, London 1837, vol. 15, app. p. 31.

46 *San Francisco Chronicle* and *San Francisco Call*, 13 May 1885, information from J. M. Sherrard, Christchurch.

47 *Launceston Examiner*, 5 July 1876. Information also from TSA. Among many claims, Brereton Watson believed he was heir to Rockingham Castle and that four sisters had married dukes. Although he was obvi-

ously well-connected, these claims have not been substantiated.

48 Hobart 1811 muster, 4/1233–4, ML.
49 Report by Judge Advocate David Collins and William Balmain of a conspiracy to seize the *Marquis Cornwallis*, 21 March 1796, in *HRA* I, i, pp. 653–61. See also Collins, *Account*, op. cit., vol. I, pp. 380–81.
50 St David's marriage register, 7 Jan. 1811, St David's burial register, 1 Sept. 1824, NS 282/8/1, TSA; Return of children, 1827–28, op. cit.
51 Proceedings of magistrates *re* Alice Blackstone, Cimitiere–Bigge correspondence including Boothman's examination, 5 Feb.–18 May 1820, in *HRA* III, iii, pp. 853–68.
52 St David's marriage register, 7 Apr. 1823, NS 282/8/1, TSA; Return of children, 1827–28, op. cit.; LSD 1/82/31a, TSA. St George's baptism and burial registers, Pitt Water, NS 229/4/5, TSA.
53 St David's burial register, 30 Dec. 1821, 19 July 1822, NS 282/8/1, TSA.
54 See *ADB*, vol. I, *re* Hibbins. St David's marriage register, 20 Feb. 1813, NS 282/8/1, TSA.
55 List of female convicts free by servitude, 29 Jan. 1844, shows that Eliza Cobb married J. Fawkner, was 5′ 2″, had light brown hair, grey eyes, was tried in London 1817, sentenced to seven years, sailed in the *Maria* 1818 and was shipped to Launceston, *Elizabeth Henrietta* 1818. Her native place was Brentford. Add. MSS 108, DL; St John's marriage register, Launceston, 5 Dec. 1822, NS 472/35, TSA.
56 *H.T.G.*, 18 Aug. 1820.
57 Petition of Sarah Skelton to Gov. Arthur 13 Aug. 1831, CSO 1/379/8600, TSA, p. 135; St John's burial register, Launceston, 24 Sept. 1831, NS 748/15, TSA.

CHAPTER 29 CRIME MARCHES ON

1 See Chapter 24; *HRA* I, vii, pp. 466 ff. See *ADB*, vol. I, Fosbrook, Boothman.
2 Knopwood, Diaries, 25 Apr. 1808, 12 Nov. 1807, Uni. of Tas.
3 Examination of Shipman 28 Oct. 1811, in *HRA* I, vii, p. 468.
4 Boothman's name re-appeared as storekeeper on a return of wheat received into public stores from Mrs Ankers (*sic*) and D. McCarty 25 Dec. 1810, in *HRA* III, i, p. 509.
5 See n. 3.
6 Macquarie to Bathurst 30 Apr. 1814, in *HRA* I, viii, p. 236.
7 Record book no. 4, George Town, 2 June 1818, MS 247, DL; J. T. Bigge, *Report of the Commissioner of Inquiry into the State of the Colony of New South Wales June 1822*, London, 1822, vol. I, p. 55.
8 Proceedings of Bench of Magistrates, Supreme Court Records, 21 Aug. 1813–12 Jan. 1814, 5/1160, AONSW.
9 Ibid. Knopwood's diary is available only from 1 Jan. 1814. The entries after 17 July 1808 have been lost.
10 *Lincoln, Rutland and Stamford Mercury*, March 1800.
11 Proceedings of Court of Criminal Jurisdiction 31 March 1807, 1152/117, AONSW; Landholders' muster, New Norfolk 1819, 4/1235, AONSW; Knopwood legal documents, 16 Apr. 1819, MS Q15/7, DL.
12 Death warrants V.D.L., 20 March 1823, C202, ML; Knopwood, 13, 14 Apr. 1823; *S.G.*, 17 Apr., 25 May 1823. For the establishment of the judicature in V.D.L. see J. N. D. Harrison (ed.), *Court in the Colony: Hobart Town May 1824*, Hobart, 1974.
13 See Chapter 28; Gaol calendar Taunton, 1 Apr. 1802; *Bath Chronicle*, 8, 15 Apr. 1802.
14 Bowden, Account book, 10 June 1810, Bowden family papers, Melbourne.
15 Proceedings of Court of Criminal Jurisdiction, 26 Sept. 1811, 1146, AONSW; *S.G.*, 16 Nov. 1811. See also Australian Joint Copying Project, Court of Criminal Jurisdiction, 1811, reel 2392, ML.
16 Letters from George and Robert Dixon, MS B425, ML.
17 *H.T.G.*, 10 Jan., 11 July 1818; *HRA* III, iii, p. 574.
18 See *ADB*, vol. II, Richard Pitt.
19 J. T. Bigge, *Report of the Commissioner of Inquiry into the State of the Colony of New South Wales June 1822*, London, 1822, vol. I, p. 143, ML; Bigge's examination of John Wade 20 March 1820, in *HRA* III, iii, pp. 310–16.
20 Lamb to Field 31 Aug. 1813, *Letters of Charles Lamb*, Everyman, London, 1909.
21 *Edinburgh Review*, 11 Apr. 1803, reviewing Collins' *An Account of the English Colony of New South Wales*, vol. II.
22 *Edinburgh Review*, 25 July 1821.
23 Ibid.
24 Earl Bathurst to Gov. Sir Thomas Brisbane 28 Aug. 1823, in *HRA* I, xi, pp. 109 ff. For further administrative and judicial reforms see legal papers, in *HRA* IV.
25 Fawkner, Reminiscences, ch. 5, LaT.
26 Landholders' muster, Clarence Plains 1819, 4/1235, AONSW; St David's birth register 17 May 1820, NS 282/8/1, TSA; St Virgil's marriage register 22 Dec. 1826, copy Uni. of Tas. archives. Dr William Ullathorne's report cited in J. W. Beattie, *Glimpses of the Life and Times of the Early Tasmanian Governors*, Hobart, 1905, p. 39.
27 Mrs Thrupp was Sarah, the daughter of Capt. John Piper and Mary Ann Shears and half-sister of David Gibson's wife; Macquarie, *Journals*, op. cit., 28 Apr. 1821.
28 N.S.W. Act, 4 Geo. IV, c. 96.
29 John West, *The History of Tasmania*, Launceston, 1852, vol. II, p. 206.
30 Knopwood, Diaries, 20 Dec. 1825, ML.
31 Ibid. Bagley had been a constable but Gov. Sorell had dismissed him for 'improper conduct'. Gen. O., 24 May 1819, A 1352, ML; CON 31/1/1042, TSA.
32 *H.T.G.*, 15 July 1825.
33 Knopwood, Diaries, Dec. 1825, 1–9 Jan. 1826 passim, ML.
34 Death warrants, V.D.L., C 202, ML; Knopwood, Diaries, 20, 23 May 1828, ML.
35 *Colonial Times*, 22 Sept. 1826; CON 23/1/C 31.
36 Sidney Baker, *The Australian Language*, Sydney, 1945, p. 44.
37 See Chapter 24; Education return, CSO 1/240/5809, TSA; *H.T.G.* 14 Feb. 1822; Gourlay's inquest 7 June

1822 and Lush's affidavit 9 Dec. 1822, Add. MSS 662, DL; Street's inquest 15 July 1823, in *HRA* III, iv, p. 191.

38 *S.G.*, 19 Aug. 1824; Ann Lush petition to Gov. Arthur 19 Sept. 1824, CSO 1/73/1539, TSA.

39 Ann Lush petition to Gov. Arthur 19 Sept. 1824, CSO 1/73/1539, TSA; Ann Lush to Gov. Arthur July 1824, MS Q996/4, ML; CSO 418/9373, TSA; CON 31/13/305, TSA.

40 Knopwood, Diaries, 19 July 1824, ML; see Daniel Sprod, *Alexander Pearce of Macquarie Harbour: Convict – Bushranger – Cannibal*, Hobart, 1977.

41 From a rare broadside 'The Awful Confession and Execution of Edward Broughton and Matthew Maccavoy . . .' cited in Geoffrey Ingleton, *True Patriots All*, Sydney, 1952, pp. 125–26.

42 Macquarie Harbour muster 1825, Add. MSS 568, DL; Memorial book, CON 45/1/305, TSA.

43 St David's burial register, 17 July 1839, NS 282/8/1, TSA.

44 See Ingleton, op. cit., pp. 127–29. The pirates took so many stores that the prisoners were left in a state of starvation.

45 *S.G.*, 17 Aug. 1824; CON 23/1/A204, TSA.

46 Avery petition to Arthur, June, 26 Oct. 1824, Mary Avery's petition 20 Nov. 1824, Attorney General's reply, CSO 1/37/663, TSA.

47 Memorial book, 5 Dec. 1831, CON 45/1, TSA; CON 31/15/A3, TSA; *H.T.C.*, 16 Dec. 1842. Raphael, who was in Sydney, received a full pardon in 1843.

CHAPTER 30 THE LEISURE HOURS

1 The *Santa Anna* was lost in the straits of Timor but all crew members were saved. See *S.G.*, 12 Dec. 1812, which gives the Captain's name as Dagg. George Miller who sailed with him called him Dregg: see Miller's *A Trip to Sea 1810–15*, Boston, Lincs., 1854.

2 *S.G.*, 6 March 1813, 3 Oct. 1814.

3 *H.T.G.*, 15 March 1817, 30 Nov. 1816.

4 Ibid., 23 May 1818.

5 Ibid.

6 Ibid., 17 Apr. 1818. There is enough evidence to show that at least twenty-five per cent of the *Calcutta* convicts were literate.

7 Harris to his brother Henry 15 Oct. 1805, Add. MSS 45156, vol. 1 BL.

8 This was the work printed by Thomas Bensley, London, 1808. See J. A. Ferguson, *Bibliography of Australia*, vol. I, pp. 184–85, no. 465.

9 Grove had not then arrived in Hobart. For a discussion of the picture see p. vi.

10 Bowden, Journal, Bowden family papers, Melbourne.

11 Fawkner, Reminiscences, cancelled passages of Book I, p. 28, LaT.

12 Knopwood, Diaries, 19 Feb. 1817, ML; *H.T.G.*, 22 Feb. 1817.

13 Knopwood, Diaries, 5 Dec. 1819, ML.

14 *H.T.G.*, 10 May 1817.

15 Ibid.

16 Ibid.

17 Ibid., 14 March 1818.

18 Ibid., 24 Apr. 1819; Knopwood, Diaries, 16 May 1819, ML.

19 *H.T.G.*, 15 May, 12 June 1819.

20 Knopwood, Diaries, 23 Oct. 1829, ML.

21 *H.T.G.*, 30 Nov. 1822.

22 According to Geoffrey Stilwell the well-known watercolour of Knopwood on the white pony that he rode for thirty years, held by the Diocese of Tasmania in Hobart, was not, as formerly believed, a contemporary work by his friend T. Gregson but by a later unknown artist.

23 Frank Bolt kindly directed me to this information in Meehan's survey book no. 16, June 1813, Tas. Lands Dept.

24 *H.T.G.*, 15 June 1816, 5, 12 Oct. 1816.

25 Knopwood, Diaries, 2 May 1814, ML.

26 Geils papers, bundles 2, 4, Allport Collection, SLT.

27 Ibid.

28 Knopwood, Diaries, 6 July, 3 Sept. 1814, ML. Stocker's horse, Ross, completed his racing career in 1830, *Colonial Times*, 7 July 1830.

29 Knopwood, Diaries, 12 Aug. 1815, ML; *H.T.G.*, 5, 12 Oct. 1816.

30 *H.T.G.*, 2, 9 Nov. 1816.

31 Geils papers, loc. cit.

32 Knopwood, Diaries, 30 Oct. 1815, ML. The 'Fairbairn style' of boat-racing was named after one of Peters' descendants.

33 'Being Xms Holydays [sic] the people [are] playing at cricket etc.', Knopwood, Diaries, 26 Dec. 1815, ML, and see also entry for 26 Dec. 1814.

34 *H.T.G.*, 14 March 1818.

35 Knopwood, Diaries, 4 June 1816, ML.

CHAPTER 31 PUTTING DOWN ROOTS

1 James Ross, *The Hobart Town Almanack*, 1830.

2 *Journals of the Land Commissioners*, op. cit., p. 25.

3 Ibid., p. 53.

4 *H.T.G.*, 11 Sept. 1819; *Colonial Times*, 29 Dec. 1826.

5 *H.T.G.*, 5 Jan. 1822.

6 *H.T.G.*, 6 Apr. 1824; *S.G.*, 9 Sept. 1824; Calder papers, p. 204, ML.

7 St David's burial register 16 June 1823, 28 May 1824, NS 282/8/1, TSA; *Journals of the Land Commissioners*, op. cit., p. 33.

8 *Colonial Times*, 15 Sept. 1826; information from Keith Grice, Brisbane, who visited his ancestor's house in 1983.

9 Morgan, op. cit., pp. 144–45.

10 Ross, op. cit., p. 25.

11 *Journals of the Land Commissioners*, op. cit., pp. 8, 9, 10.

12 Ibid., pp. 9–10.

13 *Colonial Times*, 26 Jan. 1827.

14 Information from Edith Calvert.

15 *Journals of the Land Commissioners*, op. cit., pp. 8–11.

16 Backhouse, op. cit., p. 191, 13 March 1834. Herbert Cullis has written the Hadden family history, *No Tears for Jane*, Canberra, 1982.

17 *H.T.G.*, 18 March, 13 Apr. 1820; Supreme Court records, 8 May 1820, Old Tas. Papers, vol. 271, ML; *Colonial Times*, 8 Apr. 1831.

18 *H.T.G.*, 4 March 1825; Birchall's memorial, 10 Aug. 1831, CSO 1/288/6886 and education return 1827–28, CSO 1/122/3073, TSA.

19 Pearsall's memorials 11 March 1825, 14 Nov. 1826, CSO 1/376/8585, TSA; other correspondence *re* grants, LSD 1/73/3527, LSD 1/89/207, CSO 5/162/3845, TSA.

20 Gibson had accompanied Capt. John Ritchie, commandant at Port Dalrymple, to the Derwent. Knopwood has documented his own journey to the north, leaving 24 March 1814 and returning 30 Apr., Diaries, ML. Stocker accompanied the party.

21 Knopwood, 23 March 1814; St John's Launceston marriage and baptismal register 16 Jan. 1819, NS 748/1, TSA. The position of Elizabeth Nicholls at Norfolk I., being the 'kept' woman of an official, has been as difficult to authenticate as that of the similarly situated Martha Hayes and Margaret Eddington. According to musters, she was a free woman, born at Norfolk I. about 1795. Her mother might have been Elizabeth Colley, one of the three originally sent there with Philip Gidley King in 1788. By 1812 she had a child of three, Norfolk Nicholls, Colonial Secretary papers, N.S.W., vol. VI, MSS 681, ML. His name had previously appeared on the muster of 1810 as Norfolk Piper. They were not victualled from the public stores, Norfolk I. victualling lists 1810–13, CS 4/1169, AONSW. By the 1811 Norfolk I. muster Elizabeth owned 152 male and 373 female sheep, two male and two female cattle, fifteen swine, forty goats and had fifteen acres under cultivation, A 1958, ML, 4/1169, 4/1233, AONSW. Piper also had at this time two children by Mary Ann Shears whom he married 10 Feb. 1816. Bigge, App., ML; Returns of marriages, 1816–19, Piper papers, A 254, vol. I, p. 67, ML. By 8 Jan. 1812 Elizabeth, among the settlers moved by the *Mistral* to Port Dalrymple, received £16 in compensation for her two-storeyed shingled and boarded house, List of settlers moved to Port Dalrymple, MS An 45/6, ML. In addition to Norfolk Piper she also had a daughter known as Eliza Holmes. Surveyor Evans ordered her a land grant of fifty acres adjoining David Gibson's, Return of lands, in *HRA* III, iii, p. 574. Whatever she was entitled to receive appears to have been absorbed in David Gibson's estates. There was a William Nicholls victualled at Norfolk I. 1792–96, A 1958, ML, and a John Holmes, sentenced to seven years, London 20 Sept. 1897, who arrived in the *Hillsborough* and was sent to Norfolk I. 28 June 1800, Colonial Secretary papers, MS 681, vol. III, ML. Capt. Piper's brother, Hugh Piper, who had been Deputy Commissary at Port Dalrymple from 1808, had also received a land grant of 100 acres on the South Esk River in Oct. 1809, in *HRA* III, i, pp. 752, 778. Proceedings of Judge Advocate's Court, 1809 Cornwall, indicated Gibson was his labourer. He 'lived in a house on Mr Piper's farm and sometimes they would all eat together', 5/1160, AONSW.

22 See Chapter 29; Petition to Abbott and reply 18 Oct., 19 Sept. 1819, in *HRA* III, iii, p. 527.

23 Charles Jeffreys, *Geographic and Descriptive Delineations of the Island of Van Diemen's Land*, London, 1820, pp. 90, 91. Actually, Jeffreys had seen G. W. Evans' MS report of a survey and used similar phraseology.

24 Gibson to Mr(s) Lord 10 Sept. 1818, Calder papers, p. 127, ML.

25 Landholders' muster, Port Dalrymple, 1820, 4/1235, ML.

26 Macquarie, *Journals*, op. cit., 9–25 May 1821.

27 Ibid., 29, 30 May 1821.

28 Evans published *A Geographical, Historical and Topographical Description of Van Diemen's Land* in 1822; see p. 77. Godwin had used Evans as Jeffreys had copied Evans' manuscript a few years earlier.

29 *The Diaries of John Helder Wedge 1824–1835*, eds Hon. Mr Justice Crawford, W. F. Ellis and G. H. Stancombe, Devonport, 1962, 29 Dec. 1824 and following entries, 5 Nov. 1825, 21 Oct. 1826.

30 Henry Widowson, *Present State of Van Diemen's Land*, London, 1829, pp. 116, 135.

31 Thomas Scott, Journal, 15 Jan. 1829, CSO 1/44/837, TSA.

32 James Ross, *The Hobart Town Almanack*, 1829, p. 48.

33 See Chapter 33. See also George Robinson's journal, 25 Sept. 1830, in N. J. B. Plomley (ed.) *Friendly Mission: the Tasmanian Journals and Papers of George Augustus Robinson 1829–1834*, Hobart, 1966, p. 219.

34 K. R. von Steiglitz, *Days and Ways in Old Evandale*, 1st edn, Launceston, 1946, p. 5.

35 *H.T.G.*, 24 May, 23 Sept. 1820, 23 Dec. 1826. By 1826 he was providing 20,000 lb, *Colonial Times*, 31 March 1826, and the next year 27,000 lb, 30 March 1827.

36 Petition CSO 1/4/451, pp. 714–19.

37 See Geoffrey Stilwell, 'Notes compiled for Association's excursion, Sept. 1963, to Pleasant Banks', in *THRAPP* XI, i, Oct. 1964.

38 *Colonial Times*, 17 Nov. 1840; *Cornwall Chronicle*, 27 March 1841; H. Butler Stoney, *A Residence in Tasmania*, London, 1856, p. 295.

39 *Colonial Times*, loc. cit.

40 *Launceston Examiner*, 11 Jan. 1851; *H.T.C.*, 15 Jan. 1851.

41 Petition to Gov. Franklin, CSO 5/194/4616, TSA.

42 Robert Russell to Joseph Dixon Apr. 1839. Cited in von Steiglitz, op. cit., 1967 edn.

43 Morven burial register, St Andrew's Presbyterian Church, Evandale, 15 Apr. 1858; see also Philip Brown, *Clyde Company Papers*, London, 1952, vol. II, p. 437.

CHAPTER 32 DROWNING THEIR SORROWS

1 *HRA* III, i, p. 462.

2 On 27 Nov. 1811 Macquarie noted in his journal that they found 'a comfortable farm house and a hearty rural honest welcome'. See also *ADB*, vol. II, Denis McCarty.

3 Macquarie, *Journals*, op. cit., 26 Nov. 1811; *Derwent Star and Van Diemen's Land Intelligencer*, 7 Feb. 1812; St David's marriage register, 13 June 1811, NS 282/8/1, TSA.

4 Knopwood's first available reference to Elizabeth Mary (Betsey) Mack is 18 March 1814, Diaries, ML. Years later, the day after her marriage to Henry Morrisby, Knopwood wrote that he had brought her up from the time that she was eight or nine months old; that her mother had died and her father (said to have been a marine) had left the colony. According to him she was sixteen in Aug. 1824, Knopwood, Diaries, 20 Aug. 1824, ML. There has been no satisfactory explanation of her origin but she and her children were the joys of Knopwood's life and her death shattered him.

5 Knopwood, Diaries, 29 June 1814, ML.

6 McCarty served eight months of his sentence in Sydney.

7 Macquarie to Davey 18 Aug. 1814, in *HRA* III, ii, p. 61.

8 Knopwood, Diaries, 29 June 1814, ML.

9 Ibid., 12, 13 June 1814; *Van Diemen's Land Gazette and General Advertiser*, 8 June 1814; *S.G.*, 6 July 1814.

10 Macquarie to Davey 18 Aug. 1814, op. cit., p. 63. In a private memorandum from Davey to Macquarie 6 Feb. 1813, Davey had warned Macquarie 'to be very much on his guard . . . against some designing characters . . . who will endeavour to impose upon him and mislead his judgment by artful insinuations and plausible but interested projects and Speculations'. He named Knopwood, Fosbrook, Humphrey, Loane, Bowden and Kent. 'The Chaplain is a man of very loose morals', he added. He recognised Fosbrook's corruption and advised watching Boothman.

11 Knopwood, Diaries, 30 Oct. 1815, ML.

12 Macquarie to Davey 18 Aug. 1814, op. cit., p. 65.

13 Depositions *re* robbery in March 1815 implicating John Mills and others, in *HRA* III, ii, pp. 80 ff; Knopwood, Diaries, 10 Apr. 1815, ML.

14 'He first sold spirits without licence and then purchased land at the rate of a Bottle of Rum for every acre', *Journals of the Land Commissioners*, op. cit., 25 Apr. 1827, p. 53. The *Van Diemen's Land Gazette and General Advertiser*, 2 July 1814, also implies that James Lord was involved with Whitehead in the illegal landing of spirits from the *Argo*.

15 CSO 1/112/2779, TSA; Supreme Court records, Old Tasmanian Papers, 271, 1819–20, ML; Barnes applied regularly for a renewal of his licence from 1819 to 1827. He also had a farm at the Coal River, *H.T.G.*, 11 Sept. 1819; *Colonial Times*, 17 Feb. 1826.

16 Sorell to Macquarie 28 June 1817, in *HRA* III, ii, p. 256.

17 Macquarie to Sorell 24 July 1817, in *HRA* III, ii, p. 269.

18 Supreme Court records, 7 March 1818, Old Tasmanian Papers, 196, ML.

19 See Chapter 28.

20 *H.T.G.*, 27 May 1820.

21 Ibid., 3 Oct. 1818, 5 Oct. 1822, 4 Oct. 1823.

22 Austin and Earle were licensed as partners in the Barley Mow, *H.T.G.*, 7 Oct. 1820.

23 Macquarie, *Journals*, op. cit., pp. 193–95.

24 *H.T.G.*, 7 Oct. 1820. The Derwent later became the All Nations Tavern. The Commonwealth Bank now occupies the site in Elizabeth St.

25 *H.T.G.*, 3 Oct. 1818, 16 Oct. 1819, 22 Oct. 1820. Commissioner Bigge applauded the system in V.D.L. whereby Humphrey, as Police Magistrate, had been responsible for superior regulations than those existing in Sydney. Each year memorials were presented to the Lieut.-Gov. by 29 Sept. In 1818 the number was twelve, with three in the country. Wives of convicts were not allowed licences. Only one magistrate had abused the system. J. T. Bigge, *Report of Commissioner of Inquiry on the Judicial Establishments of New South Wales and Van Diemen's Land, February 1823*, London, 1823 (Australian facsimile edn, no. 69, Adelaide, 1966), p. 81.

26 *H.T.G.*, 11 Oct. 1823; letter from James Ballance to Chief Constable Lawson at Launceston 15 Aug. 1824 and oath of James Johnson 10 Nov. 1824, MS 163(a) envelope, DL.

27 Bowden was Principal Surgeon on a salary of £182 10s when he died in 1814. He also had a 500-acre farm but Macquarie had found him 'a man of dissolute habits, prematurely old'.

28 *H.T.G.*, 3 Oct. 1818.

29 Ibid., 19, 26 Oct. 1816.

30 Ibid., 19 Oct. 1816.

31 Ibid.

32 Ibid., 26 Oct. 1816.

33 Ibid., 9 Nov. 1816. The expedition was to have a tragic result. It was well equipped scientifically and well led by Tuckey after his release in 1814 from prison at Verdun. But Tuckey and thirteen of his men died of exhaustion and fever. Tuckey's *Narrative of an Expedition to Explore the River Zaïre . . . in 1816* was published posthumously in London, 1818.

34 Inquests, 17 July 1811, 28 Dec. 1816, Old Tasmanian Papers, vol. 159, A 1188, ML.

35 Inquest, 22 Nov. 1817, Old Tasmanian Papers, vol. 159, A 1158, ML; *HTG*, 29 Nov., 6 Dec. 1817.

36 *H.T.G.*, 25 Sept. 1819.

37 Ibid., 28 Feb. 1818.

38 Ibid., 25 Sept. 1819.

39 See C. M. Goodridge, *Narrative of a Voyage to the South Seas . . .*, London, 1832.

40 Ibid., p. 128.

41 Andrew Bent, *Van Diemen's Land Almanack*, 1824, pp. 51, 53.

42 Goodridge, op. cit., p. 135; Alexander Henderson, *Early Pioneer Families of Victoria and the Riverina*, Melbourne, 1936. Although probably right in substance, it is inaccurate in the origins of the family.

43 J. T. Bigge, *Report of the Commissioner of Inquiry on the State of Agriculture and Trade in the Colony of New South Wales, March 1823*, London, 1823 (Australian facsimile edn, no. 70, Adelaide, 1966), p. 33. Bigge's examination of A. F. Kemp and George Gatehouse, in *HRA* III, iii, pp. 222, 251.

44 Dep. Asst Commissary-General George Hull to Bigge 7 Dec. 1820, in *HRA* III, iii, p. 694. See also *ADB*, vol. I, Gatehouse entry.

45 Ross, *Almanack*, 1830, op. cit.

46 Bent, op. cit., p. 89.

47 Ross, op. cit., p. 43.

48 Ross, *Almanack*, 1829, op. cit., pp. 94–103.

49 Molesworth, op. cit.

50 SC 195/15/1266, 10 Apr. 1845, TSA.

51 SC 195/15/1263, 14 Apr. 1845, TSA.

52 SC 195/19, 23 Feb. 1846, TSA.

53 SC 195/29, 2 Oct. 1851, TSA.

54 SC 195/51/6173, 5 Oct. 1867, TSA.

55 Fawkner jun. to Maria Lord 11 Oct. 1820, cited in Anderson, op. cit., pp. 49–50. Fawkner settled in Launceston in Dec. 1819, accompanied by Eliza Cobb whom he married at St John's Launceston 5 Dec. 1822, NS 472/35, TSA. Cornwall House opened in 1824. Andrew Bent, *Tasmanian Almanack*, Hobart, 1827; *H.T.G.*, 17 Sept. 1824.

56 *An Episode: Batman and Fawkner*, ed. Ian McLaren, Melbourne, 1965, pp. 3, 4 (reprint of an anonymous publication, Melbourne, 1881).

57 In spite of Batman's earlier exploration of the country surrounding the future site of Melbourne (which he did not see until later than Fawkner and his party in 1835), Fawkner could truly claim that he was the actual founder, his agent John Lancey having chosen the site which Fawkner occupied before Batman's arrival.

58 Family information from Irene Elmore.

59 Anderson, op. cit., p. 117.

60 Ibid., p. 213.

61 James Fenton, *Bush Life in Tasmania*, London, [c. 1891], p. 56.

CHAPTER 33 VIOLENCE ON THE FRONTIER

1 In his *Account* Collins frequently and objectively indicated that violence at Port Jackson was due to provocation. See also Collins' Port Orders, Port Phillip, in *HRA* III, i, p. 90.

2 Collins, *Account*, op. cit., vol. II, pp. 200–01; Hunter's instructions, in *HRA* I, i, p. 522; Hunter's Gen. O., 22 Feb. 1796, in *HRA* I, i, pp. 688–89.

3 Knopwood, Diaries, 3, 11 May 1804, ML; Collins insisted that the child must be baptised without his knowledge and must be returned to the natives, Collins to King 15 May 1804, in *HRA* III, i, p. 238. See also *Van Diemen's Land: Correspondence between Lieutenant Governor Arthur and H.M.'s Secretary of State for the Colonies*, comp. A. G. L. Shaw, Hobart, 1971.

4 Collins to King 11 Sept. 1804, in *HRA* III, i, p. 281.

5 Knopwood, Diaries, 2 Feb., 9, 12, 16 June 1806, 15 Aug. 1807, Uni. of Tas.

6 See Chapter 25; Gen. O., 1 March 1808, in *HRA* III, i, p. 563.

7 Harris to his brother Henry 14 May 1808 and to his sister Nancy 3 Oct. 1808, Add. MSS 45156, BL. For a survey of these early years of contact with the Aborigines see Marie Fels, 'Culture Contact in the County of Buckinghamshire, Van Diemen's Land 1803–11', in *THRAPP* XXIX, ii, June 1982.

8 Knopwood, Diaries, 14 Feb. 1807, Uni. of Tas.

9 Henry Ling Roth, *The Aborigines of Tasmania*, London, 1890, p. 79; H. W. Parker, *Van Diemen's Land: Its Rise, Progress and Present State*, London, 1834, p. 28. Knop-

wood might have confused him with Waring. There is no doubt that Munday from the *Calcutta* lived and became a law-abiding citizen with a family. There was also another Munday family who were free settlers in the community.

10 Knopwood, Diaries, 2 March 1807, Uni. of Tas.

11 Ibid., 19 May 1807.

12 Plomley, op. cit., p. 1041; Aboriginal papers, CSO 1/170/4072, and Bruny I. correspondence 1828, CSO 1/240/4072, TSA.

13 On 28 March 1814 Knopwood, on his journey to Port Dalrymple, noted Don's Battery between Middle Valley and Grimes Sugarloaf, Diaries, ML; Ross, *Almanack*, 1829, op. cit., p. 44; James Bonwick, *The Last of the Tasmanians*, London, 1870, p. 125.

14 Gen. O., 10 Feb. 1808, in *HRA* III, i, p. 562.

15 Evidence of James Hobbs 9 March 1830, before the Committee for the Affairs of the Aborigines, cited in *Van Diemen's Land: Correspondence between Lieutenant Governor Arthur and H.M.'s Secretary of State for the Colonies . . .*, comp. A. G. L. Shaw, Hobart, 1971, p. 49.

16 *S.G.*, 2, 16 Jan. 1813.

17 Macquarie to Geils 28 Jan. 1813, in *HRA* III, ii, p. 7.

18 See Chapters 30 and 34.

19 See *Legislative Council of Tasmania: Report 75 re Boat Expeditions round Tasmania 1815–16 and 1824*, ed. J. E. Calder, Hobart, 1881.

20 [Wells], *Michael Howe*, op. cit., pp. 8, 9. See also *HRA* III, ii, pp. 92–98; Davey's proclamation of martial law 11 March 1815, in *HRA* I, viii, p. 473; Macquarie to Davey revoking martial law 18 Sept. 1815, in *HRA* III, ii, p. 126.

21 James Stephen, London, to Gov. Arthur enclosing petition from Lewis Tombs 16 Nov. 1834, GO 2/9, pp. 229–36, TSA.

22 Principal Superintendent's office to Colonial Secretary 3 May 1835, CSO 1/789/16862, TSA, enclosing letter from Thomas Anstey and reply from Tombs; *Diaries of Wedge*, op. cit., p. xxxi, referred to Tombs investigating the Great Lake area.

23 [Wells], *Michael Howe*, op. cit., pp. 7, 9, 10; Benjamin Reardon to Capt. John Piper (his former master) gave a good eye witness account 8 Apr. 1815, cited in M. B. Eldershaw, *The Life and Times of Captain John Piper*, Sydney, 1939, pp. 131–32.

24 [Wells], *Michael Howe*, op. cit., p. 14; Knopwood, Diaries, 18 Nov. 1816, ML; *H.T.G.*, 23 Nov. 1816, 11 Jan. 1817; *S.G.*, 25 Jan. 1817.

25 [Wells], *Michael Howe*, op. cit., pp. 27–29; *H.T.G.*, 11, 18, 25 Oct. 1817; Knopwood, Diaries, 11, 13 Oct. 1817, ML. Bigge was to commend Chief Constable John Wade for being as 'remarkable for his vigorous pursuit of bushrangers . . . as for the severe losses he sustained from them', *Report into State of New South Wales*, op. cit., p. 143.

26 *H.T.G.*, 2 July 1824; Plomley, op. cit., p. 218.

27 Ibid., p. 219; Stocker's memorial to Gov. Arthur c. May 1825, CSO 1/193/4576.

28 *H.T.G.*, 17, 24 Apr. 1819.

29 Cited in Eustace Fitzsymonds (ed.), *A Looking Glass for*

Tasmania, Hobart, 1980, p. 199; *Legislative Council: Report 75*, op. cit., *re* Kelly voyage; Plomley, op. cit., p. 458.

30 Roderic O'Connor's evidence, Committee for the Affairs of the Aborigines, in *Van Diemen's Land: Correspondence*, op. cit., p. 53; *Colonial Times*, 6 June 1826; Plomley, op. cit., p. 219.

31 Plomley, loc. cit.

32 George Robinson saw the graves of the two white men Musquito killed at Oyster Bay when he visited there on 13 Jan. 1831, Plomley, op. cit., p. 314.

33 Henry Melville, *The History of Van Diemen's Land from the Year 1824 to 1835 . . .*, Hobart, 1835, pp. 38–40; Plomley, op. cit., pp. 314, 445.

34 *H.T.G.*, 3, 6, 20 Aug. 1824.

35 Melville, op. cit., p. 40. Melville's is a most perceptive account which underlines the whole problem of race relations. In speaking to his gaoler, John Bisdee, Musquito insisted that 'Hanging no good for black . . . Very good for white fellow, for *he* used to it'. See also evidence of Gilbert Robertson, Committee for the Affairs of the Aborigines, in *Van Diemen's Land: Correspondence*, op. cit., pp. 47–48.

36 *Colonial Times*, 26 Nov. 1830; George Robinson papers, Tasmanian Aborigines, MS A612, p. 283, ML; Evidence of James Hobbs, Committee for the Affairs of the Aborigines, in *Van Diemen's Land: Correspondence*, op. cit., p. 48.

37 Plomley's mammoth task of editing Robinson's Tasmanian journals covers the period from his appointment at the Bruny I. mission in 1829 until his last expedition to the remnants of the western tribes, Aug. 1834.

CHAPTER 34 SEALERS AND SAILORS

1 Keith Bowden, *Captain Kelly of Hobart Town*, Melbourne, 1964, p. 37. These children could have been only about twelve years old at this date, 1816.

2 See Stephen Murray Smith, 'Beyond the Pale: The Islander Community of Bass Strait in the Nineteenth Century', in *THRAPP* XX, iv, Dec. 1973; Lyndall Ryan, *The Aboriginal Tasmanians*, St Lucia, 1981.

3 Between 1800 and 1806 more than 100 000 seal skins filled the ships from England, the United States and the Colony.

4 See Chapter 35.

5 *OBSP*, I Sessions, 1799; HO 26/6 and 7.

6 See Chapter 33; *Legislative Council: Report 75*, op. cit., pp. 6–16; James Kelly, Journal of the whaleboat voyage, MS C 227, ML; James Kelly papers including log books, Crowther Collection, SLT.

7 Kelly, Journal of the whaleboat voyage, 25 Dec. 1815, MS C227, ML.

8 Ibid., 9 Jan. 1816. This was James Stewart of the 46th Rgt who had recently arrived as Commandant at Port Dalrymple.

9 Ibid., 13 Jan. 1816.

10 Ibid., 18 Jan. 1816. Cited in Bowden, op. cit., pp. 40–41.

11 Bowden, op. cit., pp. 40–41.

12 Kelly gave valuable evidence before J. T. Bigge on the whale and seal industry, boating, timber and trade possibilities, in *HRA* III, iii, pp. 458–66.

13 Ibid., pp. 354–58.

14 *S.G.*, 30 Sept. 1815.

15 *S.G.*, 7 Oct. 1815; Knopwood, Diaries, 4 Dec. 1815, ML.

16 His original crime was that of stealing lead, for which he received a sentence of seven years transportation which would have expired in January 1809, *Berrow's Worcester Journal*, 25 Feb. 1802; *Worcester Herald*, 27 Feb. 1802.

17 Plomley, op. cit., pp. 1002, 1019.

18 St John's Church of England baptism register, 22 Jan. 1819, no. 63, shows that Edward, son of Samuel Tomlin and Buldar (*sic*), native, born at Cape Barren 1813, was baptised by Revd John Youl, NS 748/2, TSA.

19 *H.T.G.*, 3 Apr. 1819. Prior to this voyage Tomlins had also served in the brig *Active* when it took missionaries to New Zealand. See Chapter 35.

20 Darling to Robinson 8 Dec. 1832, cited in Plomley, op. cit., p. 801, and see also p. 1002.

21 Ibid., pp. 801–02; see also pp. 276, 303.

22 Ibid., pp. 1015–16, 1018.

23 Ibid., p. 273.

24 Macquarie's proclamation 14 May 1814, in *HRA* I, viii, p. 264.

25 Knopwood, Diaries, 7 July 1814, ML.

26 Ibid., 15–17 Nov. 1815; *S.G.*, 20 Aug. 1814; Calder papers, MS A594, p. 943, ML.

27 Another version of the story is in James Bonwick, *The Lost Tasmanian Race*, London, 1884, pp. 45–50.

28 Rice's journal of exploration, 29–30 Dec. 1820, in *HRA* III, iv, p. 647.

29 St David's marriage register 22 Sept. 1823, the first entered by the Revd William Bedford, NS 282/8/1, TSA; Goodridge, op. cit., p. 127.

CHAPTER 35 MACQUARIE LAND AND BEYOND

1 *S.G.*, 9 March 1811, 17 Oct. 1812; Register of conditional pardons, 31 Jan. 1815, CO D19, AONSW.

2 See Chapters 12 and 24.

3 Windsor Govt Stores ration book 1815–17, ML; Male muster 1817 Sydney, HO 10/8; 1828 Census.

4 King to Portland 1 March 1802, in *HRA* I, iii, p. 405.

5 They appear only on the victualling list until 14 March 1804. This was the date the *Lady Nelson* arrived back at Port Jackson. There were persons named Oram on the 1828 census, possibly sons.

6 In response to Rushton's petition to King, CS 2/4/1720, 1804–06, p. 34; Agreement between J. Palmer, Commissary, and Thomas Rushton of Parramatta (then conditionally emancipated) 17 Feb. 1806, in *HRA* I, v, p. 668.

7 Gen. O. from Commissary's office, 1 March 1806, cited in *S.G.*, 19 June 1806.

8 *S.G.*, 16 Apr., 18, 26 June 1809.

9 Ibid., 1 March, 1, 15 June 1811.

10 Ibid., 15 May 1813, 5 Feb. 1814. For these years there exist many accounts and returns for the supply of grain yeast, hops etc. for the brewery at Parramatta, prisoners' barracks etc. in the Colonial Secretary's correspond-

ence, AONSW. The son received a land grant in 1824, two years after his father's death.

11 Police fund c. 1817, MS D1, Wentworth papers, p. 209, ML.

12 Raphael's petitions, 1 Dec. 1817, CS 4/1852/274, and Sept. 1818, CS 4/1856/219, AONSW. Lycett sketched views of the area. The sketches and a fine lithograph of the prison settlement at Newcastle appeared in his work *Views in Australia*, London, 1824. Noel McLachlan edited a new edition of *The Memoirs of James Hardy Vaux*, London, 1968.

13 Macquarie, *Journals*, op. cit., 28 July 1818, p. 129, and see also entry for 3 Aug. 1818; marriage register, Newcastle, 3 Aug. 1818, p. 135; Mutch Index, ML; McLachlan, op. cit., pp. lv, lvi.

14 *S.G.*, 28 Nov. 1818.

15 Bench of Magistrates 18 Sept. 1819, and Hannibal Macarthur to Macquarie 23 Oct. 1819, Bigge, App., Box 19, pp. 2921, 2974; *S.G.*, 27 March 1819.

16 Levi, op. cit., p. 122 on Solomon Solomons; *S.G.*, 10 June, 14 Oct., 4 Nov., 9 Dec. 1820, 17 Nov. 1821.

17 *S.G.*, 13 Dec. 1822, 26 June 1823; Boyes to his wife 16 Jan. 1824, cited in Levi, op. cit., p. 191.

18 *S.G.*, 5 May, 15 July 1824, 3 May 1826.

19 Ibid., 19, 28 Aug. 1826. There had been waves of anti-Semitism in Germany and England in particular in the 1820s. Interestingly, J. P. Fawkner in Launceston was wishing the Jews much success: 'They never injured England but England has been, and is obliged to them', cited in Levi and Bergman, op. cit., p. 192; in 1828 in Sydney one Jew, Walter Levi, had arranged a public meeting in protest against Czarist oppression of Jews in Eastern Europe, p. 220.

20 *S.G.*, 8 Nov. 1826. See also Levi, op. cit., p. 71 on Barnett Levey.

21 *S.G.*, 13 Dec. 1826.

22 *Monitor*, 13 March 1830.

23 *S.G.*, 31 Oct. 1835.

24 Colonial Secretary Deas Thomson sent Raphael's absolute pardon no. 1231 to Gov. Gipps 10 Feb. 1843, Colonial Secretary in-letters, A 1290, ML, pp. 427, 429.

25 Information from Rabbi Levi.

26 Of these six men, Ronaldson and Forsha were not heard of again. Wakefield decided against seafaring life and took up farming in the colony. James Price drowned soon afterwards. Allender spent some time at sea before deciding that life at the Derwent estuary with a wife and family, a lucrative ferry business and plenty of alcohol was preferable to life on the ocean wave. The sixth man, the American William Thomas, left the Derwent to join the legendary Daniel Starbuck, an American sea captain from Biddiford. Years later he did return to Hobart with a wife and family after several years on the high seas. He had married at Port Jackson and ended life as a fisherman.

27 *OBSP*, VI Sessions, 17 Apr. 1800; HO 26/7; *S.G.*, 28 Aug., 11 Dec. 1808.

28 Charles Smith would have left her to sail in the *Perseverance*, taking at least two more trips to the Feejees, as Fiji was then known.

29 Trial of Barwise unavailable; Hulk lists, HO 9; Woodriff, C 269, ML. For Williams see *OBSP*, IV Sessions, 2 June 1802; HO 26/8. See also *S.G.*, 18 Sept. 1808.

30 *S.G.*, 6 Aug. 1809. See also William Mariner's account of his adventures when stranded in Tonga. He met up with the seaman Nicholas Blake at Ha'paii. *Tonga Islands: William Mariner's Account*, Vava'u Press, Neiafu, 1981. (Originally published London, 1817.)

31 *S.G.*, loc. cit.

32 Ibid., 18 May 1811.

33 For Davis see *OBSP*, V Sessions, 2 June 1802; HO 26/8; for Kennedy, Bristol fiats, Bristol G.D., 1802; *S.G.*, 11, 18 Sept. 1808, 19 March, 9 Apr. 1809, 19, 25 Aug. 1810, 16 March 1812.

34 Margaret Steven, *Merchant Campbell 1769–1846*, Melbourne, 1965, p. 200, wrote that the wreck of the *Fox* had not been traced.

35 *OBSP*, I Sessions, Dec. 1800; HO 26/6 and HO 26/7. This was the same William Jones who was later to sail with James Kelly. See Chapter 34. *S.G.*, 9, 26 Nov. 1809. The *Active* is not to be confused with a colonial brig, of the same name, in which several *Calcutta* men later sailed.

36 *S.G.*, 24 July, 23 Dec. 1813.

37 Ibid., 24 July 1813.

38 Ibid., 23 Dec. 1813.

39 Ibid., 4, 11 Jan., 9 May 1812.

40 Ibid., 5 Jan. 1811.

41 Ibid., 2 March, 5 Oct. 1811.

42 Ibid., 26 Feb., 5 March 1814.

43 This was a recurring theme during the year when Marsden threw his energies into opening up communications with the Maoris as later recollected in his *Observations on the Introduction of the Gospel into the South Sea Islands*; see also *Proceedings of the Church Missionary Society*, London, 1808–09, app.; and Eric Ramsden, *Marsden and the Missions: Prelude to Waitangi*, Sydney, 1936.

44 *S.G.*, 10, 31 March, 21, 28 Apr., 25 Aug. 1810.

45 Ibid., 4 March 1814, 8 Oct. 1814.

46 Gospel according to St Luke, ch. 11; See also C. M. H. Clark, *A History of Australia*, vol. I, Melbourne, 1962, pp. 286–87.

47 Marsden's report on his visit to New Zealand is in *HRA* I, viii, pp. 576–82. During their visit they learned something of the fate of the brig *Venus*, one of the Campbell fleet taken by pirates at Port Dalrymple in 1806. See Chapter 24.

48 *S.G.*, 2 Nov. 1815, 5 Oct. 1816.

49 Ibid., 30 Dec. 1815, 7, 19 Oct. 1816.

50 Ibid., 23, 30 Nov. 1816.

51 Ibid., 3 June 1815, 12 Apr. 1817. William Jones had served Capt. William in *The Brothers* when he joined the *Trial* in New Zealand at the time Maoris occupied the decks of the *Trial*, killing several of the crew.

52 For Gray see HO 26/6; for Arnott see *OBSP*, VI Sessions, July 1800; HO 26/6 and HO 26/7; *S.G.*, 19 Nov. 1809; Kelly papers including log books, Crowther Collection, SLT.

53 *S.G.*, 3 June 1815; Return of shipping and cargoes, in *HRA* I, viii, p. 591. Arnott joined the *Rosetta* brig,

later known as the *Prince Leopold*, and sailed in her when she chased the *Trial*, seized by Portuguese pirates. *S.G.*, 30 Jan. 1817. Soon afterwards Arnott, tired of the sea, petitioned Gov. Sorell on the strength of his service during the *Prince Leopold* chase for a town allotment on which to erect a house. He became a chairmaker. Memorial 24 Aug. 1822, LSD 1/73/89, TSA.

54 Macquarie himself had been well aware of the effects of trading with the islander communities and in 1814 proclaimed regulations to be observed by masters and crews of all vessels engaged in trading with the Pacific Islands, hoping that the 'Rapacity and Cruelty of our sailors will be in some Degree at least restrained, and that the Intercourses of Trade with those Islands will be rendered more secure than at present'. Macquarie to Bathurst 17 Jan. 1814, in *HRA* I, viii, p. 96. See also *HRA* I, viii, pp. 96–118 for proclamation and depositions regarding the capture of the *Daphne*; deposition of John Jones, Add. MSS 185, DL.

CHAPTER 36 CONVICTS UNBOUND

1 At least 113 legal marriages took place either in England or the colony. There were numerous *de facto* relationships, including those with Aboriginal women, and second and third marriages. There were at least 77 *Calcutta* men still alive in V.D.L. in 1824 and eleven others known to be living elsewhere.

2 *H.T.G.*, 16 July 1824.

3 Ibid., 30 Nov. 1822.

4 Ibid.

5 Ibid.

6 Ibid.

7 Knopwood, Diaries, 31 Dec. 1825–21 Jan. 1826, ML.

8 J. B. Hirst, *Convict Society and its Enemies*, Sydney, 1983, traces the transformation of N.S.W. into a free society and discusses the differences between Australia's beginnings and that of a slave society. Robert Hughes, op. cit., takes an opposing view and argues that the transportation system was a model for the twentieth century Gulag. Russel Ward, *The Australian Legend*, Melbourne, 1958, had previously discussed the 'disproportionately strong influence of a convict society on working class attitudes and the nascent Australian ethos'.

9 *ADB* entries, vols I, II.

10 *H.T.G.*, 22 June 1822.

11 Sorell to Bigge enclosing distribution of pews in St David's, Sept. 1820, in *HRA* III, iii, p. 681.

12 *HRA* III, iv, pp. 532 ff.

13 Mabel Hookey, *The Chaplain*, Hobart, 1970, included a chapter 'Old Graves and a King's Secret' in which she speculated that the Desaillys, brought to V.D.L. in a chartered vessel and possessed of a large and secret pension, were derived from this royal alliance. Her argument is convincing but not proven.

14 Nor could Knopwood accept Morrisby's treatment of his wife: 'He behaved very ill to my poor dear girl. I took her part. His conduct is too bad', Knopwood, Diaries, 17 June 1829, ML. In Oct. 1830 she died in childbirth. It was her daughter Elizabeth Sarah who

erected the monument to Knopwood in the Rokeby churchyard.

15 The most interesting of the extant letters is the one which Mabel Hookey published in *Bobby Knopwood and his Times*, op. cit., written in 1830 from England by P. H. Stannard recalling events of Knopwood's youth.

16 Knopwood, Diaries, 22 Aug. 1823, ML.

17 Ibid., 28 Sept. 1826.

18 *Colonial Times*, 17 Feb. 1826.

19 Ibid., 19 May 1826.

20 *ADB*, vol. I, James Cox. Cox married Eliza Eddington, the natural daughter of David Collins and their home near Evandale is now one of the Tasmanian National Trust's finest acquisitions.

21 *Colonial Times*, 29 Sept. 1831, 27 Aug. 1830.

22 Knopwood did not attend but he noted the day — 15 March 1832 — in his Diaries, ML.

23 Knopwood hunted regularly with Gregson and his cronies throughout 1836 and 1837.

24 As a matter of interest, in later years the author of the John Peel verses, John Woodcock Graves, came to Hobart and was buried at St David's in 1886.

25 Knopwood, Diaries, 30 Oct. 1815, 24 May 1828, ML.

26 Later the Theatre Royal. See Lady Franklin's journal, Royal Soc. of Tasmania Collection, Uni. of Tas.

27 Knopwood, Diaries, 24 Feb. 1831, ML.

28 Her children Henry Morrisby and Elizabeth (later married to John Davidson) were his heirs. Knopwood's sister had left him a legacy at the end of his life. Had the Morrisby children not lived the Chases would have been his heirs.

29 See J. B. Walker, *Prelude to Federation 1884–98*, ed. Peter Benson Walker, Hobart, 1976.

CHAPTER 37 A CONVICT IN THE CUPBOARD

1 Bacon, op. cit., p. 95.

2 'Partly because it was misunderstood at home, partly because it is hopeless to rely overly on deterrence to get rid of crime.' See Shaw, *Convicts and the Colonies*, op. cit., pp. 358–60.

3 Robson, *The Convict Settlers*, op. cit., pp. 157–58. By examining the crimes of individuals and something of their lives, Robson, together with Levi and Bergman on the Jews, Rudé on the protesters, Robinson on the children of convicts and Adam-Smith on the Young Irelanders, has extended the study of the system, replacing statistics with persons.

4 Taylor and Crute.

5 Portia Robinson, *The Hatch and Brood of Time*, Melbourne, vol. I, 1985.

6 Dinham, Fawkner, Raphael and Rotchfort were at Newcastle; Avery, Bagley, Gwynn and Lush at Macquarie Harbour; and Richards served a term at Moreton Bay.

7 From his memorial at Rokeby.

8 The settlement on the Yarra in August 1835, named Melbourne when Gov. Richard Bourke arrived in February 1837, was still only a village. In the year of Knopwood's death a return of population at Port Phillip showed 3511 persons lived at Port Phillip. The

census of 1851 showed there were 39 000 persons in Melbourne alone and within the next ten years the population increased by a further 100 000. Today it is approaching 3 000 000.

9 In 1890 Henry Gyles Turner was expressing the feelings then current and, indeed, of those until recent times when he wrote 'Sorrento — Then and Now, 1803, 1890' including the verses:

> Some left their bones to bleach upon the strand,
> Some fled the lash to die in hunger's faint;
> But all, thank God, passed to another land,
> And saved this generation from their taint.
>
> . . .
>
> Ah, well for us those times we never knew,
> And well for all who love the happier lot
> No record stands of all that ghastly crew,
> To mark how once their crimes deformed this spot.

10 Refer to their genealogies in Alexander Henderson, *Early Pioneer Families of Victoria and Riverina*, Melbourne, 1936, and *Australian Families: a Genealogical and Biographical Record*, Melbourne, 1941.

11 Marjorie Butler, *Convict by Choice*, Melbourne, 1974, and other writings. Valerie Austin, 'The Austin Family in Australia', in *V.H.M.* XXXVI, iii, Aug. 1965, appears to be an accurate genealogical reference.

12 Richard Lord has compiled *The History of the James Lord Family (c. 1757–1824) in Tasmania*, (privately circulated) Hobart, 1966.

13 The present writer has found Fawkner's recollections relating to the *Calcutta* convicts and other early settlers and officials more reliable than one might have believed. His obsession with the part he played in the foundation of Melbourne has clouded the historical contribution his recollections have made to a period in which records are few.

14 As far as one can ascertain to date, John Batman appeared before magistrates in Sydney in February 1821 relating to the support of his alleged unborn child by a young orphan girl, Elizabeth Richardson. See Barry Bridges, 'John Batman: A note on his migration to Van Diemen's Land', in *THRAPP* XIII, ii, June 1976; see also letter from John Hart to A. W. H. Humphrey 2 Feb. 1822 from Swanport referring to John Batman,

one of his assigned servants who had withdrawn himself from his 'protectition' (*sic*) and 'returned stating that it was his intention to present to Hobart Town to take a complaint against Henry Lee, my overseer. There has been some affray between them . . . I have also to state that I have brought the prisoner before you long since for his misconduct . . . I shall be able to await upon you in the course of a short time when the hearing shall come to trial', Police Dept. records, Old Tasmanian Papers, ML. He added he had failed to dissuade Batman from leaving until he could find someone to whom he might deliver him up, so had provided him with provisions for five days in case he might be compelled to commit deprivations. The outcome is history. Somehow he arrived at Ben Lomond and was received as a free man and received a land grant, but his earlier career and how it had been expunged from the records remains a mystery.

15 Daniel Deniehy ridiculed the clause in William Wentworth's Constitution Bill, 1853, proposing a colonial nobility.

16 It is just possible that a child of two might have had a hazy memory of such a traumatic experience. The Armytages had lived at Ingleby, Winchelsea, from 1847, acquiring the Hermitage property in 1851 but not building the present house (later the Geelong Church of England Girls' Grammar School) on the site until c. 1860.

17 William Strutt depicted the scene in several sketches. See *Victoria the Golden*, ed. Marjorie Tipping, Melbourne, 1980, p. 32.

18 This was the same year that gold was discovered in Victoria. The face of the whole nation rapidly changed with the influx of free settlers, not only from the British Isles but from Europe and America. Terra Australis, New Holland, or Botany Bay, whatever the name, was well on the way to becoming a new and free society as transportation ceased. The newcomers and their offspring soon became the dominant influence and in the main only those of convict origin who had become well-established on the land and had their representatives elected to the colonial (and later State) legislative councils retained some influence for the next hundred odd years.

BIOGRAPHIES

*I*HAVE RECORDED THE basic details of those who sailed as convicts in H.M.S. *Calcutta* from original documents. Considerations of space have made it impossible to provide notes to the biographies supporting every statement but the extensive bibliography and notes to the main text should guide the curious reader to verification of facts where necessary. Clerical errors led to deviations in spellings and sometimes wrong entries. I have made the decision to use spellings occurring most frequently, placing the most commonly used name first. Except for Joseph Myers, all appeared on the indents of convict ships held in the papers of the Colonial Secretary, Archive Office of N.S.W. (4/4004), and in Capt. Woodriff's list of those received from the hulks in his memo book (ML C269). Twenty-five of these were not entered on the Home Office Convict Transportation register held in the Public Record Office, London (HO 11/1) but twenty were added by an unknown hand to a corresponding list now in the N.S.W. archives. These included the seven Gibraltar mutineers who came unexpectedly on board at the last minute as well as nine from Somerset and Stafford. Apart from those who died during the voyage, nine were missing from the Commissariat return of convicts victualled from 17 October 1803. The name of Joseph Myers appeared only on this list. He was victualled as a prisoner at Port Phillip as well as at Hobart Town. Later records indicate that he arrived in the *Calcutta* after a conviction in March 1802 in Shropshire.

Two hundred and eighty *Calcutta* men (including the names of some who died at Port Phillip) appeared on the Comprehensive Register of Convicts, 1804–53, held in the Tasmanian State Archives Office (CON 22). I have omitted some whose names crept into these and other records as *Calcutta* convicts, unfortunately listed as such in later histories. For instance, no William Russell came in the *Calcutta*, as stated in the Hobart muster 1811, but James Russell, a private in the marines, did and was probably the William Russell (a free man) referred to in Knopwood's diary (cited in Mary Nicholls (ed.), *The Diary of the Reverend Robert Knopwood, 1803–1838*, Hobart, 1977, pp. 66, 67 and 132. Another William Russell was sentenced at Derby in May 1802. He came in 1806 from Port Dalrymple to serve Lieut. Johnson but was a man of unruly character who became a bushranger (*HRA* III, i, pp. 359, 564 and Knopwood (cited in Nicholls, pp. 138, 141–2, 150–1)). Russell therefore could not have been the same man as William Bannister (Derby 1802). As the latter's name faded from all other records, it is likely that he was the person whom Humphries reported had been swept off the rocks.

One *Calcutta* convict called William Marsh, who died in Hobart in 1848 by that name, has sometimes been confused with William Bell also tried at Cambridge in 1802. The latter had a child of eight at the time of the 1811 muster and came to Hobart from Norfolk Island. Two other Norfolk Islanders appearing on Hobart musters as *Calcutta* men were Thomas Crowder and William Foyle, but both were First Fleeters; Crowder arrived in the *Alexander*, and Foyle in the *Charlotte*. The name William Sherrard or Shebburd also appeared on the Hobart musters as having arrived in the *Calcutta*, as did John Stephens (CON 22). But they too came free from Norfolk Island. The 1811 muster recorded that Edward Miller, who was a settler and not a convict, sailed in the *Calcutta* and not in the *Ocean*. Such discrepancies prove that after a time there was little discrimination between many of those who had arrived free and had become free. Clerks perhaps guessed at both length of service, time and ship of arrival, spelling of names and, even more frequently, ages.

Actually few name changes are known to have occurred. One of the Thomas Williamses became Charles Williams. Archibald Campbell was also known as James Campbell and William Leach as John Leach. Henry Lazarus became Henry Ellis and David Belton became William Selsby when they returned to London and were re-transported.

Details of the trials, which often included age, parish of birth, home, occupation and family information, have been taken mostly from court records, gaol calendars, and English newspapers. Names of those on the hulks at Woolwich listed occupations (CO 201/28). I have also drawn information from Colonial Secretary's correspondence, Land Department records, early newspapers and other publications, shipping logs and registers, memorials, pardons, musters, church registers, court records, inquests and some family records held among descendants. Knopwood's diaries and Fawkner's manuscripts are among valuable (although not always reliable) sources as well as the published historical records. Numerous letters from individuals and miscellaneous reports which survive have been indicated where relevant.

There are discrepancies in ages in the different records. Although there is evidence that some felons may have given reduced ages at their trials in the hope of a lighter sentence, this author has taken the age at trial to be the most accurate because it was given by the offender himself under oath. It is from this age that the date of birth was derived when no other information was forthcoming. Records show that ages at the time of marriage were often underestimated by those taking a young wife, while ages at death were sometimes overestimated by family or officials. In the earlier registers of burials the age given at the trial was used to estimate the age at the time of death. Invariably, the death was documented days after the event. In many cases there is a difference of only a year or two, but in others the variation is greater.

It seems accurate that 308 convicts embarked aboard the *Calcutta* and eight died during the voyage. Three hundred arrived at Port Phillip. Twenty-one convicts died there, including six who escaped. One escapee survived there for the next thirty-two years. But most died from scurvy or drowned. According to the Commissariat return only 268 convicts arrived in Hobart. Some went on to Port Jackson then and at later dates. By 1808 many gained their freedom and left the colony. Twenty-six who had suffered from scurvy or other weaknesses had passed on. The 1811 musters show that 99 no longer remained in southern V.D.L. or had failed to report for the muster. By 1820 seven were living in the Port Dalrymple area. At least four, apart from those in confinement, were living in Sydney. Some who had been at sea re-appeared in later musters or were on the 1828 census.

• • •

ALEXANDER, JAMES [c.1775–1804]
Weaver, aged 27. Literate.
Tried at the Spring Assizes of the Palatinate of Lancaster (Lancaster G.D.) 20 March 1802, for forging bills. Sentenced by Justice Sir Giles Rooke to transportation for fourteen years. Gaoled at Lancaster Castle, transferred to the hulks at Langston.
Died of scurvy, Hobart Town, 13 September 1804, aged 29.

ALLENDER, URIAS [c. 1769–1842]
(Uriah Allendar)
Sailor, aged 33. Claimed to have served for eighteen years in the Royal Navy, wounded twice in battle, served in H.M.S. Formidable *and with Lord Rodney.*
Tried at Kent Summer Assizes (Maidstone G. D.) 4 August 1802 for receiving and concealing slop clothing in his dwelling house, including one blue greatcoat and one blue cloth waistcoat (£2 5s 0d) which David Wakefield (*q.v.*) had stolen from John Ledwich from his ship the *Richard and Eliza* lying in the River Medway within the port of Rochester. (He had previously been committed for trial at the Canterbury S. of P.) Sentenced by Baron Hotham to transportation for fourteen years. Gaoled at Canterbury and transferred to the *Prudentia* hulk at Woolwich.

Allender served as a sailor during the voyage out, without irons. He was among those who volunteered to accompany William Collins to Port Jackson taking despatches from Port Phillip. He received a conditional pardon for his

good conduct in January 1806. He attended the Hobart musters in 1818, 1819 and 1823.

He was in Sydney in 1810 as witness in a trial and the following year joined the crew of the brig *Concord* on a sealing voyage to Macquarie I.

He received a 30-acre land grant from Gov. Macquarie at Clarence Plains near Kangaroo Point, on which by 1819 he had sown some wheat and potatoes and ran eight male and eight female cattle, 30 male sheep and 100 ewes. He employed one government servant and three free men. He provided wheat and meat for the Commissariat.

He received a ferry licence in 1816 and for many years ran a service between Hobart and Kangaroo Point. His ferries were involved in several accidents, including a bad one when his ferry capsized in 1819 and drowned three persons. He also took court action on several occasions and appears to have been a happy-go-lucky character, although quarrelsome when drunk. He subscribed to the Auxiliary Bible Society.

Allender married Elizabeth Earley in Hobart, 25 September 1815. She was the natural daughter, born on Norfolk I., of Rachel Earley, who had been transported in 1787 after being convicted for theft at Reading. She had sailed in the *Friendship* with the First Fleet, and Pte Samuel Marsden of the N.S.W. Corps was the father of her children. Another daughter, Catherine, married Charles Clark (*q.v.*) and a third daughter, Ann, married Henry Robinson (*q.v.*). The Allenders had at least nine children, six sons and three daughters, several of whom died in infancy.
Died at Kangaroo Point, buried at St Matthew's, Clarence Plains, 25 April 1842. His widow married John Evans in 1853, St Mark's, Bellerive.

Surnames of descendants have included: Atkins; Bacon; Bloomfield; Cecil; Cowburn; Challenger; Chandler; Folder; Fraser; Graham; Henwood; Hilber; Hitchins; Hudson; Jones; Kilpin; Lonergan; May; Moles; Pearsall; Pearson; Schoe; Thomas; Treganowan.

ANCHOR, DANIEL [c. 1770–1849]
(Ankers)
Butcher, aged 32, married to Frances —. Literate.
Tried at Kent Summer Assizes (Maidstone G.D.) 4 August 1802 together with a John Jones for uttering a forged promissory note (£1) with intent to defraud the Governor and Company of the Bank of England. Sentenced by Baron Hotham to transportation for life. Gaoled at Maidstone and transferred to the *Prudentia* hulk at Woolwich.

Frances (Fanny) accompanied her husband in the *Calcutta*. He was employed as a butcher and allowed on deck without irons, while she shared the gunroom with Mrs Power and the woman then known as Mrs Whitehead. Mrs Anchor soon became the mistress of the deputy commissary-general, Leonard Fosbrook. While at Port Phillip, Anchor attempted to escape but was caught and placed under guard.

Anchor attended the Hobart musters in 1811, 1820, 1823 and 1825. He had numerous small convictions in the colony.

By August 1804 his wife had some stock — a sow and six fowls, Anchor received considerable benefits through her association with Fosbrook. The latter used her as an accomplice in some of his fraudulent dealings for which he had to stand trial in Sydney in 1813. She appeared as a witness while Anchor himself had acted as a receiver of goods from the stores. Gov. Macquarie withheld his expected conditional pardon in January 1813, informing Administrator Geils that he was unworthy of great indulgence. Anchor had been in trouble a few weeks previously for 'enticing away' the wife of John Coward (*q.v.*) née Elizabeth Harkinstone. In 1813 he paid £11 4s 0d for a house in Collins St. which later had to be removed when the streets were re-arranged.

At the time of Gov. Bligh's arrival in Hobart, Anchor was sharing a cottage with James Belbin and his family. His wife was still living with Fosbrook who in 1811 purchased a good house from Susannah Grove after the death of her husband James (*q.v.*).

He claimed 100 acres of land which Gov. Davey had granted R. Gavin in 1815. That year he was a key witness in the case against Denis McCarty in which a cow was killed. Anchor claimed that the cow was his and that he had killed it for the muster of troops.

Fanny Anchor returned to England with Fosbrook in September 1814 in the *Seringapatam*. She appears to have continued living with him and in 1816 they were in Vale Place, Hammersmith, Middlesex.

Anchor bought several ponies from the Geils estate. There is no record that he re-married but he appears to have had a son, David, born about 1815 and perhaps the child of Elizabeth Coward. In 1827 David Anchor (Ankers) was living with his parents in Melville St., who were Protestant, both living, and of good character.

Anchor ultimately received a conditional pardon in 1829 and an absolute pardon in 1838.

Buried 29 September 1849, Hobart, aged 80.

The only known descendant was his son.

ANDREWS, JOHN [c. 1779–1804]
?, aged 22.
Tried at Southampton Spring Assizes (Winchester G.D.) 2 March 1801 for stealing wearing apparel from Edward White of Corhampton. Sentenced to transportation for seven years. Gaoled at Winchester Gaol, then transferred to the hulks at Langston.

Buried 16 July 1804, Hobart, aged 41 (?).

APPLETON, WILLIAM [1793 – ?]
Child, aged 9, of Westminster, where he lived with his father; 4'4", sallow complexion.
Tried at Middlesex V Sessions (Middlesex G.D.) 2 June 1802, for stealing an apron and seven shillings from Samuel Smith, milkman. Sentenced by Mr Justice Conant to transportation for seven years. Appleton had previously (in March 1802) been declared not guilty of stealing a ribbon. Gaoled at Newgate and transferred to the *Stanislaus* hulk at Woolwich.

During the voyage out he was allowed to go without irons. In Hobart he lived with Sgt Thorne and his family. Knopwood referred to him in 1806 as 'the boy Appleby'.

After serving his sentence he probably returned to England c. 1808–9.

ARMSTRONG, ROBERT, alias JOHN ARMSTRONG [c. 1772–1851]
Baker, aged 30, born Whitechapel; 5'7", dark complexion.
Tried at Middlesex V Sessions (London G.D.) 13 January 1802 for stealing a box (8d), 60 breeches balls (30s 0d) and 12 rubbers (6s 0d) from William Bellingham, keeper of the Blue Boar Inn, Aldgate. Sentence pronounced by the Recorder to transportation for seven years. Gaoled at Poultry and transferred to the *Prudentia* hulk at Woolwich.

Armstrong attended the Hobart musters in 1811 and 1818 as a free person. He received a grant of 30 acres from Gov. Brisbane in June 1823 in the district of York, adjacent to Michael Lawler's (*q.v.*) farm. He might have been the husband of Sarah Armstrong who died, 25 July 1824, aged 34. He appears to have received a further small land grant in March 1850 of 2 roods and 1 perch.

Fell from a ladder while painting the house of William Sims in Argyle St., Hobart, while greatly intoxicated and fractured his spine. Employed by Thomas Harbottle, a painter and glazier in Elizabeth St. Died at H.M. General Hospital. An inquest held 2 October 1851, found that death was accidental.

ARNOTT, THOMAS [c. 1776–1847]
(Arnet)
Watchmaker, aged 24, of London; 5'6", dark complexion, brown hair, dark eyes.
Tried at Middlesex VI Sessions (Middlesex G.D.) 9 July 1800 for stealing a gown (5s 0d), three handkerchiefs (4s 0d) and one pair of shoes (1s 0d) from the bedroom of Sarah Welsh, spinster, who said she thought he was having fun. Although Arnott was acquitted by Mr Justice Conant (and he was the only person of that name brought before the Old Bailey over a period of years) he was re-tried a week later at Middlesex S. of P. and sentenced to transportation for seven years for petty larceny. Gaoled at Newgate and transferred to the hulks at Langston.

When Arnott was free by servitude he left for Port Jackson. In December 1809 he sailed in the colonial schooner *Halcyon* to Otaheite for pork. The following March he joined the schooner *Unity* on a sealing voyage to the Bay of Islands, returning with 2 000 skins. He was a crew member of several ships over a period of years, including the brig *Rosetta*, built for inter-colonial trade and re-named the *Prince Leopold* in 1818 when acquired by Gov. Macquarie for government service. Among other ships in which he served were *The Brothers* (1813), *Governor Bligh* and *Archduke Charles* (1814), the schooner *Bligh* (1815), the sloop *Martha* (1817).

By November 1817 he had become storekeeper to Charles Williams and lived in a hut at Thomas Triffitt's property in the Macquarie district. Arnott, according to Knopwood, had threatened to kill Michael Howe. Arnott himself claimed in a memorial of 24 August 1822 to have been a member of a boat crew in search of a launch from the *Prince Leopold*. The implication is that pirates had seized the vessel and had intended to take Michael Howe along the coast.

Arnott requested a town allotment but instead of a free grant he ultimately purchased 80 acres granted originally to Richard Brown (*q.v.*) in Coal River Road near Kangaroo Point. This took place about 1824 and for several years there was a dispute between Arnott and a William Short who had occupied the land and house. It was not until January 1839 that Arnott received acknowledgement of his legal claim for all the land he had applied for. When he settled there he became a chairmaker.

Buried 5 January 1847, St Matthews, Clarence Plains, aged 65.

ASHTON, GEORGE [c. 1768 – after 1841]
Labourer, aged 33, Leyland, Lancaster. Literate?
Tried at the Summer Assizes of the Palatinate of Lancaster (Lancaster G.D.) 15 August 1801 together with Isaac Slater and Philip Porter (*q.v.*) for stealing 23 pieces of calico (£23) and 23 pieces of cotton (£23) from the drying house of John, George, William, Edward and Ralph Clayton at Leyland. Sentenced to death. Reprieved by Lord Chief Justice Alvanley and Justice Sir Alan Chambre with Porter and both sentenced to transportation for fourteen years. Slater hanged. There were two other charges concerning the theft of similar goods valued at £25, stolen from Jeremiah Gregory, and from Ellis Hunt. Gaoled in the Castle at Lancaster and later transferred to the hulks at Langston.

Ashton attended the Hobart musters in 1811, 1818, 1819 and 1823. Soon after arrival he was appointed a constable and was overseer of bricklayers until 1816 when he was dismissed for neglect of duty. The following year he was appointed a district constable at Green Ponds where he received a 60-acre land grant in addition to a 30-acre grant already held at Herdsman's Cove. He purchased a further 2 000 acres at Green Ponds in 1828 where he was one of the most successful farmers. He named his property Glenfern.

By 1819 he had married Ann (?). Among their children were Hugh, Louisa (died in 1825 aged seven weeks) and Ellen who married Robert Jones at Oatlands in 1848. Mrs Ashton, Hugh and Ellen visited England and returned in the *Adventure* in 1833.

For several years Ashton held a public pound at Green Ponds, his house acted as a post office and in the absence of a lockup he claimed to have housed hundreds of prisoners and their escorts overnight. As a constable his life was frequently endangered during bushranging days when he took part in hunting down Howe, Brady, Dunn and others. He held an excellent character and among other attributes he indicated a tolerant attitude towards Peter Harley, a native from Otaheite, when he supported his application for a land grant in 1828 at Green Ponds. He became a special constable and pound keeper at Brighton in 1832 but two years later was living in Hobart, having transferred management of the pound to a nephew. He appears to have been living at Brighton by 1839 and in August 1841 he advertised (*H.T.G.*) that interest on his property was in arrears.

Date and place of death have not been traced.

Surnames of descendants have included: Jones.

ASPDEN, JOSEPH, alias AUSTIN [c. 1775 – ?]
(Asten, Ashton, Apsden)
?, aged 27.
Tried at the Spring Assizes of the County Palatinate of Lancaster (Salford G.D.) 20 March 1802 for having stolen cotton. Sentenced by Lord Kenyon and Justice Sir Giles Rooke to transportation for seven years. Gaoled in the county gaol and transferred to hulks at Langston.

Aspden attended the Hobart musters in 1811 and 1819.
There appears to be no other record of his activities in the colony.

ATKINSON, WILLIAM [c. 1777 – ?]
Servant to a gentleman, aged 24, born Bath; 5'6", dark complexion, brown hair, grey eyes.
Tried at Middlesex IV Sessions (Middlesex G.D.) 15 April 1801 for stealing a pocket-book (1s 6d) from Capt. John Johnstone containing banknotes, lottery tickets and his regimental account. Sentenced by the Chief Baron to transportation for seven years. Gaoled at Newgate and transferred to the *Prudentia* hulk at Woolwich.

Atkinson had considerable freedom soon after his arrival in Hobart. He accompanied Harris and Knopwood during their 14-day exploration of Storm Bay, Bruny I. and the Huon in November 1804. William Collins employed him as a crew member of the *Sophia* in November 1805. The *Sophia* was engaged in whaling activities in Bass Strait, reaching Sydney with 24 tons of oil. Atkinson departed in the *William Pitt* which was sailing to London via Canton but one presumes he disembarked when it called at Port Dalrymple. He married Mary Clark, 13 April 1807, Hobart.

Atkinson's name did not appear on the muster rolls or among records of those who joined the crews of other ships, although a Mary Atkinson (his wife?) attended the muster in 1811 at Port Dalrymple.

His experience as a seaman would have enabled him to join a ship to leave the colony.

ATTENBOROUGH, JOHN [c. 1787 – ?]
(Attenborrow)
?, aged 15.
Tried at Nottingham Spring Assizes (Nottingham G.D.) for picking the pocket of John Wilcockson, druggist, 11 March 1802 and stealing several bank notes from a red leather pocket book during the funeral ceremony of the late Alderman Worthington in St Peter's churchyard. Sentenced to death by the Lord Chief Baron. Reprieved by Rt Hon. Sir Archibald Macdonald, Hon. Sir John Graham and John Balguy Esq. and sentenced to transportation for life. His colleague Thomas Soar, aged twelve, was reprieved and sent to the Philanthropic Society in London to be trained against vice. Gaoled at Nottingham and transferred to the hulks at Langston.

During the voyage out Attenborough became a messenger to Lieut. Dower and was allowed to go without irons.

After his arrival in V.D.L., there appears to be no further record of his life in the colony.

It is likely that because of his youth and apparent good behaviour he received an unrecorded pardon and returned to England.

AUSTIN, JAMES [c. 1778–1832]
Farm Labourer, aged 24. Born Church Thatch Farm, Baltonsborough, Somersetshire, second son of John Austin and his wife Sarah (née Higgens).
Tried at Somerset S. of P. (Wells) 13 January 1802 together with his cousin John Earle (*q.v.*) on two charges, for

using force and arms to steal 100 lb of honey (30s 0d) and six straw bee hives (3s 0d) from his uncle, Peter Higgens, at Hornblotten and also for stealing 100 lb of honey (30s 0d) and five straw bee hives (2s 6d) from Edward Powell at West Lydford. Found guilty on both charges and sentenced to transportation for seven years. Gaoled at Wells prison and transferred to the hulks at Langston.

Austin attended the Hobart musters in 1811, 1818, 1819 and 1823. He received land grants of 50 and 30 acres at Glenorchy from Gov. Macquarie and had a grazing licence on the west side of the Doe River run beyond New Norfolk. By 1819 he had large quantities of wheat and other crops sown, and ran 15 male horned and 15 female cattle, a horse, 350 male sheep and 350 ewes. He employed five government servants and three free men. He supplied large amounts of meat and wheat to the Commissariat (3 000 lb in three months in 1822).

In August 1804 George Harris wrote that Austin was his valet and cook. Austin was already living in a small stone cottage which he called Baltonsborough Place soon after he was free. Here Knopwood had to seek shelter overnight in 1814. Austin was in partnership with his cousin Earle in several ventures.

In 1818 they had a licence to run a ferry between Baltonsborough (Austin's ferry) and the Old Beach (Compton) and in 1819 a licence for the Barley Mow at the Black Snake. When Gov. Macquarie stayed there in 1821 he renamed the inn Roseneath. They also had the Northampton Arms at Compton but dissolved their partnership by mutual consent in 1822. Austin was noted as a brewer of porter. During the twenties he leased the Roseneath ferry, which he retained in his name, for several years. His nephews Solomon and Josiah, who arrived from Somerset in 1825, then took over the lease. Other nephews followed to enjoy the good fortune that their uncle had struck and received huge grants of land. James himself owned 1 480 acres by grant and had bought a further 1 470 acres by 1831. He owned two two-storey stone houses, which with outhouses were then valued at £2500.

He tried to buy the *Colonial Times* from Andrew Bent in 1827 but he was refused a licence to publish. He was illiterate and it was believed that he could easily become the tool of Bent who had been imprisoned for libel.

Austin subscribed to the Auxiliary Bible Society and the New Town Church. In his latter years Hannah, widow of Richard Garrett (*q.v.*) who had successfully managed her own stock and brought up two sons, came to live at Roseneath about 1828, probably more as a companion than a housekeeper. She was then about 60 years old. The fine old house was among the victims of the 1967 bush fires.

Died at Austin's Ferry, 28 December 1831, after a short but severe illness. Buried 2 January 1832, St David's. The inscribed tombstone states that he was aged 55 and that his cousin Earle was later buried in the same grave.

In a will dated 11 December 1828 he left a life interest in his estate to Hannah Garrett and after her death the estate would revert to his nephews Josiah and Solomon Austin. He appointed Andrew Bent as executor. Hannah shrewdly appointed her own attorney but soon afterwards a convict constable George Madden, aged 30, who already had a wife in England, married Hannah.

Many other Austins migrated to V.D.L. and later the Western District of Victoria, ultimately benefiting from the success and wealth of James Austin.

Among his nephews' descendants, some have been members of parliament and others notable for their public service and philanthropy. The Austin hospital in Melbourne bears the family name. Surnames of descendants have included: Bailey; Binnie; Biscoe; Black; Blomfield; Body; Bowie; Bullied; Bullivant; Butler; Cameron; Caverhill; Clack; Collins; Cook; Cortis; Cotton; Cumming; Cusack; Danvers; Darling; Darnton; Davis; Dawborn; Dickson; Dredge; Dunstan; Embling; Fairbairn; Fieldhouse; Forbes; Fraser; Gatehouse; Gillespie; Gordon; Grannum; Gray; Griffiths; Halliday; Ham; Henty; Herring; Higgins; James; Johansen; Kater; Landale; Lang; Lascelles; Lees; Lewes; Lewis; Light; Lyle; Mack; Mackenzie; Mackinnon; Maidment; Mason; McKay; Millar; Millear; Morris; Orolana; Osborne; Palmer; Pearce; Pinton; Philip; Pidgeon; Plaistow; Pocock; Porch; Richardson; Robertson; Robinson; Rowan; Rowe; Rusden; Scarborough; Shands; Smith; Storey; Symes; Turner; Umphelby; Wales; Wasey; Watson; West.

A biography of James Austin appears in the *Australian Dictionary of Biography*, vol I.

AVERY, JOHN [c. 1778–1851]
(Avory, Every)
?, aged 24, born Portsmouth. Literate.
Tried with John Lock at Southampton Assizes (Winchester) 27 July 1802 for stealing a grey mare at Stoneham from William Mansbridge. Sentenced to death. Reprieved by Mr Justice Rooke and Baron Graham and sentenced to transportation for life. Gaoled in the county gaol and transferred to the *Captivity* at Portsmouth.

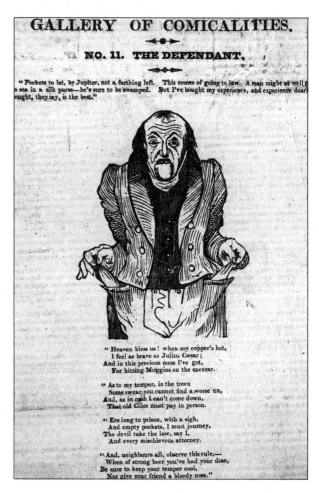

He attended the Hobart musters in 1811, 1818, 1819 and 1823.

Avery was among the prisoners whom Knopwood examined in May 1805 for attempting to escape to New Zealand in a whale boat. There was insufficient evidence to convict the men.

Avery became an overseer in April 1805 and the following month received a conditional remission.

For some unknown reason he was in Sydney in 1813.

By 1819 Avery received a 30-acre land grant at Melvill from Gov. Macquarie and purchased a further 55 acres at Herdsman's Cove on which he grew wheat and other crops and had four male cattle.

On 9 January 1815, in Hobart, he married Margaret Dann, a convict, aged 29, who had arrived in the *Catherine* the previous year from Cork and London. By 1824 they had had six children, including four sons and a daughter who had died at three months. His wife was again pregnant.

He made arrangements to educate his sons. Unexpectedly his whole life changed from one of reasonable success to disgrace. He was convicted at the Supreme Court of Criminal Jurisdiction in Hobart, August 1824 for stealing sheep and sentenced to transportation to Macquarie Harbour for fourteen years. It was his first known conviction in the colony. His description in 1832 when he gained his ticket-of-leave was 5'7", brown to grey hair, grey eyes, 55 years of age, his face somewhat wrinkled and he had a scar on top of his forehead. He had been assigned to Henry Robinson (*q.v.*), for two years.

Gained an absolute pardon in 1842. Buried 1 September 1851, Hobart, aged 84 (?).

AYLMER, JOHN (JAMES), alias ELMORE [c. 1783–1803] (Elmer)
Labourer, aged 19.
Tried at Kent Spring Assizes (Maidstone G.D.) 15 March 1802 for breaking open the dwelling-house of George Palliser, Esq., at Breadger and stealing sundry articles of silver plate. Sentenced to death. Reprieved and sentenced by Baron Hotham to transportation for life. Gaoled at Maidstone and transferred to the *Prudentia* hulk at Woolwich.
Died 18 December 1803, Port Phillip. Registered as James Elmore, aged 22.

BAGLEY, GEORGE [c. 1782–1853]
?, aged 20.
Tried at Hereford Spring Assizes (Hereford G.D.) 16 March 1802 for stealing six sheep and four lambs from Luke Kyrwood. Sentenced to death. Reprieved by Baron Thomson and Justice Sir Alan Chambre and sentenced to transportation for life. Gaoled in the county gaol and transferred to hulks to Langston.

Pateshall wrote that the Hereford convicts on board the *Calcutta* were among those he released from irons.

Bagley attended the Hobart musters in 1811, 1818, 1819 and 1823. He received a conditional pardon in May 1816. He became a constable but was dismissed from service in May 1819 for improper conduct. It appears likely that over a period of time Bagley was a useful accomplice to bushrangers. He had been before the Bench of Magistrates for some misdemeanour in July 1817 at the time when Knopwood was implicated in his alleged assistance to Michael Howe. In January 1826 a Supreme Court hearing sentenced Bagley to imprisonment for seven years, a few days after the execution of bushranger James M'Cabe with whom he might have had some association.

Bagley probably served some time at Macquarie Harbour before returning to Hobart where, in June 1835, he married Mary Mullen, a widow, at St Matthew's, New Norfolk.
Buried 25 April 1853, New Norfolk, aged 83 (?), a labourer. She was buried 3 November 1841, 'a lunatic'.

BALLANCE, JAMES [c. 1775–1825]
?, aged 27, of Bilston. Conduct orderly. Wore spectacles. Literate.
Tried at Staffordshire Spring Assizes (Stafford G.D.) 25 March 1802 for being in possession of forged £1 and £2 notes which he attempted to send in a packet to an address in Norwich. Other forged notes were found in his house when it was searched. Sentenced to transportation for fourteen years. Gaoled at Stafford and transferred to the hulks at Langston.

He attended the Hobart musters in 1811, 1818, 1819 and 1823. He received a conditional pardon in 1813 and was free by servitude in 1816.

In earlier days he was among those whom Knopwood reported missing from Hobart with dogs when they spotted a Tasmanian tiger.

He received grants of 80 acres at Clarence Plains and 40 acres in the Drummond district on which he grew wheat and other crops and ran large numbers of sheep and cattle, providing meat regularly to the Commissariat as well as wheat. He also conducted the Freemasons' Arms, an inn at Kangaroo Point, for many years.

In Hobart, 27 July 1812, he married Hannah Edwards but they were separated by 1818 when he advertised that he would not be responsible for her debts.
Died 9 September 1825, Kangaroo Point. David and Ann Lord were executors of his estate.

BANNISTER, WILLIAM [c. 1760–?]
?, aged 42.
Tried at Borough of Derby S. of P. 3 May 1802 for stealing bacon from Charles King. Sentenced to transportation for seven years. Gaoled at Derby and transferred to the hulks at Langston.
Bannister's name does not appear on the Commissariat return of prisoners of 1803–04 which indicates that he did not land at Port Phillip. He might have died on the voyage out without his death being recorded or he might have travelled on to Port Jackson. (It is unlikely that he was the man named William Russell, who in one record was mistakenly recorded as having sailed in the Calcutta after a conviction at Derby on the same date. This man came from Norfolk I. and became a bushranger.)

BARNES, FRANCIS [c. 1771–1842]
Printer, aged 30, of St Bride's, London, former soldier; 5'6", dark brown hair, grey eyes. Literate.
Tried at Middlesex IV Sessions (Middlesex G.D.) 15 April 1801 for privately stealing from Nathaniel Swan a bank post bill (£10), two banknotes (£40), other banknotes valued at £10, £25 and £2 and eleven Rochester, Chatham

and Stroud banknotes (£75). The crime took place in the second tier of boxes in the Drury Lane Theatre. He was found with £172 on him and said he found them. He was in the same box as Swan and sat out the performance. Sentenced to death by Mr Justice Heath. Reprieved and sentenced to transportation for life. He had had a previous conviction in 1795 in the name of William Barnes and had been sentenced to seven years' transportation, delivered to Southampton but pardoned so that he might serve in the 60th Rgt. He was wounded in 1801 and later discharged. Gaoled at Newgate and transferred to the *Prudentia* hulk at Woolwich.

Barnes attended the Hobart musters in 1811, 1818, 1819 and 1823. He received a free pardon on 25 January 1813. He was given 80 acres at Glenorchy on which he grew crops and ran sheep, as well as holding a grazing licence beyond Pitt Water.

He employed four government servants to run his property at Glenorchy in 1819 while he lived in Hobart.

From the earliest days in Hobart Collins used his services in many ways. He assisted with the printing of the Garrison Orders and General Orders and in 1810 the *Derwent Star and Van Diemen's Land Intelligencer*. He acted in a clerical capacity and was present as a witness at many of the marriages performed by the Revd Robert Knopwood. He received £25 as an overseer (listed as Edward Barnes) in 1810.

From 1808 he conducted a successful business as proprietor of the Hope and Anchor Inn. Apart from two minor fines for selling spirits without a licence, he was known as 'a good and lawful man'.

On 16 June 1823, Barnes married Elizabeth Ann Macklin, aged 39, a free woman (he gave his age as 43). Ceremony probably performed by newly arrived Revd William Bedford. She died 6 April 1827, apparently childless. On 24 October 1833 Francis Barnes, widower of Clarence Plains, married Mary Anne Pritchard, spinster.

Died as a farmer, 26 January 1842, Ralph's Bay where he owned 600 acres. Buried 29 January, St David's, aged 73 (?). His widow married Richard Stevens of Glenorchy in August 1843.

BARWISE, ROBERT [c. 1770–1810?]

(Barways)

?, aged 30.

Tried at Westmoreland Summer Assizes (Appleby G.D.) 28 August 1800 for grand larceny. Sentenced to transportation for seven years. Gaoled at the county gaol and transferred to the *Fortune* hulk at Portsmouth.

In September 1807 Barwise and James Davis (*q.v.*) appeared before Knopwood on charges of purchasing kangaroo meat from Dr Bowden's and George Harris' servants and together with Charles Shore (*q.v.*) and William Roberts (*q.v.*) with using an officer's boat without permission. They received an unknown number of lashes.

From September 1808 until May 1810, after he was free by servitude, Barwise advertised that he was leaving the colony. He became a sailor and served in the schooner *Mercury*, the brig *Star*, and the brig *Trial* on sandalwood and sealing expeditions.

He must have been one of the three men from the Trial *massacred*

by natives on the Palliser I. (Tuamotus) where they were left to collect pearls and shells.

BEAN, WILLIAM [c. 1774 – after 1829]

Mathematical instrument maker, aged 28, born London, married; 5'7", sallow complexion.

Tried at Middlesex III Sessions (London G.D.) 17 July 1802 together with two others for breaking and entering the house of his masters, John and Edward Troughton, mathematical instrument makers at Peterborough Court, and stealing a sextant, (8 gns), a pair of elliptical compasses (£3), one turn bench (£4), brass work of a reflecting telescope (£3). Edward Troughton used a bayonet and wounded one of the men. When Bean's house was searched his wife seemed to know nothing of the crime. Sentenced to death by the Recorder. Reprieved and sentenced to transportation for life. Gaoled at Newgate and transferred to the *Captivity* at Portsmouth.

Bean's wife did not accompany him in the *Calcutta*.

He attended the Hobart musters in 1811 and 1818. He received a conditional pardon in 1815.

In September 1805 while in Hobart he stole a gun, the property of the Crown, and received 300 lashes. During trouble with bushrangers in March 1815 he abused James Austin (*q.v.*) for searching for the bushrangers but received no punishment. At this time he was described as having brown hair, black eyes and a dislocated right hip. He was lame ever afterwards and in great pain, incapable of laborious work. David Lord gave him a home until 1828 when he petitioned for admission to the Invalid Establishment at New Norfolk as an object of charity, in great poverty and distress. The colonial surgeon in 1829 noted that he was 'scarcely capable of earning a subsistence and may be commended as a proper object for the indulgence prayed for'.

The date and place of his death have not been traced.

BEARDMORE, JOHN, alias JOHN JOHNSON [c. 1774 – after 1820]

(Beardsmore)

?, aged 28.

Tried at Staffordshire Spring Assizes (Stafford G.D.) 25 March 1802 for stealing a bay mare from John Poolton of Bilston. Sentenced to transportation for life. Gaoled at Stafford, and transferred to the hulks at Langston. His conduct was orderly.

Between 1816 and 1818 Beardmore made several attempts to escape from Hobart and received punishment in 1818.

There appears to be no further record of his activities after he was reported missing in April 1820.

BELTON, DAVID [c. 1754–1819]

?, aged 48, married to Elizabeth ?.

Tried at Berkshire Spring Assizes (Abingdon G.D.) 26 March 1802 for stealing silk ribbons from Emily Snow, milliner, together with Mary Belton (his daughter ?) and Mary Giles, on suspicion of receiving the same, knowing them to have been stolen. Belton was sentenced to death and the women acquitted. Reprieved by Justices Sir Soulden Laurence and Sir Simon Le Blanc and sentenced to transportation for life. Gaoled at the county gaol and transferred to the hulks at Portsmouth.

Belton's wife Elizabeth accompanied her husband in the *Calcutta*. In August 1806 Collins advised Gov. King that he was allowing her to proceed to Port Jackson in the *Estramina* on some private business. She returned two months later in the *King George* with two children. She died and was buried in Hobart, 23 June 1810, aged 41.

David Belton received a free pardon in October 1810. He attended the Hobart muster in 1811. In August of that year he appeared as a witness at the inquest of Pte Samuel Wiggins.

He returned to England and changed his name to William Selsby. Under that name and as a labourer he was charged at Sussex Assizes (Bury St Edmunds) 23 August 1818 with having stolen three heifers (£15) from Samuel Ireland of Gislingham. Sentenced to death by Rt Hon. Vicary Gibbs and Sir Robert Graham. Reprieved and sentenced to transportation for life.

He sailed in the Hibernia *but died during the voyage, according to a report (H.T.G., 15 May 1819) which described him as 'William Selsby, formerly a very eccentric character in this settlement by the name of David Belton.' However, a man named William Selsby, town crier, was buried 8 April 1826, St David's, aged 63. Belton probably knew him in Hobart and used his name in England.*

BEST, WILLIAM [c. 1768–1804]
Labourer, aged 44, single, of Wallingford, Berkshire; 5'7", brown or hazel eyes, warts on his nose, a claret mark on his left hand and arm, and was described as both lusty and disorderly.
Tried at Dorset Spring Assizes (Dorset G.D.) 18 February 1802 for stealing ribbons from Sarah Hawkins. Sentenced by Justice Sir Simon Le Blanc to death. Reprieved and sentenced to transportation for life. He was gaoled at Dorchester where he was employed at peg-making and transferred to the *Captivity* hulk at Portsmouth.

He must have been ill when Collins left him with the group at Port Phillip. Died 18 March 1804, aged 44 (?).

BIRCHALL, JOHN [1779–1860]
(Burchall, Birchell, Buckhall)
Labourer, aged 23, of Woore, Shropshire. Married with two children. Son of James and Elizabeth Birchall, tenant farmers, of Woore Hollows, one of five children, bap. at Woore on 6 May 1779. Literate.
Tried at City of Chester Pleas of the Session of the Crown Mote, 23 October 1802 for theft and breaking gaol, 31 March 1802 and stealing £5 worth of goods from Thomas Benbow, and retaken in London 24 April. He was found not guilty of the theft, but sentenced to death for breaking gaol. Later reprieved and sentenced to transportation for life. Gaoled at The Castle, Chester, and transferred to the *Captivity* hulk at Portsmouth.

His family did not accompany him to the colony.

Birchall attended the Hobart musters in 1811, 1818, 1819 and 1823. He received a conditional pardon in June 1810 and was free by 1818.

He received 55 acres in grants of land at Pitt Water where he farmed very successfully. He purchased a further 400 acres by 1819, employing seven servants, and 433

acres in 1831. He provided large amounts of grain and meat regularly for the Commissariat and the military.

Information about his family in England is not available, but he married Susannah Bellett on 24 October 1809. She was the daughter of ex-convict, Jacob Bellett, a First Fleeter, from Norfolk I., in Hobart. They had at least nine children between 1812 and 1828. The Birchalls educated their daughters, as well as sons, at the school at Pitt Water. His eldest son James, the first native-born white child in the area, later married Sarah Reardon, daughter of a neighbour, Bartholomew Reardon, who was also a First Fleeter from Norfolk I.

Birchall acted as district constable at Pitt Water for several years until 1819. He also built a schooner which he used as a ferry for the local inhabitants to carry provisions and passengers across the lagoon between Pitt Water and the opposite bank.

Knopwood recorded two early misdemeanours when Birchall was absent from labour for five weeks (1806) and stole a dog. He received 500 lashes. In December 1819 he was before the Deputy Judge Advocate's court on a charge that he had beaten a prisoner but there were insufficient grounds to arrest him. A week later he was relieved of his duties as district constable.

Buried 9 May 1860, St Georges, Sorell, aged 85 (?).

Surnames of descendants have included: Bannister; Hanley; Kean; Kemp; McPhee; Moore; Peacock; Reid; Riseley; Young.

BLACKFORD, BENJAMIN [c. 1778 – ?]
Biscuitmaker, aged 24.
Tried at Kent Summer Assizes (Maidstone G.D.) 4 August 1802 together with Joseph Powell (*q.v.*) for stealing, in Lewisham, one wether sheep from Robert Jennings. Sentenced to death. Reprieved by the Lord Chief Baron and Baron Hotham and sentenced to transportation for seven years. Gaoled at Maidstone and transferred to the hulks at Woolwich.

During the voyage out he was employed as a sailor.

In March 1807 he took part in a disturbance with the military patrol and was confined to the guardhouse. Several of the offenders received 200 or 100 lashes but not Blackford, who was a member of the boat crews. However, the following month he informed bushrangers that the patrol was searching for them. Knopwood sat on the bench to try Blackford and the others but there is no record of the verdict.

Soon after he had completed his sentence, Blackford, together with Urias Allender, went to Sydney to appear as witness in a trial. They returned to Hobart in the *King George* on 9 June 1810.

As Blackford's name did not appear on either the Hobart or Sydney muster rolls of 1811, it is likely that being an experienced sailor, he returned to England.

BLACKMORE, JOHN [c. 1775–1842]
Seaman, aged 27, of Bristol.
Tried at Kent Spring Assizes (Maidstone G.D.) 15 March 1802 for stealing, at Gravesend, three notes (£7) from Swithen Shepherd. Sentenced to death. Reprieved by Baron Hotham and Mr Justice Heath and sentenced to transpor-

tation for life. Gaoled at Maidstone and transferred to the hulks at Woolwich.

While at Port Phillip, Knopwood punished him with 100 lashes for 'contempt of the military'.

He attended the Hobart muster in 1811 but not later ones, although he was still in the colony. He was listed as missing from employment in August 1814. By August 1821 he had received a conditional pardon. At that time he was 5'2½", had grey hair, grey eyes, and was a seaman.

He was buried at New Norfolk on 26 November 1842, aged 85(?). He had been a hospital patient and the cause of death was 'febris'.

BLAKE, JAMES [c. 1779 – ?]
Waterman, aged 22, from Lambeth; 5'5", dark complexion, brown hair, grey eyes.

Tried at Middlesex IV Sessions (Middlesex G.D.) 15 April 1801 together with Thomas Davies (*q.v.*) and William Smith (*q.v.*) for stealing a sack (2s 0d) and four bushels of barley (30s 0d) from George Shum and others, taken from a barge in the Thames into their peterboat. Sentenced to transportation for seven years by Mr Justice Heath. Gaoled at Tothillfields and transferred to the *Fortune* hulk at Langston.

There appears to be no further record of Blake in the colony after reaching Hobart. As a sailor, he would have had no trouble returning to England c. 1808 when free by servitude.

BOLTON, JOHN [c. 1785 – ?]
Linen draper, aged 17, born Ellesmere, Shropshire; 5'5", dark complexion.

Tried at Middlesex II Sessions (Middlesex G.D.) 13 January 1802 for stealing from his employer, Phillip Gibbons, a woollen draper in Tottenham, two waistcoat pieces (8s 0d). He had pawned the goods for 3s 0d. Sentence pronounced by the Common Sergeant was transportation for seven years. He had previously been acquitted of a charge in December 1801 of embezzling £2 on account of Gibbons. Gaoled at Newgate and transferred to the *Prudentia* hulk at Woolwich.

He attended the Sydney muster in 1811. Bolton was already at Port Jackson by 1809 when he applied for a wine and spirit licence in the Hawkesbury area. He was by this time free and advertised a £10 reward for information against persons who had reported that he had uttered false information on the general muster about the number of acres of grain he had cultivated on a farm with partner, William Ezzey. In November 1810 he was warned against trespassing on other farms, allowing his sheep to graze and cutting down timber in Petersham. Twelve months later Bolton and Ezzey advertised their farm at Windsor for sale as they were leaving the colony. It comprised fourteen head of horned cattle, seven horses, a cart, chaise and harness, two harrows, pigs, and all necessary agricultural equipment.

He appears to have left the colony soon afterwards.

BOOTHMAN, JOHN BROADHURST [c. 1780–1829]
Clerk, aged 22, pa. Dean(e) near Bolton, Lancashire. Literate.
Tried at the Palatinate of Lancaster Q.S. (Lancaster) 20 January 1802 for embezzling £70, part of sum of £6 720

belonging to his employers Thomas and Joseph Ridgeway, bleachers of Norwich. Sentenced to transportation for seven years. Gaoled at Salford, then Lancaster Castle, then transferred to the hulks at Langston.

At Port Phillip he became a subordinate of the night watch.

After his arrival in Hobart he became a storekeeper, at first in charge of hospital supplies. In July 1806 an incendiarist set fire to the hospital while Boothman was in it and Collins believed it was an attempt to intimidate him as a witness called to assist in the prosecution of two confined prisoners.

For several years Boothman was a clerk assisting the Governor and signed orders from Government House.

But in 1812, from London, Francis Shipman (*q.v.*) implicated him with Fosbrook in charges of fraud and forgery between 1808 and 1809, stating that he had been imprisoned for twenty months. These accusations against Boothman were not proven, although he had to appear at Port Jackson at the court-martial of Fosbrook in 1814.

He returned to his work in Hobart and became acting secretary to Gov. Davey in 1816 and superintendent of convicts at £50 per annum. He again appeared at Port Jackson in 1817 on behalf of Davey, then retired, to give evidence against Surgeon H. St John Younge.

Boothman attended the Cornwall (Launceston) musters in 1819, 1820, 1821 and the Hobart muster in 1823. He received a grant of 100 acres from Gov. Macquarie before 1820 at Port Dalrymple where he ran 15 male sheep and 50 ewes.

Boothman married Mary Westlake in Hobart, 8 October 1810. She was born on Norfolk I., the daughter of Edward Westlake who had arrived in V.D.L. in 1808 and settled at Clarence Plains. (Her sister became mistress to Denis McCarty.) Westlake had originally been transported for seven years for sheep stealing and had arrived in the *Charlotte*, the first to arrive at Norfolk I. The Boothmans had two daughters while they lived in a fine house in Collins St. which they sold when they left in 1818 when he became principal superintendent at Port Dalrymple. They had three more daughters and two sons whom they educated at the public school. During Knopwood's journey north in 1819, Boothman was present as witness to several marriages.

Gov. Sorell gave Major Gilbert Cimitière, commandant at George Town, a good reference regarding Boothman's competence as an overseer in charge of crown prisoners. On 2 August 1819 Major Cimitière swore him in as chief district constable for George Town. He had charge of the building of Government House. Apart from taking charge of gangs of prisoners and their assignment to settlers, he had to pronounce sentence on them. He was therefore sometimes the victim of those who absconded, such as in 1820 when bushrangers stole property from him. He employed three government men.

In 1820 he was involved in a dispute with Lieut. Charles Vandermeulen of the 40th Rgt, his immediate superior as inspector of public works, and was suspended for insubordination. Vandermeulen and Boothman both gave evidence to Commissioner Bigge, each accusing the other of neglect of duty and other charges.

Boothman became clerk to the wealthy landowner James Cox of Clarendon and continued to cultivate his own land, but returned to Hobart about 1823 and lived in Liverpool St. A return of children in 1827 showed that they were of good character and Protestant but little else is known of their activities at that time. It is likely that Boothman worked as a clerk in a private capacity.

Died 11 November 1829, Hobart. Buried 3 days later at St David's, where a headstone exists. The register stated he was a clerk, aged 48. The Colonial Times *announced that his family was left destitute.*

Surnames of descendants have included: Blain; Collier; Dean; Dunsmore; Fowler; Harnett; Harris; Lade; Milne; Simmonds; Stander; Terry.

A biography of John Broadhurst Boothman appears in the *Australian Dictionary of Biography*, vol I.

BOWERS, WILLIAM [c. 1782–1807?]
Miller, aged 19, of Deptford, Surrey; 5'7", fair complexion, brown hair, and black eyes.
Tried at Middlesex I Sessions (Middlesex G.D.) 2 December 1801 for assaulting and robbing John Gale of a silver watch while he and Gale, from the *Irresistible*, had been drinking at the Pea Hen near Gray's Inn Lane. Sentenced by Justice Sir Nash Grose to death. Reprieved and sentenced to transportation for life. Gaoled at Newgate and transferred to the *Prudentia* hulk at Woolwich.

When in Hobart he escaped to the bush in 1805 and on his capture received 300 lashes and was put in irons for one year. He escaped again in August 1807 in a group armed and with plenty of dogs. Although his fellow bushrangers returned, there was no further mention of him in the records.

Presumed dead c. 1807–08.

BOWMAN, THOMAS [c. 1775–1816]
Chairmaker, aged 26, of St Luke, Middlesex; 5'4", fair complexion, brown hair, grey eyes.
Tried at Middlesex V Sessions (Middlesex G.D.) on 20 May 1801 together with Richard Hall and John Margetts (*q.v.*) for breaking and entering and stealing 104 blankets (£40) in the house of John Sylvester, manufacturer's agent. The blankets were the property of William Sellman. Bowman said he had been called to fetch a table and that the blankets had been left in the house by mistake. He called witnesses who gave him a good character. Sentenced by Baron Graham to death, reprieved and sentenced to transportation for life. Gaoled at Newgate and transferred to the hulks at Woolwich.

On the voyage out he was employed on deck as a ward-room cook.

He attended the Sydney muster in 1811. He was granted a ticket-of-leave that same year. By this time he had a son, Thomas, by Catherine Connelly, born c. 1809. There is no record of their marriage in Hobart.

Died 21 January 1816, Sydney, aged 42. Catherine applied to the male orphan school to have her child admitted. The papers stated that the father was dead and the mother a very poor and bad character.

BRADLEY, JOSEPH [c. 1780–1804]
Trunkmaker, also described as carpenter and joiner, aged 21, pa. Marylebone; 5'6", fair complexion, brown hair and grey eyes.
Tried at Middlesex II Sessions (Middlesex G.D.) 14 January 1801 for stealing a black gelding (valued £8) and a cart (£10) from Thomas Sprigmore. Acquitted of first offence and sentenced for second by Mr Justice Bond to six weeks in the house of correction and transportation for seven years. He had spent six months in the house of correction in 1799 for a previous conviction. He was gaoled at Newgate and transferred to the *Stanislaus* hulk at Woolwich.

In the *Calcutta* he served on deck as part of the carpenter's crew.

Killed 11 December 1804, Hobart, while apparently carrying on his trade. The following day Knopwood, as coroner at the inquest, conceded that he might have received blows from fighting with fellow convict Cole (q.v.), but the verdict was accidental death from Bradley's falling upon some stumps of trees and tools.

BRAY, THOMAS [c. 1787–1845?]
Twine-spinner, aged 14, of Shoreditch; 4'9", fair complexion, brown hair and grey eyes.
Tried at Middlesex III Sessions (London G.D.) 18 February 1801 for stealing 72 yards of ribbon from the shop of Anthony Harrison. Sentenced by Justice Sir Soulden Laurence to transportation for seven years. Gaoled at Newgate and transferred to the hulk *Stanislaus* at Woolwich.

He was one of the convicts who seized the *Marcia* and was sent to Sydney for trial by the Court of Vice-Admiralty in February 1808. These convicts were sentenced to death, but because they were seen to have displayed humanity towards the master and crew (the *Marcia* was owned by Kable & Co.) Major George Johnston was influenced to extend the Royal Mercy on condition of their serving as prisoners for the remainder of their lives. As some others involved in the seizure (e.g. David Gibson (*q.v.*)) received immediate benefits from the experience, there is no reason to believe Bray was not among them.

It is possible that he remained in Sydney, receiving land grants at Bunbury, Curran and elsewhere. This Thomas Bray became a respected farmer, with farms on the Parramatta River and Concord supplying meat and wheat to the government stores. He was granted a beer licence in 1815 and generously subscribed to good causes. He was still alive but did not appear on the 1828 census. He might have returned to V.D.L.

A Thomas Bray died in Launceston on 13 April 1845. An inquest disclosed he had been gaoled the previous week, was found drinking at the Scottish Chief, and removed to the colonial hospital where he died of a fever.

BREWER, GEORGE [c. 1780–1807]
Biscuit baker, aged 22, of Coleman St., London, bap.pa. St Catherine's, London, mother had lately died; 5'7", dark complexion, brown hair, hazel eyes.
Tried at Middlesex II Sessions (Middlesex G.D.) 13 January 1802 for assaulting Jeremiah Hargan at Goodman's Fields on the King's Highway (together with Michael Doyle (*q.v.*)). They had been drinking. Sentenced by the Chief Baron to death. Reprieved and sentenced to transpor-

tation for life. He had been previously (September 1801) tried and acquitted for highway robbery. He was gaoled at Newgate and transferred to the *Captivity* hulk at Portsmouth.

Brewer was one of Dr Bowden's servants.

Knopwood reported in February 1807 that while out kangaroo hunting Brewer was speared after some of his colleagues had killed four natives. They left him in the bush to die.

BRIANT, WILLIAM [c. 1761 – c. 1829]
(Bryant)
Labourer, aged 40, from Reading, of pa. Chipping Barnet, Berkshire; 5′5″, dark ruddy complexion, brown hair, grey eyes.
Tried at Hertfordshire Summer Assizes (Hertford G.D.) 20 July 1801 for stealing a truss containing two pieces of Irish linen and other articles from Thomas Watson. Sentenced to transportation for seven years. Gaoled at Newgate, transferred to the county gaol and later to the *Stanislaus* hulk at Woolwich.

During the voyage Briant was charged with drunkenness and was confined in the lower prison room.

He attended the Hobart musters in 1811, 1818 and 1819. In July 1818 he signed an address from prominent landowners supporting R. W. Loane respecting his differences with George Gunning. He appears to have received a land grant in 1821 and a William Briant was living in Liverpool St. in 1827 when a return of children showed that he had a daughter of eight, son of four and daughter of four months, that the parents were Protestant and of good character. He already had two older children.

Date and place of Briant's death have not been traced. He appears to have died in Hobart in 1829.

Surnames of descendants have included: Bryant; Hendley.

BRISCOE, BENJAMIN [c. 1781–1819]
Umbrella maker, aged 21, of Stepney; 5′6″, fair complexion.
Tried at Middlesex IV Sessions (London G.D.) 28 April 1802 for stealing a pocket-book containing two banknotes (£1 each) from James Barton, clerk to a Mr Callaghan, St Swithin's Lane. Sentence pronounced by the Recorder was transportation for seven years. Gaoled at Poultry and transferred to the *Captivity* hulk at Portsmouth.

He attended the Hobart musters in 1811 and 1818. Together with John Cruse (*q.v.*) he absented himself from labour in 1807 and was tried by Knopwood and others who sentenced him to 300 lashes.

He married Sarah Gooding (or Goodwin) in Hobart, October 1808. They had three sons and four daughters. One son died in infancy. When daughter, Mary Anne, died in 1896, aged 89, she was reported to be the oldest Tasmanian, had married four times and had fourteen children. Briscoe received a 50-acre land grant from Gov. Macquarie, which was farmed by his widow, together with a further 20 acres which she purchased after his death. By 1819 she had sown ten acres of wheat and grazed two male cattle, ten male sheep and forty ewes with the help of money subscribed from a public appeal.

Drowned when Urias Allender's ferry boat overturned between Hobart and Kangaroo Point, 24 September 1819. His widow later married a convict, Mark Bunker, aged 28, who had been transported in the Castlereagh *on 30 May 1820. An uncle, Capt. Brimstone, assisted with the upbringing of the children.*

Surnames of descendants have included: Bellinger; Carroll; Cockerill; Gregory; Hayes; Parrot; Tierney; Tuthill.

BROMLEY, THOMAS [c. 1784–1804]
Labourer, aged c.16, pa. St Thomas, Southwark.
Tried at Surrey S. of P. (Newington) 14 January 1800 for stealing five boots from Thomas Clinch. Sentenced to seven years transportation. Gaoled at the county gaol and transferred to the *Stanislaus* hulk at Woolwich.

Died of scurvy 28 October 1804, Hobart.

BROWN, CHARLES [c. 1779 – ?]
Husbandman, aged 22, brother of John (q.v.).
Tried at Berkshire Spring Assizes (Reading G.D.) 28 February 1801 with John Brown for breaking open the house of John Hobbs of Lambourn and stealing 30 lb of bacon, cheese, bread and wearing apparel; and breaking open the house of John Champ and stealing wearing apparel. Sentenced to death. They were left for execution, apparently reprieved by Justices Sir Soulden Lawrence and Sir Giles Rooke and removed from the county gaol to the *Prudentia* hulk at Woolwich.

Charles Brown attended the Hobart musters in 1811, 1818 and 1819. He received a conditional pardon in 1813 and was free by 1818. He was a gardener at Restdown for Andrew Geils in 1813 and nurseryman for Dr T. W. Birch in 1817. On 16 June 1818 he married Catherine Oates, aged 23, convict, who arrived in the *Alexander* (1816). They had a daughter, Catherine, baptised 5 August 1819, Hobart.

In August 1819 a Charles Brown advertised that he was leaving the colony.

BROWN, JAMES [c. 1781 – ?]
Sailor in the indiaman Warley, *aged 20, from Stoke's Bay, Hampshire; 5′4″, dark complexion, brown hair, dark hazel eyes.*
Tried at Middlesex III Sessions (Middlesex G.D.) 18 February 1801 for stealing wearing apparel from a chest belonging to Samuel Clarke of the *Warley*. Clothes included a greatcoat (7s 0d), three silk handkerchiefs (8s 0d), shirt (4s 0d), waistcoat (5s 0d), two pairs woollen drawers (5s 0d), trousers (6s 0d), jacket (2s 0d), etc. Brown and colleague Thomas Little pawned some while others were found at the home of Little's father. Witnesses gave them good characters, although they swore at the trial that they were fourteen years old. Sentence pronounced by the Common Sergeant was transportation for seven years. Gaoled at Newgate and transferred to the *Fortune* hulk at Langston.

During the voyage Brown served on deck as cook's mate.

Brown was among those who joined Robert Stewart (*q.v.*) in attempting to escape in the government cutter in February 1806 and was sent to Port Jackson for trial before the Court of Criminal Jurisdiction. In May he was gaoled in Sydney awaiting 'examination' but appears to have received no long-term punishment because by 1808 he was free. He appears to be the James Brown who joined the American whaler *Elizabeth* which, during a voyage lasting several months, collected 100 tons of sperm oil at King I.

In April 1810 this James Brown sailed for England via

Bengal in the Mary Ann, *a ship registered in Calcutta and carrying a cargo of spars.*

BROWN, JOHN [c. 1781–1811?]
Labourer, aged 20, brother of Charles (q.v.).
Tried at Berkshire Spring Assizes (Reading G.D.) 28 February 1801 together with Charles Brown for breaking open the house of John Hobbs of Lambourn and stealing 30 lb of bacon, cheese, bread and wearing apparel; and breaking open the house of John Champ and stealing wearing apparel. Sentenced to death. They were left for execution but apparently reprieved by Justices Sir Soulden Lawrence and Sir Giles Rooke and removed from the county gaol to the *Prudentia* at Woolwich.

Apart from the John Brown who was an associate of Richard Lemon and committed several murders in the north, there appears to have been another John Brown who went bush. He was a servant to Lieut. James Johnson in 1806–07. This Brown was wounded by a native spear while out kangaroo hunting at Pitt Water. He supplied his bushranging friends with bread and later joined them. He did not return with the others, and may be the John Brown of the *Calcutta* as he did not appear on the 1811 musters.

If so, he is probably the John Brown recorded on the St David's burial register, 22 February 1811, aged 30.

BROWN, RICHARD [c. 1777–1821?]
?, aged 25.
Tried at Berkshire Spring Assizes (Reading G.D.) 1 March 1802 for having stolen a light iron-grey gelding from Charles Jenner of Abingdon. Sentenced to death. Reprieved by Baron Thomson and Justice Sir Alan Chambre and sentenced to transportation for 14 years. Gaoled in the county gaol and transferred to hulks at Langston.

He attended the Hobart musters in 1811 and 1819. Returning to V.D.L. in the *Endeavour* after several years engaged in sea-faring expeditions, he received 30 acres of land in the Coal River area on which he ran 35 male and 55 female sheep. He is not to be confused with Richard Brown who came from Norfolk I., settled at Clarence Plains, and drowned in 1820. There are several other Richard Browns and it is likely that this Brown served in the *Nautilus*, *Rosetta* and *King George* between 1816–18. He was in the *Rosetta* (later known as the *Prince Leopold*) when it went in pursuit of the pirated brig *Trial*. He survived a violent lightning hurricane while in the *King George* en route to the Marquesas for a cargo of pork and sandalwood.

Drowned off the coast of New Zealand when engaged in a sealing expedition in the brig Hope *(Capt. Grimes), 1821.*

BROWN, THOMAS [c. 1772–1840]
Seaman, aged 29, single, born Aberdeen, lived in Chapel St., Weymouth; 5'8½", complexion and hair brown, grey eyes, and his face seamed with smallpox.
Tried at Dorset S. of P. (Blandford) 13 January 1801 for 'falsely pretending' to William Sharland of Melcombe Regis, tailor, that he was captain of a vessel, the *Elizabeth*, lying at Weymouth and that he had just arrived from Guernsey. He obtained from Sharland one pair of corduroy breeches (24s 0d), two silk handkerchiefs (13s 0d), two pairs of worsted stockings (11s 0d) and banknotes and mon-

ey to the value of 21s 0d. On the same day he made the same pretence to George Burgess of Melcombe Regis, linen-draper, and obtained seven yards of Irish linen (17s 6d), one silk handkerchief (2s 0d), one cotton handkerchief (2s 6d), one linen handkerchief (2s 0d), and a quantity of cambric (2s 3d). T. J. Browne, J.P., sentenced him to transportation for seven years. He was gaoled at the county gaol and transferred to the *Captivity* hulk at Portsmouth. His behaviour was orderly. While in the gaol he was employed picking oakum.

From 1809, when free, he sailed in the *Endeavour* and *Eliza* on sealing expeditions in Bass Strait. He returned to V.D.L. in the *Trial* in time for the 1811 muster, after which he probably returned to sea because he did not attend other musters.

Died in the hospital at New Norfolk. Buried 5 September 1840, aged 76 (?). A note recorded that he arrived in the Ocean.

BROWN, WILLIAM [c. 1765–1803?]
Husbandman, aged 37.
Tried at Nottingham Summer Assizes (Nottingham G.D.) 5 August 1802 for being at large after a previous gaol sentence of two years for stealing a gun from a Revd Clarke of Annesley. Sentenced to transportation for life. Gaoled at Nottingham county gaol and transferred to the hulks at Woolwich.

Among the prisoners who escaped at Port Phillip and did not return, presumed to have perished in the woods some time in December 1803 or later.

BUCKLEY, JOHN [c. 1757–1825?]
?, aged 45.
Tried at Somerset Spring Assizes (Taunton G.D.) 1 April 1802 for stealing a watch from John Charlton. Sentenced to transportation for life. Gaoled at the county gaol, Taunton, and transferred to the hulks at Langston.

During the voyage Buckley was Tuckey's servant. At Port Phillip he served Collins and was the successful claimant in the first litigation there when he brought a charge against Robert Kennedy (q.v.) with whom he had arranged to exchange a pair of shoes, which were too small, for a waistcoat.

Buckley received a free pardon in April 1810 and there appears to be no record of him in the colony after that date until a ticket-of-leave arrived for a John Buckley in February 1824 and a letter at the G.P.O. in March 1825. If this were the same man, he must have been the John Buckley known as Pretty Jack, an associate of the notorious Charles Routley. This Buckley wandered wherever he could get work and few would employ him. He had been living at Pitt Water and worked for Hugh M'Ginniss. He bore a bad character and had committed a previous felony in the colony. He had a very disagreeable face, large feet, was pock-pitted and was a very clumsy man.

In May 1829 Routley was charged with and later hanged for murdering this John Buckley whose body was discovered in July 1825. Buried May 1825, St George's, Hobart.

BUCKLEY, WILLIAM [c. 1782–1856]
Bricklayer by trade, former soldier in Cheshire Militia and the

4th or King's Own Rgt of Foot, serving in Holland. Wounded in right hand. Aged 20, born Marton, near Macclesfield, Cheshire, son of a farmer. Literate.

Tried at Sussex Summer Assizes (Lewes G.D.) 2 August 1802 together with William Marmon (*q.v.*) for burglariously entering the shop of a Mr Cave of Warnham and stealing two pieces of Irish cloth (8s 0d). Margaret Harris was also charged with receiving the cloth knowing it to have been stolen. She was discharged. Buckley and Marmon were sentenced to death. Reprieved by the Lord Chief Baron and Baron Hotham and sentenced to transportation for life. Gaoled at the county gaol and transferred to the hulks at Langston.

At Port Phillip, Buckley (not to be confused with John Buckley (*q.v.*), Collins' servant) is believed to have helped with the construction of a bomb-proof magazine and stone storehouse for which he made cement from the local limestone. He escaped from the settlement on Christmas Day 1803 and was still missing, believed dead, when the *Ocean* removed the last of the settlers to Hobart.

For nearly 32 years Buckley, befriended by natives of the Watourong tribe, lived a life of freedom based at his hut near Bream Creek on the coast of southern Victoria. He had at least one native wife and a daughter. He gave himself up to surveyor J. H. Wedge at Indented Head in July 1835. Wedge's description of him then was:

6'5⅞" (without shoes), age 53, trade bricklayer, complexion brown, head round, hair dark brown, visage round and marked with smallpox, forehead low, eyebrows bushy, eyes hazel, nose pointed and turned up, well-proportioned with an erect military gait; mermaid on upper part of right arm, sun half-moon, seven stars, monkey and W. B. on lower part of right arm.

Wedge obtained his pardon from Gov. Arthur hoping he would be a good intermediary between the two races, but he was confused in his loyalties more because of the time span since his contact with white people than lack of intelligence, of which his contemporaries accused him, rather unfairly when one examines how he managed to survive. For a short time he worked for John Batman as an interpreter on a salary of £50 per annum and later as government interpreter. He guided J. T. Gellibrand on some of his travels, assisted J. P. Fawkner with his house and was with Capt. Foster Fyans, Police Magistrate, at Geelong. He was outraged when he heard that white settlers had massacred blacks (in retaliation for the death of two shepherds) and raped young women.

He left for Hobart in December 1837. He made contact with an old fellow convict, Joseph Johnson (*q.v.*), at Green Ponds, who interceded on his behalf with Gov. Franklin to give him some employment. He became assistant storekeeper at the Immigrant's Home. Between 1841 and 1850, he was gate-keeper at the Female Factory. When he retired in 1850 he received a pension of £12 per annum to which the Victorian government later added £40. John Morgan, with some sponsorship from William Robertson, who had known Buckley at Port Phillip, published Buckley's story in 1852. Present day historians believe it is close to fact.

Buckley married Julia Eagers, widow of a mechanic, at St John's Church of England in New Town, 27 January 1840. She had two daughters.

They lived in Arthur's Circus, Hobart, where Buckley was killed on 30 January 1856 when he slipped under the wheels of a cart as it turned the corner.

A biography of William Buckley appears in the *Australian Dictionary of Biography*, vol. I. He has also been the subject of several other publications.

BYRNE, JAMES, alias JOHN BYRNE [c. 1762–1843] (Burn, Burne)
?, aged 40, born Northampton; 5'7", dark complexion.
Tried at Middlesex III Sessions (Middlesex G.D.) 17 February 1802 for stealing a pocket-book (6d), two 7s pieces and 2s 0d from John Lawson, a Chelsea pensioner, from a private house in Westminster where he was looking for a bed. Byrne blamed Lydia Moody, the women he was living with. The three had been drinking. Sentence pronounced by the Recorder was transportation for seven years. Gaoled at Tothillfields and transferred to the *Captivity* hulk at Portsmouth.

Byrne became a sealer in 1807. He sailed in the *Santa Anna* to the Bay of Islands and then in 1809 joined the *Pegasus* in which he appears to have worked his way to England; his name is not on any 1811 muster roll. He must have returned to V.D.L. because he attended the Hobart musters in 1818 and 1819. He was farming at Herdsman's Cove by 1817 and received a 60-acre grant at Glenorchy the following year. In 1817 Byrne found the body of William Drew (*q.v.*) murdered by Michael Howe, on his property.

Byrne had married Ann —, perhaps while in England as there is no record of their marriage in the colonies. She died in June 1818, in Hobart. On 23 October 1826, St Matthew's, New Norfolk, he married Margaret Sweetman.

Died in hospital after a catarrhal disease. Buried 27 December 1843, St Matthew's, New Norfolk.

BYRNE, STEPHEN [c. 1766–1803]
Silk weaver and sailor, aged 36, born co. of Wicklow, living at Spitalfields; 5' 10", dark complexion.
Tried at Middlesex III Sessions (Middlesex G.D.) 13 January 1802 for stealing one guinea, 4s 0d, three Ramsgate banknotes (5s 0d each), and £1 from George Trounce in the house of James Taff at Spitalfields. Byrne and Trounce were sailors just arrived from Demerara. Both had been drinking. Sentenced by Justice Sir Giles Rooke to death. Reprieved and sentenced to transportation for life. Gaoled at Newgate and transferred to the *Captivity* hulk at Portsmouth.

Died at sea during the voyage out. Knopwood reported that he 'committed the body to the deep' on 7 May 1803. Pateshall reported 'died from mere debility brought on by seasickness'.

CAMPBELL, ARCHIBALD, alias JAMES CAMPBELL [c. 1777–1829]
Husbandman, aged 23, born Glasgow. Literate.
Tried at the Court of Justiciary, Glasgow, 25 April 1800 together with George Rankin for theft and being by habit and repute a common thief. Sentenced to transportation for life. Gaoled at the Tolbooth of Glasgow, transferred to the hulks at Woolwich.

Campbell's name (as James) did not appear on the Hobart muster roll until 1823, probably because he frequently absconded from duty. He attempted to escape with

Robert Stewart in June 1805 and after his return received 300 lashes and irons for one year. In March 1807 he received a further 200 lashes and was confined after a disturbance with the military and giving information to bushrangers. In 1814 he was outlawed during his association with the bush-ranger Peter Mills but was among those to whom Gov. Davey offered an amnesty on return to Hobart.

For several years he lived with an Aboriginal woman on Furneaux I. where he discovered a crystal mine known as Jemmy Campbell's mine. Davey secured him an absolute pardon for his discovery. He had established a valuable relationship with the natives and brought a number into Hobart in 1814 who were later landed on Bruny I.

At this time he was described as 5′3¼″, fresh complexion, tall, brown hair, hazel eyes, small scar on each eyebrow and mark of gunshot wound above right ankle, free.

Campbell might have had some experience in whaling as well as sealing. He was running some cattle in the Hobart area in 1819 and was appointed a ferryman. In December of that year he and his native woman accompanied Henry Rice (q.v.) on his exploration of the east coast. During this journey the black woman died.

On 22 September 1823 Campbell married Jane Jarvis, a 40-year-old convict transported in the *Mary Ann*. It was the first marriage the Revd William Bedford conducted at St David's.

Buried 26 June 1829, St Andrew's, Hobart.

CARMICHAEL, ADAM [c. 1778–1806 ?]
Private in 5th Rgt of North British Militia, aged 23, stationed in Aberdeen. Literate.
Tried at Aberdeen Court of Justiciary 14 April 1801 for breaking into the shop of John Mennie, merchant, in Aberdeen and stealing 12-20 Scotch cheeses, a 12-pint spirit cask of gin, 12 lb of green tea, two stone of candles, a box of oranges, two rolls of tobacco, two large bottles of spirits, two pairs of worsted stockings. He should have been on guard but had gone to the house of Ann Graham to buy a bottle of gin and returned to drink with other soldiers on guard. Twenty witnesses gave evidence against him. Sentenced by Lord Methuen to transportation for fourteen years. Gaoled at the Tolbooth in Aberdeen and transferred to the *Prudentia* hulk at Woolwich.

During the voyage out he was employed as a servant.

By August 1804 he was one of the few convicts who had acquired some livestock — five fowls. In June 1805 he tried to escape in Knopwood's boat with Robert Stewart (q.v.) and others. The following December he escaped from the guardhouse with David Gibson (q.v.) and others. On 8 January 1806 the General Orders declared them to be outlaws. Knopwood reported that all had returned by 20 January 1806 and received 300 lashes and irons for one year.

It appears more than likely that Carmichael did not return because there seems to be no further reference to him in the records, apart from a letter awaiting his collection.

CARRETT, JAMES, alias THOMAS CARRETT [c. 1776–1825]
(Carrotts)
?, aged 26.
Tried at Yorkshire Spring Assizes (York G.D.) 6 March 1802 for returning from transportation before the expiration of his term. Sentenced to death. Reprieved by Lord Kenyon and Justice Sir Giles Rooke and sentenced to transportation for life. Gaoled at York Castle and transferred to the hulks at Langston.

He attended the Hobart musters in 1818 and 1819. He received a conditional pardon in January 1813 and was free by 1818. He received a grant of 30 acres at Green Ponds which he sold.

He was among those who attempted to escape with Robert Stewart (q.v.) in February 1806. In August 1807 Knopwood named him as a bushranger armed and with plenty of dogs. He joined the bushranging gang of M'Cabe and Townshend. In January 1813 he received a conditional pardon for informing on and helping secure the leaders at their headquarters at Oyster Bay. There Carrett had cohabited with an Aboriginal woman whose husband he had claimed to have killed. Soon afterwards he joined the brig *Active* then engaged in the black whale fisheries off the Derwent.

For a while Carrett was one of Capt. James Kelly's crew members in the *Henrietta Packet* trading sealskins between colonial ports. He also sailed in the schooners *Cumberland* (to New Zealand) and *Geordy* when it was wrecked at Port Davey in 1815. In April 1819 he sailed from Launceston on the maiden trading voyage of the sloop *Governor Sorell*. He became 'faithful servant' to surveyor, Thomas Scott and accompanied him on his expedition to the east coast and central Tasmania between 1822 and 1823. His likeness appears in some of Scott's sketches. He then joined James Hobbs on his circumnavigation of the island in an open boat and was accorded special mention for the exploration of the Pieman River and examining the land as far as Cape Grim. From the Colonial Revenue he received payment for services to the government in exploring the island — £23 1s 1d for the quarter ending 30 September 1924.

Carrett died in Hobart on 16 January 1825, aged 47 (?).

CASHMAN, JOHN HENRY [c. 1788–1803]
Clerk, aged 14, born London, father dead, mother kept pigs and family quite well off; 5′1″, dark complexion. Literate.
Tried at Middlesex III Sessions (London G.D.) 17 February 1802 for forgery on four counts of charging, uttering and publishing same with intent to defraud his employer John Windus, of Vere and Co., an attorney in Old Broad St. Employed for two months and absconded, buying tarts and a watch in Holborn for 1½ guineas. Eight witnesses gave him a good character. Sentenced to death by Justice Sir Simon Le Blanc. Reprieved and sentenced to transportation for life. Gaoled at Newgate and transferred to the *Prudentia* hulk at Woolwich.

During the voyage out he was employed as servant to Richard Wright, master of the *Calcutta*. While the ship was anchored off the Cape of Good Hope, Cashman stole a gold watch from Surgeon Edward Brumley and according to Knopwood four dollars (Spanish?) from the pocket-book of Mr MacDonal (Lieut. Donovan?).

He drowned in Simon's Bay, 19 August 1803, either trying to get ashore, or, more likely, by suicide. Collins described him as 'a fine youth'.

CLARK(E), CHARLES [c. 1785–after 1819]

Waiter, aged sixteen, of London; 4'2", sallow complexion, brown hair, hazel eyes.

Tried at Middlesex VII Sessions (Middlesex G.D.) 16 September 1801 for stealing a bank note (£1) from John Jordan. Clark was waiter at an eating house at Covent Garden. Jordan gave him the note for payment and waited one hour for the change. Clark disappeared. Sentenced by Justice Sir Simon Le Blanc to transportation for seven years. Gaoled at Newgate and transferred to the *Prudentia* hulk at Woolwich.

Clark was a servant to Sgt McCauley and attended the Hobart musters in 1811, 1818 and 1819.

Clark received grants of 90 acres of land at Queenborough and 30 acres at New Norfolk in 1818 from Gov. Macquarie.

He was a constable by 1812. When two soldiers were court-martialled in March of that year Clark, who was in charge of the courthouse, was dismissed for neglect of duty.

On 2 April 1812 he married Catherine Earley, daughter of Rachel Earley, a first fleeter who had been transported in the *Friendship* and had arrived from Norfolk I. with two other daughters; Elizabeth, who was to marry Urias Allender (*q.v.*) and Ann, who was to marry Henry Robinson (*q.v.*). The father of these girls was Pte Samuel Marsden, N.S.W. Corps.

Clark became manservant to William Parish who had arrived in the *Ocean* as an overseer. In September 1812 Clark assisted in the capture of bushrangers M'Cabe, Townshend and Geary when they burgled the house of Parish and was a witness in Sydney at their trial by the Court of Criminal Jurisdiction.

Clark was later tried but acquitted in January 1818 at the Supreme Court in Sydney of sheep stealing, together with Thomas Graham and others whose death sentence was commuted to life imprisonment.

In February 1818 Clark survived a ferry tragedy in the Derwent when one of Austin's ferries capsized.

The date and place of his death have not been traced.

CLARK(E), JOHN [c. 1769–1853]

?, aged 33, married 23 July 1798 in England.

Tried at Derby Spring Assizes (Derby G.D.) 13 March 1802 with John Gadsby (*q.v.*) for sheep stealing. Sentenced to death by Baron Graham. Reprieved and sentenced to transportation for life. Gaoled at Derby and transferred to the hulks at Langston.

He attended the Hobart musters in 1811, 1818 and 1819. He received a conditional pardon in January 1813 and a grant of 60 acres in the district of Drummond (Black Brush) in January 1817. He also had a grazing licence on the Spring Hill run, east of the Port Dalrymple Road, in 1819. He was supplying the Commissariat with large amounts of wheat by 1818 and 100 lb of meat by 1820.

Described as a fettler at Tea Tree Brush, Clark gave evidence against a Michael Reilly for stealing a fowling piece from his house together with others who were sent to Sydney for trial in 1820.

In 1821 Clark charged Thomas Whitaker with stealing 100 wether sheep from him. The Court of Criminal Jurisdiction in Sydney found Whitaker guilty and sentenced him to Newcastle for life. Clark, like the other John Clarke (*q.v.*), had some partnership dealings with James Lord (*q.v.*) A convict named Edward Lowndes forged Clark's signature in 1822 in an attempt to defraud Lord and was sentenced to Macquarie Harbour.

Bushrangers from the Green Ponds area, headed by Matthew Brady, raided Clark's house over Christmas 1825. By 1826 Clark was a very successful farmer in partnership with Michael Lackey. The Land Commissioners stayed for four nights on the farm which they found held a good deal of wheat, a very good slatted stable and about 1 000 sheep.

In January 1833 Clark applied for a town allotment of 10 acres at Brighton which was refused. His petition states that he had acquired by grant or purchased 540 acres and rented 900 acres of crown land, of which he had 60 acres in cultivation, 60 head of cattle, and 800 sheep. He intended building a house and retiring from business. He must have built his house, Rosewood, at this time.

Although Clark's wife did not come to Australia, his only child Mary married Thomas Lowen, whom she joined with their daughter in 1826 after Lowen was transported. They subsequently had a son Frederick and there are numerous descendants.

Died 25 January 1853, at his home, at the Tea Tree Brush. Buried 28 January, Pontville (Brighton), aged 88 (?).

Surnames of descendants have included: Ellis; Gard; Grice; Lowen; Phillips.

CLARKE, JOHN [c. 1773–1830]

Clerk, aged 29, of London. Literate.

Tried at Middlesex III Sessions (London G.D.) on two charges on 14 September and 27 October 1802: I) fraudulently embezzling from John East a banknote (£25) and two others (£10 each) and one at £5, II) while employed as clerk to James Yarraway, timber and coal merchant of Blackfriars, for taking and receiving from James Harrison, carpenter, four banknotes (£20 each), one (£5), one (£1 10s 0d) on account of Yarraway and fraudulently embezzling and secreting them. Up till then Clarke had an exceptional character and had lived with Yarraway for fourteen months. Yarraway said he had behaved as well as any young man. Sentenced by the Common Sergeant to transportation for seven years. Gaoled at Giltspur St. and transferred to the *Prudentia* hulk at Woolwich.

Clarke was allowed to go without irons during the voyage out. He attended the Hobart musters in 1811, 1819 and 1823 (presuming the two entries for John Clark (*q.v.*), *Calcutta*, Derby, was a mistake). Clarke received a grant of 50 acres of land at Herdsman's Cove on which he employed a free man.

Clarke found clerical work from the earliest days in V.D.L. He witnessed marriages, took oaths and by April 1807 he was an overseer of convicts. In October 1810 his name appears as a superintendent, replacing William Paterson, at £50 per year. The following year he became a constable and superintendent of public works to assist A. W. H. Humphrey. During a bout of ill health in 1812 the Garrison Orders referred to the 'steady and zealous attention to the duties of his station'.

He gave evidence in the case of Denis McCarty in December 1813 at the time when the cow was killed. In

November 1818 he was in Sydney when the case of *Loane* v. *Humphrey* was heard before the Supreme Court. Clarke was employed as clerk to Loane. In October 1818 he was in partnership with James Lord (*q.v.*) as licensed publican of the Dusty Miller in Elizabeth St.

He received rations for himself and his wife, Ann Grey, whom he had married on 5 September 1814. The Landholders' muster of 1819 shows they had three children, although no children are shown as rationed in February 1820.

He was probably the John Clarke who was in hospital in January 1830, and buried at St David's, 12 January, aged 54 (?).

COBB, FRANCIS [c. 1767 – after 1844?]
Cord-wainer, aged 35, pa. St Martins, Canterbury, Kent. Literate.
Tried at City of Canterbury S. of P. 3 April 1802 for stealing leather. Thomas King tried for receiving it. Sentenced to transportation for seven years. Gaoled at Canterbury and transferred to the *Prudentia* hulk at Woolwich.

Cobb had the duties of a sailor in the *Calcutta*. He attended the Hobart musters in 1811, 1818, 1819 and 1823. Cobb lost his house in Hobart in July 1805 when it caught fire as the whaler *King George* was arriving from Port Jackson. Knopwood commented that 'It is very remarkable that we always had a fire when a strange sail has been in sight, or very near the Derwent.' In March 1807 Collins sent Cobb to Sydney as witness in the trial of Thomas Jones (*q.v.*) for stealing and slaughtering a cow.

Cobb received a land grant of 50 acres in the Hobart area and by 1819 had extensive crops, nine male and seventeen female cattle and 1 000 ewes. He employed five government servants and two free men and supplied meat and wheat regularly to the Commissariat.

He also owned two houses in Bathurst St., Hobart where he carried on a bakery business. He supplied a cart and bullocks for conveying the baggage of Gov. Macquarie to Port Dalrymple, for which he received £22 in payment. He appears to have been in some financial trouble and unable to maintain his stock so he sold his land, renting instead 1 900 acres of land belonging to George Langford at Blackman's Bridge.

However, in 1818 he was able to produce £10 surety on behalf of Robert Lancaster that he keep the peace and be of good behaviour.

He left Hobart late in 1822 to reside near Ross where in 1826 he ran up to 1 500 sheep, twelve working oxen, and 160 horned cattle.

In September 1822 he served on a jury at an inquest on the body of John Hill, accidentally killed while felling a tree. He was probably one of the first of the *Calcutta* convicts to marry, perhaps before 1810, but the date of his marriage to Sarah — and the birth dates of their five children have not been traced. On 23 March 1827, he was described as a widower when Knopwood married him at Kangaroo Point to Sarah Caroline Rubery, a widow from Ross. The second Mrs Sarah Cobb died a year later, 24 March 1828. He was alive in 1844 when it was reported (*H.T.G.*, 7 December) that he, a widower, had married a Mrs C. Rubery, perhaps a daughter-in-law.

The date and place of his death have not been traced.
Surnames of descendants have included: Jones; Salmon; Watson.

COCKSWORTH, WILLIAM [c. 1772 – after 1811]
(Coatsworth, Colesworth)
Husbandman, aged 30.
Tried at Kent Spring Assizes (Maidstone G.D.) 15 March 1802 for assaulting and robbing John Berry, on the highway in Strood, of one silver watch, three £5 notes, etc. Sentenced to death. Reprieved by Baron Hotham and Mr Justice Heath and sentenced to transportation for life. Gaoled at the West Kent county gaol at Maidstone and transferred to the *Prudentia* hulk at Woolwich.

Cocksworth escaped from the guardhouse in December 1805 with David Gibson (*q.v.*) and others. On 8 January 1806 the General Orders announced them to be outlaws. Knopwood reported that all had returned by 20 January 1806 and received 300 lashes and irons for one year. In 1809 Cocksworth was a lime-burner and gave evidence in the Judge Advocate's Court that he had helped rescue George Wheeler (*q.v.*) whom Thomas Gorman had shot at and wounded. By 1810 Cocksworth must have had some small store because he was supplying goods to Dr Bowden.

Attended the Hobart muster in 1811, after which there is no further record to date.

COLE, JOHN [c. 1781–1826]
?, aged 21, born Ashburton, Devon; 5'9", dark complexion.
Tried at Middlesex II Sessions (Middlesex G.D.) 13 January 1802 for stealing three miniature pictures (21s 0d) and ten silver teaspoons (26s 0d) from Elizabeth Oliver, widow, at her house the Sign of the Standard, Wells St., Whitechapel, where he lodged. He pawned the spoons, saying he was going on board a ship, and left the pictures with Mary Seaman who gave evidence against him. Sentence pronounced by the Recorder was transportation for seven years. Gaoled at Newgate and transferred to the *Captivity* hulk at Portsmouth.

During the voyage Cole was employed in the *Calcutta* as a servant to Knopwood who discharged and double-ironed him for inattention and on strong suspicion of robbing a chest in the wardroom steward's berth.

Cole was troublesome. In December 1804 he was suspected of killing Joseph Bradley (*q.v.*) after striking him on the head but the coroner's verdict was accidental death. In 1806 he was punished for stealing a kettle from Mrs Hobbs. The following March he was involved in a disturbance with the military and received 100 lashes and confinement in the guardhouse.

Cole was one of the convicts who pirated the *Marcia*. He was sent for trial at Port Jackson in February 1808, condemned to die by the Vice-Admiralty Court, but pardoned. He must have remained at Port Jackson as he does not appear on musters held in V.D.L. He became a sailor serving in the *Campbell Macquarie* on a voyage to Macquarie I., and *Endeavour* sealing in Bass Strait. While in port in Hobart, in 1819, he witnessed the drowning of two men in Hangan's Bay. He later joined the ill-fated *Sally*, a Hobart schooner engaged in bay-whaling in the D'Entrecasteaux Channel.

During a sealing expedition to the Auckland Islands a boat from the Sally *overturned and Cole was among the six seamen drowned, 6 November 1826.*

CONNELLY, ARTHUR [c. 1767 – after 1833]
Skinner and leather draper, aged 35, married. Literate.
Tried at City of Bristol S. of P. 8 April 1802 for robbing
Thomas Browning of his goods and banknotes on the
King's Highway. Committed to gaol and tried in the Court
of *Oyer et Terminer* before the Mayor, Recorder and Alder-
man (as J.P.s) and a jury. Sentenced to death by the Mayor.
Reprieved and sentenced to transportation for life. Gaoled
at the city gaol and transferred to the *Prudentia* hulk at
Woolwich.

Connelly's wife Sarah was allowed to accompany her husband and was berthed in the prison room in the *Calcutta*.
She was employed nursing a passenger from Rio, who was
ill and who disembarked at Cape Town.

Connelly and his wife attended the Hobart musters in
1811, 1818, 1819 and 1823. They had one child in 1819.
Connelly's brothers Charles (transported 1812) and Henry
joined him in Hobart. Arthur Connelly received a conditional pardon in January 1813 and a grant of 35 acres at
Clarence Plains from Gov. Macquarie where he ran some
sheep. He also owned a house in Argyle St. for which he
received £12 in compensation when the land was resumed.
A new one in the same street cost him £5. In 1819 he
became assistant gaoler at Hobart at a salary of £25 per
annum. His brother Charles had a licence for the Bricklayers' Arms and from there began the Friendly Society for
ex-*Calcutta* persons. Charles became the second husband of
Margaret Eddington (the mistress of David Collins at the
time of his death), after Michael Howe murdered her husband, the bushranger George Watts.

A note in the Colonial Secretary's papers relating to
Charles Connelly's children describes the parents as of 'bad
character'; although one child, Annie, was presented to
Queen Victoria.

*Sarah Connelly was buried 27 June 1835, aged 66, at the
Presbyterian Church at Bothwell where Arthur had been appointed
postmaster in 1833. No record of his death has yet been traced.*

CONSTABLE, WILLIAM [c. 1768 – ?]
Sailor, late of Bengal, aged 33.
Tried at Middlesex VI Sessions (Middlesex G.D.) 1 July
1801 for stealing three pairs of unfinished gloves (4s 0d)
from John Brooks, glover, while trying on the gloves. Had
been drinking. Sentenced to transportation for seven years.
Gaoled at Newgate and transferred to the *Fortune* hulk at
Portsmouth.

During the voyage out Constable was cook's mate and
allowed on deck.

*There appears to be no further record of this Constable's
whereabouts, but he may have been allowed to go to Port Jackson
where the S.G., 19 October 1806, referred to a William Constable, on the Hawkesbury, having drawn a note for 17 bushels of
wheat in favour of a John Howarth who was offering a reward for
a case of forgery.*

COOPER, ROBERT [1745–1837]
*Labourer, aged 57, pa. Warminster, Wiltshire, a gypsy (?),
married; 5'7½", black hair, dark brown to hazel eyes, cut on
left eyebrow and another on left forehead, high cheek-boned, high
forehead, lusty, orderly behaviour in county gaol.*
Tried at Dorset Summer Assizes 5 August 1802 on sus-

picion of stealing nine he-asses and four blind halters from
William Miles of Cranborne. Sentenced by Baron Graham
to transportation for seven years. Gaoled at Dorchester and
transferred to the *Captivity* hulk at Portsmouth.

Cooper's wife did not accompany him.

He was probably the gypsy, Cooper, who helped the
Fawkners during the voyage out.

Cooper attended the Hobart musters in 1811, 1818 and
1819, when he was classed as an invalid and 1823 when 'on
charity'. He had a 30-acre land grant from Gov. Macquarie
at Clarence Plains, on which he ran a few cattle.

*Appears to have lived for several years in hospital. Buried 21
January 1837, Holy Trinity, Hobart, age stated as 103 (?)
years.*

COOPER, WILLIAM [c. 1783–1820]
?, aged 19.
Tried at Southampton Summer Assizes (Winchester) 27
July 1802 together with James Cooper and William Jacobs
(*q.v.*) and others for stealing a sheep from George Garnier at
Wickham. Sentenced to death. Reprieved by Justices Sir
Giles Rooke and Baron Graham and sentenced to transpor-
tation for life. James Cooper was executed. William Cooper
was gaoled at Winchester and transferred to the hulks at
Portsmouth.

During the voyage Cooper was servant to a gunner. The
gypsy Cooper mentioned by J. P. Fawkner was more likely
Robert Cooper (*q.v.*).

Cooper attended the Hobart muster in 1818 and 1819.

He received a conditional pardon in January 1814. He
lived with a sister of John and William Waterson who had
arrived from Norfolk I. in 1808. She was known as
Elizabeth, the daughter of James Waterson and Elizabeth
Thomas, both convicts. They had three children born
between 1815 and 1820. Cooper took out a grazing licence
at Herdsman's Cove in 1819. In the same year he purchased
10 acres at Clarence Plains and rented 400 acres at Glebe on
which he raised crops together with 56 head of cattle, 132
rams and 300 ewes. He had two government servants. He
provided meat regularly for the Commissariat and owned a
house on the corner of Argyle and Liverpool streets which
had a good baker's oven and fine garden. He was a benefactor to the Auxiliary Bible Society. He gave surety for
Thomas Ransome to take out a licence for the Joiners' Arms
and to William Atkins for Chequers at Clarence Plains. He
arranged for Gov. Macquarie's baggage to be conveyed to
Launceston at a cost of £20.

*On Christmas Eve 1819 Knopwood reported that he and little
Betsey visited William Cooper who was very ill. He died a few
days later, 6 January 1820, at his farm at Clarence Plains after
a short illness. The H.T.G. reported that he was 'much respected
as an old inhabitant of this Colony and has left an infant family
to lament his death'.*

Soon afterwards his property was put up for sale.

Surnames of descendants have included: Cleator; Myler; Osboldstone.

CORMACK, WILLIAM [c. 1757 – ?]
(McCormack)
*Plasterer, aged 44, from Tipperary, Ireland; 5'3", fair complex-
ion, brown hair, grey eyes.*
Tried at Middlesex V Sessions (Middlesex G.D.) 20 May

1801 (together with Denis Kennedy (*q.v.*)) for stealing four sheep (£4) from John Claridge, a farmer at Finchley. He was hungry. Sentenced to death by Baron Graham. Reprieved and sentenced to transportation for life. Gaoled at Newgate and transferred to the *Captivity* hulk at Portsmouth.

Attended the Hobart muster in 1811 as McCormick {sic}. There appears to be no further record of him after that date.

COWARD, JAMES (JOHN) [c. 1777–1845]
Labourer, aged 23, from Offington, Kent; 5'3", dark complexion, brown hair, grey eyes.

Tried at Middlesex I Sessions (London G.D.) 3 December 1800 for stealing two black oxen (£20) from Phillip Delaney, in Kent, one of Scotch, one of Welsh breed. Coward said he was looking for a job, he was 'out of place', and had asked to drive the oxen to Smithfield. He had already been detained for a like offence. Sentenced by the Recorder to death, reprieved and sentenced to transportation for life. Gaoled at Giltspur and transferred to the hulks at Woolwich.

Coward appears to have been absent from Hobart each time the musters were taken, but there is enough evidence to show that he lived there for many years, probably as a labourer, for he had no grant of land.

In 1807 Knopwood tried Coward for gambling on the Lord's Day and in 1810 Bowden paid him £4 for some stonework and guttering.

On 3 June 1812 John Coward married Elizabeth Harkinstone whose name appeared, without her husband's, as 'on' victuals on the Hobart muster roll of 1818. At the time of their marriage Coward was working for, and lived with, Daniel Anchor (*q.v.*), the butcher. On 26 December 1812 Coward charged Anchor with enticing away his wife but Anchor was reprimanded and discharged and appears to have kept the wife.

Coward was still in Hobart in 1818 and was able to put down sureties up to £50 for the appearance in court of various friends to keep the peace and be of good behaviour.

It is likely that he went to live in Launceston and that he was the James Coward who, while living on the George Town Road, was injured in a cart accident and died 10 April 1845.

CRAWLEY, DANIEL [c.1775–1808]
Tailor, employed as cutter, aged 27, born Cork, Ireland; 5'10", dark complexion, brown hair, dark hazel eyes. Literate.

Tried at Middlesex II Sessions (Middlesex G.D.) 13 January 1802 for stealing a yard of woollen cloth (10s 0d) from John, Nicholas and Bryce Pearce, army clothiers. Crawley was in their employ as a cutter. They found red cloth tied under his waistcoat. Sentence pronounced by the Common Sergeant was transportation for seven years. Gaoled at Newgate then transferred to *Captivity* hulk at Portsmouth. He had been acquitted of a charge of forgery and been committed briefly to Newgate awaiting trial in December 1801. As a suspected forger, he must have been literate.

Buried 19 October 1808, aged 36 (?).

CRENER, MICHAEL, alias MICHAEL McGUIRE [c.1750–1810]
Labourer, aged 52.

Tried at East Kent S. of P. (Canterbury) 30 April 1802 for assaulting Thomas Perry in the Blue Town, pa. Minster, and robbing him of a knife, six halfpennies, a handkerchief and a pair of gloves. Sentence pronounced by seventeen J.P.s, comprising a grand jury, was transportation for seven years. Gaoled at St Augustine's gaol, Canterbury and transferred to the *Prudentia* at Woolwich.

In December 1806 Crener received 100 lashes from Knopwood after being found guilty of robbing the garden of a Kennedy (*q.v.*).

Buried 8 January 1810, Hobart, aged 60.

CROFT, THOMAS [1762–1831]
(Cross, Crofts)
Brickmaker, aged 40, born in the Castle foregate, Shropshire, 1762, son of Thomas and Esther (or Hester) (née Farmer) who married at St Mary's, Shrewsbury, 4 May 1761. Thomas jun. married Mary Dudley, born Oakham, Worcestershire c. 1761. Literate.

Tried at Shropshire Spring Assizes (Shrewsbury G.D.) 20 March 1802 together with his brother Edward on suspicion of stealing a double girth and two double reined bridles and other articles from John Cadwallader, pa. of the Holy Cross and St Giles, Shrewsbury, and Thomas himself of stealing a flaxen sheet from Edward Smout of the same parish and a black gelding from Ann Lawley, of Kinlet. Sentenced to death. Reprieved by Baron Thomson and Sir Alan Chambre and sentenced to transportation for life. Gaoled at the county prison in Shrewsbury and transferred to the hulks at Portsmouth.

At the same sessions Mary Croft was acquitted of a charge of stealing, together with Richard Garrett (*q.v.*) (who was found guilty and came in the *Calcutta*) a piece of calico from William Beaumont, mercer, St Chad, Shrewsbury. She was also acquitted of uttering in payment four pieces of counterfeit coin.

Mary Croft accompanied her husband in the *Calcutta* and was berthed in the prison room.

Croft attended the Hobart musters in 1811, 1818, 1819 and 1823. He received a conditional pardon in January 1813 and held grazing licences near the Stony Hut Plains, New Norfolk, on which he ran nine horned and 51 female cattle, 150 male sheep and 350 ewes in 1819, when he had one daughter Elizabeth and employed one free man. He supplied large amounts of meat to the Commissariat.

From the earliest days in the colony Croft was one of the most useful of all the prisoners. As a brickmaker he was, for several years, fully employed overseeing other brickmakers. In September 1804 he complained to Collins about the wilfulness of those trying to destroy his work. Collins issued a General Order prohibiting such interference. In 1806 he provided Knopwood with 400 bricks for the building of Cottage Green. In 1807 and 1809 his own house in Elizabeth St. was broken into, the second time by Job Stokes who was later executed for the crime.

David Lord acquired Croft's property in Elizabeth St., probably after the deaths of Mary Croft (buried at St David's 30 December 1821) and daughter Elizabeth aged 10, who died 19 July 1822 after an accident. Croft went to live at Snake Banks on the South Esk where he leased a house and shops from E. D. Wedge. On 29 August 1831

Gov. Arthur approved of a joint petition from Croft and Sarah Skelton, transported for stealing and assigned to a neighbour, John Reece, to marry but the marriage does not appear to have taken place.

Died the following month. Buried 24 September 1831, St John's, Launceston.

CRONBURY, CHRISTOPHER [c. 1780–1805]
(Croenbury, Crombe)
Soldier, 25th Foot Rgt, aged 23, stationed at Gibraltar. Possibly Dutch.
Tried in secret (?) at an army court martial December 1802 following a mutiny at Gibraltar and sentenced to death. Commuted by H.R.H. the Duke of Kent. Embarked at Gibraltar in the sloop H.M.S. *Cynthia*, 12 January 1803. Taken aboard the *Calcutta*, 21 April at Portsmouth.
Died 13 November 1805, Hobart, of a cough, aged 25. [Knopwood added a note against his diary entry of 4 January 1804 including Crombe [sic] among the names of Gibraltar mutineers who served as members of the night watch at Port Phillip. Against the name 'Crombe' he mistakenly wrote that he had died at Port Phillip. This was apparently added much later.]

CROSS, SAMUEL, alias JOHN [c.1776 – ?]
Wheelwright, aged 25, of St Martin's-in-the-Fields; 5'5", dark complexion, brown hair, hazel eyes.
Tried at Middlesex VII Sessions (Middlesex G.D.) 16 September 1801 for stealing 10 yards of cashmere (30s 0d) from George Goodey, man's mercer, of Covent Garden. Sentenced by Baron Hotham to transportation for seven years. Gaoled at Tothillfields and transferred to the *Stanislaus* hulk at Woolwich.
During the voyage out he was employed in the carpenter's crew on deck.
There was no record after his arrival in Hobart.
He probably left the colony when free about 1808–09.

CRUSE, JOHN [c. 1788 – after 1825]
(Cruiss, Cruce)
Tried at the Spring Assizes of the Palatinate of Lancaster (Lancaster G.D.) on 20 March 1802 for being in possession of forged notes. Sentenced by Justice Sir Giles Rooke to transportation for fourteen years. Gaoled at Lancaster Castle and transferred to the hulks at Langston.
During the voyage out he was servant to Lieut. Donovan.
He attended the Hobart muster in 1811 and the Sydney muster in 1817, in which he was described as free (having completed his sentence in 1816) and a dealer, still in the colony. He must have had permission to go to Sydney several years earlier.
In 1814 he was principal overseer of government gangs of sawyers and timber fellers at Lane Cove when he was dismissed from service for supplying private individuals with timber and shingles. In 1820 he owned a timber carriage and cattle but sold the carriage.
Some time after this he left for Hobart and in October 1825 joined the Andromeda *to return to England.*

CRUTE, JOHN [c. 1777–1826]
(Cruitt)
Soldier, aged 26, 25th Foot Rgt stationed at Gibraltar. Born Ashburton, Devon; 5'8¾", dark brown hair, blue eyes, a mark of gunshot wound on his right thigh and a scar on his left cheek.
Tried in secret (?) at an army court martial December 1802, following the mutiny at Gibraltar and sentenced to death. Commuted by H.R.H. the Duke of Kent to transportation for life. Embarked at Gibraltar in the sloop H.M.S. *Cynthia*, 12 January 1803. Taken aboard the *Calcutta* on 21 April at Portsmouth.
In December 1803 Collins appointed him a subordinate of the night watch.
In October 1806 he escaped from Hobart with Thomas Tombs (*q.v.*) and others, returning the following January when he received 300 lashes as punishment.
He attended the Hobart muster in 1811, and although he remained in V.D.L. his name did not appear on other muster rolls.
In 1820 he received an absolute pardon.
He lived for a long time at Pitt Water, was a labourer, and became a notorious character who managed to evade the law for many years until detected of sheep stealing from David Lord in 1826. He appeared before Chief Justice Pedder at the Supreme Court in Hobart and was sentenced to death.
Executed 18 September 1826, aged 'nearly 50'.

CURTIS, JOHN [c. 1775–1805]
Sailor, aged 27.
Tried at Somerset Summer Assizes (Wells G.D.) together with John Waterson (*q.v.*) on 21 August 1802 for having stolen one coat, three waistcoats, a silk handkerchief and one pair of worsted stockings after breaking and entering the house of Charles Potter at Thurloxton. Sentenced to death. Reprieved by Baron Graham and Justice Sir Giles Rooke and sentenced to transportation for life. Gaoled first at Ilchester, then at Wilton and transferred to the hulks at Langston.
During the voyage out he served as a sailor.
Died 27 May 1805, Hobart, aged 28 (?), from catarrh.

DAVEY, JAMES [c. 1781–1846]
(Davie)
Husbandman, aged 21.
Tried together with Robert Davey at Essex Summer Assizes (Chelmsford G.D.) 28 July 1802 for breaking into the shop and dwelling house of Joseph Presland at Debden, stealing a piece of Irish cloth, a silk handkerchief, a pair of worsted stockings, four £1 notes and £10 in cash. Found not guilty. Tried on a second charge of stealing a flour sack. After consideration of four other indictments, Justice Baron Hotham said it was necessary for the security of the county to sentence Davey to transportation for seven years. Gaoled at Chelmsford and transferred to the *Prudentia* hulk at Woolwich.
Davey was either transferred or had means after he was free to go to Norfolk I. where he appeared on the Commissariat return, victualled for 29 days since 3 March 1810, after which he worked as a labourer. In 1811 he had five acres in cultivation and owned six swine. He was in hos-

pital at Norfolk I., treated for a wound in January 1812 and was among the settlers who embarked in the *Lady Nelson* for Port Dalrymple, arriving on 20 January 1813, free, single, and with no goods or stores. Thereafter he appeared on the Cornwall musters of 1819, 1820 and 1823.

He received a grant of 40 acres at Norfolk Plains, mostly sown with wheat, in 1820. He also had two female horses, five male horned cattle and six female cattle. He employed a government servant. When a new road and bridge were built over the South Esk near Longford the road cut through the middle of his property.

On 18 January 1819, at St John's, Launceston, he married Catherine Jordan; ceremony performed by the Revd John Youl. They already had two children, Robert born in 1816 and James born in 1818 (he died in infancy). Within the next twelve years they had another son and four daughters. The parents were not literate but appear to have contributed to the education at least of their sons.

Davey was especially proud of Ploughboy, his powerful horse, seventeen hands high and five years old. He advertised it in 1835 as a 'sure foal-getter', his terms being £3 with 4s 0d groomage fee, paddocks provided gratis but without responsibility. If wished, Ploughboy would travel occasionally within a few miles of Norfolk Plains.

Davey spent his final years in Brisbane St., Launceston. Died suddenly from natural causes, probably apoplexy, 23 February 1846, aged about 65.

Surnames of descendants have included: Barrow; Britt; Hodgetts; Larking; Lewis; Palmer; Rudd; Styles; Thorne.

DAVID, JEREMIAH [c. 1754–1803]

Labourer, aged 47, pa. Llanwrda, co. Carmarthen, Wales, married, a son, William Jeremiah.

Tried at Carmarthen Summer Assizes (Carmarthen G.D.) 12 August 1801 for stealing in the pa. Mothvey two male sheep from David Jones and three glass bottles (1s 0d) from John Rees, Bishop. Not guilty of second charge. His wife was also indicted but there was no record that she was tried. He was sentenced to death. Reprieved and sentenced to transportation for life. Gaoled at Carmarthen Shire Gaol and transferred to the hulks at Portsmouth.

His family did not accompany him.

Died at sea of dysentery, 13 September 1803.

DAVIES, THOMAS [1778 – ?]

Fisherman, aged 23, of London, born Mitcham, Surrey; 5'5", dark complexion, brown hair, grey eyes.

Tried at Middlesex IV Sessions (Middlesex G.D.) 15 April 1801 together with James Blake (*q.v.*) and William Smith (*q.v.*) for stealing a sack (2s 0d) and four bushels of barley (30s 0d) from George Shum and others, taken from a barge in the Thames into their peterboat. Sentenced to transportation for seven years by Mr Justice Heath. Gaoled at Tothillfields and transferred to the *Fortune* hulk at Langston.

There appears to be no further record of Davies in the colony. He probably returned to England c. 1808 when he would have been free.

DAVIS, JAMES [c. 1781 – ?]

Shoemaker, aged 19, of City of London; 5'5", fair complexion, brown hair, grey eyes. Literate.

Tried at Middlesex VI Sessions (Middlesex G.D.) 9 July 1800 for stealing, with William Halstead, 20 lb sugar (18s 0d) from Charles Smith. He pleaded innocent and one witness gave him a good character. Sentenced by Mr Justice Kinnard to transportation for seven years. Gaoled at Newgate and transferred to the hulks at Langston.

Davis attended the Hobart muster in 1811 but prior to that he spent some time at sea. He appears to be the Davis who accompanied Knopwood and Harris on their fourteen-day exploration of Bruny I., Storm Bay and the Huon in November 1804. He and Salmon (*q.v.*) were in some trouble in June 1807 on suspicion of having wounded a servant of William Collins but they were acquitted. Three months later he received 'severe corporal punishment' for buying or receiving kangaroo and emu meat from the servants of Bowden and Harris.

It is likely that Davis was the James Davis who in May 1809 joined the crew of the whaler *King George*, for the Auckland Islands and later sailed in the *Cyclops* to Fiji for sandalwood.

After returning to Hobart at the time of the muster he joined the American brig Aurora *which had come from Macquarie I. After calling at Sydney with a large cargo of elephant seal oil and skins, it sailed to Calcutta. His death has not been traced.*

There were several persons of the same name in the colony. Alternatively, he might have been the James Davis who received land grants of 40 and 22 acres at New Norfolk. This Davis was concerned as a witness in the case against Denis McCarty in 1813–14 when he deposed that the people of New Norfolk were dissatisfied with McCarty's conduct. McCarty had called him an informer with malicious intentions.

DAVIS, JOHN [c. 1788 – ?]

Shoemaker, aged 14, born Southwark.

Tried at Middlesex V Sessions (Middlesex G.D.) 2 June 1802 for stealing bacon (1s 6d) from Thomas Rogers, of Ratcliff, grocer and cheesemonger. Sentenced by Baron Graham to transportation for seven years. Gaoled at Newgate and transferred to the *Prudentia* hulk at Woolwich.

Davis did not appear on any of the muster rolls. There were others of his name in the colony. One absconded and was outlawed in March 1808. By 1814 one had become a bushranger with Peter Mills. It is more than likely that John Davis, of the *Calcutta*, sailed as a crew member on numerous expeditions to the islands; perhaps in the *Fox* when it discovered Foveaux Strait, and the *Mary and Sally* when James Kelly took it on a whaling voyage to Macquarie I. in 1814. He then appears to have joined the *Elizabeth and Mary* which made many voyages to Macquarie I.

A John Davis did run sheep on leased land at Clarence Plains in 1819 and a John Davis, aged 35, married Mary Brown at St David's, 9 December 1822. This John Davis was executed for sheep stealing in 1826, together with *Calcutta* convict John Crute (*q.v.*).

Because of his name, it is difficult to trace his activities with any certainty.

DAWKINS, THOMAS [c. 1769–1803]
?, aged 33.
Tried at Derby Spring Assizes (Derby G.D.) 13 March 1802 together with Joseph Johnson (*q.v.*) for horse stealing. Sentenced to death by Baron Graham. Reprieved and sentenced to transportation for life. Gaoled at the county gaol and transferred to the hulks at Langston.
Died 1 November 1803, Port Phillip, aged 33 (?), having been 'in a state of great debility'.

DAWSON, JOHN [c. 1787 – after 1827]
Post-boy, aged 15, of Bolton-le-Moors, Lancashire. Roman Catholic. Literate.
Tried at the Spring Assizes of the Palatinate of Lancaster (Lancaster G.D.) 24 March 1802 for stealing two bills of exchange (£13 and £137) while employed to carry as a post-boy. Sentenced to death. Reprieved by Lord Chief Justice Kenyon and Justice Sir Alan Chambre and sentenced to transportation for fourteen years. Gaoled at Lancaster Castle and transferred to the hulks at Portsmouth.
Dawson attended the Hobart musters in 1811, 1818, 1819 and 1823. He received a grant of 30 acres at Herdsman's Cove from Gov. Davey, half of which produced wheat while he ran cattle, 50 rams and 100 ewes on the other half in 1819. He employed one government servant.
On 1 July 1816, in Hobart, John Dawson, aged 30, married Margaret Kelley, aged 22. She was a convict who had arrived in the *Alexander*. By 1827 they had a son and three daughters, were living at New Town and described as Roman Catholics and of good character.
He has not been traced beyond this date.

DEACON, EDWARD [c. 1775–1804]
Brickmaker, aged 27.
Tried at the City of Chester Pleas of Session of Crown Mote 21 April 1802 for an unknown felony. Sentenced to transportation for life. Gaoled at Chester Castle and transferred to the hulks at Langston.
Died 8 November 1804, Hobart, of scurvy.

DENHAM, MARK [c. 1782–1803]
Gardener, aged 20, born Kensington; 5'6", dark complexion.
Tried at Middlesex III Sessions (Middlesex G.D.) 17 February 1802 together with John Heels (*q.v.*) for stealing a bay mare (£3) from William Loosely, formerly of Harrow and since gone to the West Indies. Denham and Heels had gone to look after an ass and a foal. Heels said the mare was his and he sold it to Denham. Sentenced by Justice Sir Simon Le Blanc to death. Reprieved and sentenced to transportation for life. Gaoled at Newgate and transferred to the *Captivity* hulk at Portsmouth. Three witnesses gave him a good character.
Died 20 May 1803, at sea near Tenerife, from debility brought on by seasickness.

DINHAM, JOHN [c. 1764 – after 1817]
?, aged 38.
Tried at Somerset Spring Assizes (Taunton G.D.) together with Robert Lawrence (*q.v.*) 1 April 1802 for stealing one wether sheep from the Rt Hon. Hester, Countess Dowager of Chatham, and two wether sheep from J. Michell. Sentenced to death. Reprieved by Justices Sir Soulden Laurence and Sir Simon Le Blanc and sentenced to transportation for life. Gaoled at Taunton and transferred to the hulks at Langston.
After arrival in Hobart Dr Bowden employed him as shepherd and stock keeper.
He attended the Hobart muster in 1811, the Sydney muster in 1811 and the Newcastle muster in 1817.
He was charged with stealing, using force and arms, eight ewes from Bowden 26 September 1811. He appeared before Judge Ellis Bent at the Court of Criminal Jurisdiction in Sydney, pleading that he had taken the sheep to Joseph Heatley, because they were inflicted with scab, for the purpose of curing them. William Mansfield (*q.v.*) was also involved with the crime but was acquitted.
Dinham was sent to Newcastle after being capitally reprieved.

DIXON, JOSEPH [c. 1777 – d. before 1823]
?, aged 25, born Durham.
Tried at Middlesex V Sessions (Middlesex G.D.) 2 June 1802 for stealing 28 lb sugar (12s 0d) from Francis Searle and Edward Smith, and on a second count, for charging it to be the property of John Archer. Searle was a grocer and partner of Smith. Archer said he delivered the goods to the house of a Mr Dixon in Queen St., Soho, and Joseph Dixon stole them from the cart and ran off with them. Sentence pronounced by the Recorder was transportation for seven years. Gaoled at Newgate and transferred to the *Captivity* hulk at Portsmouth.
Dixon attended the Hobart musters in 1811, 1818 and 1819 when he was described as an invalid in the general hospital.
Probably died before the muster of 1823.

DIXON, WILLIAM, alias WILLIAM SMITH [c. 1785 – after 1834?]
Labourer, aged 16, born Newcastle.
Tried at Northumberland Summer Assizes (Newcastle G.D.) 1 August 1801 for stealing a horse from Barmoor South Stead belonging to A. Forster. Sentenced to death. Reprieved by Justice Sir Alan Chambre and Lord Chief Justice Alvanley and sentenced to transportation for life. Gaoled in Morpeth prison and transferred to the *Stanislaus* hulk at Woolwich.
Dixon attended the Hobart musters in 1811, 1818, 1819 and 1823. He received a conditional pardon in May 1816 and an absolute pardon in 1817. He was employed as a sawyer and received an order for a land grant of 40 acres at Pitt Water from Gov. Macquarie on which he grew wheat in 1819, but it appears to have come into the hands of David Lord. He had a farm at Muddy Plains on one side of Ralph's Bay. Although there is no record of his marriage, Knopwood referred to visiting a Mr Dixon in the area in March 1834 and christening a child there.
He was in trouble during 1825 when, in February, he was absent from his usual place of residence after being charged with a felony. The police office in Hobart gave notice of escaped convicts still missing a month later, offering £2 reward for the capture of William Dixon, described as 5'8", with brown hair, grey eyes, a native of Newcastle, a sawyer who arrived in *Calcutta* and was free by servitude.
His death has not been traced.

DOWSING, JAMES [c. 1776–1839]
?, aged 25, of London; 5'4", fair complexion, brown hair, grey eyes.
Tried at Middlesex I Sessions (London G.D.) 2 December 1801 for stealing out of a cart a parcel containing a wrapper (1s 0d) and 35 yards of woollen cloth (£11 4s 0d) belonging to William Sutton, who kept the Salisbury Arms at Smithfield. Dowsing said he picked up the parcel in the street. Sentence pronounced by the Recorder was transportation for seven years. Gaoled at Poultry and transferred to the *Captivity* hulk at Portsmouth.

He attended the Hobart musters in 1811, 1818, 1819 and 1823. He received a 30-acre land grant at Argyle in 1820. Dowsing's Point was named after him.

He remained a bachelor until 5 November 1827 when he married a widow, Johanna Scully, at St David's. They had at least one daughter.

He died at New Town at the age of 64 (?), a farmer. Buried 15 January 1839, St David's. Johanna Dowsing died in March 1867, aged 96.

Surnames of descendants include: White.

DOYLE, MICHAEL [c. 1769–1814?]
Biscuit baker, aged 33, bap. pa. St George, East London; 5'6", fair complexion.
Tried at Middlesex I Sessions (Middlesex G.D.) 13 January 1802 for assaulting Jeremiah Hargan at Goodman's Fields on the King's Highway, together with George Brewer (*q.v.*) and stealing a watch (£5), chain (6d) and seal (2d). Doyle dressed as a sailor. He had been working as a waterside lumper. They had been drinking. Elizabeth Guelph, with whom he had lived for three months, gave witness that he was with her all day and that he had come from abroad. Sentenced to death by the Chief Baron. Reprieved and sentenced to transportation for life. Gaoled at Newgate and transferred to the *Captivity* hulk at Portsmouth.

Doyle attended the Hobart muster in 1811. He was a servant to surgeon William Hopley. He was one of the convicts who seized the ship *Argo* in May 1814 which had brought out a cargo of rice, sugar, tea, coffee, piece goods, rum, etc. The chief officer ordered them off the ship at Storm Bay into a leaky boat. They appear to have been in league with Andrew Whitehead (*q.v.*) and Denis McCarty on whose premises large quantities of illegal spirits were found. Macquarie, sending a report to the government of Bengal (*Argo* was registered in Calcutta), requested apprehension of the convicts whom Captain Dixon had seduced away from the territory.

There were other Michael Doyles in the colony but there is nothing to indicate this one returned. He probably drowned when off-loaded from the Argo.

DREW, WILLIAM, alias SLAMBO [c. 1777–1817]
Farmer, aged 23, of Southwark, 4'10", dark complexion, brown hair, hazel eyes. (A later entry states 5' and grey eyes.)
Tried at Middlesex S. of P. 28 September 1800 for stealing a quantity of wet linen hanging out to dry from Sarah Jackson. Sentence pronounced by the Common Sergeant was two months in Newgate and to be publicly whipped and discharged. Recommitted to Newgate in February 1801 and tried for petty larceny 20 February. Sentenced to transportation for seven years as 'a very old offender'. Gaoled at Newgate and transferred to the *Stanislaus* hulk at Woolwich.

Drew attended the Hobart muster in 1811. Known as Slambo, he worked as a shepherd near New Norfolk for William Williams (*q.v.*) of Hobart and was in correspondence with the bushranger Michael Howe whom he agreed with his master to take at the first opportunity.

Howe murdered Drew. Buried by Knopwood, 13 October 1817 aged 41 (?).

DUFF, JAMES [c. 1781–1818]
(Duffy)
Lapidary, aged 19, of Pancreas, Middlesex; 5', dark complexion, brown hair, grey eyes.
Tried at Middlesex VII Sessions (Middlesex G.D.) 17 September 1800 for stealing four quarter loaves of bread (5s 0d) from David Pitcairn, baker. George Longden swore he had had Duff seven times in the House of Correction for running away from his master. Sentence pronounced by the Common Sergeant was transportation for seven years. Gaoled at Newgate and transferred to the hulks at Langston.

James Duff's name did not appear on any of the Hobart muster rolls. He became a bushranger in 1806 when he was absent from labour for eleven weeks. He was charged on his return with stealing dogs, and received 300 lashes. He spent another four months in the bush in 1807 but returned to accept the Governor's amnesty. In March 1808 he was again absent and was one of those responsible for bringing in the head of the notorious murderer Lemon and his associate Brown as prisoner. Collins praised his 'spirited and successful exertions' in a General Order. Duff later worked as a labourer for Augustus Morris (*q.v.*) at the Tea Tree Brush. In April 1818, after a short illness, Mrs Morris sent him with a bundle of clothes to a neighbour's house. He did not return and Augustus Morris discovered his body.

At a coroner's inquest, 13 April 1818 A. W. H. Humphrey found he had 'died by the visitation of God'.

DUFF, PATRICK [c. 1770 – after 1816]
(Duffy, Duffey)
Discharged soldier, aged 32, born Monrath, Ireland; 5'8", dark complexion.
Tried at Middlesex II Sessions (Middlesex G.D.) 13 January 1802 for assaulting and robbing John Barclay on the King's Highway of a clasp knife (2d), 4s 0d, ten sixpences and 36 halfpennies. Barclay kept the King's Head in Islington. At night he saw two men, one in sailor's and one in soldier's dress. They tore open his coat and said it was 'bloody hard for them to be without money'. Duff held him while the sailor ran off with the money. Police found only an old pocket-book, knife and tobacco box on Duff, who said he was held up by two men. He produced his army discharge from the pocket-book. He had been wounded three times. The jury recommended him for mercy for not having used violence but the Common Sergeant read his sentence of death. Reprieved and sentenced to transportation for life. Gaoled at Newgate and transferred to the *Captivity* hulk at Portsmouth.

Duff attended the Hobart muster in 1811. In September 1816 he received a conditional pardon and later an absolute pardon.

It is likely that he returned to England or Ireland before the muster of 1818.

DUKES, RICHARD [c. 1767 – ?]
Pattern-maker, aged 35, of London, late of pa. Wormley, co. Hertford; 5'5", fair complexion, brown hair, grey eyes.
Tried at Hertfordshire Spring Assizes (Hertford G.D.) 8 March 1802 together with John Nowlan and Thomas Barnes for breaking and entering with force and arms the house of Sir Abraham Hume at Wormleybury and stealing a mocha stone box set in gold (10s 0d), a miniature picture set in enamel (5s 0d), a gold box (£1 10s 0d), and ivory pick-case set with pearls (£1), a bloodstone watch set with diamonds (£2), a gold filigree smelling-bottle (£1 10s 0d), an agate box (£1), nine silver tea-spoons (1s 0d), a silver tea-pot (£3), a plated coffee biggin (2s 0d), a cocoa biggin (2s 0d), a pair of gold-plated sleeve buttons (£2), a pair of silver buckles (£1), and three pounds of mutton. Sentenced to death by Mr Justice Conant. Reprieved and sentenced to transportation for life. Gaoled at Hertford county gaol, transferred to Newgate and later to the hulks at Woolwich.

There appears to be no record of Dukes' activities after his arrival in Hobart in 1804.

EARLE, JOHN [c. 1778–1840]
Farm labourer, aged 24, born Baltonsborough, Somerset, 1777, younger son of Samuel Earle, farmer, and his wife Mary (née Austin). Literate.
Tried at Somerset S. of P. (Wells) 13 January 1802 together with his cousin James Austin (*q.v.*) for using force and arms to steal I) 100 lb of honey (30s 0d) and six straw bee hives (3s 0d) from his uncle, Peter Higgens, at Hornblotten; II) also for stealing 100 lb of honey (30s 0d) and five straw bee hives (2s 6d) from Edward Powell at West Lydford. Found guilty on both charges and sentenced to transportation for seven years. Gaoled at Wells prison and transferred to the hulks at Langston.

During the voyage out Earle became servant to Lieut. Pateshall.

Earle attended the Hobart musters in 1811, 1818 and 1819. He received a 40-acre land grant from Gov. Macquarie at Glenorchy. By 1819 he appears to have had no listed stock but was supplying meat to the Commissariat, as much as 9 000 lb in one quarter in 1824. That year he suffered an armed hold-up and was robbed by bushrangers. In 1826 he received a further land grant of 200 acres at Glenorchy.

In the early days in Hobart, Earle was Knopwood's gardener. Although often in trouble and receiving as many as 500 lashes at a time, Knopwood continued to employ him for several years. He was good with the dogs, hunting down kangaroos, useful with a boat and made several exploratory journeys with Knopwood up the river and down Storm Bay to the Huon and Bruny I. He was also useful with timber and made a bedstead, albeit with the illegal use of timber, for Stocker (*q.v.*). On one occasion when out hunting he shot at natives who threw stones and shook spears.

Earle was in partnership with his cousin Austin in several ventures. In 1818 they had a licence to run a ferry service between Baltonsborough (Austin's Ferry) and Old Beach (Compton) and in 1819 a licence for the Barley Mow at the Black Snake. When Gov. Macquarie stayed there in 1821 he renamed the inn Roseneath. They also ran the Northampton Arms at Compton but dissolved their partnership by mutual consent in 1822. Later Charles Goodridge leased the Compton ferry, which had remained in Earle's hands, for a time.

Earle joined the Auxiliary Bible Society and later went into partnership with David Lord when they grazed stock in the Oatlands district. In 1829 he became pound-keeper at the Eastern Marshes where he had large and extensive sheep walks and a further grant of 100 acres. He also bought 30 acres at Green Ponds, where he retired, naming the property High Sunderland.

On 5 August 1822 he married a woman five years older than himself, Mary Ann Fletcher, widow of Charles Fletcher of Port Dalrymple. Knopwood rode up to Roseneath to perform the ceremony. One of the Fletcher creditors, Mr Corney, warned persons against receiving from Earle any cattle or sheep from Fletcher's estate and warned Earle, then in debt, against branding his name on any stock before the estate debts were paid. In 1830 while they were driving near New Town, Earle had what might have been a stroke and fell out of his chaise. He fractured a shoulder bone.

The Earles had at least two sons and were caring for an orphaned boy, John Weeding, aged six, whom they had adopted and were educating. They moved into Hobart and were living at 31 Elizabeth St. in 1831 but two years later they separated when a servant, Harriet Taylor, was assigned to Earle and became pregnant to Charles Brown, an overseer. Mrs Earle made unproven charges against her and she charged Mrs Earle with intrigues with other men and being constantly drunk.

Died 15 January 1840. Buried 21 January, St David's, aged 60, according to the inscription on his tombstone. He shared his grave with James Austin. Ann Earle died at Battle Hill, Green Ponds, 18 April 1838, aged 63.

Surnames of descendants have included: Reid.

EDWARDS, JOHN [c. 1780–1813]
(Edwardes)
Baker (?), aged 21, from Worcester; 5'3", fair complexion, light brown hair, grey eyes.
Tried at Middlesex Assizes VIII Sessions (London G.D.) 28 October 1801 for stealing a pocket-book (5s 0d) and silver pencil case (3s 0d) from Solomon Arden, baker. Sentence pronounced by the Recorder was transportation for seven years. Gaoled at Poultry and transferred to the *Prudentia* at Woolwich.

In June 1806 John Edwards became a baker but his name did not appear on the 1811 Hobart muster roll. He was probably the Edwards who tried to escape in Capt. Bristow's whaler, the *Sarah*, in October 1807.

Buried 16 January 1813, Hobart, aged 33.

EDWARDS, JOSEPH CHARLES [c. 1779–1809]
Clerk, aged 21, married, with one child. Literate.
Tried at Kent Summer Assizes (Maidstone G.D.) 27 July

1801 for stealing a silver watch from Matthew Mallet in Greenwich. Sentenced to transportation for seven years. Gaoled at Maidstone and transferred to the *Prudentia* hulk at Woolwich.

His name appears on Capt. Woodriff's list as a writer employed by Lieut. Houston of the *Calcutta*. Edwards' wife Elizabeth and daughter Elizabeth accompanied him on the voyage and were berthed in the prison room.

On 28 April 1804 Knopwood buried their daughter at the Derwent.

Buried 21 January 1809, Hobart, aged 30. Elizabeth Edwards was buried 6 June 1833, St David's, aged 60 and described as 'a poor woman'.

EMBLIN, JEREMIAH [c. 1760–1808]
(Emblem)
Attorney's clerk, aged 42, of Lincoln's Inn, London; 5'7", dark complexion. Literate.
Tried at Middlesex VI Sessions (London G.D.) 14 July 1802 for embezzling a banker's draft for £209 11s 0d made out to his employer, John Benbow, an attorney with chambers in Lincoln's Inn. He had cashed the draft for four £50 notes with Gosling's and Sharpe's cashier, Ewings. Emblin considerably altered his appearance. He then changed money for tens and fives at the Bank of England, endorsing the entry J. Emblin, Lincoln's Inn. Emblin, when detained by a policeman at Bath, was also in possession of Benbow's gold watch and a box. Sentenced by the Recorder to transportation for fourteen (seven?) years. Gaoled at Tothillfields and transferred to the *Prudentia* hulk at Woolwich.

During the voyage out, Emblin was allowed to go without irons.

Knopwood reported on 27 February 1808 that he had 'buried Jeremiah Emblem {sic}, formerly an eminent attorney in London'.

EVERITT, CHARLES, alias EVERARD [c. 1781 – after 1833]
?, aged 20, born London, lodging at the Swan and Pike at Enfield Marsh; fair complexion, brown hair and hazel eyes.
Tried together with brother James at Middlesex VIII Sessions (London G.D.) 28 October 1801 for breaking and entering the house of James Maze and stealing nine 7s pieces, 12s 0d, banknotes of £50, £30, £20, £10, three £5, three £2, twelve £1, bills of exchange for £6 11s 0d and £14 14s 0d, and money order £92 12s 0d from Maze's accompting house at the dockside. The Everitts had climbed up a ladder from a barge. Joel Lovell gave evidence against them. He said he was buying lottery shares and asked them to go with him. James Everitt sen., father of the boys, was also charged and found guilty of harbouring his sons after they had committed the felony. Charles and James jun. were sentenced to death by the Recorder, reprieved and sentenced to transportation for life. The brothers were gaoled at Newgate and transferred to the *Captivity* hulk at Portsmouth. Their 64-year-old father, originally from Hilton, Dorsetshire, died in prison. James Everitt sailed in the *Coromandel* for Port Jackson.

Charles Everitt attended the Hobart musters in 1811 and the Hobart convict musters of 1820, 1821 and 1833, one of the few *Calcutta* convicts who does not appear to have received a pardon.

In 1813 he was a government stock keeper at New Nor-

folk and gave evidence that he had killed some cattle for Denis McCarty in the case heard at the Supreme Court.

He had a ticket-of-leave confirmed in 1817 and his record shows that he was then aged 34, a labourer, 5'9½", brown hair, brown eyes, and pock-pitted.

Everitt has been difficult to trace after 1833 when he was engaged on public works in Hobart.

Members of the well known Bass Strait Islander family of Everitt are descended from Charles' brother James.

EVERITT, JOHN, alias EVERARD [c. 1781–1803]
(Everett)
?, aged 21. Literate.
Tried at Wiltshire Assizes (Salisbury G.D.) 13 March 1802 on four charges concerning the forgery of a £2 banknote and promissory note with intent to defraud James Cowley. Sentenced to death. Reprieved by Justices Sir Soulden Laurence and Sir Simon Le Blanc and sentenced to transportation for life. Gaoled at Salisbury gaol and transferred to the hulks at Langston.

Died 15 November 1803, Port Phillip.

FAWKNER, JOHN [c. 1772–1854]
(Falkiner, Faulkner, etc.)
Metal refiner, aged 29, born Birmingham, lived in London at 2 Parker's Lane, Drury Lane and later at 11 Whitecross St., near St Giles-without-Cripplegate Church. Married Hannah Pascoe whose parents were from Cornwall and lived in Cock Lane, one son John and one daughter Elizabeth, two children died in infancy; 5'6", sallow complexion.
Tried at Middlesex VI Sessions (London G.D.) 1 July 1801 for receiving a gold snuff box set with diamonds (£400), diamond necklace (£20), a pair of shoe buckles (£20), a pair of gold knee buckles (£11), two silver table-spoons (£1 10s 0d) and five silver tea-spoons (£2). They had all been stolen by Thomas Collett alias Putty (convicted at the last sessions and sentenced to transportation for fourteen years) from John Christian Weppler, a planter from Jamaica, out of a cart carrying his large red leather trunk from Gravesend to Billingsgate. Henry and Mary Hayes had also received goods from Collett, and were tried on 26 May 1801. Mr Justice Grose found Henry Hayes not guilty but sentenced Mary Hayes to transportation for fourteen years. Collett received a sentence of transportation for seven years. The Common Sergeant read the sentence on Fawkner — transportation for fourteen years. Gaoled at Newgate and transferred to the *Prudentia* at Woolwich.

Hannah Fawkner and the children accompanied Fawkner in the *Calcutta* and bargained with the carpenter for better accommodation, paying £20 for a berth in the fore cockpit, sharing with the Groves (*q.v.*). John Pascoe Fawkner, the son, has left his own reminiscences of the voyage and of the months at Port Phillip. They appear to have had a makeshift hut at Sullivan Bay. They acquired a chest made from the local box.

Fawkner attended the Hobart musters in 1811, 1818, 1819 and 1823, as well as the Sydney muster in 1817. He received a conditional pardon in February 1812 and was free soon afterwards.

He arrived in Hobart with a sow and was among the earliest to receive a land grant. Gov. King granted him

50 acres near the rivulet in January 1806 and the family received further grants from Gov. Macquarie — the father 50 acres, wife 50 acres, son 90 acres, and daughter Elizabeth (widow by then of Thomas Green (q.v.)) 40 acres, all on the Main Road at Glenorchy. Fawkner had five acres of wheat, one cow, one ox, one ewe, one wether, one male and two female goats, two male and six female swine. By 1807 Fawkner had grown a garden, owned three cows, two bull calves, three wethers, fifteen ewes, four lambs, one ram goat and three wether goats, and employed a government servant. By 1819 they had 76 acres sown with wheat, barley and vegetables, thirteen horned cattle, 29 female cattle, 104 male sheep and 270 ewes and employed six government servants. He provided large quantities of wheat and meat to the Commissariat. Fawkner was among those who supported and subscribed towards the construction of a bridge and road to New Town in 1807.

In 1806 Mrs Fawkner returned to England, partly to claim an inheritance. She was absent for three years. During this time Elizabeth kept house for her father and brother. Soon after her mother's return Elizabeth married Thomas Green, who had received a conditional pardon in 1807. They had two children, one born the day after her husband's death in November 1812.

It is likely that Mrs Fawkner returned to the colony with some useful materials and goods to supply John Ingle for his store. The latter held accounts for Collins' funeral expenses, showing that 39 yards of black hat ribbon, a pair of black breeches and a pair of stockings came from 'Mr Fawkner'.

Fawkner and his wife continued to live in Hobart, conducting a store at 23 Macquarie St., while their son set up a bakery business. But 1814 saw John jun. in serious trouble. Sympathetic towards eight young convicts, he helped them acquire a whale boat and tools, and assisted them in their planned escape. When brought before the magistrates he received 500 lashes and a three-year sentence at Coal River (Newcastle). He was released about a year later and returned to the bakery in Hobart and sold liquor without a licence. In the meantime his father was implicated in Commissary P. G. Hogan's court martial for robbing the government stores for which he was sentenced in August 1819 to receive 200 lashes and three years at Newcastle. Evidence before Commissioner Bigge showed that Fawkner had been providing much of his own wheat to supply troops with bread while leaving wheat in the store.

When the streets were re-aligned the Fawkners had their Macquarie St. property reduced to three instead of four allotments. Fawkner jun. built himself a comfortable seven-roomed house in Collins St. which he advertised for sale in 1825, three years after he moved to Launceston with his future wife (Eliza Cobb) and had established the Cornwall Hotel. In 1824 the father had planned to return to England but Hannah took ill and died on 17 January 1825, buried at St David's.

On 1 October 1825, at St David's, Fawkner married Ann Archer (née Jones), a 44 year old widow. She died and was buried 4 November 1841, St David's. Fawkner's third marriage was to Eliza Carr, aged 41, on 23 December 1846.

For a short time he was the nominal owner of the *Port Phillip Patriot*, which his son had transferred to his name. He and his wife came to live in Pascoe Vale, to be with John jun., then a member of the Legislative Council of Victoria. James Fenton has described Fawkner sen. in old age as a man of very slender build, with only one eye.

His house in Macquarie St., Hobart, was for sale in February 1855.

Died 24 September 1854, buried at the Melbourne General Cemetery. His widow died 15 May 1858. John Pascoe Fawkner died 4 September 1869, mourned by hundreds of persons as the father and a founder of Melbourne.

Through the second marriage of his daughter Elizabeth to Richard Lucas (13 August 1816), son of a private in the First Fleet, Thomas Lucas and his wife, née Ann Howard, John Fawkner sen. has hundreds of descendants living in various parts of Australia.

Surnames of descendants have included: Abslom; Bate; Baldwin; Cannell; Cato; Charles; Coventry; Crichton; Donaldson; Dorrie; Elmore; Ginn; Goldberg; Gregg; Hamilton; Hill; Holmstrom; Jackson; Kay; Lilley; Lonergan; Lovett; Lucas; McDonald; Pearsall; Smith; Sproule; Stace; Williamson; Yarnold. Other surnames appearing through John Pascoe Fawkner's adopted children include Springhall, Walsh and Wiseman as well as Lucas.

A biography of John Pascoe Fawkner appears in the *Australian Dictionary of Biography*, vol. I. He has been the subject of several publications.

FELL, JOHN BENJAMIN [c. 1777 – ?]
Collecting clerk, aged 25, born and living in London; 5'3", fair complexion. Literate.
Tried at Middlesex III Sessions (London G.D.) 17 February 1802 for embezzling and secreting banknotes from his employers Robert Peddir and John Henry Bluhm of Gould Sq., London, merchants and shipbrokers, to the value of £20, £1 and 12s 9d from Messrs Newman, Everitt and Drummond. Fell had been with the firm as collecting clerk for ten years and should have entered the money in the account book. Sentence pronounced by the Common Sergeant was transportation for seven years. Gaoled at Poultry and transferred to the *Prudentia* hulk at Woolwich.

At Port Phillip, Fosbrook was employing Fell to assist him with the issue of provisions. During the period of his servitude Fell continued as storeman in Hobart. On the expiration of his sentence he returned to London about 1809 to join his mother who lived in East St., Lambeth. In an examination of Fosbrook for fraudulent conduct in 1812, Francis Shipman (q.v.) gave evidence that Fell could corroborate evidence against Fosbrook regarding abuses with rice and kangaroo meat.

A Melbourne descendant claims that John Benjamin Fell later returned to Australia and lived in Bendigo where he had a son John. They later went to live in Sydney and John Benjamin founded another family there. If this were so, he must have been in his seventies when he went to Bendigo. This man might have been a son of the original John Benjamin and migratea at the time of the Gold Rush.

Surnames of descendants have included: Fisher.

FELLOWES, SAMUEL [c. 1775–1803]
Husbandman, aged 25.
Tried at Kent Spring Assizes (Maidstone G.D.) 15 March 1802 for assaulting and robbing James Hardy of £3 16s 6d on the highway in Darenth. Sentenced to death. Reprieved

Gallery of Comicalities.

NO. 9. THE PLAINTIFF.

"I've heard of the sharp between two flats (the former having eaten the oyster and given the shells to his clients), but I think I'm the flat between two sharps—for, though I've gained my cause, I've lost my rag, or, rather, have nothing but rags left. Not a feather to fly with, and the two rascally attorneys laughing in their sleeves at my folly."

"By Goles it is a foolish plan,
In Court to settle a dispute;
And I, alack! am like the man
Wot gain'd his CAUSE but lost his SUIT.

"Don't marvel that my face is long
Nor quiz me for my shoulder shruggins;
If I've one copper left I'm wrong,
And law has done for poor Mat Muggins.

"With extra costs and extra fees,
These vile attorneys always cook you;
Your last remaining coin they squeeze,
And then for Whitecross Prison book you.

"Better to let our quarrels die,
Than sink to poverty and tatters;
Better if neighbour Giles and I
Over a pot had settled matters.

"All glory to our code of laws!
Of right or wrong a sad confuser!
And if I'm floored, who gained the cause,
May Lord have mercy on the loser."

by Baron Hotham and Mr Justice Heath and sentenced to transportation for life. Gaoled at Maidstone and transferred to the *Stanislaus* hulk at Woolwich.

Died at sea near Tenerife 17 May 1803 of debility brought on by seasickness.

FERNANDEZ, JOSEPH [c. 1781 – ?]
Sailor, aged 20, from Portugal; 5'5", very dark complexion, black hair, black eyes.
Tried at Middlesex I Sessions (Middlesex G.D.) 2 December 1801 for stealing 100 lb of gum (£8) from the schooner *Bilboa* of Philadelphia in the River Thames. He was a member of the crew and knew no one in England. Sentenced by Justice Sir Alan Grose to transportation for seven years. Gaoled at Newgate and transferred to the *Captivity* hulk at Portsmouth.

During the voyage out Fernandez was employed as a sailor.

In June 1805, with Robert Stewart (*q.v.*), Archibald Campbell (*q.v.*) and others he deserted camp in Knopwood's boat. After three weeks of freedom, they were brought back from Schouten I. by marines. In January 1806 Fernandez escaped again with a party led by Stewart in a boat belonging to John Blinkworth. He became a bushranger and Knopwood recorded that he was armed and had plenty of dogs. He was away for about two years before accepting the Governor's pardon if he returned.

When his sentence expired he probably joined a ship, as a sailor, to return home.

FITZGERALD, THOMAS [c. 1777–1824]
Clerk, aged 25; 5'9", dark complexion, of London. Literate.
Tried at Middlesex III Sessions (London G.D.) 17 February 1802, together with his brother John for receiving William Fraser's banker's draft for £85 4s 6d made out to Messrs Drummond & Co., St Martin's-in-the-Fields, and embezzling £5 4s 6d, entering the £80 in the account book of his employers, George Oakley, Thomas Shakleton and John Evans. He had been in their employment as clerk for eight months. He begged them to stop the prosecution and he and his brother would transport themselves to any part of the world. Evans refused. Fitzgerald received £45 a year plus board and lodgings. Sentence pronounced by the Common Sergeant was transportation for seven years. His brother (aged twenty, 5'8", dark complexion, of London) was declared not guilty and released from Newgate. Thomas Fitzgerald was gaoled at Newgate and transferred to the *Prudentia* hulk at Woolwich.

During the voyage Fitzgerald, who claimed to have served as a captain in the Army in charge of a troop of horse, was allowed to go without irons. He engaged in teaching some of the young boys. While in the Indian Ocean Knopwood had occasion to punish him for stealing linen and other clothes from one of the officers. He received three dozen lashes.

At Port Phillip, Fitzgerald worked at drawing timber carriages and probably continued with a little teaching.

He attended the Hobart musters in 1811, 1818, 1819 and 1823. He leased land in the Hobart area and by 1819 had five male and fourteen female cattle, 100 male sheep, 500 ewes and two government servants.

From the earliest days in Hobart he was attached to the civil establishment, first assisting Surveyor Harris as clerk and clerk to the Magistrates' Court at least by 1808. He also conducted a school from his house in the public square from 1807 which, in 1814, was one Macquarie ordered to be removed from the allotment. He moved to Davey St.

He succeeded Samuel Warriner (q.v.) as government schoolmaster in June 1812, his salary of £10 per annum to be paid from the Police Fund. It was soon increased to £15 in remuneration of his services as clerk to the Bench of Magistrates and in 1814 to £25. Under Gov. Davey's instructions, he was responsible for ordering Denis McCarty to produce his public stock book and receipts in the case against McCarty in 1813–14.

On 14 August 1815, in Hobart, Fitzgerald married Mary Agnes Martin, aged 37, free, from Sydney. She was a school teacher and had been well recommended as a former convict by Revd Samuel Marsden; she was the widow of a surgeon in the Royal Navy, Abraham Martin, and had a son, William Joseph Martin, aged six. The Fitzgeralds had two children within the next five years. They both continued to teach, using labourers to run the farm. Unfortunately Fitzgerald was a heavy drinker which affected his work. Gov. Davey dismissed him from the Bench for repeated complaints over his drunkenness, neglect and being absent for several days. Davey, however, admitted he was well qualified to continue teaching and recommended the provision of Bibles, prayer books and spelling books. In 1818 Fitzgerald opened an evening school at the request of several young men employed during the day. They attended three hours nightly. Mary Fitzgerald received a salary for teaching the young women of the colony.

Evidence of A. W. H. Humphrey before Commissioner Bigge suggested that many early court records kept in Fitzgerald's small thatched cottage had been destroyed by damp and wet. Gov. Sorell criticized him for providing only 500 lb of meat to the Commissariat during the past quarter of 1820 instead of his usual 1 000 lb. He increased it to 3 000.

In 1818 he temporarily occupied Ingle Hall, home of the merchant John Ingle, but had to relinquish it to Edward Lord when a new schoolroom was finished.

In 1824 Fitzgerald retired and received some superannuation, but died that year. Buried 2 September 1824, St David's, aged 49 (?).

Mary Fitzgerald for some time afterwards received unwelcome attentions from a man named Kirby and had to appeal to James Scott, then a magistrate, for protection. She opened a day academy for young ladies near the new bridge in Campbell St. An education return of 1827 shows she lived in Goulburn St., was of good character, and cared for a child aged three, Mary Ann, probably the daughter of William Joseph Martin.

Mary Agnes Fitzgerald married William Nicholls, carpenter, who had arrived as a settler in the *Ocean*, 23 December 1829. They lived at Clarence Plains where she died and was buried, 10 July 1831.

Surnames of descendants have included: McArdell.

FLETCHER, WILLIAM [c. 1775–1850]
Labourer, aged 26 of pa. Michael-Mile-End, Colchester, Essex. Literate.

Tried at Essex Spring Assizes (Chelmsford G.D.) 9 March 1801 together with Joseph Parker for assaulting with force and arms and robbing John Snell of a silver watch and coins to the value of £1 3s 8d. Sentenced to death. Reprieved by Baron Hotham and Mr Justice Heath and sentenced to transportation for seven years. Gaoled at the county gaol and transferred to the hulks at Portsmouth.

Fletcher attended the Hobart musters in 1811, 1818, 1819 and 1823.

At Port Phillip and in Hobart he was employed as a sawyer and on expiration of his sentence in 1808 he became a constable. He carried out his duties at least until 1827 when he asked for a superannuated allowance on account of asthma and rheumatism, brought on by exposure to dampness and winter chills. After an unqualified testimony from E. Abbott as to his excellent character, he retired on the pay and allowance of a petty constable. He received £10 annually for the rest of his life. He had also received an original grant of land at Macquarie Plains.

He was a subscriber to the New Town Church in 1830.

On 26 June 1821 at the age of 46, he married Elizabeth Walton, aged 33, a convict transported in the *Morley*. They had at least one child, a daughter, Sarah, who died March 1835.

Died 6 August 1850, St Mary's Hospital, Hobart, his age then given as 60.

FORSHA, CHRISTOPHER, alias WATKINS [c. 1779 – ?] (Forshaw)
Caulker (corker), aged 21, of Whitechapel; 5'7", dark complexion, dark brown hair, hazel eyes. Literate.

Tried at Middlesex I Sessions (Middlesex G.D.) 3 December 1800 for stealing 14 lb of sheet copper (12s 0d) from Thomas Dalton, his employer, who was employed at the time by Messrs Perry in their dockyard. Forsha admitted that he had taken it from an East India ship, the *Albion*. Sentence pronounced by the Common Sergeant was transportation for seven years. Gaoled at Newgate and transferred to the *Prudentia* hulk at Woolwich.

While at Port Phillip, Collins chose Forsha as a crew member accompanying William Collins to Port Jackson with messages for Gov. King. He left on 6 November 1803 in a six-oared cutter.

When he first arrived in Hobart in February 1804 he became one of Knopwood's servants, looked after his boat, and helped build Cottage Green.

He tried to capture and escape in a whale boat to go to New Zealand in 1805, but this did not deter Collins from recommending him for a conditional pardon received in January 1806, for his general good conduct and for accompanying William Collins on their dangerous journey in 1803.

Because he was a seaman, he would have had no trouble in securing passage home, apparently soon afterwards.

FOSSETT, JAMES, alias HICKMAN [c. 1781–1809] (Fawcett, Forcett)
Drover, aged 20, of Shoreditch, London; 5'7", dark complexion, brown hair, grey eyes.

Tried at Middlesex IV Sessions (London G.D.) 15 April 1801 for stealing a sheep in Smithfield from a Mr Payne.

He had at the same sessions already been convicted of stealing two chests of tea (£40) from a wagon and premises of John Alcock, for which Lord Kenyon sentenced him to transportation for seven years. Sentenced on the second charge by Mr Justice Heath to death. Reprieved and sentenced to transportation for life. Gaoled at Newgate and transferred to the hulks at Woolwich.

Knopwood recorded in December 1806 that Fossett had taken away his bitch, Miss, some pork and an iron kettle. He joined other bushrangers and Knopwood sent his servants after them and the dog. After a fortnight the bitch was returned.

Fossett must also have returned. He was buried 19 July 1809, Hobart, aged 40 (?).

GADSBY, JOHN, alias JOHN THE MALTSTER [c. 1772–1827]

?, aged 30.

Tried at the Derby Spring Assizes (Derby G.D.) 13 March 1802 together with John Clark (*q.v.*) for sheep stealing. Sentenced to death by Baron Graham. Reprieved and sentenced to transportation for life. Gaoled at the county gaol and transferred to the hulks at Langston.

Gadsby attended the Hobart musters in 1811 and 1818 and the Port Dalrymple musters of 1820, 1821 and 1823. He received a conditional pardon in January 1814 and a free pardon soon afterwards. During his early years in Hobart he was a farm labourer for Richard Clark at Risdon.

He had received a land grant of 60 acres by 1822 at Port Dalrymple and leased at least another 30 acres from James Hill, clearing the land on which he grew extensive wheat and barley crops, had a garden and orchard, and raised some sheep, cattle and pigs.

Buried 5 June 1827, St John's, Launceston, aged 63 (?), a resident of Patterson's Plains.

GAIN, JOHN [c. 1781–1820]

(Gains)

?, aged 20.

Tried at the Spring Assizes of the Palatinate of Lancaster, 24 March 1801 for grand larceny. Sentenced to transportation for seven years. Gaoled at Lancaster Castle and transferred to the hulks at Portsmouth.

Gain attended the Hobart muster in 1811.

By December 1804 Gain was one of Knopwood's servants and during the early years he was trusted with dogs to go kangarooing. He discovered coal at Coal River. In February 1807 Knopwood discharged him for ill-treating his dogs, but he took him back into service in 1811.

In 1820 Knopwood lent Gain to assist Sgt McCauley with his harvest at Muddy Plains. While out duck shooting he appears to have collapsed after the bite of a snake and drowned in a lagoon, causing great sorrow in Knopwood's household and, indeed, throughout the whole community of those who had arrived in the *Calcutta*.

Died about 6 February 1820. Buried St David's, 15 February, aged 35 (?).

GARRETT, RICHARD [c. 1782 – ?]

(Garratt)

Spur-maker, aged 20, born in Worcestershire, de facto wife Hannah Harvey.

Tried at Shropshire Spring Assizes (Shrewsbury G.D.) 20 March 1802 for stealing with Mary Croft (acquitted — see Thomas Croft) and others a piece of printed calico from William Beaumont, mercer, a piece of brown sheeting from William Jones, and a piece of linsey from Joseph Parry, hatter, all of St Chad, Shrewsbury. Sentenced to death, reprieved and sentenced to transportation for life. Gaoled at Shrewsbury and transferred to the hulks at Portsmouth.

Hannah Harvey (free) accompanied Garrett on the voyage as Mrs Garrett. When Collins discovered they were not married, he ordered a marriage ceremony to take place. Knopwood officiated at the ceremony on 28 November 1803. It was the first registered European marriage at Port Phillip. They had a daughter, Harriet, born c. 1808 and son Edward, born c. 1809.

Appears to have died soon afterwards, although his death was not recorded. He is not to be confused with another prisoner, William Garrett, already at Risdon in 1804, who was associated with escapees and bushrangers. Richard Garrett was not on the 1811 muster roll.

Hannah Garrett remained in the colony. In 1813 she paid £13 for a skilling in Liverpool St. and after rearrangement of the streets received compensation from the government. In 1819 she had no land of her own but owned four male and eight female cattle, 100 male sheep and 200 ewes. She was supplying meat regularly to the Commissariat. By 1823 she owned a brick house on the corner of Campbell and Collins Streets, Hobart, which Capt. Kelly rented for twelve months. In 1827 her son and daughter were living in Brisbane St. The mother was said to be of good character.

About this time she moved to Roseneath, to housekeep for James Austin (*q.v.*) who, after his death in 1831, left her a substantial interest in his estate for life. In 1833 she married the police constable George Madden, a man much younger than herself. She was believed to have been more than 70 at the time; but could hardly have been more than 60.

GIBSON, DAVID [1778–1858]

Labourer, aged 24, born 26 April, Aberuthven, Perth. Son of John and Giles (née Binning), a farmer, three brothers and two sisters. Living at Kingston-upon-Hull, Yorkshire.

Tried at Yorkshire Spring Assizes (York G.D.) 4 March 1802 for stealing, with the use of force and arms, five gold watches, one French gold watch, capped, two French plain gold watches, (all valued £60), one gold locket for a lady's miniature with the figure of Peace worked in hair (40s 0d), one piece of Portugal coin (27s 0d), three £1 Bank of England notes, five guineas and a half in gold, one pair of silver knee buckles (3s 0d), one pair of silk stockings (5s 0d), one pair of cotton stockings (1s 0d), all the property of William Coles of St Paul's Churchyard, London, jeweller. Gibson stole these valuables from a portmanteau at the Neptune Inn, house of John Mansfield, pa. Holy Trinity, Kingston-upon-Hull. Gibson was pursued to Beverley where he was arrested with the goods in his possession. Sentenced by Justice Sir Giles Rooke to death. Reprieved and sentenced to transportation for life. Gaoled at York Castle and transferred to the hulks at Langston. There he became closely attached to George Lee (q.v.) a well-educated convict.

On 12 December 1803, while at Port Phillip, Gibson and Lee absconded with a gun and ammunition taken from the Governor's gardener. Gibson returned alone before Collins abandoned the settlement and informed him about the large river (the Yarra) at the head of the harbour and the fate of some of his escaped companions.

Gibson attended the Port Jackson musters in 1811 and 1817 and the Cornwall musters in 1819, 1820, 1821 and 1823. He received a conditional pardon in 1813 and an absolute pardon soon afterwards (yet for some unknown reason the Sydney muster roll of 1817 described him as a labourer holding a ticket-of-leave). He received 1 030 acres of land granted by Gov. Macquarie on the South Esk River and had a grazing licence at Humphrey's water hole. In 1820 he had planted 57 acres of wheat, three of barley, two of potatoes and owned two horses, 131 horned cattle, 276 female cattle, 1 600 male sheep, 2 200 ewes, four male and four female swine, and employed six government servants and one free man. In addition he had purchased 760 acres and his wife had a 50-acre land grant. In the same year he was supplying 6 000 lb of meat quarterly to the Commissariat at Port Dalrymple. By 1839 he had acquired many more properties: 1 500 acres from Revd R. C. Clairborne; 285 acres from Lieut. George Gunning; 720 acres from Thomas Capon; 1 220 from John Peevor; 457 at Cleveland; 175 from Elizabeth (Nicholls) Gibson. Much of this land was in the area of the South Esk River.

Yet Gibson's success was as unexpected as it was rapid, unexpected because of the nature of his early crimes in the colony. Knopwood reported, 21 December 1805, that he had escaped from the guardhouse. He appears at that time to have been Dr Hopley's servant. The absconders were outlawed for absenting themselves from public labour and returned for trial by the magistrates on 22 January 1806. He received 300 lashes and was ironed for one year.

Gibson committed a more serious crime in December 1807. He and eight others were sent to Sydney for trial by court martial for piracy of the schooner Marcia. On 13 February 1808 the Court of Vice-Admiralty met and Edward Abbott, sitting as Judge Advocate, condemned them to die, but Major Johnston pardoned them all and sentenced them to remain convicts for life.

It appears that Gibson was assigned to the merchant, Robert Campbell, while at Port Jackson. Campbell recognised in him a person with some considerable farming ability. He arranged to have him returned to V.D.L. where he appears to have been assigned to Ensign Hugh Piper, N.S.W. Corps and Deputy Commissary at Port Dalrymple. Piper received a land grant of 100 acres on the South Esk River and there Gibson threshed wheat for the Commissariat, was on government rations and lived in a house on Piper's farm. He gave evidence before the Judge Advocate's Court in 1809 at Port Dalrymple on behalf of a Pte Grant of the 73rd Rgt and another, Cornish, that they had killed and eaten a sheep believed to have been part of their rations. As government stock keeper under Capt. John Ritchie, he was in charge of driving bullock wagons between Port Dalrymple and Hobart. He later became overseer of the runs and stations of Edward Lord. Gibson's signature (usually marked with a cross until he learned to write several years later) appeared occasionally on official receipts.

When Norfolk Islanders arrived in the north in 1813 Elizabeth Nicholls and her son, Norfolk, by Capt. John Piper, brother of Hugh, were among those on board the Minstrel. She was born on Norfolk I. about 1795, probably the daughter of William Nicholls, a convict who had arrived in the Royal Admiral in 1792. Another child known as Eliza Holmes and possibly the daughter of John Holmes, a convict transported in the Hillsborough and sent to Norfolk I. in 1800, was born soon after Elizabeth arrived in V.D.L. Elizabeth received considerable favours, such as a small house and some compensation for the considerable stock she had acquired at Norfolk I.

Elizabeth was probably living with Gibson by the time he carted Knopwood's baggage on the latter's trip to Port Dalrymple in February 1814. Later the next year their first son was born, and in all they had seven sons and three daughters, as well as the two earlier children who lived with them. When the Revd John Youl arrived at Port Dalrymple he married Elizabeth Nicholls to David Gibson on 16 January 1819 and on the same day baptised two of their children.

Until this time Gibson's home appears to have been in Launceston. He had built stockmen's huts on his land and continued managing for Robert Campbell. He and Edward Lord remained in partnership and were joint owners of an enormous flock which the Trimbys, a father and two sons, raided as part of their renowned sheep stealing activities in 1818. They were sent to Port Jackson on a charge of stealing 1 000 sheep with Gibson's mark and sentenced to fourteen years at Newcastle. Bushrangers continuously preyed on his stock keepers and they in turn created their own troubles with the natives.

After his return to Launceston Gibson built the first Pleasant Banks as a public house and lodging place on the South Esk River. There the Macquaries stayed most comfortably on their journey north in May 1821. Other travellers over the years referred to the warmth of Gibson's hospitality and the splendid results of his labours. The Land Commissioners reported on the richness of his land and with much bitterness on the manner in which he, as a convict, had been favoured. G. A. Robinson reported that Gibson's stock keeper had massacred natives.

In 1828 Gibson was petitioning Gov. Arthur for more land. He already had 800 acres by grant and 6 500 by purchase, and was providing 27 000 lb of meat to the Commissariat. Arthur refused. His industry and methods were producing turnips weighing more than 50 lb to feed his fat oxen which weighed 1 200 lb each. They appeared at the cattle show in Launceston. He imported two Durham bulls at £500 each, the best in the country. When his house burnt down he built a new one costing some £10 000. He became one of the founders of the Presbyterian Church at Evandale, had subscribed to the Auxiliary Bible Society, and even as early as 1816 had been able to afford the princely sum of five guineas for the Waterloo fund for the relief of families of soldiers.

Gibson and his large family continued to prosper and gain general approval in the community. A fire occurred in 1851 at Pleasant Banks but did no serious damage. He sent wheat to the Paris Exhibition in 1855. Artists painted his portrait, one possible itinerant artist being Ludwig Becker. Of his appearance we know that he was of medium height and had gingery hair. J. H. Wedge wrote of his 'laughing Caledonian voice'. His children married well and built some of the finest houses in northern Tasmania and his many descendants have occupied some of the highest positions in the land.

Died 15 April 1858, of 'debility' at his home, a 'gentleman'. Buried St Andrew's Presbyterian Church in Evandale four days later aged 82 (?). His seven sons and three daughters were alive when he died. His widow also survived him. She died 28 January 1872, aged 77, and was buried at St Andrew's.

Surnames of descendants have included: Abbott; Andrews; Archer; Armitage; Armstrong; Arthur; Bailey; Baird; Banham; Barnes; Barnett; Blazeley; Bond; Boon; Bowering; Boyce; Boyd; Brookes; Brown; Burrows; Butler; Button; Chen; Chugg; Cockerill; Cookman; Coones; Cowell; Crawford; Creedon; Crosby; Daniel; De Pury; Dennis; Dickens; Dickenson; Douglas; Dowl; Dowling; Downer; Dufour; Dunn; Edgell; Edwards; Farquharson; Field; Fleming; Fletcher; Fox; Gatenby; Gillespie; Gillette; Gray; Hall; Halligan; Hamilton; Hanliss; Harper; Harris; Harrison; Hawkins; Headlam; Hempel; Henty; Hinman; Hogarth; Hooper; Jago; Keach; Kelly; Kirkby; Knights; Layton; Leichney; Links; Luckman; Ludwyche; Lyle; MacDonald; McDougall; McGee; Mackinnon; McLean; Males; Marshall; Maynard; Mills; Mitchell; Morgan; Morris; Murray; Myler; Nicolson; Nye; O'Farrell; Ormond; Osboldstone; Osborne; Padman; Peipers; Philip; Phillips; Price; Rae; Rex; Riley; Ritter; Robe; Roberts; Rogers; Roxburgh; Sayer; Seager; Shaw; Shore; Smith; Smyth; Staley; Stewart; Taylor; Terry; Thirkell-Johnson; Thorold; Tomlinson; Tovell; Tuckett; Turnbull; Vigors; Vincent; Walker; Walters; Watkins; Wayne; Whitehouse; Widdowson; William; Williams; Wilson.

A biography of David Gibson appears in the *Australian Dictionary of Biography*, vol. I.

GODWIN, RICHARD [c. 1777–1804]
Husbandman, aged 25.
Tried at Essex Spring Assizes (Chelmsford G.D.) 10 March 1802 for stealing 26 sheep from the Rt Hon. Dowager Lady Ann Dacre, of Belhus, Aveley. Sentenced to transportation for life. Gaoled at the county gaol and transferred to the *Prudentia* hulk at Woolwich.

During the voyage out Godwin was employed on deck as a poulterer.

Died 9 March 1804, Port Phillip.

GRAY, SAMUEL [c. 1784 – after 1815]
Labourer, aged 17, of St Saviour, Southwark; 5'6", dark complexion, brown hair, dark eyes.
Tried at Surrey S. of P. (Newington) 24 February 1801 for stealing a tub of butter from Joseph Topham at St Saviour's, Southwark. Sentenced to transportation for seven years. Gray had previously been charged in December 1800 and acquitted of stealing three lb of coffee for persons unknown. Gaoled first at Poultry, then the county gaol, and transferred to the hulks at Woolwich.

Gray was among the first of the *Calcutta* convicts to engage in sealing and whaling. He served in the *Perseverance*, *Halcyon*, *Active*, the *Governor Macquarie*, the schooner *Brothers*, the *Earl Spencer*, the *Governor Bligh*.

Appears to have returned to London in March 1815 in the Sydney Packet.

GREEN, JOHN, alias ROBERT LAWRENCE [c. 1780 – ?]
Labourer, aged 21, of St George's, Southwark.
Tried at Surrey S. of P. (Reigate) together with John Johnson alias Clement Lawrence (q.v.), 14 April 1801 for stealing a quantity of sugar from William Phillips of St George's, Southwark. Sentenced to transportation for seven years. Gaoled at Reigate and transferred to the hulks at Portsmouth.

He may be the John Green who, during 1805–06, advertised that he was leaving the colony and appears to have left for England in the Sophia, *5 October 1806. This would have been possible, although unusual, if he had received an early pardon.*

GREEN, THOMAS [c. 1784–1812]
?, aged 18. Literate.
Tried at Warwickshire Spring Assizes (Warwick G.D.) 23 March 1802 for stealing a horse, together with B. Davis. Sentenced to death. Reprieved by the Lord Chief Baron and Baron Graham and sentenced to transportation for life. Gaoled at Warwick Castle and transferred to the hulks at Portsmouth.

In July 1804 Green received 100 lashes for an unknown misdemeanour in Hobart. In February 1805, together with Richard Wright (who had arrived with Denis McCarty), he escaped in a boat of the American ship *Myrtle* which traded between Bengal and the north-west coast of America. They reached Port Jackson and Gov. King ordered them back to Hobart in the *Mary*. In spite of this, Collins made Green one of his gamekeepers and had a boat made for him. He received a conditional pardon in May 1807.

On 30 October 1809 Knopwood married him to Elizabeth, daughter of John Fawkner sen. (q.v.). They had two children; the son Thomas was born 31 October 1810 and daughter Sarah Elizabeth was born just after the death of their father.

Buried 11 November 1812, Hobart.

Elizabeth Green later married Richard Lucas, of Brown's River, on 13 August 1816 at Cottage Green. They had several children and many descendants (see Fawkner, John (q.v.)).

GROVE(S), JAMES [c. 1770–1810]
Die-sinker and engraver, aged 32, born Birmingham; 5'4", fair complexion, living in Church St., Birmingham, married to Susannah, one son. Literate.
Tried at Warwick Spring Assizes (Warwick G.D.) 13 March 1802 for engraving a set of plates and counterfeiting a large quantity of Bank of England notes. Sentenced to death. Reprieved by Chief Baron and Baron Hotham and sentenced to transportation for life. Gaoled first at Newgate while under interrogation by Bank of England officials to whom he supplied important information on the detection of future forgeries. Removed to the county gaol at Warwick and transferred to the *Captivity* hulk at Portsmouth.

While in Newgate Thomas Bensley, a leading London printer, visited Grove and gave Susannah and their son board and lodging in London. Grove began writing letters to him in a newly found spiritual vein but many were destroyed by fire. The existing letters indicate that his wife had a dowry of £3 000 which should have yielded an annual income of £150.

Susannah Grove and their son Daniel accompanied him in the *Calcutta*. During the voyage he was allowed to go without irons. Mrs Grove was quite sea-sick but reasonably well berthed in the fore cockpit; Grove together with Fawkner (*q.v.*) had bargained with the carpenter for better accommodation, which cost £20.

At Port Phillip, Grove became a subordinate of the night watch. He remained there until May 1804, after a fall which had somewhat incapacitated him, but he continued with the manufacture he had begun in making thirteen casks of alkali from seaweed with the help of five men in his charge. He tended some sheep he had bought from the Cape and manufactured tea from the black tea-tree. He planned also to make soap with the alkali and tallow he had bought at the Cape.

From the beginning both Collins and Knopwood showed more favours to Grove than perhaps any other convict. Collins was able to get Gov. King to pardon him conditionally in 1806. Macquarie in June 1810, somewhat warily, accepted Edward Lord's recommendation for an absolute pardon.

The Groves' first habitation in Hobart was a two-roomed house with kitchen, the best in Hobart, which appears to have been built by Samuel Gunn (*q.v.*). The Groves later received a town allotment on which they were able to build a good house, ultimately acquired by the government when Captain Murray became commandant. Grove assisted in the building of the second Government House for Collins as well as helping his friend Knopwood.

Grove was an assistant to Thomas Clark as store-keeper in 1808 and in 1810 received £70 per annum. He continued to make soap, some of which was sent to Sydney, cut a stamp for bills for the government, and did some painting and carving.

Knopwood spent more time with Grove than with any other convict in those first years and treated him as an equal. He accompanied Knopwood's party exploring Bruny I. and the Huon River in 1804 and had every reason to write to Thomas Bensley in London of the great respect in which he was held and how happy he was with his lot.

Distraught after the sudden death of his friend Gov. Collins (for whose coffin he probably engraved an inscription on the silver-plated lid), Grove himself died on 17 April 1810, aged 41. Buried in Hobart near Collins' own grave.

Susannah Grove sold their house and interests, and with her son returned to England in the *New Zealander*, September 1811.

Benjamin, son of Thomas Bensley, published James Grove's surviving letters in 1859: *Lost and Found; or, Light in the Prison. A Narrative, with original letters, of A Convict condemned for forgery.* Only one known copy of the work exists. It is in the British Library. In *All the Year Round* Charles Dickens published a review article of the work in the issue of 20 August 1859, entitled *A Piece of Blood Money.*

GROVER, RICHARD [c. 1783 – after 1813]
Butcher, aged 18, of St Anne's, Soho; 5'5", dark complexion, brown hair, grey eyes.
Tried at Middlesex VIII Sessions (Middlesex G.D.) 28 October 1801 for assaulting and robbing Sophia Price on the King's Highway of a cloak (2s 0d). Sentenced to death by Mr Justice Heath. Reprieved when four witnesses gave him a good character and sentenced to transportation for life. Gaoled at Liptrap and Newgate, then transferred to the *Stanislaus* hulk at Woolwich.

In August 1807 Grover became a bushranger whose gang was armed and had plenty of dogs. He returned the following December after Gov. Collins promised an amnesty. He escaped again in March 1808 and Collins offered £10 reward for the capture of bushrangers. He must have returned sometime, although not for the 1811 muster roll, because he received a conditional pardon in 1813.

Beyond that date his activities have not been traced.

GUEST, EDWARD [c. 1782–1817]
Labourer, aged 30, of Manchester.
Tried at the Palatinate of Lancaster S. of P. 20 January 1802 for stealing two yards of linen wrapper (1d), six dozen worsted stockings (2d), 100 pairs of stockings (2d) from Richard Mawdsley of Manchester. Sentenced to transportation for seven years. Guest had previously been charged on 5 January 1802 together with James Swan with an assault on James Nadin, constable, of Manchester, but his indictment shows 'nothing done' as he was transported on the later indictment. Gaoled at the county gaol and transferred to the hulks at Langston.

Guest attended the muster in 1811 in Hobart where he was principal blacksmith from 1807. He had a two-roomed house in Elizabeth St. near Wellington Bridge, with a blacksmith's shop attached. Dr Bowden's store accounts showed he bought regularly from him and that he kept a woman. He also employed Guest to do 'sundry iron work' in 1810.

Died after long illness. Buried 2 April 1817, Hobart, aged 46 (?). Thomas Newby and James Mitchell managed his estate, arranging for the sale of his house and business and paying his creditors.

GUNN, SAMUEL [c. 1780–1859]
Shipwright, formerly Royal Navy, aged 22, widower. Literate.
Tried at Norfolk Summer Assizes (Norwich G.D.) 9 August 1802 for stealing a saddle and bridle out of the stable of John Wright of Fordham and offering them for sale to Mr Glasscock of Downham Market who suspected him and sent for a constable. Sentenced by Lord Chief Justice Alvanley and Justice Sir Nash Grose to transportation for seven years. Gunn had served on board a man-of-war for three years and was at the Battle of Copenhagen. Gaoled at the county gaol and transferred to the hulks at Portsmouth.

During the voyage out he served on deck as part of the carpenter's crew and was allowed to go without irons. At Port Phillip he was appointed to direct the shipwrights.

Gunn attended the Hobart musters 1811, 1818, 1819 and 1823. He received an original grant of 50 acres at Hangan's Point over which there was some dispute in 1818. The following year he was running stock and employing one government servant. On 23 July 1804, in Hobart, he married his second wife, Jane(t) (the daughter of Supt. Patterson). She had received 30 acres in 1807 on which she grew wheat and barley.

Gunn became the first master builder of boats in V.D.L. while employed in public works. In February 1813 R. W. Loane engaged him to build the first square-rigged vessel, the brig *Campbell Macquarie*, 133 tons, in Hobart. He built many other vessels during the course of the next twenty years.

By September 1817 Gunn had become a seaman in the brig *Sophia* under James Kelly, master. He was charged with absconding, failing to report for duty, and sent to work in the gaol during the present engagement of the *Sophia*. Soon afterwards he acquired a large boat from T. W. Birch to convey cattle or luggage in the Derwent.

By 1818 he had built a good house on the site of an earlier one in Bridge St. worth between £400 and £500, but there was a dispute with George Guest over the ownership of the land.

The Gunns had three daughters and two sons between 1805 and 1813, after which Janet died in 1826 and was buried 4 April, aged 46.

Samual Gunn's third marriage was to Ann Hart, convict, 14 February 1827, St David's. In 1831, when Gunn was designated a superintendent, they were living at 10 Campbell St. and later lived in New Norfolk. In 1837, with their daughter Elizabeth, they sailed for South Australia in the *Emma*. There he became an agent for Lloyd's of London, but committed an unknown minor crime for which he was pardoned, 1 October 1838. The Gunns later returned to Tasmania.

Drowned in a state of intoxication while living at New Norfolk. Buried 24 March 1859, St Matthew's, aged 77. The St David's register records the burial of a Sarah Gunn, boatbuilder's wife, 4 April 1859, aged 46, but she was probably the wife of Samuel jun.

Surnames of descendants have included: Bradshaw; Brown; Daley; Green; Jillett.

GWYNN(E), JOHN [c. 1790–1859]
No trade, aged 12, from Montgomery, Wales, living in London; 4' 10", fair complexion, brown hair, light eyes. Literate.
Tried at Middlesex II Sessions (Middlesex G.D.) 14 July 1802 for stealing two neck handkerchiefs (2s 0d) and a child's spencer (2s 0d) from John Hathaway at Bury Place, Bloomsbury, while in his house and later burglariously breaking out of the house to escape when Charles Greece, a visitor, heard a noise upstairs and pursued him. Sentenced by Justice Sir Giles Rooke to transportation for seven years for stealing but not guilty of burglary. He had been confined in Clerkenwell and sentenced to a whipping in December 1801 for stealing a stewpan from the shop of Edward Robinson and had also been in custody on a previous occasion under another name. Gaoled at Newgate and transferred to the *Prudentia* hulk at Woolwich.

During the voyage out he was twice punished: once for theft and once for stabbing a man in the hand with a penknife.

He attended the Hobart musters 1811, 1818, 1819 and 1823. He was grazing cattle and sheep on land in the Hobart area in 1819. He had the services of a government servant and free man. He received a grant of 30 acres at Carlton River from Gov. Macquarie in 1822 when he bought two bullocks and agricultural implements and peti-

tioned for the help of another government man. But there was lengthy argument and litigation over the rights to the land.

In 1819 the government compensated him for acquisition of a skilling (valued at £30) near the water's edge. From there he had traded produce between Hobart and the other settlements, using the cutter which J. P. Fawkner (*q.v.*) and others had built in 1814 when they were arrested and tried to escape. In 1820 he replaced this with a fine large schooner brought from Sydney in the *Atlas*. At the end of that year he proposed to return to England in the brig *Robert Quayle*. It is likely that he might have spent two to three years away from Hobart at that time. He could have worked his way as a crew member as his name is not on the passenger list. There is no record of him in the colony during those years. This was unusual, because he made both before and after those years many appearances before the magistrates for crimes ranging from theft, drunk and disorderly to assault for which he had received quite minor punishments.

On 10 December 1817, in Hobart, John Gwynn, then aged 28, was married to Ann Bass, aged twenty, a convict transported in the *Canada*, after he had been fined £5 for attempting to inveigle her from her place of assignment. There is no record of any children.

By 1827 Gwynn was living in Campbell St., Hobart, his occupation given as fisherman. He spent a short time at Macquarie Harbour between mid-1824 and mid-1825, returning to Hobart with a load of Huon pine. It must have been about this time that he was re-classified as a convict but he was free again by 1829 when he petitioned for more land and compensation for his losses. In October 1846 he was with William Keep (*q.v.*) when the latter suffocated and died while working down a well.

Died at Forcett, occupation still listed as fisherman. Buried 11 August 1859, St George's, Pitt Water, aged 72 (?).

HALL, JOHN [c. 1774–1808?]
?, aged 28.
Tried at Warwick Summer Assizes (Warwick G.D.) 14 August 1802 for burglary in the house of J. Hewitt, at Warwick. Sentenced to death, reprieved and sentenced to transportation for life. Gaoled at Warwick Castle and transferred to the hulks at Portsmouth.

Knopwood reported the death of a person named Hall by drowning, 16 July 1808.

HANGAN, JOHN [c. 1779 – after 1819]
Stonemason, aged 23, born in Kent. Literate.
Tried at Middlesex VII Sessions (Middlesex G.D.) 15 September 1802 for stealing two waistcoats (18s 0d), one pair breeches (20s 0d) and one pair stockings (2s 0d) from Benjamin Pritchard, journeyman bricklayer. Hangan came to the house of John and Frances Hunt to ask for lodging. He had been two days in London sleeping in a public house. He stayed two days with the Hunts (Hunt was a cooper) sharing a room with Pritchard. He asked for a pen and ink. He left with Pritchard's clothes and was found at Hackney. Sentenced by the Common Sergeant to transportation for seven years. Gaoled at Newgate and transferred to the *Captivity* hulk at Portsmouth.

Hangan was among those who escaped at Port Phillip in November 1803 and returned voluntarily after experiencing much privation. Collins commented on his wretched appearance and need for medical treatment and decided against punishment.

Hangan attended the Hobart musters in 1811, 1818 and 1819.

On 30 July 1804, in Hobart, Hangan married Jane Heels, the widow of convict John Heels (*q.v.*) who had died at Port Phillip. They had seven sons and one daughter. Fawkner noted that he was a stone mason by trade and the marriage was not a happy one.

By July 1807 Hangan had a 50-acre land grant at Hangan's Point from Gov. King on which he was growing grain and vegetables. R. W. Loane bought the property in 1813 but Gov. Sorell assumed the title and marked it out for the establishment of the Government House and gardens in 1818. Gov. Macquarie and Knopwood both refer to the case before a Bench of Magistrates in which Hangan appeared in July 1814 respecting a letter Hangan wrote but without elaborating on the circumstances or the outcome. It probably had something to do with Loane's claim on the land.

Geils employed Hangan at Geilston as manager until the arrival of William Broughton in 1816. Macquarie ordered Hangan and his family to Sydney to appear as witnesses in an inquiry into Broughton's conduct but they appear to have remained in Hobart where Hangan was practising his trade as a stonemason.

Hangan had problems with some of his sons. William went missing in 1817 for sixteen days when aged 11, and the following year was found dead in the woods. His son John Edward was hanged, 23 May 1828, attended by Knopwood who noted that he was the first native born youth in the colony to be executed.

Hangan does not appear to have been alive at this time. The last Hangan child was born in 1819 and Hangan's name was not on the 1823 muster roll.

His wife (then known as Ann) appeared as the sole parent on the education return of 1820–21 in which she stated that she had a son aged five and daughter aged 13 who could read and would attend public school. The other sons appear to have been a butcher and a dealer. Her third marriage was to Peter Copeland, an inn-keeper at the Tea Tree Brush.

HARFIELD, JAMES [c. 1778–1853]
?, aged 23, of Twickenham, Middlesex; 5'5", dark complexion, brown hair, grey eyes.
Tried at Middlesex I Sessions (Middlesex G.D.) 2 December 1801, together with Joshua Thatcher, (*q.v.*) for stealing a pig from Thomas May, publican and shopkeeper. Both had been drinking. Sentenced by Justice Sir Nash Grose to transportation for seven years. Gaoled at Newgate and transferred to the *Captivity* hulk at Portsmouth.

Harfield attended the Hobart musters in 1811, 1818 and 1819 as a free person. He was among those who found Pte Samuel Wiggins dead from excessive alcohol in July 1811. He was employed as a cartwright by Geils at Restdown between 1812 and 1814. He then lived at Native Corners in the Richmond area.

On 7 March 1807, in Hobart, James Harfield married Mary Bills. She was a convict, convicted in Shropshire in 1801 and had arrived at Port Jackson in the *Glatton*. When she died in January 1821 she was free, aged 48.
Buried 19 August 1853, St Luke's, Richmond, aged 63 (?), occupation carpenter.

HARRISON, FINCH [c. 1780–1839]
Husbandman, aged 22.
Tried at Kent Spring Assizes (Maidstone G.D.) 15 March 1802 for stealing, in Eastling, a watch and other articles from John Dunk. Sentenced to transportation for seven years. Gaoled at the county gaol and transferred to the *Prudentia* hulk at Woolwich.

Harrison attended the Hobart musters in 1811, 1818, 1819 and 1823. His name was on a return of settlers living in Pitt Water in 1820.

In 1806 he was among those whom Knopwood reported were with Robert Stewart (*q.v.*) and others when attempting to abscond in the black cutter. Again in March 1807 he was among those confined in the guardhouse for a disturbance among the prisoners and military patrol, receiving 200 lashes. He was also on a charge for not keeping the peace, 1 June 1818. He provided £15 and his friend John Coward (*q.v.*) £50 surety, to be of good behaviour.
Buried 24 July 1839, aged 55 (?), labourer.

HAY, ROBERT, alias JAMES COLVIN [c. 1773–1839]
Carrier, aged 28, of Alyth, Scotland. Literate.
Tried at Perth Court of Justiciary 23 October 1801 on a charge of sheep stealing and a further charge of burglary and theft of £9–£10, mostly Perth guinea notes from a locked chest, the property of Joseph Dryburn at Boat of Bardmoney, Alyth. Lords Cullen and Dundennan heard his trial. Sentenced him to transportation for fourteen years. Gaoled at the Tolbooth, Perth, and transferred to the *Prudentia* at Woolwich.

Hay remained at Port Phillip to assist Lieut. Sladden's group during the removal. The *Ocean* log reported that while there he had a conviction for theft and received 80 lashes.

He attended the Hobart musters in 1811, 1818 and 1819. He received an absolute pardon in February 1812 and a land grant from Gov. Macquarie from Jones Springs to the Fat Doe River run at Elizabeth Town, New Norfolk, in 1818. By the following year he was growing mostly wheat crops and running 50 male and 50 female cattle, 200 male sheep, and 200 ewes. He employed a government servant and a free man and supplied the Commissariat with meat.

In March 1805 he was among those whom Knopwood reported were missing for three months and who saw a Tasmanian tiger. By 1813 he was a constable in the New Norfolk district and gave evidence at the case against Denis McCarty when the local inhabitants expressed their distrust in McCarty and his business methods. In April 1815 he deposed at the inquest on the body of Charles Carlisle who was murdered by Hugh Burn, one of Howe's associates. He had collected and armed men to hunt down the bushrangers.

On 20 November 1815, in Hobart, Hay, then aged 40, married the widow Maria Hopper, aged 20. Maria, born on

Norfolk I., 15 November 1796, had had a daughter as early as August 1810 when she was 14 and married to William Hazelwood, a convict. The Hays had ten more children and some living descendants claim descent from William de la Haye who came from Normandy in 1160, married a Celtic heiress and became Baron of Erroll.

In August 1827 Hay advertised a 30-acre property for sale with house and farm. The title showed it was a Norfolk I. grant which must have been made originally to his wife or her family. He cautioned persons against buying the farm through Mr Butler or Mr Wells and that no other person but himself had any claim to the farm.

Died at Back River, New Norfolk, a farmer. Buried 8 June 1839, St Matthew's, aged 69 (?).

Surnames of descendants have included: Brooks; Connor; Reynolds; Richardson; Robinson; Tate; Triffit; Ward; Warren; Young.

HAYNES, JOHN [? – ?]
(Haines, Hines, Hynes)
Soldier, aged ?, 25th Foot Rgt, stationed at Gibraltar.
Tried in secret (?) at an army court martial December 1802 following a mutiny at Gibraltar and sentenced to death. Commuted by H.R.H. the Duke of Kent to transportation for life. Embarked in H.M.S. *Cynthia*, sloop, 12 January 1803. Taken aboard the *Calcutta*, 21 April at Portsmouth.

In December 1803, at Port Phillip, Collins appointed him as a subordinate of the night-watch.

He attended the Hobart musters in 1811, 1818 and 1819. He received a conditional pardon in 1816 and was free by 1818. By 1819 he received a grant of 30 acres from Gov. Macquarie at Clarence Plains on which he ran 100 male and 100 female sheep. At that time he was unmarried.

The John Haines who died in Hobart aged 46 on 2 August 1829 was a clerk in the Colonial Secretary's Office who had arrived in the colony in 1821.

The ultimate fate of John Haynes, the Gibraltar mutineer, has not been traced.

HAYWARD, THOMAS [c. 1777 – ?]
(Haywood, Heywood)
Carpenter, aged 25.
Tried at Sussex Spring Assizes (Horsham G.D.) 27 March 1802 for stealing from the house of Richard Swaine, one iron cleaver, one tin saucepan, two coffee mills, etc. Sentenced by Baron Hotham to death. Reprieved and sentenced to transportation for life. Gaoled at Horsham and transferred to the hulks at Langston.

During the voyage out he was engaged as a member of the carpenter's crew and allowed on deck without irons.

He was one of the party who, in May 1805, attempted unsuccessfully to escape in a new whaleboat to New Zealand. In December 1807 he was, with David Gibson (*q.v.*) and others, involved in the piracy of the *Marcia*. The Court of Vice-Admiralty sentenced them to death in February 1808 but Major Johnston pardoned them on condition of their serving as convicts for life because of their humanity towards the crew.

There is no record to date that he returned to V.D.L. from Port Jackson.

HEATH, THOMAS [c. 1787–1814]
?, aged 15.
Tried at Warwick Summer Assizes (Warwick G.D.) 14 August 1802 for stealing linen together with Ann Pearce from the house of Mr James Smith of Warwick. Sentenced to death, reprieved and sentenced to transportation for life. Gaoled at Warwick Castle and transferred to the hulks at Portsmouth.

Heath attended the Hobart muster in 1811.

Thomas Heath and Susannah Riseley were married in Hobart, 5 May 1810. She was probably a sister of Maria Lord.

Knopwood described an event in September 1814 as 'a very melancholy accident. A young man Heath, lately married, and two more coming from Kangaroo Bay with a bullock in the boat. It was upset and the three men drowned.'

A headstone at St David's recorded that Heath was drowned, 15 September 1814, aged 25 (?).

HEDFORD, JOSEPH, alias PACKFORD [c. 1780 – ?]
Seaman, tallow chandler, aged 21, of Bridgewater, Somerset; 5'5", fair, light brown hair, grey eyes.
Tried at Middlesex VII Sessions (London G.D.) 15 September 1801 for stealing a pocket-book (1s 6d), banknote (£5) and eleven banknotes (£11) from Richard Hadrill, Canterbury, retired businessman. Hedford, by trade a tallow chandler, had been selling pens on the streets. Sentence pronounced by the Recorder was transportation for seven years. One witness gave him a good character. Gaoled at Giltspur St. and transferred to the *Fortune* at Langston. He had previously, in December 1797, been convicted under the name of Packford and sentenced to transportation for seven years, delivered to the hulks at Woolwich in 1798 and pardoned in March 1799 on finding security for his good behaviour.

There is no further record of him after his arrival in Hobart. As a seaman, he probably left the colony when his sentence expired in 1808.

HEELS, JOHN [c. 1779–1804]
(Eiles)
?, aged 23, born Ealing, Middlesex, had lived at Harrow some years before, married; 5'5", dark complexion.
Tried at Middlesex III Sessions (Middlesex G.D.) 17 February 1802 together with Mark Denham (*q.v.*) for stealing a bay mare (£3) from William Loosely, formerly of Harrow and since gone to the West Indies. Denham and Heels had gone to look after an ass and a foal. Heels said the mare was his and he sold it to Denham. Sentenced to death by Justice Sir Simon Le Blanc. Reprieved and sentenced to transportation for life. Gaoled at Newgate and transferred to the *Captivity* at Portsmouth.

Jane Heels accompanied her husband during the voyage out, berthed in the prison room. There were no children.

Died 3 January 1804, Port Phillip, aged 24 (?). Jane Heels married a fellow prisoner, John Hangan (q.v.), 30 August 1804, Hobart.

HENLEY, VALENTINE [c. 1763–1808]
Apothecary, aged 38, born Ireland; 5'7", light brown hair, grey eyes.
Tried at Middlesex IV Sessions (London G.D.) 15 April 1801 for stealing two handkerchiefs from George Ensor in the street. Two witnesses gave him a good character. Sentenced by the Recorder to transportation for seven years. Gaoled at Giltspur St. and transferred to the *Prudentia* hulk at Woolwich.

In Hobart he was appointed as overseer at the General Hospital, April 1808 (when free).

Burial registered on Christmas Day 1808 as Valentine Hindley, aged 62.

HOBERMAN, JOHN [c. 1765–1847]
(Obleman, Ogleman)
Tobacco manufacturer, aged 37, from Germany, married; 5'8", dark complexion. Literate.
Tried at Middlesex IV Sessions (Middlesex G.D.) 28 April 1802 for stealing 13 lb tobacco and 14s 0d from Ann Kemp, widow and manufacturer of tobacco in Whitechapel Road, his employer. Mrs Kemp's son gave evidence that Hoberman had been absent for a long time from work, saying his own child had had an accident falling in the fire. He was tried before a jury of whom half were foreigners. He spoke good broken English. Sentenced by Baron Thomson to transportation for seven years. Gaoled at Newgate and transferred to the *Captivity* hulk at Portsmouth. His wife did not accompany him.

Hoberman attended the Hobart musters in 1811, 1818, 1819 and 1823. He claimed 30 acres of farmland in 1812 which became part of Geils' land at Old Beach and receipts show he sold a farm for £90. The claim was taken to the Supreme Court in Equity and the case dragged on until 1825. He had 38 acres in Carlton by 1838.

On 1 January 1810, in Hobart, he married Ann Doyle, a convict from Dublin who had arrived at Port Jackson in the *Rolla*. He gave his marital status as single. They had at least one child, a daughter, Sarah.

He was a faithful storekeeper and servant to Kemp and Gatehouse at the brewery at New Town. Until November 1810 he was a constable at New Town, then was demoted to watchman. He made a donation to Mrs Briscoe's fund when her husband drowned (*q.v.*).

Hoberman was living in Goulburn St. when he died 14 June 1847, aged 85 (?).

Surnames of descendants have included: Makepeace.

HOLDHAM, ROBERT, alias WILLIAM KNAPP [c. 1776–1823]
(Oldham, Holdshaw)
Gardener, aged 24.
Tried at Lincolnshire Spring Assizes (Lincoln G.D.) 8 March 1800 upon the oath of Susanna Graham of Bicker for having married her on 19 August 1799, calling himself William Knapp a bachelor, having another wife alive. Sentenced to transportation for seven years. Gaoled at Lincoln and transferred to the *Prudentia* hulk at Woolwich.

He attended the Hobart musters in 1811, 1818, and 1823.

Holdham was witness appearing against Anne Allen at a trial in Sydney in 1806. She had committed arson in the house of Thomas Peters (*q.v.*). Holdham got into bad company and was in debt, which contributed in 1812 towards the loss of 80 acres of land which he had purchased at New Norfolk. There he had sown mostly wheat and potatoes and ran 23 male and 30 female sheep. In February 1823 Holdham was charged as the principal in a theft of 150 sheep belonging to Thomas Wells. The *H.T.G.*, 1 March 1823, lengthily reported the case.

Convicted at the Court of Criminal Jurisdiction for sheep stealing by Judge John Wylde during the Court's circuit in Hobart. Executed 14 April 1823, aged 50 (?).

HOPKINS, ALEXANDER [c. 1780 – ?]
Gun-maker, aged 21.
Tried at Kent Assizes (Maidstone G.D.) 27 August 1801 for stealing a metal watch from Thomas Jones in Greenwich. Sentenced to transportation for seven years. Gaoled at Maidstone and transferred to the *Prudentia* hulk at Woolwich. He is not to be confused with Thomas Hopkins, who was a servant to Gov. Collins and later became a publican.

As there appears to be no other record of Alexander Hopkins after his arrival in Hobart, it is likely that he returned to England after his sentence expired in 1808.

HORNE, WILLIAM [c. 1763–1847]
?, aged 39. Literate.
Tried at Warwick Summer Assizes (Warwick G.D.) 18 August 1802 for sheep stealing. Sentenced to death. Reprieved by Baron Thomson and Mr Justice Heath and sentenced to transportation for life. Gaoled at the county gaol and transferred to the hulks at Portsmouth.

Horne attended the Hobart musters in 1811, 1818, 1819 and 1823 and his name was on a return of settlers living at Pitt Water in 1820. He received a conditional pardon in January 1814 and an absolute pardon soon afterwards. He received a 30-acre land grant at Pitt Water (and appears to have acquired 50 more) where he grew several crops. In 1819 he had two male and six female cattle, thirty male sheep and seventy ewes. He had a government servant. But by July 1820 he almost lost his freehold farm and a good house when R.W. Loane sued him.

In May 1805 he was one of the prisoners examined for trying to escape in a whaleboat to New Zealand but there was insufficient evidence to convict them. In 1829 he was charged with breaking and entering the house of the late A. Simpson and stealing various articles. He was discharged through lack of proof.

On 22 May 1809 he married Hannah, the mother of Bartholomew and John Reardon, Norfolk I. settlers (sons of a first fleeter). She would have been 53 at the time (see Williams, Thomas (*q.v.*)).

Buried 19 April 1847, St George's, Pitt Water, aged 87 (?), his occupation then given as butcher. She was buried 4 November 1829, St George's, Pitt Water, aged 73.

HUNTER, JOHN [c. 1770 – after 1824]
Labourer, aged 32, of Manchester.
Tried at the County of the Palatinate of Lancaster S. of P. (Salford) 21 June 1802 for theft of one wood handboard

(ld), one japanned handboard (ld), two pairs worsted stockings (ld) and one book (ld) from Philip Houghton at Manchester. Sentenced to transportation for seven years. Gaoled at the county gaol and transferred to the hulks at Langston.

During the voyage Hunter was given duties as a sailor.

He attended the Hobart musters in 1811, 1818, 1819 and 1823 and the Port Dalrymple muster of 1820.

Early in his career he had been in some trouble, escaping from the watch house in May 1806 and spending the next five months in the woods before surrendering. In January 1807 he took to the bush and burnt down the house of Surgeon Mountgarret at Risdon.

Between 1814 and 1818 he appears to have been the John Hunter who sailed in the brig *Active*, which took the Revd Samuel Marsden and missionaries to New Zealand, the Revd and Mrs William Crook to the Society Islands, and returned with sandalwood and pork from Otaheite.

Hunter, although listed as a free person in 1823, was granted a ticket-of-leave in 1824, apparently having been in further trouble.

There appears to be no further record of him after that date.

HURLEY, TIMOTHY [c. 1769–1803]
Travelling merchant, aged 30, of Scotland.
Tried at Court of Judiciary, Ayr, 13 April 1799, together with Patrick Hurley (his brother?), for tendering false and uttering counterfeit money. Sentenced to a whipping by Lord Eskgrove and transportation for seven years. Gaoled at the Tolbooth in Ayr, transferred to the *Laurel* and then the *Fortune* hulk at Langston.

Died 10 December 1803, Port Phillip, aged 35 (?).

ISAACS, JOHN [c. 1788–1804]
Sailor, aged 14, of Newcastle-on-Tyne, Jew; 5'0", fair complexion.
Tried at Middlesex IV Sessions (Middlesex G.D.) 28 April 1802 with stealing a silver watch (15s 0d), gold chain (10s 0d), and gold seal (10s 0d), from Joseph Hall; a jacket (2s 0d), and trousers (1s 0d), from John Turner; and a silk handkerchief (6d) from James MacPherson, all on board the *Commercial Treaty* at the Leith and Berwick Wharf. Hall was the captain, Turner the foremastman, and MacPherson a servant. Isaac said he'd won the watch in a raffle. Sentence pronounced by the Recorder was transportation for seven years. Gaoled at Newgate and transferred to the *Prudentia* hulk at Woolwich.

During the voyage out he served as a sailor.
Died of scurvy, 2 October 1804, Hobart.

JACOBS, SAMUEL [c. 1782–1841]
Tailor, aged 18, of Norwich, Jew; 4'11", dark brown hair, dark complexion, hazel eyes.
Tried at Middlesex VII Sessions (Middlesex G.D.) 17 April 1800 for stealing a pair of leather shoes (2s 10d) from Ann Maddocks, who kept a shoe shop on Tower Hill. Sentence pronounced by the Common Sergeant was transportation for seven years. Gaoled at Newgate and transferred to the *Stanislaus* hulk at Woolwich.

His name did not appear on any of the Tasmanian muster rolls.

According to Rabbi Levi, this Samuel Jacobs lived for many years in Sydney, where he was buried 22 September 1841, Jewish Cemetery, Devonshire St.

JACOBS, WILLIAM [c. 1762–1852]
?, aged 40, married, possibly Jewish. Literate.
Tried at Southampton Summer Assizes (Winchester G.D.) 27 July 1802 with James Cooper for stealing a fat cow from William Parnham of Southwick. Sentenced to death. Reprieved by Justices Sir Giles Rooke and Baron Graham and sentenced to transportation for life. Gaoled at Winchester and transferred to the hulks at Portsmouth. His wife did not come out.

By August 1804 Jacobs had two fowls.

He attended the Hobart musters in 1811, 1818 and 1819. He received a conditional pardon in 1813 and was free by 1818. He received a land grant of 40 acres at Clarence Plains in 1819 on which he ran ten male and 30 female sheep, two male cattle, and grew wheat and barley. He had a wife and government servant.

In a memorial to Gov. Arthur in May 1828 he described his farm on which he had built a substantial weatherboard house of four rooms and a good barn. Thomas Lascelles described him as an 'industrious good old man' and the district constable Edward Boultbee, as a 'steady and upright character'.

He was a widower when he married Silena Lawrence, 7 July 1812 in Hobart. They had at least two children, Samuel and William. His wife died in April 1825, aged 44 and the following January he married a convict woman, Sarah Thorn, who had arrived in Hobart in the *Lord Sidmouth* in 1823. Jacobs appears to have made a fourth marriage to one Anne, described as a gentlewoman when she died in 1836. A note refers to her as the *widow* of William Jacobs (*Calcutta*).

Buried 6 June 1852, St David's, Hobart, aged 90 (?).

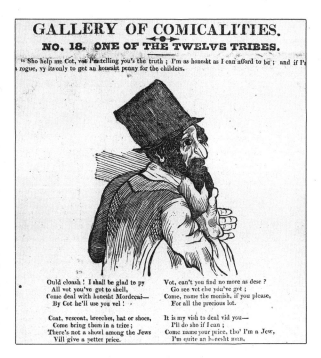

JAMMISON, JOHN [c. 1771–1820]
(Jamieson, Jemmison)
?, aged 29, married.
Tried at Devonshire Summer Assizes (Exeter G.D.) 4 August 1800 together with Sarah Jammison for stealing sundry articles of wearing apparel. They had been apprehended and charged with several felonies over a long period of time. Sentenced to death. Reprieved by Lord Chief Justice Eldon and Justice Sir Alexander Thomson and sentenced to transportation for seven years. Sarah Jammison (wife ?) appears to have been acquitted of this latest charge and was probably the Sarah Jamieson who had already been sentenced and arrived at Port Jackson in the *Nile* in 1799, and later in Hobart. Gaoled at Exeter and transferred to the hulks at Langston.

He attended the Hobart musters in 1811, 1818 and 1819. By 1818 he had a land grant of 30 acres in the Hobart area (Humphrey's River) at which he grazed 200 male and 300 female sheep, six male and four female cattle, and grew wheat, barley and vegetables. He employed a convict and a free man and had a child but no wife. He contributed to the Auxiliary Bible Society.

In May 1820 he had a serious accident when a heavy piece of timber fell on his leg and shattered it in 'a most dreadful manner'. A report in the *H.T.G.* noted that amputation was necessary.

He died on 2 June 1820 in the Hobart General Hospital, aged 48 (?), respected as an honest and industrious man.

JARRETT, EDWARD [c. 1782 – ?]
(Jarratt, Jarrott)
Husbandman, aged 20.
Tried at Kent Spring Assizes (Maidstone G.D.) 15 March 1802 for assaulting Daniel Solomon on the King's Highway and robbing him of goods and money. Sentenced to death. Reprieved by Baron Hotham and Mr Justice Heath and sentenced to transportation for life. Gaoled at Maidstone and transferred to the *Prudentia* hulk at Woolwich.

Escaped from Hobart, October 1806. Appears that he did not return. In March was declared an outlaw in the General Orders, £10 offered as reward for apprehension. No record that he returned.

JOHNSON, JAMES [c. 1767–1804]
Blacksmith, aged 35.
Tried at Essex Assizes (Chelmsford G.D.) 28 July 1802 for stealing a steel trap. Sentenced to transportation for seven years. Gaoled at Chelmsford and transferred to the *Prudentia* hulk at Woolwich.

During the voyage out he was employed on deck as an armourer's mate.

Died soon after arrival in V.D.L., 3 March 1804, Risdon Cove, aged 36 (?).

JOHNSON, JOHN, alias CLEMENT or EMMET LAWRENCE or LAURENCE [c. 1780 – ?]
Labourer, aged 21, of St George's, Southwark.
Tried at Surrey S. of P. (Reigate) 14 April 1801 together with John Green alias Robert Lawrence (*q.v.*) for stealing a quantity of sugar from William Phillips at St George's,

Southwark. Sentenced to transportation for seven years. Gaoled at the county gaol and transferred to the hulks at Portsmouth.

John Johnson's name did not appear on the Commissariat return during the time of the settlement at Port Phillip, but there was a note in the records of John Clark (*q.v.*) and James Lord (*q.v.*) that James Ballance (*q.v.*) witnessed a promissory note for a John Johnson, 22 April 1810.

He appears more than likely to have been the John Johnson who sailed in the brig *Perseverance* to Macquarie I. in 1812, later joining the brig *Cyclops* and other vessels engaged in the Pacific trade. This Johnson was a member of the crew of the *Governor Macquarie* on a pearling expedition when they discovered deserters from the *Favourite* who were planning an act of piracy, and he was a member of Capt. Kelly's crew in 1819 when he gave witness against Urias Allender (*q.v.*) and Henry May for assaulting Kelly. He had settled in Hobart by the time of the 1823 muster, named as having arrived with Capt. Woodriff in the *Calcutta*. He was not the John Johnson, a Dublin man executed in 1826, who was one of the M'Cabe's bushranging gang.

Beyond 1823 Johnson's activities have not been traced.

JOHNSON, JOSEPH [c. 1776–1852]
(Johnstone)
Labourer, aged 26, from Tissington, Monegash, Derbyshire.
Tried at Derby Spring Assizes (Derby G.D.) 13 March 1802 at the County Hall, Crown End, for horse stealing, together with Thomas Dawkins. Both sentenced by Justice Sir Robert Graham to death. Reprieved and sentenced to transportation for life. Gaoled at the county gaol and transferred to the hulks at Langston.

Johnson attended the Hobart musters in 1811, 1818 and 1819. He was one of the earliest to receive a conditional pardon (1809) and later an absolute pardon. He received a 30-acre land grant at Herdsman's Cove from Gov. Macquarie and a further 110 acres at Herdsman's Cove in addition to purchasing a further 100 acres. By 1819 he was growing large quantities of wheat and vegetables and owned two horses, fourteen male and sixteen female cattle, 600 male sheep and 1 200 ewes. He employed three government servants. He sold the land at Glenorchy to buy 100 acres at Green Ponds before 1821.

Johnson married Elizabeth Smith, aged 30, a convict transported for seven years from Dublin in the *Catherine*, arriving first in Sydney in 1814. She could write well, and Johnson, who had been illiterate, taught himself to read and write. They had one child but it must have died in infancy. In 1827 they had an orphan, Owen Clark, aged twelve, living with them, perhaps adopted.

The Land Commissioners reported favourably on Johnson's land and his farm but in 1825 J. H. Wedge found much of it poor and rocky. In 1834 James Backhouse stayed with Johnson and found him most industrious and sober, possessing some 5 000 acres. William Buckley (*q.v.*) visited him on his return to Tasmania and Johnson assisted Buckley to get a job.

Johnson was so successful that several members of his family came to Tasmania to share in his good fortune. Some lived with him at the fine house he built, Tissington, in the Castle Hill area at Green Ponds. His nephew William, with his wife and three children, arrived in 1821 and received a land grant at Green Valley. Another nephew, Edmund, arrived in 1827 with his sons Edmund and Joseph, and the family rapidly expanded.

Johnson leased his stockyard to other large stockholders including James Lord (*q.v.*). Thieves stole 120 of Lord's sheep from it in 1820. He was not averse to giving a good recommendation for a Polynesian settler, Peter Harley from Otaheite, for a land grant so that he could settle at Green Ponds.

When Elizabeth Johnson was old and failing, Joseph Johnson sen. took Jane Baird alias Hadden (or Haddow)* as housekeeper. After Elizabeth's burial at Green Ponds, 30 April 1845, Johnson married his housekeeper at the Church of Scotland in Hobart, 13 May 1846. She had arrived in the *Garland Grove* in 1841 and was assigned to Capt. William Clark at Bothwell. She had barricaded his house against Martin Cash and his gang after which she received a ticket-of-leave. But the 'marriage' to Johnson was not a success. Jane's husband William Hadden arrived in V.D.L. to claim his wife. She deserted Johnson and he had to disclaim her debts. One of his nephews, Edmund, married, first, Jane's daughter and, on her death, another daughter, Jean (or Jane), no doubt to make sure of holding some of the property which Jane successfully claimed when Joseph died.

Died 19 December 1852, Green Valley, Brighton, probably at the home of his nephew William, of 'debility', aged 80 (?). Buried at Green Ponds two days later.

Surnames of Johnson's nephews' descendants have included: Bowman; Calvert; Evans; Fletcher; Harvey; Hurley; Kellock; Luttrell; Maxwell; Moore; Nichols; Piesse; Pike; Purbrick; Reynolds; Sadler; Sale; Sidney; Steane; Vanrenan.

*G. Cullis, *No Tears for Jane: A Hadden Family History*, Canberra 1982.

JONES, GEORGE [c. 1761–1823]
Shoemaker, aged 39, of Marylebone; 5'6", fair complexion, brown hair, grey eyes.
Tried at Middlesex II Sessions (Middlesex G.D.) 15 January 1800 for stealing several handkerchiefs in a shop from Catherine Chapman. Sentenced by Justice Sir Soulden Laurence to death. Reprieved and sentenced to transportation for life. Gaoled at Newgate and transferred to the hulks at Woolwich.

This George Jones attended the Hobart musters in 1811, 1818 and 1819.

By 1816 he had received a conditional pardon and by 1818 was free. Some time before he was married and according to the landholders' muster of that year, although he had no land grant, he owned eighteen female cattle, fourteen male sheep and 80 female sheep.

He appears to be the George Jones who took to the bush with fellow *Calcutta* convicts for a few months in 1814. He had escaped in May, joined the bushranger Peter Mills, and was outlawed. Gov. Macquarie proclaimed those who returned to their establishments would be granted an amnesty.

Buried 4 December 1823, St David's, Hobart, aged 64 (?).

JONES, JOHN [c. 1751–1804]
Labourer, aged 51, born in Steviouk, co. Flint, Wales.
Tried at Shropshire Spring Assizes (Shrewsbury G.D.) 20 March 1802 for stealing a black mare from John Simpson of Pantyblythen, co. Flint. Sentenced to death. Reprieved by Baron Thomson and Justice Sir Alan Chambre and sentenced to transportation for life. Gaoled at Shrewsbury and transferred to the hulks at Portsmouth.

On 3 January 1804, at Port Phillip, Jones absconded, but returned to camp on 23 January in a very weakened state. Collins described him as 'an infirm old man' and had to leave him behind when the larger contingent sailed for V.D.L.

Died 17 February 1804, Port Phillip, 'from fatigue', aged 51 (?).

JONES, JOHN, alias HUGHES [c. 1781 – ?]
Labourer, aged 19.
Tried at Bedfordshire Summer Assizes (Bedford G.D.) 24 July 1800 for having aided and assisted James Hughes alias Jones, under sentence for transportation, and three other prisoners in making their escape from the county gaol at Bedford on 6 January 1800. Sentenced by Baron Hotham to transportation for seven years. Gaoled first at Chelmsford, Essex, removed to gaol at Bedford and transferred to the *Stanislaus* hulk at Woolwich. While in gaol Jones had bad eyes and needed special nourishment and care.

Jones helped capture the bushrangers Lemon and Brown, the Port Dalrymple murderers, in March 1808. He helped bring in the head of Lemon.

Likely that he returned to England when his sentence expired in 1808. There were other John Jones in the colony but none appears to be the Calcutta *John Jones whose name was not on the 1811 muster rolls.*

JONES, THOMAS [c. 1777 – after 1817?]
?, aged 25.
Tried at Sussex Spring Assizes (Horsham G.D.) 27 March 1802 for stealing a valuable chestnut mare from a stable belonging to Jasper Bates, of Fernhurst, the property of William Fennemore. Sentenced to death by Baron Hotham. Reprieved and sentenced to transportation for life. Gaoled at Horsham and transferred to the hulks at Langston.

In October 1806 Knopwood informed Collins that Thomas Jones had stolen and killed a cow (£25). He was sent in the *Estramina* to Port Jackson to stand trial at the Court of Criminal Jurisdiction but was acquitted in May 1807.

He received a conditional pardon in February 1812. He does not appear to have returned to V.D.L.

It is likely that he was the Thomas Jones who, in August 1812, joined the brig Atlanta *on a whaling expedition. In 1815 this Thomas Jones was in the crew of the* Geordy *which was blown through Bass Strait towards the entrance of Port Phillip. In 1817 he joined the sloop* Martha *which traded with the Fiji Islands.*

JONES, WILLIAM [c. 1788 – after 1817]
No trade, aged 12, of St Sepulchre's, London; 3'11", dark complexion, brown hair, hazel eyes, very crooked legs.

Tried at Middlesex II Sessions (Middlesex G.D.) 3 December 1800 for stealing a cloth wrapper (2s 0d), brown Irish cloth (£2 18s 0d), and printed cotton (£1 5s 0d) out of the wagon of William Sutton, carrier. Sentenced to transportation for seven years by Justice Sir Giles Rooke. Gaoled at Newgate and transferred to the *Prudentia* hulk at Woolwich.

During the voyage out Jones was employed as a servant in the ward-room.

By May 1805 Jones was one of Knopwood's trusted servants in V.D.L. He was allowed regular use of Knopwood's boat, sailing up and down the Derwent with John Gain (*q.v.*) (another servant) on numerous occasions, accompanied by dogs, to acquire kangaroos, emus, swans and anything that could provide food for the people. In two months they brought back 66 kangaroos and coal from the Coal River. He also assisted with a little farming.

Although nearing the end of his sentence, Jones deserted on October 1806, spending four months away from the camp and managing to survive off the land with Jarrett, Tombs and Crute. He was taken by Supt. Clark 3 February 1807.

William Jones became a sailor first with Campbell & Co., serving in the brig *Perseverance* in 1808–09 on two voyages to Fiji to collect sandalwood. He appears to have thought of returning to England in the *Atlanta* in 1809 but instead sailed in the brig *Active* with a sealing gang for Bass Strait. He joined the brig *Mary and Sally* (Capt. Kelly), August 1813. It was owned by William Collins and sailed for Macquarie I.

In April 1815 he was in the schooner *The Brothers*, of which William Hovell was master. While in New Zealand natives attacked the ship and several of the crew were killed. Jones survived and in October 1815 he was a deserter from the *Baring*, described as 26 years of age, fresh complexion, 5'2½". He re-joined Kelly in Hobart, December 1815 and was one of his crew in a five-oared whale boat, *Elizabeth*, which Dr T. W. Birch sent to explore the harbours of south-west Tasmania.

In June the following year he sailed in the *Elizabeth and Mary*, one of Campbell's schooners captained by Richard Siddons, on a voyage to Macquarie I. In April 1817 he left in the *Campbell Macquarie* with a cargo of wool for Batavia.

There appears to be no further record of this William Jones.

JORY, JOHN [c. 1784–1804]
Miner, aged 17, of Gwennap, Wales.
Tried at Cornwall S. of P. (Truro) 14 April 1801 for stealing 2 lb of candles (6d) from William Hichens. Sentenced by thirteen J.P.s to transportation for seven years. Gaoled at Truro and transferred to the hulks at Langston.

Jory was too ill to leave Port Phillip when the larger contingent sailed for V.D.L.

Died 17 February 1804, Port Phillip, aged 19.

KEEP, WILLIAM [c. 1788–1846]
Postal clerk, aged 13, from Brentwood, Staffordshire. Dark complexion, brown hair, dark eyes. Literate.
Tried at Middlesex VIII Sessions (London G.D.) 28 October 1801 for stealing banknotes for £15 and £2 while employed sorting letters at the G.P.O., London. He went to buy cloth for pantaloons, coat and two waistcoats. He was dressed in a blue coat, leather breeches, white stockings and had an apron on. Sentenced to death by Mr Justice Heath who recommended mercy on account of his youth. Reprieved and sentenced to transportation for life. Gaoled at Poultry and transferred to the *Prudentia* hulk at Woolwich.

During the voyage out he became a servant to Lieut. Gov. Collins.

He attended the Hobart musters in 1811, 1818 and 1819. He received a conditional pardon in April 1815 and an absolute pardon soon afterwards. At this time he was a brickmaker, described as 5'7", dark complexion, black hair, dark brown eyes.

He received a 30-acre land grant at Pitt Water from Gov. Macquarie before 1819 when he was farming wheat and barley and preparing 22½ acres for pasture. He must have received a further 30 acres when a court order in 1824 threatened to put up and sell the property by public auction unless he carried out several executions. His farm then had only 20 acres in cultivation.

On 26 December 1814, in Hobart, he married teacher Eleanor Johnson, a convict. They had at least four children, two of whom died in infancy. One surviving son was on the education return of 1824, aged six, and could read.

In later life Keep provided James Bonwick with some information on the settlement at Sullivan Bay and the persons he remembered there.

An inquest held, 24 October 1846, showed that William Keep, while going down a well — 'accidentally, casually and by misfortune by foul air . . .' choked and suffocated at the house of Ann Keep, his widow.

Surnames of descendants have included: Drury.

KEMP, RICHARD [1769–1847]
Labourer, aged 29 (33?), son of William Kemp of Eynsford, Kent, and Mary (née Rivers) of St Mary Cray, Kent. Bap. 17 December 1769, pa. St Mary Cray where he attended school. Married Anne Toler of Wilmington, Kent, at Wilmington, 14 February 1792, one son. Literate.
Tried at Kent Spring Assizes (Maidstone G.D.) 15 March 1802 together with Samuel Toler for using force and arms and stealing one wether sheep from Thomas Harman and others in Wilmington. Sentenced to death. Reprieved by Baron Hotham and Mr Justice Heath and sentenced to transportation for life. Gaoled at Maidstone and transferred to the *Prudentia* hulk at Woolwich. His wife did not accompany him.

Kemp attended the Hobart musters in 1811, 1818, 1819 and 1823, and was on the census of 1842. He received a conditional pardon in January 1813 and an absolute pardon soon afterwards. Knopwood employed Kemp as one of his servants in Hobart until 1818. He received a 30-acre land grant from Gov. Macquarie before 1819 when he had 20 rams and 50 ewes, providing meat for the Commissariat. He employed three servants in 1842 and there were ten persons living on his property, Green Hills, Forcett.

On 7 April 1823, at St David's, he married Mary Deal, aged 24, a convict transported in the *Janus* from Cork.

They had at least one son and six daughters and numerous successful descendants.

Buried 14 August 1847, St George's, Sorell, aged 79, his occupation given as farmer and abode as Forcett. Mary Kemp was buried 14 October 1865, St. George's, aged 85.

Surnames of descendants have included: Allen; Barwick; Bedwell; Chambers; Cooper; Denning; Harland; Haydon; Hudson; Jones; Murray; Ring; Sapwell; Smith; Watson; Westerman; Wiggins.

KENNEDY, DENIS [c. 1777 – after 1823]
Tailor, aged 24, from Ernley, Tipperary; 5'6", dark brown hair, grey eyes, dark complexion. Literate.
Tried at Middlesex V Sessions (Middlesex G.D.) 20 May 1801 for stealing, together with William M'Cormack (Cormack (*q.v.*)) and a Thomas Jones four sheep (£4) from John Claridge, a farmer at Finchley. Kennedy said M'Cormack wanted some mutton and he was hungry. Kennedy had three witnesses who gave him a good character. All were sentenced to death by Mr Justice Graham. Reprieved and sentenced to transportation for life. Gaoled at Newgate and transferred to the *Captivity* hulk at Portsmouth.

Kennedy attended the Hobart musters in 1811, 1818, 1819 and 1823. He does not appear to have received any land grant. He received a conditional pardon in January 1813 and an absolute pardon soon afterwards.

Kennedy probably carried on his trade as a tailor for a few years. By 1810 Dr Bowden noted that he was a stonecutter and his purchases from Bowden's store were those of a comfortable person. He acquired a well situated and good house in Collins St. which he advertised for sale or for rent in 1820 on good terms.

He married Ann Burn, a free woman from Dublin, aged about 37, 7 January 1811, Hobart. She had originally arrived from Cork in the transport *Marquis Cornwallis*, which had arrived at Port Jackson in February 1796.

Kennedy's death has not been traced but it is possible that a Jane Kennedy, aged 13, an orphan living at New Norfolk about 1827 (and not an object of charity) might have been their daughter. Ann Burn was buried 1 September 1824, St David's, aged 50.

KENNEDY, JAMES [c.1785 –]
?, aged 17 years, lived at Bowlyard, Southampton, with mother and father, in a lodging house; 5'5", dark complexion, and suggestion that he was deaf.
Tried at Middlesex VI Sessions (Middlesex G.D.) 14 July 1802 for assaulting and robbing Elizabeth Butcher of two pairs of stockings (10s 0d), shawl (5s 0d), slippers (2s 0d), scissors (1s 0d) and two handkerchiefs (2s 0d) on the King's Highway, High Street, St Giles. Sentenced by Justice Sir Soulden Laurence to transportation for seven years for stealing but not guilty of violence. Gaoled at Newgate and transferred to the *Captivity* hulk at Portsmouth.

As there is no further record of Kennedy after his arrival in V.D.L., it is likely that he returned to England after his sentence expired in 1809.

KENNEDY, ROBERT [c. 1775–1812]
(Cannady)
Labourer, aged 26.
Tried at City of Bristol S. of P. 20 October 1801 for committing an unknown felony (all reliable records miss-

ing). (Kennedy told A. W. H. Humphrey that his conviction was for buying a watch, knowing it to be stolen.) Sentenced by the Mayor, Recorder and Aldermen as J.P.s to transportation for seven years. Gaoled at Bristol and transferred to the hulks at Woolwich.

During the voyage out he was a servant to Mr Bromley, surgeon of the *Calcutta*. At Port Phillip he was, according to Knopwood, servant to A. W. H. Humphrey. He was a party in the first litigation at Port Phillip when John Buckley (*q.v.*), convict servant to Gov. Collins, charged him with keeping a waistcoat he had promised to exchange for a pair of shoes. Knopwood, as a magistrate, ordered Robert Cannady [*sic*] to give the waistcoat to Buckley.

Robert Kennedy joined the brig *Fox*, sailing from Port Jackson in May 1809, to go sealing. He appears to have remained in the *Fox* and been one of the party left at Foveaux Strait for six months.

He was probably among those drowned when the ship was wrecked, 26 September 1810, Amsterdam I.

KEOGH, OWEN [c. 1773 – ?]
(Kegho)
?, aged 29, probably from Wales.
Tried at Southampton Q.S. (Portsmouth) 9 October 1802 for an unknown petty larceny. Sentenced to transportation for seven years. Gaoled at Portsmouth and transferred to the hulks at Portsmouth.

Keogh attended the Hobart muster in 1811. He was employed as a servant to G. P. Harris in May 1805, when Knopwood recorded that he and Lieut. Sladden 'sat upon some business' relating to Keogh.

He probably returned to England when his sentence expired about 1809.

KIDMAN, RICHARD [c. 1761–1832]
Clock-mender, aged 40, born Waterbeach, Cambridge, of labouring people. Had also been a plumber, gardener, shoemaker and glazier. Lived in Bell Lane, St Giles, Cambridge, with his wife Sarah. Literate.
Tried at Cambridge Assizes (Cambridge G.D.) 11 March 1801 for a burglary at Caius College, Cambridge, stealing large amounts of silver plate including candlesticks and cutlery. Kidman had received prior and minor convictions for robbery and had served at the bridewell, the Castle, and had been publicly whipped in the market place. For several years Kidman in association with William Grimshaw (executed March 1801) had been engaged in numerous burglaries in several of the Cambridge colleges but their ingenuity had prevented their being apprehended. They had allegedly been able to dispose of much of their loot when melted to Henry Cohen, who was charged as an accessory.

After a very short trial, Kidman, who had pleaded guilty, was sentenced to death by Justice Sir Nash Grose. Reprieved and sentenced to transportation for life. After a very long trial Cohen was declared not guilty. Kidman was gaoled at Cambridge and transferred to the *Prudentia* hulk at Woolwich.

His wife did not accompany him in the *Calcutta*

Kidman was among the prisoners missing with dogs for three months in 1805 at the time they saw a Tasmanian tiger. He might have been a useful man employed in some public works. There is no certainty what his actual employment was but he must have been close to or trusted by Collins who recommended him for a free pardon — one of the first — received October 1810. He returned to England in the *New Zealander* in 1811. A book published in Cambridge in 1840, *The Trials of W. Grimshaw and R. Kidman for burglary (with a sketch of their lives) and of H. Cohen as an accessory before and after the fact*, records that he received his pardon for disclosing a plot to murder the Governor and gave a brief account of his subsequent career in Cambridge and the United States.

After returning once more to Cambridge he died. Buried January 1832, St Giles.

Any descendants, as yet, are unknown, but Sir Sidney Kidman, whose father came from within twenty miles of Richard's birthplace, appeared to be a kinsman and there are Kidmans still living in and around Cambridge.

See Chapter 6 for a fuller account of Kidman's career.

KING, GEORGE [c. 1783–after 1837 ?]
(James King)
Farmer, aged 19.
Tried at Berkshire Spring Assizes (Reading G.D.) 1 March 1802 for breaking in to the house of John Marlow of Barkham and stealing two golden guineas, a knife and other articles. Sentenced to death. Reprieved by Baron Thomson and Justice Sir Alan Chambre and sentenced to transportation for fourteen years. Gaoled at Reading and transferred to the hulks at Langston. King attended the Hobart musters in 1811, 1818 and 1819.

He was appointed a government stock keeper in September 1804, a position he held for some years. At one time, he was a government servant to Richard Clark at Risdon and later to Samuel Humphrey, a settler from Norfolk I. There is some evidence that he was neglectful of duty and Andrew Whitehead (*q.v.*) gave him a bad character at the time he, King, brought charges against Denis McCarty in 1813. But he appears to have been a foolish rather than a bad man.

In 1815 he was a servant with a ticket-of-leave to William Abel of New Norfolk. During an inquest on the body of Charles Carlisle, murdered by bushrangers, he gave intelligent answers to questions and a lengthy deposition regarding robbery at the house of James Triffitt at Macquarie Plains.

By 1824 he owned 100 sheep which, in a memorial for a land grant, he declared he had obtained by 'honest and industrious means'. A police report of the time shows that he had not been convicted of any offence since he arrived in 1803 and was, at that time, shepherd to James Triffitt. There appears to be no record that he received the land but a Hobart court record shows that in June 1829 a George King, free by servitude and known as 'Jimmy Jackass' was fined 5s 0d for being drunk and disorderly in the streets of Hobart.

On 19 October 1835, St Matthew's, New Norfolk, a George King, bachelor, of Macquarie Plains, was married to Emma Mallett, widow, also of Macquarie Plains; ceremony performed by the Revd William Garrard. In 1837 Governor Franklin allowed him 200 acres bounded on the

north by Green Point to Port Cygnet for the payment of £50.

Date of death has not been traced.

LANGLEY, JAMES [c. 1782–1807 ?]
Plasterer, aged 20, of Middlesex. 5'6", fair complexion.
Tried at Middlesex VI Sessions (Middlesex G.D.) 14 July 1802 for stealing a pair of boots (12s 0d) from Thomas Kennedy, boot and shoe maker of Oxford St. Sentenced by Justice Sir Giles Rooke to transportation for seven years. Gaoled at Newgate and transferred to the *Captivity* hulk at Portsmouth.

Escaped from Hobart, July 1807 and was believed to be at large in the woods. As there is no record of his return, he probably perished within the year.

LAWLER, MICHAEL [c. 1778–after 1827]
(Lawlor)
Labourer, aged 34, from Tipperary, Ireland, late of Ealing, Roman Catholic; 5'8", dark complexion. Literate.
Tried at Middlesex Commission of *Oyer et Terminer* 5 June 1802 on four counts of false pretences: I) to Isaac Greentree, a servant and shopman of Michael Fowler and John Tucker of Ealing, ironmongers, that the Revd Dr George Nicholas had sent him to obtain one saw (5s 0d), one spade (4s 0d), two pruning knives (2s 0d), and one scythe (4s 6d); II) to Samuel Blake of Ealing, linen-draper, that he was a servant of Revd George Nicholas and had brought a counterfeit note from his wife Elizabeth Nicholas to obtain 12 yards of linen cloth (£1 16s 0d) and two pairs of stockings (7s 0d); III) to John Godwin, servant and shopman of William St., Ealing, that he was the Revd George Nicholas' gardener and that his name was John Maxwell, thereby obtaining two pairs of stockings (7s 0d); IV) to John Beck of Ealing, linen-draper, for the same except that the stockings were valued at 9s 0d. Sentenced by the Senior Police Magistrate on the last indictment to transportation for seven years. Gaoled at Newgate and transferred to the *Captivity* hulk at Portsmouth.

Lawler attended the Hobart musters in 1811, 1818 and 1819.

In 1810 Lawler signed a contract with Edward Lord to lease two acres of land in Hobart on the River Derwent for 2s 6d per annum for fourteen years. By 1817 he was producing wheat for the Commissariat and in 1818 he received his own grant of 40 acres at Clarence Plains on which he raised wheat and vegetables. He and his wife employed two government servants, one named Christopher Keegan. Soon after his assignment to Lawler, Keegan was found dead a mile from the house after a heavy night's drinking at the Chequers Inn at Clarence Plains.

A Mary Lawler from Clonmel, Ireland, who had been convicted in 1802, had arrived in the *Atlas* and died in June 1814, free, in Hobart. She appears to have been his wife. Her name appeared on the 1811 Hobart muster rolls.

For a time Lawler was a gardener to Geils at Restdown. On 19 July 1817 he married Rosan McLane, aged 32, a convict who arrived in the *Alexander*.

It is not surprising to find Lawler had trespassers on his property for he appears to have been an industrious farmer who had some noteworthy successes in fruit growing, as in

1827 when a newly grafted apple tree produced thirty apples within a year. He was friendly with Knopwood and subscribed to the Auxiliary Bible Society.

Rosan Lawler died May 1827, Muddy Plains. The date of Lawler's own death has not yet been traced.

LAWRENCE, JOHN [c. 1781–1815]
(Laurence)

Labourer, aged 20, of Halstock, Dorset, single; 5'6", brown hair, fair complexion, grey eyes, lusty appearance.
Tried at Dorset Spring Assizes (Dorchester G.D.) 12 March 1801 for stealing two sheep from John Gerrard of Beaminster. Sentenced to death by Justice Sir Simon Le Blanc. Reprieved and sentenced to transportation for life. Gaoled at Dorchester where he was employed at hatting and transferred to the *Captivity* hulk at Portsmouth.

Although his name did not appear on the 1811 Hobart muster roll, Lawrence was living in Hobart in 1813 when he received first a conditional and then an absolute pardon.

He was a servant to Edward Lord and had engaged in a fight with John Marsden, one of Knopwood's servants. Knopwood called to see him to find him dying. He read prayers and soon afterwards Lawrence died. An inquest on 1 December 1815 showed that three ribs were broken. The jury charged Marsden with manslaughter. Edward Lord arranged for the funeral on 1 December in Hobart and he was buried aged 36 (?).

LAWRENCE, ROBERT [c. 1778–after 1829]
(Laurence, Lurance)

?, aged 24.
Tried at Somersetshire Spring Assizes (Taunton G.D.) together with John Dinham (*q.v.*) 1 April 1802 for stealing one wether sheep from the Rt Hon. Hester, Countess Dowager of Chatham, and two wether sheep from J. Michell. Sentenced to death. Reprieved by Justices Soulden Laurence and Sir Simon Le Blanc and sentenced to transportation for life. Gaoled at Taunton and transferred to the hulks at Langston.

Lawrence attended the Hobart musters in 1811, 1818 and 1819. He received a conditional pardon in 1816 and full pardon in 1821. On 13 March 1819 Gov. Sorell announced his appointment as a constable. By this time he had married (21 April 1817) a free settler, Lucy de Peete, in Hobart but she died, March 1820. The following May he married Susanna House, a convict who had arrived in the *Maria*, aged 48. (Lawrence was not literate and the ages given at the two marriages were inconsistent.)

In 1824 he was living in Bridge St., Hobart, when he advertised a 'good house' for sale, with 'two rooms, a good garden, neatly laid out and cropped.'

Advertised in May 1824 that he was leaving the colony with his wife. However, he was probably still alive in 1829, whether in Hobart or not, when he received a long overdue grant of 30 acres originally ordered for him by Gov. Macquarie.

LAZARUS, HENRY, alias HENRY ELLIS [c. 1779 – after 1836]

Pedlar, aged 22, of London, married, one child, Jew; 5'6", dark complexion, brown hair, grey eyes.
Tried at Middlesex VII Sessions (Middlesex G.D.) 16 September 1801 for stealing four handkerchiefs (13s 0d) and a napkin (2s 0d) from James Coe and James Brown, linen-drapers, Oxford St. Sentence pronounced by the Common Sergeant was transportation for seven years. Two witnesses gave him a good character. Gaoled at Newgate and transferred to the *Prudentia* hulk at Woolwich.

During the voyage out Lazarus served as a sailor and at some stage might have been a servant to Lieut.-Gov. Collins.

His name does not appear on the muster rolls of 1811.

After the expiry of his sentence he returned to England in 1817, changing his name to Henry Ellis. He probably found no family left. He was later charged at Warwick Assizes 30 March 1822 for highway robbery and sentenced to transportation for life. The gaol report from Warwick showed that he behaved well and was orderly while there for four months.

He returned to Hobart in the *Morley*, 7 February 1823. He attended the Hobart convict muster in 1825 as Henry Ellis (assigned to R. Maunder) and 1830 (assigned to O. Smith (*q.v.*)). He received a ticket-of-leave in 1833.

Was still alive in 1836 when he received a conditional pardon.

LEACH, WILLIAM, alias JOHN LEACH [c. 1774–1853]
(Leech)

Watchmaker, aged 27, pa. St Luke, Golden Lane, London; 5'5", fair complexion, brown hair, grey eyes. Literate.
Tried at Middlesex VI Sessions (Middlesex G.D.) 1 July 1801 for stealing a copper pot (6s 0d) from George Brandburg of Islington. He pleaded that he was ill for some time. The doctor had ordered him to bathe early in the morning and he was returning home from the New River. Sentence pronounced by the Common Sergeant was transportation for seven years. He had previously been convicted in December 1791, sentenced to transportation for seven years and sailed in the *Albermale* to Botany Bay. He returned to England at an unknown date. In February 1801 he had served a month in Newgate and received a public whipping for stealing two shirts from George Burns. Gaoled at Newgate and transferred to the hulks at Portsmouth.

He attended the Hobart musters in 1811, 1818, 1819 and 1823. He received a 40-acre land grant at Glenorchy from Gov. Macquarie on which he grew a variety of crops and was raising 57 male sheep and 200 female sheep by 1819. He employed one government servant and supplied meat to the Commissariat.

William Leach was among those in a disturbance with the military patrol in 1807 and received 200 lashes.

On 3 June 1816, in Hobart, he married Mary Burn, aged 40, a free woman. They had four children. One daughter died in 1825. The name of only one son appears in the return of juveniles of 1827 when he was living at Argyle St. with Protestant parents of good character.

Buried 29 September 1853, St David's, aged 83 (?). Mary Leach was buried 1 May 1827, St David's, aged 51 and described as a 'poor woman'.

LEE, GEORGE [c. 1780– after 1803]

Clerk, aged 22, well-educated and able. Literate. Possibly Irish.
Tried at Worcester Spring Assizes (Worcester G.D.) 6 March 1802 for trying to pass forged bank notes. Sentenced to transportation for fourteen years. Gaoled at Worcester

and transferred to the hulks at Langston, from where he corresponded with Sir Henry Mildmay, M.P., regarding the state of the hulks.

At Port Phillip, Lee accused Supt Clark and overseer, John Ingle, of 'infamous conduct', according to Collins, 'which he could not support by any one evidence.' (Lee was Ingle's clerk at Port Phillip.) Thereupon, he decided to steal a gun and food, and escape with David Gibson (*q.v.*), 'with whom he was intimate at the hulks.' Collins wrote that he was a young man of education and abilities and did not believe he would be foolish enough to try to reach Port Jackson. Collins had not employed him at hard labour, hoping to use his abilities, and had allowed him to construct a small hut. He had abused the privileges, creating dissatisfaction among the prisoners with illiberal reflections on the officers. Knopwood had investigated his conduct and found he had brought malicious accusations against John Manning (*q.v.*) for coining. After reaching the River Yarra he refused to return to camp with Gibson.

He presumably died in the woods at Port Phillip in 1803–04.

LEONARD, RICHARD [c. 1784–1804]
(Lennard)
Labourer, aged 17, of London; 5', fair complexion, brown hair, grey eyes.
Tried at Middlesex VII Assizes (London G.D.) 16 September 1801 for stealing a book (2s 0d) and pocket-book (6d) from James Angier, manufacturer, of Norwich, in the street at Cheapside. Sentence pronounced by the Recorder was transportation for seven years. Gaoled at Poultry and transferred to the *Prudentia* hulk at Woolwich.

During the voyage out he served as a sailor.
Died 22 January 1804, Port Phillip, aged 19 (?).

LEWIS, WILLIAM [c. 1746–1804]
(Lewes)
Yeoman, aged 55, of Llandyssul, Cardigan, Wales. Married.
Tried at Cardigan G.S. 24 May 1801 for stealing with force and arms one ewe (5s 0d) from John Thomas, farmer of Llandyssul. Sentenced by the High Sheriff of the county, John Lloyd, to death. Reprieved and sentenced to transportation for life. Gaoled at county gaol, Carmarthen and transferred first to the hulks at Portsmouth and later to Langston. Lewis's wife did not accompany him.
Soon after arrival in V.D.L. Lewis died, 12 May 1804, Risdon Cove.

LORD, JAMES [c. 1757–1824]
Labourer, aged 44, born Bradford, Yorkshire (?) but living at Wakefield, Yorkshire. Married Grace Hayley at Halifax, 14 July 1785. Children David born c. 1785 and Ann born c. 1790. Believed by family to have descended from Flemish weavers and to be a fustian maker who was politically active. Literate.
Tried at Yorkshire Q.S. (Bradford G.D.) 16 July 1801 together with John Green for stealing three bushels of oats (10d) from James Moore of Halifax, using force and arms. Sentenced by the adjutant to transportation for seven years (Green received a sentence of two years' gaol). Gaoled at York Castle and transferred to the hulks at Portsmouth. His wife did not leave England.

Fawkner noted that Lord was first working in Hobart in charge of those burning charcoal for the blacksmiths.

He attended the Hobart musters in 1811, 1818, 1819 and 1823. Soon after he was free in 1808 he appears to have begun trading in a small way when Gov. Bligh purchased goods from him in Hobart. In 1810 he purchased the allotment and house in Collins St. owned by Francis Shipman (*q.v.*) prior to the latter's departure for England. At that time he employed an assigned servant, William Holsgrove, as clerk and allowed him to live there until 1827.

He received 120-acre land grants from Gov. Macquarie at the Coal River and 60 acres at Clarence Plains. In 1816 he was supplying 4 000 lb of meat a quarter to the Commissariat. By 1819 he was holding 420 acres in the Hobart area on which he grew wheat, owned four male horses and grazed 110 horned cattle, 190 female cattle, 700 male sheep and 1 800 ewes. He purchased a 40-acre farm from James Mayberry at the Coal River, the 60-acre Sweetwater Farm at Eastern Blue Hill (which was the beginning of the town Richmond), and owned a cottage and small farm near the bridge at Sandy Bay. He appears to have paid cash for all his transactions but for a time did owe Michael Michaels (*q.v.*) £250 which he repaid in 1816.

He also received a small town allotment in 1818 on the corner of Macquarie and Elizabeth Streets (known as Lord's corner) on which he guaranteed to build a good and sufficient dwelling and to pay annual rent to the Crown of £2 (the house was demolished in 1900 when the present G.P.O. was built on the site). He had to surrender a house in Davey St. (which had been occupied by Lieut. Lord when he was commandant) in 1819 when the streets were re-aligned. He received £50 compensation with a lease of two acres near the Barracks.

In a memorial to Gov. Davey dated 5 September 1815, Lord asked that his son, daughter-in-law and their five children, living in Halifax, be permitted to come as settlers. He outlined his extensive property interests, that he had nearly £2 000 out in mortgages and above that in book debts, a heavy stock-in-trade and livestock, 1 200 sheep and 100 head of horned cattle. He had plans to erect a dwelling-house costing upwards of £2 000. Under-Secretary Goulburn refused the strong recommendation which came from Davey but the family managed to get a passage by Royal Warrant in 1817.

He was involved in the incident of illegally landing spirits from the *Argo* in 1814 with Denis McCarty and Andrew Whitehead (*q.v.*). This kind of money was undoubtedly the source of his ready capital to buy so much property and to lend money. He had several properties mortgaged to him, including William Maum's 30-acre farm at Clarence Plains and purchased 50 acres from Elizabeth Hall, widow of John Hall, a Norfolk I. settler, in Sandy Bay for the sum of £100. He and Thomas Clark, who had come in the *Calcutta* as a superintendent of convicts, were partners in the general store they conducted from the property on the corner of Collins and Elizabeth Streets. He was also in partnership with John Clarke (*q.v.*) as a publican conducting the Dusty Miller on the opposite corner. After 1820 James Lord was the sole licensee.

James Lord was a principal creditor in several estates which he applied to administer, including those of Robert

Nash (in conjunction with Edward and Maria Lord), John Taylor and Anthony Lowe (q.v.).

Lord was a subscriber and member of the Auxiliary Bible Society but he appears to have given little time to activities outside his extraordinary capacity to accumulate money and land. He imported goods from Simeon Lord in Sydney, but he disputed that the latter sent woollen manufactures when he desired payment in tannin from wattle bark.

David Lord was soon one of the leading pastoralists and merchants in the country. When he built a palatial house on the Sweetwater Farm, Gov. Sorrell named it Richmond Park after the royal residence in England. It was a victim of the 1967 bush fires. By 1830 he had acquired 11 500 acres of land. The Lords had received many favours, despite James being a convict and David the son of a convict, which attracted much criticism from the Land Commissioners. They were also subject to robberies, such as when their farm at Sandy Bay was burgled in 1820 and 120 sheep held at Joseph Johnson's (q.v.) stockyard were stolen in the same year.

In 1823 James and David Lord both announced they were retiring from business and were visiting England, but James still acquired further land grants amounting to 600 acres from Gov. Brisbane at York Plains. He was, however, in ill health and unable to make the proposed visit to England.

Died 4 August 1824, Hobart, aged 69. Buried at St David's, the largest funeral in Hobart to that date.

There were several obituaries and Knopwood noted that he had accumulated a fortune of £50 000. David Lord died in 1847, having acquired great wealth. Many descendants have achieved distinction in the history of Tasmania.

Surnames of descendants have included: Aitken; Bezette; Burley; Butler; Campbell; Champion; Coke; Cole; Dudgeon; Fawcett; Fish; Fry; Guthrie; Hannaford; Hawley; Hickmer; Hutchins; Ibbott; Ivey; Jeffries; Johnstone; McMahon; O'Meagher; Peberty; Pettman; Potter; Purves; Rule; Simonds; Singleton; Smith; Swan; Waller; Walpole; Weedon; Wells; Westbrook; Wilcock; Wilkinson; Wilson.

A biography of his son, David Lord, appears in the *Australian Dictionary of Biography*, vol II.

LORING, JOHN [c. 1770 – ?]
(Laring)
Sailor (?), aged 32, of Middle Cummock, Somerset.
Tried at Somerset Summer Assizes (Wells G.D.) 21 August 1802 with breaking and entering house of Thomas Collard at Middle Cummock and stealing hat (5s 0d), coats (10s 0d) two waistcoats (6s 0d), two shirts (6s 0d), three handkerchiefs (3s 0d). Sentenced to transportation for seven years for stealing but charge of breaking and entering dismissed. Gaoled at Ilchester and transferred to the hulks at Langston.

During the voyage out Loring was employed on deck as a sailor.

There was no further record of him after his arrival in V.D.L. With his experience as a sailor he probably left the colony to return to England when his sentence expired.

LOWE, ANTHONY [c. 1773–1818]
Blacksmith, aged 28, of Great Bolton, Lancashire.
Tried at the County Palatinate of Lancaster S. of P. (Sal-

ford) 22 April 1801 for stealing 100 lb of flour (1d), 100 lb of meal (1d), one linen bag (1d) and one bag (1d) from Elizabeth Ainsworth and the theft of similar articles from William Irlam at Great Bolton. Sentenced to transportation for seven years. Gaoled at Salford and transferred to the hulks at Langston.

At Port Phillip, Lowe was put in charge of the blacksmiths.

In Hobart he was classified as a superintendent.

He attended the Hobart musters in 1811 and 1818. He grazed a quantity of an improved breed of horned cattle at Kangaroo Point, supplying meat to the Commissariat. He also carried on his trade as blacksmith from his own shop in Elizabeth St. which contained two forges and a quantity of excellent tools. He had a fine garden extending to Bathurst St.

He was recommended for a land grant of 50 acres but died before he could take it up. Buried 27 December 1818, St David's Hobart, aged 46 (?), after a few hours' illness. James (q.v.) and David Lord administered his estate, including the sale of the blacksmith's shop and tools as well as the stock at Kangaroo Point.

LUSH, SYLVESTER [c. 1774–1839]
Labourer, aged 28, of Cuckleton, near Wincanton, Somerset, married; 5'7", brown hair, fair complexion, hazel eyes, lusty, old bruise on the left side under the jaw near ear. Literate.
Tried at Dorset Spring Assizes (Dorchester G.D.) 18 March 1802 for stealing sheep, together with James Ware, from Edward Hawkins of Gillingham, yeoman. Sentenced to death by Justice Sir Simon Le Blanc. Reprieved and sentenced to transportation for life. Gaoled at county gaol, Dorchester and employed at hat-making. Behaviour there somewhat disorderly. Transferred to the *Captivity* hulk at Portsmouth. His wife did not accompany him.

Lush attended the Hobart musters in 1811, 1819, 1823, a Macquarie Harbour convict muster in 1825 and Hobart convict muster in 1833. He had received a conditional pardon in January 1814 and absolute pardon soon afterwards, but was in further trouble in 1824. He received a 30-acre land grant from Gov. Macquarie at Glenorchy adjoining the farms of Austin (q.v.) and Earle (q.v.) and was growing varied crops in 1819. He had acquired four mares, 50 ewes and employed a government servant. He supplied wheat to the Commissariat and subscribed to the Bible Society.

Early in his career in Hobart he had appeared before the Court of Criminal Jurisdiction in Sydney on a charge of stealing one wether sheep from John Downes at New Town on 4 December 1806. He was sent in the *Estramina* but absconded and there appears to be no record of any punishment. On his return to Hobart he kept out of trouble for many years.

On 8 December 1812, in Hobart, he married Ann Burrows, a 12 year old daughter of Elizabeth Cole (or Nicholls) from Norfolk I. They had at least four daughters, two of whom might have died before 1824 when they indicated a wish to educate two younger ones who both knew their letters.

In February 1822 Lush was charged with assaulting and beating up his wife. He was bound to keep the peace on

bonds of £50 and two of £25. He transferred the farm to
her name and she left him later in the year to live with John
Vale, an assigned servant. In June 1824 he was charged
with having received 36 ewes (value £36) knowing them to
have been stolen from William Walkinshaw and received a
sentence of fourteen years at Macquarie Harbour. A repent-
ant Ann Lush petitioned for his return which was effected
in 1829 when a report on his good conduct allowed him to
return to Hobart assigned to his wife. In the meantime the
property had been sold by the Sheriff Beaumont under an
execution for private debt. He received a ticket of leave in
1832.

*Buried 17 July 1839, St David's, Hobart, a free settler, aged
74 (?).*

Surnames of descendants have included: Burrows; Danvers; Fisk; Frost;
Goodwin; Shirbert.

MCALLENAN, DANIEL [c. 1782 – ?]
(Michael Allonan, MacAllenon, McAlones, etc.)
*Sailor (?), aged 20, living at Moorgate Coffee House, London,
born Ballimony, Ireland; 5'4", dark complexion. Literate.*
Tried on two counts at Middlesex III Sessions (Middlesex
G.D.) 17 February 1802 I) for stealing on 13 August 1801
a mare (18s 0d), saddle (14s 0d), bridle (5s 0d) and bit
(1s 0d) from Joseph Pring. These had been delivered to him
at the Moorgate Coffee House in London. They were ultimately discovered at the stables of one Fairer in Liverpool,
for which four guineas had been paid to McAllenan, posing
as a Captain Lynn, who said he was going to the Isle of
Man. In contradictory evidence McAllenan said he was
going to Dartford in Kent to meet his brother who was a
lieutenant in H.M.S. *Charlotte*. McAllenan said himself
that he was supposed to join his ship the *Charger* and had
asked his brother to return the mare to Pring. He then
went by coach to Plymouth. He later discovered that his
brother had gone to Liverpool, sold the mare there, and lost
his commission, and subsequently left for America.

Verdict: not guilty after the jury had sat for five hours.

II) Charged at the same sessions with stealing on 29
November a silver boat (30s 0d) and tablespoon (16s 0d)
from Christopher Ibbotson at the George and Blue Boar in
Holborn. Waiter Francis Moody said he had ordered smelts
and flounders in the coffee room. He had taken butter in a
silver boat and he had asked for a tablespoon. He was
confused. Sentenced to seven years transportation. Gaoled
at Newgate and transferred to the *Captivity* hulk at
Portsmouth.

During the voyage out he became a servant to Knopwood. He deserted camp at Port Phillip but returned to
surrender after five miserable days. In Hobart Knopwood
tried to punish him for insolently refusing to repair the
road opposite his house but Collins, who appears to have
thought well of him, intervened.

McAllenan was among those who seized the *Marcia* in an
act of piracy and received the sentence of death at the Court
of Vice-Admiralty at Port Jackson in February 1808. They
were pardoned later that month.

*As his name did not re-appear in colonial records, he probably
returned to England as he would have been free by servitude soon
afterwards.*

MCCARTHY, PATRICK [c. 1779–1823]
(Macarthy, McCarty, etc.)
*Soldier, aged 24, 25th Foot Rgt, stationed at Gibraltar, prob-
ably Irish, Roman Catholic. Literate.*
Tried in secret (?) at an army court martial December 1802
following a mutiny at Gibraltar and sentenced to death.
Commuted by H.R.H. The Duke of Kent to transportation
for life. Embarked at Gibraltar in the sloop H.M.S.
Cynthia, 12 January 1803. Taken aboard the *Calcutta*, 21
April, at Portsmouth.

In December 1803 Collins appointed him a subordinate
of the night-watch.

He attended the Hobart musters in 1811, 1818, and
1819. For a time he was a boatman and hired out his boat.
He bought 30 acres at Elizabeth Town, New Norfolk, and
in 1819 had planted wheat, potatoes and had 10 female
sheep. He received a conditional pardon in 1816 and was
free by 1818.

On 26 March 1821, in Hobart, he married Mary Walsh,
convict transported in the *Canada* from Cork. They had
already had two sons and one daughter. Another daughter
arrived after their marriage. McCarthy agreed to pay £20
towards the education of his eldest son in 1821.

*Killed by Black Jack, one of the Oyster Bay tribe, 1824. One
of the first victims to cause escalation of the war against the
Aborigines. Buried 22 May 1823, Silas Gatehouse's farm,
Oyster Bay.*

[The subsequent execution of Black Jack and the Sydney
native Musquito, who had incited him, saw the beginnings
in V.D.L. of the Black War.]

MAGGOTT, JOHN [1783 – ?]
(Maggett)
*Labourer, aged 18, of St George, Hanover Sq. (elsewhere records
pa. Marylebone); 5'2", fresh complexion, brown hair, hazel eyes.*
Tried at Westminster S. of P. 25 June 1801 for stealing
one check brace (10d) from George, Marquis of Townsend,
nephew of Viscount Sydney. Witnesses against Maggott
were Watson Seymour, of White Hard Yard, Tichbourne
St., coachmaker, and Richard Levett of Great Marlborough
St., yeoman, bound by £40 each in recognizance. Sen-
tenced by twelve J.P.s to transportation for seven years.
Gaoled at Newgate and transferred to the *Fortune* hulk at
Langston.

*There is no further record of Maggott after his arrival in
V.D.L. It is likely that he returned to England soon after his
sentence expired in 1808.*

MAHONEY, ARTHUR [c. 1782 – ?]
(Mahaney, Mahy)
Labourer, aged 17.
Tried at Middlesex VIII Sessions (Middlesex G.D.) 13 September 1799 for stealing a set of bed furniture (8s 0d), quilt
(2s 0d), tablecloth (2s 0d), pair of silk stockings (8s 0d),
and shawl (1s 0d), the property of Mary Marsh, cheesemonger, whose husband John was abroad. Sentenced to
transportation for seven years. Gaoled at Newgate (?) and
transferred to the *Prudentia* hulk at Woolwich.

*As there is no further record of Mahoney after his arrival in
Hobart, he probably returned to England c. 1807 when his sentence expired.*

MANBY, JOHN [c. 1763–1828]
Butcher, aged 40, of Windlesham, Surrey, married.
Tried at Surrey Spring Assizes (Kingston G.D.) 22 March 1802 for stealing, together with George and Ann Row, a mare (£30), a saddle and stirrups (10s 0d) and a set of harness (£1) from John Simons. Sentenced to death. Reprieved by Baron Hotham and Mr Justice Heath and sentenced to transportation for life. Manby was tried also for stealing two barrows of pigs (£14) from Henry Lipscomb, also of Windlesham, but was acquitted. Gaoled at the county gaol and transferred to the *Prudentia* hulk at Woolwich.

Mrs Sarah Manby accompanied her husband in the *Calcutta* and was berthed in the prison room.

Manby attended the Hobart musters in 1811, 1818, 1819 and 1823. He was one of the first to receive a conditional pardon, in 1807, and an absolute pardon in January 1813. In August 1804 he owned a boar and a fowl and by July 1807 was already noted as a 'settler'. He had acquired more than an acre on which he was raising three male sheep, 20 ewes and seven female goats. He had a land grant, probably 30 acres, from Gov. Macquarie, on which, in 1819, he ran 200 male sheep and 300 ewes, but sold it to Alfred Thrupp.

By 1808 Manby was a stock keeper and, according to William Maum, a 'very decent man' who was building a house with two rooms and a skilling which he would sell to Robert Nash, due to arrive from Norfolk I., for upwards of £150. He was employed as an overseer for the government in 1810 at £25 per year. In 1813 he bought a house in Collins St. valued at £20 for which he was compensated in 1820 after the survey of the town.

He then built a house in Macquarie St. which he advertised for sale in October 1816 and another house adjoining Davey St. which he advertised for sale in 1819. He had a publican's licence for the Crooked Billet New Inn in Hobart in 1820.

Robert Manby, aged 22, who married Hannah Frully on 13 October 1818, might have been this Manby's son. There was also an Elizabeth Manby on the 1819 muster roll, possibly a daughter.
Buried 18 January 1828, St David's, Hobart, aged 65 (?), described as a housekeeper. Eleanor (?) Manby was buried 7 August 1829, St David's, aged 71, a settler's widow.

MANN, WILLIAM [c. 1760 – after 1833]
Carrier, aged 40, of London, from Stevenage, Herts; 5'9", fair complexion, flaxen hair, hazel eyes.
Tried at Middlesex VII Sessions (Middlesex G.D.) 17 September 1800 for stealing a cauldron of coals (50s 0d) from William Thrappitt and others in a barge on the River Lea. Mann kept a horse and cart and carried goods of all description. Several gave witness against him and three others gave him a good character. Justice Sir Simon Le Blanc sentenced him to transportation for seven years. Gaoled at Newgate and transferred to the *Prudentia* hulk at Woolwich.

Mann remained in V.D.L. after his sentence expired in 1807. He attended the Hobart muster in 1811. He must have brought with him some capital or gained substantial capital from some source because he bought a 60-acre farm at Cornelian Bay from Michael Michaels (*q.v.*) when the latter returned to England. He made some expensive purchases at the auction sale of Andrew Geils at Restdown in 1814. He also bred horses, and owned considerable stock and fine household goods which he mortgaged to James Lord (*q.v.*) and Thomas Clark for £300 in 1817, with the agreement that if repaid with interest by March 1820 the property would revert to Mann. It had still not been paid off by 1833, when David Lord, son of James, allowed Mann to continue occupying the land for which he had never drawn any rent.
He was still living at Clarence Plains in 1833.

MANNING, JOHN [c. 1782 – after 1839]
Baker (?), aged 20.
Tried at Warwickshire Spring Assizes (Warwick G.D.) 23 March 1802 for a burglary at Meriden. Sentenced to death. Reprieved by the Lord Chief Baron and Baron Graham and sentenced to transportation for life. Gaoled at Warwick Castle and transferred to the hulks at Portsmouth.

At Port Phillip George Lee (*q.v.*) accused Manning of coining but Knopwood decided it was a 'malicious transaction'.

He attended the Hobart muster in 1811 but not those of 1818 and 1819.

He received a conditional pardon in 1814 but his free pardon took 25 years longer. He became a baker for William Presnell in Argyle St. and later for John Fawkner (*q.v.*) in Macquarie St. He then provided biscuit for the Commissariat and by 1819 was advertising 'fancy biscuits and cakes of all sorts' and supplying ships as well.

Manning had several convictions; for repeated neglect of duty and insolence to his master, punished with 100 lashes in 1806, and picking the pocket of John Taylor, for which Knopwood allowed him some lenience if he made the money good.

A Sarah Manning, perhaps his wife, farmed on her 30-acre land grant at Glenorchy.
He was still alive in 1839.

MANSFIELD, WILLIAM [c. 1778–1852]
?, aged 24.
Tried at Somerset Spring Assizes (Taunton G.D.) 1 April 1802, after removal from Dorset, for knocking down Henry Bythesea on the King's Highway and robbing him of a silver watch. Sentenced to death. Reprieved by Justices Sir Soulden Laurence and Sir Simon Le Blanc and sentenced to transportation for life. Gaoled at Taunton and transferred to the hulks at Langston.

Mansfield attended the Hobart musters in 1811, 1818, 1819 and 1823. He received a conditional pardon in 1816 and an absolute pardon in 1818. By 1819 he had a grant of 30 acres at Glenorchy from Gov. Macquarie and had taken out a grazing licence at the Black Snake Run. He grew wheat and other crops, grazed 57 male sheep and 200 female sheep and employed a government servant. By 1818 he was supplying substantial quantities of meat to the Commissariat. He received a further 30 acres when a friend, Robert Lancaster, died, and successfully applied for 50 more acres in 1828 at Glenorchy. By this time he owned 350 sheep, twenty head of cattle and three horses, and lived in a weatherboard two-storey house with outhouses. Some time between 1838 and 1841 the family moved to Mount Pleasant, Bridgewater.

Mansfield was earlier employed as an agricultural labourer on Dr Bowden's farm. He became involved in 1811 in a sheep stealing case from which, after hearing at the Court of Criminal Jurisdiction in Sydney, he was acquitted of all charges.

Between 1812 and 1816 Mansfield visited New Zealand and Macquarie I. in whalers. He served in the *Active* when missionaries appointed by the Revd Samuel Marsden went to New Zealand and was, for a time, a crew member of the *Elizabeth and Mary*.

On 4 December 1809 he married Maria Nicholls. She was the daughter of William Nicholls, from Norfolk I., who had arrived in the *Royal Admiral* in 1792 as a convict and who might have been the father of Elizabeth Nicholls, married to David Gibson (*q.v.*). The Mansfields had seventeen children, from whom there have been hundreds of descendants.

Died in 1852, Mount Pleasant, Bridgewater, aged 74, of 'decay of nature'. Maria died 7 May 1858, aged 64, same cause.

Surnames of descendants have included: Faddie; Gay; Jones; Jordan; Stump; Thomas.

MARGETTS, JOHN [c. 1772 – ?]
(Margett)
Silversmith, aged 29, of Cripplegate, London, married; 5'4", fair complexion, flaxen hair, grey eyes.
Tried at Middlesex V Sessions (Middlesex G.D.) 20 May 1801 together with Richard Hall and Thomas Bowman (*q.v.*) for breaking and entering and stealing 104 blankets (£40) in the house of John Sylvester, manufacturer's agent. The blankets were the property of William Seliman. A loaded pistol was found in Margetts' house. He said the blankets had been left in the house by mistake. Sentenced by Baron Graham to death, reprieved and sentenced to transportation for life. Gaoled at Newgate and transferred to the *Captivity* hulk at Portsmouth.

Rebecca Margetts, who was charged with receiving the stolen goods, was found not guilty. She was 25, 5'4", fair complexion, brown hair, grey eyes, from Wandsworth, Surrey. She did not accompany him in the *Calcutta*.

During the voyage out Margetts was employed on deck as a cook's mate. By August 1804 he had acquired some livestock — two fowls. His name did not appear on the 1811 muster roll, nor is there any record that he died, escaped or received an early pardon.

It is possible that, because he had a wife in England, a trade, and had been given some trust, he was allowed to return, his pardon unrecorded.

MARMON, WILLIAM [c. 1777 – after 1821]
(Warner)
?, aged 25.
Tried at Sussex Summer Assizes (Lewes G.D.) together with William Buckley (*q.v.*) 2 August 1802 for burglariously entering the shop of John Cave of Warnham, shopkeeper, and stealing two pieces of Irish cloth (8s 0d). They passed them over to Margaret Harris who was charged with receiving the cloth. Sentenced to death by Baron Hotham. Reprieved and sentenced to transportation for life. Gaoled at Lewes and transferred to the hulks at Langston.

At Port Phillip Marmon deserted camp, December 1803, but returned suffering from scurvy before the *Ocean* sailed for V.D.L.

He seems to have caused no further trouble. He attended the Hobart musters in 1811, 1818 and 1819. He received a conditional pardon in May 1816 and was free by 1818.

He probably returned to England towards the end of 1821 when he advertised that he was leaving the colony.

MARSH, WILLIAM [c. 1779–1848]
(March)
Servant, aged 23, at Trinity College, Cambridge.
Tried at Cambridge Summer Assizes 2 August 1802 for stealing from rooms of a gentleman at Trinity College, Cambridge, several articles of wearing apparel. Sentenced to transportation for seven years. Gaoled at Cambridge and transferred to the hulks at Woolwich.

Marsh received 200 lashes during a disturbance between prisoners and the military patrol in 1807. He had supplied the other prisoners with spirits. Later that year he was a bushranger, armed and had plenty of dogs. When he returned he received 300 lashes.

Although not on the 1811 muster roll in Hobart, he attended the Hobart musters in 1818 and 1819 as a free person with a land grant at Pitt Water on which he farmed wheat and vegetables.

Buried 24 April 1848, St George's, Sorell, aged 80, having become a carpenter.

MARSHALL, GEORGE [c. 1762–1804]
Sawyer, husbandman, aged 40, of Southwell, Nottingham, married there to Ann Revill 19 February 1784. Details of baptisms at Southwell of four sons and four daughters are recorded. Two sons died.
Tried at the S. of P. of the Liberty of the Archbishop of York of Southwell and Scrooby in the County of Nottingham 17 July 1802 for stealing a piece of iron (10d) from John Jackson of Southwell. Sentenced by four J.P.s to transportation for seven years. Gaoled at Nottingham and transferred to the *Prudentia* hulk at Woolwich.

Marshall's family did not accompany him in the *Calcutta*.

Died 19 October 1804, Hobart, of scurvy.

MELLOWES, JOHN [c. 1770–1816]
?, aged 32. Literate (?).
Tried at Northampton Summer Assizes (Northampton G.D.) 27 August 1802 for stealing a bay gelding from Benjamin Drayton of Cow Meadow, Northampton. Sentenced to death. Reprieved by Mr Justice Heath and Sir Alexander Thomson and sentenced to transportation for life. Gaoled at Northampton and transferred to the hulks at Langston.

He attended the 1811 muster in Hobart.

In 1812 Mellowes petitioned for a free pardon which he received in January 1813. He could sign his own name, as seen in a receipt for payment for rent of a house to the inspector of public works as an office, occupied in May and June 1812, for £2 4s 6d.

Buried 13 August 1815, Hobart, age 45 (?). {Note: Bigge's Appendix gives death date 11 August 1816, buried 13 August.}

MERRIDEW, RICHARD [c. 1763–1804]
(Meredow, Meriden)
Labourer, aged 39 of London; 5'6", dark complexion.
Tried at Middlesex III Sessions (Middlesex G.D.) 17 February 1802 for stealing a sheet (4s 0d), shift (4s 0d), apron (1s 0d) and cuffs (6d) from the house of Francis Wright. He was caught by Charlotte Atkins and was very frightened. Sentenced by Mr Justice Hotham to transportation for seven years. Gaoled at Newgate and transferred to the *Captivity* hulk at Portsmouth.
Died 7 November 1804, Hobart, aged 40 (?), of scurvy.

MICHAELS, MICHAEL [c. 1776 – alive 1819]
Brickmaker, aged 26, born Liverpool, brother D. Michaels, Jew; 5'7", dark complexion.
Tried at Middlesex III Sessions (London G.D.) 17 February 1802 firstly for making and uttering a piece counterfeit money to the likeness of a 7s piece and offering it to John Lucas, and secondly for trying to sell a watch to Capt. Lucas, master of a coastal vessel, living in Essex county. He received two good 7s pieces for the watch and exchanged two bad pieces for its return. He had already served a year in the county gaol in Surrey, having been convicted at the Surrey S. of P., Guildford, 15 July 1800, for a similar crime. Sentence pronounced by the Common Sergeant was death. Reprieved and sentenced to transportation for life. Gaoled at Poultry, then Newgate, and transferred to the *Prudentia* hulk at Woolwich.

While at Newgate his brother visited him. While presenting Michael with a guinea the prisoner ripped open his brother's belly with a knife. The brother was taken to the St Bartholomew's Hospital.

He attended the Hobart muster in 1811 after receiving a free pardon in 1810. He had a farm of 60 acres at Cornelian Bay but gave his address as Elizabeth St. and appears to have carried on an extensive business as a money lender.

Soon after arrival in Hobart, Michaels became an overseer and at his hut Collins mustered other convicts for inspection preparatory to issuing clothing for the following six months. By August 1804 he owned thirteen fowls. Unfortunately he lost his house through fire the following January. By 1807 he had acquired seven ewes. He was apparently one of Collins' most trusted men. In January 1810 Collins' young mistress Margaret Eddington applied through him for the services of Kitty Belbin, daughter of the fiery Norfolk Islander (then confined in the guard house) to live at Government House and nurse her young child.

Michaels returned to England in 1812 after selling his farm to William Mann (*q.v.*). He left his power of attorney with Knopwood and later transferred it to Thomas Newby to collect £780 owed to him in Hobart. These debts ranged from the estate of the late Lieut. Breedon and £103 3s 9d from Capt. Murray to money lent to ex-convicts for much smaller amounts. In 1819, Newby had to threaten court action against those who did not pay up.

By this time Michaels was living at 2 Swan St., East Smithfield in London and described his occupation as a merchant. He encouraged other Jews to go to Australia as free settlers and gave Aaron Abraham, who married his niece, access to the money owed him in Hobart. But by 1825 Knopwood had acquired the money himself and Abraham did not argue about it.
Date and place of death are unknown.

MILES, JOHN [c. 1773–1831]
(Mills)
?, aged 29.
Tried at Sussex Summer Assizes (Chichester G.D.) 13 July 1802 for an unknown felony. Sentenced to death. Reprieved and sentenced to transportation for fourteen years. Gaoled at Chichester and transferred to the hulks at Portsmouth.

He attended the Hobart musters in 1811, 1818 and 1819 and received a conditional pardon on 25 January 1813. He might have been the John Mills fined in Hobart, September 1818, for retailing spirits without a licence.

By 1819 he was farming at Herdsman's Cove where he rented 500 acres on which he produced large quantities of wheat, barley and vegetables, and ran 19 male and 33 female cattle, 200 male and 500 female sheep and employed four government servants. He renewed a grazing licence at the Black Marsh later that year and received a 30-acre land grant between Queenborough and Glenorchy in 1820. He provided meat regularly for the Commissariat. He had troubles dealing with sheep stealers when 200 of his sheep were missing from the Tea Tree Brush in 1819.
In spite of his early success he appears to be the labourer John Mills [sic] who was buried 14 March 1831, St Matthew's, Pitt Water, aged 59 (?).

MILLS, JOHN alias POLLARD [c. 1790–1821 (?)]
(Millis)
Painter (?), aged 12, born in London.
Tried at Middlesex IV Sessions (Middlesex G.D.) 2 June 1802 together with Thomas Williams alias Long (*q.v.*) and a Thomas Smith for stealing five planes (5s 0d), a handsaw (1s 6d), gauge (6d), two chisels (6d) and a turn-screw (1d) from John Masters, carpenter at Tottenham Place. Sentenced to transportation by Baron Graham for seven years for stealing working tools valued at 1s 0d. Gaoled at Newgate and transferred to the *Prudentia* hulk at Woolwich.

During the voyage out Mills was a messenger boy but remained in irons.

He was absent from the Hobart musters in 1811, 1819 and 1823 but attended in 1818.

In July 1814 he was missing from employment with others who were known to have joined Michael Howe's bushranging gang, including John Blackmore (*q.v.*) and John (*q.v.*) and George Jones (*q.v.*). John Mills, during one of their plunderings, threatened to rob and rape Mrs Denis McCarty. This man was not the John Mills who had arrived with Howe in the *Indefatigable*.
Likely he was the John Mills who was convicted of highway robbery and sentenced to death, August 1821. Executed 24 August.

MOORE, WILLIAM, alias STONE [c. 1780 – ?]
Shoemaker, aged 22, of London; 5'4", fair complexion.
Tried at Middlesex V Sessions (London G.D.) 2 June 1802

for stealing a 34 lb basket of butter (£1 16s 0d), a blanket (2s 0d), and linen cloth (6d) from Levi Edwards, storekeeper at Battle Bridge, Newgate Market. Sentence pronounced by the Recorder was transportation for seven years. Gaoled at Newgate and transferred to the *Captivity* hulk at Portsmouth. He had previously been convicted in May 1800 and gaoled at Newgate for one year under the name of Stone.

As there is no further record of Moore after his arrival in Hobart, he probably left the colony when his sentence expired in 1809.

MORRIS, AUGUSTUS [c. 1784–1824]

Labourer, aged 18, of pa. St Thomas, New Sarum, Wiltshire. Literate.

Tried at Wiltshire Summer Assizes (Salisbury G.D.) 31 July 1802 for using force and arms to steal from his master, James Hughes of St Thomas, in the city of New Sarum, six shirts (30s 0d), four pairs of stockings (20s 0d), three pairs of pantaloons (20s 0d), two waistcoats (8s 0d) and one coat (5s 0d). Sentenced to transportation for seven years. Hughes had formerly been a cornet in the 16th Light Dragoons but neither he nor Morris had served in Egypt as Morris later claimed. Nor does Morris' name appear on any army list. Gaoled at Salisbury gaol and transferred to the hulks at Langston.

Morris remained in irons during the voyage out. According to Fawkner, he was a young stalwart man of about 5'10", known as Don Morris, who was useful at Port Phillip in guiding the timber carriages.

He attended the Hobart musters in 1811, 1818, 1819 and 1823. He soon became a successful farmer, receiving 40 and 50-acre land grants from Gov. Macquarie in the Ulva and Strangford districts. He had a licence to graze at the Hanging Sugarloaf run, Macquarie River, and he was in partnership with W. T. Stocker (*q.v.*) in several ventures, including a farm known as the Judge's Farm. In 1819 their stock keeper on the Macquarie River was in a struggle with natives. By 1819 he had purchased a further 153 acres at Herdsman's Cove and had 78 acres planted with wheat, seven with potatoes, owned two horses, 60 male and 92 female cattle, 600 male sheep and 1 200 ewes. He employed three government servants and a free man. He built a commodious slaughterhouse at the Herdsman's Cove as well as a stockyard and supplied enormous amounts of wheat and meat to the Commissariat.

He had at first been a troublesome person in the colony, escaping by boat with Robert Stewart (*q.v.*) and others in May 1805 and again with Stewart in September of the same year. He made a third attempt to escape from the guardhouse in December 1805. When caught he received 300 lashes and was ironed for a year.

Some time before March 1814, when Knopwood listed the known localities on the old track to Port Dalrymple, Morris defended himself from hostile natives on a dome-shaped hill known afterwards as 'Don's Battery'.

On 20 February 1813, in Hobart, he married Constantia Hibbins, daughter of a drunken Norfolk Islander, the former Deputy Judge Advocate, Thomas Hibbins. They had four children.

Morris was proprietor of the Cove Ferry Inn at Cove Point and also ran a ferry service between Cove Point and the Black Snake, later leased by Charles Goodridge. He gave evidence in favour of R.W. Loane in the latter's case against George Gunning. He was himself in court in 1820 to answer charges by his boatman, John Patterson, of assault and was fined £20. He was also the employer of James Duff (*q.v.*) who was found dead in the bush.

After several months illness, during which he lived in Hobart, Morris gave his power of attorney to Ambrose Boyd and made A. W. H. Humphrey his executor. Died 28 May 1824, aged 36 (?), buried at St David's. Constantia Morris died at Cove Point, buried 16 June 1823, St David's, aged 29. The youngest child, Martha, died in 1825.

The young children who were well provided for were educated in Hobart and made good marriages. Augustus Morris jun. later sailed in 1835 with John Aitken to Port Phillip and became one of the founders of Colac. He then sought lands further afield and became an M.P.

There are many descendants, mostly in N.S.W. and Qld, where they have held vast properties. Surnames of descendants have included: Parker; Gilbertson.

A biography of Augustus Morris jun. appears in the *Australian Dictionary of Biography*, vol. II.

MUNDAY, GEORGE [c. 1778–1867]
(Mundy, Monday)

?, aged 24.

Tried at Devonshire Spring Assizes (Exeter G.D.) 22 March 1802 for burglary and stealing spirituous liquors from the house of Edward Beer at Plymouth. Sentenced to death. Reprieved by Justices Sir Simon Le Blanc and Sir Soulden Laurence and sentenced to transportation for life. Gaoled at Exeter gaol and transferred to the hulks at Langston.

Munday attended the Hobart musters in 1811, 1818, 1819 and 1823, although early reports show that a George Munday (probably Munder) was killed by Aborigines in 1809. Munday received a conditional pardon in January 1813 and an absolute pardon soon afterwards. In 1818 he received a 50-acre land grant from Gov. Macquarie in the Hobart area on which he grazed two male sheep and 28 ewes.

By 1812 Munday had been appointed an overseer. On 1 May 1811, in Hobart, he married Ann Reading but she died, 4 January 1812, aged 16. He then married Sarah, daughter of Samuel Free, a settler from Norfolk I. who was living at Sandy Bay. She was 16, and they had eight sons and three daughters. In 1821 they had a house in Argyle St. which was burgled.

They were still in Hobart until about 1820 when they were registering their children for attendance at a public school. They appear to have moved about that time to Clarence Plains where several of their children appear on the St Matthew's baptismal register. George Munday subscribed towards a new chapel there.

In 1831 a Mr Mundy occupied a house in Goulburn St. Hobart.

Buried 1 June 1867, St George's, Pitt Water, his age given as 101 (?) and home as Cherry Tree Opening.

Surnames of descendants have included: Nash.

MYERS, JOSEPH [c. 1777–1814]
(Meyers, Meers)
?, aged 25.
Tried at Shropshire (probably Spring Assizes held at Shrewsbury) in March 1802 for an unknown felony. Sentenced to transportation for seven years. His name appears on only one official list of *Calcutta* convicts, showing he was victualled at Port Phillip where he became an overseer.

In V.D.L. he was missing for three months in 1807. He gave evidence before the Bench of Magistrates, December 1813 in the case against Denis McCarty.

Buried 6 October 1814, Hobart, aged 37.

NELSON, MATTHEW [c. 1788 – after 1811]
?, aged 14, of Greenwich; 5'1", fair complexion.
Tried at Middlesex IV Sessions (Middlesex G.D.) 28 April 1802 for assaulting John Howard, aged 11, on the King's Highway and stealing from him five silver boxes for watches (£2), the property of James Hallam. Sentence pronounced by the Recorder was transportation for seven years. Gaoled at Newgate and transferred to the *Prudentia* hulk at Woolwich. Nelson had previously been acquitted on the same date of stealing six silk handkerchiefs (36s 0d) from George Oliver's shop.

On 20 December 1805, after his arrival in V.D.L., Nelson absconded to the woods and was outlawed. He was taken on 9 January 1806 and on 22 January Knopwood reported that the magistrates met to try Nelson and Bowers (*q.v.*), his companion. They received 300 lashes each and were ordered irons for one year. Nelson escaped again, 11 March 1808, and was once more declared an outlaw; £10 was offered for his apprehension. He must have returned to camp as he attended the Hobart muster in 1811.

His activities after that date have not been traced.

NEWLAND, JOHN [c. 1771–1822]
(Nowland, Nowlan, Knowlan(d), etc.)
Sailor (?), aged 30, pa. Westham, Stratford, Essex.
Tried at Essex Summer Assizes (Chelmsford G.D.) 22 July 1801, together with Edward Brooks, for breaking into the workshop of William Munday at Westham and stealing one pair of iron arms for an axletree (£1) and 1s 0d. Sentenced to transportation for seven years. He was gaoled at Chelmsford and transferred to the hulks at Langston.

Newland served as a seaman in the *Ocean* while it removed the party from Port Phillip. While still at Sullivan Bay, 13 May 1804, he received 50 lashes on the back for smoking in the lower prison room and nearly setting fire to the ship. Two days later he committed the same offence and received a further 50 lashes.

He attended the Hobart musters in 1811, 1818 and 1819.

On 9 April 1812, in Hobart, he married Catherine Murphy. They lived in a hut in Collins St. for which the government paid £10 compensation when the streets were re-arranged. He ran a ferry service between Hobart and Kangaroo Point in 1816, but got into financial difficulties and had to advertise it for sale in April 1820 as 'a large ferry boat' in order to pay his debts to W. T. Stocker (*q.v.*). He appears to have supplied the Commissariat with wheat in 1817 but there was no record of a land grant.

Buried 29 December 1822, St David's, his age given as 59.

NORTH, JAMES [c. 1779 – after 1811]
Brickmaker, aged 21, of St Giles, Camberwell.
Tried at Surrey Spring Assizes (Kingston-upon-Thames G.D.) 19 March 1800 for highway robbery and assault on Isaac Green at St Giles, taking from him a silver watch (£1) and watch-chain (6d), watch key (1d) and coins (1s 6d). Sentenced to death. Reprieved by Sir Beaumont Hotham and Mr Justice Heath and sentenced to transportation for seven years. Gaoled at Newgate and transferred to the *Prudentia* hulk at Woolwich.

In Hobart he was before the magistrates in January 1807 with a party of prisoners who had killed a goat. They received 500 lashes each.

Some time after that he must have gone to Port Dalrymple as he attended the muster of free persons there in 1811. In December 1811 a person named North at Port Dalrymple received an extra 40-acre grant of land from Gov. Macquarie in compensation for land needed for government purposes. As a brickmaker, North would have been a useful person at a time when the principal settlement in the north was being moved lower down the river.

There appears to be no further record of him after 1811. Whether he remained at Port Dalrymple, died without record of death, or returned to England is uncertain.

NOWLAND, JAMES PATRICK [c. 1783 – ?]
Apprentice to a fustian broker, aged 19.
Tried at Middlesex I Sessions (London G.D.) 4 December 1802 for stealing 40 yards of woollen cloth (£10) from Daniel Britten, packer, of Basinghall St. Nowland had been employed as an apprentice to Thomas Martin, a broker in Spanish wool, and claimed that Martin's brother (since gone away) had asked him to pawn the goods. Sentence pronounced by the Recorder was transportation for seven years. Gaoled at Poultry and transferred to the *Prudentia* hulk at Woolwich.

Nowland appears to be the 'Cowlan' whom Knopwood records on 9 February 1806, as one of the prisoners trying to escape with Robert Stewart (*q.v.*) in John Blinkworth's boat. Knopwood reported on 29 July 1807 that he was engaged on magistrate's business regarding Newland [*sic*]. There had been a robbery at the house of William Collins, and Nowland, according to fellow-prisoner Strickland (*q.v.*), was implicated. Those accused threatened to kill Strickland. This trouble occurred at the time the first public house was opened in Hobart. Nowland probably received some form of punishment which has not been recorded.

He escaped from custody in March 1808 and £10 was offered as a reward for his apprehension. There is no further record of him in the colony.

ORAM, WILLIAM [c. 1772 – ?]
?, aged 28.
Tried at Leicester Summer Assizes (Leicester G.D.) 14 July 1800 for sheep stealing. Sentenced to transportation for life. Gaoled at Leicester and transferred to the hulks at Langston.

On 4 March 1804, after arrival in V.D.L., Oram left for Port Jackson in the *Lady Nelson* in company with Thomas Rushton (*q.v.*), who was skilled in both brewing and hemp manufacture. It is possible that Oram had some experience in a related occupation that would be useful to Gov. King.

His later activities have not been traced, but the names of possible sons appeared on the 1828 census for Sydney.

PAGE, THOMAS [c. 1772–1804]
Framework knitter, aged 30, of Melbourne (Littleover), who had a child by Sarah Offyflow.
Tried at Derby Spring Assizes (Derby G.D.) 13 March 1802 for highway robbery of unknown goods. Sentenced by Justice Sir Robert Graham to death. Reprieved and sentenced to transportation for life. Page had previously been convicted for poaching with a gun at Melbourne, fined £5, and discharged from a bond at the Derby Easter Sessions of 1801. He had indemnified the inhabitants of Shirley against the maintenance of a bastard child he had fathered by Sarah Offyflow, single woman. Gaoled at Derby and transferred to the hulks at Langston.

On 27 December 1803 Page escaped at Port Phillip, but was taken the next day.

Died 27 January 1804, Port Phillip, aged 31 (?).

PEARSALL, JOHN [c. 1777–1843]
(Piercall, Pearseall, Piercell, etc.)
Nailer, aged 24.
Tried Staffordshire Summer Assizes (Stafford G.D.) 22 July 1801 with others for stealing a bull calf, two tame cocks, six tame hens and two cheeses from John Dean of Bushbury. Sentenced to death. Reprieved by Baron Thomson and Justice Sir Soulden Laurence and sentenced to transportation for life. Gaoled in the county gaol and transferred to the hulks at Langston. His conduct was orderly.

He attended the Hobart musters in 1811, 1818, 1819 and his name appears on the census of 1842. He received a conditional pardon in January 1813 and an absolute pardon in 1838. He had received a 35-acre grant from Gov. Macquarie at Clarence Plains by 1819 on which he grew wheat and grazed four male and one female cattle, 30 male sheep and 70 female sheep. He employed a government servant. By 1825 he had a further grant of 70 acres adjoining his farm. In 1839 he purchased 203 acres also at Clarence Plains, where he was a subscriber for the new chapel.

Pearsall was employed in his trade as a nailer from early times. He kept a forge at Clarence Plains.

On 1 January 1816, in Hobart, he married Maria, aged 19, daughter of William and Frances Nicholls who had arrived as settlers in the *Ocean* in 1803. William Nicholls had been a superintendent at Port Phillip and in Hobart. In 1804 he had received a land grant of 100 acres at Stainsforth Cove.

John and Maria Pearsall had six sons and five daughters but most died in infancy, leaving only two adult daughters and two baby sons by the 1842 census in which the parents and daughters were listed among land proprietors, merchants, bankers and professional persons. By then Pearsall was employing three single men as gardeners, stockmen and agricultural labourers.

Buried 22 December 1843, St Matthew's, Clarence Plains, aged 61 (?). His wife died 26 March 1860, aged 64, buried at St Matthew's.

There are many descendants, some of whom have held prominent positions in Tasmania. Surnames of descendants have included: Blegg; Gillian; Lucas; Ludberg; Williams.

PEEL, WILLIAM [c. 1765–1804]
(Peale, Peal)
?, aged 37.
Tried at Yorkshire Spring Assizes (York G.D.) 6 March 1802 for stealing one ewe and one lamb from James Brigg of Easington. Sentenced to death. Reprieved by Lord Kenyon and Justice Sir Giles Rooke and sentenced to transportation for life. Gaoled at York Castle and transferred to the hulks at Langston.

Died 13 May 1804, Hobart.

PENDALL, JOSEPH [c. 1768–1833]
(Pendle, Pendell, etc.)
Horse doctor, aged 34. Literate.
Tried at Cambridge Spring Assizes (Cambridge G.D.) 17 March 1802 for stealing a horse (£4) from Nathaniel Weld of Trumpington. Sentenced to death. Reprieved by Lord Chief Justice Alvanley and Justice Sir Nash Grose and sentenced to transportation for life. Gaoled at the county gaol and transferred to the *Prudentia* hulk at Woolwich.

Pendall attended the Hobart musters in 1811, 1818, 1819 and 1823. He received a conditional pardon in May 1816 and an absolute pardon soon afterwards. He had received a 50-acre land grant at Pitt Water from Gov. Macquarie by 1819 on which he grew wheat and grazed four male sheep and ten ewes.

In 1811 he attended a trial at the Court of Criminal Jurisdiction in Sydney to give evidence on behalf of James Clissold in his prosecution against John Willis (*q.v.*) for stealing sheep. He was employed at Geilston for several years before taking up his own property. In 1823 he was before the Lieutenant-Governor's Court for debt and was forced to sell his land in 1824 to pay creditors.

In a memorial of November 1824 to Gov. Arthur asking for a further grant he indicated that by perseverance and industry he had acquired 50 sheep and two working bullocks. He was then at Macquarie River. There is no record that he received any further grant.

On 2 April 1819, in Hobart, he married Mary Hambelton, aged 25, a convict transported in the *Alexander*. They had one daughter.

Buried 26 December 1833, St David's, aged 60 (?), a labouring man.

PENDRIDGE, JOSEPH [c. 1773 – ?]
(Pentridge)
Soldier, aged 26.
Tried at Bedford Spring Assizes (Bedford G.D.) 7 March 1799 for stealing a black mare from William Green of Bolnhurst and a black horse from John Mee of Highham Ferrers. Sentenced to death. Reprieved by Lord Chief Justice Eldon and Mr Justice Askhurst and sentenced to transportation for seven years. Gaoled at Bedford and transferred to the *Stanislaus* hulk at Woolwich. During his gaol term he was ill and fed 'on mutton broth and other nourishments'.

During the voyage out he was employed on deck as a

wardroom baker. In V.D.L. he acquired some livestock (three fowls) in August 1804.

There appears to be no further record of him in the colony. As he would have been free by 1806 he probably returned to England soon afterwards.

PETERS, THOMAS [c. 1776–1839]

Labourer, aged 26, married to Ann Hews (Hughes?) of Warwick, daughter Elizabeth.

Tried at Yorkshire Summer Assizes (York G.D.) 31 July 1802 for stealing old silver plate, including ten pints or cups, together with William Jones, William Douglas, John Armitage and others from John Gamble of Leeds. Richard Howarth, pawnbroker of Leeds, gave evidence that Malcolm Wright, shopkeeper of Liverpool, had received the goods and that they, with constables, went to a public house near the old dock at Liverpool. Howarth admitted he had agreed to give £16 10s 0d for the silver. Sentenced to death by Lord Chief Justice Ellenborough. Reprieved and sentenced to transportation for life. Gaoled at York Castle and transferred to the hulks at Portsmouth. Ann Peters was allowed to accompany her husband, who remained in irons, in the *Calcutta*. She and her daughter were berthed in the prison room.

During their stay at Port Phillip Ann Peters became pregnant. Their daughter Martha was baptised in Hobart on 23 September 1804.

Peters attended the Hobart musters in 1811, 1818, 1819 and 1823. He received a conditional pardon in 1813 and an absolute pardon soon afterwards.

Gov. King granted Mary [*sic*] Peters 40 acres of land on the brook (River Derwent) in 1805. As a female proprietor she sowed wheat and potatoes and had her husband assigned to her as a government servant. A return of 1804 showed he held four fowls in his own name. In 1807 the property was mistakenly returned in his name as a settler with three children, one servant and no wife. They had wheat, barley and potato crops, two cows, two bull-calves, two ewes and a female goat. By 1809 they had added to their stock a bull and three oxen. In October 1808 the Peters had a fourth daughter. The name of the mother was omitted from the baptismal register. Three later daughters and one son born between 1810 and 1815 were registered as the children of Thomas Peters and his wife née Mary Ann of Warrick [*sic*] adding that they were married in England.

By 1820 Peters had received a 600-acre land grant from Gov. Macquarie at Herdsman's Cove. He already held grazing licences between Bagdad and Constitution, where he had a farm house known as Baker's Farm. He had increased his stock to 40 male and 110 female cattle, 200 male sheep and 400 ewes and employed three free persons. He provided large quantities of meat and wheat for the Commissariat.

From the beginning Peters was one of the most successful of all the *Calcutta* convicts. As well as his farming interests, he had, from early days, a lucrative blacksmith's business in Elizabeth St. where he kept a small stud and occasionally raced his horses. He had licences for the Plough Inn and the Duke of York at the foot of Wellington Bridge which he advertised for sale in June 1819 just after the death of his wife in May, from inflammation of the throat. Thomas Peters was 'an inhabitant much respected in this settlement for many years'; his wife had left eight children, 'four or five of them at a time they most need a mother's care'. (*H.T.G.*, 29 May 1819)

By this time Peters' eldest daughter had married a young settler, George Armytage, who had arrived in Hobart in 1816 from Yorkshire; perhaps the son, or a kinsman, of the John Armitage with whom Peters had committed his crime. He received a 200-acre grant of land at Bagdad adjoining Peters' run. Peters and his family moved from Hobart to live in Bagdad. He had acquired other farms, including that owned by Thomas Tarratt (*q.v.*) and one at York Plains.

Peters was in trouble on several occasions during the time he lived in Hobart. Several times he was before the court for debt but other times for misdemeanours of a violent nature, such as when he was fined for threatening persons with a pistol in 1818 and 1820.

An education return of 1822 indicated that he was prepared to educate his children and that his twelve-year-old daughter could write. Two of his daughters, Sophia and Ann, were speared by blacks in 1830. Ann died, but Sophia recovered to marry James Pillinger. Peters' daughter Charlotte married Francis Flexmore.

Died at Bagdad, aged 64 (?). Buried 21 July 1839, Green Ponds. Ann was buried 26 May 1819, St David's (her tombstone says April), aged 39.

Among the thousands of descendants have been some of Australia's most prominent families. Surnames of descendants have included: Alexander; Armytage; Bailey; Balmain; Bell; Bere; Bird; Braithwaite; Brookes; Byron-Moore; Campbell; Carmichael; Clarke; Colquhoun; Dobson; Dyce-Murphy; Erwin; Fairbairn; Farran; Fekete; Fitzpatrick; Flexmore; Galletly; Galloway; Glover; Graham-Smith; Grey-Smith; Guest; Hayes; Hearne; Herbert; Holt; Hopkins; Hovelt; Kerslake; Kininmonth; Landale; Lumsden; Mackinolty; McDonald; McFadden; MacFadyen; McIntosh-Smith; McIntyre; Miller; Mockford; Molesworth; Muirhead; Page; Paxton; Pearce; Pillinger; Pincott; Purves; Pyke; Richards; Richmond; Russell; Rust; Seton-Williams; Sinclair; Staughton; Thordd; Vallentyne; Van Katwyk; Warford-Mein; Warner; Watt; Wheatley; Whitehead; Williams.

PHIPPS, GEORGE [c. 1774–1839]

?, aged 28. Literate.

Tried at Berkshire Spring Assizes (Reading G.D.) 1 March 1802 for having stolen a silver cream jug, a silver teapot and a plated candlestick from the dwelling house of Mrs Emma Elliott in the parish of Bray. Sentenced to death. Reprieved by Baron Thomson and Justice Sir Alan Chambre and sentenced to transportation for fourteen years. Gaoled at Reading and transferred to the hulks at Langston.

Phipps attended the Hobart musters in 1811, 1818, 1819 and 1823. He received a conditional pardon in January 1813 and an absolute pardon soon afterwards.

He became the government gardener and in the early days in Hobart supplied the inhabitants with a good variety of vegetable roots, fruit and other trees.

On 24 June 1816, in Hobart, he married Elizabeth Mac-Away, aged 23, a convict transported in the *Alexander*, but within six months advertised that he was not responsible for his wife's debts. They had been separated since 27 September.

A George Phipps living in Launceston with a young family appears to be a different man.

Buried 18 March 1839, St David's, aged 70 (?), a house-keeper. Elizabeth was buried 22 February 1821, St David's.

PIROELLE, NICHOLAS [c. 1757–1804]
(Pirioele)
Confectionery maker, aged 44, of Burgundy, France, married; 5'4", dark complexion, brown hair, hazel eyes.
Tried at Middlesex I Sessions (London G.D.) 2 December 1801 for stealing 10 lb preserved apricots (50s 0d), 100 lb caraways (30s 0d), 2 lb apple jelly (8s 0d), 12 lb sugar (6s 0d), a wooden box (1s 0d), 12 sheets of foil (6s 0d), 12 jars (12d) and 12 galli-pots (6d) from his employers Martha Hoffman (widow), Charles-Godfrey Hoffman and James Rix Hoffman, a firm of confectioners at Bishopsgate St. He said through an interpreter that he had bought the apricots from a Joseph Fondière. Four witnesses gave him a good character. Sentence pronounced by the Recorder was transportation for seven years. Gaoled at Poultry and transferred to the *Prudentia* hulk at Woolwich.

Piroelle's wife Sarah and their son Henry were allowed to accompany him. They slept in the prison room during the voyage out.

Died suddenly 22 May 1804, Hobart. Surgeon Bowden's report suggested that he was poisoned. He opened his body and found that 'Upon opening the thorax, the pericardium and both sides of the chest contained a large quantity of water which had stopped the action of the lungs. The heart was unusually large, but not otherwise diseased. In the abdomen I examined the stomach and intestines particularly, which were perfectly healthy, and contained a small quantity of half digested food, in which there was nothing remarkable. The liver was also much enlarged from some former disease.'

A livestock return of August 1804 shows that Mrs Piroelle owned two fowls. In June 1806 she was appointed as a public baker for six months. There appears to be no further record of her or her son in the colony. They probably returned to Europe.

PIZZEY, HENRY [c. 1782 – after 1823]
(Pazey, Pizey, etc.)
?, aged 20.
Tried at Berkshire Spring Assizes (Reading G.D.) 1 March 1802 for stealing a pair of shoes and a pair of breeches from John Maynard, carter to James Cooper of Binfield, and with stealing a loaf of bread from Cooper. Sentenced to transportation for seven years. Gaoled at Reading and transferred to the hulks at Langston.

During the voyage out Pizzey was punished for insolence. In September 1807 he received severe corporal punishment for absenting himself from labour for several days. Some time after this he must have moved to Port Dalrymple because he attended the musters there in 1811, 1818, 1819, 1820, 1821 and 1823. He also appears on the landholders' muster rolls of Port Dalrymple for 1818 and 1820, indicating that he had a grant of 30 acres from Gov. Macquarie. By 1820 he had under cultivation wheat and barley and owned some cattle and swine.

On 29 January 1816 he was in Sydney when he married Hannah Robertson at St Phillip's. He returned to V.D.L. in the schooner *The Brothers* soon afterwards. The musters indicate that he had a wife and kept a servant.

The records are too faint to indicate whether they had any children and Pizzey's later activities have not been traced. But it is believed that there are descendants.

PLUNKET(T), PATRICK [c. 1777 – ?]
?, aged 25. Irish.
Tried at Devonshire S. of P. (Exeter) 5 October 1802 for petty larceny. Sentenced to transportation for seven years. Gaoled at Exeter and transferred to the hulks at Langston.

During the voyage out he was twice punished — firstly for insolence and secondly for fighting.

In October 1804, in V.D.L., he received 100 lashes at a court martial of Pte Woolley with whom he was found drinking. Woolley received 200 lashes. In December 1806, after having escaped for three weeks and stealing a dog, he received 300 lashes for fighting with the marines. In June 1807 he and Vasey (*q.v.*) escaped to the bush and on their return received 400 lashes.

In March 1808 he absconded and attempted to kill a settler at the Falls. A reward of £50 was offered for his apprehension. There appears to be no further record of him.

POOLE, THOMAS [1774–1839]
Baker, aged 26, bap. 28 August 1774 pa. Gloucester, of Ashleworth, Gloucestershire, son of Robert Poole.
Tried at Gloucester Spring Assizes (Gloucester G.D.) 25 March 1801 for burglariously entering the dwelling house of William Roberts and stealing and carrying away with the use of force and arms one cloth great coat (15s 0d), one man's hat (5s 0d), one pair of leather shoes (5s 0d), part of a linen shirt (6d), two pairs of worsted stockings (1s 0d) and one linen sheet (1s 0d). Sentenced to death. Reprieved by Justices Sir Soulden Laurence and Sir Giles Rooke and sentenced to transportation for life. Gaoled at the county gaol and transferred to the *Prudentia* hulk at Woolwich.

Poole attended the Hobart musters in 1811, 1818 and 1819. He received a conditional pardon in April 1815. A register of these pardons in 1825 describes him as 5'5", dark complexion, dark hair and dark eyes.

Poole received a 30-acre land grant at Herdsman's Cove from Gov. Davey on which he was growing wheat, barley and vegetables by 1819 and grazing two male and two female cattle, 150 male sheep and 350 ewes. He supplied meat to the Commissariat.

A memorial of 1820 must have given him a good grant of land at Green Ponds where he farmed successfully for many years.

On 20 September 1820, in Hobart, he married Mary Molony, aged 25, a convict transported in the *Broxenbury*. They had four children.

Buried 26 August 1839, Green Ponds, aged 64 (?).

His widow married John Dowdy, shoemaker, at Brighton, in March 1843.

Surnames of descendants have included: Addison; Goble; Hart; Hughes.

POPE, WILLIAM [c. 1767 – ?]
Able seaman, aged 34, of St James, Westminster; 5'5", dark complexion, brown hair, hazel eyes, stout.
Tried at Westminster S. of P. 22 October 1801 together with Alexander Farrell for stealing four iron bars (10d) attached to house of Arthur Robinson Chauwell, clerk, of

St James. The patrols of the Watch House at St James, Rice Evans, John Murphy and Arthur Hayden, gave evidence against them. Pope sentenced to transportation for seven years and Farrell to imprisonment for two months. Gaoled at Newgate and transferred to the *Fortune* hulk at Langston.

Pope had previously served in Newgate when, in April 1795, Mr Justice Rooke had sentenced him to death for stealing velveteen in London from Robert Crofts. He was reprieved and sentenced to transportation for life to the West Indies but did not leave England. A magistrate's letter noted that 'William Pope is a very old offender, that he has been considered a very dangerous man to society.' On 14 May 1794 he was charged with several other notorious persons suspected of committing 'foul robberies' in Surrey, but he was discharged when he seemingly pretended he had hurt his head which disabled him in his work as a seaman.

During the voyage out Pope served as a sailor.

A return of livestock in August 1804 shows William Pope kept three fowls. This appears to be the last record of him in the colony.

He was a sailor who would have become free by servitude in 1808; probably returned to England.

PORTER, PHILIP [c. 1775–1804]
Labourer, aged 26, of Leyland, Lancaster.
Tried at the Summer Assizes of the County Palatinate of Lancaster (G.D.) 15 August 1801 together with Isaac Salter and George Ashton (*q.v.*) for stealing 23 pieces of calico (£23) from the drying house of John, George, William, Edward and Ralph Clayton at Leyland. Sentenced to death. Reprieved by Lord Chief Justice Alvanley and Justice Sir Alan Chambre and sentenced to transportation for fourteen years. Gaoled at Lancaster Castle and transferred to the hulks at Portsmouth.

Died 11 August 1804, Hobart, aged 30 (?), of dropsy.

POTASKI(E), JOHN [c. 1762–1824]
(Patoskey, Potaskee, Potasky, etc.)
?, aged 40, born Poland, married Catherine Sullivan from Ireland, one son born in England. Roman Catholic.
Tried at Sussex Spring Assizes (Horsham G.D.) 27 March 1802 for stealing, together with John O'Brien, a hair shawl and other articles in the shop of Mrs Pollard at Newhaven. Sentenced by Baron Hotham to transportation for seven years. Gaoled at Horsham and transferred to the hulks at Langston.

Potaski's wife and their son John accompanied him in the *Calcutta*. They were berthed in the prison room. On 17 February 1804 Mrs Potaski gave birth to a daughter, Catherine, in the *Ocean* as it lay in Risdon Cove.

Potaski attended the Hobart musters in 1811, 1818, 1819 and 1823.

By 1807 he had acquired some pigs and sold two to Knopwood. Catherine Potaski received a 30-acre land grant from Gov. Davey at Clarence Plains, and her husband was renting farms at Kangaroo Point, Geilston and Risdon by 1816, growing more corn on them than was needed for a year's supply in the whole colony, according to Surveyor George Evans. They had a comfortable house at Kangaroo Point. In 1819 he grazed four male and ten female cattle

and twenty ewes, while the land his wife owned grew wheat and provided additional pasture. He supplied the Commissariat with wheat.

Potaski tried to buy Geilston when it was still owned by Andrew Geils. A new agent, Alfred Thrupp, restrained him, and chose to take large quantities of wheat in place of rent over which there were disputes when Thrupp did not issue receipts for the delivery of wheat. The Potaski's son Joseph burgled the Thrupp household, committing rape on Mrs. Thrupp, for which he was executed, 19 May 1821.

Potaski advertised in February 1818 that he was sailing in the *Frederick* to the Ile de France but it is unlikely that he went. In August 1820 he put his house at Kangaroo Point up for auction. His daughter Catherine married Edward McDonald at St Virgil's, on 29 June 1824.

Buried 31 August 1824, St David's. A stone in the burial ground names a 'Peter Patoskey who departed this life August 29th 1824 aged 50 years'.

Surnames of descendants have included: Brady; Connor; Dunlop; Gatland; Geehman; Hardy; Hickey; Kenna; McDonald; Milledge; Miller; Morcillin; Murphy; O'Loughlin; Paul; Pownall; Purcell; Robins; Steynes; Sparling.

POWELL, JOSEPH [c. 1766–1808]
Coachman, aged 36.
Tried at Kent Summer Assizes (Maidstone G.D.) 4 August 1802 together with Benjamin Blackford (*q.v.*) for stealing one wether sheep from Robert Jennings at Lewisham. Sentenced to death. Reprieved by the Lord Chief Baron and Baron Hotham and sentenced to transportation for seven years. Gaoled at Maidstone and transferred to the hulks at Woolwich.

Powell was one who accompanied Knopwood and Harris, in 1804, in the government boat to explore Storm Bay, Bruny I. and the Huon with provisions for fourteen days.

Buried 6 July 1808, Hobart, aged 39 (?).

POWER(S), MATTHEW [c. 1775 – ?]
Printer, aged 27, born in Dublin, living in Thanington, Kent; 5'10", dark complexion, married to Hannah, aged 26, 5'2", fair complexion, Irish but had lived in Middlesex. Literate.
Tried at Kent Summer Assizes (Maidstone G.D.) 4 August 1802 together with his wife for uttering a counterfeit £5 banknote made out to Abraham Newland or bearer with intent to defraud James Warren. Power was declared guilty and his wife discharged. They had both been confined to Newgate on a previous charge when Urias Allender (*q.v.*) was convicted. Power was declared guilty and his wife discharged. He was sentenced by Baron Hotham to transportation for fourteen years. He was gaoled at Maidstone and transferred to the *Prudentia* hulk at Woolwich.

During the voyage out Mrs Power was berthed in the gunroom and her husband allowed to go without irons. They received special treatment as she soon became mistress to Lieut.-Gov. Collins after an earlier affair with Lieut. Lord. While they were at Rio de Janeiro, Power bought stock to the value of £27 11s 7d for Dr Bowden.

At Port Phillip Collins and Mrs Power stood for the child of Sgt Thorne at a baptismal ceremony. J. P. Fawkner's Reminiscences and Knopwood's diaries over the years mention their association from Port Phillip days. Collins appointed Power a subordinate of the night watch at Port Phillip.

After arriving in Hobart, Collins sent out a General Order erasing Power's name from the list of prisoners and inserting it in the class of free people, an action allowed by Gov. King in a letter of October 1804. Power and Lieut. Lord were continually in dispute, and Collins at one stage sided with Power and arrested Lord. Power leased two acres of town land next to Collins in December 1805 for fourteen years at 2s 6d a year and had a 50-acre grant at Sullivan Cove from Gov. King the following month. Returns of livestock and agriculture showed that Mrs Power held six fowls in July 1804 and that by October 1806 the Powers had a bull, four cows, one male sheep and six ewes, and a government servant. The following July they had increased their stock to two cows, two calves, two rams, ten wethers, 35 ewes and had two servants. George Harris wrote to his mother in October 1805 that Collins had built elegant houses for convicts where the wife was a favourite.

Power began to trade in spirits. Campbell & Co. in Sydney warned against receiving bills drawn on his credit. Power was meeting ships and arranging credit with ships' captains calling at Hobart. He and William Collins had inspected invoices of goods sent from Port Jackson by Simeon Lord and Kable & Co. by the whaler *King George*. They were suspected of defrauding the Commissariat. It was suggested Power should go to trial at Port Jackson but the Bench of Magistrates, under David Collins' instructions, gave him the benefit of the doubt because there was no evidence of any fraud, although there were bills to the value of £661 11s 0d drawn by the Commissary Fosbrook to the credit of Matthew Power.

Power was among those who encouraged the building of a bridge and road from Hobart to New Town in 1807 and subscribed towards its construction. Collins was also able to use Power as a printer, and while Bligh was at the Derwent in April 1809 he had asked for his Proclamation to be printed. Collins had agreed but when Power came to print it the ink had mysteriously disappeared.

By this time Collins' interest in Hannah Power had waned and he had a new mistress from Norfolk I. In 1809 the Powers decided to return to England, perhaps anticipating that Bligh might make trouble for them.

In 1808 Power assigned all rights to the title of his lease of the Hobart allotment to Capt. Samuel Chase, who had married Collins' daughter by his Sydney mistress. In 1809, on his arrival in Hobart, R. W. Loane bought the land from Power and erected a house costing £3 000, presumably because Chase had not taken up the rights.

In London, Francis Shipman (*q.v.*) named Power as one who could corroborate his charges against Fosbrook. In May 1812 he stated that the Powers lived in London and had six weeks previously left their address in Upper Marylebone St. They were not contacted.

There are no details traced of their later career. Perhaps they suspected what might happen to Shipman and did not wish to be involved.

PRESTAGE, JOHN [c. 1764–1833]
(Priestedge, Prestige, Priesage, also Thomas P.)

On unemployed relief since January 1865, son of John and Elizabeth Prestidge {sic}, pa. Moreton Pinkney, Northampton.
Tried at Northampton Assizes (Northampton G.D.) 1 March 1802 for stealing one wether sheep from William Painter, farmer, of Sulgrave. Sentenced to death. Reprieved by the Lord Chief Baron and Baron Graham and sentenced to transportation for life. Prestage's father was in receipt of relief almost weekly from 1780 onwards and other members of the family also received relief. Gaoled at Northampton and transferred to the hulks at Langston.

Prestage attended the Hobart musters in 1811, 1818, 1819 and 1823. He was granted one of the earliest conditional pardons, in 1807, and an absolute pardon many years later. He received a 40-acre land grant at Pitt Water from Gov. Macquarie on which he had a good farmhouse. By 1819 most of his acreage was producing wheat and other crops with large supplies on hand. He ran twelve male cattle, twelve female cattle, 30 male sheep, 70 female sheep and employed four government servants, one of whom might have been the parent of a child mentioned as part of his establishment. There appears to be no record that Prestage had married and no wife mentioned, although he had a brother-in-law named Heatley. He supplied the Commissariat with wheat and the *H.T.G.* referred to him as an industrious settler.

In Hobart's early days he had tried to escape with others when, in May 1805, they hoped to reach New Zealand in a whale boat. He was not convicted. When he appeared in 1811 to give evidence at an inquest on the body of Pte Samuel Wiggins, he was described as 'a free and lawful man'. During the same year he appeared at the Court of Criminal Jurisdiction in Sydney as a crown witness for the prosecution of James Clissold against John Willis (*q.v.*) for sheep stealing. In 1820 he was the victim of incendiarism when he lost 500 bushels of wheat.

He advertised the farm, which he had extended to 60 acres, for sale in 1831 and died at Pitt Water, aged 62 (?). Buried 16 March 1833, St George's.

PRICE, JAMES [c. 1774–1805]
Labourer, aged 26, of Farnham, Surrey; 5'4", dark complexion, brown hair, hazel eyes.
Tried at Middlesex VIII Sessions (Middlesex G.D.) 28 October 1801 for stealing two geldings (£18) from William Townsend at Riverhead. He and his colleague Henry Ellis, hardware carrier, were both sentenced to death by Mr Justice Heath. Reprieved and sentenced to transportation for life. Gaoled at Newgate and transferred to the hulks at Woolwich.

During the voyage out James Price was occupied as a sailor. In November 1803 he was one of the convicts who volunteered to accompany William Collins in the six-oared cutter to Port Jackson.

He tried to escape, 17 February 1805, from Hobart by swimming out to an East India ship, the Myrtle, *bound for the north-west coast of America, but was drowned, aged 32 (?), before reaching the ship, body washed ashore at Sandy Bay.*

PRICE, JOHN [c. 1760–1803]
Labourer, aged 40, of Newtown, Montgomery, Wales.
Tried at Montgomery G.S. (Spring) 1800 for driving away

two oxen (£20), property of Thomas Ashford of Newtown in November 1799. Sentenced to death. Reprieved and sentenced to transportation for fourteen years. Six persons appeared as witnesses against him. Gaoled at Newtown (?) and transferred to the hulks at Portsmouth.

Died 25 November 1803, Port Phillip, aged 42 (?).

PRICE, THOMAS [c. 1753–1803]
Labourer, aged 48, of Llanhew (?) Brecon, Wales.
Tried at Brecon G.S. 28 March 1801 together with Thomas Williams (*q.v.*) for breaking and entering the house of Thomas Pritchard of Pentwyn, Llanvigan, county of Brecon and stealing one sheet, one gown, six yards flannel, eight cheeses, tea, gin, etc. (a long list). Guilty of stealing but not of breaking and entering. Sentenced to transportation for fourteen years. Eleven persons appeared as witnesses. Gaoled at Brecon and transferred to the hulks at Portsmouth.
Died 17 November 1803, Port Phillip, aged 48 (?).

PRITCHARD, THOMAS [c. 1780 – after 1803]
Millwright, aged 22, of St Oswald, Chester.
Tried at Pleasure of the Session of Crown Mote, Chester 21 October 1802 for stealing one gelding (£5) from Samuel Jackson out of a field at Ellesmere and selling it at Chester. Sentenced to death. Reprieved and sentenced to transportation for fourteen years. Gaoled at Chester Castle and transferred to the *Captivity* hulk at Portsmouth.
During the voyage out Pritchard was punished for insolence.
On 19 December 1803 he escaped from the camp at Port Phillip; did not return and presumably died soon afterwards.

PYE, GEORGE [c. 1772 – after 1803]
?, aged 30.
Tried at Nottingham Assizes (Nottingham G.D.) 11 March 1802 for stealing one ewe from Samuel Kitchener of Mansfield. Sentenced to death. Reprieved by the Lord Chief Baron and Baron Graham and sentenced to transportation for life. He was supposedly one of an organised gang of sheep stealers. Gaoled at Nottingham and transferred to the hulks at Langston.
By December 1803 he had escaped from the camp at Port Phillip, probably with William Buckley (q.v.); did not return and presumably died soon afterwards.

QUIN(N), THOMAS [c.1776–1807]
Plasterer, aged 24, of Dublin; 5'7", dark complexion, brown hair, hazel eyes.
Tried at Middlesex VI Sessions (Middlesex G.D.) 9 July 1800 for stealing a portable writing desk (£5 5s 0d) from Thomas Hanford, deskmaker. Sentenced by Justice Sir Soulden Laurence to transportation for seven years for stealing goods valued at 39s 0d. Two witnesses gave him a good character. Gaoled at Newgate and transferred to the *Fortune* hulk at Portsmouth.
In 1807 Quinn escaped from Hobart and, after being away for a very long time, accepted the Governor's offer of an amnesty and returned on 6 December.
It is possible that he was married for a short time to Martha Hayes, as he was the only person named Quinn in

Hobart. On her marriage to Andrew Whitehead (*q.v.*) in June 1811 she signed as Martha Hayes Quinn.
Knopwood entered name on register of burials, Hobart, 28 December 1806 instead of 1807, aged 30.

RAPHAEL, JOSEPH [c. 1785–1853]
(Raphell)
Hatter, aged 17, born pa. St Dunstan's, Stepney, and living near the corner of Flower and Dean St. Spitalfields with his father, Jew; 5'4", dark complexion, black hair and eyes. Literate.
Tried at Middlesex IV Sessions (Middlesex G.D.) 28 April 1802 for having, together with three colleagues, attacked Peter Theodory, a foreigner, on the King's Highway and robbed him of a silver watch and chain as well as clothes. Sentenced to death by Lord Chief Justice Ellenborough. Reprieved and sentenced to transportation for life. Gaoled at Newgate and transferred to the *Prudentia* hulk at Woolwich.
Raphael attended the Sydney muster in 1811 and he appeared on the Sydney census of 1828. He received a conditional pardon before 1811 which he lost when convicted in 1817 and sent to Newcastle. He did not receive an absolute pardon until 1842.
In earlier times in Hobart he had been troublesome, trying to escape in the *Sarah* in 1807. He must have had permission to live in Sydney where he engaged for many years in various trades and partnerships, mostly in Pitt St., amidst much litigation. During a spell at Newcastle he married a Protestant, Ann Clements, aged 22, a convict transported in the *Mary Ann*. They had a daughter, Jane and an adopted son. In 1824 during a visit to Sydney, G.T.W.B. Boyes described him as among those Jews who were 'rich, keeping a handsome Tilbury . . . Raphael, rather stout and not too tall . . .'
He was always a troublesome yet generous-hearted man.
Buried 26 September 1853, Sydney, by a Methodist minister (although he was always known as a Jew who had contributed substantially towards the building of the Sydney Synogogue).
See ch. 35 for a fuller account of Raphael's career.

REEVES, GEORGE [c. 1761 – ?]
Tradesman, aged 40, of St George, Hanover Sq; 5'3", dark complexion, brown hair.
Tried at Middlesex V Sessions (Middlesex G.D.) 20 May 1801 for stealing a black gelding (£5) from John Hanscom of Hackney. The horse was taken to Soho for slaughtering. Sentence pronounced by the Recorder was death. Reprieved and sentenced to transportation for life. One witness gave him a good character. Gaoled at Tothillfields and transferred to the *Captivity* hulk at Plymouth.
There is no further record of him after his arrival in Hobart.

REYNOLDS, JOHN [c. 1780 – after 1819]
Private soldier in 18th Rgt of Light Dragoons, aged 21.
Tried at Yorkshire Summer Assizes (Rotherham G.D.) 18 July 1801, with three other soldiers, for stealing cotton handkerchiefs and other goods from Messrs Pitt and Richardson of Beverley. Sentenced to transportation for seven years. Gaoled at York Castle and transferred to the hulks at Portsmouth.
On 11 March 1808 his name appeared in the General

Orders as an absconder from Hobart and an outlaw. On 24 March £10 was offered for his apprehension. He returned and attended the Hobart muster in 1811. A notation on the muster rolls showed that he had been fined in the settlement. By this time he would have been free.

He appears to have joined the crew of the brig *Active* in May 1813, which was engaged in whaling and sealing expeditions in New Zealand and Tasmanian waters. He probably spent several years as a sailor, because he was not present at any 1818 musters. In October 1818 he advertised that he was leaving the colony, but he attended the muster in Hobart in 1819.

After that there is no further record of his whereabouts. Perhaps he joined the crew of a ship returning to England. He might have been married to one named Mary Reynolds (1819 muster of free persons at Hobart).

RICE, HENRY [c. 1758–1833]
?, aged 43, from Ireland, married with children? Roman Catholic. Literate.
Tried at Chester Pleas of Session of Crown Mote 31 August 1801 for uttering a forged £2 note at Latchford. Sentenced to death, reprieved and sentenced to transportation for fourteen years. Gaoled at Chester Castle and transferred to the hulks at Langston.

Rice attended the Hobart musters in 1811 and 1818. He received a free pardon in 1812 and a land grant of 80 acres at the Coal River from Gov. Davey. In 1816 this land was the subject of a dispute which Rice lost against Roger Gavin. By 1819 Gov. Macquarie had restored his land and he had crops on five acres and five horned and ten female cattle grazing on the rest. He employed a government servant. In 1823 the *Sydney Gazette* reported that he had built a 'house of earth' (presumably mud brick).

In earlier days he had escaped twice from custody. In June 1805 he was among the escapees who saw a Tasmanian tiger. Collins had offered £10 reward for his apprehension in March 1808. He became a servant to George Gunning, a former officer in the 73rd Rgt who was living in New Town, but had also acquired large grants in the Coal River area. On two occasions in 1818 Rice found himself in dangerous situations while protecting his employer and his property. In April he helped secure James Mahoney who had attempted armed robbery at the house at New Town. In June R.W. Loane forcibly took a musket from Rice when he (Loane) and his servants removed cattle which Rice claimed were his. Loane threatened that he would see Rice hang if it cost him £1 000. The Bench of Magistrates investigated several of the charges against Loane and committed him for trial in Sydney. The court ordered him to find sureties up to £200 for twelve months.

In 1829–20 Gov. Sorrell put Henry Rice in charge of a party to explore the east coast. They set out from the Coal River on 13 December. The successful journey, of which Rice left a daily account, took four weeks. Rice was then ordered a land grant of 150 acres at Glenorchy, but there was some confusion over the measurements and ultimately Gov. Arthur allowed him 160 acres.

Rice possibly had sons named Henry, transported for life from Dublin in the *Bencoolen* (1816) and Terence who received seven years, also from Dublin. They were probably brothers and both ultimately married women named McShane or McShean. If they were Rice's sons, it was probably this Henry (jun.?) who farmed the Glenorchy property. In 1824 his housekeeper, Mary Davis, by whom he had a child, was tragically killed when a cart overturned. This Henry Rice died in Sydney in 1829.

Henry Rice sen. continued to live at the Coal River. Impoverished in his old age, he became a servant to George Burn who built his house, Roslyn, at Richmond.

Buried 18 May 1833, St Matthew's, Pitt Water, aged 82 (?).

There was a sequel to the Rice story which raises an interesting question, as yet unanswered satisfactorily. A James Rice, of Abbey St., Dublin, corresponded with the Colonial Secretary in 1837 about a possible land grant given his father, an ex-convict, now deceased and left by his late father in V.D.L. James Rice believed that his father came from Tanderagee, co. Armagh, and was transported for life in 1798. (He might have left Ireland then). James claimed that about ten or twelve years later the Governor of V.D.L. deputed him to take charge of presents of animals and birds to the Prince Regent who in return presented him with ten acres of land in the centre of Hobart. When he arrived in London he wrote to his wife (actually then dead) asking her to return with their children, but the children were then living in Dublin. James Rice believed his father died about 1825 or 1826 in Hobart possessing a considerable amount of land and property. James could well have been the brother of Henry jun. and Terence, both of Dublin, and all too young to know for certain whether Henry sen. was tried in Dublin or Chester, and when. The naturalist George Caley visited Hobart in October 1805, collecting specimens which he took to Sir Joseph Banks, returning to England in the *Hindostan* in 1810 with Bligh. He took with him an assistant known as Rae. Could this have been a misreading of the old writing for Rice? We know Rice was a literate man. He was interested in the Tasmanian tiger. Sir Joseph Banks received the collection for which Frederick William III of Prussia offered the sum of £350 for the 'extensive and valuable collection of birds and reptiles . . .' But it remained in England, presented to the Linnean Society. There is nothing available in the records to confirm or deny the family legend. Collins could well have assigned Rice, already an experienced bushman, to act as a guide to Caley and allowed him to accompany him to England.

Surnames of those claiming descent have included: Fisher.

RICHARDS, JOSEPH [c. 1767 – after 1828?]
?, aged 34, from Bristol; 5'3", fair complexion, light hair, grey eyes.
Tried at Middlesex Commission of *Oyer et Terminer* 4 July 1801 for petty larceny and perjury. Sentenced to transportation for seven years. Gaoled at Newgate and transferred to the *Captivity* hulk at Portsmouth. A note on the Home Office list records that he had previously been tried at Hick's Hall (London sessions were held at Clerkenwell until 1779 when Hick's Hall was demolished). It would appear from this that Richards had had a prior conviction by the time he was twelve years old.

During the voyage out Joseph Richards was employed on deck as an armourer's mate, without irons.

Some time after his arrival in V.D.L., probably after he was free by servitude, Richards went to Port Jackson. He attended the 1811 muster there. In August 1813 he was living in the district of Windsor when, according to a note in Bigge's Appendix, he was fined 5s 0d for assault. On 26 March 1814 the *Sydney Gazette* reported that he was found guilty of theft. In June 1819 he advertised that he was leaving the colony. He appears to have returned to Hobart where, in December 1824, he appeared before the Supreme Court and was sentenced to death for stealing wheat from Urias Allender (*q.v.*). If this were the same Joseph Richards, he must have received a capital reprieve and been sent to one of the secondary penitentiaries.

However, a Joseph Richards was in Sydney in 1828, when tried at the Supreme Court, was found guilty of stealing 40s 0d from a dwelling house, and transported to Moreton Bay for seven years.

RICHARDSON, WILLIAM [c. 1775–1858]
Private soldier in the 3rd Rgt of Guards, aged 27, from Lincoln; 5'8", dark complexion.
Tried at Middlesex III Sessions (Middlesex G.D.) 17 February 1802 for entering the house of James James of Princes St., Westminster, vintner, at midnight and burglariously stealing a canvas bag (1d), £16 in monies numbered, three banknotes (£2 each), and eight other banknotes (£1 each). Richardson had lodged with James for three to four months. A colleague, Duncan, from his regimental company, gave evidence that they had been paid and were drinking all the evening. Although very drunk, Richardson managed to climb up to a high window. He had on him his own silver watch and chain and a purse he had found, for which he was not charged. Sentenced by Mr Justice Hotham to death. Reprieved and sentenced to transportation for life. Gaoled at Tothillfields and transferred to the *Captivity* hulk at Portsmouth.

Richardson attended the Hobart musters in 1811, 1818, 1819 and 1823 and his name appears on the 1842 census. He received a conditional pardon in 1813 and an absolute pardon soon afterwards. He purchased 50 acres of land at Muddy Plains in 1822 on which he built a house, stockyards, barn and pig sties. This was subject to a minor dispute when he unwittingly cultivated ten adjoining acres belonging to Robert Mather. There was an amicable agreement when, because of a recommendation to Gov. Arthur that he was a man of good character and very industrious, he was allowed to keep the ten acres as a grant. In 1819 he had 114 male sheep and 241 ewes.

From the earliest days he was one of Knopwood's servants and accompanied him on the exploration of Storm Bay, Bruny I. and the Huon. On one of his many hunting expeditions he was nearly killed by a native. Knopwood allowed him considerable freedom with dogs and a gun. In a further affray with the natives in 1807 he shot one who was about to spear him. There is a tradition in the family that he was once saved by sheltering behind the body of a beached whale. Knopwood kept in touch with his former servant, who appears to have also worked for Sgt McCauley for a time.

William Richardson married Elizabeth Winrow, aged 21, a convict who had arrived in the *Mary* in 1823. She had received a sentence of seven years at the Liverpool Peace Sessions on 6 May 1822. They had five sons and three daughters. Descendants, of whom there were many, have continued to farm in the area for generations.

He was possibly the William Richardson whom George Robinson described as a veteran in charge of rationing the natives at Bruny I. for a few months before George Robinson took control in 1829.

Died at Muddy Plains. Buried 2 August 1858, St Matthew's, Rokeby, described as a 'farmer, one of the first persons to land in the colony', aged 102 (probably 82).

Surnames of descendants have included: Bignell; McComb.

RIDEOUT, AMBROSE [c. 1755–1836]
(Ridought, Ridiout, Ridout, Ridcourt)
Labourer, aged 45, pa. Manston, Dorset, married; 5'7½", dark brown hair, grey eyes, brown complexion.
Tried at Dorset Summer Assizes (Dorchester G.D.) 1 July 1800 on suspicion of breaking and entering the house of Richard Foot of Manston and stealing 65½ guineas. Sentenced by Baron Thomson to death. Reprieved and sentenced to transportation for life. Gaoled at Dorchester where he was employed at hatting then transferred to the *Captivity* hulk at Portsmouth. His behaviour was orderly.

He attended the Hobart musters in 1811 and 1819. He received a conditional pardon in June 1810. He received a 30-acre land grant at Herdsman's Cove. By 1819 he was growing wheat and vegetables and had 25½ acres in pasture with his partner Lambert.

In 1820 he appeared before the Lieutenant-Governor's Court in Hobart. He gave evidence against John Hill, Thomas Atkinson and Michael Riley, escapees from Hobart, found armed at Jericho. He described himself as a fettler. The prisoners had committed armed robbery. They had stolen tobacco, cutlery and other articles from Rideout after breaking and entering his home. They were committed for trial at the Court of Criminal Jurisdiction.

Died while visiting Joseph Johnson (q.v.) at Green Ponds. Buried there, 19 October 1836, aged 63 (?).

RILEY, JAMES [c. 1777–1804]
(Ryley)
Cabinetmaker, aged 25, of Clerkenwell; 5'6", fair complexion.
Tried at Middlesex IV Sessions (Middlesex G.D.) 28 April 1802 for stealing a silk handkerchief (1s 6d) from George Naylor of the *York Herald*, in the Strand near St Clement's Church. Sentence pronounced by the Common Sergeant was transportation for seven years. Gaoled at Newgate and transferred to the *Prudentia* hulk at Woolwich.
Died 16 September 1804, Hobart, aged 26, from catarrh.

RILEY, THOMAS [c. 1774–1839]
(Ryley)
Soldier in the Royal Artillery but stocking weaver by trade, aged 27, from Berwick-upon-Tweed, married with one son.
Tried at Northumberland Summer Assizes (Newcastle G.D.) 1 August 1801 for burglariously entering, together with a fellow private in the Royal Artillery named Ridley Brown, the house of Mr Leslie, baker, near the ferry boat landing at North Shields, Tynemouth, and stealing seven hens and a cock. Sentenced to death. Reprieved by Lord

Chief Justice Alvanley and Justice Sir Alan Chambre and sentenced to transportation for seven years. Gaoled at Morpeth gaol and transferred to the *Prudentia* hulk at Woolwich.

Isabella Riley and their son Thomas accompanied Riley on the voyage. They were berthed in the prison room. She was convicted of a theft while on board ship and received two dozen lashes in punishment.

In 1806 Riley became a public baker. He attended the Hobart musters in 1811, 1818, 1819 and 1823. He received a conditional pardon in January 1813 and an absolute pardon soon afterwards. He, his wife and his son had all received 30-acre land grants at Pitt Water from Gov. Macquarie and a further 40 acres in 1826. They supplied wheat and meat to the Commissariat.

In May 1812, he visited Sydney to appear before the Court of Criminal Jurisdiction as witness in a murder trial but the details have not been traced.

Thomas Riley jun. disappeared from home in 1817. His parents advertised that if he returned home he would be kindly treated and that any person harbouring him would be prosecuted. There appears to be no record of what happened except that James Lord (*q.v.*) and Bernard Walford lost £10 each in security when he failed to appear before the court in February 1818. Riley sen. had some contracts with Lord, including one in which he provided a number of skins to keep as ballast in the *Sinbad* on a voyage between Launceston and Sydney in 1819. This became the subject of a dispute between Lord, who had contracted to fill the ship, and the owner George Barnard. In 1819 Riley provided surety for Charles Connelly when he was granted a licence to run the Bricklayers' Arms.

In 1820 servants of Thomas Riley accused him of lighting fire to the haystacks of John Prestage (*q.v.*) at Pitt Water but he was declared not guilty. One servant, Thomas Welsh, said Riley owed him money and Riley admitted stopping part of his wages because he owed him money.

On 5 April 1824, at St David's, Thomas Riley jun., having returned to the family fold, married Hannah (or Ann) Bryant. She was aged 36 and a convict. They had at least two children as well as one before marriage. Thomas Riley sen. appears to have had at least one other son, George.

Thomas Riley sen. of Forcett, arrived Ocean, was buried 7 January 1839, St George's, aged 66 (?). Ann (Isabella?) Riley was buried 1 June 1838, St George's, aged 63.

Surnames of descendants have included: Bendar; Watson; Wiggins; Williams.

ROBERTS, JAMES [c. 1779–1820]

Button-maker, aged 23, born Birmingham.
Tried at Shropshire Spring Assizes (Shrewsbury G.D.) 20 March 1802 together with William Baker, Thomas Storey (*q.v.*) and Ann Storey, for stealing a quantity of cheese from John Davies of Wellington. Sentenced to death. Reprieved by Baron Thomson and Justice Sir Alan Chambre and sentenced to transportation for life. Gaoled at Shrewsbury and transferred to the hulks at Portsmouth.

His name does not appear on the Hobart muster rolls but he lived in or near Hobart, where he had a number of minor convictions. He was probably the Roberts who escaped and spent five months in the woods in 1806. In 1808 he was acquitted of killing a pig, and between 1816 and 1818 he was convicted on several occasions of neglect of duty and drunkenness. One conviction in 1817 was concerned with his absence from the muster. Roberts escaped from Hobart in January 1818 and arrived in Sydney where he attempted to board the ship *Frederick* in Sydney Cove without a pass. He was returned to gaol in Hobart and kept in irons. The Judge Advocate's Court returned him to trial before the Supreme Court in Sydney.

Must have returned once more to Hobart for punishment as he was still a prisoner in Hobart on 13 September 1820 when he died. His description then was 5'3½", brown hair, grey eyes, his occupation given as brick-maker.

ROBERTS, WILLIAM THOMAS [c. 1786–1860]

Chimney sweep, aged 16, born and lived in Spitalfields, London; 5'3", fair complexion.
Tried at Middlesex II Sessions (Middlesex G.D.) 13 January 1802, together with another chimney sweep known as Billy the Sweep, for breaking a window and entering the ironmongery shop of Thomas Revell and stealing two axes (2s 0d), a saw (2s 0d), five knives (5d), and five forks (5d). Roberts begged Revell to let him be sent to sea. Sentenced by Justice Sir Soulden Laurence to death. Reprieved and sentenced to transportation for life. He had previously been sentenced by Mr Justice Hotham (17 September 1801) to gaol for six weeks and to be publicly whipped. Gaoled at Newgate and transferred to the *Captivity* hulk at Portsmouth.

He attended the Hobart muster in 1811. He received a conditional pardon in 1815 and an absolute pardon in 1819. At that time he was described as a labourer by trade but who had a farm and a family and bore a good character, 5'4½", fair ruddy complexion, dark sandy hair and hazel eyes. He and William Roberts (*q.v.*) (Gloucester 5 August 1801) were called to Sydney in January 1819 because of confusion about their sentences.

Roberts received a 30-acre land grant from Gov. Macquarie at Clarence Plains where in 1819 he grew wheat and other crops and grazed two male cattle and 50 ewes. He employed a government servant and provided both meat and wheat for the Commissariat. By 1820 he was supplying 5 000 lb of meat. He also had a brick dwelling house and a weatherboard house on a farm of 200 acres which he appears to have bought at Green Hills, Pitt Water, over which he had some legal dispute with Bartholomew Reardon. The Lieutenant-Governor's Court ordered that it be sold by public auction in 1824.

In 1826 he petitioned Gov. Arthur for a further land grant, informing him that he had his original 30 acres in cultivation with four working bullocks, a cart, ploughs, farrows and all farming utensils and 400 ewes. William Gellibrand testified to his good character but a note on his memorial suggested 'no additional land at present'. By this time he was able to write.

On 4 May 1818, in Hobart, William Roberts, aged 37, married Martha Hudson, aged 29, free. She had arrived at Port Jackson in the *Experiment* in 1804, tried at the Borough of Leeds S. of P. 23 April 1803 and transported for seven years. She appears to have arrived in Hobart before 1807 and attended the 1811 muster there. She was flogged by order of Lieut. Lord, because of her public pronouncements against Maria Lord whom she had known in Sydney. The Roberts had one son, James, born in 1822 and a daughter, Sarah, born in 1826.

Knopwood recorded that he christened two further children of a 'Mr' Roberts in 1833. He was also paying rent to the Roberts. Martha Roberts was killed on 17 January 1830 when a cart overturned as the family was returning from a church service held by Knopwood at Kangaroo Point. She was buried 20 January, St Matthew's, Clarence Plains. A fortnight later William Roberts ordered a three gallon keg from D.W. Bush.

On 23 February 1852, he married Phebe [sic] Ann Callaghan when he was aged 70, at St Matthew's, Clarence Plains.

Buried 31 August 1860, St Matthew's, aged 79 (?).

ROBERTS, WILLIAM [c. 1786 – ?]

Bricklayer, also named as a shoemaker, aged 16, late of Christchurch, Middlesex, and living at Haysend; 5′1″, fair complexion.
Tried at Middlesex IV Sessions (Middlesex G.D.) 28 April 1802 for highway robbery, assaulting George Gregory jun. and stealing one silver watch (£4) and one steel watch chain (1s 0d). Found guilty of stealing but not violently. Sentence pronounced by the Recorder was transportation for seven years. Gaoled at Newgate and transferred to the *Prudentia* hulk at Woolwich.

During the voyage out he served as a servant on the starboard side of the gun-room.

He was not on any of the muster rolls, and probably left the colony when free about 1809.

ROBERTS, WILLIAM [c. 1779–1867]

Husbandman, aged 22, of Churchtown, Gloucester.
Tried at Gloucestershire Summer Assizes (Gloucester G.D.) 5 August 1801 for breaking and entering the house of Elizabeth Hooke at Arle, Cheltenham, and stealing one deal box, one tin cannister, twelve guineas in gold, two half crowns, 3s 0d, two sixpences and 3s 4d. Sentenced to death. Reprieved by Baron Thomson and Sir Soulden Laurence and sentenced to transportation for life. He had also appeared at the previous sessions, charged with stealing a scythe, scythe handle, a hammer and two rubbers but was found not guilty. Gaoled at the county gaol and transferred to the *Prudentia* hulk at Woolwich.

Roberts attended the Hobart musters in 1811, 1818, 1819 and 1823. He received a conditional pardon in 1813 and an absolute pardon in 1819 when his occupation was given as sawyer. He was then described as aged 34, 5′4″, dark complexion, black hair, dark hazel eyes.

As a sawyer, he was probably the William Roberts who provided Dr Bowden with 8 000 laths at a cost of £6 for additional rooms to his house in 1810 and W. Colquhoun on behalf of Geils with 140 bushels of lime at a cost of £7 for use at Restdown in 1812–13.

He and William Roberts (q.v.) (Middlesex 13 January 1802) were called to Sydney in January 1819 because of

confusion about their sentences. He spent his entire servitude and up until 1825 working for William Nicholls, settler, who farmed at Clarence Plains but had a grazing licence between York Plains and Blackman's River where Roberts was stock keeper. In 1825 Roberts petitioned Gov. Arthur for a land grant. He had accumulated property worth £200 and was recommended as a 'very deserving man brought up in agriculture'. In 1826 when a tenant of 40 acres at Broad Marsh, he received a poor grant of 30 acres near the lower Jordan. He applied for more land in 1828 but for some reason the Land Board then considered him unworthy to be granted more.

Appears to have spent his latter years at Brighton where he died in 1867 at the Sign of the Crown Inn kept by William Sharp. An inquest found he 'died by the visitation of God from natural causes.' The Brighton burial register stated that he was a messenger and small dealer by common warrant, buried 7 January 1867, aged 97 (87 ?).

ROBINSON, HENRY [c. 1780–1845]

(Robertson)
Calico-printer, aged 22. Roman Catholic (?).
Tried at Kent Summer Assizes (Maidstone G.D.) 4 August 1802 together with Dorton and William Robertson for breaking open the dwelling house of Edward Overright in Cliffe and stealing sundry articles of wearing apparel. Sentenced to death. Reprieved by the Lord Chief Baron and Baron Hotham and sentenced to transportation for seven years. Gaoled at Maidstone and transferred to the *Prudentia* hulk at Woolwich.

During the voyage Robinson was given the duties of a sailor.

He attended the Hobart musters in 1811, 1818, 1819 and 1823. He received a 30-acre land grant at New Norfolk in 1818 from Gov. Macquarie. He might have sold this land because he was renting eleven acres at Pitt Water in 1819 where he had ten sown with crops and ran four male cattle and 33 ewes. He employed a government servant. By 1830 John Avery (q.v.), an old *Calcutta* man who had since been convicted, came to him as his assigned servant. (Another Henry Robinson, with whom he may be confused, was a seaman from 1805, engaged in sealing. He became harbour master and pilot at Port Dalrymple in 1810.)

On 27 April 1821, at St David's, Robinson married Ann Earley, aged 23, who was born free on Norfolk I., a natural daughter of Rachel Earley, a First Fleet convict, and Pte Samuel Marsden. His brothers-in-law were Urias Allender (q.v.) who had married Elizabeth Earley, and Charles Clark (q.v.) who had married Catherine Earley. The Robinsons had at least one child, William, who was baptised at St Virgil's on 2 June 1829.

A.W.H. Humphrey charged Robinson, Finch Harrison (q.v.) and John Walsh with breaking into his house at Pitt Water in March 1817 but Robinson was discharged as not guilty.

Died at Pitt Water. Buried 8 February 1845, St George's, a labourer from Carlton, arrived Calcutta, *aged 70 (?). Ann Robinson was buried 30 June 1851, St Matthew's, Clarence Plains, aged 60 (?), a farmer's wife.*

ROGERS, JOHN [c.1783 – after 1823]
?, aged 19.
Tried at Sussex Spring Assizes (Horsham G.D.) 27 March 1802 with Robert Mongford for stealing eleven watches and sundry articles of plates and trinkets from the shop-window of Mr Holman, silversmith at Lewes. Sentenced to death by Baron Hotham. Reprieved and sentenced to transportation for life. Gaoled at Horsham, receiving bread for 79 days, and transferred to the hulks at Langston.

He attended the Hobart musters in 1811, 1818 and 1819. In 1813 he received a conditional pardon and later an absolute pardon. According to the landholders' muster of 1819 he held a grant of 30 acres at Clarence Plains on which he ran 50 male and 100 female sheep and two male cattle. He supplied meat to the Commissariat.

Rogers became a servant to Dr Hopley in the colony. In July 1804 Knopwood reported that he had punished him with 100 lashes. The following March, Rogers and four others took some dogs and were missing in the bush for three months but there is no record of punishment. Rogers spent a fortnight in the bush the following January and received 300 lashes and irons for one year after his return.

When Rogers married Mary Ward, free, in Hobart, on 2 December 1819, his age was 49. In spite of the discrepancy of age he appears to be the *Calcutta* convict rather than the John Rogers who died on 21 December 1815. He had to caution the public against giving credit to his wife Mary in 1820 and refused to be responsible for her debts. John Rogers of the *Calcutta* attended the Port Dalrymple musters of free persons in 1821 and 1823.

After that date his record has not been traced.

RONALDSON, JOHN [c. 1772 – ?]
(Rawlinson)
Distiller, aged 29, of St George's in the East, Middlesex, married; 5'6", fair complexion, brown hair, grey eyes.
Tried at Middlesex VI Sessions (Middlesex G.D.) 1 July 1801 for stealing three gallons of turpentine from his employer, John Shuttleworth, a manufacturer of turpentine in Sun Tavern Fields. Since the charge he discovered Ronaldson had robbed him of half a ton during his three years' employment. He took the oil in bladders and sold it to a man in an oil and colour shop in Shadwell. He earned only 16s 0d a week and said his master allowed him some 'perks'. Having been found guilty on four charges, he was sentenced to transportation for seven years. Ronaldson was married and his mother-in-law, who lived with them as a servant, gave witness on his behalf. Gaoled at Newgate and transferred to the *Prudentia* hulk at Woolwich. His wife did not accompany him.

During the voyage out Ronaldson was employed as a sailor. At Port Phillip he was one who volunteered to accompany William Collins in the six-oared cutter to take despatches to Gov. King at Port Jackson, for which he received commendation and, in 1806, conditional emancipation for his good conduct.

In August 1804 a return of livestock at Hobart showed that he held one sow.

As there appears to be no further record of him after 1806, he probably returned to England; his experience as a sailor would have ensured him a passage home.

ROSE, JOSEPH, alias SADLER, JOHN SADLER ROSE [c. 1772–1804]
Labourer, aged 30. Jew?
Tried at Leicester Spring Assizes (Leicester G.D.) 18 March 1802 for horse-stealing. Sentenced to transportation for life. Gaoled at Leicester and transferred to the hulks at Langston.

Died 2 October 1804, Hobart, aged 36 (?), of scurvy.

ROTCHFORT, JAMES [c. 1790–1833]
(or Joseph, Rochford, Rockfort)
Blacksmith, aged 12, of London; 4', dark complexion.
Tried at Middlesex V Sessions (Middlesex G.D.) 2 June 1802 for stealing a wooden till (1s 0d) and 8s 0d in money from Elizabeth Milton, widow, of Soho, who kept a chandler's shop. Rotchfort had a pick-lock in his pocket. Sentence pronounced by the Common Sergeant was transportation for seven years. Gaoled at Newgate and transferred to the *Prudentia* hulk at Woolwich.

During the voyage he was employed as a messenger boy with irons.

Rotchfort attended the Hobart musters in 1818 and 1823. In 1823 he received a 30-acre land grant in the York district.

He had several convictions in the colony and did not receive a ticket-of-leave until 1823, although he was recommended for a free certificate in 1819. He received 200 lashes in 1808 for losing a wether sheep belonging to William Nicholls, then his master. He appears to have been working for William Anderson in the Queenborough district in 1816 when he charged Bridget Lamb, a convict, with stealing a shirt from him. In 1819 he was a sawyer and described as 5'4½", brown hair, dark grey eyes.

On 25 November 1820 he was committed for trial at the Court of Criminal Jurisdiction in Sydney where he was found guilty of attempting to commit a rape on Sarah Ann Bryan, under twelve. He received a sentence of two months' hard labour at Newcastle.

On his return to V.D.L. Rotchfort settled down as a farmer at Pitt Water. On 1 November 1828, at St Luke's, Richmond, he married Eleanor Phillips of Sorell. They had male twins baptised in May 1831 who both died within five days at Orielton.

Buried 9 March 1833, St George's, Pitt Water, aged 44, described as a farmer of Sorell, arrived Calcutta.

RUSHTON, THOMAS [c. 1746–1822]
Brewer, aged 56, possibly from the pedigreed family of Rushton of Macclesfield, married? Literate.
Tried at Chester Pleas of the Session of Crown Mote 21 April 1802 for forgery of twenty £1 and ten £2 notes found in his possession together with a certain implement and materials at Stockport. Sentenced to transportation for fourteen years. Gaoled at Chester Castle and transferred to the hulks at Langston. A Thomas Rushton, farmer of Macclesfield, married Mary Johnson by special licence on 7 November 1785 at Prestbury. If she were Rushton's wife, she did not accompany him to the colony.

Soon after arrival at Hobart, Collins sent Rushton (mid-March) to Port Jackson to advise on supplies of barley for the brewery at Parramatta. Rushton remained at Port Jackson where he attended the musters in 1811 and 1817. He received a conditional pardon in 1809 and absolute pardon in 1812. He owned a house in Clarence St. which he sold in 1811 and a brewery with a house attached at 12 Hunter St. He also owned a farm near Parramatta.

His petition, undated but before 1806, to Gov. King for restoration to his former situation in life and forgiveness for his former errors apparently impressed King. He received many favours, even before his pardon.

He rented the brewery at Parramatta and had business agreements with John Palmer, the Commissary, and Absolom West, brewer. He had a regular contract to supply yeast and beer to the prisoners' barracks. By 1814 he was contracting for 6 000 bushels of barley at 7s 0d a bushel.

In 1818 he was among the leading merchants who signed a memorial to Gov. Macquarie requesting that articles of British manufacture brought on convict transports should be allowed to land.

He was a generous subscriber to several funds, including the Benevolent Society, the Auxiliary Bible Society, for enclosure of the burial ground at Sydney, and victims of the Hawkesbury floods.

Probably because he had a wife still alive in England, Rushton never married in the colony. But, in spite of his age he became the father of two sons, John and Henry, to two different women, Elizabeth Graham and Harriet Cross, in 1815 and 1821.

Died 21 November 1822, Sydney. Buried at St Phillip's, aged 78 (?).

Among the many items advertised for sale from his estate, which was administered by an Elizabeth Smith, was a chamber organ. In 1824 a Charles Rushton, also of Hunter St., married Mary Ann Wilkinson Talmadge of O'Connell St. He was probably a son or even a grandson who had arrived from England and received a land grant in 1824.

See also ch. 35 for a fuller account of Rushton's career.

SALMON, THOMAS [c. 1780 – ?]
Carpenter, aged 20. Literate.
Tried at Norfolk Summer Assizes (Norwich G.D.) 4 August 1800 for stealing a Bank of England note (£200) from John Adey of Aylsham. Sentenced to transportation for seven years. Gaoled at Norwich and transferred to the hulks at Woolwich.

Salmon became one of Knopwood's faithful servants from the time of arrival at Sullivan Cove. He was among the most successful men to hunt kangaroos and emus. He accompanied Knopwood and Harris on the exploration of Storm Bay, Bruny I. and the Huon. He rescued Dr Hopley when he was lost in the bush. In April 1805 Knopwood noted that he dismissed Salmon from his service but he must have repented soon afterwards, lending him to James Grove (*q.v.*) to cut rafters for his house. Salmon was briefly in trouble for being among those who, in March 1807, were creating a disturbance among the military patrol. Knopwood tried the prisoners and punished all except Salmon who was drunk. The following June, Knopwood again liberated Salmon after a charge that he had cut one of William Collins' men.

By this time he was about to become free by servitude. Knopwood noted that on 2 October 1807 Salmon went on board the *Sarah*, a whaler, which sailed to Sydney. There might have been some trouble there with his papers because a Thomas Salmon appeared before the Court of Criminal Jurisdiction on 30 June 1808 on a charge of absconding on a whaler.

He appears to have been released and probably returned to England.

[This writer and other researchers are not satisfied that he was not the Thomas Salmon of the same age, who described himself as a carpenter and builder, when seeking permission to settle at the Derwent and Port Jackson in 1812-13. This man had arrived in Hobart in a whaler, then returned home to arrange for his brother and family to emigrate. He was in touch with Stocker (*q.v.*) in 1812 and was present at the marriage, in Hobart, of James Waterson, an ex-convict from Norfolk I. The *Calcutta* Thomas Salmon obviously had access to a large amount of money and was no fool. If they were the one person, some statements in the entry (Salmon, Thomas) in the *Australian Dictionary of Biography* will need revision.]

SCHOLER, GEORGE [c. 1782 – after 1813]
(Schuller)
Sailor, aged 20, born in Middlesex.
Tried at Middlesex V Sessions (Middlesex G.D.) 2 June 1802 for stealing a box of coins from Mark Currie, carman, the property of John Clarke, Currie's employer. The box was found in Susannah Wright's disorderly house in Spitalfields. Scholer had taken the money from a cart and was preparing to go to sea the next morning. Sentenced by Justice Sir Nash Grose to transportation for seven years. Gaoled at Newgate and transferred to the *Prudentia* hulk at Woolwich.

During the voyage out Scholer was employed as a sailor.

In November 1804 he was in the crew of the government boat accompanying Harris and Knopwood on a fourteen-day exploration voyage to Storm Bay, the Huon and Bruny I. In April 1807 he was tried by the Bench of Magistrates as a member of the boat crews who had alerted bushrangers that the patrol was aware of their plans to rob the stores.

Apart from an account for two rams he sold for £10 to Lieut.-Col. Geils at Restdown in 1812 and 1813, there appears to be no further record of Scholer.

SCHOLFIELD, JOHN [c. 1775–1807]
(Schofield)
Labourer, aged 27, of Ashton.
Tried at the Spring Assizes of the County Palatinate of Lancaster (Lancaster G.D.) 24 March 1802 for stealing four yards of linen cloth (6s 0d), one crimson cloak (10s 0d), another cloak (10s 0d), three pairs worsted stockings (1s 0d), one pair women's shoes (2s 0d), one pair man's shoes (5s 0d), one flannel waistcoat (2s 0d), and one hat (3s 0d) from the house of William Buckleton of Ashton. Sentenced to death. Reprieved by Lord Kenyon and Justice Sir Giles Rooke and sentenced to transportation for fourteen years. Gaoled at Lancaster Castle and transferred to the hulks at Portsmouth.

Buried 21 January 1807, Hobart, aged 31 (?).

SCOURCE, JOHN [c. 1778–1839]
(Secours, Scours, etc.)
?, aged 24.
Tried at Wiltshire Spring Assizes (Salisbury G.D.) 13 March 1802 for stealing a mare (£10) at Chippenham from John Frankling. Sentenced to death. Reprieved by Justices Sir Soulden Laurence and Sir Simon Le Blanc and sentenced to transportation for life. Gaoled at Salisbury and transferred to the hulks at Langston.

He attended the Hobart musters in 1811, 1818, 1819 and 1823. He received a conditional pardon in 1816 and was free by 1818. Two men were sentenced to six months in a chain gang for committing a robbery on Scource and Capt. William Blyth in 1817. Scource had no land grant. Possibly he worked for Blyth at Humphries River.

He might have been the person named Scores who accompanied George Robinson on his mission to the sealers in 1830, leaving him in January 1831 to join James Parish, the pilot at the Tamar.

Buried 1 June 1839, Trinity Church, Hobart, 'an object of charity'.

SCULLER, JOHN ALEX [?]
(Scullar, Scouller, Schuyler)
Soldier, aged ?, 25th Foot Rgt, stationed at Gibraltar. Probably Dutch.
Tried in secret (?) at an army court martial December 1802 following a mutiny at Gibraltar and sentenced to death. Commuted by H.R.H. the Duke of Kent to transportation for life. Embarked at Gibraltar on the sloop, H.M.S. *Cynthia* on 12 January 1803. Taken aboard the *Calcutta* on 21 April at Portsmouth.

In December 1803 Collins appointed him a subordinate of the night watch at Port Phillip.

Sculler was one of Knopwood's trusted servants by 1806 and in April 1808 he captured the bushranger John Williams alias Rush (*q.v.*).

There is no further record of his activities. He probably returned to Europe.

SHIPMAN, FRANCIS [c. 1782–1813]
Clerk, aged 20, from Yorkshire; 5'10", dark complexion. Literate.
Tried at Middlesex III Sessions (London G.D.) 17 February 1802 for embezzling £1 11s 0d from his employers Francis, Joseph and Jonathan Sills for which he gave a receipt for that amount to George Willett. He had previously been charged and acquitted at previous trials for embezzling warrants for £5 7s 0d and 14s 8d, saying he had forgotten to enter them in the books. Three witnesses gave him a good character. Sentence pronounced by the Recorder was transportation for seven years. Gaoled at Giltspur and transferred to the *Prudentia* hulk at Woolwich.

During the voyage out he was allowed to go without irons.

At Port Phillip, Shipman served as a subordinate of the night watch.

In Hobart, Collins appointed Shipman as a clerk on 18 March 1804. From the beginning he also assisted Surveyor Harris with the measuring of land, including Knopwood's original plot, and two acres of a town grant and a 400-acre grant at Ralph's Plains (Rokeby) in 1807. He had his own

servants to hunt kangaroos after being granted a free pardon in January 1805. At this time he held a rood of land in Collins St. on which he raised one wether, two ewes, three lambs and two hogs.

In 1807 he was discharged from office as storekeeper but continued his survey work as a deputy surveyor of the interior until December 1809.

In 1810 Shipman received permission to visit Sydney before his return to London. He sold his house in Collins St. to James Lord (*q.v.*) who later allowed William Holgrove, his assigned servant, to live in it.

After his arrival in London, he gave his address as care of Mr Thacker at the King's Arms, Poland St. Perhaps to ingratiate himself with the authorities, he made an anonymous charge against Leonard Fosbrook, his former employer, which led to the latter's court martial at Port Jackson for fraudulent conduct in 1813. This disclosed other charges of embezzlement which ultimately led to Fosbrook's dismissal for neglect of duty and examination of John Boothman's (*q.v.*) position. Shipman admitted that he had disclosed the frauds in expectation of a monetary reward and that he was totally destitute.

Shipman himself was tried in London on unknown charges presumably connected with his own allegations and was publicly executed some time in 1813 in London.

SHORE, CHARLES [c. 1773–1815?]
(Shaw)
?, aged 29, of Box.
Tried at Wiltshire Spring Assizes (Salisbury G.D.) 13 March 1802 for burglariously entering a fowl house and stealing six hens (6d) and a cock (12d) from William Lacey, victualler, at Box adjoining his own dwelling-house. Sentenced to transportation for seven years. Gaoled at Salisbury and transferred to the hulks at Langston.

During the voyage out Shore was punished for insolence and double-ironed. While at Port Phillip, he was among the six convicts who escaped over the Christmas period. He was shot and wounded. A cart and men were sent to bring him in and Dr Bowden attended him. Knopwood took a deposition from him before leaving Port Phillip. He was still suffering from the effects of the shot in July 1805, according to Collins.

Shore attended the Hobart muster in 1811. In October 1815 he sailed in Denis McCarty's schooner the *Geordy* with James Carret (*q.v.*). McCarty told Knopwood of the loss of the schooner on the South Cape after a gale during which she parted her cables and he ran her on shore.

It appears likely that Shore drowned at the time, although McCarty himself and Carret, if on board, survived.

SMITH, CHARLES [c. 1781 – after 1816?]
Shoemaker, aged 19, of St Martin's-in-the-Fields; 5'6", dark complexion, black hair, black eyes, loss of sight in left eye.
Tried at Middlesex VI Sessions 17 April 1800 for stealing a cheese from the shop of James Jackson, chandler. Sentence pronounced by the Common Sergeant was transportation for seven years. Gaoled at Newgate and transferred to the hulks at Langston.

Soon after he was free by servitude in 1807 he left for Port Jackson and joined the crews of many ships between

1808 and 1816, including the brigs *Favourite, Daphne, Active, Perseverance,* and *Cyclops.* He sailed in the *Mary and Sally* with James Kelly for Macquarie I. in August 1813. When the *Queen Charlotte* called at the Marquesas in 1816 to acquire pork and sandalwood, he returned with the first pawpaw seeds for the colony.

The last trace of his activities appears to be that he, as Mr Charles Smith, left Sydney in the brig Daphne, *December 1816, en route for the Marquesas and China.*

SMITH, CHRISTOPHER [c. 1783–1803]
?, aged 19.
Tried at Norfolk Summer Assizes (Norwich G.D.) 9 August 1802 for stealing five ewes and six lambs from Ann Youngs of Tilney. While driving them to Wisbeck Market, he sold them to one Juson for £2 2s 0d. Sentenced to death. Reprieved by Lord Chief Justice Alvanley and Justice Sir Nash Grose and sentenced to transportation for life. Gaoled at Norwich and transferred to the hulks at Portsmouth.

Smith died at sea off the South Australian coast on 3 October 1803.

SMITH, EDWARD, alias BIDDLE [c. 1771 – ?]
Labourer, aged 28, of Manchester.
Tried at the Q.S. of the Palatinate of Lancaster (Preston) 4 April 1799 together with Thomas Morley, Samuel and Richard Terry, all of Manchester, for the theft of one Bank of England bill (£20), notes to the value of £5 and £2, and other pieces of paper each valued at one halfpenny, all the property of William Lancaster of Preston. All but Smith acquitted. Smith sentenced to transportation for seven years. Eight persons gave evidence. Gaoled at Preston and transferred to the *Fortune* hulk at Langston.

Edward Smith remained at Port Phillip after the main contingent left for Hobart. The *Ocean* log, 8 May 1804, reported that he was punished with 50 lashes while at Sullivan Bay for contempt of the centinel [*sic*].

There appears to be no further record of his activities after arrival in Hobart. It is probable that he left the colony after he became free by servitude in 1806–07.

[See later career of Samuel Terry, 'the Botany Bay Rothschild' in the *Australian Dictionary of Biography*, vol. II]

SMITH, JOHN, alias HENRY WILLIAMS [c. 1781 – alive 1818]
Labourer, aged 20, of London; 5', fair complexion, light brown hair, dark eyes.
Tried at Middlesex V Sessions (Middlesex G.D.) 20 May 1801 for stealing from his person a silk handkerchief (2s 0d) from a Mr Wall at Charing Cross. Sentenced by Baron Graham to transportation for seven years. Smith had had a previous conviction in the name of Henry Williams in May 1800 and had been sent for two years to the House of Correction. Gaoled at Newgate and transferred to the *Prudentia* hulk at Woolwich.

Smith attended the Hobart muster in 1818. On 22 December 1817, in Hobart, a John Smith, aged 35, free, married Sarah Cann, aged 24, a convict transported in the *Canada.*

His name makes him difficult to trace any further.

SMITH, OLIVER [c. 1759–1852]
Labourer, aged about 40. Literate.
Tried at Norfolk S. of P. (Norwich) on 21 January 1801 for stealing a deal box (2s 0d) and 70 silk and worsted shawls (£10) from Messrs Marsh of St George, Tombland, who were carrying the goods manufactured by Nicholas Mallett of St George, Colegate. Sentenced by Robert Harvey, M.P., mayor, to transportation for seven years. Gaoled at Norwich and transferred to the *Prudentia* hulk at Woolwich.

During the voyage Smith served as a loblolly boy.

He attended the Hobart musters in 1811, 1818, 1819 and 1823. He became an overseer of convicts in February 1808 and by 1812 was designated an overseer of public works at £25 a year. He received a 50-acre land grant from Gov. Macquarie in the Hobart area where in 1819 he employed a government servant. Returns show that he had no grain or stock at that time.

He lived in Collins St. in 1813 and had to relinquish the house valued at £20 in 1817 when the re-arrangement of streets took place.

He married Sarah —, some time before 1818 and became a constable in charge of the market at the end of Davey St. He continued to live in Collins St. where he had an extensive vegetable garden. He was a subscriber to the Bible Society. When Henry Lazarus (*q.v.*) was re-convicted in England and returned to Hobart as Henry Ellis, Smith engaged him as his servant.

He retired in 1826 and for many years afterwards received a pension of £25 a year voted by the Legislative Council and approved by the Crown.

In 1830 and 1834 he received minor fines for leaving his horse and cart unattended in the street in Hobart.

In October 1845 one of the Canadian rebels Elijah Woodman, visited him and found him very feeble but hospitable. Smith supplied the hapless exile with two and sixpence for medicine and later housed several of the exiles awaiting their return to Canada.

Died 21 March 1852, Hobart, aged 90 (?), buried four days later at St David's. His widow died 26 September 1853, aged 83, also buried at St David's where their deaths were commemorated by a memorial stone. They do not appear to have had any children.

SMITH, THOMAS [c. 1774 – after 1831]
Bricklayer, aged 26, pa. St Giles-in-the-Fields, born Leake, Staffordshire; 5'6", dark complexion, dark brown hair, dark eyes.
Tried at Middlesex I Sessions (Middlesex G.D.) 3 December 1800 for stealing from a cart a chest containing 52 lb of tea (£20) belonging to Thomas Bryon and William Brandon, partners of 262 Oxford St. Sentenced by Justice Sir Giles Rooke to transportation for seven years. Gaoled at Tothillfields and transferred to the *Fortune* hulk at Portsmouth.

Smith attended the Hobart musters in 1818 and 1823.

He was still alive in 1831 when, in a memorial to Gov. Arthur, he advised that he had been renting a farm at Glenorchy at £30 a year from Hugh McShean which had been sold by the sheriff to H. Bilton after an order of execution. McShean had insisted on paying Bilton rent to keep faith with Smith but Bilton had taken action against him and the enormous expense was contributing to his total ruin. Smith, who had paid Gellibrand £39 1s 1d and Butler £40, had a wife and five children wholly dependent on his industry, but the government order was that it could not interfere in a private transaction.

He might have been the Thomas Smith who married Esther Gibbons, 28 September 1822, at St David's.

His name makes it difficult to trace any later descendants.

SMITH, THOMAS [c. 1780–1821?]
?, aged 22.
Tried at Warwickshire Spring Assizes (Warwick G.D.) 23 March 1802 for stealing linen out of a bleaching ground. Sentenced to transportation for fourteen years. Gaoled at Warwick Castle and transferred to the hulks at Portsmouth.

Smith attended the Hobart musters in 1811, 1818, 1819 and 1820, but not 1823. He received a grant of 30 acres at Clarence Plains in 1820 and prior to that lived in the Hobart area where in 1819 he owned two male horned cattle.

On 4 September 1817, Thomas Smith, aged 38 (?), free, had married Martha Fagan, aged 25, a convict transported in the *Alexander*. They appear to be the parents of three children at the lower settlement at Pitt Water in 1827, but if so, the two elder ones would have been born before their marriage.

He was possibly the Thomas Smith who died in Hobart and was buried 1 February 1821, aged 37 (?).

SMITH, THOMAS SCOTT [c. 1778–1803]
Rider to a wholesaler, clerical impostor, aged 23, of Southwark; 5'7", dark complexion, brown hair, hazel eyes, thin, and stared 'with an unmeaning eye'. Son of an 'indulgent father', Robert Smith. Literate.
Detained at Bow St. and tried, it appears, at a special court sitting in London 22 October 1801 for forging and uttering an order for payment of £10, purporting to be the order of Robert Smith, his father, on Messrs Smith, Payne and Smith, bankers near the Mansion House, which he had cashed with a Mr Copper of Hungerford Coffee House, the Strand, who believed him to be a curate of St Martin's-in-the-Fields. Sentenced to death by Mr Justice Graham. Reprieved and sentenced to transportation for life. Smith was well educated at Peckham School and his father purchased for him an estate well cultivated and stocked for him on his arrival in New Holland. The English newspapers of the day exposed him as the 'sham parson' who had officiated at St Martin's-in-the-Fields and who claimed to be a nephew of Lord Eldon. He said he had been educated at Queen's College, Cambridge, where he received a B.A. degree. He had ordered a set of canonicals from a mercer's shop in Holywell St., borrowing a set in the meantime. He was gaoled at Tothillfields and transferred to the *Prudentia* hulk at Woolwich.

Smith, however, never left England. While at Spithead, although he had been given every indulgence on board, according to Pateshall, he poisoned himself. Died 13 March 1803, aged 23 (?).

SMITH, WILLIAM [c. 1773 – ?]
Drover, aged 27, of Enfield, Middlesex.
Tried at Middlesex IV Sessions (Middlesex G.D.) 2 April 1800 on three counts of stealing eight silver spoons (6d), four silver dessert spoons (£3), five dozen silver teaspoons (£4), two pairs of silver sugar tongs (15s 0d), five silver chains (30s 0d), three silver watches (£6), one wooden box (1s 0d), three double-bottomed glass bottles (6s 0d), three glass mugs (3s 0d), two pairs of glass bellows (2s 0d), one wooden box (6d), three pieces of printed cotton each 21 yards (£10), two men's hats (10s 0d), four pieces of silk handkerchiefs (30s 0d), from William Mountain, John Wallis, Joseph Butt, Thomas Hennessy, Eusebius Dandy, Richard Miller and Thomas Dancer Markham. Thirteen persons including a coachmaker, silversmiths, watchmaker, linen-draper, glassblower and constables gave evidence against him but he was found guilty on only one count and sentenced to transportation by Justice Sir Giles Rooke for seven years. He was gaoled at Newgate and transferred to the *Prudentia* hulk at Woolwich.

He appears to have been the most likely of the three William Smiths to have joined in the disturbance between the prisoners and the military patrol in March 1807, confined to the guardhouse and given 100 lashes.

He probably left the colony at the expiration of his sentence, c. 1807-08. His name makes it difficult to trace him further.

SMITH, WILLIAM [c. 1777–1846]
Fisherman, aged 24, of Battersea; 5'7", dark complexion, brown hair, hazel eyes.
Tried at Middlesex IV Sessions (Middlesex G.D.) 15 April 1801 together with James Blake (q.v.) and Thomas Davies (q.v.) for stealing a sack (2s 0d) and four bushels of barley (30s 0d) from George Shum and others, taken from a barge in the Thames into their peterboat. Sentenced to transportation for seven years by Mr Justice Heath. Gaoled at Tothillfields and transferred to the *Fortune* hulk at Langston.

Smith attended the Hobart muster in 1811. He might have been the William Smith who, between 1812 and 1814, served as a crewman in the *Mary Ann*, *Governor Macquarie*, *Mary and Sally*, *Earl Spencer* and *Elizabeth and Mary*.

He rented 50 acres of land in the Hobart area and by 1819 was producing several crops and owned four male and four female cattle, twenty male sheep and 40 ewes and had a government servant. He received a 30-acre land grant at Clarence Plains from Gov. Macquarie in 1820. He helped care for Knopwood in 1834, during the latter's illness.

William Smith had married Sarah —, about 1815, which might account for his return to Hobart.

Died 16 September 1846, aged 70. Sarah Smith died 28 October 1826, aged 36, six months after the birth of their second daughter. The Smiths were buried at St David's where the family names are inscribed on a tombstone.

SMITH, WILLIAM [c. 1774 – ?]
?, aged 28.
Tried at Borough of Derby S. of P. (Derby) 18 January 1802, for stealing sugar from William Watson. Sentenced to transportation for seven years. Gaoled at Derby and transferred to the hulks at Portsmouth.

He probably left the colony at the expiration of his sentence, c. 1809. His name makes it difficult to trace him further.

SPENCER, JONATHAN, alias JOHN SMITH [c. 1781–1804]
Butcher, aged 21, of Braunston near Oakham, Rutland.
Tried at Rutland Summer Assizes (Oakham G.D.) 30 July 1802 for stealing 45 sheep and 45 lambs from a Mr Robinson and others at Braunston. Sentenced to death. Reprieved by Mr Justice Heath and Baron Thomson and sentenced to transportation for life. Gaoled at Oakham and transferred to the hulks at Woolwich.

During the voyage out Spencer was employed on deck as a poulterer.

Died 5 March 1804, Risdon Cove, aged 22 (?).

STEEL, WILLIAM, alias STEVENS [c. 1793–1815]
Child's pump maker, aged 9, born London.
Tried at Middlesex V Sessions (Middlesex G.D.) 2 June 1802 for stealing 25 yards of Irish cloth (50s) from linen-drapers Thomas Foster and John Brown of Oxford St. Sentence pronounced by the Recorder was transportation for seven years. Gaoled at Newgate and transferred to the *Prudentia* hulk at Woolwich.

During the voyage out Steel served as a servant to the boatswain and went without irons.

In March 1808 Steel absconded and was outlawed. £10 was offered as a reward for his apprehension.

He did not attend the 1811 muster, but he appears to be the William Stevens, a *Calcutta* convict (according to the St David's burial register) who was a stock keeper to Robert Nash and assisted bushrangers attached to Michael Howe's gang. He exchanged jewellery and other goods which he had stolen from the house of Arnold Fisk at Pitt Water for kangaroo skins. A sitting of the Magistrates' Court in Hobart on 22 May 1815, sentenced Stevens to death but spared his two younger associates. There was also a William Stevens who came in the *Indefatigable* in 1811.

He was executed on 25 May, 'hung in chains', on Hunter's I., aged 26 (?). Knopwood found the affair very upsetting and recalled it twelve months later.

STEWART, ROBERT, alias MICHAEL or ROBERT SEYMOUR [c. 1773 – ?]
(Stuart)
Sailor, claimed to have been in the Royal Navy, aged 28, Scottish; 5'7", dark complexion, dark hair, grey eyes. Literate.
Tried at Middlesex V Sessions (Middlesex G.D.) 20 May 1801 firstly for forging and counterfeiting a bill of exchange with intent to defraud Thomas Boote, grocer, in the course of buying stores for a ship; secondly, uttering and publishing, as true, a bill of exchange with the like intention; and six other similar accounts on various persons. He posed as Michael Seymour, captain of a frigate *Prudentia*. In defence he said Capt. Seymour, an army officer, had endorsed the bills, given them to him and gone to Minorca. Sentenced to death by Mr Justice Graham. Reprieved and sentenced to transportation for life. Gaoled at Newgate and transferred to the *Prudentia* hulk at Woolwich.

At Port Phillip Stewart became an overseer and went fishing with Knopwood and Harris, but soon after his arrival in V.D.L. he was in trouble, making several attempts to escape by boat. In 1806 he was gaoled at Port Jackson and later escaped, being the ring-leader of the pirates who seized the brig *Harrington*.

The last definite news of him was that he was in gaol in Calcutta in 1809.

See ch. 25 for a fuller account of Robert Stewart's career.

STOCKER, WILLIAM THOMAS [c. 1776–1837]
Former lieutenant in the Dragoons, aged 26, of Broadcliff, Devon, married to Ann, daughter of Capt. Pemberton, R.N.; 5'7", dark complexion. Literate.
Tried at Middlesex IV Sessions (Middlesex G.D.) 28 April 1802 together with his wife Ann, aged 29, 5'4", fair complexion of Chester, for having in their possession forged and counterfeited banknotes, each of £5. Stocker sentenced by Baron Thomson to transportation for fourteen years. Ann Pemberton was not convicted. Stocker was gaoled at Newgate and transferred to the *Prudentia* hulk at Woolwich.

Ann Stocker accompanied her husband in the *Calcutta* but died 3 May 1803, on the passage to Tenerife, advanced in pregnancy.

At Port Phillip, Stocker became one of Collins' most trusted men when he became principal of the night watch. He also became friendly with Knopwood, accompanying

IRISH WHISKEY.

Och! Judy dear, a fig for beer,
The pleasure, sure, is greater,
When you are dry, to bung your eye
With quarterns of the "cratur."

him by boat searching for escapees. Knopwood referred to him as 'Mr' Stocker.

Stocker attended the Hobart musters in 1811, 1818 and 1819. He received one of the earliest absolute pardons (date unknown) and was always treated as a free man. He owned, mostly purchased or acquired by his later marriage, an enormous acreage, largely in the Macquarie River and Quamby's Brook areas. By 1819 the 555 acres he had purchased were producing good crops while his stock included four male and five female horses, 65 male cattle, 111 female cattle, 818 male sheep (including four merino rams) and 1 350 ewes. He employed two government servants and a free man. His wife owned eleven male and 32 female cattle, 480 male sheep and 155 ewes. He had a grazing licence also for land on the west side of the Macquarie River and over the years, gained further properties in the Ross-Longford area.

On 27 June 1816, at St David's, Stocker had married Mary, aged 46, widow of the settler Henry Hayes who had sailed in the *Ocean* to join his wife. Mary Hayes had arrived in the *Glatton* as a convict in March 1803, at Port Jackson, with their daughter Martha. The Hayes had both been implicated in the crime for which John Fawkner sen. (*q.v.*) had been sentenced. Although Stocker's name appears on an education return stating that he was educating a daughter at Stone's, the child was more likely to be his step-granddaughter, Mary Whitehead, the child of his good friend Andrew Whitehead (*q.v.*) and his wife née Martha Hayes.

While still Mary Hayes, Mrs Stocker had conducted the Derwent Hotel, Elizabeth St., from about 1808. Under Stocker's management it became the leading hotel until 1838. Stocker did not confine his publican interests to Hobart because he later held the licence for the Man o'Ross which he built on the west bank of the Macquarie River. The first races in the area were held in his paddock nearby. His property was also the site of a serious confrontation with natives in 1819.

Stocker also provided a cartage service between Hobart and the settlements north as well as holding the first postal contract inaugurated by Gov. Davey. He was one of the many victims of robberies by bushrangers, including Michael Howe and Matthew Brady. He opened a butcher's shop in Collins St. with adjoining slaughterhouse to retail some of his surplus meat and became an agent to sell bullocks and other stock on behalf of others. He established a public ferry at Stony Point to cross to Cove Point.

Stocker acted as security for Edward Miller, the settler, as an agent for Andrew Geils during a cattle sale at Sorell Springs in 1822. Although Miller discharged him from liability for losses, charges and expenses regarding the purchase of cattle, Miller was to take Stocker to the Supreme Court in January 1824 demanding that Stocker render a debt of £3 000 which he had borrowed. Justice Francis Forbes directed that Stocker re-pay the debt and costs of £3.

Stocker and his wife joined the Auxiliary Bible Society, subscribed to the New Town Church, the Wesleyan Methodist Chapel for a Sunday School, and were alloted a pew at St David's. He became the administrator of several estates and an original proprietor of the Bank of V.D.L.

Died 20 October 1837, Hobart, aged 63 (?), licensed victualler, and was buried 2 November, St David's. Mary Maria Stocker was buried 14 January 1843, St David's, aged 82. They shared the same tomb with Henry Hayes and Andrew Whitehead.

Surnames of Mary Stocker's descendants have included: A'Beckett; Ballard; Bowen; Bryant; Devine; Garrett; Hayes; Herring; Knight; Lambert; Lyle; Millear; Terry; Whitehead.

See also chs. 28, 32 and 33 for a fuller account of Thomas Stocker's career.

STOKES, THOMAS [?]
Stocking trimmer.
Tried at Nottinghamshire Summer Assizes (Nottingham G.D.) 31 July 1800 for an unknown crime. Sentenced to transportation for seven years. Gaoled at Nottingham and transferred to the hulks at Woolwich.

During the voyage out Stokes acted as a wardroom cook, on deck.

By April 1805 Knopwood had employed him as one of his servants. He was adept at catching large kangaroos and emus, and for two years Knopwood allowed him freedom to go hunting. On one occasion he had to confine Stokes for insolence and reported him to Collins, but he was not punished.

As his name faded from the Knopwood diary and he did not attend the Hobart muster in 1811, it is probable that he left the colony soon after he was free from servitude c. 1807. His experience as a cook could have ensured him a passage home.

STOREY, THOMAS [c. 1782 – after 1824]
(Story)
Whitesmith, aged 20, born Birmingham, married to Ann —.
Tried at Shropshire Spring Assizes (Shrewsbury G.D.) 20 March 1802 together with James Roberts, (*q.v.*) William Baker, and wife Ann Storey (acquitted) for stealing cheese from John Davies of Wellington. Sentenced to death. Reprieved by Baron Thomson and Justice Sir Alan Chambre and sentenced to transportation for life. Gaoled at Shrewsbury and transferred to the hulks at Portsmouth. His wife did not accompany him.

On 24 November 1805 Storey absconded from Hobart and returned five weeks later. He received a punishment of 300 lashes and was put in irons for one year. He escaped again in the winter of 1806 and was absent for five months before surrendering in November. In May 1807 he made a further escape and, with a number of colleagues, was declared a bushranger, armed, and with plenty of dogs. He returned and accepted the Governor's pardon in December 1807 but by March 1808 was declared an outlaw with £10 reward offered for his apprehension.

After what appeared to be a few quieter years, Gov. Sorell sent him to Sydney in the Greyhound *in March 1818, describing him as a crown servant in bad health, certified by Surgeon Edward Luttrell that a change of climate was necessary. He received his ticket-of-leave in 1824.*

STRATEN, SANDER(S) VAN [?– after 1834]
(Saunders, Straghter, Starten, Stratten)
Soldier, aged ?, 25th Foot Rgt stationed at Gibraltar. Dutch.
Tried in secret (?) at an army court martial in January 1803 following the mutiny at Gibraltar and sentenced to death. Commuted by H.R.H. Duke of Kent to transportation for

life. Embarked at Gibraltar on the sloop, H.M.S. *Cynthia* on 12 January 1803. Taken aboard the *Calcutta* on 21 April at Portsmouth.

In December 1803 Collins appointed him a subordinate of the night watch.

In 1805 van Straten erected a kitchen chimney, oven and stove for Knopwood. By 1810 he had established good credit as a customer at Dr Bowden's store. He received a free pardon in 1813 when he was living with an unknown woman at New Norfolk. By 1820 he had a land grant of 34 acres.

He attended the Hobart musters in 1811, 1818 and 1819.

He appears to have married twice. Ann van Straten, aged 50, was buried at St Matthew's, New Norfolk, on 7 August 1834. On 19 November 1834, at St Matthew's, Sander van Straten married Mary Cole, a widow who was literate.

His activities in the colony after 1834 have not been traced.

STRICKLAND, PHILIP [c. 1784 – after 1817]
(Stickland)
Labourer, aged 17, of Corfe Mullen, Dorsetshire; 5'8", brown hair, fair complexion, hazel eyes, wart on ball of right thumb.
Tried at Dorset Spring Assizes (Dorchester G.D.) 12 March 1801 for stealing three pieces of gold coin and other articles from Thomas White of Corfe Mullen. Sentenced by Justice Sir Simon Le Blanc to death. Reprieved and sentenced to transportation for life. Gaoled at Dorchester where employed at hatting. Transferred to the *Captivity* hulk at Portsmouth. Orderly behaviour.

Strickland attended the Sydney musters in 1811 and 1817. He received a conditional pardon in January 1813 and an absolute pardon before 1816 when he received a land grant in the Castlereagh district.

In earlier days in Hobart, Strickland had been a servant to William Collins at a time a robbery occurred. Strickland was implicated and informed on his associates when a free pardon and passage to England were offered. He was then in fear of his life and taken in the *Albion* to Sydney.

Strickland married Maria, née Collitts, the mother of three children and widow of Evan Field, in Sydney. She appears to have had two more children by Strickland. The Windsor government stores ration book shows most of the family were on rations between 1815 and 1817. In 1816 Strickland was a subscriber to the Waterloo fund. Three children were on the census of 1828 but the parents were not.

Ann Miller, alias Strickland, who appears to have been Maria's daughter, had advertised that she was leaving the colony in March 1818. There appears to be no record of Maria's death or of Philip Strickland's.

Surnames of descendants have included: Chisholm.

TAGG, JOHN [c. 1782 – after 1824]
?, aged 19, St Giles, Middlesex; 5'5", dark complexion, brown hair, hazel eyes.
Tried at Middlesex IV Sessions (Middlesex G.D.) 15 April 1801 together with John Williams (*q.v.*) for stealing an umbrella in the shop of Jervis Wells, Venetian blindmaker in Piccadilly. Sentence pronounced by the Common Ser-

geant was transportation for seven years. Gaoled at Newgate and transferred to the *Fortune* hulk at Portsmouth.

He was in Sydney in November 1811, free by servitude, and joined the colonial vessel *Cumberland*, which was engaged in whaling at Macquarie I. He sailed in the *Somersetshire*, for Calcutta in December 1814 and returned to Sydney, whence he sailed in the brig *Campbell Macquarie*, again to Calcutta, on 10 July 1815, with a cargo of coal, spars and whale oil. By March 1818 he had joined the *King George* which traded in the South Sea Islands.

He was again in Sydney in April 1824, advising that he was about to leave the colony.

TARRATT, THOMAS [c. 1789 – after 1824]
(Tarrett)
Lamplighter, aged 12, of Marylebone; 4'1", dark complexion, dark hair, hazel eyes.
Tried at Middlesex IV Sessions (Middlesex G.D.) 15 April 1801 for stealing a gun (£4), fowling piece (30s 0d), pair of pistols (30s 0d), silver tea ladle (2s 0d), silver tea strainer (1s 0d), and a plated milk ladle (1s 0d) from the house of Thomas Moore. Sentenced by Mr Justice Heath to transportation for seven years. Gaoled at Newgate and transferred to the *Prudentia* hulk at Woolwich.

During the voyage out Tarratt was employed as a messenger but remained in irons.

Tarratt did not attend any of the Hobart musters. A return of land grants (1820) shows that a Thomas Terrett [*sic*] had received 80 acres in the Kingborough district.

In earlier days Tarratt was tried before the magistrates for 'gambling on the Lord's Day' in February 1807. Soon afterwards, in May 1807, he absconded to the woods and was outlawed in March 1808 as a desperate character.

He occupied a farm known as Tarratt's farm in 1817 adjoining that of Thomas Peters (*q.v.*) in the Kingborough district. On 1 November 1822 Tarratt petitioned Gov. Sorell, stating that he had never received an allotment and wished to build. He stated that he had arrived in the *Calcutta* as a marine. Surveyor Evans approved his request, which was apparently in his own handwriting but there appears to be no record that he received it. However, a return of juveniles (1824) needing education in the southwest part of Norfolk Plains included a son, aged twelve, of Thomas Tarratt, who could read. There was a Thomas Ferrett who came in the *Calcutta* as a private but the records distinctly showed the name in the petition spelt as Tarratt or Tarrett.

Neither his activities in the colony, nor his marriage, have been traced beyond 1824.

TAYLOR, JAMES [? – after 1817]
Soldier, aged ?, 25th Foot Rgt stationed at Gibraltar, born Worcester; 5'3", fair complexion, sandy hair, hazel eyes, quite attractive.
Tried in secret (?) at an army court martial December 1802 following a mutiny at Gibraltar and sentenced to death. Commuted by H.R.H. Duke of Kent to transportation for life. Embarked at Gibraltar on the sloop, H.M.S. *Cynthia*, on 12 January 1803. Taken aboard the *Calcutta* on 21 April at Portsmouth.

In 1803 Collins appointed him a subordinate of the

night watch. Soon afterwards Knopwood punished him for contempt of the military with 100 lashes. With David Gibson (*q.v.*) and others he seized the *Marcia* at Hobart and was sent to Port Jackson for trial by the Court of Vice-Admiralty in February 1808. The men, condemned to die, were reprieved and pardoned by Major Johnston because they had shown mercy towards the crew.

Taylor remained in Sydney, according to the muster rolls of 1811 and 1817. He appears to have been a constable for a short time in 1811 but was dismissed the following year for 'gross neglect of duty'. He received a conditional emancipation in 1815 when he was described as a carpenter and was free by 1817, described as a labourer.

His activities in the colony have not been traced beyond 1817.

TAYLOR, JAMES [c. 1782 – after 1803 (?)]
Labourer, aged 20, pa. Flixton, Lancashire.
Tried at the Palatinate of Lancaster Summer Assizes (Lancaster G.D.) 28 August 1802 for stealing a gelding (£18) from Allen Beckett at Flixton. Sentenced to death. Reprieved by Lord Ellenborough and Justice Sir Alan Chambre and sentenced to transportation for fourteen years. Gaoled at Lancaster Castle and transferred to the hulks at Langston.

This James Taylor was victualled at Port Phillip for only 35 days. He would have been one of the escapees who did not return.

Collins reported in the General Orders, 28 July 1805, that James Taylor perished at Port Phillip.

THATCHER, JOSHUA [c. 1771–1841]
?, aged 30, pa. Shepperton, Middlesex; 5'6", fair complexion, light hair, grey eyes.
Tried at Middlesex I Sessions (Middlesex G.D.) 2 December 1801 together with James Harfield (*q.v.*) for stealing a pig from Thomas May, publican and shopkeeper. Both said they were much in liquor. May called Thatcher a blackguard and scoundrel, although he had been a friend. Thatcher said: "You may be damned; damn my eyes, if I live to come back, if I don't do you." Sentenced by Mr Justice Grose to transportation for seven years. Gaoled at Newgate and transferred to the *Captivity* hulk at Portsmouth.

Thatcher attended the Hobart musters in 1811, 1818, 1819 and 1823. He received a 34-acre land grant from Gov. Macquarie on which in 1819 he grew wheat and grazed seven male horned cattle, twenty female cattle, 100 male sheep and 300 ewes. He kept two servants and supplied large quantities of meat regularly to the Commissariat. By January 1822 he was district constable as well as pound keeper at New Norfolk. At a date unknown he married Mary —, who died in April 1837, aged 67.

Buried 23 October 1841, New Norfolk, labourer, aged 70.

THOMAS, JOHN [c. 1775–1803]
Butcher, aged 26.
Tried at Surrey Spring Assizes (Kingston G.D.) 25 March 1801 for stealing, together with John Pearzley and William Abbott, a quantity of seed and several stacks and bags from Malcolm and Doughty of Lambeth. Sentenced to transportation for seven years. Gaoled at Kingston and transferred to the hulks at Woolwich.

Died 5 May 1803, at sea near Tenerife, aged 28.

THOMAS, WILLIAM [c. 1779–1830]
Sailor, aged 23, from America; 5'7", dark complexion.
Tried at Middlesex VI Sessions (Middlesex G.D.) 14 July 1802 for stealing 45 lb of sugar (22s 0d) from James Stranach, master of a ship in the Thames. Stranach had engaged him as a lumper in the hold. He had said he was starving and worked well. Thomas said a customs house officer had said he could take a little sugar for his seastock. Sentence pronounced by the Common Sergeant was transportation for seven years. Gaoled at Newgate and transferred to the *Captivity* hulk at Portsmouth.

During the voyage out he served as a sailor. At Port Phillip, he volunteered as a member of the crew accompanying William Collins to Port Jackson with despatches for Gov. King. He was praised for his conduct and in December 1805 received a conditional emancipation for his good behaviour.

By July 1806, William Thomas was free to join the crew of a whaling ship. He sailed out of Sydney in the American whaler *Aurora* owned by the noted Daniel Starbuck of New England. The *Aurora*, during four months in Bass Strait, returned to Sydney with 44 tons of sperm oil and 500 seal skins.

He joined another American ship, the brig *Hannah and Sally*, owned by Henry Kable jun. of Philadelphia. It had brought a huge cargo from America and Canton, and on 26 July 1807 Thomas sailed in it to Canton, together with 19 300 seal skins. He returned to N.S.W. and attended the Sydney muster in 1811; the rolls noted that he arrived in the colony originally in the *Calcutta* and had been a resident of Sydney from September 1808.

By 1818 he had married Mary —, and had a family. Gov. Macquarie notified Sorell that he was sending the family to Hobart as free settlers. They left in the merchant ship *Duke of Wellington*, which arrived in Hobart in February 1818. He became a fisherman.

Died 9 August 1830, Hobart, aged 57 (?), of apoplexy brought on by intoxication. Mary Thomas died 6 May 1823, Hobart, aged 48. Both were buried at St David's.

THOMAS, WILLIAM [c. 1779–1804]
?, aged 22.
Tried at Wiltshire Summer Assizes (Salisbury G.D.) 18 July 1801 for stealing, together with Isaac Box, a cow and calf from John Kempster of Highworth. Sentenced to death. Reprieved by Justice Sir Simon Le Blanc and Baron Graham and sentenced to transportation for life. Gaoled at Salisbury and transferred to the hulks at Langston.

Died 1 January 1804, Port Phillip, aged 24 (?).

THOMPSON, RICHARD [c. 1768–1804]
(Thomson)
?, aged 34. Literate.
Tried at the Summer Assizes of the County Palatinate of Lancaster (Lancaster G.D.) 28 August 1802 for forgery. Sentenced by Justice Sir Giles Rooke to life imprisonment. Gaoled at Lancaster Castle and transferred to the hulks at Langston.

Died 18 January 1804, Port Phillip, aged 35.

TIT(T), THOMAS [c. 1776 – after 1823]
Plasterer, aged 25, of Pancreas, Middlesex. A dwarf of 3', dark complexion, dark brown hair, hazel eyes.
Tried at Middlesex IV Sessions (Middlesex G.D.) 15 April 1801 for burglariously breaking and entering the house of William Summers and stealing a cotton gown (5s 0d), a silk cloak (5s 0d), pair of pockets (6d) and handkerchief (4d) from Ann Dell. Acquitted of burglary but sentenced by Mr Justice Heath to transportation for seven years for stealing. Gaoled at Newgate and transferred to the *Prudentia* hulk at Woolwich.

Little of his life in the colony is known except that he attended the Hobart musters in 1811, 1818, 1819 and 1823 as a free person.
His activities after that date have not been traced.

TOMBS, THOMAS [1776 – after 1837]
(Tooms)
Sailor, aged 26, born Henley-on-Thames. Married to Philippa, one son, Lewis. Literate.
Tried at Berkshire Summer Assizes (Abingdon G.D.) on 26 July 1802 for stopping Elizabeth Macklow and Martha Collins of Broad Hinton, Wiltshire, on the highway in Twyford field in the liberty of Whistley and robbing them of various pieces of silver coin. Sentenced to death. Reprieved by Justices Sir Soulden Laurence and Sir Simon Le Blanc and sentenced to transportation for life. Gaoled at Abingdon and transferred to the hulks at Portsmouth. His family did not accompany him.

During the voyage Tombs performed duties as a sailor.

Tombs attended the Hobart muster in 1811. He received a conditional pardon in 1813 and an absolute pardon in 1816. He was allocated a land grant of 30 acres in the Launceston area in 1826 and was said to have sold it for the proverbial bottle of rum. John Barefoot owned his grant in 1829. There is some sad correspondence from his son Lewis of Great Marlow, County of Bucks, labourer, who believed the father was worth a fortune which he, the son, expected to claim.

Early in his career Tombs deserted the settlement at Hobart and after eight weeks' freedom in the bush appeared before the Bench of Magistrates and received a punishment of 300 lashes for absenting himself from labour and stealing. While engaged again in bushranging activities in 1813 he apprehended M'Cabe and Townshend, assisting in their capture, for which he received his emancipation.

He wrote to his family in England that he intended to return and advertised on several occasions that he was leaving the colony, but chose to stay. He was with Denis McCarty's party in New Norfolk in April 1815 when the search for John Whitehead and bushrangers connected with the robbery and murder of Charles Carlisle took place. The following December he joined Kelly in the *Henrietta Packet* on the voyage of circumnavigation of Tasmania when they discovered Port Davey and Macquarie Harbour.

In 1816 he was winning races as a jockey at Orielton Park. It was said that he had once ridden in England for Lord Barrymore.

For a time he was a sheep shearer in the Campbelltown district. He explored the area between Maloney's Sugar Loaf and the east coast, discovering the lake called after him. For a time he lived at Green Ponds. He had a number of dogs with which he hunted kangaroos in the Kelso district, selling their meat and skins.
He later made his headquarters at Michael Howe's marsh and was last seen in 1837 by J. E. Calder on Table Mountain.

TOMLIN(S), SAMUEL [c. 1782–1819)]
?, aged 20.
Tried at Worcestershire Q.S. (Worcester) 18 January 1802 for stealing lead from the house of F. Williams in Bridge St. Sentenced to transportation for seven years. Gaoled at Worcester and transferred to the hulks at Langston.

In July 1807 Samuel Lightfoot fired at Tomlins and William Russell as they tried to escape, taking dogs, and joining other bushrangers who were absent from Hobart for several weeks. At one stage they broke into the overseer Clark's stockyard. Ultimately Sgt McCauley caught up with Tomlins at New Town. Knopwood pronounced punishment on 13 October 1807 but does not state what it was.

Tomlins, when free by servitude, became a sealer. In 1814 he joined the crew of the *Active* when it visited New Zealand with missionaries hoping to establish friendly intercourse with the natives. He returned to spend the next five years in Bass Strait where he co-habited with Bulra (= POOL.RER.RE.NER), a native woman. Their rendezvous was Hunter I. They had a son, Edward, born at Cape Barren I. in 1813 and baptised by the Revd John Youl at St John's, Launceston on 22 January 1819. Edward later lived with Little Mary (NICK.ER.EM.POW.ER.RER.TER), a native of Ben Lomond. As 'Ned' Tomlins he was an associate of William Dutton in the early days of whaling at Portland and became a famous harpooner.
Samuel Tomlins was drowned together with Chief Officer C. Feen of the brig Jupiter *at Kangaroo I. during a sealing voyage early in 1819.*

Among descendants are Bass Strait Islanders with the surname Tomlins.

TOUCHFIELD, JOHN [c. 1777–1838]
(Tuckfield, Tutchfield)
?, aged 24, living in his own house in Hoxton, London; 5'4", fair complexion, brown hair, grey eyes, blind in left eye.
Tried at Middlesex V Sessions (Middlesex G.D.) 20 May 1801 for stealing 70 lb of lead (12s 0d) from Harris and Martha Rees from a building and affixing it to his own house at Hoxton. Sentenced by Baron Graham to transportation for seven years. Gaoled at Newgate and transferred to the *Captivity* hulk at Portsmouth.

Touchfield attended the Hobart musters in 1818, 1819 and 1823. He received a 30-acre grant from Gov. Macquarie at Elizabeth Town, New Norfolk on which in 1819 he grew wheat and vegetables and grazed eight male and twelve female cattle, 20 rams and 60 ewes. He kept two government servants. He supplied meat to the Commissariat.

On 27 March 1826, Touchfield married Mary Thorp at St Matthew's, New Norfolk.
Died in hospital at New Norfolk. Buried 27 September 1838, St Matthew's, aged 60.

TRAHERNE, THOMAS [c. 1768–1804]
(Treehorn[e], Treherne, etc.)
Carpenter, aged 34.
Tried at Hereford Spring Assizes (Hereford G.D.) 16 March 1802 for trying to escape from Hereford county gaol while under sentence of transportation for life. (There appears to be no record of his previous crime.) Sentenced to death. Reprieved by Baron Thomson and Justice Sir Alan Chambre and sentenced to transportation for life. Gaoled at Hereford and transferred to the hulks at Langston.

Pateshall wrote that the Herefordshire convicts on board the *Calcutta* were among those whom he released from irons.
Died 2 March 1804, Risdon Cove, aged 35.

TRIM(M), WILLIAM, alias DAVIS or DAVIES [c. 1781–1818]
?, aged 21.
Tried at Devonshire Summer Assizes (Exeter G.D.) 9 August 1802 for breaking into the dwelling house of Thomas Langford Brown and stealing a looking glass, four silver spoons and other articles. Sentenced to death. Reprieved by Justice Sir Giles Rooke and Sir Robert Graham and sentenced to transportation for life. Gaoled at Exeter and transferred to the hulks at Langston.

In 1806 Collins employed Trim as a government gamekeeper. He received a free pardon in October 1810.

He must have been absent from the 1811 muster although he remained in the Hobart area and was employed by Mrs Maria Sergeant. In February 1818 he was committed to trial on charges of stealing 200 sheep from Stynes and Troy at the Coal River. He arrived in Sydney in the *Henrietta Packet* to appear before the Court of Criminal Jurisdiction and was found guilty.
Returned to Hobart in the Minerva *for execution, 10 June 1818. Buried in Hobart the following day.*

VASEY, WILLIAM [c. 1781– after 1809]
Sailor, aged 21, of Norwich, staying with an aunt and uncle; 5' 3", dark complexion.
Tried at Middlesex VI Sessions (London G.D.) 14 July 1802 for stealing a pocket-book (2s 0d) from William Newhouse, a worsted weaver, in Leadenhall St. Sentence pronounced by the Recorder was transportation for seven years. Gaoled first at Newgate, transferred to Poultry and later to the *Prudentia* hulk at Woolwich.

In V.D.L. Vasey was one of three prisoners punished with 500 lashes for killing a goat in January 1807. The following June he took to the bush but returned. Knopwood sentenced him to receive 400 lashes.
Appears to be no further record of him in the colony; he probably left about 1809 after he had gained his freedom by servitude. As a sailor, he would have been able to obtain a passage home or elsewhere.

VOSPER, WILLIAM [c. 1767–1803 (?)]
(Veosper[s])
?, aged 35.
Tried at Devonshire Spring Assizes (Exeter G.D.) 22 March 1802 for stealing a feather bed and other articles of bedding from Grace O'Meily of St Thomas. Sentenced to death. Reprieved by Justices Sir Simon Le Blanc and Sir Soulden Laurence and sentenced to transportation for life. Gaoled at Exeter and transferred to the hulks at Langston.
Escaped at Port Phillip 20 November 1803. Later in Hobart, Collins used his case as a warning against absconders, noting that Vosper had perished miserably in the woods.

WADE, JOHN [c. 1776–1829]
Shoemaker, cordwainer, aged 24, of St Saviour's, Southwark. Literate.
Tried at Surrey S. of P. (Newington) 14 January 1800 for stealing one caulk and one firkin of butter from Richard Muggeridge. Sentenced to transportation for seven years. Gaoled at Newington and transferred to the hulks at Woolwich.

Wade attended the Hobart musters in 1811, 1818, 1819 and 1823. He received a 200-acre land grant from Gov. Macquarie at Pitt Water and 300 acres at Breadalbane in the Port Dalrymple district. He sold the latter grant in 1820 and bought 700 acres at Pitt Water, including a 400-acre farm from R. W. Loane for £800. By 1819 he had 65 acres growing wheat, barley on six, peas and beans on four, potatoes on three acres and owned two horses, 80 male and 100 female cattle, 330 male sheep and 620 ewes. He employed eleven government servants and provided large quantities of wheat and meat to the Commissariat.

On arrival in Hobart, Collins appointed him government shoemaker and farmer. As soon as he was free in March 1807 he appears to have visited Port Jackson where he applied to join the crew of the *Governor Bligh*, one of Andrew Thompson's ships, to go on a sealing voyage. He probably worked at Thompson's tannery before the ships sailed for the Straits, but perhaps the life did not appeal to him because he was soon back in Hobart.

On his return he married Catherine Morgan at St David's on 21 February 1808. She was literate and had been born free on Norfolk I., the daughter of two First Fleeters. The Wades had five daughters and three sons. Two sons were to go to New Zealand, one of whom, John, then became a 'Forty-niner' and was well remembered as a pioneer of San Francisco.

From 1810–18 Wade served as chief constable of the county of Buckinghamshire and lived in Argyle St.

In 1816 he charged Assistant Surgeon H. St John Younge with neglect of duty but refused to give witness in Sydney when legal action against Younge was taken. When Lieut. Jeffreys arrived in the *Kangaroo* in Hobart in 1817 to land large quantities of illegal spirits and he was harbouring convicts and the rum-running bankrupt merchant Garnham Blaxcell. Wade boarded the ship, released Capt. Jones whom Jeffreys had ironed and reported back to Gov. Sorell.

He was continually harassed on his grazing lands by bushrangers, including Howe and Geary who threatened his life. Others stole his sheep and other property. He decided to resign from the position of constable and concentrate on his farm and other interests. In 1820 he sold his valuable property and stores in Argyle St. (with its excellent cellar). He moved for a short time to Launceston before settling permanently on his property at Pitt Water, where, among other interests, he operated a boat service to Hobart.

He was a benefactor and committee member of the Auxiliary Bible Society, a keen supporter of and participant in horse-racing, and a proprietor of the newly established Bank of V.D.L. in 1824. He contributed both financially and as a committee member during an appeal for the erection of the Methodist chapel school.

Commissioner Bigge praised him for his 'well cultivated farm and decent habitation' and for his activities which were 'as remarkable for his vigorous pursuit of bushrangers . . . as for the severe losses he sustained from them'.

Buried 6 May 1829, St Matthew's, Pitt Water aged 54 (?). His wife died 5 July 1876, Launceston, after a notable career in which she carried on her husband's agricultural pursuits with considerable success.

There are many well known descendants in Tasmania, New Zealand and the United States, as well as one who married an English baronet. Surnames of descendants have included: Allen; Chittleburgh; Farmer; Lamond; Reddy; Robinson; Watson; Withers.

See ch. 28 for a fuller account of Catherine Wade's career.

WAKEFIELD, DAVID [c. 1777 – after 1823]
Fisherman, aged 25.

Tried at Kent Summer Assizes (Maidstone G.D.) 4 August 1802 for stealing, together with William Wrigglesworth, three bales and one handkerchief containing various articles of slop clothing (£70 and upwards) from John Ledwich from the *Richard and Eliza* lying in the River Medway within the port of Rochester. They had previously been committed for trial for the offence at the Canterbury S. of P. Sentenced to transportation for seven years. Gaoled at Canterbury and transferred to the *Prudentia* hulk at Woolwich.

During the voyage Wakefield acted as mate on deck to the Captain's cook. At Port Phillip he was among those who volunteered to accompany William Collins to Sydney with despatches from Port Phillip, and received a conditional pardon for his good conduct in January 1806.

He attended the Hobart musters in 1811, 1818, 1819 and 1823. He had a 30-acre farm at Geilston which he sold for £50 in 1812 to Lieut. Col. Geils through the agency of James Gordon. A dispute arose and a memorial supported by Gov. Davey caused Macquarie to declare that Wakefield (and William Collins who had also sold an adjoining acreage to Geils) deserved no pity 'as they ought not to have sold or parted with their farms to him or anyone'.

Wakefield continued to farm and provided meat for the Commissariat in 1818-19.

His activities after 1823 have not been traced and it is probable he worked his passage back to England. Several unclaimed letters had continued to arrive for him at the G.P.O.

WALL, RICHARD [c. 1779–1805]
Sailor (?), aged 23, native of Exeter.

Tried at Devonshire Summer Assizes (Exeter G.D.) 9 August 1802, together with Matthias Jewell and William Hockaday, for burglariously entering the house of Richard Honey, armed with bludgeons and their faces blackened, beating and wounding Richard Honey and robbing him of two pistols and a sabre. All were sentenced to death. Wall

was reprieved by Justices Sir Giles Rooke and Sir Robert Graham and sentenced to transportation for life. The others were executed. Wall was gaoled at Exeter Castle and transferred to the hulks at Langston.

During the voyage out he was given the duties of a sailor.

Soon after his arrival in Hobart, Wall must have been allowed considerable liberty. He was probably an experienced sailor because William Collins had engaged him as a crew member of the *Sophia*. He was one of eight men left sealing at Oyster Cove when Aborigines set fire to their camp and robbed them of provisions as well as 2 000 skins. Capt. Demaria, of the *Nancy*, discovered their plight and took them on board.

The ship ran into a hurricane before reaching Jervis Bay and was wrecked 18 April 1805. Wall was the only person to lose his life.

WALSH, ROBERT [c. 1776–1804]
Printer, aged 25, of Wicklow, Ireland, Roman Catholic. A former Irish rebel; 5'10", dark complexion, brown hair, dark hazel eyes. Literate.

Tried at Middlesex I Sessions (Middlesex G.D.) 2 December 1801 for stealing, together with Thomas Blake alias Evans, a satin cloak (5s 0d) and gown (6s 0d) from Robert Thompson at the house kept by Mary Thompson, the Plough, in Rochester Row, Tothill Street. Thompson was a sailor from the *Kent*. Blake said he was a captain and had come to rent the Plough. He returned with Walsh in a coach, saying he was the mate on his ship. Walsh said he had a house at Bristol which he leased for £500 and wanted Mary to take care of it. She refused because she was a married woman with a family. After some drinking, she apparently took Blake upstairs. She denied she had met him by agreement and called him her 'dear husband'. Mrs Blake had come to see Mary while Blake was in gaol and offered her £20 or £30 not to appear in court as she had three children and was with child. Walsh and Blake were both declared guilty. Sentence pronounced by the Common Sergeant was transportation for seven years. Walsh was gaoled at Tothillfields and transferred to the *Captivity* hulk at Portsmouth.

Too ill to be removed from Port Phillip with the first contingent. Died 27 September 1804, Hobart, aged 26 (?), of scurvy.

According to George Rusden, he was a United Irishman who, during his stay at Port Phillip, wrote to political prisoner 'General' Joseph Holt, in Sydney, a former colleague. One of the convicts accompanying William Collins with despatches to Gov. King must have carried the letter, which was found after the rising of March 1804 among Holt's papers.

Walsh claimed that he had been tried for sedition. He named several of the rebels who had been put to death in Ireland and others at Port Jackson to whom he sent greetings: Phill [sic] Cunningham (then about to die at the Castle Hill uprising), Bill Leonard, John Bowen, and all those transported from Clonmell in 1799.

WALTHAM, JAMES [c. 1776–1842]
Sawyer, aged 24, of Boston, Lincolnshire.
Tried at the Borough of Boston S. of P. 21 April 1800

together with John Troughton for stealing 3 lb of cheese (10d) from French Johnson. Sentenced to transportation for seven years. Gaoled at the Lincoln county gaol and transferred to the hulks at Woolwich.

Waltham attended the Hobart musters in 1811, 1818, 1819 and 1823. He received a 50-acre land grant from Gov. Macquarie at Green Ponds some time after 1819 when he was already grazing four male and 20 female cattle.

The Land Commissioners discovered his grant had been wrongly surveyed and had to settle a dispute between him and Philip Pitt in 1826. In 1828 he was compensated with £7 for having his bullocks impressed to convey military baggage to Hobart. One ox died. He was described then as blind, old and poor, depending in great measure on the bullocks for support. He requested further land and produced witnesses declaring he was an honest man and of good character. In 1829 he was given a further 100-acre grant on condition of actual residence. His home was known as Waltham Abbey.

On 6 November 1816, in Hobart, he had married Jane Murray, aged 39. The Walthams had no children but they had a boy of ten, James Every who was orphaned, living with them in October 1827 whom they presumably had adopted.

Buried 9 February 1842, Green Ponds, aged 60 (?). Jane Waltham was buried 29 June 1842, Green Ponds, aged 60.

WARING, ROBERT [c. 1761–1807]
(Waringe, Warring)
Labourer, aged 40, of Chorley, Lancashire.
Tried at the Summer Assizes of the Palatinate of Lancaster (Lancaster G.D.) 15 August 1801 for stealing out of the bleaching croft of John Mellor, of Chorley, 20 yards of calico (20s 0d) and 20 yards of cotton (20s 0d). Sentenced to transportation for fourteen years. Gaoled at Lancaster Castle and transferred to the hulks at Portsmouth.

Waring became a servant to Fosbrook.

According to Knopwood, while out hunting in February 1807, natives forced him into his hut and speared him. He shot at one of the natives and killed him. He managed to reach the first falls. A boat brought him to Hobart but he died from spear wounds, 12 February 1807, aged 44 (?).

WARRINER, GEORGE SAMUEL [c. 1784–1813]
(Wariner)
Clerk, aged 38; 5′5″, dark complexion. Literate.
Tried at Middlesex IV Sessions (Middlesex G.D.) 28 April 1802 for embezzling a banker's draft for £11 1s 6d on account of George Hayes while employed as a clerk to William Bayley and William Blew, perfumers in Cockspur St. Warriner failed to enter the sum in their books. A young girl came to say Warriner was not well enough to attend business. Blew pursued him to Deal, Dover and Folkstone. He was found at Liverpool. Four witnesses gave him a good character. Sentence pronounced by the Common Sergeant was transportation for seven years. Gaoled at Tothillfields and transferred to the *Prudentia* hulk at Woolwich.

During the voyage, Warriner was employed on deck as a schoolmaster and allowed without irons.

He attended the Hobart muster in 1811. Knopwood noted in November 1806 that he had occasion to send for Warriner for his misconduct without elaboration. At all other times he was obviously one of the most favoured convicts. He became Collins' chief clerk, drawing up and witnessing all major documents. He read the proclamation and General Orders from Collins to Bligh in the lumber yard to the convicts. He was appointed superintendent in 1810 at £50 a year, town clerk in August 1812 and postmaster in September 1812. By September 1813 he was superannuated and, according to Macquarie who referred to him as 'Old Warriner', was still equal to the duties of Clerk to both the Naval Officer and Treasurer of the Police Fund which required little writing.

Buried 18 October 1813, Hobart, aged 51 (?).

WATERSON, JOHN, alias WALTERS [c. 1768 – after 1824]
(Waters)
Sailor, aged 34, born Biddiford, Devon.
Tried at Somerset Summer Assizes (Walls G.D.) 21 August 1802, together with John Curtis (*q.v.*), for having stolen one coat, three waistcoats, a silk handkerchief and one pair of worsted stockings after breaking and entering house of Charles Potter at Thurloxton. Sentenced to death. Reprieved by Justice Sir Giles Rooke and Baron Graham and sentenced to transportation for life. Gaoled first at Ilchester then Wilton and transferred to the hulks at Langston.

During the voyage out he served as a sailor.

In 1812 he petitioned for a free pardon but this apparently was not granted. His name did not appear in any of the muster rolls. A description of him c. 1824 shows that he was 5′10″, had grey hair, hazel eyes, feather left eye, seaman. He was then known as Walters and was still classed as a convict who had arrived in the *Calcutta* and *Ocean*.

His activities in the colony have not been traced beyond 1824.

WEBB, RICHARD, alias WILLIAMS [c. 1786 – after 1823]
Labourer (?), aged 15, born Dudley, Staffordshire.
Tried at Staffordshire Summer Assizes (Stafford G.D.) 22 July 1801 for stealing two guineas, two linen shirts, two books, three razors and a paper case from the house of Thomas Davis at Enville. Sentenced to death. Reprieved by Baron Thomson and Justice Sir Soulden Laurence and sentenced to transportation for life. Gaoled at Stafford and transferred to the hulks at Langston. His behaviour was orderly.

His description in 1815 was 5′3″, brown complexion, brown hair, hazel eyes, strong impediment in his speech and scar on his upper lip. His occupation was that of a labourer.

He attended the Hobart muster of free persons in 1818, having received a conditional pardon in 1815 and absolute pardon in 1823.

He appears to have left the colony soon afterwards.

WHEELER, GEORGE [c. 1781 – after 1817]
?, aged 21.
Tried at Berkshire S. of P. (Abingdon) 22 October 1802 for stealing a piece of sackcloth and 20 yards of hemp sacking from Joseph Frogley of Abingdon. Sentenced to transporta-

tion for seven years. Gaoled at Abingdon and transferred to the hulks at Portsmouth.

Wheeler attended the Sydney musters in 1811 and 1817. He had arrived there in February 1810 to bear witness against Thomas Gorman before the Court of Criminal Jurisdiction. Gorman was charged with shooting at and wounding Wheeler, one of his fellow limeburners, and was convicted, but because he was a useful labourer escaped the death sentence. Wheeler appears to have remained in Sydney where, in 1811, he was already described as a landholder.

He has not been traced beyond 1817. There were several persons of the same name, including one who treated blacks badly and was burned to death on Bruny I. (date unknown) according to J. B. Walker.

WHITEHEAD, ANDREW [c. 1769–1832]
Clerk, aged 32, from co. Stirling, Scotland, living in London, de facto wife; 5'10", dark complexion, brown hair, dark eyes. Literate.
Tried Middlesex IV Sessions (Middlesex G.D.) 15 April 1801 for embezzling a bill for £40 received from his masters John and William Hamilton and Thomas Pinkerton. He was a collecting clerk and kept the wharfage book. He did not enter the amount, absconded in February and was apprehended in the American ship *Industry* bound for New York. Sentenced by Justice Lord Kenyon to transportation for fourteen years. Gaoled at Newgate and transferred to the *Prudentia* hulk at Woolwich.

During the voyage he was allowed to go without irons. He was accompanied by Mary, who was known as 'Mrs' Whitehead. She shared the gun room of the *Calcutta* with Mrs Power and Mrs Anchor and for a time was mistress to Fosbrook. At Port Phillip she was one who stood for the son of Sgt Thorne at his baptism. At Port Phillip, Whitehead was appointed as a subordinate of the night watch.

When, after arrival in Hobart, Collins discovered that the Whiteheads were not married, he arranged for her despatch to Sydney in the *Ocean* in August 1804.

Whitehead attended the Hobart musters in 1811, 1818, 1819 and 1823. He received a free pardon in 1807 and was appointed overseer at the Government's Prospect Farm at New Town in October 1807. Collins granted him land there, confirmed in 1813 as 1 105 acres which the government purchased in 1818 for £1 300, with compensation of 600 acres. The premises were needed to complete the track to the New Town rivulet. He received further large grants including 200 acres near Brighton, 2 000 acres on the South Esk River in 1820 and 100 acres on the Ouse River in June 1823. By 1819 he was also grazing on the Blackman's River. On his farm at Herdsman's Cove he was growing vegetable crops, grazed 200 male sheep and 540 ewes, employed five government servants and one free man. His wife owned three male and nineteen female cattle, 40 male sheep and 200 ewes. They supplied large quantities of meat and wheat to the Commissariat.

On 13 June 1811 he had married Martha Hayes, daughter of the *Ocean* settler Henry Hayes and his wife Mary who had been transported in the *Glatton*, arriving at Port Jackson with her daughter in March 1803. Martha had two daughters by Lieut. Bowen who had ensured she was well provided for when he returned to England in 1804. Whitehead provided for them further by transferring some of Martha's stock to their name after marriage. He and Martha had one daughter, Mary; their son died in infancy.

Early in his career in Hobart, Whitehead became a valuable government servant, acting first as overseer, and later superintendent of stock at £50 a year and manager of the Government Farm. Knopwood reported some business involving his ill-conduct to Fosbrook, which is not surprising, but the two had to work together in the interests of producing enough food at a time of near-starvation. He was also named for a time as a constable. He held one of the earliest liquor licences when he was allowed to sell spirits and beer at Herdsman's Cove House.

He was closely associated with Denis McCarty and others at the time of the smuggling of spirits from the *Argo*. His sentence was remitted to house arrest only, which upset Gov. Macquarie, even though the latter had stayed with him in 1811.

For many years the Whiteheads were close friends of Robert Knopwood but relations became strained. Knopwood made few references to the Whiteheads after he himself received a land grant at the Cove. Perhaps they had arguments about some cattle which had strayed. It is more likely that the effects of Bigge's report, in which Bigge was critical of the power in the land exerted by ex-convicts,

GALLERY OF COMICALITIES.
NO. 12. EVENING DIVERSIONS.

Come lads, let's push the bowl about
These are the times for jovial parties;
We'll drink the ruling powers out,
And sing the new ones in, my hearties.

'Tis true I'm getting rather queer,
But now's the time to drink, or never,
A bumper toast I'll volunteer—
For Colonel ARTHUR's new successor.

Down with the old Executives,
The radicals are now victorious,
And while such punch our landlord gives,
We'll every man of us get glorious!

God save the King! upon my soul,
I feel I'm getting rather muzzy;
Betsy! we want another bowl—
Why don't you bring it in you huzzy?

might have created a cooling of the friendship, because
Knopwood chose to move across to Clarence Plains, far
away from his old friends, although he occasionally saw the
daughters.

Whitehead's farms produced spectacular results. The following years saw him at first financially embarrassed and
then adding to his wealth, robbed by Michael Howe's
gang, gaining a pew at St David's, and educating the girls.

*Died 29 November 1832, aged 64 (?). Buried at St David's
in a tomb acquired by his mother-in-law, Mary Stocker, for the
Hayes family. In January 1836 Martha Whitehead married a
20-year-old constable, Bernard Williamson, when she was aged
50. She was buried 17 May 1871, St David's, aged 85.*

Surnames of descendants of Martha Whitehead have included: A'Beckett;
Ballard; Bowen; Bryant; Devine; Garrett; Hayes; Herring; Knight;
Lambert; Lyle; Millear; Terry.

WHITEHEAD, JOHN, alias COUNTRY JACK [c. 1767–
1804]
*Gardener, aged 34, of Beverley, Yorkshire, married to Sarah,
alias Griffiths; 5'6", dark complexion, brown hair, hazel eyes.*
Tried at Middlesex III Sessions (Middlesex G.D.) 18 February 1801, together with Sarah Whitehead, for stealing two
pairs of breeches (30s 0d) from the shop of Judah Moles at
Russell Court and secondly for both stealing one pair of
leather breeches (10s 0d) from the shop of Rowland Allen at
Seven Dials. Both sentenced by Mr Justice Hotham to
transportation for seven years. Whitehead had previously
been transported by the name of 'Country Jack' and had
served out his term. Another conviction in October 1800,
when living in Beverley, Yorkshire, was for stealing two
salt fish from the shop of John Groves. For this he was
publicly whipped and discharged. On each occasion he was
gaoled at Newgate. In May 1801 (December 1802?) he was
transferred to the *Minorca* hulk at Woolwich. His wife was
aged 28, 5'6", dark complexion, blue eyes, from Shrewsbury, who was delivered on board the *Nile*.

At Port Phillip, Whitehead became an overseer during
the loading of stores aboard the *Ocean* prior to departure for
V.D.L.

*Died 20 September 1804, Hobart, aged 38 (?), of scurvy; he
had the job of waterman.*

WILKINSON, JOHN [c. 1767–?]
Shoemaker, aged 33, of Blakesley, Northampton, twice married.
Tried at Northampton Summer Assizes (Northampton
G.D.) 22 July 1800 for stealing from William Shepheard
of Blakesley, a chandler of Broughton, a pocket-book containing two draft stamps (2s 0d) and papers of little or no
value. Sentenced to transportation for seven years. Gaoled
at Northampton and transferred to the hulks at Woolwich.

The Blakesley parish registers show that John was the
son of Jonathan and Martha Wilkinson. He was baptised on
19 May 1767. He married Mary Brown of Woodend, on 14
November 1794. She died and was buried on 13 February
1798. On 14 February 1799 John Wilkinson married
Elizabeth Hall of Blakesley. John and Mary had a daughter
Elizabeth (baptised 19 February 1797). John and Elizabeth
had a daughter Alice (baptised 21 July 1799) and a son
John (baptised 18 March 1804), by which time John sen.

was in Hobart. None of the family appears to have joined
John Wilkinson in the colony.

Wilkinson was for a time a servant to Dr I'Anson. He
must have been given some kind of house, for according to
Knopwood, William (?) Russell broke into it in April
1807.

Knopwood reported in July and August 1807 some
details of a sad occurrence concerning Wilkinson but some
of the diary concerned with the events has been mutilated.
One gathers that Wilkinson was before the Bench of Magistrates for having committed an assault, presumably sexual,
on Sarah Lewis, a child aged five years and three months.
For this he was sentenced to be pilloried for one hour.

*As this episode occurred during the month that he would have
become free from servitude, and there is no further record of him in
the colony, he probably returned to his family in England soon
afterwards.*

WILLIAMS, JOHN [c. 1784–before 1823]
*Cooper, aged 16, born Cork, Ireland, living in pa. St John's,
Westminster; 5'1½", fair complexion, dark hair.*
Tried at Middlesex V Sessions (London G.D.) 28 May 1800
together with John Newman for a burglary at the Glaziers'
Arms, Blackfriars, the house of Robert Williamson, with
intent to steal. Sentence pronounced by the Recorder was
death. Reprieved and sentenced to transportation for life.
Gaoled at Giltspur and transferred to the *Prudentia* hulk at
Woolwich.

During the voyage out Williams was employed as a
cooper on deck.

He attended the Hobart muster in 1819 as an invalid.
He received a conditional pardon in 1818 and a free pardon
in 1821, when he was then described as 5'1½", florid
complexion, black hair and grey eyes.

*He probably died sometime after 1821 and before the 1823
muster.*

WILLIAMS, JOHN, alias JOHNSON [c. 1784–after 1808]
Sailor, aged 18, born in London; 5'5", dark complexion.
Tried at Middlesex VI Sessions (Middlesex G.D.) 14 July
1802 for stealing a coat (3s 0d), breeches (14s 0d), three
waistcoats (8s 0d), jacket (3s 0d), shirt (3s 0d), silk handkerchief (2s 0d), one pair of shoes (3s 0d), one pair of
stockings (1s 0d), a towel (6d), from his employer, Samuel
Payne, a waterman, to whom he had been apprenticed for
about a week. He had been to visit an uncle, returned to
rob, then burglariously broke out of the house. Sentenced
by Justice Sir Giles Rooke to transportation for seven years.
Gaoled at Newgate and transferred to the *Captivity* hulk at
Portsmouth.

During the voyage he was probably the John Williams
allowed to go without irons.

In May 1805 he was among the prisoners who planned to
escape in the new whaleboat to New Zealand but there was
insufficient evidence to convict them. Williams did escape
later when he was among those who seized the *Marcia* in
December 1807 and were sent for trial by the Vice-Admiralty Court in Sydney. Found guilty of piracy and sentenced
to death but Major Johnston reprieved them all on condition of their serving as convicts for life.

His name makes it difficult to trace him further.

WILLIAMS, JOHN, alias RUSH or RUST [c. 1785–?]
Labourer, aged 16, of pa. St Luke, Middlesex; 5'3", dark complexion, brown hair, dark hazel eyes.
Tried at Middlesex IV Sessions (Middlesex G.D.) 15 April 1801 for stealing together with John Tagg (q.v.) an umbrella (6s 0d) from Jervis Wells, venetian blind-maker, at his shop in Piccadilly. Tagg was said to have taken it and given it to Williams. Sentence pronounced by the Common Sergeant was transportation for seven years. Gaoled at Newgate and transferred to the *Prudentia* hulk at Woolwich.

In January 1807 he was one of those suspected of burning Dr Mountgarrett's house to the ground.

The following May he absconded from the settlement and was at large in the woods. By August, Knopwood had named him as a bushranger with arms and plenty of dogs. He was captured by Sgt McCauley at New Town and received punishment. In March 1808 he was outlawed as a desperate character when he escaped once more and £10 was offered for his apprehension. John Sculler (q.v.) captured him on 12 April but there appears no further record of his career.

He might have escaped again and ultimately died in the woods or been sent to Sydney for trial. His name makes it difficult to trace him further.

WILLIAMS, JOHN (CHARLES) [c. 1768–after 1821]
Labourer, aged 34, of pa. St John the Baptist, Chester.
Tried at City of Chester Pleas of the Crown Mote, 9 September 1802, for stealing one Bank of England note (£1), one pocket book (6d) and one pair of scissors (6d) from the pocket of Samuel Daully of Netherpool. Sentenced to transportation for seven years. Gaoled at Chester Castle and transferred to the hulks at Langston.

He attended the Hobart musters in 1811, 1818, 1819 and 1823. He appears to have been the Charles Williams who accompanied William Hovell in the *Governor Macquarie* to the Marquesas in August 1814. He received a 30-acre land grant from Gov. Macquarie at Clarence Plains in 1820. Prior to that he had leased grazing land for 170 male sheep and 300 ewes at Parson's Valley run, New Norfolk. He supplied meat to the Commissariat. He employed Thomas Arnott (q.v.) as stock keeper while he lived in Elizabeth St. where he kept a file-cutting business and was employed by the government.

In earlier times Williams had been one of Knopwood's servants who accompanied him on trips up and down the rivers. In 1806 he appears to have made a brief escape when Knopwood reports that he took him as prisoner but he was to become a good friend of Knopwood in later years and accompanied him on several of his boat journeys. In September 1819 he gave surety for Francis Barnes (q.v.) when he took out a licence for the Hope in Macquarie St.

Williams became a member of the Auxiliary Bible Society. He had been one of the first of the *Calcutta* convicts to marry but the date has not been traced. He had been visiting his farm at New Norfolk with Knopwood and was staying overnight at Andrew Whitehead's when he received the news of his wife Margaret's suicide on 15 November 1819. Knopwood buried Margaret Williams at Sandy Bay. They had a ten-year-old daughter according to the Educa-

tion return in 1821. She could read and wished to attend public school.

His name makes it difficult to trace him further.

WILLIAMS, JOSEPH [c. 1757–1834]
?, aged 45. Literate.
Tried at Berkshire Spring Assizes (Reading G.D.) 3 March 1802 on suspicion of having stolen a sheep from Thomas Pocock of Chievelly. Sentenced to death. Reprieved by Justices Baron Thomson and Sir Alan Chambre and sentenced to transportation for life. Gaoled at Reading and transferred to the hulks at Langston.

Joseph Williams attended the Hobart musters in 1811, 1818, 1819 and 1823. He received an absolute pardon in 1813.

On 24 June 1816, in Hobart, he married Ann Bennett, a convict who had arrived in the *Alexander*. Two months after his marriage his wife left him and he advertised that he would not be responsible for her debts.

He became an assistant to the government printer, Andrew Bent. But he appears to have been implicated in James McCabe's bushranging activities; in 1825 he was sentenced to transportation, presumably to Macquarie Harbour, for seven years.

He was farming at Clarence Plains when he died in 1834. Buried 5 April, St Matthew's by Knopwood, his age given as 81 (?).

WILLIAMS, THOMAS [c. 1769–1854 (?)]
(Wheeler)
Cordwainer, aged 32, of pa. Llanvillo, co. of Brecon, Wales.
Tried at Brecon G.S. 28 March 1801, together with Thomas Price (q.v.) for burglariously stealing from the dwelling house of Thomas Pritchard of Pentwyn, parish of Llanvigan, Brecon, one sheet, one gown, six yards of flannel, eight cheeses, tea, gin and many other goods. Found guilty of stealing but not burglariously. Sentenced to transportation for fourteen years. Gaoled at Brecon and transferred to the hulks at Portsmouth.

Williams attended the Hobart muster in 1811, 1818, 1819 and 1823. He would have been free by servitude in 1815. He received a 60-acre land grant from Gov. Macquarie at the Black Brush in the Strangford district where, in 1819, he grazed 60 horned cattle and two female cattle. By 1826 he had a further 30 acres in the same area, 50 acres producing wheat. There he had built a dwelling house, large barn and other buildings, and had 24 working bullocks, 150 horned cattle, 800 sheep. In a memorial dated 9 January 1826 he asked for a further grant.

While still a convict he had received permission to marry Frances Reardon on 8 April 1808, in Hobart. She had arrived with her family from Norfolk I., her father was Bartholomew Reardon, a First Fleeter, her mother married William Horne (q.v.). The Williams had six sons and four daughters. In 1821 four of the sons attended Darley's evening school and in 1827 a return of children showed eight of the children were still living and that the parents were Protestant and of good character. By this time they were living in Collins St.

Williams died in 1851. Buried at St David's where a headstone recorded that he died 29 May 1854 (1851 in register), arrived Calcutta, *aged 87. Frances Williams was also buried in the same vault 7 September 1857, as well as their son William (1856, aged 35) and grandson Edwin (1853, infant), son James (1862, aged 54), his wife Susannah (1870, aged 55), and a Christina Williams (1843, aged 34) who might have been a daughter-in-law.*

WILLIAMS, THOMAS [c. 1766–1812]
Labourer, aged 36, of pa. St Thomas, Southwark.
Tried at Surrey S. of P. (Newington) 12 January 1802 for stealing two £5 banknotes and other notes from G. Fournier, pa. St Thomas, Southwark. Sentenced to transportation for seven years. Gaoled at Newington and transferred to the hulks at Portsmouth.

Williams attended the Hobart muster in 1811. He was a constable in Hobart but was dismissed in April 1812.
Buried 8 June 1812, Hobart, aged 45 (?).

WILLIAMS, THOMAS [c. 1777–1827]
?, aged 24.
Tried at Hereford Summer Assizes (Hereford G.D.) 30 June 1801 for stealing unknown goods in the house of Herbert Lipputt. Sentenced to transportation for seven years. Gaoled at Hereford and transferred to the hulks at Portsmouth.

Pateshall wrote that the Hereford convicts on board the *Calcutta* were among those he released from irons.

Williams attended the Hobart musters in 1811, 1818, 1819 and 1823. Although he had no land grant in 1819 he was grazing 25 male sheep and 125 ewes in the Hobart area. He was stated to have a wife but there is no definite knowledge of the woman he married. His name makes his career difficult to trace.

Williams worked in earlier days as a stock keeper for Dr Bowen, who paid him 20s 0d a week, at New Norfolk. He was probably the Thomas Williams who gave evidence against Denis McCarty in December 1813. Knopwood mentioned one stock keeper named Williams whose brother was a magistrate at Marlborough in Wiltshire. A Thomas Williams was also employed as a drover at Geilston in 1816.
Died 30 April 1827, Hobart. Buried St David's. A headstone marked his grave. An inscription informs that he 'arrived in the colony in 1804 with His Honor Governor Collins' and that he was aged 48.

WILLIAMS, THOMAS, alias LONG [c. 1786–1853]
Copperplate printer, aged 15, born in Middlesex; 5'2", dark complexion.
Tried at Middlesex IV Sessions (Middlesex G.D.) 2 June 1802, together with John Mills alias Pollard (*q.v.*) and a Thomas Smith, for stealing five planes (5s 0d), a handsaw (1s 0d), a gouge (6d), two chisels (6d) and a turn screw (1d) from John Masters, carpenter, at Tottenham Place. Sentenced by Mr Justice Graham to transportation for seven years. Gaoled at Newgate and transferred to the *Prudentia* hulk at Woolwich.

Williams was servant to Gammon, the *Calcutta* master's mate, and was allowed to go without irons.

He attended the Hobart muster in 1818. In January 1807, Williams (alias Long) received 500 lashes together

with North (*q.v.*) and Vasey (*q.v.*), for killing a goat. He was not on the 1811 muster and seems to have been the Thomas Williams who spent several years as a sealer, shipwrecked when serving in the *Active* in 1809 and stranded for more than four years on Solander's I.
Buried 12 February 1853, Brighton, aged 67 (?), described as Calcutta farmer.

WILLIAMS, WILLIAM [c. 1783–1853]
?, aged 19.
Tried at Middlesex IV Sessions (Middlesex G.D.) 15 April 1801 for stealing 200 lb of lead (40s 0d) from Robert Ladbroke, Robert, Charles and Felix Calvert and William Whitmore from that which was fixed to their house in the Strand. Three witnesses gave him a good character. Sentenced by Mr Justice Heath to transportation for seven years. Probably gaoled at Newgate. Transferred to the hulks at Portsmouth.

During the voyage out he was servant to Surgeon I'Anson.

He attended the Hobart muster in 1819. He had received no land grant by 1819 but had a grazing licence granted at Big Hill in the upper part of and west of the Macquarie district. Here he ran the ten male cattle, 20 female cattle, 300 male and 500 female sheep he had acquired as a landholder. He was supplying meat to the Commissariat.

At this time he was living in Macquarie St. on a valuable allotment which Capt. J. M. Johnson had leased. After the latter's return to England in 1809 Williams married Johnson's mistress, Mildred Harrison alias Rose, whom Johnson had brought from Sydney in 1806. She and Johnson had two children; one was burnt to death. The Williams had four children, one of whom drowned in a ferry accident in 1818. Another was still-born. Mildred died of burns after a long illness following an accident in 1817. In 1817 Williams also lost his servant William Drew (*q.v.*), whom Michael Howe murdered. In June 1823 he received a 60-acre land grant at New Norfolk.

Williams belonged to the Auxiliary Bible Society. He gave donations to the Methodist Chapel for a Sunday School for children. He educated his two surviving children, sending the son to Stone's for private tuition.
Died at New Norfolk on 24 April 1853. Buried 28 April, St Matthew's, aged 76 (?).

WILLIAMS, WILLIAM [c. 1774–after 1823]
Servant, aged 27 from Caernarvon, Wales; sallow complexion, dark hazel eyes.
Tried at Middlesex VI Sessions (Middlesex G.D.) 1 July 1801 for breaking and entering the house of Henry, Lord Mulgrave, and stealing two cloth coats (30s 0d), a great coat (10s 0d), breeches (1s 0d), leather breeches (5s 0d), a waistcoat (1s 0d), four shirts (10s 0d), nine pairs of stockings (9s 0d), from John Doling, groom to Lord Mulgrave. Williams said Doling had worked with him at another place and was visiting him in Hartley Mews where he slept over the stable. Thomason Kendrew, a soldier's wife, said that she had washed for Williams for five or six months. He had asked to leave a trunk with her. Her husband took it to Marlborough St. Sentenced by Justice Sir Giles Rooke to

death. Reprieved and sentenced to transportation for life. Gaoled at Newgate and transferred to the *Prudentia* hulk at Woolwich.

Williams attended the Hobart musters in 1811, 1818, 1819 and 1823. He received a conditional pardon in 1813 and an absolute pardon soon afterwards. He appears to have received no grant but in 1819 grazed seven male and five female cattle, 60 male sheep and 140 ewes at Herdsman's Cove. At that time he was not married.

He might have been the William Williams who advertised he was leaving the colony in February 1825. His name makes it difficult to trace him further.

WILLIS, JOHN [c. 1777–1841]

Women's shoemaker, aged 23, of Marylebone, born Richment, near Woburn, Bedfordshire; 5'9", fair complexion, brown hair, dark eyes. Literate.

Tried at Middlesex I Sessions (Middlesex G.D.) 3 December 1800 for stealing 26 yards of woollen cloth (£11 4s 0d) from dwelling-house of Christopher Talbot, 64 Edgeware Rd, tailor. George Wright, shoemaker, gave evidence against him. Sentenced by Justice Sir Nash Grose to death. Reprieved and sentenced to transportation for life. Gaoled at Newgate and transferred to the *Prudentia* hulk at Woolwich.

During the voyage out Willis was employed as a servant on the larboard side of the gun-room.

In March 1808 Willis was among a number of absconders from the settlement for whom Lieut.-Gov. Collins offered a reward of £10 each for knowledge of their whereabouts.

Willis attended the Hobart musters in 1819 and 1823. He received a conditional pardon in June 1810 and a 40-acre land grant at Pitt Water from Gov. Macquarie on which, by 1819, he was growing wheat and potatoes and raising fifteen male cattle, 25 female cattle, 80 male and 340 female sheep. He employed two government servants.

He was sent to Sydney in 1811 (thereby missing the Hobart muster) on a charge of stealing a ewe (£2), with the use of force and arms, from James Clissold. He was then a labourer, found guilty, sentenced to death. This was obviously reprieved but he might have served two or three years at Newcastle. He had returned to Hobart by December 1816 when he was witness at an inquest on the body of Richard Francis.

He was probably married about this time — perhaps in Sydney as there is no record in Hobart except that he had a wife at the time of the 1819 landholders' muster. She must have died because on 6 August 1821, at St David's, he married Bridget Keep, aged 24, a convict transported in the *Alexander*. They had at least two children, both of whom died in infancy in 1828 and 1829.

An inquest on Bridget Willis at Sorell on 16 July 1834, found that she had died at her home from the effects of drinking. There were no marks of violence. There is other evidence that Willis himself was involved in events concerned with excessive drinking. It is probable that this and his wife's death contributed to his losing his farm and good livelihood.

Buried 29 April 1841, St George's, Sorell, a labouring man.

WISDOM, EDWARD [c. 1782–?]
(Abraham Wisdom)

Sailor (?), aged 19, of Clerkenwell, Middlesex; 5'5", fair complexion, light hair, grey eyes.

Tried at Middlesex S. of P. 31 October 1801 for an unknown petty larceny. Sentenced by Justice Baron Thomson to transportation for seven years. Gaoled at Newgate and transferred to the *Captivity* hulk at Portsmouth.

When in Hobart, Knopwood named Wisdon [*sic*] as one of the men taking the government black cutter *Flinders* and John Blinkworth's boat to try and escape from Sandy Bay on 9 February 1806. His colleagues all survived, some to take part in further escapades.

It is likely that, as a minor offender, and possibly a sailor, he left the colony when he became free by servitude in 1808. Alternatively, it is possible that he changed his name to Edward West and remained in Hobart until a person of that name was buried 27 April 1840, Holy Trinity, aged 62, Calcutta convict.

WOOLLEY, EDWARD, alias WILLIAM BRADFORD [c. 1779 –before 1860]

Shoemaker, aged 23, of West Chester.

Tried at City of Chester Sessions of the Pleasure of the Crown Mote 8 April 1802 for burglariously entering and stealing from the house of Robert Barlow, of Macclesfield, a silver watch, a pair of stockings, 2s 0d in silver, and pieces of copper money. Sentenced to death. Reprieved and sentenced to transportation for seven years. Gaoled at Chester Castle and transferred to the hulks at Langston.

Woolley attended the Cornwall (Launceston) musters in 1818, 1819, 1820, 1821 and 1823. He was to receive a 30-acre land grant at Port Dalrymple in 1820. By 1820 he was providing meat regularly for the Commissariat and was in partnership with George Jubb.

He appears to have left for northern Tasmania soon after he became free in 1809. He made one escape from Hobart in October 1805 when he was absent for several weeks. He received 300 lashes and had to work in irons for one year.

He was probably married to Mary Woolley, a widow, of Young Town near Launceston who was buried 2 June 1860, St John's, Launceston. His own death has not been traced.

WOOLLEY, WILLIAM [c. 1780–1844]

?, aged 22, of pa. St Thomas in the city of New Sarum.

Tried at Wiltshire Spring Assizes (Salisbury G.D.) 13 March 1802 for stealing with force and arms one purse (6d) and seven guineas from John Charles at St Thomas in New Sarum. Sentenced to transportation for seven years. Gaoled at New Sarum and transferred to the hulks at Langston.

Woolley attended the Hobart musters in 1811, 1818, 1819 and 1823. He received a 30-acre land grant from Gov. Macquarie at Green Hills, Pitt Water. By 1819 he was growing wheat and potatoes and grazing 50 male sheep and 150 ewes.

In earlier years in Hobart, Woolley worked as a sawyer. He was employed by Geils at Geilston from whose estate he bought ten old ewes in 1814 and a further 21 sheep during the next three years. Among several payments he received were £47 1s 4d for building a hut at Old Beach and £38 18s 4d for erecting a stockyard and sheepfold at Pitt Water.

On 30 March 1818, in Hobart, William Woolley, aged

37, married Mary Robin, aged 30, a convict transported in the *Canada*. They had two sons, William and George.

The Woolleys were engaged in a court dispute with John Gould who lived with them in 1820. He said Woolley had stolen notes from him. Woolley was placed on a bond of £20. On another occasion, in 1819, Woolley provided surety of £25 for John Brady in a case against him.

Buried 23 September 1844, St George's, Sorell, aged 65 (?), 'after a painful illness of three years', a farmer of Sorell Bottom, Canning, arrived Calcutta.

There are many descendants.

WRIGHT, JAMES [c. 1778–1820]
Labourer, aged 23, born Hampstead, Hertfordshire.
Tried at Middlesex III Sessions (Middlesex G.D.) 18 February 1801 for stealing a pair of drab cloth breeches (12s 0d), swansdown waistcoat (8s 0d) and cloth great coat (21s 0d), from Richard and Lydia Angel. She kept an old clothes shop. Wright tried on the clothes, ran away and she pursued him, caught him by the skirt of the coat and he fell down. A neighbour called "Stop, thief." Wright said he had put down the money for the clothes and a mate had taken the money and ran away with it. He had one witness who gave him a good character. Sentenced by Baron Hotham to transportation for seven years. Gaoled at Newgate and transferred to the *Prudentia* hulk at Woolwich.

Wright attended the Hobart musters in 1811, 1818 and 1819. He had purchased ten acres of land at Pitt Water by 1819 on which he grew wheat and vegetables and grazed 30 ewes.

Knopwood mistakenly reported James instead of Richard Wright as escaping in the *Myrtle* in 1805.

James Wright was unmarried at the time of the landholders' muster of 1819 although there is a Jane Wright and a Mary Wright on the muster roll of that year.

Accidentally killed 4 July 1820 when an inquest disclosed that he had fallen off the pathway into a stone quarry in Bridge St. He was in 'a state of inebriation' and died on the spot. Buried at St David's two days later, aged 46 (?).

APPENDIX A: Shipping personnel

H.M.S. *CALCUTTA* COMPLEMENT WHEN SAILING FROM SPITHEAD, APRIL 1803:

Captain Daniel Woodriff*
James Tuckey, first lieutenant
Richard Donovan, second lieutenant
Nicholas Pateshall, third lieutenant
William Dowers, fourth lieutenant
John Houston, fifth lieutenant
Richard Wright, master {replaced at Cape of Good Hope by ?Purchis}
Edward Bromley, surgeon*
Edward White, purser
Henry Wyatt, boatswain
Ephraim Robinson, gunner
William Langley, purser's steward
Michael McCarty, ship's cook
——— Stone, master's mate
Edward Cunningham, boatswain's mate
Samuel Innis, assistant boatswain
David Evans, gunner's mate
Thomas Patrick, sailmaker
Thomas Stone, quartermaster
N. Course, warrant officer
Midshipmen: Daniel James Woodriff, James Robert Woodriff, Frederick Edward Vernon-Harcourt, William Gammon.

Midshipman Robert Matthews Woodriff, listed on the original muster, did not sail. Knopwood also listed Stone and Gammon as master's mates; Stevens (Henry Stephens), Vicary, Armstrong and Wiseman as midshipmen; and Vernon and Harcourt as two persons. Vernon-Harcourt, who became an admiral, was the grandson of Baron Vernon and the son of a future Archbishop of York.

Fifty-nine Royal Marines attached to the *Calcutta* included Charles Menzies* (first lieutenant), John Murray McCulloch (second lieutenant), and the following sixteen who assisted Collins at Port Phillip, viz. Sergeant Timothy Marshall and Privates Thomas Robinson, John Pegg, George Winsley, Thomas Hodgeman, William Heydon, William Hutton, James Smith, James Buzant, William Evert, George Wagstaff, James Russell, John Collier, Denis Dunn, Thomas Eaves and William Whiley.

About 150 seamen included John Jackson, Thomas Gilligan, Christopher Stanhope, James Carman, John Smith, George Calgar, Sol. Thomas, John Owen, Charles Templeton, John Blacklow, Francis Burgis, James Bryant, Samuel Hinds, John Greaves. Four who deserted at Cape Town were Richard Southey, John Brown, James Henley and Stephen Tolburn. (Carman died during the voyage out.)

OCEAN MUSTER, APRIL 1803, LONDON:

Captain John Mertho, commander
Mr David Souter, chief mate
Mr John Walker, second mate
Mr William Irwin, third mate
Mr Jno. Serverne, surgeon
Richard Dodd, gunner
John Melvill, carpenter
John Thomas, cook
Thomas Molony, ship's steward
Seamen: John Webber, John (?Robert) Mason, James Giles, Joseph Silvester, John Osborne, John Hysom, Thomas Naystrum (?Noestrum).

There is evidence that the following were also members of the crew during the *Ocean*'s stay in Australian waters:
John Williams, Anthony Cable and William Fisher, who drowned at Port Phillip; Richard Nelson (boatswain), Michael Mansfield (who became a pilot in Hobart), Richard Lucas, Charles Lewis, Charles Morris, John Camp, Joseph Bento, Emmanuel Joseph, —— Davis, Joseph Sawfield, Joseph Truckston, William Tulloch, Abraham Moseley, —— Gibbs, Michael Patterson, Richard David.

*Indicates those whose biographies appear in *Australian Dictionary of Biography*, vols I and II.

APPENDIX B: Marine personnel

ROYAL MARINES WHO SAILED IN H.M.S. *CALCUTTA*, AND
THEIR FAMILIES:
Lieutenant Colonel David Collins (see also under Civil
Officers).

Captain Lieutenant William Sladden and his wife Susannah
— returned to England in 1806 soon after he became
a captain.

Lieutenants James Michael Johnson and Edward Lord —
Johnson returned to England in 1807; Lord married Maria
Riseley and became a wealthy landowner and trader. He
died London, 1859.*

Sergeants Robert Allomes, James McCauley, Richard Sergeant and Samuel Thorne, with wives Mary McCauley,
Maria Sergeant and Ann Thorne. Richard Sergeant was
demoted to private at Port Phillip and his wife (she died in
1855 aged 72) became the de facto wife of Dr Bowden. The
Thorne's son William was the first child born at Port
Phillip. Allomes was later demoted to private. All these
families remained in Van Diemen's Land and had moderate
success, mostly in farming.

Corporals John Bellingham, Thomas Cole, William Davis
and William Gangell. The last replaced Richard Sergeant
as a sergeant and married Ann, the widow of John Skelthorn, Hobart, March 1804; they remained in the colony.
Bellingham was later demoted to private and returned to
England in 1812. Davis became a sergeant and also remained in the colony.

Drummers John Brown and William Hughes — returned
to England in 1812 together with the latter's wife Mary.

Privates Robert Andrews, William Bean, John Blacklow,
Richard Bowden, Richard Buckingham, Patrick Carroll,
William Catford, William Clesshold, George Curley or
Kearley, John Downs, Robert Evans, Thomas Ferratt,
Hugh Germain, Thomas Green, Thomas Hodgeman
(?Hoge), William Johnson, John Keeling, Thomas
Pennington, William Perry, John Price, Price Pritchard,
James Ray, Richard Rowell, George Smith, James
Spooner, Job Stokes, Samuel Sudrick, John Taylor, John
Topley, Richard Walton, Edward Westwood, John Whalley,
Samuel Wiggins, Joseph Woolley and Allan Young —.

Susannah Wiggins (née Welch) arrived at Port Phillip
with her husband and children, Ann (who died there aged
three) and Thomas (born at sea in July 1803). Hodgeman
(?Hoge) also died at Port Phillip. Sarah Spooner and
Elizabeth Bean also arrived with their husbands. Bean
became a corporal in 1805 and was a sergeant by 1812
when the family returned to England. Mary (née Cook), the
wife of George Curley, gave birth to a son in Hobart in July
1804; he lived for one day. Another baby died the following year. Richard Sergeant returned to England in 1812 as
a corporal. His wife remained with Dr Bowden. Other
privates who returned to England in 1812 were Andrews,
Bellingham, Catford, Green, Johnson, Rowell (who had
been servant to Edward Lord), Spooner, Walton and Woolley.

Stokes was executed in Hobart in July 1810. Other
deaths traced of marines and their wives include Patrick
Carroll, Thomas Cole and Samuel Wiggins (1811), John
Blacklow (1812), Ann Gangell (1816), Ann (Susannah)
Thorne (1820), and Hugh Germain (1857) and his wife
Mary (1860).

The following, because of their good character, were among
those who remained in Van Diemen's Land and received
land grants: Allomes, Clesshold (?Clysold), Davis, Downs,
Evans, Gangell, Germain, Keeling, McCauley, Pennington, Pritchard, Sudrick, Taylor, Thorne, Topley, Westwood, Whalley and Young. There are many descendants
among those who married and had families.

*A biography of Edward Lord appears in *Australian Dictionary of
Biography*, vol. 2.

APPENDIX C: Civil officers and their families

DAVID COLLINS*

Lieutenant-Governor. Married to Maria Stuart Proctor, who remained in England. Their only child died in infancy. His de facto wives were 1) Ann Yeates at Port Jackson, by whom he had two children, Mariamne Laetitia and George; 2) Hannah Power at Port Phillip and Hobart Town, wife of convict Matthew Power; and 3) Margaret Eddington, by whom he had two children, John and Eliza, both baptised, Hobart, January 1810.

THE REVEREND ROBERT KNOPWOOD*

Chaplain, who lived at Cottage Green and later at Clarence Plains, where he died, 18 September 1838.

WILLIAM I'ANSON

Surgeon, had a land grant on the Derwent. Died, Hobart, November 1811.

MATTHEW BOWDEN*

First Assistant Surgeon. His de facto wife was Maria Sergeant (née Stanfield); their eldest child was born, June 1805. Bowden became a storekeeper and farmed near Humphrey's rivulet. Died, Hobart, October 1814.

WILLIAM HOPLEY*

Second Assistant Surgeon. Married to Judith Hobbs in England, who arrived with daughter Julia; other children born in Hobart. Died, Hobart, August 1815.

LEONARD FOSBROOK*

Deputy Commissary. His de facto wife was Frances (Fanny) Anchor, wife of convict Daniel Anchor. He had land at Humphrey's rivulet and at Sullivan Cove. He returned with Fanny to England in 1814.

GEORGE PRIDEAUX HARRIS*

Deputy Surveyor. Married Ann Jane Hobbs, Hobart, July 1804. He had land at Sandy Bay, and died in Hobart in October 1810. His widow married George Gunning, a lieutenant in the 73rd Regiment.

A. W. H. (ADOLARIUS) HUMPHREY*

Mineralogist. Married Harriet Sutton, free, from Port Jackson in 1812. He became chief magistrate, a member of the first Legislative Council and a very successful farmer Died, June 1829.

THOMAS CLARK*

Superintendent and storekeeper at the government farm at New Town. He had a farm on the Derwent and later at Campania. Died, December 1828, unmarried.

WILLIAM PATTERSON

Superintendent, with a wife and two children, Frederick and Janet who married convict, Samuel Gunn.

JOHN INGLE*

Overseer of convicts. Married to Rebecca Hobbs in Hobart in July 1804. Their daughter Elizabeth had been born at Port Phillip in April 1804. He became a successful merchant and shipowner and in 1818 the family returned to England, where he died in 1872.

WILLIAM PARISH

Overseer of convicts. He had land on the west side of the Derwent.

*Indicates those whose biographies appear in *Australian Dictionary of Biography*, vols I and II.

APPENDIX D: Settlers and their families who left England aboard the *Ocean*

JOHN BLINKWORTH
Former convict at Port Jackson. Returned to rejoin his de facto wife Elizabeth Cummings. They married in Hobart in March 1804; had one son, then aged nine. The father became a superintendent and successful farmer at Stainsforth Cove. When his wife died he married Vienna Eades in July 1815.

WILLIAM CAW
Missionary and ex-ship's carpenter, went on to Port Jackson from Port Phillip.

SOPHIA CHILVERS
Niece of Elizabeth Cockerill. Married Michael Mansfield, an *Ocean* seaman, February 1805, Hobart; he then became the harbour pilot.

WILLIAM COCKERILL
Whitesmith, with his wife Elizabeth and their children William, Arabella and Ann. He became a successful farmer at Stainsforth Cove.

WILLIAM COLLINS*
Seaman, late Master in the Royal Navy. Married Charity Hobbs in 1808 and became a shipowner and trader.

WILLIAM PASCOE CROOK*
Missionary, and his wife Mary; they went on to Port Jackson from Port Phillip. Died, Melbourne, June 1846.

JOHN DACRES
Gardener. Married Annabella [*sic*] Cockerill, January 1811 and farmed at Stainsforth Cove. Died, May 1836.

ANTHONY FLETCHER
Stonemason, and his wife Sarah (?). Two children, one child died at Tenerife and one at Port Phillip heads. They went to Port Jackson but later settled in Hobart.

JOHN JOACHIM GRAVIE
Cutler and armourer, employed by John Hartley. Later went to Port Jackson.

EDWARD FORD HAMILTON
Son of Sir Charles Hamilton Bart. Arrived in the care of John Hartley and later joined a whaler.

JOHN HARTLEY
Seaman, with his wife Hezekiah and son Joseph. They went to Port Jackson in August 1804, later returned to England, then emigrated to Port Jackson, August 1809. The family again returned to England in 1814.

HENRY HAYES
Carpenter, to rejoin his convict wife Mary and their daughter Martha at Port Jackson. The family settled as farmers at Stainsforth Cove. Died, Hobart, May 1813.

THOMAS HAYES
Millwright, his wife Elizabeth and children Thomas, William and Henrietta; went on to Port Jackson but later settled and farmed at Stainsforth Cove and Bagdad.

JANE HOBBS
American-born widow of Lieutenant William Hobbs, R.N., with son James* (who became an explorer and wharfinger) and daughters Judith (see under Hopley), Rebecca (who married John Ingle, July 1804), Ann Jane (who married G. P. Harris, July 1804) and Charity (who married William Collins, October 1808). Jane Hobbs lived in Hobart and died, February 1813.

THOMAS ISSELL
Miller, who farmed at Stainsforth Cove.

SAMUEL LIGHTFOOT
Former convict at Port Jackson, and his wife. He became a hospital assistant. His wife might have died on the voyage out.

THOMAS FIGGETT LITTLEFIELD
Servant to Robert Littlejohn. Married Ann Elizabeth Cockerill, January 1807, farmed at Stainsforth Cove.

ROBERT LITTLEJOHN*
Limner, school teacher and naturalist. He farmed at Miller's Bay. Died October 1818.

EDWARD MILLER
Cordwainer, with his wife Elizabeth and daughter Jane. He farmed near Humphrey's rivulet and Macquarie River. He acted as agent for Andrew Geils, and later W. T. Stocker employed him as his butcher in Hobart.

ROBERT MILLER
Shipwright, went on to Port Jackson from Port Phillip.

JOSEPH MOULDING
Servant to the Hartleys.

EDWARD NEWMAN
Carpenter, transferred to the *Calcutta* as ship's carpenter.

WILLIAM NICHOLLS
Carpenter, with his wife Frances and children John, William and Maria (who married the convict John Pearsall). He farmed at both Clarence Plains and York Plains.

RICHARD PITT*
Painter, with children Francis, Philip and Salome; his wife and one child remained in England. Successful farmer at Stainsforth Cove and later at Clarence Plains. He was also Chief Constable. Died in May 1826.

THOMAS PRESTON
Pocketbook maker, farmed at Stainsforth Cove. Died July 1818.

JOHN CAREYS SKELTHORN
Cutler, with wife Ann and daughter Mary. Died, Port Phillip, October 1803; Ann married Corporal William Gangell in Hobart in March 1804.

*Indicates those whose biographies appear in *Australian Dictionary of Biography*, vols I and II.

APPENDIX E: Deaths prior to removal from Port Phillip, 20 May 1804

BEFORE LEAVING ENGLAND:
Thomas Scott Smith, at Spithead, 13 March 1803.

BURIED AT SEA:
Ann Stocker, wife of convict, on passage to Tenerife, 4 May (aged 29).
John Thomas, on passage to Tenerife, 5 May.
Stephen Byrne, on passage to Tenerife, 7 May.
Samuel Fellowes, on passage to Tenerife, 17 May.
Mark Denham, at Tenerife, 20 May.
John Henry Cashman, drowned himself, Cape of Good Hope, 19 August.
Jeremiah David, Southern Indian Ocean, 15 September.
Christopher Smith, Southern Ocean, 3 October.

BURIALS AT PORT PHILLIP, 1803–04:
Thomas Dawkins, 1 November.
John Everitt, 15 November.
Michael McCarty, cook on the *Calcutta*, buried on shore, 15 November.
Thomas Price, 17 November.
John Price, 25 November.
Timothy Hurley (register states Thomas), 10 December.
James Aylmer (Elmore), 18 December.
William Thomas, 1 January 1804.
John Heels, 3 January.
Richard Thompson, 18 January.
Richard Leonard, 22 January.
Ann Wiggins, daughter of Pte Samuel Wiggins and Susannah (née Welch), 23 January (aged 3).
Thomas Page, 27 January.
John Jones, 17 February.
John Jory, 21 February.
Thomas Hoy, private of marines, 7 March.
William Best, 18 March.
Richard Godwin, 19 March.

DEATHS DURING THE *OCEAN* VOYAGE, 1803–04:
John Careys Skelthorn, settler, 10 October, (aged 33).
Two babies of Anthony Fletcher and wife: one baby died at Tenerife and daughter, born 5 July, died Port Phillip heads 8 October.

DEATHS OF *OCEAN* SEAMEN:
Anthony Cable, William Fisher, John Williams drowned near Swan I., Port Phillip, 15 January 1804.

ESCAPEES FROM PORT PHILLIP PRESUMED TO HAVE DIED THERE:
James Taylor, escaped 20 November.
William Brown, 20 November.
William Vosper, 20 November.
George Lee, 12 December.
George Pye, 27 December.
Thomas Pritchard, 27 December.
At least one person drowned off the rocks on the Ocean Beach at Port Phillip. According to Humphrey, after the first contingent sailed to the Derwent, a prisoner lost his life there.

Today the Collins Settlement Historic Site at Sullivan Bay near Sorrento, administered by the National Parks Service, commemorates this first European settlement in Victoria.

In 1864 John Gunn, grandson of *Calcutta* convict Samuel Gunn and his wife, née Janet Patterson, visited the settlement. He painted a small watercolour of the graves (see p. 100), five marked with their crosses, and inscribed the work 'Painting of Pioneer Graves at Sorrento, 1864. To Jane Gunn from her loving brother John'. This would appear to be, apart from oral history, the most reasonable explanation that the graves date back to the 1803–04 settlement rather than that they are the final resting-place of early limeburners. The watercolour is in the Queen Victoria Museum and Art Gallery in Launceston. As well as the five graves marked by headstones it depicts some twenty mounds which appear to be the graves of others who died during the early settlement. The numbers tally with those known to have died there. The more prominent headstone might well be that of the marine, Thomas Hoy. Of course limeburners might well have been buried there also.

Four graves still exist, believed to contain the remains of four of the five said to have died after Collins left for V.D.L. The fifth grave, remembered by elderly inhabitants of the area, is apparently beneath the existing house. An earlier burial ground was undoubtedly close to the Heads and became the cemetery at the Quarantine Station but erosion long ago caused the disappearance of the first graves. Among these were the baby Fletcher, John Skelthorn and probably Michael McCarty.

ACKNOWLEDGEMENTS

*T*O CHRONICLE THE history of many individuals is only possible when original records survive and when a historian has the opportunity to study them, as I have done in detail, although intermittently, by drawing on all my reserves of patience over a period of thirty-five years, and to view them with the perspective, if not the tyranny, of distance.

Long before some of the material had become more readily accessible on card indexes, microfilm, and other technological devices, I haunted British and American, as well as Australian and Pacific repositories. Unravelling rolls of yellowed and dusty vellum recording the depositions, indictments, trials, gaol and hulk reports of the *Calcutta* convicts tried in the Assize courts, took many long hours in the old Public Record Office in London.

Fortunate to have lived in New England during a year's study at Harvard University (1951–52), and later working in the Library of Congress in Washington D.C. (1968–69), I was able to extend my study beyond Australian shores. I have browsed through whalers' logs in the burgeoning museums of New England in the hope of discovering some escapees from custody in an Australian colony. I have also worked in dark and dank conditions in freezing church crypts, and stewed in over-heated archives throughout Australia. I have also travelled widely to meet or correspond with many descendants to try to portray the history of these 308 men in my life. Their stories had been there in scattered records awaiting discovery by someone interested in the history of penology.

I recall the many discussions in the late nineteen-forties and fifties when the late Sir John Barry, Justice of the Supreme Court of Victoria, the young Norval Morris, now Professor of Law and Criminology at the University of Chicago, and my husband were among those who gathered for hours on end to talk on penal reform. Sir John, who was writing his own historical biographies on John Price and Alexander Maconochie, guided me to basic texts and discussed problems arising from unexpected judgments, particularly in Peace and Quarter Sessions.

I have since revisited the United Kingdom and Eire on several occasions to continue research into the crimes of the *Calcutta* convicts and must acknowledge the help of many persons and institutions as follows:

The officers of the Public Record Office in Chancery Lane and later at Kew.

Archivists at the County Records Offices at Bedford, Berkshire, Carmarthen, Cheshire, Cornwall, Derbyshire, Devonshire, Dorset, Essex, Hereford, Gloucester, Greater London Record Office (for Middlesex), Kent, Lancashire, Leicester, Middlesex (the Guildhall), Northamptonshire, Norfolk, Northumberland, Nottingham, Somerset, Shropshire, Staffordshire, Surrey, Sussex (East), Sussex (West), Warwick, Westmoreland, Wiltshire and Worcestershire.

Archivists at the City Records offices at Bristol, Chester, Norwich, Newcastle-upon-Tyne, Worcester and Wakefield.

Librarians at the City or Borough Records offices at Bath, Birmingham, Boston, Bradford, Brighton, Cambridge, Derby, Exeter, Lincoln, Reading, Shrewsbury, York, and the Central Library, Maidstone, the Central Public Library, Northampton, the County Library, Oakham, and the Taunton Public Library.

Librarians and archivists at the British Library, Cambridge University, Canterbury Cathedral, Genealogical Society (London), India Office, National Maritime Museum (Greenwich), Royal Commonwealth Society, West Register House (Edinburgh) and Wiltshire Archaeological Society.

The Director of the National Library of Ireland; the Keeper of Manuscripts and Records, Aberystwyth; the Keeper of the Public Record Office of Ireland; the Registrar-General, New Register House, Edinburgh; the Office of the Chief Herald of Ireland, Dublin Castle; the Librarian of Trinity College, Dublin; the Editors of the *Chester Courant, Chester Observer* and *Shrewsbury Chronicle*.

Among individuals who were particularly helpful were Joan Sinar (Derby), Hilda Stowell (Hampshire), Meryl Jancey and A. M. Wherry (who first led me to the Pateshall Diary) (Hereford), R. Sharpe France (Kent), Judy Egerton (London), Mary Hill (Shropshire), F. J. T. Tyzack (Lancashire), G. M. Jones (Cardiganshire), Elizabeth Berry (Norwich), Morpeth Verco (Dorset), E. Cave (Cambridge), who alerted me to the unusual publication on the trial of Richard Kidman, and Gerald Slevin (Dublin Castle), who guided me to several repositories in Eire, unfortunately with little to show for the effort involved.

Apart from studies of log-books at the Peabody Museum

and Essex Institute, both in Salem, I read copies of others held in the Library of Congress, Washington, D.C., where the Librarian of Congress, Dr L. Quincy Mumford, allocated me a carrel in which I was able to work for several months. During this time (1968–69) I wrote much of the present study, and acknowledge the help and support of many of the Library staff, who arranged for material from England and Australia to be accessible. Dr Stephen McCarthy, Executive Director of the Association of Research Libraries, and Louis E. Martin, his Associate Executive Director, were also supportive. Likewise, I thank Dr Andrew Osborn, former assistant librarian of the Widener Library at Harvard; archivists at the U.S. National Archives, Washington, D.C.; staff at the Bernice B. Bishop Museum, Hawaii; and the Archivist at the Library and Museum, Raratonga.

The many persons and institutions I would like to thank in Australia include the Literature Board of the Australia Council who provided a small Special Projects Grant in 1977, which helped with interstate travelling and typing expenses. The State Librarian of New South Wales, R. F. Doust, encouraged me to apply successfully for a Dr C. H. Currey fellowship in 1981. I have always been most grateful for the support I have had from many librarians at that institution, beginning with Mitchell Librarians Phyllis Mander-Jones, Marjorie Hancock, Suzanne Mourot, and others at the Mitchell including Patricia Jackson, Shirley Humphries, and Dianne Rhodes (now Dixson Librarian). Many of these persons provided me with State archival material before the removal of the archives to the State Archives Office in George Street, Sydney.

At the National Library of Australia, Canberra, the former Librarian Allan Fleming, Pauline Fanning and more recently John Thompson have assisted.

In Tasmania, as all historians acknowledge, no-one could be more helpful, supportive and knowledgeable than Geoffrey Stilwell, Curator of the Allport Collection at the State Library, who kindly checked some of this manuscript. State archivists who have helped by answering queries over the years have included M. J. Saclier, R. C. Sharman and Mary McRae. Few persons however could ever have absorbed more knowledge about 'convictism' than the late Peter Eldershaw, whom it was a privilege to know during early visits to the Tasmanian Archives. His widow Shirley, now in the Archives Office, has lately been most helpful, together with Mary Nicholls and several others unknown by name.

Others to whom I owe thanks in Tasmania include the Professor of History at the University of Tasmania, Michael Roe, whose support when publication of this work was delayed gave me fresh impetus to continue and who spent precious time reading and commenting on my manuscript; John McPhee, former Curator at the Queen Victoria Museum, Launceston (now at the National Gallery, Canberra); Richard Lord (President of the Tasmanian First Settlers' Association); also Alison Alexander, Frank Bolt,

Roma and the late Graham Blackwood, Dr Clifford and the late Edith Craig, the late Dr W. L. Crowther, Edith Calvert, Janice Daley, Vera Fisher, the late Francis Foster, Patricia Foster, A. Gard, Edward Gibson, James Stuart Gibson, the late E. R. Henry, Shirley Hughes, Janice Hickey, Anne McKay, Glen Richardson, Irene Schaffer, Adrienne Steane and Lilian Watson.

The late John Feely, former Chief Librarian of the State Library of Victoria, and many others within the Library have assisted me over many years. These have included the late Phil Garrett and La Trobe librarians Patricia Reynolds (now Wilkie), Diane Reilly, and manuscript officer Tony Marshall. At the Baillieu Library, University of Melbourne, Mary Lugton and Patrick Singleton in particular have unearthed excellent background material. The libraries and collections at the Royal Historical Society of Victoria and the Genealogical Society of Victoria and the Royal Australian Historical Society, Sydney, have provided the answers to some queries.

Individuals in Victoria whom I must thank include Patsy Adam-Smith, Marie Allender, Hugh Anderson, the late Dame Valerie Austin, Sandra Bardwell, the late Marnie Bassett (who kindly spent some of her own valuable time in London researching some queries), Geoffrey Bowden, the late O. Bowden, Paul Callender, Dr Phillip Brown, Peter Collins, John Currey, Professor Greg Dening, Irene Elmore, Marie Fels, Bill Gibson, Rollo Hammet, Dorothy Haughton, Win Jones, the late Victor Keating, Elizabeth Larking, the late J. Le Souef, Rabbi Levi, Betty Miller (formerly Mrs Douglas Bowden), Betty Miller (née Hayes), the late John Osboldstone, Lech Paszkowski, Warren Perry, John Ritchie, John Ross, Mary Rusden, Stuart Sayers, Jessie Serle, Emeritus Professor Bernard Smith, June Stewart, Beryl Thomas, the late Hal Warren and Morris Williams.

In other parts of Australia correspondents have included Dr John Cumpston, Dr W. Hudson, the late Nan Phillips and Dr T. G. Vallance, all of Canberra; Keith Grice, Brisbane; John Earnshaw, Dr Brian Fletcher, the late A. J. and Nancy Gray, and Dr Hazel King, all of Sydney; Douglas Tilghman, of Penrith; as well as J. M. Sherrard of Christchurch in New Zealand. I thank also many descendants of the *Calcutta* convicts who prefer to remain anonymous.

Those who have shared the typing and retyping of manuscript material over the years have included the late Beris Jellis and Mary Whitham, while Helen Williams has most capably put it into its final shape. I am only too aware of the difficulties of publication and thank my publisher Lloyd O'Neil and his staff for their patience, especially Robert Sessions, Felicity Anderson, Helen Duffy and Lesley Dunt, and, designer, Sandra Nobes.

This work, however, would never have been completed without the tremendous encouragement given me by some academic historians and by many friends and family. Professor Manning Clark, Dr Lloyd Robson and Professor Geoffrey Blainey all examined my work in progress during the 1960s and gave me the confidence to continue, which I maintained in spite of many interruptions and the knowledge that I still had a long way to go.

Other good friends who have given much support are the late Hazel de Berg, Jim Campbell, Clem and Nina Christesen, Jessie Clarke, the late Andrew Fabinyi, June Helmer, Ian McLaren, Mr Justice Else Mitchell, Dr Stephen Murray-Smith, Dr Tom Perry and Professor A. G. L. Shaw. Margaret Carnegie, Neilma Gantner and John Leslie have been more than patient with their friend who never appeared to be near the end of her research.

On the day he died in April 1970, soon after Sir John Barry died, my husband said, 'You must finish the convict book!' I am happy that he had enough confidence in me to believe that the discussions we had so long ago with Jack Barry and Norval Morris might lead to the publication of some unusual research. But not only my late husband and other good friends had that confidence. My brothers, John and David McCredie and my sons Paul and Tony, always expected me to finish some time; but without the encouragement of Paul, who in the past year has advised on the legal terminology and given general criticism, the book might well have been further delayed. Above all others, I thank him for the precious time taken from his own family, and thank my daughter-in-law Lesley for her understanding.

PICTORIAL ACKNOWLEDGEMENTS

The author and publishers gratefully acknowledge the assistance of the following individuals and institutions who gave their permission to reproduce works in their collections. We also wish to thank McKenzie Gray Photography for their excellent photographic work and Phillip Belfrage for the illustrated map.

Jacket illustrations (details):

Attrib. G. P. Harris, *Sullivan Cove, Tasmania, 1804. First settlement at the River Derwent*, watercolour 20.6 × 34 cm on mount 23.5 × 35.9 cm, Mitchell Library, State Library of New South Wales.

ii-iii: Thomas Whitcombe, *H.M.S. Calcutta of 52 guns*, oil on canvas, relined on masonite, 53.5 × 76.3 cm, one of a series of three paintings, National Library of Australia.

vii: G. P. Harris, *Camp at Sullivan Cove, Derwent, Van Diemen's Land*, pencil, British Library.

xii: G. P. Harris, ink sketch, British Library.

1: Walter Thornbury, *Old and New London*, vol. III, London, p. 301, Baillieu Library.

4: Jorgen Jorgenson, drawing of Sir Joseph Banks, from his allegorical autobiography, *The Adventures of Thomas Walter*, British Library.

5: Walter Thornbury, *Old and New London*, vol. III, London, p. 199, Baillieu Library.

10: Ibid, pp. 66-7.

11: Ibid, p. 451.

16-17: William Redmore Bigg, *Soldiers boarding a prison hulk*, c. 1800, watercolour 33 × 50.5 cm, Rex Nan Kivell Collection, National Library of Australia.

22: Walter Thornbury, *Old and New London*, vol. VI, p. 79, Baillieu Library.

26: Charles Whiting, *James Gillray from the Original Plates*, Baillieu Library.

29: Engraving from George L. Craik and Charles Mac-Farlane, *Pictorial History of England During the Reign of King George the Third*, vol. VIII, p. 647.

37: Pencil drawing by Hanslip Fletcher.

40: Engraving from George L. Craik and Charles Mac-Farlane, *Pictorial History of England During the Reign of King George the Third*, vol. VIII, p. 705.

41: Walter Thornbury, *Old and New London*, vol. II, London, p. 462, Baillieu Library.

42-43: British Library.

46: Pencil drawing 26.8 × 18.5 cm, National Library of Australia.

48: Charles A. Lesueur, *Nouvelle-Hollande: Ile King, L'Elephant – Marin ou Phoque A Trompe. Vue de la Baie des Elephants*, hand coloured lithograph taken from composite sketches Lesueur made at King Island in December 1802, 24.3 × 31.5 cm, Rex Nan Kivell Collection, National Library of Australia.

50: A. Cardon, *Lieutenant-Governor David Collins (1756–1810)*, engraving from a miniature by I. T. Barber, 12.4 × 7.5 cm, La Trobe Library Collection, State Library of Victoria.

55: State Library of Tasmania.

58: Mitchell Library, State Library of New South Wales.

64: La Trobe Collection, State Library of Victoria.

66: Private collection.

71: Private collection.

75: Private collection.

78: James Tuckey, cartouche attached to the chart of Port Phillip, British Library.

82: Unknown artist, portrait of Capt. William Collins, oil on canvas 53.0 × 40.5 cm, Queen Victoria Museum and Art Gallery, Launceston.

88: British Library.

92: Private collection.

96: Charles Henry Theodore Constantini, William Buckley, supplement to the *Cornwall Chronicle*, September 1837, lithograph 24.5 × 20 cm, Dixson Library, State Library of New South Wales.

100: Attrib. John Gunn, *Pioneer Graves at Sorrento*, c. 1864, watercolour on paper 7.1 × 11 cm, Queen Victoria Museum and Art Gallery, Launceston.

102-3: Private collection.

107: Unknown artist, *Major Johnston with Quarter Master Laycock, one Sergeant and 25 private marines . . . 5 March 1804*, watercolour 27.5 × 40.2 cm, Rex Nan Kivell Collection, National Library of Australia.

116: George Prideaux Harris, *G. P. Harris' Cottage, Hobart Town*, 1806, watercolour 15.3 × 19.5 cm, Rex Nan Kivell Collection, National Library of Australia.

120: C. A. Lesueur, *Nouvelle Hollande. Navigation*, from *Voyage De Découvertes Aux Terres Australes . . . Partie Historique Redige Par M. F. Péron. Atlas Pas M. M. Lesueur Et Petit. Diragé Par J. Milbert*, 1804, plate 23, copper engraving 24 × 31.5 cm, Rex Nan Kivell Collection, National Library of Australia.

127: William Duke, *The Rounding*, 1848, lithograph 42.5 × 27 cm, W. L. Crowther Collection, State Library of Tasmania.

130: G. P. Harris, ink sketch, 1806, 11.4 × 18.4 cm, Rex Nan Kivell Collection, National Library of Australia.

138: G. P. Harris, *Pipra m. & f. speckled manakins, 1806*,

watercolour showing Hunter's Island and the Derwent from Hospital Hill, 24.5 × 19 cm, Mitchell Library, State Library of New South Wales.

140: Garrison Orders, 8 July 1810 – 2 December 1812, 15.4 × 19.2 cm, Dixson Library, State Library of New South Wales.

145: *Settlement Norfolk Island – from North East*, pencil 20 × 31.8 cm, Rex Nan Kivell Collection, National Library of Australia.

147: Fearn Rowntree, *Hobart Town Van Diemen's Land*, Hobart, 1966.

148-9: G. W. Evans, *South-west view of Hobart Town*, 1819, watercolour 35.5 × 53.8 cm, Dixson Library, State Library of New South Wales.

154: Allport Library and Museum of Fine Art, Hobart.

157: *Hobart Town Gazette*, 12 September 1818.

165: Attrib. Thomas Lempriere, *South West View of Macquarie Harbour, Tasmania*, 1830s, pencil and watercolour drawing 21.9 × 72.3 cm, Petherick Collection, National Library of Australia.

170: *Port Phillip, First Survey and Settlement of*, a paper ordered by the Legislative Assembly to be printed 21 November 1878, Melbourne.

175: Photograph by Keith Grice, Brisbane.

176: Courtesy of Mrs Edith Calvert, Tasmania.

177: Ludwig Becker (?), *Portrait of David Gibson*, oil on canvas 73 × 68 cm, Gibson family.

183: *Views in Van Dieman's* [sic] *Land*, c. 1822, 20.3 × 32.3 cm, Dixson Library, State Library of New South Wales.

186: Ibid, 19.1 × 32.5 cm, Dixson Library of New South Wales.

190: Thomas Scott, *A Breakfast in the Bush*, woodcut from James Ross, *Hobart Town Almanack*, 1830.

192: Thomas Scott, William Stocker's hut on the Macquarie River, 1821, pencil sketch, Mitchell Library, State Library of New South Wales.

193: Augustus Earle, *Hobart Town*, 1821, watercolour 36.8 × 54.6 cm, Dixson Galleries, State Library of New South Wales.

196: Frontispiece to Charles Medyett Goodridge, *Narrative of a Voyage to the South Seas*, 6th edition, London, 1847.

209: William Strutt, J. P. Fawkner (jun.), watercolour 22 × 13.2 cm, from *Victoria the Golden*, Parliamentary Library of Victoria.

209: Marble bust of Augustus Morris jun., National Library of Australia.

215: *Views in Van Dieman's* [sic] *Land*, c. 1822, 14.8 × 21.3 cm, Dixson Library, State Library of New South Wales.

252: W. L. Goodwin (?), woodcut from the *Cornwall Chronicle*, Launceston, 1836.

273: Ibid.

283: Ibid.

313: Ibid.

321: Ibid.

BIBLIOGRAPHY

Manuscripts in the United Kingdom

BOROUGH ARCHIVES
Boston   Quarter Sessions indictments 1800
BRITISH LIBRARY
Maps and charts
Government Orders, Hobart Town 1813–16, Add. MSS 37840
G. P. Harris letters, maps and papers, Add. MSS 45 156 and 45157
Robert Brown's correspondence from Sullivan Bay
Hamilton and Greville papers, vol. iv, Add. MSS 42071
CITY ARCHIVES
Canterbury   Gaol calendars 1801–02
Norwich   Quarter Sessions indictments 1800
Nottingham   Gaol calendar 1802
Wakefield   Quarter Sessions indictments 1801
COUNTY ARCHIVES
Bedford   Gaol registers, calendars of prisoners, gaolers' bills 1799–1800
Brecon   Gaol file 1801
Cardigan   Gaol file, indictments and Great Sessions register 1801–02
Carmarthen   Gaol file, calendar of prisoners 1801
Chester   Register of Quarter Sessions and Crown Mote 1802, indictments and proceedings
Cornwall   Quarter Sessions rolls 1801
Derby   Quarter Sessions order-book 1801
Devon   Quarter Sessions order-books 1800–02
Dorset   Quarter Sessions order-books, calendars of prisoners, gaol registers, sessions rolls 1800–03
Gloucester   Calendar of prisoners 1801
Hereford   Pateshall papers
Kent   Gaol calendars 1801–02 (Maidstone)
Lancashire   Quarter Sessions indictments 1799–1802
Middlesex   Middlesex indictments 1800–02; Westminster indictments and Quarter Sessions order-books 1801
Montgomery   Great Sessions gaol file 1800
Nottingham   Date-book 1802; minute-book for the Liberty of Southwell and Scrooby Quarter Sessions 1802
Shropshire   Gaol calendars 1802
Somerset   Calendar of prisoners 1802; Quarter Sessions indictments and minute-books 1801
Stafford   Gaol registers 1801–02
Surrey   Quarter Sessions order-books and Surrey process-book 1800–02

Sussex East   Gaolers' bills 1802
GENEALOGICAL SOCIETY, LONDON
Boyd's Marriage Index
GUILD HALL LIBRARY, LONDON
Delivery Sessions book, September 1800–02
London Oyer et Terminer and Gaol Delivery records
Miscellaneous records of London Court
Miscellaneous records of London prisoners upon orders
INDIA OFFICE RECORDS
East India Company papers
Ocean log-book 1803–04
LONDON COUNTY COUNCIL
Old Bailey Sessions book 1800–02
LONDON MISSIONARY SOCIETY
South Seas correspondence
William Pascoe Crook papers
NATIONAL LIBRARY OF WALES
Miscellaneous papers including calendar of prisoners, indictments 1800–02 of Brecon, Carmarthen, Cardigan and Montgomery
NATIONAL MARITIME MUSEUM, GREENWICH
Naval register
PUBLIC RECORD OFFICE, LONDON
Admiralty
Letters from Secretary of State
Logs of Captain and Master, H.M.S. *Calcutta*, 1803–04
Muster books, H.M.S. *Calcutta*, 1802–03
Board of Trade papers
Whale fisheries, hemp and flax 6/93–6/97
Colonial Office
Papers including Governors' and Colonial Secretarys' despatches, general and miscellaneous correspondence (N.S.W.); entry books, N.S.W., 1786; entry books *re* convicts, N.S.W., 1788–1868; miscellanea 1803–1900; V.D.L. original correspondence
Home Office
Documents including records of the Clerks of Assize 1799–1802; agenda books, depositions, indictments, Crown minute books, etc. for gaol books relating to Essex, Gloucester, Hertford, Lancashire, London, Somerset, Southampton, Surrey, Wiltshire and Yorkshire; records of the County Palatinates of Chester, Durham and Lancaster; Old Bailey reports
War Office
Court martial records, Gibraltar 1802–03
Muster rolls and books of the 16th Regiment of Dragoons 1801–03
Records of the 25th Regiment 1802–03
Sundry Army lists, muster books

WEST REGISTER HOUSE, EDINBURGH
  Assize records of the High Court of Judiciary, including indictments, minute books, 1799–1802
WESTMINSTER GUILD HALL
  Records of Court of Common Pleas 1800–03

Manuscripts in other Overseas Repositories

EIRE
Dublin Castle
  Family records
UNITED STATES OF AMERICA
  Bernice P. Bishop Museum, Honolulu
    Fuller Collection
  Essex Institute, Salem
    Log-books of American whalers
  Library of Congress, Washington, D.C.
    Facsimiles of log-books
  Nantucket Whaling Museum
    Log-books of American whalers
  Peabody Museum
    Log-books

Manuscripts in Australia

NATIONAL LIBRARY OF AUSTRALIA, CANBERRA
  Banks papers
  Fawkner's journal
  Knopwood miscellaneous papers
  Woodriff papers
NEW SOUTH WALES STATE ARCHIVES
  Colonial Secretary's Office
    Correspondence: Norfolk Island musters and victualling lists; Newcastle musters and victualling lists; Van Diemen's Land books including Buckingham and Cornwall musters 1811–23; Norfolk Island list of settlers embarking on *Lady Nelson* for Port Dalrymple 1813; shipping indents of the Principal Superintendent of Convicts
  Supreme Court
    Records containing proceedings of Hobart Bench of Magistrates 1806–, Judge Advocate's Court, Hobart 1809– and Cornwall 1809; Court of Appeal and Civil Jurisdiction case papers 1810–11; N.S.W. Court of Criminal Jurisdiction, miscellaneous papers 1807–16; courts martial papers; miscellaneous papers Moreton Bay, Newcastle, including registers of pardons, petitions, etc.
PRIVATE COLLECTIONS IN AUSTRALIA
  Matthew Bowden's journal and account book (Bowden family, Melbourne)
  Hobbs family tree and papers (A.S. Collins, Geelong)
  Fawkner papers (Mrs Irene Elmore and Walsh family, Drouin)
  James Lord family papers (Richard Lord, Hobart)
  David Gibson family tree (James Stuart Gibson, Hobart)

QUEEN VICTORIA MUSEUM AND ART GALLERY, LAUNCESTON
  Beattie collection
  Thomas Scott papers and sketches
ROYAL HISTORICAL SOCIETY OF VICTORIA
  George Gordon McCrae papers
STATE LIBRARY OF NEW SOUTH WALES
  Dixson Library
    Calder papers
    John Clark diary
    Court records, George Town
    Fawkner files
    General and Garrison order-books 1810–12, V.D.L.
    Knopwood letter-book, sermons and legal documents
    Macquarie Harbour muster and return of prisoners, 1825
    Marriage affidavits, Hobart, 1837
    Police Office records, Hobart
    Settlers' agreements, New Town, 1807
MITCHELL LIBRARY
  Official papers
    Bigge's appendix
    Bonwick transcripts
    Census 1828
    Commissariat returns 1803–05
    Government Orders ration book 1812–18
    Governors' papers and despatches: Governor King (correspondence and pardons); Governor Bligh (1808–10); Governor Macquarie (letter-books, pardons, etc.); Governors Arthur, Bourke and Gipps (many from Bonwick transcripts)
  Military papers
  New South Wales Colonial Secretary's papers: Tasmania 1801–
  Old Tasmanian Papers:
    Vols 17-20 Lieutenant-Governor's Court proceedings 1820–23
    Vol. 27 Supreme Court records 1818–20
    Vol. 159 Coroner's Court and petitions 1811, 1816, 1818
    Vols 178-9 Civil suits, etc. 1815–24
    Vols 196-7 Bench of Magistrates, Hobart, 1818, 1829, 1832
    Vols 206-7 Convicts, N.S.W.
    Vol. 212 Petitions and convicts' correspondence
    Vols 234, 265-70 Police Department records 1810–
    Vol. 271 Bench of Magistrates, Hobart, licences granted and court proceedings 1819–20
    Vol. 272 Supreme Court proceedings, Hobart, 1829
  Register of deaths in Van Diemen's Land 1803–20
  Transport Commission papers: invoices for stores for Port Phillip, petitions
  Van Diemen's Land books, including musters of convicts and free persons, Hobart, Port Dalrymple and Norfolk Island, 1811; population, male and female convicts, Buckingham, 1818; land and stock, Hobart, 1819; population, Hobart, 1819; land and stock, Port Dalrymple, 1819; popula-

tion, Port Dalrymple, 1819; convicts, Hobart, 1820; population, Port Dalrymple, 1820; land and stock, Port Dalrymple, 1820; prisoners, Hobart, 1821; population, Port Dalrymple, 1821; land and stock, Port Dalrymple, 1822; muster, Hobart, 1823; convicts in Van Diemen's Land, 1825, 1830, 1832, 1833

Private papers

Governor Arthur papers

Banks papers, including Tuckey's Memoir of his Chart of Port Philip (*sic*)

Governor Bligh papers

Governor Bourke papers

Bowes Smyth journal

Brabourne collection including Tuckey papers

Campbell and Co. papers

David Collins papers

Collins family papers

Calder papers

Fisher collection: civil suits 1815–24

G.P. Harris papers

Reverend Rowland Hassall papers

Robert 'Buckey' Jones, Recollections of Thirteen Years Residence in Norfolk Island

Kenison James Index

Governor King papers

Knopwood diaries 1801–02, 1803–04, 1814–20, 1822–34, 1836–38, including his journal of proceedings on board H.M.S. *Resolution* 1 January 1801–22 July 1802 and on board H.M.S. *Calcutta* 24 April 1803 to Derwent December 1804

Knopwood miscellaneous papers including correspondence and sermons

Reverend Samuel Marsden papers

Mutch Index of baptisms, marriages and deaths at St Phillips, Sydney

William Paterson papers

John Piper papers

George Robinson papers

Thomas Scott papers 1820–28

Tuckey, miscellaneous papers including Sketch of the Present State of New South Wales and Observations on the most Eligible Routes from Port Jackson

J. B. Walker, notes on Tasmania

J. Helder Wedge diary

William Wentworth papers

Woodriff papers including memo book

STATE LIBRARY OF TASMANIA

Allport collection

George Collins papers

Geils papers

Miscellaneous papers and cuttings

Crowther Collection

James Kelly log-books

James Kelly papers

STATE LIBRARY OF VICTORIA

La Trobe Collection

Bonwick papers

J. E. Calder papers

Fawkner reminiscences and other papers

James Hobbs papers

Knopwood letters

Langhorne papers including Buckley's reminiscences

Captain Tregurtha log-book

Shillinglaw collection

Todd papers

TASMANIAN STATE ARCHIVES

William Allison notebook

Auxiliary Branch Bible Society of Van Diemen's Land papers and reports

Census 1837, New Town

Census 1842, Richmond

Church registers:

Brighton (Pontville): St Mark's

Clarence Plains: St Matthew's

Colebrook: St James'

Green Ponds: St Mary's

Hobart: St David's, St Virgil's, St George's, St Andrew's, Holy Trinity

Launceston: St John's, St Paul's

New Norfolk: St Matthew's

New Town: St John's Trinity

Richmond: St Luke's

Sorell and Pitt Water: St George's

Colonial Secretary's Office

Papers including musters of 1811; return of purchases and exchanges of buildings and lands 1813–19; returns of juvenile population needing education, Hobart c.1820; return of children 1827–28 (Hobart, Launceston, New Norfolk, Brighton, Green Ponds, Pitt Water, Glenorchy and New Town)

Convict Department records

Comprehensive register of convicts, vols I, II (CON 22)

Alphabetical register of male convicts, 3 vols (CON 23)

Conduct registers of male convicts (CON 31)

Convicts' memorials for indulgences (CON 44)

Alphabetical registers of applications for indulgences (CON 45)

Governors' letter-books and memoranda

Land Department

Memorials, land grants

Edward Lord, letter-book 1821–22

George Robinson papers

Supreme Court records

Inquests

Wayn Index

William Williamson, letters 1820

UNIVERSITY OF TASMANIA

Royal Society Collection

James Belbin diary

G. T. W. B. Boyes papers and diary

Knopwood diaries 1805–17 July 1808

B.C. Mollison, Tasmanian Aboriginal Genealogies, Part I, unpublished thesis, 1974

Roman Catholic register of baptisms, marriages and deaths 1820–56, transcript

St Joseph's register of baptisms, marriages and deaths

Printed Documents

——, *Report of the Commissioner of Inquiry into the State of the Colony of New South Wales, June 1822*, London, 1822 (Australian facsimile ed., no. 68, Adelaide, 1966).

——, *Report of the Commissioner of Inquiry on the Judicial Establishments of New South Wales and Van Diemen's Land, February 1823*, London, 1823 (Australian facsimile ed., no. 69, Adelaide, 1966).

——, *Report of the Commissioner of Inquiry on the State of Agriculture and Trade in the Colony of New South Wales, March 1823*, London, 1823 (Australian facsimile ed., no. 70, Adelaide, 1966).

Clark, C. M. H. (ed.), *Select Documents in Australian History*, 2 vols, Sydney, 1950.

Eldershaw, Peter, *Guide to the Public Records of Tasmania. 1. Colonial Secretary's Office Record Group*, Hobart, 1857, *2. Governor's Office Record Group*, Hobart, 1958, *3. Convict Department, Hobart, 1965.*

The Evidence of the Bigge Reports, ed. John Ritchie, 2 vols, Melbourne, 1971.

Fitzsymonds, Eustace (ed.), *Mortmain, Van Diemen's Land*, Hobart, 1977.

Historical Records of Australia, series I, III, IV, ed. Frederick Watson, Sydney, 1914–25, including General and Garrison Orders of Port Phillip, 1803–04.

Historical Records of New South Wales, vols I-VII, eds Alexander Britton and F. M. Bladen, Sydney, 1893–1901.

Hull, Hugh, *A Statistical Account of Van Diemen's Land . . . 1804–1823*, vol. I, Hobart, 1856.

Journals of the Lands Commissioners of Van Diemen's Land 1826–28, ed. Anne McKay, Hobart, 1962.

Legislative Council of Tasmania: Report 75 re Boat Expeditions round Tasmania 1815–16 and 1824, ed. J. E. Calder, Hobart, 1881.

Molesworth, William, *Report from the Select Committee of the House of Commons on Transportation . . .*, London, 1838.

Old Bailey Sessions Papers, London, 1799–1802.

Port Phillip: First Survey and Settlement of, with a preface and notes by J. J. Shillinglaw, Melbourne, 1878.

Report of the Select Committee [of the Parliament of Great Britain and Ireland] *. . . with Observations on the System of Transporting Convicts to Botany Bay . . .*, London, 1799.

Reports on the Historical Manuscripts of Tasmania, vols 1-5, Hobart, 1964.

Rules and Orders of the Lieutenant Governor's Court in Van Diemen's Land, Hobart, 1819.

Statistical Returns of Van Diemen's Land 1824–36, John Montagu (comp.), Hobart, 1836.

Statutes [of the Parliament of Great Britain and Ireland] *. . . Convicts and Transportation 43 Geo III*, London, 1802.

The Trials of W. Grimshaw and R. Kidman for Burglary (with a Sketch of their Lives) and of H. Cohen as an Accessory before and after the Fact, W. Rowton, Cambridge, 1850.

Van Diemen's Land: Correspondence between Lieutenant Governor Arthur and H.M.'s Secretary of State for the Colonies . . . Military Operations . . . against the Aboriginal Inhabitants, comp. A. G. L. Shaw, Hobart, 1971.

Votes and Proceedings of the Legislative Council of Victoria, Paper 15, Melbourne, 1878.

Published Material

Abbot, G. M. and Nairn, Bede (eds), *Economic Growth of Australia 1788–1821*, Melbourne, 1969.

Anderson, Hugh, *Out of the Shadow*, Melbourne, 1962.

Anon., *An Old Bailey Experience*, London, 1833.

Australian Dictionary of Biography, Vols I, II, ed. Douglas Pike, Melbourne, 1966, 1967.

Australian Encyclopaedia, 10 vols, Sydney, 1958.

Backhouse, James, *A Narrative of a Visit to the Australian Colonies*, London, 1843.

Baker, Sidney, *The Australian Language*, Sydney, 1945.

Barker, E. H. (ed.), *Geographical, Commercial and Political Essays . . .*, London, 1812.

Barrett, W. R., *History of Tasmania to the Death of Lieutenant-Governor Collins in 1810*, Hobart, 1936.

Barton, G. and Britton, A. (eds), *New South Wales from the Records 1789–94*, Sydney, 1894.

Barton, G. and Britton, A., (eds), *New South Wales from the Records 1789–94*, Sydney, 1894.

Bateson, Charles, *The Convict Ships*, Glasgow, 1939.

Baudin, Nicolas, *The Journal of Post Captain Nicolas Baudin . . .*, ed. Christine Cornell, Adelaide, 1974.

Beaglehole, J. C., *The Exploration of the Pacific*, London, 1947.

Beattie, J. W., *Glimpses of the Life and Times of the Early Tasmanian Governors*, Hobart, 1905.

Beccaria, C., *Dei Delitti e delle Pene* (1764), trans. J. A. Farren, London, 1880.

Bensley, Benjamin (ed.), *Lost and Found or Light in the Prison: narrative and letters of James Grove from Port Phillip and the Derwent 1803–4*, London, 1859.

Bentham, Jeremy, *Collected Works*, 11 vols, Edinburgh, 1843.

——, *Discourses on Civil and Penal Legislation*, London, 1802.

——, *A Plea for the Constitution*, London, 1803.

Besant, Walter, *London in the Eighteenth Century*, London, 1925.

Bethall, L. S., *The Story of Port Dalrymple*, Launceston, 1958.

Billis, R. V. and Kenyon, A. S., *Pastoral Pioneers of Port Phillip*, Melbourne, 1932.

Blackstone, William, *Commentaries on the Laws of England*, 4 vols, London, 1765–69.

Blainey, Geoffrey, *The Tyranny of Distance*, Melbourne, 1966.

Bolger, Peter, *Hobart Town*, Canberra, 1973.

Bonwick, James, *The Bushrangers*, Melbourne, 1856.

——, *Curious Facts of Old Colonial Days*, London, 1870.

——, *The Last of the Tasmanians*, London, 1870.

——, *The Lost Tasmanian Race*, London, 1884.

——, *The Wild White Man and the Blacks of Victoria*, Melbourne, 1863.

Bowden, Keith, *Captain Kelly of Hobart Town*, Melbourne 1864.

Boys, R. D., *First Years at Port Phillip*, Melbourne, 1935.

Bride, T. F. (ed.), *Letters from Victorian Pioneers*, Melbourne, 1898.

Brown, Philip, *Clyde Company Papers*, vols I–VI, London, 1941–68.

———, *The Narrative of George Russell of Golf Hill*, London, 1935.

Brown, Robert, *Prodromus Florae Novae Hollandiae*, London, 1811.

Burford, Robert, *Description of a View of Hobart Town, Van Diemen's Land . . . exhibiting at the Panorama, Strand*, London, 1831.

Burke, J. L. (ed.), *The Adventures of Martin Cash, comprising a faithful account of his exploits . . .*, Hobart, 1870.

Burke's Landed Gentry, vol. 11, London, 1847.

Button, Henry, *Flotsam and Jetsam: Floating Fragments of Life in England and Tasmania*, Launceston, c.1909.

Calder, J. E., *Some Account of the Wars, Extirpation, Habits, etc. of the Natives of Tasmania*, Hobart, 1875.

Caley, George, *Reflections on the Colony of New South Wales*, ed. J. E. B. Currey, Melbourne, 1966.

Clark, C. M. H., *A History of Australia*, vols 1–2, Melbourne, 1962, 1968.

Cobley, John, *The Convicts*, Sydney, 1965.

———, *The Crimes of the First Fleet Convicts*, Sydney, 1970.

———, *Sydney Cove*, vols I–III, London and Sydney, 1962–65.

Collins, C. R., *Saga of Settlement*, Perth, 1956.

Collins, David, *An Account of the English Colony in New South Wales*, vols I–II, London, 1798–1802. (Also reissued ed. Brian Fletcher, Sydney, 1975.)

———, *An Account of a Voyage to establish a Settlement in Bass's Straits . . .*, ed. from the despatches of David Collins by John Currey, Melbourne, 1986.

Colquhoun, Patrick, *Treatise on the Police of the Metropolis*, London, 1795, 1806.

Coutts, P. J. F., *An Archaeological Survey of Sullivans* [sic] *Bay, Sorrento*, Melbourne, 1982.

———, *Victoria's First Official Settlement, Sullivans* [sic] *Bay, Port Phillip*, Melbourne, 1981.

Crawford, Mr Justice, Ellis W. F. and Stancombe, G. H. (eds), *The Diaries of John Helder Wedge 1824–1835*, 1962.

Croker, T. C. (ed.), *Memoirs of Joseph Holt*, 2 vols, London, 1838.

Crook, William Pascoe, *An Account of the Settlement at Sullivan Bay, Port Phillip, 1803*, ed. John Currey, Melbourne, 1983.

Cullis, Herbert G., *No Tears for Jane: a Hadden family history*, Canberra, 1982.

Cumpston, J. H. L., *First Visitors to Bass Strait*, Canberra, 1973.

———, *Shipping Arrivals and Departures, Sydney 1788–1825*, Canberra, 1963.

Curr, Edmund, *An Account of the Colony of Van Diemen's Land*, London, 1824.

Dakin, W. J., *Whalemen Adventurers*, Sydney, 1934.

Dallas, K.M., *Trading Posts or Penal Colonies*, Hobart, 1969.

Delano, Amasa, *A Narrative of Voyages and Travels*, Boston, Mass., 1817.

Derry, John, *Cobbett's England*, London, 1968.

Dictionary of National Biography, 63 vols, London, 1885–1900.

A Dictionary of the Vulgar Tongue, London, 1811.

Earnshaw, John, 'Select letters of James Grove, convict: Port Phillip and the Derwent', *Tasmanian Historical Research Association Papers and Proceedings*, VIII, i, Aug., and ii, Oct. 1959.

Eden, F. M., *State of the Poor*, vols I–III, London, 1797.

Eden, William, *Principles of Penal Law*, London, 1771.

Eldershaw, M. Barnard, *The Life and Times of Captain John Piper*, Sydney, 1939.

Ellis, M. H., *John Macarthur*, Sydney, 1955.

———, *Lachlan Macquarie*, Sydney, 1947.

An Episode: Batman and Fawkner, ed. Ian McLaren, Melbourne, 1965.

Evans, G. W., *A Geographical, Historical and Topographical Description of Van Diemen's Land*, London, 1822.

Evatt, H. V., *Rum Rebellion*, 4th ed., Sydney, 1944.

Fenton, James, *Bush Life in Tasmania*, London, 1891.

———, *A History of Tasmania*, Hobart, 1884.

Ferguson, J. A., *Bibliography of Australia*, vol. 1, Sydney, 1941.

Flinders, Matthew, *Observations on the Coasts of Van Diemen's Land, on Bass's Straits and its Islands . . .*, London, 1801.

———, *A Voyage to Terra Australis 1801–03*, London, 1814.

Forsyth, W. D., *Governor Arthur's Convict System: Van Diemen's Land 1824–1836*, London, 1935.

Fortescue, J. W., *A History of the British Army*, vol. IV, part II, 1789–1801, London, 1889.

Frost, Alan, *Convicts and Empire: A Naval Question 1776–1811*, Melbourne, 1980.

Geographical, Political and Commercial Essays, London, 1812.

Giblin, R. W., *The Early History of Tasmania: the Geographical Era 1642–1804*, London, 1928.

Giusseppi, M. S., *A Guide to the Mss preserved in the Public Records Office*, vols I–II, London, 1923–24.

Griffiths, Arthur, *Chronicles of Newgate*, 2 vols, London, 1884.

Godwin, Thomas, *The Emigrants' Guide*, London, 1823.

Goodridge, C. M., *Narrative of a Voyage to the South Seas . . . Eight Years' Residence in Van Diemen's Land*, London, 1832.

Grant, James, *The Narrative of a Voyage of Discovery, Performed in His Majesty's Vessel the Lady Nelson*, London, 1803.

Griffiths, Arthur, *Chronicles of Newgate*, 2 vols, London, 1884.

Hague, Thomas, *Appeal to His Majesty on the State of the Nation*, London, 1810.

———, *Letter to the Duke of York: Inquiry*, London, 1808.

Hammond, J. L. and Barbara Hammond, *The Village Labourer*, London, 1911.

Harding, Alan, *A Social History of English Law*, London, 1966.

Hay, Douglas, and other contributors from University of Warwick, *Albion's Fatal Tree: Crime and Society in Eighteenth-century England*, London, 1975.

Hazzard, Margaret, *Punishment Short of Death: A History of the Penal Settlement at Norfolk Island*, Melbourne, 1984.

Henderson, Alexander, *Australian Families: a Genealogical and Biographical Record*, Melbourne, 1941.

Hirst, J. B., *Convict Society and Its Enemies*, Sydney, 1983.

Hogan, J. F., *The Convict King (Jorgen Jorgensen)*, Hobart, n.d.

Hodsworth, W. S., *A History of English Law* (13 vols), vol. IV, London, 1932–52.

Hookey, Mabel, *Bobby Knopwood and His Times*, Hobart, 1929.

——, *The Chaplain*, Hobart, 1970.

Howard, John, *The State of Prisons in England and Wales, with an Account of Some Foreign Prisons*, 4th ed., London, 1790.

Hudspeth, W. H., *Hudspeth Memorial Volume: An Introduction to the Diaries of the Rev. Robert Knopwood, A. M., and G. T. W. B. Boyes*, Hobart, 1954.

Humphrey, A. W. H., *Narrative of a Voyage to Port Phillip and Van Diemen's Land . . . 1803–04*, ed. John Currey, Melbourne, 1984.

Hunter, John, *An Historical Journal of the Transactions at Port Jackson and Norfolk Island*, London, 1793.

Ingleton, Geoffrey, *True Patriots All*, Sydney, 1952.

Inscriptions in Stone: St David's Burial Ground 1804–1872, comp. R. Lord, Hobart, 1976.

James, William, *The Naval History of Great Britain from the Declaration of War in 1793 to the Accession of George IV*, London, 1837.

Jeffries, Charles, *Geographic and Descriptive Delineations of the Island of Van Diemen's Land*, London, 1820.

Kiddle, Margaret, *Men of Yesterday*, Melbourne, 1961.

Kiernan, T. J., *Irish Exiles in Australia*, Dublin, 1854.

King, Jonathan and King, John, *Philip Gidley King*, Melbourne, 1981.

Labilliere, F. P., *Early History of the Colony of Victoria*, vols I–III, London, 1878.

Lawson, Will, *Blue Gum Clippers and Whale Ships of Tasmania*, Melbourne, 1949.

Leask, Brian, *Genealogical Guide to Some Australian Families . . .*, Adelaide, 1979.

Lee, Ida, *The Log-books of the* Lady Nelson, London, 1915.

Levi, J. S., *The Forefathers: a Dictionary of Biography of the Jews of Australia 1788–1830*, Melbourne, 1976.

—— and Bergman, G. F. J., *Australian Genesis: Jewish Convicts and Settlers 1788–1850*, Adelaide, 1974.

Lycett, J., *Views in Australia*, London, 1824.

Mackaness, George, *The Life of Vice-Admiral William Bligh*, 2 vols, Sydney, 1931.

McKay, Anne (ed.), *Journals of the Land Commissioners for Van Diemen's Land 1826–1828*, Hobart, 1962.

Mackay, David, *A Place of Exile: the European Settlement of New South Wales*, Melbourne, 1985.

McLachlan, Noel (ed.), *The Memoirs of James Hardy Vaux, including his Vocabulary of the 'Flash Language'*, London, 1964.

McNab, Robert, *Muruhiku: a History of the South Island of New Zealand . . .*, Invercargill, 1907.

——, *The Old Whaling Days*, London, 1913.

Macquarie, Lachlan, *Journals of his Tours in New South Wales and Van Diemen's Land 1810–1822*, Sydney, 1956.

Mahan, A. T., *The Influence of Sea Power upon the French Revolution and Empire*, vol. II, London, 1837.

Mann, William, *Six Years' Residence in the Australian Provinces, Ending in 1839 . . .*, London, 1839.

Marshall, John, *Royal Naval Biography*, vol. VIII, part iv, London, 1830.

Martin, Ged (ed.), *The Founding of Australia: the Argument about Australia's Origins*, Sydney, 1978.

Mayhew, Henry, *London Labour and London Poor*, London, 1851.

Melville, Henry, *The History of Van Diemen's Land from the Year 1824 to 1835 . . .*, Hobart, 1835.

Micco, Helen, *King Island and the Sealing Trade 1802*, Canberra, 1971.

Miller, E. Morris, *Pressmen and Governors: Australian Editors and Writers in Early Tasmania*, Sydney, 1952.

Miller, George, *A Trip to Sea 1810–15*, Boston, Lincs., 1854.

Montague, John, *Statistical Returns of Van Diemen's Land 1824–36*, Hobart, 1836.

Morgan, John, *The Life and Adventures of William Buckley*, Hobart, 1852.

Mowle, L. M., *A Genealogical History of Pioneer Families of Australia*, Adelaide, 1978.

Naval Chronicle, vol. 32, London, 1814.

Neale, Erskine, *Life of Field-Marshal H.R.H., Edward, the Duke of Kent*, London, 1850.

Nicholls, Mary (ed.), *The Diary of the Reverend Robert Knopwood 1803–1838*, Hobart, 1977.

Nicholson, Ian H., *Shipping Arrivals and Departures: Tasmania 1803–1833*, Canberra, 1983.

Norman, L., *Sea Wolves and Bandits*, Hobart, 1946.

O'Brien, Eris, *The Foundation of Australia*, Sydney, 2 eds, 1950.

O'Byrne, William, *A Naval Biographical Dictionary*, London, 1849.

O'May, Harry, *Wooden Hookers of Hobart Town and Whalers out of Van Diemen's Land*, Hobart, n.d.

Parker, H. W., *Van Diemen's Land: Its Rise, Progress and Present State*, London, 1834.

Pateshall, Nicholas, *A Short Account of a Voyage round the Globe in H.M.S. Calcutta 1803–04*, ed. Marjorie Tipping, Melbourne, 1980.

Pelham, Camden, *Chronicles of Crime*, 2 vols, London, 1887.

Péron, M. F., *A Voyage of Discovery to the Southern Hemisphere . . . 1801, 1802, 1803 and 1804, trans. from the French*, London, 1809.

Phillips, Richard, *A Collection of Modern and Contemporary Voyages and Travels*, vol. I, London, 1805.

Plomley, N. J. B. (ed.), *Friendly Mission: the Tasmanian Journals and Papers of George Augustus Robinson 1829–1834*, Hobart 1966 and Supplement 1971.

——, *The Tasmanian Aborigines*, Launceston, 1977.

Plucknett, Theodore, *A Concise History of the Common Law*, London, 1956.

Poynter, John, *Society and Pauperism*, Melbourne, 1969.

Radzinowicz, L., *A History of the English Criminal Law and Its Administration from 1730*, 4 vols, London, 1948.

Ritchie, John, *Punishment and Profit*, Melbourne, 1970.

Robertson, E. Graeme, *Early Buildings of Southern Tasmania*, 2 vols, Melbourne, 1970.

——, and Craig, E. N., *Early Houses in Northern Tasmania: an Historical and Architectural Survey*, 2 vols, Melbourne, 1964.

Robinson, Portia, *The Hatch and Brood of Time*, Melbourne, 1985.

Robson, Lloyd, *The Convict Settlers of Australia*, Melbourne, 1965.

——, *A History of Tasmania*, vol. I, Melbourne, 1983.

Roe, Michael, *Quest for Authority in Eastern Australia 1835–1851*, Melbourne, 1965.

Romilly, Samuel, *Observations on the Criminal Law of England*, London, 1811.

Ross, James, *The Settler in Van Diemen's Land*, Hobart, 1836.

Roth, Henry Ling, *The Aborigines of Tasmania*, London, 1890.

Rudé, George, *Protest and Punishment: the Story of the Social and Political Protesters Transported to Australia 1788–1868*, London, 1978.

Rusden, G. W., *Discovery, Survey and Settlement of Port Phillip*, Melbourne, 1871.

Ryan, Lyndall, *The Aboriginal Tasmanians*, St Lucia, 1982.

Savery, Henry, *The Hermit in Van Diemen's Land*, Hobart, 1829.

Sayer, Captain, *The History of Gibraltar and of Its Political Relation to Events in Europe*, London, 1862.

Scott, Ernest, *The Life of Captain Matthew Flinders, R.N.*, Sydney, 1914.

——, *Terre Napoleon: a History of French Explorations . . . in Australia*, London, 1910.

Shaw, A. G. L., *Convicts and the Colonies: a Study of Penal Transportation . . .*, London, 1966.

——, *Sir George Arthur, Bart, 1784–1854*, Melbourne, 1980.

Shillinglaw, John, *Historical Records of Port Phillip*, Melbourne, 1879.

Smee, G. J. and Provis, J. Selkirk, *Pioneer Register*, vol. II, Netley, S.A., 1979.

Smith, Bernard, *European Vision and the South Pacific 1768–1850*, London, 1960.

Smith, Sydney, *Essays, Social and Political*, London, n.d.

Stackpoole, A., *The Sea-Hunters*, Philadelphia, 1953.

Stancombe, G. Hawley, *Highway in Van Diemen's Land*, Launceston, 1974.

Starbuck, Alexander, *History of the American Whaling Industry*, vols I–II, New York, 1964.

Steven, Margaret, *Merchant Campbell 1769–1846*, Melbourne, 1965.

Stieglitz, Karl von, *A History of Local Government in Tasmania*, Hobart, 1958.

——, *The Pioneer Church in Van Diemen's Land*, Hobart, 1954.

—— (ed.), *Sketches in Early Van Diemen's Land by Thomas Scott*, Hobart, 1966.

Stone, Caroline and Tyson, Pamela, *Old Hobart Town and Environs 1802–1855*, Melbourne, 1978.

Stoney, H. Butler, *A Residence in Tasmania*, London, 1856.

Swan, R. A., *To Botany Bay*, Canberra, 1973.

Thornbury, Walter, *Old and New London: a Narrative of its History, its People and its Places*, vols II, III, VI, London, 1872–78.

Tuckey, James Hingston, *An Account of a Voyage to Establish a Colony at Port Philip {sic} in Bass's Strait*, London, 1805.

——, *Narrative of an Expedition to Explore the River Zaïre . . . in 1816*, London, 1818.

Turnbull, Clive, *Black War*, Melbourne, 1948.

Turner, Henry Gyles, *A History of the Colony of Victoria*, vol. I, London, 1904.

Vallance, T. G., 'The Start of Government Science in Australia: A. W. H. Humphrey, His Majesty's Mineralogist in New South Wales, 1803–12', *Proceedings of the Linnean Society of New South Wales*, 1981.

Walker, James Backhouse, *Early Tasmania: Papers Read before the Royal Society of Tasmania . . . 1888–99*, Hobart, 1950.

Walker, Peter Benson (ed.), *Prelude to Federation: 1884–1898. Extracts from the Journal of James Backhouse Walker*, Hobart, 1976.

Wells, [Thomas], *Michael Howe the Last and Worst of the Bushrangers of Van Diemen's Land . . .*, Hobart Town, 1818.

Wentworth, W. C., *A Statistical, Historical and Political Description of the Colony of New South Wales and its Dependent Settlements in Van Diemen's Land*, London, 1820.

West, John, *The History of Tasmania*, vols I–II, Launceston, 1852.

Widowson, Henry, *Present State of Van Diemen's Land . . .*, London, 1829.

Windeyer, W. J. V., *Lectures on Legal History*, 2nd ed., Sydney, 1957.

Almanacks

Bent, Andrew, *Tasmanian Almanack*, 1825–30.

——, *Van Diemen's Land Almanack*, 1824, 1827.

Melville, Henry, *Almanacks*, 1831–1836.

Murray's Almanack, 1829.

Ross, James, *Almanacks*, 1829–1838.

Wood, James, *Van Diemen's Land Almanack*, 1839.

Newspapers and Periodicals

BRITAIN

All the Year Round; Aris' Birmingham Gazette; Bath Chronicle; Bath Journal; Bell's Weekly Messenger; Country Gentleman and Farmer's Journal; Berrow's Worcester Journal; Cambridge Chronicle; Cambridge Intelligencer; Chelmsford Chronicle; Cheshire Courant; Cornwall Chronicle; Derby Mercury; Dublin Evening Post; Dublin Review; Edinburgh Advertiser; Edinburgh Review; European Magazine and London Review; Exeter Flying Post; General Evening Post; Gentleman's Magazine; Hampshire Chronicle; Hereford County Press and Shropshire Mail; Hereford Journal; Hereford Times; Lancaster Gazeteer; Leicester Journal; Lincoln, Rutland and Stamford Mercury; London Observer; Maidstone Journal; Newcastle Chronicle; Newcastle Courant; Northampton Mercury; Norfolk Chronicle; Norwich Mercury; Nottingham Journal; Penny Magazine of the Society for the Diffusion of Useful Knowledge; Quarterly Review; Reading Mercury; Salisbury and Winchester Journal; Staffordshire Advertiser; Sussex Weekly Advertiser; The Times; Transactions of the Linnean Society; Western Flying Post; Worcester Herald; York Courant; York Herald.

AUSTRALIA

Newspapers

Australian–Asiatic ('Murray's') Review; Australian (1824–); Church of England Messenger; Colonial Advocate; Colonial Times; Colonist; Cornwall Chronicle; Cornwall Press; Derwent Star and Van Diemen's Land Intelligencer (1810 and 1811); Hobart Town Advertiser; Hobart Town Courier; Hobart Town Gazette and V.D.L. Advertiser; Hobart Town Gazette and Southern Reporter; Independent; Launceston Advertiser; Morning Post; Monitor; Sydney Gazette and New South Wales Advertiser; *Tasmanian; True Colonist; Van Diemen's Land Gazette and General Advertiser.*

Periodicals

Australian Genealogist; Ancestor; Historical Studies; Journal of the Royal Australian Historical Society; Medical Journal of Australia; Proceedings of the Linnean Society of New South Wales; Royal Society of Tasmania Papers and Proceedings; Tasmanian Historical Research Association Papers and Proceedings; Victorian Genealogist; Victorian Geographical Journal; Victorian Historical Magazine.

INDEX

BASS

Hunter I^D

Cape
Grim

Lady

THIS PART OF THE COUNTRY UNKNOWN

Well Wooded

THIS PART OF THE COUNTRY

High

SOUTHERN OCEAN

Cape Sorell

Macquarie Harbour

N

UNINHABITED RAIN FOREST

Port Davey

VAN DIEMEN'S LAND

South West Cape